RISK AND NEGLIGENCE IN
ESTATES, AND TRUST

RISK AND NEGLIGENCE IN WILLS, ESTATES, AND TRUSTS

SECOND EDITION

MARTYN FROST
PENELOPE REED QC
MARK BAXTER

OXFORD
UNIVERSITY PRESS

OXFORD

UNIVERSITY PRESS

Great Clarendon Street, Oxford, OX2 6DP,
United Kingdom

Oxford University Press is a department of the University of Oxford.
It furthers the University's objective of excellence in research, scholarship,
and education by publishing worldwide. Oxford is a registered trade mark of
Oxford University Press in the UK and in certain other countries

First edition published in 2009
Second edition published in 2014

Impression: 1

Published in the United States of America by Oxford University Press
198 Madison Avenue, New York, NY 10016, United States of America

British Library Cataloguing in Publication Data
Data available

Library of Congress Control Number: 2013949968

ISBN 978–0–19–967292–9

Printed and bound by
Lightning Source UK Ltd

FOREWORD

Sir Alastair Norris
Vice Chancellor of the County Palatine

To those browsing the stationer's shelves for a pre-printed form or reading the blandishments on the website it all seems so straightforward: what could possibly go wrong? The practitioner asked to prepare a will, or to resolve the differences in a fractured family knows only too well. It is not a question of simply complying with the formalities, but of ensuring that the sundry potential challenges can be forethought and forestalled.

Many a dispute over a will is a proxy for some other battle. Many a dispute is caused by disappointed expectations raised by a testator who was not as circumspect as Hilaire Belloc's 'Aunt Jane'

> Her fortune is large; though we often remark
> On a modesty rare in the rich,
> For her nearest and dearest are quite in the dark
> As to what she will leave, or to which.

Many a dispute over a will arises out of a straightforward inability to accept that a testator could have exercised a free disposing power in the way reflected in the will. The emotional engagement in the dispute is why the number of disputes over wills continues to grow even as litigation becomes more expensive; in the last five years the number of cases commenced doubled.

The same is true of the administration of estates and trusts. The increasing costs of administration invite greater scrutiny and challenge. The greater complexity of personal affairs and of the fiscal regime provides greater scope for oversight and error. The range of potential claimants grows. But here the increasing costs of litigation and more prominent commercial considerations mean that (sensibly) fewer of these cases proceed to a full hearing. A consequence of these private compromises is that in general there is less opportunity for the law to develop in a public way.

The careful professional knows of these perils and puts in place procedures to address them. To do so she or he needs a clear exposition of the relevant law supplemented by practical guidance.

This new edition of the book will be a great aid to such professionals. It speaks out of a depth of practical experience of will preparation and probate and trust administration and it thoroughly reviews judicial comment on the actual circumstances that have produced the disputes and the litigation. I commend the authors on their diligence and on the clarity of their presentation.

PREFACE TO THE FIRST EDITION

The leading rule for the lawyer, as for the man of every other calling, is diligence. Leave nothing for tomorrow which can be done today. Never let your correspondence fall behind. Whatever piece of business you have in hand, before stopping, do all the labour pertaining to it which can then be done.

A lot of the advice in this book is summarized in the above extract from notes prepared by President Abraham Lincoln for a law lecture in 1850. I think we can assume that if Mr Lincoln (as he then was) was sufficiently troubled by delays and lack of diligence to write out this note then he considered that he had an important problem to address—it is a lot of words for a man whose most famous speech was only 208 words longer.

What we have attempted to do is to highlight the areas of risk in will preparation, although the infinite ingenuity of clients and draftsmen will, in time, show us new possibilities that we did not contemplate during our researches. The administration of estates and trusts also presents us with the impossibility of covering every possible risk of a negligent action. In some cases, such as that of taxation, the dearth of case law has meant we can only suggest how the practitioner may seek to exclude any duty to the client in relation to such matters, or where such a duty is unavoidable, point out the common pitfalls that await him and how they may be avoided. Our collectively lengthy experience of the subject has taught us nothing if it has not taught us that there will always be new ways of getting it wrong.

We have therefore tried to approach much of the subject matter from the point of view of avoidance of risk and, where possible, promoting general awareness of risk and policies to reduce it. 'Reduce' is important in this context as we do not believe that elimination of risk is possible.

PREFACE TO THE SECOND EDITION

We are living in a time when wills have a greater importance than ever before. Greater wealth is now more widely held by a greater proportion of the population than ever before. Hand in hand with this goes an increase in will and estate disputes. There are many reasons for the rise in disputes, including changes in the composition and structure of society (significantly mobility and longevity), all of which make the draftsman's work more challenging. Despite this, the work involved in wills seems to be valued less by the clients that need them. Perhaps this might be better expressed as the value of the work, knowledge, and skill involved in a will is not recognized by the clients.

This paradox creates a dangerous market for the product. It is one where expectations and needs are high, but these are expected by clients to be met at unrealistically low prices. Lack of profit from wills forces reductions in training and qualifications in order to try to deliver the product with any chance of a profit, however small it might eventually be. This in turn leads practitioners to complain that the stance of the court over issues of negligence and practice for wills is unrealistic given the lack of reward for preparing them. While we understand this point of view, we wholeheartedly believe that the court must be right to try to maintain appropriate standards of practice.

The unregulated nature of the wills market does not help, nor does the lack of any mandatory standard of knowledge or training. But, because education and service levels cost money that may well not be recouped through increased fees, there is not a lot of hope for higher standards until regulation forces it. Regulation will raise fee levels, but is this not a realistic price for a person's last will, one of the most important financial documents that they will ever sign? A sound and well-planned will involves far more knowledge than the average client realizes. The growth in the number of disputed wills suggests to us that the present position is not working.

This is not to argue for wills to be a reserved legal activity. However, given the central importance of wills to property and inheritance, it does seem dangerous to support the present position which leaves the court alone in maintaining standards.

ACKNOWLEDGEMENTS

Thanks are due to all those who have been generous with their time and knowledge in providing us with information and, especially, materials.

Thanks are also due to our families who have yet again shown great patience and understanding with the disruption caused by the time demands that writing makes.

The *Wills and Trusts Law Reports* continues to be a leading source of materials in this area and great use has been made of these reports.

Lincoln and Lincoln's Inn
September 2013

CONTENTS

C ADMINISTRATION OF ESTATES AND TRUSTS

D TAXATION

F STATUTES AND APPENDICES

TABLE OF CASES

TABLE OF LEGISLATION

NATIONAL LEGISLATION

Australia

PART A

NEGLIGENCE AND WILL PREPARATION

1

AN INTRODUCTION TO TORT

A. Introduction

'Mistakes in the preparation of a will give no cause of action to the intended beneficiary since   **1.01**
the solicitor owes no duty to anyone other than his client, the testator'.[1] This observation from
Cordery on Solicitors in 1968 reflects the old, and long-standing, rejection of a draftsman's liability for his will preparation. It describes an approach that to the current age of extensive tortious
liability is quite startling in the absence of any beneficiary remedy for negligent work. Had it
remained a correct statement of the law today much of this book would not have been written.
That this quotation should now look out of place today helps to illustrate the change within society and its current, and growing, expectation that perceived wrongs will always have a remedy.

In 1979 the decision of Sir Robert Megarry V-C in *Ross v Caunters*[2] began a process of change   **1.02**
in the law's approach to this particular area of negligence. To understand why this change was
necessary, and how the modern law has then developed, it is helpful to look at why solicitors'
liability for negligent wills was previously viewed as impossible.

B. Privity of contract

Before *Ross v Caunters*, the question of liability for the actions, or inactions, of the will drafts-   **1.03**
man was considered to be a matter strictly defined by the application of privity of contract
to the contract between the draftsman and his client. Privity of contract is the concept that

---

[1] Graham J Graham-Green and Duncan S Gordon, *Cordery on Solicitors*, 6th edition (Butterworths
Law, 1968).
[2] [1979] 3 All ER 580; although ironically, Lord Goff's judgment in the House of Lords in *White v Jones*
[1995] 1 All ER 691 at 710c regarded the *ratio* in *Ross v Caunters*, although definitely not the result, as incorrect.

only those who are party to a contract may sue on it. When applied to will preparation in the past, this meant that

- only the testator and the draftsman were able to sue on the contract for the preparation of the will, ie the solicitor was solely responsible to his client;
- if the actions of the draftsman had been negligent, the loss to the testator was likely to be negligible (for negligence actions it is, of course, necessary for the claimant to show loss, not merely that something was done incorrectly); and
- the intended beneficiaries under the will who failed to benefit were not parties to the contract and could not sue on it.

The judgment in *Robertson v Fleming*

1.04 The judgment of the House of Lords in the Scottish case of *Robertson v Fleming*[3] epitomized the restrictive approach to any duty of care that the application of privity of contract produced. This mid-nineteenth century case did not concern the preparation of wills,[4] but its importance lies in the firm *dicta* of their Lordships.

1.05 Lord Campbell LC stated that a solicitor's duties in the preparation of a will could give rise to a cause of action 'only by showing privity of contract between the parties'. He went on to deny any assertion that a disappointed beneficiary could sue where a contractual relationship did not exist, and observed that

> If this were the law a disappointed legatee might sue the solicitor employed by a testator to make a will in favour of a stranger, whom the solicitor never saw or before heard of, if the will were void for not being properly signed and attested. I am clearly of the opinion that this is not the law of Scotland, nor of England, and it can hardly be the law of any country where jurisprudence has been cultivated as a science.[5]

1.06 His colleague Lord Cranworth also firmly endorsed this view:

> The doctrine contended for ... is evidently untenable. Such a doctrine would, as is pointed out by my noble friend, lead to the result, that a disappointed beneficiary might sue the testator's solicitor for negligence in not causing his will to be duly signed and attested, though he might be an entire stranger both to solicitor and the testator.[6]

1.07 Clearly, these wholehearted endorsements of privity of contract were a bar to will negligence actions then, and would remain so for some considerable time to come. Both of these speeches (which were in turn endorsed by their two other colleagues in the House) focus on the idea that someone unknown to the solicitor would make a claim, although in reality, as we now know, it is far more likely that the claimant would be a close relative of the testator and would quite probably be known to the solicitor in the sense that he is clearly identified by name in the instructions. Despite the remarks of their Lordships being *obiter*, *Robertson v Fleming* was seen as providing a binding precedent for privity of contract being a bar to action by any beneficiary, however close to the testator.[7]

---

[3] (1861) 4 Macq 167.

[4] Much of the issue depended on the meaning of the expression 'for behoof of'.

[5] *Robertson v Fleming* (n 3) at 177.

[6] *Robertson v Fleming* (n 3) at 185.

[7] From a modern perspective, it is strange to see negligence addressed as solely a contractual issue without consideration of tort. However, in 1938, in *Groom v Crocker* [1938] 2 All ER 394, it was held that at that time a solicitor's duty to his client was in contract only and not in tort.

Robertson v Fleming remained unchallenged on this point for over 100 years.[8] In theory, this   **1.08**
case should have put an end to the issue until such time as the House of Lords reviewed the
matter.[9] The answer as to how a lower court was able to develop the issue, notwithstanding
Robertson v Fleming, began with a bottle of ginger beer allegedly containing the remains of
a decomposing snail. However, before examining this unsavoury contribution to the law of
tort, there is one further privity of contract aspect which should be examined.

Modern reform of privity of contract

Privity was reformed by the Contracts (Rights of Third Parties) Act 1999,[10] which provided   **1.09**
for contracts to be enforceable by non-contracting parties who had benefit conferred on
them by the contract.

It is interesting to note at the outset that the Law Commissioners, when proposing this   **1.10**
reform, did not intend that it should extend to claims by disappointed beneficiaries.[11]

> The wording of our proposed reform is therefore not intended to include negligent will draft-
> ing... The crucial words are that the promise must be one to confer a benefit on the third party.
> The solicitor's express or implied promise to use reasonable care is not one by which the solici-
> tor is to confer a benefit on the third party. Rather it is one by which the solicitor is to enable
> the client to confer a benefit on the third party.

However, the question is possibly still open, at least to a degree, as to whether or not the   **1.11**
terms of the Act are in fact sufficiently wide to include contracts to prepare wills. While it is
arguable that s.1 is drawn in sufficiently wide terms potentially to catch such contracts, closer
scrutiny creates problems. Lord Mustill's dissenting House of Lords' judgment in *White v
Jones*[12] (expressed before this reform of contract law) identified a crucial issue:

> even under a much expanded law of contract it is hard to see an objection that what the testator
> intended to confer on the new beneficiaries was the benefit of his assets after his death; not the
> benefit of the solicitor's promise to draft the will.[13]

Separating the document from its effect in this way does not necessarily assist, as the issue of   **1.12**
the consequences of the contractual act must surely be what this problem is all about.

Greater help in rebutting the application of the 1999 Act can be obtained from looking at   **1.13**
what is actually conferred on the beneficiary, and this cannot reasonably be described as a
benefit. A solicitor's work is aimed at putting the client in a position whereby he can benefit
the beneficiaries if he chooses (and continues to choose to do so, as there is of course nothing
irrevocable about most wills). There is at this stage no benefit permanently conferred on the
beneficiary.

---

[8] 'I remember Roxburgh J, no doubt mindful of these authorities, once expressing the view, in a case in the
early 1950s, that the moral responsibility of a lawyer entrusted with the preparation of a will was a particularly
high one, since no one would be likely to have an effective legal remedy if he did the job badly' (Sir Christopher
Slade, 'Professional Liability in the Will-Making Process', in J Getzler (ed), *Rationalizing Property, Equity and
Trusts—Essays in Honour of Edward Burn* (LexisNexis, 2003).
[9] The House of Lords (now the Supreme Court) is not necessarily bound by its own previous decisions.
[10] Based on the Law Commission's recommendations in Law Comm 242 (1996).
[11] Law Comm 242 [1.9] and [7.20].
[12] [1995] 1 All ER 691.
[13] [1995] 1 All ER 691 at 723D.

1.14 Such benefit as there is conferred on the beneficiary is freely revocable by the testator without notice to the solicitor (the other party to the contract) and of no value during the testator's life. It does therefore seem that the nature of what is conferred on a third party, under a contract to prepare a will, is outside of the type of benefit contemplated by the draftsman of this act. This view was supported by the New Zealand Court of Appeal in *Gartside v Sheffield Young & Ellis*,[14] when they reviewed s.4 Contract (Privity) Act 1982 (New Zealand) and its possible application to a contract for a will (s.4 is similarly phrased to s.1 of the English Act). Cooke J observed:

> on an ordinary reading of the key s.4 of that Act, a prospective beneficiary under a proposed will could not invoke the Act. For the contract between the testator and the solicitor would not itself contain a promise conferring or purporting to confer a benefit on the prospective beneficiary. Putting the point in another way, the solicitor has not promised to confer a benefit on him.[15]

1.15 At present, whilst it is conceded that an argument could lie that this Act does confer a right on the disappointed beneficiary, it looks unlikely that such an argument would succeed. The issue is probably most safely dealt with within the contract to provide a will, by specifying that the terms of this Act are not applicable to the contract.

C. The growth of the tort of negligence

1.16 This book is not the place to attempt a detailed analysis of the growth of the tort of negligence, but a survey of the main features and issues involved is appropriate in order to explain and illustrate the way in which tort has developed and become capable of application to will preparation. It is also necessary in order that the features of liability in respect of will preparation can be more easily understood.

1.17 The tort of negligence can be held as being complete when three conditions are satisfied:

- the defendant owes a duty of care to the plaintiff;
- the defendant has acted or spoken in such a way as to breach that duty of care; and
- the plaintiff has suffered damage as a consequence of the breach.[16]

Donoghue v Stevenson

1.18 The 1932 House of Lords decision in *Donoghue v Stevenson*[17] is considered to have laid the foundations of the modern tort of negligence. A shop assistant's friend purchased for her a bottle of Stevenson's ginger beer at Mr Mingella's Wellmeadow café in Glasgow and she became ill after drinking it (along with the remains of a decomposing snail that it was alleged to have contained). The ensuing litigation, against the manufacturer of the drink as opposed to the vendor, by a party who did not directly purchase the product but consumed it, started the law on the course of liability for negligence where there is no contractual relationship between the parties,[18] but where there is such a degree of proximity that, as in this case, the manufacturer should reasonably have foreseen the consequences of his negligence:

---

[14] [1983] NZLR 37.
[15] [1983] NZLR 37 at 42.
[16] *Jackson & Powell on Professional Liability*, 7th edition (Sweet & Maxwell, 2011) [2-020].
[17] [1932] All ER Rep 1.
[18] Reportedly Mrs Donoghue's claim was settled for £200 before final trial of the issue.

The rule that you are to love your neighbour becomes, in law, you must not injure your neighbour; and the lawyer's question, Who is my neighbour? receives a restrictive reply. You must take reasonable care to avoid acts or omissions which you can reasonably foresee would be likely to injure your neighbour. Who then in law is my neighbour? The answer seems to be—persons who are so closely and directly affected by my act that I ought reasonably to have them in contemplation as being so affected when I am directing my mind to the acts or omissions which are called into question.[19]

This view originally contemplated physical damage or harm to the plaintiff. Therefore, although this decision started the development of modern tort in the direction that would eventually dispose of the privity of contract restriction on liability for will preparation, it had not yet travelled nearly far enough.   **1.19**

Hedley Byrne and economic loss

Liability in tort for purely financial harm was established with the House of Lords' 1963 decision in *Hedley Byrne & Co Ltd v Heller & Partners Ltd*.[20] It is true to say that the extent of the duty in financial loss cases had caused the courts difficulty and, despite this decision, was to continue to do so.   **1.20**

I consider that it follows and that it should now be regarded as settled that if someone possessed of a special skill undertakes, quite irrespective of contract, to apply that skill for the assistance of another person who relies upon such skill, a duty of care would arise. The fact that the services to be given are by means of or by the instrumentality of words can make no difference. Furthermore, if in a sphere in which a person is so placed that others could reasonably rely upon his judgement or skill or upon his ability to make careful enquiry, a person takes it upon himself to give information or advice to, or allows his information or advice to be passed on to, another person who, as he knows or should know, will place reliance upon it, then a duty of care will arise.[21]

In *Hedley Byrne*, the possible injustice of the liability extending to all misstatements was recognized, and their Lordships favoured the nature of the relationship as being a controlling factor in determining the extent of the duty. This nature of relationship test has also been described as the assumption of responsibility, ie 'Had the person making the misstatement assumed responsibility towards the party suffering loss?' That is to say, did he know, or should he reasonably have known, that his statement would be relied upon by the third party? Reliance on the statement by the third party was seen as an important element of this decision; indeed almost an essential element. However, in the cases considered later, concerning beneficiaries failing to benefit under wills, it was clear that the beneficiaries could not have placed any reliance on the solicitor's work as they need not have known about it, nor could they have reasonably relied on their legacy, being as it is before the testator's death, a mere *spes*.   **1.21**

Generally speaking the intended beneficiary will   **1.22**

- be unaware of the testator's intentions;
- will have done nothing in reliance of the testator's intentions;
- will not have changed their position to their detriment in reliance of the testator's intentions;
- have been given no assurances of any kind by the solicitor.

---

[19] Per Lord Atkin [1932] All ER Rep 1 at 580.
[20] [1963] 2 All ER 575.
[21] Per Lord Morris, *Hedley Byrne* (n 20) at 594.

1.23 These aspects were to cause difficulty in the beneficiary cases, although in the first will negligence case, *Ross v Caunters*, Megarry V-C found that reliance was not an essential part of the *Hedley Byrne* principle.[22]

1.24 The decision in *Hedley Byrne* overruled the earlier majority decision in *Candler v Crane, Christmas & Co*[23] on this particular issue, and supported the dissenting judgment of Denning LJ in that case. *Hedley Byrne* established that there was liability for words as well as deeds, and for pure economic loss as well as physical damage.[24] It was not necessary that these words were spoken or written directly to the party who claimed the injury.

1.25 The view of economic loss in *Hedley Byrne* was not restricted to misstatements, and was extended to economic loss from actions and omissions through the decisions in *Caparo Industries plc v Dickman*[25] and *Henderson v Merrett Syndicates*.[26] However, these decisions did not, either singly or collectively, reach the point that it was axiomatic that liability for negligence in will preparation was established. The decisions in *Ross v Caunters* and *White v Jones* both required reconsideration of these preceding cases before their principles were extended to will preparation, but it was not always clear how they were being extended and to what extent.

Tests of relationship

1.26 The nature of the relationship and assumed responsibility are only part of the continuing judicial angst regarding testing the relationship between the two parties.[27] However, this particular area lies outside the scope of this book as the decision in *White v Jones* clearly established that the intended beneficiaries were sufficiently proximate to the draftsman for it to be reasonable that they were owed a duty of care.

1.27 The editors of *Jackson & Powell*[28] set out the following principles as underlying the current law of negligence:

1. A tortious duty is imposed by law on *A* in relation to *B*. *A* does not himself agree to the imposition of the duty, although it may result from his voluntary acts or agreement. A finding that *A* owes *B* a duty of care is therefore a legal conclusion drawn from the relevant facts.

2. At the heart of liability for negligence is that *A* should reasonably have foreseen that carelessness on his part could result in damage to *B* or to a 'relevant' class to which *B* belongs. It does not follow that *A* owes a duty of care to *B*, but absent reasonable foreseeability of damage, he will not do so.[29]

---

[22] [1979] 3 All ER 580 at 592.

[23] [1951] 1 All ER 426.

[24] The *Hedley Byrne* principle has also been described as 'the rationalisation or technique adopted by English law to provide a remedy for the recovery of damages in respect of economic loss caused by the negligent performance of services' (Lord Steyn in *Williams v Natural Life Health Foods Ltd* [1998] 1 WLR 830 at 834F).

[25] [1990] 1 All ER 568.

[26] [1994] 3 All ER 506.

[27] 'The more I think about these cases, the more difficult I find it to put each into its own proper pigeon hole. Sometimes I say: "There was no duty". In others I say "The damage was too remote". So much so that I think the time has come to discard those tests which have proved so elusive. It seems to me better to consider the particular relationship in hand, and see whether or not, as a matter of policy, economic loss should be recoverable' (Lord Denning in *Spartan Steel Alloys Ltd v Martin & Co (Contractors) Ltd* [1972] 3 All ER 557).

[28] *Jackson & Powell on Professional Liability* (n 16) at [02-081].

[29] *Hamilton v Papakura DC* [2002] UKPC 9; 3 NZLR 308. There is no single fixed standard of reasonable foreseeability. The degree of foreseeability required is related to the consequences which might be foreseen. The

3. While careless infliction of reasonably foreseeable physical injury, or reasonably foreseeable damage to goods or other property, requires to be justified if A is not to be required to compensate B for having inflicted it, that is not the case where the damage suffered does not involve personal injury or damage to goods or other property.[30]

4. In the latter case (which covers both pure economic loss and the failure to confer a benefit), the law of tort recognizes both the difficulties in imposing a potentially wide liability on A and that it may be entirely legitimate and consistent with public policy for A to cause pure economic loss[31] or fail to confer a benefit.

5. Whatever the nature of the damage, a duty of care should be found where, and only where, it is reasonable for A to be liable to compensate B for having negligently caused the damage in question.[32]

It is not suggested that these principles provide a framework to evaluate any novel situation: **1.28** they explain where the development of the law has reached today.

Evolution of the law of torts in the area of wills

In considering the application of the law of tort to the area of wills, it is important to remem- **1.29** ber that tort is an area of law that continues to develop and that the urge to do practical justice to new types of claims leads to new developments.[33] It is also unwise to take an unduly rigid view of the legal principles involved given this evolving nature of torts[34] and the degree of willingness, on the part of the judiciary, to blur the boundaries between different areas. This means that where there are areas of will preparation in which the court has not yet considered questions of liability, it is unwise to assume that a court might not at some future date find a duty of care that develops existing features of the duty of care in a new way. Tort is a judge-developed area of law and nothing in the decisions commented on in this work would lead the authors to conclude that it will not develop further in time.

---

more serious the damage, the lesser the degree of likelihood of its occurrence that is needed (*Jolley v Sutton LBC* [2000] 1 WLR 1082; *Attorney-General of the Virgin Islands v Hartwell* [2004] UKPC 4; 1 WLR 1273).

[30] Lord Oliver in *Murphy v Brentwood DC* [1991] 1 AC 398 at 487B–C: 'The infliction of physical injury to the person or property of another universally requires to be justified. The causing of economic loss does not. If it is to be categorised as wrongful it is necessary to find some factor beyond mere occurrence of the loss and the fact that this occurrence could be foreseen.' But Cooke P in *South Pacific Manufacturing Co Ltd v New Zealand Security Consultants and Investigations Ltd* [1992] 2 NZLR 282 at 296: 'The first concern of the law is naturally personal safety. Injury to the person is a kind of damage in a class of its own. Or at least most people would, I think, say so. On the other hand, a plaintiff awarded damages for harm to property is being compensated essentially for economic loss. It would be a crude system of law that drew a vital distinction for this purpose between tangible and intangible property interests.'

[31] Lord Reid in *Dorset Yacht Co Ltd v Home Office* [1970] AC 1004 at 1027B: 'For example causing economic loss is a different matter; for one thing, it is often caused by deliberate action. Competition involves traders being entitled to damage their rivals' interests by promoting their own, and there is a long chapter of law determining in what circumstances owners of land can and in what circumstances they may not use their proprietary rights so as to injure their neighbours.'

[32] Lord Reid in *Hedley Byrne* (n 20): 'The law ought so far as possible to reflect the standards of the reasonable man'.

[33] 'Just as equity remedied the inadequacies of the common law, so has the law of torts filled gaps left by other causes of action where the interests of justice so required' (Bingham LJ in *Simaan General Contracting Co v Pilkington Glass Ltd (No 2)* [1988] 1 All ER 791).

[34] 'The law of contract and the law of tort are, in a modern context, properly to be seen as but two of a number of imprecise divisions, for the purpose of classification, of a general body of rules constituting one coherent system of law' (Deane J in *Hawkins v Clayton* [1988] 164 CLR 539 at 584).

D. Negligent actions

1.30 The standard definition of negligence is to be found in McNair J's direction to the jury in *Bolam v Friern Hospital Management Committee*:[35]

> I must explain what in law we mean by 'negligence'. In the ordinary case which does not involve any special skill, negligence means this:
>
> Some failure to do some act which a reasonable man in the circumstances would do, or doing some act which a reasonable man in the circumstances would not do; and if that failure or doing of that act results in injury, then there is a cause of action. How do you test whether this act or failure is negligent? In an ordinary case it is generally said, that you judge that by the action of the man in the street. He is the ordinary man. In one case it has been said that you judge it by the conduct of the man on the top of the Clapham omnibus. He is the ordinary man. But where you get a situation which involves the use of some special skill or competence, then the test whether there has been negligence or not is not the test of the man on the top of the Clapham omnibus, because he has not got this special skill. The test is the standard of the ordinary skilled man exercising and professing to have that special skill. A man need not possess the highest expert skill at the risk of being found negligent. It is well established law that it is sufficient if he exercises the ordinary skill of the ordinary competent man exercising that particular art. I do not think I quarrel much with any of the submissions in law which have been put before you by counsel. Counsel for the plaintiff put it this way, that in the case of a medical man negligence means failure to act in accordance with the standards of reasonably competent medical men at the time. That is a perfectly accurate statement, as long as it is remembered that there may be one or more perfectly proper standards; and if a medical man conforms with one of those proper standards then he is not negligent.

1.31 This passage deals with failures and omissions that fall short of acceptable standards and in examining this subject it is important to differentiate between these and errors of judgement for which a professional need not be culpable.

> The onus of proving professional negligence over and above errors of judgement is a heavy one.[36]
>
> [T]he duty of care is not a warranty of a perfect result.[37]
>
> Many would wish that the right to recovery . . . did not depend on proof of negligence. But as long as it does, defendants are not to be held negligent unless they are in truth held to have fallen short of the standards I have mentioned.[38]
>
> It is of equal importance that the actions which are being judged are judged in accordance with prevailing knowledge and circumstances and not in retrospect and with the benefit of hindsight.[39]

---

[35] [1957] 1 WLR 582 at 586–7.

[36] Per Simon Brown LJ in *Martin Boston and Co v Roberts* [1996] PNLR 45, CA, citing *Rondel v Worsley* [1969] 1 AC 191. See also: 'At best, the case against the defendant is marginal, and a marginal case does not make negligence' (Megarry J (as he then was) in *Duchess of Argyll v Beuselinck* [1972] 2 Lloyd's Rep 172 at 185).

[37] *Wilsher v Essex Area Health Authority* [1987] AC 1074.

[38] Bingham LJ in *Eckersley v Binnie* (1988) 18 Con LR 1.

[39] 'In this world there are few things that could not have been better done if done with hindsight. The advantages of hindsight include the benefit of having a sufficient indication of which of many factors present are important and which are unimportant. But hindsight is no touchstone of negligence. The standard of care to be expected of the professional man must be based on events as they occur, in prospect and not in retrospect' (Megarry J in *Duchess of Argyll v Beuselinck* (n 36) at 185).

The standard to be applied does not encompass the solicitor being faultless in his judgement[40] (except perhaps in basic or extremely simple matters) nor is it expected that the solicitor should have an all encompassing knowledge of the law.[41] But, the view has been expressed in Canada that a solicitor 'must have sufficient knowledge of the fundamental issues or principles of law applicable to the particular work he has undertaken to enable him to perceive the need to ascertain the relevant point'.[42]

1.32

The clear implication of this is that, in terms of will preparation, a sound knowledge of the fundamentals of the law relating to wills is required of the will-preparer.[43]

1.33

During the post-war period, in parallel to the growth of the tort of negligence, there has also been an examination and re-examination of the question of whether or not a solicitor can owe a duty to a client in tort as well as in contract. Despite earlier decisions to the contrary,[44] it is currently regarded as settled that the duties in contract and tort coexist[45] in so far as a client is concerned. For a breach of either duty to occur, the solicitor must have been negligent in the sense that he failed to meet the standard which can reasonably be expected of him: 'The basic rule is that negligence consists in doing something that a reasonable man would not have done in that situation or omitting to do something that a reasonable man would have done in that situation.'[46]

1.34

In considering whether or not a solicitor's actions or inactions amount to negligence, it should be borne in mind that professionals are not to be liable for damage caused by, what in the light of events, transpires to have been an error of judgement in a matter where the opinions of reasonably well-informed and competent members of the same profession might have differed. Such professionals should only be liable for matters that no member of the profession who was reasonably well informed and competent would have done or omitted to have done.[47] However, the difference between an act of negligence and an error

1.35

---

[40] *Godefroy v Dalton* (1830) 6 Bing 460: 'he is not answerable for error in judgement upon points of new occurrence, or of nice or doubtful construction, or of such as are usually entrusted to men in the higher branch of the profession of the law'; approved in *Fletcher & Son v Jubb, Booth & Helliwell* [1920] 1 KB 275.

[41] 'No attorney is bound to know all the law; God forbid that it should be imagined that an attorney, or a counsel, or even a Judge is bound to know all the law; or that an attorney is to lose his fair recompense on account of an error, being such an error as a cautious man might fall into' (*Montriou v Jefferys* (1825) 2 C & P 113); 'it is not the duty of a solicitor to know the contents of every statute of the realm. But there are some statutes which it is his duty to know' (*Fletcher & Son v Jubb, Booth & Helliwell* (n 40)).

[42] *Central Trust Co v Rafuse* [1987] 31 DLR (4th) 481.

[43] See later at Chapter 5 Part A regarding who should draft wills.

[44] Notably *Groom v Crocker* [1938] 2 All ER 394, but also *Clark v Kirkby-Smith* [1964] 2 All ER 835, *Bagot v Stevens Scanlan & Co Ltd* [1966] 3 All ER 577 and *Cook v Swinfen* [1967] 1 All ER 299 wherein Lord Denning MR observed 'an action against a solicitor is always one for breach of contract'.

[45] *Henderson v Merrett Syndicates Ltd* [1994] 3 All ER 826 approving *Midland Bank Trust Co Ltd v Hett, Stubbs & Kemp* [1978] 3 All ER 571 on this point; see also Lord Denning MR in *Esso Petroleum Co Ltd v Mardon* [1976] QB 801 where he considered *Groom v Crocker* to be wrong. However, note also *Holt v Payne Skillington* [1995] 77 BLR 51 where an act beyond the contractual retainer can give rise to a liability in tort that is greater than the liability under the contract.

The coexistence of contractual and tortious liability for solicitors is also to be found in Canada (*Central Trust Co v Rafuse* [1987] 31 DLR (4th) 481), in Australia (*Astley v Austrust Ltd* [1999] Lloyd's Rep PN 758), in New Zealand (*Mouat v Clark Boyce* [1992] 2 NZLR 559), and in Ireland (*Finlay v Murtagh* [1979] IR 249).

[46] Per Lord Bridge in *Hazell v British Transport Commission* [1958] 1 WLR 169 at 171.

[47] *Saif Ali v Sidney Mitchell* [1980] AC 198 at 218D (per Lord Diplock).

of judgement is difficult.[48] In the latter, the circumstances under which advice was given (particularly time pressure) can be a factor,[49] as can the degree of risk attached to the original advice.

Test for standard to be applied to the duty

1.36 The standard of 'the reasonable man' is traditionally expressed as being that of the ordinary citizen,[50] unless this test is being applied to a specialist defendant (as in the subject of this book), when the standard must be that of the reasonably competent practitioner in the profession in question.

1.37 McNair J explained this as:

> Where you get a situation which involves the use of some special skill or competence, then the test as to whether there has been negligence or not is not the test of the man on the top of the Clapham omnibus, because he has not got this special skill. The test is the standard of the ordinary skilled man exercising and professing to have that special skill. A man need not possess the highest expert skill; it is established law that it is sufficient if he exercises the ordinary skill of an ordinary competent man exercising that particular art.[51]

1.38 In addition, Oliver J observed in *Midland Bank v Hett, Stubbs & Kemp*[52] that a solicitor must not be judged by the standard of a 'particularly meticulous and conscientious practitioner. The test is what the reasonably competent practitioner would do having regard to the standards normally adopted in his profession'.

1.39 However, in applying this standard is it to be the standard that is

- ordinarily achieved by members of the profession;[53] or
- in the view of the court, the standard which members of the profession ought to achieve?[54]

1.40 The difference between these two possibilities might, on occasion, be difficult to see. In practice, as the court is the arbiter of the standard, the second view is the one that will ultimately prevail, albeit that the court will at least be informed of the former and may choose to apply

---

[48] 'Merely to describe something as an error of judgement tells us nothing about whether it is negligent or not. The true position is that an error of judgement may, or may not be, negligent; it depends on the nature of the error' (*Whitehouse v Jordan* [1981] 1 WLR 246).

[49] *Griffin v Kingsmill* [2001] Lloyd's Rep PN 716.

[50] The famous man on the Clapham omnibus from *Hall v Brooklands Racing Club* [1933] 1 KB 205, although he seems to have appeared earlier in *McQuire v Western Morning News* [1903] 2 KB 100, a libel case, in which Sir Richard Henn Collins MR attributed the term to Lord Bowen, who had died nine years earlier. Wikipedia suggests, without citation, that it is derived from the phrase 'the bald-headed man at the back of the omnibus', coined by the nineteenth-century journalist Walter Bagehot to describe the normal man of London.

[51] See the direction to the jury in *Bolam v Friern Hospital Management Committee* (n 35) at 586. It is suggested in *Jackson & Powell on Professional Liability* (n 16) at [11-111] that nineteenth-century decisions on the standard of skill and care expected of solicitors should now be treated with caution except to the extent that they set out matters of principle that may have been approved more recently. Clearly, both the nature of practice and the standards expected have changed considerably since then.

[52] [1978] 3 All ER 571; subsequently approved in *Martin Boston & Co v Roberts* [1996] 1 PNLR 45.

[53] *Bolam v Friern Hospital Management Committee* (n 35); *Halsbury's Laws of England* (4th edition) Vol 34 [12].

[54] *Midland Bank Trust Co Ltd v Hett, Stubbs & Kemp* (n 45): 'The extent of the legal duty in any given situation must, I think, be a question of law for the court'; *Bown v Gould & Swayne* [1996] PNLR 130; *X v Woollcombe Yonge* [2001] WTLR 301.

it as their appropriate standard if there is no foreseeable risk.[55] In *Bolitho v City and Hackney HA*[56] it was observed in the House of Lords that:

> The court is not bound to hold that a defendant doctor escapes liability for negligent treatment or diagnosis just because he leads evidence from a number of medical experts who are genuinely of the opinion that the defendant's treatment or diagnosis accorded with sound medical practice ... responsible, reasonable and respectable—all show that the court has to be satisfied that the exponents of the body of opinion relied upon can demonstrate that such an opinion has a logical basis.

This was later applied in *Patel v Daybells*[57] with the explanation: **1.41**

> If a practice in the profession exposes clients or patients to a foreseeable and avoidable risk, the practice may not be capable of being defended on rational grounds, and in those circumstances the fact that it is commonly (or even universally) followed will not exclude liability for negligence.

This means that evidence of what constitutes the standards set and widely attained in the   **1.42**
profession is of prime importance.[58] Non-compliance with professional standards is not in
itself proof of negligence, but is clearly a significant factor for the court to take into account.[59]
Interesting issues are raised by this test when, as for wills, different professions provide the
same service. There is little judicial comment on this issue, apart from *Esterhuizen v Allied
Dunbar*[60] (where it was accepted that the standards applying to solicitors should apply to
a non-solicitor will-preparer). It seems reasonable that a uniform standard is applied to
will-preparers, and the only practical standard is that which is applied to solicitors.

Different standards of care within the same profession

There is a difference in the standard of care expected of a remunerated trustee and unremu-   **1.43**
nerated trustee,[61] but as yet there is no definitive answer to the question as to whether or not
within the legal profession there are differences based upon claimed expertise (which will
often be reflected in different levels of remuneration). However, there is a real prospect of a
court imposing on certain members of the profession a higher duty than might be imposed
upon the rest of that profession. The Trustee Act 2000 introduced a statutory duty of care[62]
in respect of the exercise of certain designated powers of trustees and personal representatives.[63] This duty of care expressly requires that regard must be had to any special knowledge
or experience that the trustee or personal representative has, or holds himself out as having.

As far as the administration of trusts is concerned, this point was approached earlier by Brightman   **1.44**
J in *Bartlett v Barclays Bank Trust Company Ltd*[64] when he held that he was of the opinion 'that

---

[55] *Simmons v Pennington* [1955] 1 WLR 183.
[56] [1997] 4 All ER 771.
[57] [2002] PNLR 6; see also from Eire *Roche v Peilow* [1986] ILRM 189 and *Donovan v Cork County Council* [1967] IR 173 and from Hong Kong *Edward Wong Finance Co Ltd v Johnson Stokes & Master* [1984] AC 296 (Privy Council).
[58] See, eg the expert evidence on behalf of the plaintiff referred to in *Esterhuizen v Allied Dunbar* [1998] 2 FLR 668.
[59] *Johnson v Bingley Dyson & Furey* [1997] PNLR 392.
[60] [1998] 2 FLR 668.
[61] '[A] paid trustee is expected to exercise a higher standard of diligence and knowledge than an unpaid trustee' (per Harman J in Re *Waterman's Will Trusts* [1952] 2 All ER 1054).
[62] Section 1 Trustee Act 2000.
[63] Schedule 1 Trustee Act 2000.
[64] [1980] 1 All ER 139.

a higher duty of care is plainly due from someone like a trust corporation which carries on a specialised business of trust management'.[65] Although, in this instance, this view was used to distinguish between the level of expertise expected from a trust corporation and a prudent man or woman, there is clear notice being taken of claimed levels of expertise.

1.45 This view was developed further by Harman J in *Cancer Research Campaign v Ernest Brown & Co*[66] when he drew a distinction between the tax planning abilities of members of chambers in Lincoln's Inn and 'ordinary people in the ordinary way of [legal] business or…a legal executive in a small high street firm of solicitors'.[67] By commenting on the legal executive and the small high street firm of solicitors, he left unanswered the question of the experienced and knowledgeable legal practitioner when compared to the small high street firm.

1.46 This same question had earlier been left unanswered by Megarry J (as he then was) in *Duchess of Argyll v Beuselink*:[68]

> No doubt the inexperienced solicitor is liable if he fails to attain the standard of a reasonably competent solicitor. But if the client employs a solicitor of high standing and great experience, will an action for negligence fail if it appears that the solicitor did not exercise the care and skill expected of him, though he did not fall below the standard of a reasonably competent solicitor? If the client engages an expert, and doubtless expects to pay commensurate fees, is he not entitled to expect something more than the standard of the reasonably competent? I am speaking not merely of those experts in a particular branch of the law, as contrasted with a general practitioner, but also of those of long experience and great skill contrasted with those practising in the same field of law but being of a more ordinary calibre and having less experience.… If, as is usual, the retainer contains no express term as to the solicitor's duty of care, and the matter rests upon an implied term, what is that implied term, what is that term in the case of a solicitor of long experience and standing or specialist skill?…I wish to make it clear that I have not overlooked the point which one day may require further consideration.

1.47 It is unfortunate that, having so well expressed the question, it was not necessary for Megarry J to then go on and answer it.[69]

1.48 There are very pertinent remarks in *Nederlandse Reassurantie Groep Holding NV v Bacon & Woodrow and Ernest & Young*[70] on special skills:

> having undertaken to provide that advice (they) were obliged to exercise all reasonable professional care in their work.… The standard of care to be expected is to be measured by reference to the quality of work reasonably to be expected from a professional firm…possessed of the skills which by undertaking the work in question that firm…warranted that it had.

---

[65] [1980] 1 All ER 139 at 152c.

[66] [1997] STC 1425.

[67] Whether or not the ability to handle tax saving deeds of variation is correctly treated as a specialist skill must be open to question given their current widespread and everyday use by probate practitioners.

[68] [1972] 2 Lloyd's Rep 172 at 183 (concerning a contract for the publication of the memoirs of Margaret, Duchess of Argyll who the court acknowledged, with some considerable understatement, 'was much in the public eye' at the time of the contract).

[69] As was again the case when the Court of Appeal heard *Martin Boston and Co v Roberts* [1996] PNLR 45, CA: 'It may be, as a passage in Megarry J's judgment in the Duchess of Argyll case suggests, that different standards apply, depending upon the different level of experience, expertise and, indeed, expensiveness of individual solicitors. For present purposes, however, it seems to me immaterial to explore the accuracy of that proposition or how far it may be taken' (per Simon Brown LJ). Canada has explored this in *Elcano Acceptance Ltd v Richmond, Richmond, Stambler & Mills* [1985] 31 CCLT 201 and *Confederation Life v Shepherd, McKenzie* [1992] 29 RPR (2d) 271 and accepted different standards for a specialist and a general practitioner.

[70] [1997] LRLR 678.

If the skill that is warranted is a specialist skill, the client is entitled to the standard of work reasonably to be expected of a specialist professional possessed of that skill. To measure the standard of care in such a case by reference to a non-specialist professional would be wrong in principle because it would involve a dislocation between the skill that was contractually assumed and the quality of work to be expected.

The standard of care is further to be measured by reference to the purpose for which the client required the advice. The magnitude of the loss that the client might suffer if the advice given turned out to be wrong is a material factor in setting the standard of professional care to be expected.

Also in *Hicks v Russell Jones & Walker*,[71] Henderson J observed that

the standard to be applied is in my judgment that of a reasonably competent solicitor with experience in the fields of commercial litigation and insolvency, including the conduct of complex appeals. RJW are a well-known City of London firm, and it would be absurd to judge them by the same standard as a small country firm.

This goes some considerable way to addressing Megarry's question (above) in *Duchess of Argyll v Beuselink*. Whilst the question is to some extent unsettled, we consider that it would be imprudent not to try to act to the accepted standard (the reasonably competent practitioner) for the area of work in which the solicitor specializes,[72] whilst at the same time being aware that a court will, quite possibly, hold the solicitor accountable for any higher expertise that he has claimed in that area of work. Although it does not yet appear to be a factor in liability, it must be open to question that a court could expect a higher standard from a solicitor whose charging rate was higher than his peers in order to reflect claimed skills and experience above those usually exhibited by his peers. **1.49**

In this connection it should not be assumed that undertaking work for a reduced, or small, fee reduces the standard of care expected of the draftsman;[73] a point which for will preparation deserves to be underlined for all draftsmen, given the level of fees too often charged.

In *Matrix Securities v Theodore Goddard*,[74] however, the standard applied to a city firm giving corporate tax advice was that which could be expected of a reasonably competent firm with a specialist tax department, ie that there was no higher duty expected within those specializing in the same field. **1.50**

The Court of Appeal in *Balamoan v Holden & Co*[75] held that a small country solicitor instructed by a legally aided client in a comparatively small claim should not be the subject **1.51**

---

[71] [2007] EWHC 940 (Ch).
[72] *Matrix-Securities Ltd v Theodore Goddard* [1998] PNLR 290: 'such skill and care as a reasonably competent solicitor in the relevant sector of the profession'. See also *Elcano Acceptance Ltd v Richmond, Richmond, Stambler & Mills* (n 69); also Etherton J in *Grimm v Newman* [2002] STC 84: 'the way in which a reasonably competent accountant tax adviser, with the same specialism as the First Defendant, would have responded to the request for advice'.
[73] *Johnson v Bingley, Dyson & Furey* (n 59); *Investors' Friend Ltd v Leathes Prior* [2011] EWHC 711 QB: 'When solicitors undertake work at a specific fee, they are generally speaking obliged to complete it exercising the ordinary standard of care, even if it has become unremunerative'; *Paratus AMC Ltd v Countrywide Surveyors Ltd* [2011] EWHC 3307 (Ch): 'a valuer is not excused from doing what is necessary to provide a competent valuation merely by the low level of his remuneration'; *Hicks v Russell Jones & Walker* (n 71): 'As [the claimants] were legally aided, RJW were bound to act on their behalf as if they were private clients of moderate means'.
[74] [1998] PNLR 290.
[75] (1999) 149 NLJ 898.

of too rigorous a standard of care in those particular circumstances as the solicitor was anxious not to incur costs which could not be recovered from the other side. It was held to be of 'critical importance' that too rigorous a standard was not applied. However, notwithstanding this, the Court of Appeal also observed that

> it is necessary to apply the standard of care reasonably to be expected of a reasonably careful litigation solicitor who holds himself out as competent to practise in the field of law in which his client has engaged his services. A one man firm cannot expect a lower standard of care to be applied to it merely because it delegates the conduct of its client's affairs to an unqualified member of its staff, however experienced. If the conduct of that member of staff falls below the standard appropriate for a solicitor, and he does not seek appropriate advice from counsel or from a solicitor in the firm when need arises, then the firm cannot complain about a finding of negligence against it. (per Brooke LJ)

1.52 The latter part of this passage highlights an additional area of risk for the practitioner who may overlook that the standard of care will remain that of the solicitor despite delegation to others of his staff.[76]

1.53 The Court of Appeal has also examined the reliance or otherwise that may be placed by a solicitor on counsel's views. If a solicitor having properly instructed counsel acts in accordance with that advice, he will not usually be negligent even if counsel's advice proves to be mistaken or misconceived. However, he will be at fault if he does not reject advice from counsel that is obviously or glaringly wrong.[77]

1.54 The latter point was considered and accepted in *Estill v Cowling Swift & Kitchen*.[78] Here the court quoted with approval Sir Thomas Bingham MR in *Ridehalgh v Horsefield*:[79]

> We endorse the guidance given on the subject in *Locke v Camberwell Health Authority*.[80] A solicitor does not abdicate his professional responsibility when he seeks the advice of counsel. He must apply his mind to the advice received. But the more specialist the nature of the advice, the more reasonable is it likely to be for a solicitor to accept and act on it.

1.55 The court in *Estill* cited the principles from *Locke* as being:

1. In general a solicitor is entitled to rely upon the advice of counsel properly instructed.
2. For a solicitor without specialist experience in a particular field to rely on counsel's advice is to make normal and proper use of the Bar.
3. However, he must not do so blindly but must exercise his own independent judgement. If he reasonably thinks counsel's advice is obviously or glaringly wrong, it is his duty to reject it.

---

[76] *Richards v Cox* [1943] 1 KB 139 involved a question of the solicitor's liability for the actions of his clerk. The Court of Appeal in *Balamoan* described it as 'an example of the principle that a solicitor may be acting at his peril if he creates unnecessary risks for his client by letting his clerk act in matters beyond his competence by advising on points which ought to be referred to counsel'. There is an Australian authority which found for the opposite view: that the standard applicable to a managing clerk was that of a managing clerk and not a solicitor: *Shigeva v Schafer* [1984] 5 NSWLR 502.

[77] 'He is not entitled to rely blindly and with no mind of his own on counsel's views', May LJ in *Davy-Chiesman v Davy-Chiesman* [1984] Fam 48 and also Dillon LJ in the same case: 'The solicitor is highly trained and expected to be experienced in his particular fields of law and he does not abdicate all responsibility whatever by instructing counsel.'

[78] [2000] WTLR 417 (a case involving the preparation of a trust deed).

[79] [1994] Ch 205 at 237G.

[80] [1991] 2 Med LR 249.

This will not assist where the instructions to counsel are wrong or inadequate and such defects led to defective advice.

An example of the risks of acting outside of a solicitor's area of knowledge and expertise is to **1.56** be found in *Credit Lyonnais v Russell Jones & Walker*[81] where the defendant firm were found to have breached their duty of care. They assigned responsibility for the claimants' property work to a corporate lawyer who the court found to be 'a lawyer who was not, and never claimed to be, a property lawyer'. The court observed that there was no reason to doubt that the solicitor concerned was

> an able and industrious corporate lawyer. No lawyer can hope to be an expert in all areas of law and he has never claimed to be an expert in property law. The fault which led to [the claimant's] problems can be traced back to the [defendant firm's] decision to assign a corporate lawyer to a property case.

Similarly in *Hurlingham Estates Ltd v Wilde & Partners*,[82] Lightman J held that a solicitor who had 'next to no knowledge of tax law and was quite unqualified to give tax advice' breached his duty of care to the client in failing to appreciate and advise on an exposure to tax in a property transaction.

E. The court as the arbiter of standards within the legal profession

When considering the standard of knowledge and expertise to be attributed to solicitors, **1.57** one should consider both how this refers to what a competent solicitor would have done in a particular set of circumstances and how a standard is established. This was set out clearly by Oliver J in *Midland Bank Trust Company v Hett, Stubbs & Kemp*, where he observed:

> The extent of the legal duty in any given situation must, I think, be a question of law for the court. Clearly if there is some practice in a particular profession, some accepted standard of conduct which is laid down by a professional institute or sanctioned by common usage, evidence of that can and ought to be received. But evidence which really amounts to no more than an expression of opinion by a particular practitioner of what he thinks he would have done had he been placed, hypothetically and without the benefit of hindsight, in the position of the defendants is of little assistance to the court, whilst evidence of the witnesses' view of what, as a matter of law, the solicitor's duty was in the particular circumstances of the case is, I should have thought, inadmissible, for that is the very question which it is the court's function to decide.[83]

The last point in the above quotation also highlights an issue on which courts have taken **1.58** differing views in wills negligence cases.

The purpose of expert evidence has been defined by the Court of Appeal as being 'that the **1.59** Court should reach a fully informed decision'[84] and it is for any party seeking to call expert evidence to satisfy the court that such evidence is available, relevant, and would assist the court. Relevance is the key, and this has been addressed as follows:

---

[81] [2002] EWHC 1310 (Ch).
[82] [1997] STC 627.
[83] [1978] 3 All ER 571.
[84] *United Bank of Kuwait v Prudential Property Services Ltd* [1995] EGCS 190.

although I am satisfied that both experts were doing their best to assist me, I found their evidence of limited value...A substantial part of their evidence appeared to be directed to establishing...a matter of law...That, it seems to me, is a matter for the court and not one for expert evidence.[85]

1.60 In *The Guild (Claims) Ltd v Eversheds*[86] (a matter concerning negligence in a company takeover) no expert evidence was introduced regarding the advice which should, or should not, have been given regarding a banking report. In considering this issue, Jacobs J noted the lack of expert evidence on the point:

> I was told that no solicitor expert evidence was provided because it was thought that the court would have the necessary expertise. Quite why, I do not know. Judges are unlikely to have had much experience of this sort of thing. Whilst they are equipped to decide points of law, practice in a field of expertise is something quite different.

1.61 It would seem that, as far as legal practices are concerned, the more esoteric or specialized an area of practice becomes, the more likely it is that a court would accept expert evidence to aid their understanding.

Admissibility of expert evidence in wills negligence cases

1.62 Neuberger J (as he then was) in *X v Woollcombe Yonge*[87] clearly disapproved of the value of such evidence in wills negligence cases, citing the above passage from Oliver J in *Midland Bank Trust Company v Hett, Stubbs & Kemp*. Neuberger J would not go so far as to accept that such evidence was inadmissible, given s.3 Civil Evidence Act 1972,[88] but was clearly disinclined to give it any weight, citing the following:

1. Jacob J in *Routestone Ltd v Minories Finance Ltd*: 'it by no means follows that the court must follow it'.[89]
2. Millett LJ in *Bown v Gould & Swayne*: 'I deplore the suggestion that it is either helpful or necessary to call evidence from high street solicitors whose individual practices may be eccentric and differ and whose practices certainly do not make the law of the land.'[90]
3. Brown LJ in the same case: 'What the solicitors should properly do in the very particular and highly individualistic circumstances of this case is by no means a matter of practice. It is a matter of law to be resolved by the judge.'[91]

---

[85] Etherton J in *Grimm v Newman* (n 72).

[86] [2000] Lloyd's Rep PN 910.

[87] [2001] WTLR 301 at 310.

[88] '3(1) Subject to any rules of Court made in pursuance of Part I of the Civil Evidence Act 1968 or this Act, where a person is called as a witness in any civil proceedings, his opinion on any relevant matter on which he is qualified to give expert evidence shall be admissible in evidence....

(3) In this section "relevant matter" includes an issue in the proceedings in question.'

Rule 35.1 CPR now limits expert evidence to that which is reasonably required to resolve the issue. Rule 35.4 CPR sets out the powers of the court to restrict expert evidence. The court's permission is required to adduce an expert report. Any application for permission must identify the particular area concerned and the expert responsible for the report.

[89] [1997] 1 EGLR 123.

[90] [1996] PNLR 130 at 137; also at 136: 'that is a matter of law and not practice. It does not require to be established by an expert witness. It is also a question of law whether the purchasers' solicitor was under a duty to inspect the property.'

[91] [1996] PNLR 130 at 135 and also: 'the evidence sought to be adduced falls foul of Oliver J's dictum. It would amount to no more than an expression of opinion by the expert, either as to what he himself would have done, which would not assist, or as to what he thinks should have been done, which would have been the very issue for the judge to determine.'

Evans-Lombe J in *Barings plc v Coopers & Lybrand*[92] expressed the view that admitting evidence under s.3(1) Civil Evidence Act 1972 was at the court's discretion if the court found that it would be relevant and helpful. This is a slightly stronger approach to admissibility than that shown in *X v Woollcombe Yonge*, but clearly with the same end result. **1.63**

In *X v Woollcombe Yonge*[93] Neuberger J observed that as neither expert before him relied on textbooks or practitioners' books to establish the basis of the practice that they were advocating, their evidence was of 'very limited value'. Although the experts gave opinions as to what was the right general practice in this area, the judge was left with the impression that all he was told was what either one would have done in the circumstances.[94] These remarks point clearly to the value of being able to demonstrate compliance with universal practice such as is established by accepted textbooks of practical guidance. **1.64**

This robust assertion of the court's function to decide such issues can be contrasted with the approach taken by Longmore J (as he then was) in *Esterhuizen v Allied Dunbar*,[95] when the court was faced with expert evidence only on behalf of one party. This expert's views were 'roundly attacked' in cross-examination by counsel for the defendant, but the defendant was not able, or perhaps chose not, to put forward their own expert. There is no suggestion in Longmore J's judgment that the expert's views in evidence were supported by 'text books or practitioners' books'. The judge instead found the expert's experience **1.65**

> entirely appropriate for the purpose of assisting me as to solicitor's practice in this area. I also find the substance of his evidence to be correct, partly because it was inherently convincing and partly because no evidence was called to challenge it.[96]

This does seem to be a very different approach to the more forceful line in *X v Woollcombe Yonge* and *Bown v Gould & Swayne*. Indeed one gets the impression when reading the *Esterhuizen* judgment that 'partly because no evidence was called to challenge it'[97] is of equal weight to the expert evidence itself. Therefore, far from being the determiner of practice, the court has in part gone against the defendant in default of it producing an expert (whose views would perhaps have mattered little in another court) and in part accepted the expert's evidence rather than weighing it more critically. **1.66**

Did the expert's evidence in *Esterhuizen* amount to any more than what Neuberger J had characterized as being no more than what the expert would have done in the circumstances? If this is the case, it might explain why some of the more controversial aspects of what was adopted from the expert evidence do not seem to be supported by contemporary 'text books or practitioners' books'.[98] Are we indeed faced with the possibility that the expert's evidence, now adopted and approved in *Esterhuizen*, was founded on views that in other courts would, if they had been admitted, have been treated as being of 'very limited value'? **1.67**

---

[92] [2001] EWHC Ch 17.
[93] Dealing with the inability of the two experts from either side to agree on whether or not the circumstances of the testatrix required the immediate preparation of a codicil or the rapid preparation of a new will.
[94] However, in *May v Woollcombe Beer & Watts* [1999] 1 PNLR 283 the court was inclined to admit expert evidence on conveyancing procedure because the textbooks provided no answer.
[95] [1998] 2 FLR 668.
[96] [1998] 2 FLR 668 at 673H.
[97] [1998] 2 FLR 668 at 674A.
[98] Part of Neuberger J's test in *X v Woollcombe Yonge* (n 54).

In *X v Woollcombe Yonge* the expert evidence was admitted but given very little if any weight as opposed to the evidence being a major factor in *Esterhuizen*.

1.68 It has been argued that both *Midland Bank Trust v Hett, Stubbs & Kemp* and *Bown v Gould & Swayne* were decisions *per incuriam*.[99] This appears to have been rejected in the way that Neuberger J has handled the issue of s.3 and support for his views can also be found in *Portman Building Society v Bond & Ingram*[100] where it was held that expert evidence is irrelevant to the legal test which is to be applied to the issue and that test remains the issue for solely the court to decide.

1.69 More recently, Rimer J considered the issue in *Football League Ltd v Edge & Ellison*:[101]

> The basic principle is that, with one exception, expert evidence on the duties of a solicitor is not admissible: it is a question of law for the court. It is then a question of fact for the court whether the duty, once identified, has been breached. The exception is that expert evidence is admissible to prove some 'practice in a particular profession, some accepted standard of conduct which is laid down by a professional institute or sanctioned by common usage'.[102]

1.70 How and when it may be appropriate to use expert evidence in will disputes will be looked at in more detail in Chapter 20.

---

[99] In error, through not having had s.3 Civil Evidence Act 1972 drawn to the courts' attention.

[100] [1998] CLY 320. See also *Franks v Sinclair (costs)* [2007] WTLR 785 where expert evidence on will preparation and solicitors' practice in taking instructions had been ruled out after argument before the Master.

[101] [2007] PNLR 2 at [278].

[102] Citing *Midland Bank Trust Co Ltd v Hett, Stubbs & Kemp* (n 45) and *Bown v Gould & Swayne* (n 54).

2

THE DUTY OF CARE IN RELATION
TO WILL PREPARATION

A. *Ross v Caunters*

Ross v Caunters,[1] somewhat surprisingly, came almost fifty years after *Donoghue v Stevenson*, **2.01** and on the face of it this seems a long interval before negligence in will preparation was looked at as a tort. Other jurisdictions had already started to look at this issue in this light and had found that in some circumstances a duty was owed to the beneficiary.[2] Within England during this period, although the principle from *Donoghue v Stevenson*[3] was clearly being developed in other areas of negligence, it was *Hedley Byrne & Co Ltd v Heller & Partners Ltd*[4] that had opened the way to the development of remedies, fashioned out of *Donoghue v Stevenson*, for purely financial losses arising out of a breach of a duty of care.

The emergence and development of the modern law of negligence, particularly since the decision in *Hedley Byrne & Co Ltd v Heller & Partners Ltd*, inevitably led to a reappraisal of the isolation of a solicitor from the reach of the ordinary law of negligence in relation to his professional dealings with a client. The clear trend of modern authority is to support the approach that the

---

[1] [1979] 3 All ER 580; the case involved the failure of the solicitor when sending a will to the client to advise correctly on the form of valid execution and attestation (the advice did not include a full explanation of the effect of s.15 Wills Act 1837). There is, however, *Hall v Meyrick* [1957] 2 All ER 722, which was unsuccessful in establishing a solicitor's liability, but this decision is probably only of historic importance. The current editors of *Theobald on Wills*, 17th edition (Sweet & Maxwell, 2010) suggest that as this case pre-dates *Hedley Byrne* it is unlikely to be followed. The facts and the argument in *Hall v Meyrick* are quite curious, especially as reading the judgment today it appears that the arguments were contrived so as not to examine the tort issues later examined in *Ross v Caunters*.
There was also *Otter v Church, Adams, Tatham & Co* [1953] 1 All ER 168 where the testator was not advised to execute a disentailing deed or will if certain settled property was to form part of his estate. It was held that damages could flow from this contract and that they should be ascertained at the time of death, ie when the free estate lost value. This was not a finding in tort.
[2] Considered in *White v Jones* [1995] 1 All ER 691 at 697F.
[3] [1932] All ER Rep 1.
[4] [1963] 2 All ER 575.

duty of care owed by a solicitor to a client in respect of professional work prima facie transcends that contained in the express or implied terms of the contract between them and includes the ordinary duty of care arising under the common law of negligence. That approach is also supported by principle in that, in the context of the general scope of the modern law of negligence to which members of this court have long to give effect, there are no acceptable grounds for refusing to recognize the liability of a solicitor in tort for negligence in the performance of professional work for a client.[5]

2.02 In *Ross v Caunters*, Megarry V-C found that:

1. It was not correct that privity of contract absolutely excluded a beneficiary from taking any action should they have suffered loss (as distinct from the testator suffering loss).
2. It was correct that the solicitor will-preparer owed the beneficiary a duty of care to see that the testator's instructions were implemented in a valid will.[6]
3. The beneficiaries could look to the law of tort to provide a remedy for loss.
4. The liability to the beneficiary existed notwithstanding that the beneficiaries had not relied on anything that had been said or done by the solicitors.

2.03 There were substantial doubts at the time as to whether or not this decision was good law, in part because Megarry V-C based his decision, to some degree, on the 'two-stage test' for negligence set out in *Anns v Merton London Borough Council*.[7] This test had been decisively overturned by the House of Lords in *Murphy v Brentwood District Council*.[8] Also, the House of Lords in *Leigh & Sillivan Ltd v Aliakmon Shipping Co Ltd*[9] considered that this test should not be applied to situations where it had previously been repeatedly held that a duty of care does not exist. But, as the Court of Appeal subsequently observed in *White v Jones*,[10] although Megarry V-C commented that the facts in *Ross v Caunters* did pass the two-stage test of *Anns*, he clearly based his conclusion on *Donoghue v Stevenson*.[11] The *Anns* test is absent from Megarry V-C's own summary of the reasons for his decision (which are set out below).

2.04 Megarry V-C provided the following summary for his decision:[12]

1. Despite the *obiter dicta* in *Robertson v Fleming*[13] and the decision in *Groom v Crocker*,[14] there was no longer a rule that a solicitor who is negligent can be liable only to his client in contract: he may be liable both to his client and others in tort.[15]
2. The basis of a solicitor's liability to others is either an extension of the *Hedley Byrne* principle or, more probably, a direct application of the principle in *Donoghue v Stevenson*.

---

[5] Brennan J in *Hawkins v Clayton* (1988) 164 CLR 539.
[6] This does not imply any more general duty to act in the beneficiaries' interests, especially those that the testator chooses not to benefit, when preparing a will. See *Clarke v Bruce Lance & Co* [1988] 1 All ER 364; *Trusted v Clifford Chance* [2001] WTLR 1219; *Sutherland v The Public Trustee* [1980] 2 NZLR 536. See later at Chapter 3 Part D.
[7] [1977] 2 All ER 492, the two tests being: (1) whether or not the relationship between the parties was sufficiently close that it was reasonably foreseeable that damage would be caused; and (2) if the first part is answered affirmatively, are there any particular considerations which should prevent or limit the duty?
[8] [1991] AC 398; [1990] 2 All ER 908.
[9] [1986] 2 All ER 145.
[10] [1993] 3 All ER 481.
[11] [1932] All ER Rep 1.
[12] [1979] 3 All ER 580 at 599 and note that he correctly characterized the statements regarding solicitors' lack of duty towards beneficiaries as such.
[13] (1861) 4 Macq 167.
[14] [1938] 2 All ER 394.
[15] Since confirmed by the House of Lords in *Henderson v Merrett Syndicates* [1995] AC 145.

3. Where a solicitor is instructed to carry out a transaction that will confer a benefit on an identified third party, the solicitor owes a duty of care to that third party, if that third party is one within his direct contemplation as one who is likely to be so closely and directly affected by his acts or omissions that he can reasonably foresee that the third party is likely to be injured by his acts or omissions.
4. The loss caused need only be financial and no physical injury need be caused to give rise to liability, following, on this point, the view that *Hedley Byrne & Co Ltd v Heller & Partners Ltd*[16] had already confirmed that damages in negligence for purely financial loss was possible.
5. In these circumstances there are no considerations which would suffice to negate or limit the scope of the solicitor's duty.

It is important to understand that the liability for a breach of duty determined in this way **2.05** is a burden on the solicitor, and that the actual distribution of the estate is not varied by the court's decision. Compensation flows from the solicitor to the beneficiary who has suffered loss; there is no question of the will being rectified to put right the solicitor's error (unless an action for rectification under the specific provisions of s.20 Administration of Justice Act 1982 is possible[17]) by depriving the 'windfall' benefit which passes to the unintended beneficiary.[18]

The judgment in *Ross v Caunters* also contained a review of relevant Californian and British **2.06** Columbian cases.[19] The support that these gave to the argument for liability was persuasive. This illustrates that the international aspects of this subject are of some significance and that not only would English decisions (including *Ross v Caunters*) be looked at critically overseas, but future English cases (notably *White v Jones*) would survey the progress of foreign jurisdictions and the relevance of their findings.

The British Columbian case of *Whittingham v Crease & Co*[20] was in particular considered **2.07** by Megarry V-C to show that the Canadian court had considered that *Donoghue v Stevenson* and *Hedley Byrne* had 'set the court free' from the restrictions of *Robertson v Fleming* and its consequences.

Following *Ross v Caunters* there was considerable debate about the correctness of the deci- **2.08** sion and some concern as to whether or not a higher court would accept the apparently innovative reasoning. It is probably not that the reasoning per se was innovative, but that its result was to overturn such a long-held belief that no cause of action existed. The Court

---

[16] [1963] 2 All ER 575.
[17] See *Walker v Medlicott* [1999] 1 WLR 727 and *Horsfall v Haywards* [1999] Lloyd's Rep 332. See Chapter 23 on the question of mitigation of loss through rectification where that route is appropriate.
[18] Although the Court of Appeal judgment in *Corbett v Bond Pearce* had the effect of reducing the windfall by leaving costs against it; see later at Chapter 3 Part B.
[19] Megarry V-C also commented on two Californian cases, *Biakanja v Irving* (1958) 320 P 2d 16 and *Lucas v Hamm* (1961) 11 Cal Rep 727 and on appeal (1961) 364 P 2d 685, which illustrated that this type of negligence had been embraced by Californian courts at a significantly earlier time than *Ross v Caunters* was considered in England. It is interesting to speculate that, if this area of law was undeveloped at the present time, the increased availability of overseas judgments, both through the Internet and greater number of professional journals, would have meant that the Californian decisions would have prompted a more swift *Ross v Caunters* case being attempted. Ultimately, such speculation is probably fruitless other than in serving to highlight the greater pace of change through easier access to information today.
[20] [1978] 5 WWR 45.

of Appeal in *Clarke v Bruce Lance*[21] had pointed the way forward with their endorsement of *Ross v Caunters*, although it was distinguished on the facts of *Clarke*. Full consideration of *Ross v Caunters* and its application came later with *White v Jones*, which eventually reached the House of Lords in 1995.[22] *White v Jones* is considered in the next section of this chapter. In the Court of Appeal in *White v Jones*[23] the result in *Ross v Caunters* was expressly approved. In the House of Lords, despite Lord Goff's view that 'as far as I am aware, *Ross v Caunters* has created no serious problems in practice since it was decided nearly 15 years ago',[24] he had doubts as to the correctness of the *ratio* of Sir Robert Megarry's solution.[25] Lord Nolan's judgment expressly approved the Court of Appeal's views.[26] This issue will be returned to in the consideration of *White v Jones* (next section below), but given the now accepted *ratio* of the House of Lords' decision,[27] Sir Robert Megarry's groundbreaking views given in his judgment may no longer be valid as to reasoning, but still valid as to result.

B. *White v Jones*

2.09   In 1993 the Court of Appeal returned to the issue in *White v Jones*[28] and there are a number of features to the decision. Given modern trends towards an increase in the number and nature of negligence actions generally, it is perhaps surprising that there was such a time lag between *Ross v Caunters*[29] and this next crucial development in this area of negligence.[30] *White v Jones* concerned loss of benefit, not through defective execution as in *Ross v Caunters*, but through failure to prepare a will within a reasonable time.[31]

Issues in the Court of Appeal

Time taken

2.10   The court, while not specifying any reasonable time, found that the time lapse, of approximately forty-four days between instructions and the testator's heart attack, was unreasonable in the particular circumstances, given that the testator was aged seventy-eight. None of the

---

[21] [1988] 1 All ER 364.
[22] [1995] 1 All ER 691.
[23] [1993] 3 All ER 481.
[24] [1995] 1 All ER 691 at 697.
[25] [1995] 1 All ER 691 at 710.
[26] [1995] 1 All ER 691 at 735.
[27] See, in particular, the Court of Appeal's views in *Carr-Glynn v Frearsons* [1994] Ch 326 at 333D–F, *Worby v Rosser* [1999] Lloyd's Rep PN 972 at 977 or *X v Woollcombe Yonge* [2001] WTLR 301 at 308F.
[28] [1993] 3 All ER 481.
[29] [1979] 3 All ER 580.
[30] Although in 1990 the first instance decision in this case found for the solicitors, in the following year there was *Smith v Claremont Haynes & Co* The Times, 3 September 1991. In this case it was found that in circumstances where the solicitor had instructions and might reasonably have been expected to be aware of the urgency created by the testator's health, the solicitor was liable for his failure to act promptly and prepare a will, thus depriving the beneficiaries of their intended benefit. There is no evidence in the judgment that the first instance decision in *White v Jones* was cited (nor for that matter does *Smith* appear in the Court of Appeal or House of Lords judgments). Judge Barnett QC referred at some length to *Ross v Caunters* and also *Gartside v Sheffield Young & Ellis* [1983] NZLR 37 (with approval of both cases) and decided that he could find for the disappointed beneficiary by extension of the *Ross v Caunters* principle. This, as appears later, is the basis on which the Court of Appeal decided *White v Jones* (but not the House of Lords).
[31] This type of breach of the duty of care had been reviewed earlier by the New Zealand courts in *Gartside v Sheffield Young & Ellis* (although *White v Jones* had a much longer delay than that which occurred in *Gartside*).

three courts that heard *White v Jones* specified at what point (how many days) the delay ceased to be reasonable and became excessive. The delay in this case was clearly found to be excessive and the court did not need to go further than that.

The irrelevance of Robertson v Fleming[32]

Sir Donald Nicholls V-C dealt robustly with one of the persistent criticisms of *Ross v Caunters*: **2.11** that of it being wholly inconsistent with the House of Lords' view in *Robertson v Fleming*. His view was that the law had plainly changed since 1861 and to follow the *dicta* in that case (which dealt solely with the privity of contract point) would be to ignore the whole development of tort stemming from *Donoghue v Stevenson*. As Steyn LJ forcefully put it:

> the exhumation of the obscure decision in *Robertson v Fleming* was not a fruitful exercise. This case was decided when the law of negligence was wholly undeveloped. The decision was founded on the privity of contract fallacy i.e. the theory that because there is no liability in contract there can be no liability in tort. That fallacy was authoritatively laid to rest 70 years later in *Donoghue v Stevenson*, which was the foundation of modern negligence. The basis of the reasoning in *Robertson v Fleming* has disappeared. In my view it is no longer useful to cite this case on questions of English law.[33]

These sentiments were confirmed in the House of Lords; as, in Lord Goff's words, 'the law **2.12** has moved on since then'.[34]

The need for the law to acknowledge the reality of the claim and the 'Lacuna' problem

Sir Donald Nicholls V-C regarded it as being of the utmost importance for the court to keep **2.13** in mind that if there was no liability to the disappointed beneficiary, then the only person who had a valid claim against the solicitor (the testator or his personal representatives) had suffered no loss and the disappointed beneficiary, who had suffered loss, had no claim: 'It would be a sorry reflection on English law if, indeed, that is the position today.'[35] This point was re-emphasized by Lord Goff in his leading speech in the House of Lords.[36]

The possibility was, therefore, that if the court found that there was no liability then there **2.14** would be a serious lacuna, or gap, in the protection offered by the law. The possibility of such a gap had previously been commented on by Cooke J in *Gartside v Sheffield Young & Ellis*[37] when he observed:

> To deny an effective remedy in a plain case would seem to imply a refusal to acknowledge the solicitor's professional role in the community. In practice the public relies on solicitors...to prepare effective wills. It would be a failure of the legal system not to insist on some practical responsibility.

---

[32] (1861) Macq 167.
[33] [1993] All ER 481 at 500.
[34] [1995] 1 All ER 691 at 701.
[35] [1993] 3 All ER 481 at 487. Lord Nolan was also troubled by the possibility of a lacuna in the law: 'In the forefront stands the extraordinary fact that, if such a duty is not recognised, the only persons who might have a valid claim (ie the testator and his estate) have suffered no loss, and the only person who has suffered loss (ie the disappointed beneficiary) has no claim...It can therefore be said that, if the solicitor owes no duty to the intended beneficiaries, there is a lacuna in the law which needs to be filled. This I regard as being a point of cardinal importance in the present case.'
[36] *White v Jones* (n 2) at 705A: 'The real reason for concern...lies in the extraordinary fact that, if a duty owed by the testator's solicitor to the disappointed beneficiary is not recognised, the only person who may have a valid claim has suffered no loss, and the only person who has suffered loss has no claim.'
[37] [1983] NZLR 37 at 43.

2.15 If it was the case that such a lacuna existed, then Sir Donald Nicholls V-C was minded to quote, with approval, the approach of Bingham LJ in *Simaan General Contracting Co v Pilkington Glass Ltd (No 2)*:[38] 'Just as equity remedied the inadequacies of the common law, so has the law of torts filled gaps left by other causes of action where the interests of justice so required.'

2.16 In Steyn LJ's words on the same subject, 'it seems just and reasonable' that a remedy is fashioned, if it does not in fact exist. All three judges found the liability was there on other reasoning, but they made this point to refute the defence's contention and to point to the injustice that would otherwise have to be addressed if there was no remedy for the beneficiaries.

Proximity

2.17 At first instance, there was some question of whether or not *Ross v Caunters* should be distinguished because it concerned failure of benefit under an existing will, whereas in the present case the testator's bounty had not been conclusively determined (ie he could have changed his mind before executing a will if it had been prepared, or he could simply have changed his mind during the period of delay) as the will was not prepared and executed. This was directly dealt with by Sir Donald Nicholls V-C: 'In my view there is no distinction in principle between this case and a case, such as *Ross v Caunters*, where the solicitor's failure lies in not warning the client about formal witnessing requirements.'[39]

2.18 The Court of Appeal found that there was liability on the grounds that the facts passed the threefold test in that

- it was foreseeable by the solicitor that a disappointed beneficiary would suffer loss;
- there was a sufficient degree of proximity between the solicitor and the intended beneficiary;
- that it was fair, just, and reasonable that liability should be imposed in these circumstances.

2.19 *White v Jones* was then appealed and the House of Lords found for the claimant 3–2.[40]

Issues in the House of Lords

Future development

2.20 Lord Goff, in giving what is considered to be the leading speech, declined to draw boundaries on the principle of this type of liability, but plainly acknowledged that there must be some, although he felt that this must be left to other courts and other cases to work out the limits.[41] This idea of the limits of the application being worked out on a case-by-case basis does seem to follow the spirit of Lord Denning's view in *Spartan Steel Alloys Ltd v Martin & Co (Contractors) Ltd*.[42] It also seems to have been correct in practice, in that this approach has

---

[38] [1988] 1 All ER 791.

[39] *Simaan General Contracting Co v Pilkington Glass Ltd (No 2)* (n 38) at 496.

[40] *White v Jones* (n 2). As an aside it is noted that between the death of the testator, Mr Barratt, and the House of Lords judgment, over eight years elapsed—a warning that litigation of this nature, particularly involving appeals, will rarely offer a quick (or cheap) solution.

[41] [1995] 1 All ER 691 at 711.

[42] 'The more I think about these cases, the more difficult I find it to put each into its own proper pigeon hole. Sometimes I say: "There was no duty". In others I say "The damage was too remote". So much so that I think the time has come to discard those tests which have proved so elusive. It seems to me better to consider the particular relationship in hand, and see whether or not, as a matter of policy, economic loss should be recoverable' (*Spartan Steel Alloys Ltd v Martin & Co (Contractors) Ltd* [1972] 3 All ER 557).

enabled later courts to define the limits of the principle on the facts of each case presented to them, without the necessity of attempting to draw conclusive limits.

Death of the testator

It would appear from the judgment that it is essential for the testator to have died before **2.21** liability can arise. Until that point either the testator can change his mind or, in the case of delay, the solicitor can complete his contracted work. Either instance must defeat a claim as no loss can reasonably have arisen before the death of the testator. Once death has occurred there is usually no alternative remedy but this. Their Lordships did not decide on the ability or the duty of the plaintiff to mitigate liability. This point has subsequently been considered by the Court of Appeal and will be examined later.[43]

Defective wills only

It was not considered that this judgment initially created any more general right applying to **2.22** third parties and professional work other than will preparation.[44]

The question of the possibility of wider application of *White v Jones* has been closely examined **2.23** since the House of Lords judgment.[45] Unsuccessful attempts include *Reeman v Department of Transport*,[46] *Wells v First National Commercial Bank Ltd*,[47] and *Goodwill v British Pregnancy Advisory Service*.[48] In this context Lord Browne-Wilkinson observed in *White v Jones* that

> the fact that the defendant assumed to act in the plaintiffs' affairs pursuant to a contract with a third party is not necessarily incompatible with the finding that, by so acting, the defendant also entered into a special relationship with the plaintiff with whom he had no contract. . . . this factor should not lead to the conclusion that a duty of care will necessarily be found to exist even where there is a chain of contractual obligations designed by the parties to regulate their dealings.[49]

In *Hemmens v Wilson Browne*,[50] in the particular circumstances the High Court declined **2.24** to extend this duty to the donee of an intended gift *inter vivos*. The solicitor had drawn a document purporting to give rights that the donee could not enforce and that the donor refused to enforce. The court found that, applying the principles from *Caparo Industries plc v Dickman*,[51]

- there was foreseeability of damage;
- there was a sufficient degree of proximity;
- this was not a situation where it would be fair, just, and reasonable to impose a duty on the solicitor.

---

[43] See Chapter 23.

[44] Although the decision in *Ross v Caunters* was noted with approval, and arguably applied to a relationship between an insurance underwriter and a bank in *Punjab National Bank v de Boinville* [1992] 3 All ER 104.

[45] See also Michael Tennet, 'The Duties of Care Owed by Pension Scheme Actuaries', *British Pension Lawyer* No 80 (May 1999), which argues that this principle could be applied to negligent advice by a pension scheme actuary that causes loss to the scheme's members.

[46] [1997] PNLR 618 (certificates of seaworthiness of vessels).

[47] [1998] PNLR 552 (instructions to a bank).

[48] [1996] 2 All ER 161 (successful vasectomy operation).

[49] [1995] 1 All ER 691 at 716F–G.

[50] [1993] 4 All ER 826.

[51] [1990] 1 All ER 568.

2.25 The last point was decided because the intended donor was still alive and could therefore make the gift, if he still wished to do so, which clearly he did not.[52] In addition the intended donor had a remedy against the solicitor if he had wanted to use it. Third, although there was some dispute as to the exact circumstances of the solicitor's instructions, the judge preferred the evidence that indicated that the solicitor had told the donor that he was acting for the donor and that the donee should take her own legal advice.

2.26 It has been found that a solicitor, when advising trustees, has assumed a relationship of responsibility towards the beneficiaries and is liable where his negligence causes loss to them.[53]

2.27 Financial advisers potentially owe a duty of care, not only to their client who instructed them, but also in some circumstances to that client's dependants. The Court of Appeal has considered this point[54] in connection with the client's pension benefits for his family after his death. Several interesting points arose.

1. The court declined to accept that a self-regulatory body's code of conduct for its members determined the scope of its member's duties.
2. What degree of proximity must there be to the client for the dependants to claim?
3. What would be the decision in future if the client was seeking to maximize his benefit at the expense of his dependants' possible benefits? The Court of Appeal recognized that such a case[55] would not be easy to deal with.

2.28 In *Killick v PricewaterhouseCoopers*,[56] *White v Jones* was applied in determining the liability of an accountant in a private company share valuation that was to be used for compulsory acquisition of shares from shareholders where the contractual agreement was with the company.

2.29 The Court of Appeal has considered *White v Jones* in the context of a property transaction[57] where the solicitor acted for borrowers, but the lender was not legally advised (nor was he widely experienced in business). After the default of the borrowers (and the mortgage security having been discovered to be ineffective[58]) there was acceptance that there was no contractual relationship between the solicitor and the lender, but the court found that there was a duty in tort in the particular circumstances.

2.30 Although there is not yet an example of this in England, there are at least two Canadian decisions where *White v Jones* has been considered and applied in a commercial context.[59]

---

[52] This approach fits with the view of Lord Goff in the House of Lords in *White v Jones*: 'Let me take the example of an *inter vivos* gift where, as a result of the solicitor's negligence, the instrument in question is for some reason not effective for its purpose. The mistake comes to light some time later during the lifetime of the donor, after the gift to the intended donee should have taken effect. The donor, having by then changed his mind, declines to perfect the imperfect gift in favour of the intended donee...I, for my part, do not think that the intended donee could in these circumstances claim against the solicitor. It is enough, as I see it, that the donor is able to do what he wishes to put the matter right' ([1995] 1 All ER 691 at 704G–J).

[53] *Yudt v Leonard Ross & Craig (a firm)* [1998] All ER (D) 375; see Chapter 15 para 15.31.

[54] *Gorham v British Telecommunications plc* [2000] 4 All ER 867.

[55] But perhaps *Clarke v Bruce Lance & Co (a firm)* [1988] 1 All ER 364 may assist as that examined the primacy of the duty to the client.

[56] [2001] PNLR 1.

[57] *Dean v Allin & Watts (a firm)* [2001] All ER (D) 288 (May); see also *Penn v Bristol & West Building Society* [1996] 2 FCR 729 and *Searles v Cann Hallett* [1999] PNLR 494.

[58] A mere deposit of deeds, which method had become ineffective as a result of s.2 Law of Property (Miscellaneous Provisions) Act 1989.

[59] *Burnett v Took Engineering* [2000] BCSC 1630 (a building dispute) and *JA Industries (Canada) Ltd v Highfield Development Ltd* [1998] ABQB 817 (a dispute over bailiffs' actions).

Relationship of beneficiaries to the testator

Lord Nolan's judgment contains a reference to proximity of relationship being a factor in **2.31** *White v Jones*, but he specifically comments that he does not mean that less close relatives are to be denied a remedy. He regards this as simply being something that is 'relevant to the pragmatic case-by-case approach which the law now adopts towards negligence claims'.[60] In many ways, the key phrase is 'pragmatic case-by-case approach' and it is one that should not be lost sight of in considering both this case and its later applications. The question of the proximity of the beneficiary to the testator is an issue that was extensively reviewed in the leading Australian case of *Hill v Van Erp*[61] where it was found that liability was not affected by the familial relationship to the testator.

The basis of the House of Lords decision

A substantial difficulty with the *White v Jones* decision in the House of Lords has been the **2.32** precise basis on which the majority arrived at their conclusion. In the Court of Appeal there was a fair degree of unanimity in the acceptance of both the *ratio* of *Ross v Caunters* and the application of a threefold test. The House of Lords not only lacked this unanimity among the majority, but Lord Goff also expressed some doubts as to the *ratio* in *Ross v Caunters* (but not the decision itself) and he did not apply the same threefold test as the Court of Appeal.[62] However, it does seem fair to say that the majority did accept that the solicitor's liability arose under the principle in *Hedley Byrne & Co Ltd v Heller & Partners Ltd* [63] and probably that there was an assumption of responsibility.

White v Jones is not without its critics (including the dissenting judgments in the Lords) **2.33** and some have argued that the House of Lords went a long way to circumvent previously accepted views on negligence and the law of tort in order to reach the conclusion that it did (only just at 3–2). On the other hand, we do not believe that we are alone in thinking that if the House of Lords had not decided on this issue the way that it did, there may well have been Parliamentary intervention in order to protect the position of the beneficiaries who would have been left with no redress. However, in the event, the House of Lords decision meant this was not necessary.

In the House of Lords there were two strong dissenting judgments and there is the clear **2.34** impression that, despite the argument about the boundaries of the law of tort, the House of Lords was making new law (as quite conceivably Megarry V-C had done before them in *Ross v Caunters*). In case this view should be thought to be unduly irreverent, the article on the case in the *All England Annual Review* (1995) comments:

> … it seems particularly unfortunate that the law in a sensitive and difficult area should be made 'on the hoof' by the judiciary rather than as a result of a much broader and calmer deliberation by, for example, the Law Commission, which might result in well-considered legislation… But this criticism is unfair in the sense that judges have no option—where a point requires decision and the parties can somehow pay for the luxury of having it made by five senior judges, they are under a duty to do the best they can.[64]

---

[60] [1995] 1 All ER 691 at 736.
[61] (1997) 71 ALJR 487.
[62] [1995] 1 All ER 691 at 735; Lord Nolan expressed the view that 'I agree with the unanimous judgments of the Court of Appeal'.
[63] [1963] 2 All ER 575.
[64] Professor BW Harvey at 470.

C. Who is the duty owed to?

2.35 This is an issue which has perhaps become clearer in light of the way that *White v Jones* has been applied subsequently, but it cannot yet be said to be wholly convincingly defined. Does the will-preparer

- owe a direct and independent duty of care to the disappointed beneficiary? or
- owe a duty of care only to the testator and, if this is breached with no loss to the testator, but with a resulting loss to the disappointed beneficiary, then the beneficiary's damages arise out of that breach?

2.36 In *X v Woollcombe Yonge*, Neuberger J's analysis of the *Lenesta Sludge* passage in Lord Goff's judgment in *White v Jones*[65] came down in favour of the second approach.[66] He found that this was consistent with the analysis of *White v Jones* in subsequent cases,[67] despite the difficulty when reading the *Lenesta Sludge* passage, in Lord Goff's judgment, of finding the duty of care described in these terms. Indeed, it appears that this aspect is not directly approached in that passage, apart from the concluding reference to *Ross v Caunters* that 'we can say with some confidence that a direct remedy by the intended beneficiary against the testator appears to create no problems in practice'.[68] As a matter of plain English, the words '*direct remedy*' have to be stretched more than a little to be taken to describe a remedy that is not independent and relies primarily on a duty owed to another. For all that this issue has become a matter of concern to the judiciary, it is difficult to see in practice that it has had much practical application, as neither approach denies a remedy to the disappointed beneficiary.[69] However, this is commented on later in Chapter 3 Part B in regard to the decision in *Corbett v Bond Pearce*.

2.37 In *Carr-Glynn v Frearsons*,[70] the estate had a potential remedy against the solicitors for negligence, in that it had suffered loss through an interest in a beneficial joint tenancy not having been severed. However, if the personal representatives recovered damages in respect of this loss, the benefit would accrue to the residuary beneficiaries and not the legatee of the half share of the property who had suffered loss. The approach of the Court of Appeal was to find that there were in fact two complementary duties which coexisted:

- a duty to take care that effect is given to the testator's testamentary intentions; and
- a duty to the testator's chosen beneficiaries not to cause them loss through failing to do what was required to give effect to those intentions.

2.38 If the first duty is not met by severing a joint tenancy, the property the testator intends to bequeath is not secured as an asset of the estate. The loss to the estate would give rise to a loss and a breach of duty on which the personal representatives could sue. The second duty is not met where effect cannot be given to the testamentary intentions (in this case the will contained the bequest, but not the interest in the property through the failure to sever).

---

[65] [1995] 1 All ER 691 at 710C.
[66] [2001] WTLR 301 at 307E. See also Part D of this Chapter.
[67] *Carr-Glynn v Frearsons* [1998] 4 All ER 225 and *Worby v Rosser* [1999] Lloyd's Rep PN 972 at 977.
[68] [1995] 1 All ER 691 at 710H.
[69] See Professor Michael A Jones, 'Third Party Beneficiaries—Disappointed Again' (2001) 17(2) *Professional Negligence*.
[70] [1998] 4 All ER 225; see later at Chapter 7 para 7.16 onwards for a fuller discussion of practical aspects of this case.

The apparently competing nature of these two duties was resolved by Chadwick LJ who sug-   **2.39**
gested that, in the circumstances of *Carr-Glynn*, the personal representatives could recover
only the loss suffered by those entitled to the residue (which was in fact no loss at all) while
the beneficiary was entitled to recover for the loss she suffered under the second duty.

> The duties owed by the solicitors to the testator and to the specific legatee are not inconsistent.
> They are complementary. To the extent that the duty to the specific legatee is fulfilled, the duty
> to the testator is fulfilled also. If and to the extent that the relevant property would have been
> distributed to the specific legatee in the ordinary course of the administration, the other per-
> sons interested in the estate can suffer no loss. In so far as the relevant property or any part of
> it would have been applied in the ordinary course of the administration to discharge liabilities
> of the estate, the specific legatee can suffer no loss.[71]

A novel approach to a similar issue was taken by Neuberger J (as he then was) in *Chappell v*   **2.40**
Somers & Blake,[72] a case regarding the liability for loss caused by a firm's delay in obtaining
probate for a client.

> there are, at least as a matter of logic, three possible answers to the present conundrum. The
> first…is…that the executrix is entitled to sue the solicitors, but has to account for any dam-
> ages to the beneficiary. The problem with that argument…is that the…executrix is not the
> person who has suffered any loss as a result of the solicitors' breach of duty.
>
> The second possibility is that the beneficiary is entitled to sue the solicitors for any loss suf-
> fered. The problem with that argument is that the solicitors plainly owed no contractual duty
> to the beneficiary, and there must be considerable doubt as to whether it would be right, as a
> matter of principle, to impose any tortious duty to the beneficiary on the solicitors.
>
> The third possibility is that, as the solicitors' duty was owed to the executrix and any loss result-
> ing from the breach of duty was suffered by the beneficiary, there is… 'a black hole' and the
> solicitors, in effect, escape from having to pay damages.
>
> Considering this issue by reference to general policy, as opposed to legal principle, I am of the
> view that there are two main points. The first is that it would be wrong if the solicitors escaped
> any liability for damages in a case such as this, merely because they could identify a dichotomy
> between the person who can claim against them for a breach of duty, namely the executrix, and
> the person who can be said to have suffered the damage, namely the beneficiary. I believe that
> this principle, 'which is identified as the impulse to do practical justice', is supported by *White
> v Jones*…to the effect that it would be 'unacceptable' if a solicitor escaped liability in that case.
>
> The second policy principle appears to me that, given that any damages would ultimately
> come to the beneficiary, irrespective of who has the right to sue, the *question of whether it is the
> executrix or the beneficiary who can bring the proceedings is not of great significance*.
>
> It seems to me…that it is appropriate to treat the executrix as representing the interest of the
> owner of the property.[73]

White v Jones concerns the consequences for intended beneficiaries when the draftsman   **2.41**
breaches his duty of care. In the Scottish case of *Fraser v McArthur Stewart*[74] negligent advice
was given by the draftsman that the intended bequest of a croft to three people was not legally
possible and that he could only leave it to a single beneficiary. As a result of this incorrect
advice, the testator changed his instructions (after considerable time, and also it is alleged,

---

[71] [1998] 4 All ER 225 at 235D.
[72] [2003] WTLR 1085.
[73] *Chappell v Somers & Blake* (n 72) at 1090A–G (authors' emphasis), but for an apparently less cogent
approach to this whole question of loss see *Daniels v Thompson* [2004] WTLR 511.
[74] [2008] COSH 159.

most reluctantly) in favour of a single beneficiary. The Scottish court held that the principle in *White v Jones* did not extend to the claim by the disappointed intended beneficiaries and that the last will must have represented the wishes of the testator. In England it is quite conceivable that the threefold test of foreseeability, proximity, and reasonableness[75] being applied might have led to a different result. The solicitor in the position in *Fraser* would have been aware that his advice would impact severely on the intended beneficiaries in that it would prevent at least two from inheriting. Negligent advice that alters the testator's instructions must remain a risk, but that risk is outside of the *White v Jones* principle and much more in line with that in *Caparo Industries*.[76]

D. The *ratio* in *White v Jones*

2.42   In seeking to understand the *ratio* of *White v Jones* it is essential to look at what the courts have made of the decision subsequently. In particular, the Court of Appeal has commented twice[77] that one key passage of Lord Goff's speech in the House of Lords is regarded by them as providing the *ratio* of the judgment:

> I therefore return to the law of tort for a solution to the problem. For the reasons I have already given an ordinary action in tortious negligence on the lines proposed by Sir Robert Megarry V-C in *Ross v Caunters* must, with the greatest respect, be regarded as inappropriate, because it does not meet any of the conceptual problems which have been raised. Furthermore for the reasons I have previously given the *Hedley Byrne* principle cannot, in the absence of special circumstances, give rise on ordinary principles to an assumption of responsibility by the testator's solicitor towards an intended beneficiary. Even so it seems to me that it is open to your Lordships' House, as in the *Lenesta Sludge*[78] case, to fashion a remedy to fill a lacuna[79] in the law which would otherwise occur on the facts of cases such as the present. In the *Lenesta Sludge* case, as I have said, the House made available a remedy as a matter of law to solve the problem of transferred loss in the case before them. The present case is, if anything, a fortiori, since the nature of the transaction was such that, if the solicitors were negligent and their negligence did not come to light until after the death of the testator, there would be no remedy for the ensuing loss unless the intended beneficiary could claim. In my opinion, therefore, your Lordships' House should in cases such as these extend to the intended beneficiary a remedy under the *Hedley Byrne* principle by holding that the assumption of responsibility by the solicitor to his client should be held to in law to extend to the intended beneficiary who (as the solicitor can reasonably foresee) may, as a result of the solicitor's negligence, be deprived of his intended legacy in circumstances in which neither the testator nor his estate will have a remedy against the solicitor. Such liability will not of course arise in cases where the defect in the will comes to light before the death of the testator, and the testator either leaves the will as it is or otherwise continues to exclude the previously intended beneficiary from the relevant benefit. I only wish to add that, with the benefit of experience during the 15 years in which *Ross v Caunters* has been regularly applied, we can say with some confidence that a direct remedy by the intended beneficiary against the solicitor appears to create no problems in practice. That is therefore the solution which I would recommend to your Lordships.[80]

---

[75] *Smith v Eric S Bush* [1990] 1 AC 831; *Caparo Industries plc v Dickman* [1990] 2 AC 605.

[76] *Gray v Buss Murton* [1999] PNLR 882.

[77] *Carr-Glynn v Frearsons* (n 67) at 231–3, per Chadwick LJ: 'It is Lord Goff's approach, set out in the passage that I have just read, which represents the *ratio* of the decision of their Lordships in *White v Jones* for the reasons explained in the analysis in this court in the later decision in *Carr-Glynn v Frearsons*.' See also *Worby v Rosser* (n 67) and Neuberger J in *X v Woollcombe Yonge* (n 27).

[78] *Linden Gardens Trust Ltd v Lenesta Sludge Disposals Ltd* [1993] 3 All ER 417.

[79] See earlier para 2.13 for this issue.

[80] [1995] 1 All ER 691 at 710C.

The key points from this passage appear to be: **2.43**

1. The decision in *Hedley Byrne* is not, by itself, capable of resolving this type of claim, as in the absence of special circumstances there cannot be the necessary assumption of responsibility towards the beneficiaries.
2. The House had previously accepted that it had the power to fashion a remedy where there was a lacuna in the law and that the circumstances in *White v Jones* were just such a case.
3. It was therefore appropriate for the House to find that in these circumstances it was just for the House to extend expressly *Hedley Byrne* and find that the assumption of responsibility to the testator/client extended to his beneficiaries.

E. Conclusions

There is a considerable degree of difficulty in establishing a common theme through the six   **2.44**
judgments of both the Court of Appeal and the House of Lords which were in favour of the
claimants.

1. The result in *Ross v Caunters* was clearly approved but some doubts were expressed as to the validity of its reasoning in the House of Lords.
2. All agreed that to find against the plaintiffs would give a result that lacked justice and which would point to a lacuna in the law.
3. It was possible to argue that to find in favour of the claimants was a straightforward extension of *Hedley Byrne* and there was clearly a degree to which it was accepted that there was an assumption of responsibility.
4. It is arguable that the threefold test applied unanimously by the Court of Appeal was supported by Lord Nolan in the House of Lords.
5. There would be dangers in trying to use this decision as authority for negligence in other transactions. It clearly is restricted to the circumstances surrounding wills. A senior Chancery counsel has referred to this decision as standing like an 'island'.[81] A good description, in that the decision is undoubtedly there, but its connection with other areas of negligence may depend upon the state of the judicial tide at any given time.
6. Lord Mustill's dissenting speech in the House of Lords referred to the limitations of the law of contract and its inability to assist the disappointed beneficiary. This objection in all probability has not been removed by the Contracts (Rights of Third Parties) Act 1999.

The Australian approach

In case the difficulty of extracting a single common *ratio* from the judgments in *White v*   **2.45**
Jones should seem disconcerting, similar difficulties are encountered in the lengthy judgment on the final appeal in *Hill trading as RF Hill & Associates v Van Erp* in the High Court
of Australia.[82,83]

---

[81] The *White v Jones* decision has also been described as 'unclassifiable'; GH Treitel, *The Law of Contract*, 10th edition (Sweet & Maxwell, 1999) 569.

[82] The highest Appellate court in Australia.

[83] (1997) 71 ALJR 487. See also the judgment of Pincus JA in *Queensland Art Gallery v Henderson Trout* [2000] QCA 93: 'It is not possible from the reasons given in *Hill v Van Erp* for a rule or principle adopted by a majority of the judges, which may be applied in solving the, no doubt increasingly common, problem of the liability of professional people ... to persons other than their clients, injured by defective work done under contract with the client. In my view, the fundamental basis of the duty being as yet unascertained, one must proceed by analogy.'

2.46   In *Hill v Van Erp* the High Court decided to uphold, on a 5–1 majority, a claim involving defective execution where a spouse of a beneficiary had witnessed the will.[84] The court considered in detail the judgments in *White v Jones* and drew attention to Lord Goff's recognition of what he called 'difficulties of a conceptual nature' with this type of claim. However, the court did not find agreement on why they should uphold liability. Three of the majority rejected extending the *Hedley Byrne* principle, although the other two did accept that there was an assumption of responsibility. The majority gave careful consideration to the proximity of relationship between the solicitors and the beneficiary and concluded that it was of sufficient proximity to bring the beneficiary within a class to which the solicitors owed a duty.[85] The effect of the judgment was to approve liability in those circumstances and having, in effect, approved *White v Jones*, it is probably safe to assume that it would have been applied had a will not been prepared.

The wider effect of *White v Jones*

2.47   *White v Jones* is quite patently of paramount importance to this area of the law. In the sixteen years between *Ross v Caunters* and *White v Jones*, *Ross* had been doubted by some commentators and some other Commonwealth jurisdictions had refused to follow it on the grounds that they considered it to be wrongly decided. The current position is:

1.   A strong High Court of Australia decided in *Hill v Van Erp* that the earlier *Seale v Perry*[86] was wrongly decided and approved the result in *White v Jones* on different reasoning (see para 2.46 above).[87]
2.   Scotland also refused to follow *White v Jones* in *Weir v Hodge (JM) & Son*[88] but it was later followed in *Davidson v Bank of Scotland*.[89]
3.   The New Zealand Court of Appeal applied *Ross v Caunters* in *Gartside v Sheffield Young & Ellis*.[90]
4.   Lord Goff in his *White v Jones* judgment observed that more recently *Ross v Caunters'* type of liability had also been accepted in Canada, California, Germany, France, and the Netherlands. *White v Jones* was later approved in Canada in *Earl v Wilhelm*.[91]

2.48   The House of Lords decision effectively stopped the debate about the validity of *Ross v Caunters* as far as the English courts are concerned, and emphatically confirmed the principle involved.

> the decision in *Ross v Caunters* has stood unchallenged for 15 years and has achieved a measure of international and academic support. The moral that solicitors, when preparing a will,

---

[84] Section 15(1) Succession Act 1981 (Queensland) makes similar provision on this point to s.15 Wills Act 1837.

[85] The issue in *Hill v Van Erp* was more similar to that in *Ross v Caunters* than that in *White v Jones*. The solicitor witnessed execution of the will and was aware, without realizing the significance, of a beneficiary's spouse acting as the other witness.

[86] [1982] VR 193.

[87] The Supreme Court of Victoria had earlier refused to follow *Ross v Caunters* in *Seale v Perry* [1982] VR 193, but see also *Watts v Public Trustee for Western Australia* [1980] WAR 97 (the Supreme Court of Western Australia) and *Findlay v Rowlands, Anderson & Hine* [1987] Tas R 60, neither of which found against liability and applied *Ross v Caunters*.

[88] 1990 SLT 266; see also *MacDougall v MacDougall's Executors* 1994 SLT 1178.

[89] [2002] PNLR 740: 'Although *White v Jones* is an English case, the law of negligence in the two jurisdictions has tended to progress as one' (per Lord Kingarth).

[90] [1983] NZLR 37.

[91] [2001] WTLR 1275; (2000) 183 DLR (4th) 45.

owe a duty to intended legatees as well as to the testator must by now have become familiar to them and to their insurers. To reverse the decision in *Ross v Caunters* at this stage would be, in my judgment, a disservice to the law.[92]

The effect of *White v Jones* on past events

A fundamental point regarding a court's decision is that it does not state what the law should **2.49** be considered to be from the date of the judgment, but rather it is the court stating what it regards the law to have always been.[93] On this basis, there can be a current or future liability for wills that were

- not prepared;
- incorrectly prepared; or
- incorrectly executed

before the time of the decisions in *Ross v Caunters* or *White v Jones*.

---

[92] Lord Nolan [1995] 1 All ER 691 at 735.

[93] See, eg *R v Governor of Brockhill Prison, Ex parte Evans No 2* (The Times, 6 July 1998) where Lord Woolf MR is quoted as referring to a principle embedded in law that any authoritative decision of the courts, stating what the law is, is operated retrospectively. The decision not only states what the law was from the date of the decision, but it states what it had always been. This is the position even if in setting out the law the courts over-ruled an earlier decision which took a totally different view of the law. This has been reaffirmed on appeal to the House of Lords (see [2000] 4 All ER 15) but with some reservations about the retrospective nature of decisions and human rights principles.

3

OTHER ASPECTS OF THE DUTY OF CARE

A. Firmly fixed intention

It is reasonably clear that if there is evidence that the testator's intention did not remain fixed **3.01** and that therefore he cannot be shown with sufficient certainty to wish to benefit the claimant, a claim on a *White v Jones* basis (for the failure to prepare a will) is going to fail.[1]

This issue was examined in in *Bacon v Howard Kennedy*.[2] This case was extraordinary because **3.02** of the great length of time that elapsed between the will instructions first being given (13 June 1986) and death (2 June 1995). There was some evidence that the testator thought that the matter had been completed, and the judge found that there was no evidence that the testator had changed his mind from the repeated instructions that he had given to the solicitors. It would seem clear that in such circumstances the court believed that the solicitor's liability continued unless, or until, there was evidence of a change of mind, or there was the preparation of a new will, or conceivably because the client had realized that matters were awry (which was not the case in *Bacon*) and had a will prepared by another solicitor. There are no direct remarks of the judge on this point, but that must be implicit in his findings.

In some contrast to *Bacon v Howard Kennedy* there is the Australian decision in *Queensland* **3.03** *Art Gallery Board of Trustees v Henderson Trout (a firm)*.[3] The facts of this case are complex and they concern delays in preparing a will for a difficult client who is described at one point in the first instance judgment as a professional will-maker. The disputed bequest concerned what was claimed to be one of the finest private art collections in Australia and one that was

---

[1] *Queensland Art Gallery Board of Trustees v Henderson Trout (a firm)* [1998] QSC 250 was confirmed on appeal; see [2000] QCA 93.

[2] [2000] WTLR 169.

[3] [1998] QSC 250.

eventually sold for A$11.6m. The case is of interest because of the fairly rigorous approach taken to establishing if there was a fixed and continuing intention to benefit the art gallery (which the court found to be absent). The period under question was much shorter than that in *Bacon*, but the court found that there was more persuasive evidence of the testatrix not having formed a fixed and continuing intention. In *Bacon*, in the absence of convincing evidence to show there was no fixed and continuing intention, the English court was inclined to accept that there was a continuing intention, while in *Queensland Art Gallery* the Australian court, with the benefit of more evidence against, was inclined to find against a fixed and continuing intention. It is suggested that the two decisions can be distinguished on their facts regarding intention. In addition, in *Trusted v Clifford Chance*[4] it was held that there could be no liability towards the disappointed beneficiary until the testator had decided upon the extent of the benefit that was to be conferred on the disappointed beneficiary.

3.04 In contrast, where a will has been prepared, albeit with defective terms, the position is clearer. Where the claim against the will draftsman is on the basis of a defective will or provision, there would be no need to prove continuing intention to benefit as the testator's decision not to alter his will evidences his wishes. In *Humblestone v Martin Tolhurst Partnership*,[5] continuing intention was looked at in terms of a will that was defectively executed. It was claimed on the part of the defendant that the claimant must prove her contention by showing that the testator's intention to benefit her continued until his death. Mann J found that the evidence did not show a positive change of mind (there may have been some equivocation on the part of the testator but not nearly enough to show that he addressed his mind to the issues and changed his wishes) and he would not accept that the burden to prove intent lay with the claimant:

> where one starts from a position where the testator does intend a disposition in favour of a given beneficiary, it does not suffice for [the defendant's] purposes to show that a degree of equivocation has crept in. It has to be apparent that there was some actual change of mind.[6]

3.05 In *Feltham v Freer Bouskell*[7] the judge raised issues of probability in examining the loss, without firmly concluding the issue. His point was whether in estimating loss to the intended beneficiary he should approach the probability of the testator executing the document on a percentage basis or on the balance of probabilities. In recognizing that ultimately, if this should be a factor, it was for another court to decide, the judge expressed the view that taking the categories from *Allied Maples Group v Simmons & Simmons*[8] a disappointed beneficiary

---

[4] [2000] WTLR 1219.

[5] [2004] WTLR 343.

[6] In reaching this conclusion Mann J concluded that remarks of Blackburne J regarding causation in *Gibbons v Nelsons* [2000] WTLR 453 provided no stronger test of continuing intention than his own did. Counsel for the defendant had been seeking to show the opposite, but was seeking to make too much of remarks that were neither detailed enough nor sufficiently addressed to this particular point.

[7] [2013] EWHC 1952 (Ch).

[8] [1995] 1 WLR 1602—three separate principles:

> [1] Questions of quantification of loss dependent on future uncertain events, such as whether the claimant would have been promoted at work, which were decided on the court's assessment usually expressed in percentage terms.
>
> [2] Questions as to what the claimant would have done, where the claimant must prove on the balance of probabilities that he would have taken action to obtain the benefit or avoid the risk.
>
> [3] Questions as to what a third party would have done, which if the claimant shows that there was a substantial rather than a merely speculative chance, are evaluated as questions of quantification of damages, and thus in percentage terms.

claim fell into category 3 and it was for the claimant to prove in percentage terms. This approach seems to be at odds with earlier cases, especially *Humblestone*.

Where the testator is still alive, there can be no liability on the part of the will-preparer for **3.06** either a failure to prepare a will or for its defective terms. As the testator is still alive, no continuing intention up to death to benefit the beneficiaries on his death can be shown (there is still time for a change of mind before death[9]).

An argument against the testator's intention was raised in the Canadian case of *Earl v* **3.07** *Wilhelm*.[10] The testator had attempted to bequeath as specific gifts certain fields which the will draftsman knew well were not in the testator's ownership; they were in fact owned by a farming company that the testator owned. It was argued in the appeal hearing that the loss arose not because of the solicitor's negligence, but through the inability of the testator to devise the parcels of land. It was further argued that if the testator had been aware of the true situation, and in particular the legal costs and possible adverse tax consequences of taking the land out of the farming company, then he might well have bequeathed his estate differently. This was rejected, the court holding that with competent legal advice (and 99 per cent ownership of the company) he would have been capable of giving effect to his wishes. That there would have been legal or taxation costs was rejected as the court believed that there are 'legal expenses and tax consequences involved in any testamentary disposition'.

B. The duty of care may well not extend to persons (or a class of persons) that the solicitor is not told about

The approach of courts has often been coloured by the question of how liability can exist **3.08** when the beneficiary may be unknown to the will-preparer.[11] This was examined closely in *Gibbons v Nelsons*[12] where Blackburne J observed:

> Given the approach of the House of Lords in *White v Jones*, how can the solicitor be held to be in breach of a duty to a person (the intended recipient of a particular benefit) of whom the solicitor is unaware? In the passage from Lord Goff's speech in *White v Jones* ... there is a reference to the assumption of responsibility 'to the intended beneficiary who (as the solicitor can reasonably foresee) may as a result of the solicitor's negligence be deprived of his intended legacy'. While acknowledging that it may not be necessary for the solicitor to be aware of the precise identity of the intended beneficiary (he may, for example, be aware that the testator intends to make a gift to someone identified only as 'my son' or to a defined class, e.g. 'my children and grandchildren') I am of the view that the law requires, at the very least, that the solicitor should know: (1) what the benefit is that the testator-client wishes to confer; and (2) who the person or persons or class of persons are (in each case ascertainable if not actually named) on whom the client-testator wishes to confer the benefit. I have seen nothing in any of the authorities which justifies an extension of the assumption of responsibility to cases where these two elements are not present.[13]

---

[9] But thereafter, as Eve J delightfully put it in *Cumins v Bond* [1927] 1 Ch 167 at 173, as far as the testator is concerned 'I have no jurisdiction extending to the sphere in which he moves'.
[10] 2000 SKCA 1; (2000) 189 Sask R 71 (CA).
[11] Starting with *Robertson v Fleming* [1861] 4 Macq 167: 'a stranger whom the solicitor never saw or heard of before'.
[12] [2000] WTLR 453.
[13] [2000] WTLR 453 at 471C–E.

3.09   When expressed in the terms above, the principle is more easily understood as not being about the duty of care extending to persons (or a class of persons) that the solicitor is not told about, and more clearly defined as being about the certainty of the testator's wishes. The two limbs in Blackburne J's approach demonstrate that the precise identity of a beneficiary may well be unknown, but as long as he is defined adequately for the purpose of the will, that is sufficient knowledge for the draftsman.

Proximity of beneficiary

3.10   It is curious how knowledge of the beneficiary and proximity has been a factor in much of the judicial reasoning, even as far back as *Robertson v Fleming*.[14] In *Gibbons v Nelsons*,[15] proximity of, or at least the solicitor's knowledge of, a beneficiary was found to be a relevant factor. The relevant passage from the judgment of Blackburne J is quoted in full above. In general terms it is difficult to dispute the conclusion he arrived at in connection with bequests under a will, in that the two-part test he sets out is necessary in order for will instructions to be given, ie

- what the benefit is that the testator-client wishes to confer; and
- who the person or persons or class of persons are (in each case ascertainable if not actually named) on whom the client-testator wishes to confer the benefit.

3.11   Without a bequest passing this test it is difficult to see how a will could be prepared by a draftsman.

3.12   However, does this test limit or exclude liability to beneficiaries of, for example, an earlier will? In the words quoted from *Gibbons* it certainly would. The issue of a duty towards beneficiaries of an earlier will (earlier than the will involving the negligent solicitor), whose benefits are harmed by the negligence of the solicitors when instructed in a later will, is another matter. Such a claim was initially attempted in *Worby v Rosser*.[16]

3.13   In *Worby* the solicitor had been found negligent in respect of the preparation of an invalid 1989 will[17] and some of the beneficiaries under the 1983 will sought to claim the costs of the probate action, which established the invalidity of the 1989 will, from the solicitor involved.[18] The Court of Appeal rejected this approach as in their view the personal representatives, not the beneficiaries of the estate, had the right of action,[19] given that the estate had suffered loss. The Court of Appeal took the view that the *White v Jones* remedy had been fashioned to fill a lacuna in the law where no remedy existed. Here there was a remedy for the estate, and if the personal representatives would not—or could not—use it, it did not fall to the court to extend the remedy to the beneficiaries.

3.14   The court in *Worby* did not need to consider the question as to whether or not the costs could have been recovered by the personal representatives against the solicitor (that was not how the action was based), but counsel for the defendant did suggest that such recovery could

---

[14]   (1861) 4 Macq 167.

[15]   [2000] WTLR 453.

[16]   (1999) 2 ITELR 59.

[17]   The will was invalid for want of both testamentary capacity and knowledge and approval, and it was also found that its execution had been procured through the undue influence of the testator's accountant.

[18]   They were arguing for a duty of care to them that was breached by preparing a will when the testator lacked the necessary capacity and was subject to the malign influence of a third party.

[19]   Why the personal representatives did not take the action is not wholly clear.

never be the case. Chadwick LJ in his judgment drew attention to this submission, but commented that he did not accept counsel's proposition that

> there were no circumstances in which such a claim would lie. It seems to me that such a submission goes too far. But as I have said it is not necessary to decide what the relevant circumstances would be.

He further observed:　　　　　　　　　　　　　　　　　　　　　　　　　　　　　　**3.15**

> If the solicitor's breach of duty under his retainer has given rise to the need for expensive probate proceedings, resulting in unrecovered costs, then, prima facie, those costs fall to be borne by the estate . . . If the estate bears the costs thereby and suffers loss then, if there is to be a remedy against the solicitor, it should be the estate's remedy for the loss to the estate. There is no need to fashion an independent remedy for a beneficiary who has been engaged in the probate proceedings. His or her costs, if properly incurred in obtaining probate of the true will, can be provided for out of the estate. If there has been a breach of duty by the solicitor, the estate can recover from the solicitor the additional costs (including the costs to which the beneficiary is entitled out of the estate).

Worby was, while rejecting the direct duty to the beneficiaries of the earlier will, leaving open **3.16** the question of costs being recovered at the legal personal representatives' action, and the *obiter* remarks of Chadwick LJ are persuasive.[20]

The question of costs recovery made in this way was revisited in *Sifri v Clough & Willis*[21] **3.17** where liability was, to a degree, accepted by the court. In an earlier action, the claimant had succeeded in overturning two wills made by her father on grounds of want of knowledge and approval, although with no order as to costs. The second action was for recovery of the costs of the first action in so far as they related to the grounds on which she was successful in challenging the wills.[22] Although the court ordered that letters of administration be granted to the claimant to administer the estate, no grant had been obtained and the claimant sued in her personal capacity. The defendant firm admitted negligence in the preparation of the will and accepted liability, but disputed the quantum. This judgment does not contain any detailed consideration of *Worby* or *Corbett v Bond Pearce* (considered below).

The Court of Appeal reconsidered the duty of care to beneficiaries of an earlier will, after **3.18** *Worby*, in *Corbett v Bond Pearce*,[23] which, whilst it clarified some aspects, has left some substantial issues unclear. In *Corbett* there were[24] substantial costs in the earlier probate action[25] and the burden of these costs had fallen on the estate. However, unlike *Worby*, the

---

[20] A similar action to *Worby* can be found in the New Zealand Court of Appeal case *Knox v Till* [2000] Lloyd's Rep PN 49. There was the same refusal to extend the duty to the beneficiaries of the earlier valid will, but there was no examination comparable to *Worby* of the rights of the personal representatives of the earlier will.

[21] [2007] WTLR 1453 (Ch).

[22] The claimant had failed in claims of want of capacity and undue influence.

[23] [2001] WTLR 419; for an excellent analysis of the Court of Appeal judgment, see Sue Carr and Graham Chapman, 'Where There's a Will, There's a Damages Claim' (2001) 2 *The TACT Review* 3 available at <http://www.trustees.org.uk>.

[24] The invalidity of the will was established in *Corbett v Newey* [1996] 2 All ER 914. The will failed because of its ineffective conditional execution. This is a form of execution that is far from common and the execution of the will was held to be valid in the first instance. It is worth asking if the solicitors were really negligent, or merely committed an excusable error of professional judgment given that the first instance decision was in their favour even though the Court of Appeal was against them.

[25] These have variously been estimated between £150,000 and £250,000.

disappointed beneficiaries under the failed will agreed *White v Jones*-based compensation, without trial, for the loss of benefit—the will would have validly represented the testatrix's intentions but for the negligent supervision of its execution. The disappointed beneficiaries were paid, by the solicitors' insurers, the value of the residue of the estate without any deduction for the costs of the action, ie they were placed in the same position as they would have been with no negligent execution of the later will and no costs left in the estate.

3.19   The personal representative of the earlier will, which was the only valid will and thus contained the dispositions effective on death, sought the recovery of the probate action costs on the grounds of the solicitors' negligence and, implicitly, that they were of sufficient proximity to their actions to have suffered a recoverable loss. At first instance this argument was successful.

3.20   The Court of Appeal, in reversing the first instance decision, found against the personal representative on the basis that to reimburse the probate action costs would amount to a double recovery of these costs against the negligent solicitors (after the first compensation sum to the disappointed beneficiaries did not deduct these costs in calculating the value of residue).

3.21   In the analysis of *Worby* in the *Corbett* Court of Appeal judgment Sir Christopher Slade commented:

> For present purposes the significance of [*Worby*] lies in the fact that the Court of Appeal accepted that in a case where a solicitor's negligence in regard to the preparation or execution of a will was the cause of expensive probate proceedings after the testator's death, this could give rise to a claim for damages against the solicitors at the suit of the testator's personal representatives for the benefit of the estate generally. On the particular facts of [*Worby*], the testator's personal representatives would have had a good cause of action for the loss suffered and, if they had pursued this claim, the solicitor would have been exposed to no double liability.[26]

3.22   The issue of double recovery is significant. If, as in *Corbett*, the costs are borne by the estate those entitled to the estate will have suffered loss. The disappointed residuary beneficiaries of the failed will are compensated on the basis of residue not being diminished by the costs, ie they will have been compensated in full for what they should have received. But recovery of the actual costs by the personal representatives is prevented on the grounds that this would amount to a double recovery of the same amount. This is notwithstanding that the negligent action of the solicitors will have caused loss to two separate parties, ie on a normal analysis have given rise to two separate claims for loss.[27] It does seem as though viewing the issue as liability for costs, as opposed to compensation for financial loss under two separate heads, leads into difficult areas.[28]

3.23   On the facts of *Worby* there was no possibility of double recovery as the testator lacked the testamentary capacity to make the later will.[29] However, if the testator had had capacity, but

---

[26] [2001] WTLR 419 at 430D–E; interesting to note the Court of Appeal not merely approved of Chadwick LJ's views but regarded the *Worby* claim, if made by the PRs, as being 'a good cause of action'.

[27] This was the analysis adopted at first instance by Eady J [2000] WTLR 655.

[28] As well as moving further away from the famous definition of the measure of damages by Lord Blackburn in *Livingstone v Rawyards Coal Co* [1880] 5 App Case 25: 'that sum of money which will put the party injured, or who has suffered, in the same position as he would have been if he had not sustained the wrong for which he is now getting his compensation or reparation'.

[29] The judgment does not reflect any action against the solicitor by those disappointed because of the later will's invalidity. Indeed, given that the testator not only lacked testamentary capacity but also had no knowledge or approval of the will's contents, and that the terms of the will were procured by the undue influence of the

the will failed through a breach of duty on the part of the solicitors, then by applying *Corbett* and compensating the disappointed beneficiaries, there would have been no recovery of the cost burden suffered by the estate. The position of the estate would therefore vary in terms of recovery, although its position remains the same in bearing the costs. This seems to introduce a major element of randomness into the personal representatives' right of recovery that is not related to their loss or actions.

It was argued at first instance that the compensation paid to the disappointed beneficiaries **3.24** in fact contained no element of costs in that it was simply the amount that would be properly payable to the beneficiary whether or not the probate action had occurred. It is the sum necessary to compensate for loss. Costs are a separate issue borne by the estate for which the personal representatives have a right of recovery.

It is not difficult to conceive of terms of wills which would give further difficulty in apply- **3.25** ing the Court of Appeal's view in *Corbett*, for example where the gifts of residue remain constant between the earlier and later wills and only specific gifts are varied. There would be no double recovery element along *Corbett* lines (the compensation for the loss of specific gifts would not be calculated to exclude the probate cost unless there had been an abatement) and the residuary legatees, albeit under the earlier will, would have suffered a real loss through the actions of the solicitor by the burden of the probate action costs. Under such circumstances, would the costs of the probate action be recoverable against the solicitor? Applying *Worby* they would, and the double recovery element of *Corbett* would fall away. To not recover them would result in an injustice to the residuary legatees, whilst recovery would make the solicitor's liability variable depending upon whether or not there were 'windfall' benefits.[30]

It is suggested that, notwithstanding the Court of Appeal's views, there is still much to be **3.26** explored in this area and that the duty to the legal personal representatives (it appears to be settled that there is no duty to the beneficiaries[31]) of an earlier will is likely to be re-examined when suitably different circumstances arise.

There are also issues of retainer involved in looking at the potential for liability to the legal **3.27** personal representatives under an earlier will. In *Worby*-type cases, retainer cannot be an issue given the testator's lack of knowledge, approval, and capacity. Therefore the potential limitation of liability through the retainer, explored in *Corbett* with the testator, did not arise in *Worby*.

The possible nature of the duty owed by the solicitor, if he owed a duty to the legal personal **3.28** representatives under an earlier will, was also reviewed in *Corbett*. This was looked at in the light of earlier decisions,[32] with the analysis that their retainer required the solicitor

---

testator's accountant (who was found to have acted fraudulently), it is difficult to see that compensation to the beneficiaries of the latter could have become an issue.

[30] But of course there will always be inconsistencies, the residuary legatees under the failed *Corbett* will were better off by losing the probate action. Had they won that action, there would have been found to have been no solicitor's negligence and the costs of the action would, in all probability, have been left in the estate, ie against the residue to the detriment of the residuary legatees, who would therefore have received less than they did after losing the action.

[31] See the *Lenesta Sludge* passage from Lord Goff's judgment in *White v Jones* [1995] 1 All ER 691 at 710C.

[32] *Banque Bruxelles Lambert SA v Eagle Star* [1997] AC 191 and *British Racing Drivers Club Ltd v Hextall Erskine & Co* [1996] 3 All ER 667.

to prevent the loss which could accrue to those interested in her estate either as creditors or as beneficiaries under the will which they were to prepare. Further, this duty could not extend to those who would benefit under the earlier will, as it was the intention that the will should have no further effect. This analysis of the limitation of the retainer may well prove to be an obstacle in any future re-examination of liability, although it is apparently inconsistent with Chadwick LJ's remarks (above) in *Worby* on the breach of duty to personal representatives.

3.29   In Sir Christopher Slade's judgment, there is a concluding passage:

> In the events which have happened, if there proves to be a residue for distribution, the two residuary beneficiaries (under the earlier will) will be better off than they would have been if there had been no breach of duty on the part of the defendants, because they would have received no part of the residuary estate if the September will had been effective. In reaching my conclusions, I am fortified by the consideration that if there proves to be a residue, justice scarcely demands that these benefits, unintended by the testatrix, to whom alone the defendants owed the duty of care now invoked by the claimant, should be received by the claimant at the expense of the defendant.[33]

3.30   The Court of Appeal's attitude towards 'windfall' benefits is unusual considering the usual absolute attitude of the courts towards the formal validity of wills. The earlier will was accepted in the probate action as being the valid disposition of the testatrix's estate. Looking behind that finding to say that the testatrix did not intend the benefit so that it may be eroded by the costs following from the negligent actions of the solicitor, lies very uneasily with the validity of the bequests.

3.31   The possibility of windfall gains by those entitled under an earlier will has always been acknowledged to be a part of the *White v Jones* solution but, at the same time, one that was of no relevance to the damages awarded. Lord Goff dismissed the argument against a disappointed beneficiary recovering loss on the grounds that this would effectively increase the size of the estate. He observed:

> I cannot see what impact this has on the disappointed beneficiary's remedy. It simply reflects the fact that those who received the testator's estate, either under an unrevoked will or on an intestacy, were lucky enough to receive a windfall; and in consequence the estate is, so far as the testator and the disappointed beneficiary are concerned, irretrievably lost.[34]

3.32   In the Court of Appeal in *White v Jones*, Sir Donald Nicholls V-C, as he then was, also dismissed the windfall argument:

> The damages are payable to the disappointed intended beneficiary, not to the deceased's estate. Those entitled to the deceased's estate receive a windfall in the sense that the deceased did not intend the estate should go to them. But that does not assist the solicitor's case. That is a direct and foreseeable consequence of the solicitor's breach of his duty to the client. Because of his negligence the client's money did not reach the right pockets. The law is requiring him to put that right in the only way it can be done.

---

[33] [2001] WTLR 419 at 434C–D. Sir Christopher Slade has subsequently downplayed the significance of this in his decision; see 'Professional Liability in the Will-Making Process', in J Getzler (ed), *Rationalizing Property, Equity and Trusts—Essays in Honour of Edward Burn* (LexisNexis, 2003).
[34] Lord Goff in *White v Jones* [1995] All ER 691 at 700F.

What is the position after *Worby*, *Corbett*, and *Sifri*?

Worby accepts the possibility that costs can be recovered by the estate against the draftsman **3.33**
of a later invalid will, and *Sifri* actually awarded the claimant the costs that related to the
successful grounds of the claim against the later will.

Both *Worby* and *Sifri* concerned work by draftsmen regarding invalid later wills, where the **3.34**
grounds of invalidity prevented any *White v Jones* claim being made by the disappointed
'beneficiaries' of the later will. By contrast, in *Corbett* there were clear grounds for a *White
v Jones* claim arising, once negligence was admitted. On the face of it, the differences in the
two approaches to recovery by the estate could be reconciled by saying that recovery of costs
by the estate depends upon whether or not there is a valid *White v Jones* claim in which compensation for costs to the beneficiary is an element and, in such a case, recovery of costs by
the personal representative is prevented on double recovery grounds. But is a reconciliation
of the court's approach on this basis reasonable?

That the claim on behalf of the testator's estate only exists if there is no *White v Jones* claim **3.35**
from disappointed beneficiaries seems an arbitrary approach—the estate suffers loss in both
instances. The difference in the two approaches then appears to make the estate's claim in
some way secondary to the beneficiaries' *White v Jones* claim, ie that the estate can only recover
costs if there is no disappointed beneficiary claim that benefits from the costs liability of the
draftsman—as in *Corbett*. If this is a correct analysis of the court's approach, then the *Corbett*
decision apparently turns on its head the reasoning used in *White v Jones*, in the House of
Lords, when creating a solution to beneficiaries' loss where the estate had suffered no loss.[35]

The position becomes a little more odd if, as in *Corbett*, the later will had given the residue to **3.36**
the same legatees as the previous will, but contained substantial specific bequests to others.
Applying *White v Jones*, the disappointed specific legatees would receive compensation for
their loss of benefit, but the residuary legatees would have no claim as they would have no
loss. The compensation for the specific legatees would not be affected by costs and then, in
the absence of the double recovery aspect, the estate could presumably recover the costs for
the benefit of the estate.

There does seem to be considerable scope to explore these issues further if a suitable case **3.37**
arises. In the meantime, the apparent inconsistency in approach between *Sifri* and *Worby*
serves to highlight the difficulties that still attach to the *Corbett* judgment.

C. No duty while testator is alive and can rectify

It is clear from both the Court of Appeal and the House of Lords judgments in *White v Jones* **3.38**
that the liability for a breach of the duty of care in will preparation can only arise where the
testator has died and cannot voluntarily rectify. A refusal by the testator to voluntarily rectify,
once the issue has been brought to his attention, must, in all usual circumstances, be sufficient evidence in itself to show a lack of continuing intention on the testator's part for the
disappointed beneficiary to benefit.[36]

---

[35] But not where the estate has a recoverable loss; see the lacuna question in *White v Jones* [1995] 1 All ER
691 at 710C.
[36] See the *Lenesta Sludge* passage from Lord Goff's speech (see Chapter 2 Part D above).

3.39 Being alive, but mentally incapable of rectification, raises rather interesting issues; as presumably rectification by way of a statutory will[37] is possible and potentially cheaper for the negligent will-preparer if there is time. However, as far as we are aware, this particular set of circumstances has not yet come before a court in a reported decision but, given the increasing age of the population, it cannot be long before it does.

D. Duty towards the beneficiary

3.40 The House of Lords in *White v Jones*[38] clearly considered that their decision only applied to a solicitor's duty towards a beneficiary under a will in which they were, or should have been, a beneficiary, and that the court was not creating any duty capable of wider application.[39]

3.41 This has not stopped attempts to persuade the courts otherwise, but, as yet, there has been no success in the area of private client work. In *Hemmens v Wilson Browne*[40] the court refused to find that any duty was owed by the donor's solicitor to the donee of a failed gift that the donor would not perfect. There had, prior to *White v Jones*, been an unsuccessful attempt to argue for a wider *Ross v Caunters*-based duty to the intended legatee in *Clarke v Bruce Lance & Co.*[41] In *Clarke* there was claimed to be a responsibility where post-execution transactions carried out by the testator with the solicitor's assistance affected interests under a will[42]—it is not surprising that it was distinguished from *Ross v Caunters*. It was alleged that where a solicitor was involved in such a transaction after the execution of the will that defeated one of the legacies in the will, the solicitor owed a duty of care to the beneficiary to advise the testator that what he was doing was contrary to the beneficiary's interests. This contention was rejected by the court.[43] In distinguishing the case from *Ross*, the court in *Clarke* expressly stated that in arriving at their decision they did not question the validity of *Ross v Caunters*.

3.42 The court in *Clarke* accepted that a solicitor can owe a duty to someone other than his client[44] and accepted, as did counsel for the solicitors, that solicitors owe a duty to beneficiaries under a will:

> This is not to suggest in any way that we question the correctness of the decision of Megarry V-C in *Ross v Caunters* . . . and of the Court of Appeal of New Zealand in *Gartside v Sheffield Young & Ellis*[45] . . . it is just that the point is unnecessary for our decision in this case . . . the duty of care alleged in this case is far wider than that found to exist in *Ross v Caunters* and accepted as arguable in Gartside's case . . . In both those cases solicitors had been instructed to prepare a will. In *Ross v Caunters* they failed to warn the testator that a will should not be signed by the spouse of a beneficiary . . . In *Gartside* . . . the negligence was a failure to comply promptly with the instructions of an aged testatrix . . . In our judgment none of the factors which were

---

[37] Sections 16 and 18 Mental Capacity Act 2005.
[38] [1995] 1 All ER 691.
[39] *Trusted v Clifford Chance* [2000] WTLR 1219.
[40] [1993] 4 All ER 826—this pre-dates *White v Jones* and was argued on *Ross v Caunters* grounds.
[41] [1988] 1 All ER 364.
[42] An option having been granted by the testator over a service station that was a specific bequest in an earlier will.
[43] The *All England Annual Review* (1988) at 295 observed that: 'This must be correct since otherwise the solicitor would face an impossible conflict of interest because the testator's interest and the beneficiaries' interests do not march hand in hand.'
[44] *Wilson v Bloomfield* (1979) 123 SJ 860.
[45] [1983] NZLR 37.

considered to be material in *Ross v Caunters* and *Gartside v Sheffield Young & Ellis* are present in the instant case.[46]

In *Clarke*, the testator had bequeathed a property to his wife for life with part of the remain- **3.43** der to a nephew. Subsequently, the testator granted a lease over the property with an option to purchase by the tenant at a fixed price. It was claimed that the solicitor knew, or ought to have known, that the plaintiff's interest as a beneficiary under the will would be adversely affected by the option and that they owed the beneficiary a duty of care similar to that owed to the testator. The court considered that, in the grant of the option, the transaction did not have as its object the benefit of the plaintiff. It was a transaction intended for the testator's benefit and, in that, his interests and those of the beneficiary were in conflict. Under such circumstances the solicitors could not owe a duty to the plaintiff without being placed in an intolerable position towards their client.[47]

The Court of Appeal also considered that if the testator had been negligently advised regard- **3.44** ing the granting of the option, as was additionally alleged by the plaintiff (but which the court did not concede was correct), then there would be a remedy for the legal personal representatives against such negligence. However, if they were to concede that the plaintiff also had a remedy in tort, then there would be the possibility of the solicitors being doubly at risk from two claims. This was on the basis that any remedy for the personal representatives would accrue for the residuary estate and not the devised fund.[48]

A similar issue to *Clarke v Bruce Lance & Co* was considered in the later *Punford v Gilberts* **3.45** *Accountants*[49] but it ended with the same result, again in the Court of Appeal. However, in this case the court could not accept that the testator did not understand that by executing the transfer of the property (to place in joint names with another) he was making it impossible for the terms of his will regarding it to take effect. The court believed that the testator was quite free to take the action he did and that it was not arguable that the defendant had any duty to the plaintiff or anyone else to point out the obvious to the testator.

Clarke v Bruce Lance & Co would have been distinguished in *Punford* if the claim that the tes- **3.46** tator's intention was that his wishes for his will would continue notwithstanding the transaction under scrutiny (as was claimed by the plaintiff) had succeeded. On the basis that the court's ultimate finding was that they did not accept this contention, *Clarke v Bruce Lance & Co* was not distinguished and by implication was reinforced by this decision.

This aspect of a later transaction being made in the testator's belief that his wishes for the **3.47** distribution under his will should remain unchanged, ie that the later transaction would reinforce and not undo the terms of his will, is an area of risk for the draftsman. Clearly in *Punford* the court did not fully explore this aspect, as they found that the continued intention that the terms of the will should continue were missing. Had this been conclusively found to be present, the judgment indicates that there could have been a duty to the beneficiary:

---

[46] Balcombe J [1988] 1 All ER 364 at 367J.
[47] See n 43 above.
[48] This issue of potential double liability would prove problematic for future consideration of negligence and will preparation (see earlier at para 3.10 onwards).
[49] [1998] PNLR 763.

a professional man, who has undertaken the preparation of a will or who has advised in regard to a will intending to benefit a third party, owes a duty of care to that third party when giving subsequent advice to the testator which is intended to ensure that his instructions as expressed in the will continue to benefit the third party, in the event that such advice is found to have been given negligently and the benefit to the third party is defeated.[50]

3.48 In the light of this, transactions which diminish the estate or alter the nature of property owned should be considered carefully and, where suitable, accompanied by a recommendation that the terms of the will are reviewed in order to establish if

- they are affected by the transaction; and
- if the testator wishes to make alternative provision.

3.49 Clearly, if the testator declines such advice, the solicitor will have been released from the duty envisaged in *Punford*. Alternatively, if the client requests the advice then the provision of the advice satisfies the duty. That is to say, either the refusal releases the solicitor from the duty or the acceptance provides the solicitor with the prospect of further fee earning for the advice (and either answer is preferable to not asking the question).

3.50 It is important to note that the duty, as framed in the above quotation, is not simply a duty owed to the beneficiary of the previously drawn will, as such a duty has already been rejected in *Clarke v Bruce Lance & Co.*[51] The duty will only arise where the testator intends 'that his instructions as expressed in the will continue to benefit the third party'. In order to avoid the difficulties encountered by the defendant, it now appears to be best practice to enquire about the testator's intentions for his will when an *inter vivos* disposal is being considered.

E. Who does the duty of care apply to?

3.51 Although *Ross v Caunters* quite clearly dealt with the liability of the solicitor will-preparer, most responsible non-solicitor will-preparers recognized that, although the court had not examined their position, it was most unlikely that any future court would decide that the principle did not apply to non-solicitor will-preparers and that a different standard of care would be applied. This view was subsequently found to be correct in *Esterhuizen*,[52] which was the first time that a court was asked to rule on this point.[53]

> I do not however accept that *White v Jones* is confined to solicitors. The essence of the decision was that the solicitor's assumption of responsibility carried with it an assumption of responsibility to prospective beneficiaries of whom he was aware. The solicitor had assumed responsibility in their case because it was part of a solicitor's business to assume that sort of responsibility. If however a non-solicitor assumes the same sort of responsibility I see no reason why such a person should be exempt from the general principle there laid down ... It seems to me in this case Allied Dunbar did assume responsibility in the same way.

3.52 The view expressed in this case was on the legal liabilities and duties involved in will preparation, but it did not attempt to impose more widely any professional rules governing the

---

[50] [1998] PNLR 763 at 767 (per Sir Christopher Slade).
[51] [1988] 1 All ER 364.
[52] [1998] 2 FLR 668 at 676C.
[53] [1998] 2 FLR 668: 'From the consumer's point of view it would be a trap for the unwary if the law imposed a significantly lower duty on non-solicitors' (per Longmore LJ).

conduct of solicitors in will preparation on non-solicitor will-preparers. Having said this, it is quite conceivable that a court might look to such rules for guidance on particular points of good practice when considering practice for non-solicitor will draftsmen.

The position of barristers who are instructed to prepare wills must also be the same as that of solicitors, the general bar immunity having been removed in *Arthur JS Hall & Co v Simons*.[54] **3.53**

The question of a professional preparing a will without charge for either a client or non-client has not been considered in the context of wills. The will prepared for an existing client without charge (perhaps as part of a larger client relationship exercise) would seem to contain the same duty of care as a will that is charged for. Where a will is prepared on a voluntary basis there is less guidance.[55] **3.54**

There is no authority in this area in respect of will preparation by a non-professional which is not for gain. It is difficult to see the same duty of care being imposed upon the lay person. **3.55**

F. Duty of a claimant to mitigate

Where the beneficiary seeks to show that there is a liability on the part of the will-preparer, he must be prepared to take all reasonable steps, in the circumstances of the particular claim, to mitigate his loss (as he would in any other action). The implications of this general principle are examined more closely in regard to litigation in Chapter 23. **3.56**

This was stated quite clearly by the Court of Appeal in *Walker v Medlicott*[56] when considering if a claimant's possible right to seek rectification of a will under s.20 Administration of Justice Act 1982 could be ignored or discounted.[57] No claimant has a duty to mitigate by following an unduly complex or speculative course of litigation (see *Pilkington v Wood*[58]), but the Court of Appeal found that a rectification action under s.20 Administration of Justice Act 1982 did not fall into the category of an unduly complex or speculative action, on its particular facts. **3.57**

Horsfall v Haywards[59] followed swiftly after *Walker v Medlicott*, and in this case the Court of Appeal made it clear that it did not view *Walker v Medlicott* as laying down an absolute rule regarding mitigation, and that any requirement to mitigate will depend upon the facts of each case. **3.58**

Although there is no English decision on it, mitigation will almost certainly be required of a beneficiary, by that beneficiary bringing into account any benefits which were received under intestacy or an earlier valid will, against that which is claimed as having been lost under the later failed bequest.[60] Whilst the court will not seek to recover 'windfall' benefits from those **3.59**

---

[54] [2000] 3 WLR 543.

[55] In *Waters v Maguire* [1999] Lloyd's Rep PN 855 the court declined to rule that a barrister undertaking pro bono work did not owe the same duty of care as when fully retained.

[56] [1999] 1 WLR 727.

[57] See *Chittock v Stevens* [2001] WTLR 643 on the criteria for applications later than six months after grant of probate (similar to those for I(PFD)A 1975 claims set out *Re Salmon* [1981] Ch 167).

[58] [1953] 2 All ER 810.

[59] [2000] WTLR 29. The estate had been distributed, because of the will's defective drafting, to the surviving spouse who was, together with her inheritance, living in Canada. There was no evidence that the defect in the will was capable of being remedied under s.20 Administration of Justice Act 1982.

[60] *Whittingham v Crease* [1978] 5 WWR 45 (Canada).

who receive them, it would be inequitable not to bring them into account if the claimant and windfall beneficiary are one and the same.

3.60 There is as yet no comprehensive judicial comment on the interaction of such claims with the Inheritance (Provision for Family and Dependants) Act 1975 (I(PFD)A 1975). But it does seem reasonable for such litigation to be required to be undertaken to mitigate a claim following the reasoning in *Walker v Medlicott*, in a very clear case for the Act to apply, such as the omission of benefit for a spouse. Thus, if the valid will makes insufficient provision for a dependant and that dependant has a right of action under the I(PFD)A 1975, then the inheritance action should be satisfied first, before looking to the solicitors for the costs of the action and any excess, over the value of the decided claim, that the disappointed beneficiary would have received but for the solicitors' negligence.[61]

3.61 It is legitimate to ask the question of whether or not the amount claimed for loss of benefit by a disappointed beneficiary could be reduced by the court, if the terms of a failed will would manifestly not have survived an I(PFD)A 1975 claim by another. This point was submitted in defence of the solicitor-defendant in *Horsfall v Haywards*[62] and was clearly considered. In *Horsfall*, however, the court (both at first instance and in the Court of Appeal) did not accept that it was realistic to assume that the widow's possible I(PFD)A 1975 claim would have had a realistic chance of upsetting the terms of the will. The inference of the Court of Appeal's remarks must be that such an issue must be considered in future if a possible I(PFD)A 1975 claim would have reasonable prospects of reducing the disappointed beneficiary's lost benefit.

3.62 It can be possible, where an error has occurred in the will or the will failed, that the beneficiaries entitled to the estate may be prepared to voluntarily correct the problem through a deed of variation. Willingness to do this on the part of the beneficiaries is of course most helpful, and will operate to mitigate or even remove completely the claim against the draftsman. However, the draftsman should be careful about promoting this as a solution, unless he is quite sure that the beneficiaries are

- fully aware of their legal position;
- fully aware of the position of the draftsman and the effect that their action could have on his liability; and
- advised that independent advice should be taken as he is unable to advise them because of his conflict of interest.[63]

3.63 The perils of approaching this without such caution were illustrated in the Canadian decision in *Hatch v Cooper*.[64] The claimant, the deceased's widow, was persuaded to rectify a defect in a will to her disadvantage, without the advantage of independent advice. When the

---

[61] This proposition was not followed in *Whittingham v Crease* where the court decided that the loss was not the difference between the benefit on intestacy and the benefit under the will, but the difference between a successful claim under Canadian family provision legislation and what was received under intestacy. The value of the family provision claim was calculated by the court without action. However, it is suggested that *Walker v Medlicott* would now require such a claim to be actually heard.

[62] [2000] WTLR 29.

[63] To remove any taint of conflict, the rectifying deed of arrangement should be prepared independently.

[64] 2001 SKQB 491.

claimant subsequently became aware of what her rights regarding the estate were, she successfully claimed for compensation from the draftsman.[65]

G. Acting in accordance with the client's instructions

A solicitor has a general duty to act in accordance with his client's instructions.[66] The solicitor **3.64** has a duty to advise on the matter on which he is instructed,[67] but it is not part of this duty '*to force his advice on his client*'.[68] Thus, if correct advice is given,[69] and the client instructs the solicitor to act against it, the solicitor, being required to follow his client's instructions,[70] will have a valid defence if that course of action ultimately causes loss[71] to the beneficiaries of the client's will. This underlines the necessity to clearly record the advice given and the instructions received.

H. Failure to revoke a will

Although all of the litigation to date has concerned the preparation of wills, the duty regard- **3.65** ing the preparation of a will could, in some circumstances, by extension, apply to the revocation of a will. For example, where a solicitor is given instructions to secure the revocation of a will on the grounds that, say, it is inappropriate and the testator is content for his estate to pass on intestacy, a failure to secure revocation through negligent advice or action could expose the solicitor to a claim from those who would have benefited from the intestate provision. Under such circumstances, it would seem that there is no real difference between the testator seeking to benefit his beneficiaries either through a will or through the intestate provisions.

I. Liability

Where loss has been caused through a breach of the draftsman's duty of care, the liability is **3.66** that of the solicitor's firm (or their insurer). The court does not have the power to alter the actual distribution on intestacy or under the will. Although the testator may have intended to have a will prepared, the fact that this was not put into effect gives rise to no power for the court to implement the wishes (see the subsequent section for comment on other jurisdictions where this is possible). The law of unjust enrichment[72] does not play a role in this and

---

[65] The position became worse because the solicitor was bound by his actions to have placed himself in relation to the claimant as an adviser (in seeking her signature to the deed) and the court further disapproved of his conduct as her adviser in not advising her of her rights under the Province's family provision legislation.

[66] *Re Graham & Oldham* [2000] BPIR 354; *Fraser v Gaskell* [2004] PNLR 32.

[67] In *McMullen v Farrell* [1993] 1 IR 123: 'A solicitor cannot ... fulfil his obligations to his client merely by carrying out what he is instructed to do. This is to ignore the essential element of any contract involving professional care and advice ... a solicitor ... has an obligation to consider not only what the client wishes him to do but also the legal implication of the facts which the client brings to his attention.'

[68] *Dutfield v Gilbert H Stephens & Sons* [1988] 18 Fam Law 473.

[69] *Morris v Duke-Cohen & Co* [1975] 119 SJ 826 where the defence to the claim failed because of inadequate advice.

[70] Alternatively the retainer could be ended if there are suitable grounds for the solicitor to do so.

[71] *Waine v Kempster* [1859] 1 F&F 744.

[72] See *Lipkin Gorman v Karpnale Ltd* [1991] 2 AC 548.

the benefits received by the beneficiaries cannot be recovered. Their benefit has been lawfully obtained under the valid disposition of the estate.

3.67 The position of an employee of a firm preparing a will does contain an element of uncertainty. The courts have, in a number of cases, resolved the issue of liability of the employee by refusing to find in favour of such liability.[73] However, a contrary result was reached in *Merrett v Babb*[74] where an employed surveyor was found to be liable to the client.[75] The Court of Appeal was satisfied that there was a duty owed by an employee to his firm's client[76] but:

> It is, of course, unfortunate for Mr Babb, if he is not insured against this claim. It is not, I think, relevant ... that Mr Babb ... is not insured, although it is a material consideration that there may be circumstances in which employed professionals may find themselves personally liable for claims against which they are uninsured. Since professional employers will normally be vicariously liable for their professional employees' breaches of duty, it may be supposed that a solvent employer's professional indemnity policy will normally cover claims against their professional employees. *Prudent professional employees will obviously want to ensure that they are covered personally by their employer's insurance and may need to take steps to obtain personal insurance if that cover does not continue after their employment ends.* (per May LJ (authors' emphasis))

3.68 The law in this area is not without its problems until the conflict between this view and that in *Williams v Natural Life Health Foods Ltd* is resolved. It may be possible that *Merrett v Babb* is capable of being viewed as arising out of special facts, but until the conflict of decisions in this area is resolved it may well be unwise to rely on that view.

3.69 This is obviously a most important area for any professional without personal indemnity cover, who has relied on his employer's insurance both during his employment and for the appropriate limitation[77] period for claims after it ends. It is a major issue for anyone who provides will drafting[78] while relying on his employer's professional insurance cover to ensure that there is run-off cover for his work.

3.70 An alternative approach would be for firms to safeguard their employees by the inclusion, with their client terms of engagement, of a condition that claims arising out of the work undertaken will only be pursued against the firm and specifically that the client will not pursue claims against employees personally.

J. Substantial compliance with formalities

> The rule of literal compliance with the Wills Act is a snare for the ignorant and the ill-advised, a needless hangover from a time when the law of proof was in its infancy. In the three centuries since the first Wills Act, we have developed the means to adjudicate whether formal defects are harmless to the statutory purpose. We are reminded that

---

[73] *Williams v Natural Life Health Foods Ltd* [1998] 1 WLR 830; *Standard Chartered Bank v Pakistan National Shipping Corp (Nos 2 & 4)* [2002] 1 AC 959; *Harris v Wyre Forest DC* [1988] 1 All ER 691; *London Drugs Ltd v Kuehne & Nagel International Ltd* [1992] 97 DLR (4th) 261.
[74] [2001] PNLR 29.
[75] His employer had ceased trading and the trustee in bankruptcy had cancelled the insurance cover without providing run-off cover.
[76] *Smith v Eric S Bush* [1990] 1 AC 831; *Phelps v Hillingdon Borough Council* [2000] 3 WLR 776.
[77] See later in Chapter 21 for a discussion of limitations.
[78] Professor John Murdoch in 'Negligent Advice: Whose Duty is It?' (2001) 17(2) *Professional Negligence* 123 more graphically describes it as 'the stuff of nightmares'.

'legal technicality is a disease not of the old age, but of the infancy of societies'. The rule of literal compliance has outlived whatever utility it may have had. The time for the substantial doctrine has come.[79]

Finding sufficient grounds to admit a will to probate, even if the formalities might be lacking, is a feature of some other jurisdictions. This has become known as 'substantial compliance' and effectively operates a statute-authorized mitigation process, but one with much wider scope than the two limited grounds in s.20 Administration of Justice Act 1982.[80] An example of this can be found in Wills Act 1997 (Victoria):   **3.71**

s.9 ...
(1) The Supreme Court may admit to probate as the will of a deceased person—
   (a) a document which has not been executed in the manner in which a will is required to be executed by this Act; or
   (b) a document, an alteration to which has not been executed in the manner in which an alteration to a will is required to be executed by this Act—
   if the Court is satisfied that that person intended the document to be his or her will.
(2) The Supreme Court may refuse to admit a will to probate which the testator has purported to revoke by some writing, where the writing has not been executed in the manner in which a will is required to be executed by this Act, if the Court is satisfied that the testator intended to revoke the will by that writing.
(3) In making a decision under sub-section (1) or (2) the Court may have regard to—
   (a) any evidence relating to the manner in which the document was executed; and
   (b) any evidence of the testamentary intentions of the testator, including evidence of statements made by the testator.

Provisions of similar effect are to be found, for example, in: **3.72**

s.10 Wills Act (Northern Territory)[81]
s.18A Wills, Probate and Administration Act 1898 (New South Wales)
s.12 Wills Act 1936 (South Australia)

The Australian experience of substantial compliance is generally thought to have been positive.[82]

Although the desirability of relaxing formal requirements in this way can be argued from several standpoints, court discretion to admit wills to probate in this way can reduce the potential cost for a breach of duty in relation to the preparation of a will. If *Ross v Caunters* was viewed in this light, there seems little doubt that the will would have been admitted to probate. There was, after all, sufficient evidence of intention on which to found a successful negligence claim and that should therefore have been sufficient to admit the will to probate under one of the Australian state provisions above. Whilst one could understand that a claim   **3.73**

---

[79] Professor John H Langbein, 'Substantial Compliance with the Wills Act' (1975) 88 *Harv L Rev* 489 at 531.

[80] Clerical error or failure to understand the testator's instructions.

[81] Somewhat challengingly, s.10(1) defines a document constituting a will as meaning 'a record of information' which includes: '(a) anything on which there is writing; (b) anything on which there are marks, figures, symbols or perforations having a meaning for persons qualified to interpret them; (c) anything from which sound, images or writings can be reproduced with or without the aid of another device; and (d) a map, plan, drawing or photograph.'

[82] Professor John H Langbein, 'Crumbling of the Wills Act: Australians Point the Way' (1979) 65 *American Bar Association Journal* 1192; Christopher Bevan, 'Admitting to Probate Informal Wills—An Australian Success Story' (2004) 1(2) *Trust Quarterly* 7.

might well lie against the solicitor for any probate action costs, those would, on the *Ross v Caunters* facts, have been less expensive. Similar results could be achieved on the evidence shown in other cases in which the English court has explored breach of duty.

3.74   Given the increased tendency to litigate on alleged will negligence and the relative strictness of the formal requirements of a will, it does seem worth considering if a more practical and equitable solution could be arrived at by reforming the Wills Act 1837 to allow the court a discretion to admit 'wills' where formal requirements are lacking by present standards (even if it would mean departing from the greater degree of certainty which the Wills Act 1837 provides)[83] but there is provable intention on the part of the testator.

---

[83]   For an interesting discussion of the implications of this type of legislation, see John H Langbein, 'Excusing Harmless Errors in the Execution of Wills: A Report on Australia's Tranquil Revolution in Probate Law' (1987) 87 *Colum L Rev* 1. See also Hilary E Laidlaw, 'Sills v Daley and the Doctrine of Substantial Compliance: Is "Close" Good Enough?' (2004) 4(1) *Trust Quarterly Review* 6, which deals with the Canadian position and concludes that there is much uncertainty as to the extent that substantial compliance applies in Canada.

PART B

THE PROCESS OF WILL PREPARATION

4

CLIENT ISSUES

A. Who is the client?

There is increasing concern about financial abuse of the elderly, and therefore correct iden- **4.01** tification of the client is becoming an ever more important question for will preparation.

There has been at least one case of impersonation of a testatrix that has received media public- **4.02** ity.[1] This concerned the conviction at Basildon Crown Court of fraudsters who had arranged for the impersonation of an elderly lady, who was in their care, in order to give instructions for a new will (for their benefit). Such impersonation may not be common, but anecdotal evidence is that it happens. The press reports of the case made it quite clear that there was no question of the will instructions having been taken in any way negligently by the will draftsman involved, but it is not hard to envisage that, if the process was in any way carelessly undertaken, the costs of any probate action occasioned might be claimed against the solicitor.[2]

The advent of anti-money-laundering (AML) checks on the identity of clients has helped to **4.03** prevent impersonation. Although such checks on a client's identity are not required for the

---

[1] *R v Spillman, Spillman & Russill* [2001] 1 Cr App R (S) 139: for an interesting commentary on this, see Peter Jeffreys, 'Uncovering Probate Fraud' (*TACT*, October 2000) </http:www.trustees.org.uk/review-index/Fraud-Probate-fraud.php> accessed 4 December 2013. More recently, from Nova Scotia, see *Re Willis, Willis v Wilson* [2010] WTLR 169.

[2] By analogy with *Worby v Rosser* [1999] 2 ITELR 59. See also, by analogy, *Sheik Ahmed Jaber Al-Sabah v Fehmi Mohamed Ali* [1997] PNLR 393 (Ch, per Ferris J), where a firm of solicitors was liable in negligence for having carried out various property transactions based on a forged power of attorney. They accepted the instructions from a person claiming to represent the supposed client without ascertaining the true position. The transactions involved the sale of the supposed client's property to the person with ostensible authority and thus the duty imposed on the solicitors was heavier still.

preparation of a will (as it is not a relevant financial transaction[3]), many firms standardize their anti-money-laundering checks and apply them to their will preparation business.

4.04 Where a will is invalid, by reason of undue influence or want of the testator's knowledge and approval, there can be exposure to a claim for the costs of the probate action if the solicitor's role in the matter was carried out carelessly and below the expected standards of good practice.[4] This points up an obvious danger in taking instructions from anyone except the testator himself, however well meaning or concerned the other parties or intermediaries may be.

4.05 *Richards v Allen*[5] highlighted several aspects of the problems of wills for the elderly, but in fact contained no judicial comment on the position of the will-preparer who prepared a will through third party instructions, where the third party would benefit (and where the court found the will to be invalid because of want of knowledge and approval and lack of testamentary capacity[6]). Concern about the risks of third party instructions was earlier expressed by the Privy Council in *Battan Singh v Amirchand*.[7] More recently, third party instructions have been reviewed in *Re Morris (deceased)*[8] and Rimer J's judgment makes most salutary reading for anyone tempted to cut corners when presented with 'clear warning signs that this was a frail and elderly lady about whose mental capacity questions were being raised' and third party instructions. In *Sifri v Orrell*[9] instructions through a third party clearly failed to result in the testator having sufficient knowledge and approval of two wills.

4.06 There is a clear risk to the will-preparer if he acts on third party will instructions

1. without confirmation, independent of the third party, from the client that the instructions are indeed the client's true wishes;
2. without confirmation from the second party where the instructions are joint but are given by only one party;
3. where there are reasonable grounds to suspect duress or undue influence in the will instructions.

4.07 A will prepared in this manner will, in all probability, be invalid and also expose the preparer to the costs of the probate action.[10]

---

[3] Paragraph 1.4.5 of the *Law Society Practice Note*, 22 February 2008, although consideration should be given as to whether or not any tax planning advice given with the will is a regulated transaction requiring customer due diligence.

[4] *Worby v Rosser* [1999] 2 ITELR 59; *Sifri v Clough & Willis* [2007] WTLR 1453. In *Re Key, Key v Key* [2010] WTLR 623 the tenor of the judge's remarks leaves little doubt that there will have been a number of issues post-trial as to the solicitor's liability for a considerable part of the costs of the action.

[5] [2001] WTLR 1031. This was an action regarding the validity of the will and there is no comment in the judgment about the duty of care, or otherwise, of the solicitor who prepared the will (without seeing the elderly testatrix) where the instructions benefited the solicitor's sister-in-law, who procured the preparation and execution of the will (which was found to be invalid).

[6] See *Sifri v Clough & Willis* (n 4) for an example of such costs being successfully recovered.

[7] [1949] AC 161; an appeal from Fiji regarding the application of the rule in *Parker v Felgate* (1883) 8 PD 171 where the will instructions came via a third party.

[8] *Re Morris (deceased), Special Trustees for Great Ormond Street Hospital for Children v Rushin* [2001] WTLR 1137.

[9] [2007] WTLR 1453; the judge distinguished between (a) where a testator knows and approves the terms of a will, but mistakenly, from explanations or otherwise, believes them to have a different effect and (b) where the testator does not know the actual wording, but believes the wording to be in terms which achieve a different result. In the former, the will takes effect as the contents were known and approved *Re Beech's Estate, Beech v Public Trustee* (1923) PD 46. In the latter case the will cannot take effect.

[10] *Sifri v Clough & Willis* (n 4).

All too often members of a family are keen to convey or 'interpret' the wishes of elderly rela-   **4.08**
tives for the will-preparer. They 'know best' what auntie wants and very often what auntie
is said to want will be of benefit to those very same members of the family. Such wishes can
often be a genuine reflection of what auntie does want, but equally there are very different circumstances where it is far less clear what the relative actually wants and the family
members may well not have auntie's interests at heart. Therefore, it is good practice that the
person taking instructions should always try to avoid any other persons being present, even
if they do not actively participate in the meeting, as mere presence can substantially inhibit
free discussion. It can sometimes be difficult to achieve this, but doing so will help to remove
suspicion of influence if there is a later challenge.[11]

Knowing who the client is should also give some information to the draftsman as to the   **4.09**
urgency of the will. Again, it may appear obvious that the sick and elderly require priority
of service, but their needs for wills are not always established at the outset, although it is
essential that this is done. In the New Zealand case of *Gartside*[12] a seven-day delay was found
to be excessive for a client, aged eighty-nine (who had recently had a fall) in a nursing home.
It is therefore vital to establish such information at the outset. This point matches generally
with the need to know the client's circumstances (see later at para 6.51 onwards for a more
detailed discussion of timing).

Assessing the urgency of a will necessitates some degree of training for secretaries or others   **4.10**
who may place appointments in the draftsman's diary. Unless the draftsman is to assess the
client and make the appointment himself, the person making the appointment must be sufficiently trained to make an informed assessment and thus control ongoing risk.

Identification of the client becomes particularly difficult when Internet will provision is   **4.11**
considered, and the lack of a satisfactory way of doing this should be covered in the Internet
service's terms and conditions of business (see later at para 7.07 onwards).

B. Language

If the client's first language is not English, to what extent can they speak and read English?   **4.12**
The difficulty with their English may be that an understanding sufficient for basic conversa-
tion is insufficient to cope with the detail of a will or with the legal concepts involved in an
English will. Other difficulties may be an absence of written or spoken English (or both).

Of particular difficulty is the explanation of the whole concept of testamentary freedom   **4.13**
(albeit circumscribed to an extent by the Inheritance (Provision for Family and Dependants)
Act 1975). This might well conflict with the cultural or religious views of the testator, or represent an idea outside his previous experience. Nonetheless, it is important to establish the

---

[11] See *Buckenham v Dickinson* [2000] WTLR 1083 for an example of instructions being taken from others
and the testator not being questioned constructively. Also, Templeman J, as he then was, in setting out the
'Golden Rule' in *Re Simpson* (1997) 127 NLJ 487. However, in the recent *Hawes v Burgess* [2013] WTLR 453,
while the Court of Appeal did not express any general disapproval of the will instructions being taken in the
presence of the testatrix's daughter (at a meeting the daughter had organized with a solicitor of her choice), this
was clearly a factor in the finding of want of knowledge and approval (as was her contribution to the dispositive
directions for the will).
[12] *Gartside v Sheffield Young & Ellis* [1983] NZLR 37.

extent he is aware of testamentary freedom as any assumption by testators that it is absent, or is constrained, can radically affect the terms of the will.

4.14 The question of the testator's domicile is one which is particularly difficult to discuss, even where English is the first language, given the nuances of the words used in its explanation.[13] It must not be overlooked that the law relating to wills contains technical words and issues that are often difficult to explain even to someone whose first language is English.

Practical pointers

4.15 Practical pointers for this issue are:

1. If the client can understand sufficient English, use simple words and phrases and replace technical terms with simpler explanations.
2. If the client can understand sufficient English, explain the legal issues involved (testamentary freedom and its limits, joint property, formality requirements, etc): do not assume any knowledge of them.
3. If the client can understand sufficient English, ensure that there is a full written record of the advice given. This is probably best done by letter evidencing what was said and agreed, but if the client cannot read English then much more emphasis is going to be placed on ensuring that the verbal advice has been adequately understood (or having the letter and your client care letter translated).
4. Where the client's English is not adequate, a professional interpreter is best (but more expensive and not always available). Very often a member of the testator's family will accompany him to translate. This is potentially dangerous if the family member (or the member's spouse) stands to benefit. It is very difficult to escape issues of knowledge and approval and undue influence when a family member provides this assistance in this way.
5. Where an interpreter is being used, ensure that questions are put to the client and that they are not responded to by the interpreter.
6. Where an interpreter is used, adapt the attestation clause accordingly and similarly adapt the execution where the testator is illiterate in English.[14]
7. Where the testator is able to execute the will himself without an interpreter, take extra time over explaining the terms of the will as standard clauses will contain words or expressions that will be unfamiliar.[15]

C. Conflicts of interest

4.16 The dangers of a conflict of interest between clients or failing to act in the client's interests are well known in general practice, but they can occur in the preparation of wills. In the case of

---

[13] See, eg the Court of Appeal in *Agulian v Cyganik* [2006] WTLR 565: 'Although it is helpful to trace Andreas's life events chronologically and to halt on the journey from time to time to take stock, this question cannot be decided in stages. Positioned at the date of death in February 2003 the court must look back at the whole of the deceased's life, at what he had done with his life, at what life had done to him and at what were his inferred intentions in order to decide whether he had acquired a domicile of choice in England by the date of his death. Soren Kierkegaard's aphorism that "Life must be lived forwards, but can only be understood backwards" resonates in the biographical data of domicile disputes' (per Mummery LJ).

[14] *Williams on Wills*, 9th edition (Lexis Nexis, 2008) precedent at [222.15] Form 22.13.

[15] *Franks v Sinclair* [2007] WTLR 439.

taking instructions from husband and wife together, a joint interview such as this contains potential difficulties for both undue influence and want of knowledge and approval.[16] The problems for the draftsman will usually centre on:

- The extent to which either party is expressing their own intentions:
  - Are they letting the other speak for them because they are already in agreement and it is easier that way?
  - Is one speaking for both, without prior discussion, because that party takes all the decisions and the other habitually acquiesces?
  - Is the party that is silent, silent through fear?
- Is the information on family and assets reliable or are there secrets?
- The two previous points are made more complex where there are family from previous relationships (of either or both) and protecting property for issue can be seen as disloyalty or untrusting towards the new partner.

Difficult though it may be to explain tactfully, it is necessary to consider whether a married couple are likely to present conflicts of interest and need to be separately represented. Obviously a solicitor must not act where a conflict of interest (or a significant risk of conflict) arises between two or more clients. Outcome 3.6 in the SRA Code of Conduct 2011 says: **4.17**

> Where there is a client conflict and the clients have a substantially common interest in relation to a matter or a particular aspect of it, you only act if:
> (a) you have explained the relevant issues and risks to the clients and you have a reasonable belief that they understand those issues and risks;
> (b) all the clients have given informed consent in writing to you acting;
> (c) you are satisfied that it is reasonable for you to act for all the clients and that it is in their best interests; and
> (d) you are satisfied that the benefits to the clients of you doing so outweigh the risks.

For married couples it may therefore make sense to ensure that both parties to the marriage sign separate terms of business. On its own, this is not sufficient and an explanation should be given as to how each is entitled to separate representation should a conflict arise or the risk that it could arise becomes apparent. Also, it may be prudent to obtain their informed consent in writing to your acting on behalf of them both. This takes on greater importance for those not yet married or for those who are married but where there is a great disparity in wealth.

The situation where the same solicitor is used by both husband and wife was examined by the Court of Appeal in *Hines v Willans*.[17] The facts were very unusual, and created a set of circumstances which it is not easy to anticipate being repeated. The court rejected the notion that there was any general ongoing retainer[18] that would produce a duty of care (referring to this as the 'family solicitor' duty). Such a retainer cannot be implied, but must be expressed. However, the court found that there was evidence in this particular case of a retainer from the series of transactions undertaken. This conclusion was supported by the solicitor's continued **4.18**

---

[16] eg *Gill v Woodhall* [2011] WTLR 251.

[17] [2002] WTLR 299.

[18] This had been rejected earlier by Oliver J in *Midland Bank Trust Co v Hett, Stubbs & Kemp* [1979] Ch 384 at 402: 'There is no such thing as general retainer ... The expression "my solicitor" is as meaningless as "my tailor" or "my bookmaker" in establishing a general duty apart from that arising out of a particular matter.'

willingness to accept appointments to see the widow. It seems fairly clear from the court's reasoning that it was the particular factors present in this case which led to this conclusion. It cannot be taken as general authority that, where wills have been prepared for a husband and wife, the solicitor cannot act to vary one of the wills later.

4.19 Even where there is a retainer, the causation argument is that there is no loss to the other party caused by the solicitor continuing to act, for if the solicitor refused, the testator would find another solicitor to effect the changes. The danger comes when, as in this case, the unusual nature of the testator's behaviour defeats the causation defence. The uncomfortable aspect is the duty owed to the other client-spouse. The solicitor clearly cannot tell the other spouse of the change of the first spouse's will. It would seem that to avoid the appearance of conflict, and where there is a retainer on behalf of the other spouse as well, the solicitor under these circumstances should decline to act any further for the other spouse.

4.20 The problem of instructions being taken jointly from husband and wife at the same meeting has received little attention in this country, but it has prompted reform in Ontario. The Law Society of Upper Canada has introduced a new conflict rule into its professional code of conduct.[19] Where a solicitor has prepared wills in these circumstances for spouses, he cannot prepare a new will or codicil for just one of them without the consent of the other. This recognizes the difficult position of later altering a will for one spouse when the will was originally prepared as a result of a joint interview.

---

[19] Rule 2.04(6):

> Where a lawyer accepts employment from more than one client in a matter or transaction, the lawyer shall advise the clients that
> (a) the lawyer has been asked to act for both or all of them,
> (b) no information received in connection with the matter from one can be treated as confidential so far as any of the others are concerned, and
> (c) if a conflict develops that cannot be resolved,
> the lawyer cannot continue to act for both or all of them and may have to withdraw completely.

The commentary on this provision explains:

> A lawyer who receives instructions from spouses or partners ... to prepare one or more wills for them based on their shared understanding of what is to be in each will should treat the matter as a joint retainer and comply with subrule (6). Further, at the outset of this joint retainer, the lawyer should advise the spouses or partners that if subsequently only one of them were to communicate new instructions, for example, instructions to change or revoke a will:
> (a) the subsequent communication would be treated as a request for a new retainer and not as part of the joint retainer;
> (b) in accordance with rule 2.03, the lawyer would be obliged to hold the subsequent communication in strict confidence and not disclose it to the other spouse or partner; but
> (c) the lawyer would have a duty to decline the new retainer, unless:
>   (i) the spouses or partners had annulled their marriage, divorced, permanently ended their conjugal relationship, or permanently ended their close personal relationship, as the case may be;
>   (ii) the other spouse or partner had died; or
>   (iii) the other spouse or partner was informed of the subsequent communication and agreed to the lawyer acting on the new instructions.
> After advising the spouses or partners in the manner described above, the lawyer should obtain their consent to act in accordance with subrule (8).

D. Retainers, contractual limitations on service, and engagement letters

Retainers

If a solicitor decides that he will decline instructions from a potential client there must be no **4.21** delay in communicating this to him or he may have assumed a limited duty of care to the client.[20] Where it is decided to terminate an existing retainer, this can only be done on reasonable notice of termination being given to the client.[21] In the context of will instructions, the necessity to act with appropriate speed in preparing a will points towards speedy decisions as to whether to accept or decline instructions in order to give the potential client adequate time to instruct others if he still wishes to proceed with the will. It is clearly not safe to exhaust a good part of the acceptable period in which to prepare a will before deciding not to accept the instructions. This will in turn clearly point to any refusal being immediate where a potential client is elderly or in ill health and requires a will. Similarly having accepted the retainer to prepare a will, termination should only be with good reason and with reasonable notice. But what is reasonable notice in the context of will preparation? Reasonable notice in these circumstances must be as quickly as possible in order to allow the client time to make other arrangements to obtain a will within a reasonable time period. Where a retainer is terminated without a will being prepared but after an unreasonably long passage of time[22] the solicitor terminating the retainer may well still be at risk until a new will is in place.

Where the solicitor is approached by a lay client who seeks advice in imprecise or non-legal **4.22** terms, the solicitor is bound to clarify the exact extent and nature of the advice that is sought. The extent of the retainer and the duty of care will then be determined by the extent and nature of the advice that the client requires.[23]

The terms of a retainer will be the initial point of reference for a court in determining what **4.23** the retainer required and the extent of the duty of care applicable.[24] Where there is doubt as to what is included in the retainer, there is authority from Canada to suggest that one of the duties of the instructed solicitor is to clarify areas of doubt with the client.[25] Where the

---

[20] *Whelton Sinclair v Hyland* [1992] 2 EGLR 158 where a telephone call to the solicitor's office was found to have brought the retainer into existence.
[21] SRA Code of Conduct 2011, Chapter 1: a retainer must not be terminated except with good reason; *Underwood, Son & Piper v Lewis* [1894] 2 QB 306; *Richard Buxton v Mills-Owen* [2010] EWCA Civ 122.
[22] Unreasonably in the context of the passage of time being sufficient for a will to have been prepared within sufficient time to meet the duty of care.
[23] *Gray v Buss Murton* [1999] PNLR 882; *Groom v Cocker* [1939] 1 KB 194; 'it is an incident of that duty that the solicitor shall consult with his client on all questions of doubt which do not fall within the express or implied retainer.'
[24] 'In identifying what are the solicitor's responsibilities the starting point must always be the solicitor's retainer' (*Royal Bank of Scotland v Etridge (No 2)* [2001] UKHL 44 at [64]). 'The extent of duties which the solicitor owes to his client depends upon the terms and limits of that retainer and any duty of care to be implied must be related to what he is instructed to do' (*Midland Bank Trust Company v Hett, Stubbs and Kemp* (n 18). 'If the solicitor does not take the precaution of getting a written retainer, he has only himself to thank for being at variance with his client over it and must take the consequences' (*Griffiths v Evans* [1953] 1 WLR 1424).
[25] *Tiffin Holdings Ltd v Millican* (1964) 49 DLR (2d) 216:

> The obligations of a lawyer are, I think, the following: (1) To be skilful and careful; (2) To advise his client on all matters relevant to his retainer, so far as may be reasonably necessary; (3) To protect the interests of his client; (4) To carry out his instructions by all proper means; (5) To consult his

solicitor identifies risk when considering the matter he is retained in, but that risk is outside of the retainer, he has a duty to draw that issue to the client's attention.[26]

Can any of the risk be limited by contract?

4.24 Although none of the cases on negligence and wills so far provide a conclusive answer to this question, there are strong indications that liability can be limited, to a degree, by the terms of the contract between client and solicitor.[27] The scope of the duty should be established from the retainer:

> The scope of duty . . . is that which the law regards as best giving effect to the express obligations assumed by the professional, neither cutting them down so that the [client] obtains less than he was reasonably entitled to expect, nor extending them so as to impose on the [professional] a liability greater than he could reasonably have thought he was undertaking.[28]

4.25 The liability of the will-preparer for a breach of his duty generally is to the client, and in the absence of a direct relationship between the will-preparer and the beneficiary, no disclaimer or contractual limitation of liability agreed directly with the beneficiary is possible. However, the duty owed to the beneficiary cannot be greater than that owed to the testator, through whom the beneficiary's claim arose. Therefore limitation of the duty of care in the retainer from the testator must operate to reduce the duty of care to the beneficiary. In *White v Jones*, Lord Goff [29] clearly seemed to accept that contractual limitation in this way is possible for the duty of care in preparing a will, although Lord Nolan's views were a little more tentative. Nicholls V-C in the Court of Appeal decision in *White* also accepted the principle of contractual limitation of loss.[30] Although the defendant in *Esterhuizen v Allied Dunbar*[31] did not assert contract limitation as a defence, Longmore J's judgment does envisage that this could be a possibility.[32]

---

client on all questions of doubt which do not fall within the express or implied discretion left to him; (6) To keep his client informed to such an extent as may be reasonably necessary, according to the same criteria.

Approved on appeal by the Supreme Court of Canada at (1967) 60 DLR (2d) 469.

[26] *Credit Lyonnais v Russell Jones & Walker* [2002] EWHC 1310 (Ch):

> He is under no general obligation to expend time and effort on issues outside the retainer. However, if in the course of doing that for which he is retained, he becomes aware of a risk or potential risk to the client, it is his duty to inform the client. In doing that he is neither going beyond the scope of his instructions nor is he doing extra work for which he will not be paid. He is simply reporting back to the client on issues of concern that he learns as a result of and in the course of carrying out his instructions.

Boyce v Rendells (1983) 268 EG 278; *Mason v Mills & Reeve* [2011] WTLR 1589.

[27] See [1996] Sept/Oct *Private Client Business* 345. See also Sir Brian Neill's judgment in the Court of Appeal in *BCCI International (Overseas) Ltd (in liquidation) v Price Waterhouse and Ernst & Young* [1998] PNLR 564. In examining the factors to be taken into account in deciding if the threefold test and assumption of responsibility are met, one relevant factor is whether or not the adviser (the defendant) was given an opportunity to issue a disclaimer. Admittedly this is in different circumstances, but it is nonetheless a clear indication that limitation by disclaimer is considered to be a possibility.

[28] This quotation is adapted from the words of Lord Hoffmann in *South Australia Asset Management Corporation v York Montague Ltd* [1997] AC 191E–F, substituting 'client' for lender and 'professional' for valuer, and is taken from the judgment in *Phelps v Stewarts* [2007] EWHC 1561.

[29] [1995] 3 All ER 704B and 711A–B.

[30] [1993] 3 All ER 491C–D.

[31] [1998] 2 FLR 668.

[32] [1998] 2 FLR 668 at 678D–F.

The SRA Code of Conduct 2011 forbids the contractual exclusion of all liability to the **4.26** client, but accepts that limitation of some liability is permissible provided

- the limitation is not below the minimum level of cover required by the SRA Indemnity Insurance Rules for a policy of qualifying insurance;[33]
- it is brought to the client's attention; and
- it is in writing.[34]

With contractual limitation of the extent of the duty of care there are three possible **4.27** approaches:

- limiting the service that is to be provided;
- excluding part of the duty of care; and
- capping liability that can arise.

Whether or not they are equally effective is open to doubt.

Limiting the service provided

If the service provided to the client is limited, those to whom there is an indirect duty,[35] **4.28** the beneficiaries, cannot claim that they are owed a wider duty that includes any services originally not contracted for by the client. This may be the safest approach, provided the client is aware of the extent of the service that is being provided and agrees to it.

Excluding parts of the duty of care

Unlike limiting the service as in para 4.28 above, this approach does not restrict the service **4.29** provided, but, with the client's agreement, excludes liability for breaches of specified parts of the duty of care. Such an exclusion would in all probability be construed strictly against the solicitor.

Capping liability

The contract to cap the monetary amount of liability will have been entered into with only **4.30** the client, and it could be argued that this will leave the extent of the duty unlimited— thereby leaving the liability for the breach of duty to the beneficiaries uncapped as they are not a party to the voluntary limitation.[36] At the present time the point is best described as uncertain.

However, if there is to be a contractual limitation of the duty to the client in any of the above **4.31** ways, it should only be used subject to

- communication;
- reasonableness;
- appropriateness.

---

[33] Outcome 1.8.

[34] Indicative Behaviour 1.8.

[35] 'Indirect' to follow the conventional analysis of the nature of the duty owed to the beneficiaries in *White v Jones* in that the duty is not direct to the beneficiaries, but indirect through the duty to the testator; see Chapter 2 para 2.36.

[36] *Killick v PricewaterhouseCoopers* [2001] WTLR 699 concerned a contract for a share valuation entered into between the company and the valuers when a third party would be bound to sell their shares at the value ascertained to the company. The 'cap' on the valuers' liability was £10m, but the claim was that the shares were undervalued by as much as £30m.

4.32 It is of course necessary that the simple elements of contract are in place, including offer and acceptance, in order for the contract to exist. Therefore, if the terms on which the service is to be provided are to be limited (such as no supervision of execution), it is vital that this is specifically drawn to the client's attention before the instructions are accepted and the work is undertaken. The draftsman will then have the client's agreement to these terms, preferably in writing, before the work commences. Communication of these issues must be clear and precise as in the event of a dispute as to the terms of the retainer prima facie it is the client's version that will prevail.[37]

4.33 Agreement may be implied, for example by the client instructing the will-preparer to proceed subsequent to being advised clearly of the terms of the service. If limitations are imposed on the service provided, it is suggested that it is not safe to 'hide' them in any way among a mass of other information or small print. Safety lies in clearly drawing the terms of business to the attention of the client so that his consent is seen to be informed consent.[38]

4.34 This process of communication and consent should not, in itself, be a delaying factor in the preparation of a will; and if conditions of service are an issue the will-preparer must be ready with them at the meeting with the testator (or before if possible) so that delay is not occasioned. To take the instructions and then to impose conditions is not a safe option, nor can it be safe to delay preparation of a will while contractual limitations are negotiated.

4.35 If the terms on which a service is to be provided are to be limited, there should be a degree of reasonableness in the will-preparer's conduct, especially as regards charging. If the service is restricted in some way, as against no limitations being specified, it is unreasonable for the same fee to be applied in both circumstances.

4.36 Reasonableness is also an issue as far as the Unfair Contract Terms Act 1977 and the Unfair Terms in Consumer Contracts Regulations 1999[39] are concerned, and either or both can apply to a contract to provide a will. Section 2(2) Unfair Contract Terms Act 1977 requires that any contract term that excludes liability is of no effect unless it satisfies the reasonableness test set out in s.11 of the Act. Section 11 requires that the term must be fair and reasonable having regard to the circumstances which were, or ought reasonably to have been known to, or in the contemplation of, the parties when the contract was made. Schedule 2 to the Act uses the following guidelines to test the question of reasonableness:

1. The strength of the bargaining positions of the parties relative to each other, taking into account (among other things) alternative means by which the customer's requirements could have been met.
2. Whether the customer received an inducement to agree to the term, or in accepting it had an opportunity of entering into a similar contract with other persons, but without having a similar term.

---

[37] *Gray v Buss Merton* (n 23) and *Re Payne* (1912) 28 TLR 201.

[38] See (1) *Republic International Trust v Fletcher Ramos* [2000] 1 All ER 183 on the perils of not bringing exclusion clauses expressly to the client's attention; (2) the *obiter* remarks of Lightman J on the necessity for fully informed consent in *Hurlingham Estates v Wilde & Partners* [1997] 1 Lloyd's Rep 525: 'any such agreement to limit the solicitor's duties must, if it is to have any legal effect, be clear and unambiguous. The client must be fully informed as to the limit of reliance he may place on his solicitor and the reason for it (i.e. the solicitor's lack of any basic knowledge or competence)'.

[39] SI 1999/2083.

3. Whether the customer knew or ought reasonably to have known of the existence and the extent of the term (having regard, among other things, to any custom of the trade and any previous course of dealing between the parties).
4. Where the term excludes or restricts any relevant liability if some condition was not complied with, whether it was reasonable at the time of the contract to expect that compliance with that condition would be practicable.
5. Whether the goods were manufactured, processed, or adapted to the special order of the customer.

Section 11(4) further provides that, where a term seeks to limit liability to a specific sum, the reasonableness must then include consideration of the resources available to meet the liability and the availability of insurance.

The Unfair Terms in Consumer Contracts Regulations 1999 contain further provisions **4.37** relating to the unfairness of contract terms:

1. A contractual term which has not been individually negotiated shall be regarded as unfair if it causes a significant imbalance in the party's rights and obligations to the detriment of the consumer.
2. A term of a contract will always be regarded as not having been individually negotiated where it was drafted in advance and the consumer was not able to influence the substance of the term.

Schedule 2 to the Regulations contains a non-exhaustive list of terms which may be regarded **4.38** as unfair and these include:

> Inappropriately excluding or limiting the legal rights of consumers vis à vis the seller or supplier or another party in the event of total or partial non-performance or inadequate performance by the seller or supplier of any of the contractual obligations.[40]

The combined effect of the tests of reasonableness under the Unfair Contract Terms Act **4.39** 1977 and the Unfair Terms in Consumer Contracts Regulations 1999 makes it unlikely that a standard approach to excluding liability for breach of the duty of care in preparing a will can work. This appears to be the case whether or not the exclusion relates to the testator, the beneficiaries, or both. It may, however, be the case that in rare circumstances, where at the client's request work is to be undertaken in circumstances which make it impossible for the solicitor to work safely to his normal standards, an individually negotiated disclaimer will be effective.

Appropriateness of the limitation to the client's needs seems self-evident, and limiting the **4.40** service provided to a client who has a high degree of need for a greater level of service— because of age, lack of experience or worldly knowledge—hardly seems to be offering a worthy standard of client care. There is also the danger that where the client's circumstances dictate that a higher standard of care is needed, an attempt to limit the service becomes unreasonable. The corollary to the earlier comment about limited fees is that higher fees are appropriate to reflect the 'fuller' service.

Where the disclaimer in a retainer to prepare a will purports to exclude all liability to third par- **4.41** ties there must be serious grounds for considering that this is unreasonable. Such a disclaimer

---

[40] Paragraph 1(b).

would, by virtue of the problem that was posed in *White v Jones*, mean that the will-preparer would rarely ever have any liability to the testator/client (no loss arising) but would instead be attempting to bar the actual loss to the beneficiaries that would arise through breach of the duty of care on almost every occasion. No reported case in this area is known to the authors.

Client engagement letters

4.42 In the context of a solicitor's practice, there will be clients who are local or who need advice and supervision who can receive a service that is not limited (and this may be reflected in any letter of engagement), but there will be those who are not local to the practice or whose understanding is such that a limited service (particularly omitting supervision of execution) is appropriate. For the latter, a different letter of engagement specifying what will and will not be done is the practical approach. This opens up the use of various exclusions and inclusions to cover in greater detail what is being offered, as opposed to retainers drawn in wide terms that might encompass matters that are not to be delivered. Contracting out of having a duty to supervise should avoid the risk in *Esterhuizen v Allied Dunbar*[41] or *Ross v Caunters*,[42] but it would still seem to be safer (and better client care) to provide written information as to how to validly execute the will. To restrict a service to providing documents only, without giving any guidance as to how they can be validly executed, does not seem reasonable.[43]

4.43 It may be that a client declines assistance with the supervision of the will, despite it being offered. In these circumstances it is suggested that a letter along the following lines is sent:

> When your will is ready for execution, I will forward it to you together with a comprehensive note setting out how it should be signed and witnessed. At our meeting you indicated that it was your preference for your will to be dealt with in this way and by sending your will to you in this way I cannot take responsibility for supervising its execution. If this does not fairly reflect what was agreed please let me know.

4.44 The purpose of this is to set out the terms agreed between both parties in the event that what was agreed becomes an issue.

E. Testamentary capacity

Background

4.45 In many ways dealing with the question of the capacity of the testator is one of the most tricky and potentially embarrassing areas with which the will draftsman has to contend. In many cases, the question will never arise, but in the case of an elderly testator, or even a much younger one who appears to have mental health problems, the issue cannot be ignored. Capacity is almost always thought of in terms of someone suffering from a mental illness, whether that be dementia of some kind or some other mental illness. However, it should not be forgotten that a testator may lack capacity through his own acts, such as drunkenness or executing a will under the influence of drugs. Recent cases have emphasized the effect on

---

[41] [1998] 2 FLR 668.
[42] [1979] 3 All ER 580.
[43] See Chapter 6 para 6.99 onwards on duty to supervise execution.

the ability of the testator to make decisions of affective disorders such as depression[44] and illnesses that cause personality changes.[45]

The ramifications for the estate if the will draftsman does not address the question of **4.46** capacity properly at the outset cannot be overestimated. As Templeman J (as he then was) said in *Re Simpson*:[46]

> when a question of testamentary capacity is raised it falls on the chancery division of the High Court to ascertain the powers of memory and rational thought of a testator at the date he made his will. The dispute as to his state of mind is often bitter, protracted and expensive. It is sometimes difficult to put in its proper perspective evidence given in good faith which derives from the testator's condition before he made his will, or derives from the testator's condition after he made his will. Sometimes the testator creates confusion by making contradictory promises; sometimes his friends and relations are blind to his failings or exaggerate his eccentricities.

The full nightmare of the contentious probate case, as extrapolated by Templeman J, should **4.47** always feature in the mind of the solicitor drawing up a will in cases of any doubt. Most challenges to wills do turn on the question of the testamentary capacity of the deceased and it is one of the hardest questions for a court to have to decide, frequently having to rely on the retrospective judgement of medical experts[47] and the anecdotal evidence of often less than disinterested witnesses.[48]

The test of capacity

The test of capacity which is most often applied in practice is that set out eloquently by **4.48** Cockburn CJ in *Banks v Goodfellow*:[49]

> It is essential to the exercise of such a power that the testator shall understand the nature of the act and its effects; shall understand the extent of the property of which he is disposing; shall be able to comprehend and appreciate the claims to which he ought to give effect; and with a view to the latter object that no disorder of the mind shall poison his affections, pervert his sense of right, or prevent the exercise of his natural faculties—that no insane delusion shall influence his will in disposing of his property and bring about a disposal of it which, if the mind had been sound, would not have been made.

Therefore, to have capacity to make a will the testator needs to satisfy the following tests:[50] **4.49**

1. He needs to be able to understand that he is making a will, and it will have the effect of carrying out his wishes on death.
2. He must be capable of knowing the extent of his property and what it consists of.
3. He must be able to recall those who have claims on him and understand the nature of those claims[51] so that he can both include and exclude beneficiaries from the will and to that end no disorder of the mind should poison his affections, pervert his sense of right,

---

[44] *Key v Key* [2010] 1 WLR 2020.
[45] *Sharp v Adams* [2006] WTLR 1059.
[46] (1977) 121 Sol J 224.
[47] In *Hawes v Burgess* (n 11) the Court of Appeal doubted how useful such evidence was.
[48] See *Key v Key* (n 44) for a striking example of this and trenchant criticism of the solicitor who drew up the will.
[49] (1870) LR 5 QB 549 at 565.
[50] There is some debate as to whether they split into three or four issues.
[51] *Boughton v Knight* [1873] 3 P&D 64.

or prevent the exercise of his natural faculties and no insane delusions should influence his will or poison his mind.

4.50 The Court of Appeal recently considered a review of this test, but decided it could not be improved.[52] One factor which must never be forgotten is the fact that the court is looking for capacity to understand the above matters, not proof of actual understanding.[53] It is also important to emphasize the level at which the test is set. In *Den v Vancleve*[54] it was said:

> By the terms 'a sound and disposing mind and memory' it has not been understood that a testator must possess these qualities of the mind in the highest degree; otherwise, very few could make testaments at all; neither has it been understood that he must possess them in as great a degree as he may have formerly done; for even this would disable most men in the decline of life; the mind may have been in some degree debilitated, the memory may have become in some degree enfeebled; and yet there may be enough left clearly to discern and discreetly to judge, of all those things, and all those circumstances, which enter into the nature of a rational, fair, and just testament. But if they have so far failed as that these cannot be discerned and judged of, then he cannot be said to be of sound and disposing mind and memory.

Timing

4.51 The relevant time for assessing the capacity of the testator is at the date when the will is executed.[55] Of course this may not be an occasion at which the solicitor is present. Best practice would suggest that if the solicitor is in any doubt that the testator will have capacity at the date of execution, he should attend in person and follow the best practice with regard to obtaining the opinion of a medical practitioner set out below.

4.52 The exception to this general principle is where the testator has testamentary capacity at the time when he gives instructions for the preparation of the will to the will draftsman and the will is prepared in accordance with those instructions; and the testator when he executes the will is capable of understanding that he is executing a will for which he has given instructions.[56] This exception was confirmed as being good law by the Court of Appeal in *Perrins v Holland*,[57] which was an extraordinary case where there was a delay of eighteen months between the giving of instructions and the execution of the will. Clearly, if reliance is to be placed on this exception, then it is important that the solicitor makes sure that the testator really does have testamentary capacity when instructions are provided.

4.53 It has been pointed out that, in cases where instructions are given to the solicitor through a lay intermediary, it is not safe to rely on this principle.[58]

Delusions

4.54 The *Banks v Goodfellow* test specifically relates to the issue of a testator who suffers from insane delusions. It might also be thought by a solicitor that no client suffering from a delusion could have capacity. However, the test is by no means so cut and dried. The delusion

---

[52] *Sharp v Adam* [2006] WTLR 1059.
[53] *Hoff v Atherton* [2005] WTLR 99.
[54] (1819) 2 Southard 589 at 660, cited in *Banks v Goodfellow* (1870) LR 5 QB 549 at 565.
[55] *Banks v Goodfellow* (n 54).
[56] *Parker v Felgate* (1883) 8 PD 171; *Clancy v Clancy* [2003] WTLR 1097.
[57] [2011] Ch 270.
[58] *Battan Singh v Armichand* [1948] AC 161, 168–9.

must be such that it influences the testator in the making of the dispositions under his will.[59]

This area was explored recently in the decision of Henderson J in *Kostic v Chapman*,[60] it being   **4.55**
common ground that the testator suffered from a delusional disorder causing him to believe
that there was an international conspiracy of dark forces against him in which he believed
family members were implicated. He left his £8m estate to the Conservative Party, and the
judge notably found that his attachment to that political party was to an extent fed by his
delusional state. The real issue, however, was whether the delusions brought about a disposal
of the testator's estate that he would not have made if of sound mind. However, the point
was also raised as to whether it only has to be shown, in order for the will to be valid, that the
delusions did not in fact exercise any influence on the dispositions in the will, or it also has to
be shown that the delusions were not likely to influence the dispositions in the will, whether
or not they actually did so. In the end the judge did not have to decide the question because
he found there was overwhelming evidence that the delusions did influence the testator in
excluding his son from the will and in favouring the Conservative Party. This point therefore
remains open, but the will draftsman dealing with a client who suffers from a delusional
disorder will need to take care that there is capacity at all.

There is of course a fine line between eccentricity and unreasonable and capricious feelings   **4.56**
on the one hand and delusion on the other. It is the unenviable task of the practitioner to
decide whether the client before him is merely foolish and eccentric or lacking capacity. Of
course in matters of doubt a medical practitioner may need to be involved.

Mental Capacity Act 2005

It is an interesting question as to whether the statutory test for capacity introduced by the   **4.57**
Mental Capacity Act 2005 has affected the test for testamentary capacity. The test is as set
out in s.2 of the Act:

> For the purposes of this Act, a person lacks capacity in relation to a matter if at the material
> time he is unable to make a decision for himself in relation to the matter because of an impair-
> ment of, or a disturbance in the functioning of, the mind or brain.

However, in s.1 it is stated that   **4.58**

> A person is not to be treated as unable to make a decision unless all practicable steps to help
> him to do so have been taken without success.

How far is the statutory test of general application? In a sense it may not matter in that it will   **4.59**
not differ from the *Banks v Goodfellow* test apart from the fact that, in assessing whether a

---

[59] So, in *Smee v Smee* (1879) 5 PD 84 the fact that the testator thought that he was the child of George IV
was material as it influenced him to make a bequest in his will to set up a library in Brighton. The judgment
described the delusion thus:

> It is important to bear in mind the nature of the deceased's delusions. He had an idea that he was the
> son of George IV; that when he was born a large sum of money was placed in his father's hands in
> trust for him; that he was robbed by his father by the diversion of a large part of that trust fund from
> him to his brothers; and that all that his father really had to give to his brothers was a sum of 1000
> each, the rest of the property (about 50,000) left by his father and divided by will between his chil-
> dren, being part of the imaginary trust fund, to which the deceased believed he alone was entitled.

[60] [2007] EWHC 2298.

testator lacked capacity, the issue of whether all practicable steps have been taken to help him make a will has to be taken into account.

4.60 In the case of *Scammell v Farmer*,[61] which involved a claim against a will where the testator suffered from Alzheimer's disease, the judge held that the Mental Capacity Act 2005 did not have retrospective effect but that if it did apply (and the implication was that it would for future deaths) the main difference was that under the Act capacity was always presumed. Notably in *Saulle v Nouvet*[62] in a different context concerning capacity, it was held that the test in this section applied only to decisions made by the Court of Protection. It seems clear to us that is not correct and the test will permeate testamentary capacity as well as all other areas where capacity is in issue. However, in practical terms, the approach to the question of capacity should not alter.

4.61 The 2005 Act gives statutory force to the rule that capacity is issue specific.[63] This is an important factor to bear in mind. Capacity has to be viewed not only as far as the individual is concerned, but also in the context of the transaction into which he is intending to enter. Therefore a testator may have capacity to enter into a simple will where his estate is uncomplicated, but lack the ability to enter into a complex will or deal with a complicated estate. This is an interesting point to note when dealing with a will that is of necessity complex because of tax planning objectives. A testator with doubtful capacity might be able to execute a simple will, but be incapable of understanding the terms of a will containing complex provisions designed to avoid tax. In looking at this issue, of course, it is proof of the capability that is required and not actual understanding, which is something that pertains to knowledge and approval rather than capacity.[64]

The duty of the practitioner

4.62 So, what is the duty of the practitioner in assessing the mental capacity of his client who wishes to make a will? Often the questions which are asked in the usual process of taking instructions will make it clear whether there is a potential problem or not. The importance of keeping a clear and full attendance note cannot be stressed too highly in this context. The will draftsman should have in mind that in any contentious probate claim each party is entitled to ask him to provide a statement.[65] The impressions of the solicitor who attended the testator on the taking of instructions for the preparation of the will, and on the execution of the will, are of vital importance in contentious probate proceedings where capacity is in issue.[66] In *Hawes v Burgess*[67] Mummery LJ went so far as to say that a judge should be slow to find that a testator lacked capacity where the will draftsman considered that he or she was capable:

> That said, it is, in my opinion, a very strong thing for the judge to find that the Deceased was not mentally capable of making the 2007 will, when it had been prepared by an experienced and independent solicitor following a meeting with her; when it was executed by her after the

---

[61] [2008] EHWC 1100; WTLR [2008] 1261.
[62] [2008] WTLR 729; [2007] EWHC 2902 (QB).
[63] *Masterman-Lister v Bruton & Co* [2003] 3 All ER 162.
[64] *Hoff v Atherton* (n 53).
[65] *Larke v Nugus* [2000] WTLR 1033.
[66] *Jones v Jones* [2006] WTLR 1847 where the evidence of the solicitor who took instructions, although he did not take a good attendance note, won the day in favour of the validity of the will.
[67] [2013] WTLR 453.

solicitor had read through it and explained it; and when the solicitor considered that she was capable of understanding the will, the terms of which were not, on their face, inexplicable or irrational...

My concern is that the courts should not too readily upset, on the grounds of lack of mental capacity, a will that has been drafted by an experienced independent lawyer. If, as here, an experienced lawyer has been instructed and has formed the opinion from a meeting or meetings that the testatrix understands what she is doing, the will so drafted and executed should only be set aside on the clearest evidence of lack of mental capacity. The court should be cautious about acting on the basis of evidence of lack of capacity given by a medical expert after the event, particularly when that expert has neither met nor medically examined the testatrix, and particularly in circumstances when that expert accepts that the testatrix understood that she was making a will and also understood the extent of her property.

4.63 The above should not be taken as giving comfort to solicitors who do not do a good job, however experienced they might be. The Court of Appeal still found the will to be invalid, albeit that it preferred to do so on the grounds of want of knowledge and approval. In each case where there might be any doubt about the matter, and that includes testators of whatever age who are terminally ill and perhaps on a great deal of medication as well as the elderly client, the solicitor should consider whether the *Banks v Goodfellow* criteria are fulfilled, and record his impressions.

4.64 There has been a considerable amount of judicial assistance on the way in which practitioners should approach the question of capacity. The leading case is the decision of Templeman J (as he then was) in *Re Simpson*[68] where he said:

In the case of an aged testator or a testator who has suffered a serious illness, there is one golden rule which should always be observed, however straightforward matters may appear and however difficult or tactless it may be to suggest that precautions be taken: the making of a will by such a testator ought to be witnessed or approved by a medical practitioner who satisfied himself of the capacity and understanding of the testator, and records and preserves his examination and finding.

There are other precautions which should be taken. If the testator has made an earlier will this should be considered by the legal and medical advisers of the testator, and if appropriate, discussed with the testator. The instructions of the testator should be taken in the absence of anyone who may stand to benefit, or who may have influence over the testator. These are not counsels of perfection. If proper precautions are not taken injustice may result or be imagined and great expense and misery may be unnecessarily caused.

4.65 Templeman J had earlier made similar comments and had described them as 'the golden if tactless rule'.[69]

4.66 This rule has attained the more recent approval of Rimer J in *Re Morris (deceased), Special Trustees for Great Ormond Street Hospital for Children v Rushin*.[70] Having described the behaviour of the solicitor who had drawn up the will of a frail, elderly testatrix who was confused as 'deplorable',[71] he went on to say:

She claimed to have experience of probate matters, and her activities at the meeting on 22nd February 1996 were also devoted to Mrs Morris's will. It should have been obvious to her

---

[68] (1977) 121 Sol J 224, better recorded at (1977) 127 NLJ 487.
[69] *Kenward v Adams* The Times, 29 November 1975.
[70] [2001] WTLR 1137.
[71] *Re Morris* (n 70) at 1197.

that this was a case in which in accordance with the guidance of Templeman J in Re Simpson deceased . . . and embarrassing though it might have been to press for it, she should have insisted that some medical assistance was invoked as to Mrs Morris's capacity to enter into this unusual transaction and make the proposed will.

In the *Morris* case there were clear indications that Mrs Morris might not have capacity. However, Templeman J's Golden Rule goes further than that. It suggests that a medical practitioner witnesses or approves the will of every elderly testator and of anyone who has suffered a serious illness.

4.67 The difficulty with this is that it is a counsel of perfection. It is in reality impracticable for every testator over a certain age to be subjected to a mental examination. The fact of the matter is that in most cases it will be clear when the testator is so incapable that he cannot provide instructions. It will be equally clear that the octogenarian who wishes to make a will is just as competent to do so as the will draftsman. It is the grey area in between where difficulty can arise. If there is any doubt the will draftsman needs to err on the side of caution.

4.68 It should be emphasized that even if a will draftsman follows the Golden Rule it will not mean that the will is upheld as a matter of course[72] and the failure to observe it will not render the will invalid[73] but a probate dispute might be avoided if it is followed and a failure to do so may impose liability on the draftsman in question for the costs of expensive proceedings.

Medical opinion

4.69 The importance of contemporaneous, competent medical evidence cannot be overestimated. It will, in almost all cases, head off a challenge to the will. The difficulties facing experts of even the highest calibre, attempting to judge retrospectively the testamentary capacity of the deceased whom they have never met, are not to be underestimated.[74]

4.70 In some cases the testator's general practitioner will be the appropriate person to approach. This is particularly the case if the GP has had a long relationship with the patient and has been able to observe any deterioration. However, some caution does need to be exercised. Some GPs have no training in assessing capacity and may need to have careful guidance through the *Banks v Goodfellow* test. Even then, some are reluctant to perform the assessment. The administration of a mini mental-state test, which is a useful tool in the diagnosis of dementia, does not ask the right questions to be a useful test of testamentary capacity unless it is clear that capacity has fallen to such a low level that making a will would be impossible. Indeed, a diagnosis of dementia does not automatically render someone incapable of making a will unless it is severe.[75]

4.71 If the testator is in hospital or a nursing home, the registrar or consultant attending on him may well be more appropriate if prepared to provide an opinion. It is important that the medical practitioner concerned is aware of the test of capacity, and records that he has considered the test and the opinion he has reached.

4.72 If none of these options proves promising, then consulting a psychiatrist is almost certainly the best course. It will almost certainly be good practice to consult the medical practitioner at

---

[72] See *Sharp v Adam* discussed below.
[73] See *Key v Key* (n 44).
[74] See *Hawes v Burgess* (n 11).
[75] See *Blackman v Man* [2008] WTLR 389.

an early stage to ensure that the testator is capable of giving instructions, and then to involve
the doctor again at the stage of execution, in cases where there is any real doubt.

Even strict adherence to the Golden Rule will not necessarily avoid a probate case. In *Sharp v*   **4.73**
Adam,[76] which involved a testator with secondary progressive multiple sclerosis, the solicitor
who drafted the will was praised for the care she had taken and the fact that she had involved
a medical expert; but the fact that the will cut out the testator's daughters with whom he had
a good relationship, and there was medical evidence that he might not have had capacity,
resulted in the will not being admitted to probate. The disorder from which he suffered
affected his personality, which led the court to conclude that he lacked capacity and therefore
failed the fourth limb of the *Banks v Goodfellow* test. The case is worrying in some respects,
in that it was the terms of the will which provided evidence of incapacity. This might be
regarded as undermining the general rule that a testator can make as capricious and eccentric
a will as he likes. The quality of the medical evidence is also important—the doctor must
have applied the right test and be able to justify his opinion that the testator has capacity.[77]

It is also clear that the need to obtain medical evidence does not relieve the solicitor from get-   **4.74**
ting on and preparing a will expeditiously for an elderly testator. In *Feltham v Freer Bouskell*[78]
a solicitor received instructions from the step-granddaughter of the testatrix, who was nearly
ninety, to draft a will in the granddaughter's favour. He complied with the Golden Rule and
asked a medical practitioner to examine her to establish testamentary capacity as there was
evidence she was suffering from dementia. The doctor took a while to produce a report but
even when he did the solicitor, who was worried about whether the testatrix really did want
to change her will, failed to act. The court held that the duty on the solicitor was to chase the
doctor for the report and if necessary instruct another doctor but in any event he could not
rely on the doctor's delay to justify his own delay in drafting the will.

But what does the solicitor do if the testator point blank refuses to be examined by a doc-   **4.75**
tor and insists that the solicitor follows his instructions and drafts a will for him? Both *Re
Simpson* and *Re Morris* suggest that the solicitor should insist on a medical practitioner
being involved, and presumably imply that the solicitor should refuse to act if the client is
uncooperative.

However, the position was put rather differently by the New Zealand Court of Appeal in   **4.76**
Knox v Till[79] where negligence was alleged against a solicitor who had drawn up wills which
were held to be invalid owing to the lack of capacity of the testator. Henry J said:

> The further duty was framed by Mr Parmenter as being to refuse to prepare a will for execu-
> tion if testamentary capacity was not established to the solicitor's reasonable satisfaction. No
> basis for the imposition of such a duty, which could still remain compatible with the ordinary
> features and ramifications of the solicitor/client relationship was proffered. There is generally
> an obligation to carry out a client's instructions. In the situation now under discussion no
> disqualifying factor such as illegality, unlawfulness or breach of ethical responsibilities arises
> to negate that duty. The giving of advice on the question of testamentary capacity and record-
> ing that advice which would appear to be possible appropriate responses to a situation where
> capacity is apparently in question, are far removed from a possible refusal to act.

---

[76] [2006] EWCA Civ 449; [2006] WTLR 1059.
[77] *Williams v Wilmot* [2012] WTLR 1635.
[78] [2013] EWHC 1952 (Ch).
[79] [2000] Lloyd's Rep PN 49.

4.77   *Knox v Till* spawned further litigation in *Public Trustee v Till*[80] where the estate attempted to claim the costs of the probate proceedings where the beneficiaries had failed. There, counsel for the estate framed the duty rather differently as being a duty to consider the question of testamentary capacity and to advise on it. On the facts, the estate failed to establish any breach of duty, but Randerson J held the following:

1. The extent of the legal duty on a solicitor is to consider and advise upon the issue of capacity where the circumstances are such as to raise a doubt in the mind of the reasonably competent practitioner.
2. However, the duty will in all cases be circumscribed by the solicitor's retainer and his duty to follow his client's instructions.
3. The solicitor has to be authorized by his client to make inquiries in cases where he thinks it necessary (a very valid point, which perhaps was not considered in *Re Simpson* and *Re Morris*).
4. If inquiries confirmed lack of capacity or some doubt, his only duty was to advise the client as to the pitfalls of executing a will in such circumstances and if the client wished to proceed in any event, he was obliged to do so. This of course must be regarded as subject to the general point that if medical evidence confirms that the testator lacks capacity, the solicitor may have good grounds for not proceeding on the basis that the client is not mentally capable of providing instructions to him.

4.78   A similar approach was taken by the English High Court in *Feltham v Freer Bouskell* where the judge, Charles Hollander QC, pointed out that the solicitor could have refused to act but had in fact accepted instructions to draft the will subject only to satisfying himself on the issue of capacity. The English courts have also considered the duty of solicitors to ascertain the capacity of a client to contract in *Thorpe v Fellowes Solicitors LLP*[81] where it was held that it would be insulting if a solicitor had to obtain medical opinion on capacity every time they were instructed by an elderly client. This perhaps rather emphasizes that the Golden Rule does not mean that medical evidence is required in the case of all elderly testators. In that case there was found nothing to lead the solicitor to suspect that the elderly client lacked capacity.

4.79   However, in circumstances where the solicitor suspects lack of capacity, and has followed the Golden Rule and obtained medical advice to the effect that the testator does not have capacity, can it really be right that there is no ethical reason why he should not go ahead and execute a will which is invalid? Should the solicitor continue to act? The danger of course is that if he does not act and the testator dies without having a will, he could find himself on the receiving end of a negligence action. This is precisely what happened in the New Zealand case of *Ryan v Public Trustee*,[82] where the public trustee was sued successfully for failing to prepare a will for an elderly testatrix whose capacity was in doubt.

4.80   This highlights another point that, in some cases, there will simply not be time for the Golden Rule to be followed and in those circumstances a will ought to be prepared—even if intended as a stop gap while the appropriate medical opinion is sought. Again, if all this is properly documented, it is hard to see how a negligence action could succeed. Indeed even if medical

---

[80]   [2002] WTLR 1169.
[81]   (2011) 118 BMLR 122; [2011] PNLR 13.
[82]   [2000] 1 NZLR 700.

reports cannot be obtained until after the will has been made, that is better than nothing; although it may not be entirely satisfactory for a testator who slips in and out of capacity.

We do not at present have any English authority to this effect, and the implication from **4.81** *Re Simpson* and *Re Morris* is that if the Golden Rule is observed and the mental capacity of the testator in doubt, then a will should not be made that would lead to expensive probate proceedings. This is not just an idle fear. The question arose in *Worby v Rosser*[83] whether beneficiaries under an earlier will could claim against a solicitor who drew up the later will of a testator who lacked testamentary capacity, which gave rise to extremely expensive probate proceedings.[84] In the Court of Appeal, Chadwick LJ considered the proposition that solicitors drawing up a later will owed a duty to beneficiaries under an earlier will as 'startling'. He said:

> In the present case there is no lacuna to be filled. If the solicitor's breach of duty under his retainer has given rise to the need for expensive probate proceedings, resulting in unrecovered costs, then, prima facie, those costs fall to be borne by the estate for the reasons which I have already sought to explain. If the estate bears the costs thereby and suffers loss then, if there is to be a remedy against the solicitor, it should be the estate's remedy for the loss to the estate. There is no need to fashion an independent remedy for a beneficiary who has been engaged in the probate proceedings. His or her costs, if properly incurred in obtaining probate of the true will, can be provided for out of the estate. If there has been a breach of duty by the solicitor, the estate can recover from the solicitor the additional costs (including the costs to which the beneficiary is entitled out of the estate). The practical difficulties which would be likely to arise if solicitors were held to owe duties directly to beneficiaries under earlier wills provide powerful support for the view that it would not be appropriate to provide a remedy in circumstances in which it is not needed. For those reasons I would dismiss this appeal.

The suggestion, therefore, in that case was that the estate might well have a remedy against **4.82** the solicitors, but beneficiaries under an earlier will would not. Therefore, in circumstances where a contentious probate claim was on foot, and it could be alleged that the solicitor who had drawn up the challenged will had failed in his duty to the testator, there could well be a claim by the estate for the costs of the probate action.

Want of knowledge and approval and undue influence

In the ordinary case if testamentary capacity and due execution of the will can be established, **4.83** knowledge and approval will be inferred. However, in cases where the circumstances are such as to arouse the suspicion of the court, the person setting up the will must prove affirmatively knowledge and approval on the part of the testator so as to satisfy the court that the will represents the wishes of the deceased.[85] In most cases the fact that a will has been professionally drawn and read over to the testator will be enough but that will not always be conclusive.[86]

The involvement of a major beneficiary in the preparation of the will is often precisely the **4.84** suspicious circumstance that will excite the attention of the court as in the famous House of Lords case of *Wintle v Nye*.[87] In *Feltham v Freer Bouskell* a solicitor who had failed to draw up

---

[83] [1999] Lloyd's Rep PN 972.
[84] Rather remarkably, the costs of a county court action amounted to £250,000; although the probate claim had taken 48 days to hear!
[85] *Barry v Butlin* (1838) 2 Moo PC 480.
[86] *Wharton v Bancroft* [2012] EWHC 91 (Ch); *Hawes v Burgess* (n 11).
[87] [1959] 1 WLR 284 and see also *Franks v Sinclair* (n 15) where the involvement of the Testatrix's solicitor son in preparing his mother's will partially in his favour, which marked an unexplained change in testamentary direction, was considered so suspicious that the will was not admitted to probate.

a will for a testatrix who had capacity and who, tired of waiting for him to do so, asked her step-granddaughter, who was the major beneficiary, to do so instead, was held liable for the compromise sum paid and costs arising out of a challenge to the will on the grounds of want of knowledge and approval. That challenge would not have arisen, the court found, if he had drawn the will himself.

4.85 Will draftsmen need to be alive to the fact that the will may not only be challenged for lack of capacity. In *Gill v Woodall*[88] the will, whereby the testatrix left her residue to the RSPCA rather than her only daughter, was prepared by a solicitor, albeit not executed before him, but there was expert evidence that the testatrix suffered from such a severe anxiety disorder that she would not have been able to take in what was going on at the meeting with the solicitor, albeit that she had capacity in the strict sense. If the draftsman had perhaps taken more care to take proper instructions from her, the outcome might have been very different.

4.86 Undue influence rarely succeeds in probate cases but there have been a number of recent successes.[89] There is no presumption of undue influence in relation to wills as Proudman J pointed out in *Hubbard v Scott*.[90] A contention of undue influence will only succeed if it can be shown that the mind of the testator has been so dominated that the will is not his own 'will' at all but that of the person influencing him.[91] In cases where a will is professionally drawn the scope for pleading undue influence is very small but even so it should be emphasized that will draftsmen should always see the testator in the absence of beneficiaries under the will and indeed alone, unless that is simply impracticable, to avoid any suggestion that there has been undue influence.

Costs in probate actions

4.87 While strictly outside the scope of this book, it is perhaps useful for the will draftsman to consider how the costs of probate cases involving lack of capacity usually fall. This whole area was considered recently by Henderson J in *Kostic v Chapman*[92] where he referred to the principles laid down in *Speirs v English*.[93] In general the costs of a contentious probate claim, like any other civil claim, are within the discretion of the court and CPR rr.43 and 44 will apply. However, although the general rule is that costs follow the event, there are two substantial and well-known exceptions to this rule in contentious probate claims, namely

1. Where the testator or those interested in the residue, have been the cause of the litigation: in such a case the costs of the unsuccessful party will usually be ordered to be paid out of the estate.
2. Where the circumstances led reasonably to an investigation in regard to a propounded document: in such a case the costs will usually be left to be borne by those who respectively incurred them.

4.88 As to the exception at (1), lack of capacity—although not obviously the fault of the testator—can render them the cause of the litigation. As to (2), in doubtful cases of capacity this might apply.

---

[88] [2011] Ch 380.
[89] For example *Schrader v Schrader* [2013] EWHC 466 (Ch); [2013] WTLR 701.
[90] [2011] EWHC 2750.
[91] *Hall v Hall* (1868) LR 1 P&D 481.
[92] [2008] Costs LR 271.
[93] [1907] P. 122.

In any event, the practitioner is most exposed where costs are to come out of the estate and **4.89** it therefore might be said that the estate has suffered loss and a claim against the draftsman might lie in the appropriate circumstances.

In *Feltham v Freer Bouskell* the claimant recovered the costs of defending a challenge to the **4.90** will as she had to bear them herself as part of a compromise reached in mediation.

F. The Equality Act 2010 and will preparation

This Act codified various previous Acts that comprised the anti-discrimination law of the **4.91** United Kingdom.[94] A provider of services to the public must not discriminate against a person when providing the service.[95] In addition, solicitors have the SRA Code of Conduct 2011, which contains:

- Principle 9—'run your business or carry out your role in the business in a way that encourages equality of opportunity and respect for diversity';
- Chapter 2 Equality and Diversity with five outcomes and indicative behaviours on the application of Principle 9.

Part 2 of the Act sets out the key concepts of the Act. There are characteristics of individuals **4.92** that are made protected characteristics:[96]

1. Age
2. Disability
3. Gender reassignment
4. Marriage and civil partnership
5. Pregnancy and maternity
6. Race
7. Religion or belief
8. Sex
9. Sexual orientation.

Discrimination against an individual on the grounds of any of these protected characteristics is unlawful.

The main area that is likely to arise for the will draftsman is the provision of services to the **4.93** disabled. Disability is more generally defined under this Act than it was under the Disability Discrimination Act 1995. A person has a disability if they have

1. a physical or mental impairment, and
2. the impairment has a substantial and long-term adverse effect on that person's ability to carry out normal day-to-day activities.[97]

In providing wills for the disabled, the issue of greater cost must be considered. Generally **4.94** the Act does not permit surcharges upon disabled persons for the extra expenses involved in

---

[94] Equal Pay Act 1970, Sex Discrimination Act 1975, Race Relations Act 1976, and Disability Discrimination Act 1995 plus Employment Equality (Religion or Belief) Regulations 2003, Employment Equality (Sexual Orientation) Regulations 2003, and Employment Equality (Age) Regulations 2006.

[95] Section 29.

[96] Section 4.

[97] Section 6.

providing services to them.[98] Hence, a service provider should not charge blind customers for the additional cost of providing Braille sales literature; the additional cost should be met, if necessary, by the service provider increasing the charge for services to all members of the public, including those who have a disability. However, arguably there may be some scope for justifying an increased charge or premium if the service provider is a small business and/ or a special one-off requirement is necessary.

4.95 For the will draftsman, if additional hours are expended in providing the service because of an individual's disability, it is possible that the cost of those hours can be charged to the disabled person, as long as it is clearly not a surcharge directly related to the disability. Arguably, this would depend on the pricing strategy for the service itself. If pricing is based on time spent, it would seem reasonable to charge more if more time is expended. If the service provider offers an option of an additional service or difference in the service which results in the service being more expensive and that option is offered to all members of the public, it would appear to be lawful to charge disabled people who take advantage of this option, so long as the option is not effectively an adjustment which enables the disabled person to use the service. If the disabled person could not access the service without the option, it is not lawful to charge for it regardless of whether members of the public who are not disabled do, in fact, have to pay for the charge.

4.96 In the context of will preparation, several possible fee-charging policies need to be considered:

- Where wills are prepared for non-disabled clients for a fixed fee irrespective of whether instructions are taken at the will-preparer's office or the client's home, it would be discriminatory to have a different charging basis purely for the disabled.
- If there is a differential fee charged depending on whether instructions are taken at the will-preparer's office or the client's home, then it must be clearly demonstrable that the same policy is applied to the disabled as the non-disabled.
- If wills are prepared for a fixed fee (whether flat-rate or differential as described above) there would appear to be no scope for charging an additional fee on a time basis for preparing a will for a disabled person even though instructions have taken longer to obtain than they would have done from a non-disabled person.
- In the authors' view, the cost of obtaining a medical opinion as to the client's testamentary capacity is not a discriminatory charge as it could apply to all clients, whether disabled or not.

4.97 Examples that may arise in practice include:

(1) *Home or hospital visits*
     If a solicitor charges a premium to members of the public for such visits, it is lawful to charge a disabled person for them unless the disabled person could not otherwise have access to the service as a direct consequence of his disability. If the disabled person is wheelchair bound but the solicitor's office is accessible, it would seem that a charge can be made for a home visit. If the disabled person is bedridden as a result of his disability or suffering from a sickness related to the disability or exacerbated by the disability, it would seem that it would not be lawful to charge a premium for a home or hospital visit because it is a reasonable adjustment. But, as mentioned above, the increased time spent

---

[98] Section 15.

might be charged depending on the pricing strategy for the service. If a disabled person is suffering from a sickness which would not otherwise fall within the Act, for example a hearing- or mobility-impaired person who has influenza, it would seem lawful to charge if members of the public would also be charged.

(2) *Provision of a will in Braille*

If the sight-impaired person has some other disability with the effect that it is necessary for him to be able to read a will himself in order to understand it (a highly theoretical example), a charge for a Braille will can seemingly not be justified. Otherwise, provided the will can be read and fully explained to a sight-impaired person, it would seem that this is a sufficiently reasonable adjustment so that if a Braille will is requested, a charge for it may be justified.

(3) *Dealing with an individual with learning disabilities*

If greater time is spent, it would seem that it is reasonable to charge for that time as long as the pricing strategy does not lead to the conclusion that an unjustified surcharge is being levied for a reasonable adjustment.

(4) *Obtaining the services of a specialist signer for a hearing-impaired client*

The service provider would be entitled to see if the service can be provided by written explanation—this would appear to be a reasonable adjustment. If the individual is sight and hearing impaired, it would seem likely that no charge could be made, other than, arguably, the greater time involved in providing the service because the provision of the specialist signer is a reasonable adjustment.[99]

(5) *Preparing deathbed wills*

The authors are aware that some firms have a policy not to take instructions for deathbed wills. At least arguably, such a policy falls foul of the Equality Act and such firms ought to take specialist opinion as to whether it is lawful.

---

[99] If the will-preparer has a policy of charging for translation in general, ie for clients for whom English is not their first language, a charge for a signer may not be discriminatory.

5

THE WILL DRAFTSMAN

A. Experience and knowledge

5.01 Both taking instructions and drafting require a sufficient degree of up-to-date knowledge and training for the complexities of the will in question. To undertake either task with a lack of knowledge, qualification, or recent experience, is to accept a level of risk that should normally be regarded as unacceptable by a practice.[1] There is, however, no legal restriction on who may prepare a will for profit.[2]

5.02 Since the risks of will preparation have started to be more widely understood, a number of solicitors' practices have decided to

- restrict both processes to those within their private client department; or
- restrict both processes to those who are competent to undertake the work; or
- bar all others within the practice from this work, unless supervised by their private client department (and therefore working to the firm's standard practices and controls for that department).[3]

5.03 Whilst these policies may offend the *amour-propre* of some traditionalists, they do seem to be reasonable steps in the context of controlling risk. For solicitors, preparing wills without up-to-date training or qualifications runs the risk of offending Chapter 7 of the SRA Code of Conduct 2011.[4]

---

[1] *Zurich @risk* newsletter, May 2008: 'Both taking instructions and drafting wills require knowledge and skill. Some claims notified to us have resulted from solicitors who do not usually have anything to do with the preparation of wills, dabbling in will drafting and getting it wrong. It may sound blindingly obvious but both taking instructions and the actual drafting should be restricted to those within your firm who have the necessary expertise.'

[2] Section 12 and para 5(3)(a) Sch 2 Legal Services Act 2007.

[3] *Zurich @risk* newsletter (n 1): 'Where you have will precedents available on your system why not limit access to these to only those authorised to draft wills? This will prevent others, who don't have the necessary experience and expertise, from using the precedents to "have a go" at will drafting.' See more generally Chapter 8 on Risk.

[4] Outcome 7.6.

5.04 In addition, the abilities, competence, and training of any member of staff, whether a qualified solicitor or not, should be considered not only for taking instructions and drafting wills generally, but also in relation to the complexities of each particular matter[5] they are asked to undertake.[6]

5.05 The partners of a firm will of course retain responsibility

- for the work that they delegate;[7] and
- for ensuring that the delegate is competent for the task delegated.[8]

5.06 The SRA Code of Conduct 2011, Rule 7, imposes a requirement of effective management, which includes appropriate supervision of staff and adequate supervision of clients' matters.

5.07 Although there is no direct authority for imposing the standard of competence of a solicitor on an unqualified member of his staff, this would appear to be the appropriate standard where the work so delegated was properly delegated, ie within the competence of the person to whom it was delegated.[9] Where there is delegation, control of the work remains important, in particular if the work involves more than two members of staff or two separate departments. One person must be in overall control.[10]

5.08 In *Re Parsons, Borman v Lel*[11] there is judicial disapproval for the unqualified or inexperienced taking instructions, drafting, or supervising execution in circumstances demanding experience, judgement, and knowledge.

> whether it is appropriate for someone who is neither a solicitor nor a legal executive qualified in probate matters, but a licensed conveyancer, ever to accept instructions to participate in the drafting of a will and in the supervision of its execution is doubtful at best. But at all events, in my view, where a would-be testator is of advanced age or has been seriously ill or is under some other incapacity, it should always be correct practice that (in addition to the need for ensuring the report and attendance of a doctor) the instructions for the will should be taken, and the execution of the will supervised, by a qualified solicitor with experience of wills. Failure to do so can readily lead to problems which could otherwise be prevented.[12]

---

[5] For the risks inherent in using those qualified, but inexperienced, in a specialist area, see *Credit Lyonnais v Russell Jones & Walker* [2002] EWHC 1310 (Ch) or *Hurlingham Estates Ltd v Wilde & Partners* [1997] STC 627. See Chapter 1 para 1.56.

[6] *Hicks v Russell Jones & Walker* (n 5): 'He was a young and still relatively inexperienced lawyer, with many excellent qualities...What he needed was effective support and supervision, but on the evidence...this seems to have been signally lacking.'

[7] *Richards v Cox* [1943] 1 KB 139 involved a question of the solicitor's liability for the actions of his clerk. The Court of Appeal in *Balamoan v Holden & Co* (1999) 149 NLJ 898 described it as 'an example of the principle that a solicitor may be acting at his peril if he creates unnecessary risks for his client by letting his clerk act in matters beyond his competence by advising on points which ought to be referred to counsel'.

[8] *Law Society v Waterlow, Law Society v Skinner* [1883] 8 App Cas 407; *Arbiter Group plc v Gill Jennings & Every and RWS Information Inc* [2000] Lloyd's Rep PN 669.

[9] 'A professional man is entitled in appropriate circumstances to delegate tasks. Whether he is entitled to delegate a particular task will depend upon the nature of the task. He is entitled to delegate some tasks to others but is not entitled to delegate others. It all depends on the nature of the task involved. If he does delegate he must delegate to a suitably qualified and experienced person' (*Arbiter Group plc v Gill Jennings & Every* (n 8) at [20]).

[10] *Summit Financial Group Ltd v Slaughter & May* The Times, 12 March 1999 where the defendants breached their duty of care in the lack of control over the work of two departments involved in the same drafting work.

[11] [2002] WTLR 237.

[12] Nigel Davies QC sitting as Deputy Judge in *Borman v Lel* [2002] WTLR 237. Consider also Goddard LJ in *Richards v Cox* [1943] 1 KB 139 at 143: 'it seems to me that the only negligence which can be alleged against [the solicitor's clerk] is that he took it upon himself to decide a somewhat difficult question'.

The above quotation highlights the risk inherent in the unqualified taking instructions, but it **5.09** also focuses on the knowledge and experience required in taking instructions from the elderly. This concern underlines the importance of using appropriately trained, experienced (and, where necessary, supervised members of a firm) for the circumstances of the testator. The opening part of the extract from this judgment contains a clear warning about the inadequately trained being involved in will preparation. The SRA Code of Conduct 2011, IB(1.7), directs that a solicitor cannot act in a matter where he has 'insufficient resources or lack[s] the competence to deal with the matter'. Whilst such a rule is not binding on will draftsmen outside solicitors' practices, it is a quite clear and sensible benchmark of acceptable practice for all draftsmen.

The latter part of the quotation above indicates that, in the judge's view, certain types of will **5.10** instructions should only be dealt with by qualified solicitors with experience. Whether that would be followed precisely in other cases has yet to be seen, but another court may find that a legal executive, suitably trained and experienced, could undertake the work instead of a solicitor. Experience of the issues involved may be more important than the qualification.

Where the testator's requirements, once established, call for greater expertise than the person **5.11** taking the instructions has, then referral to a more experienced draftsman within the firm should be made without delay.[13]

B. Gifts to the draftsman

Where a draftsman prepares a will that contains significant benefit for him (either in abso- **5.12** lute terms or in relation to the value of the estate), it raises issues of want of knowledge and approval such that affirmative evidence of the testator's knowledge and approval is required.[14] The provision of independent legal advice on the gift to the draftsman, which is clearly evidenced, should be sufficient to dispel the suspicion. However, where a probate action is necessary because a professional draftsman has neglected this straightforward precaution, there must be a real risk that he is exposed to a claim for the costs of the action notwithstanding that eventually the will is upheld.

The Solicitors' Code of Conduct 2007, Rule 3.04, provided: **5.13**

> Where a client proposes to make a lifetime gift or a gift on death to, or for the benefit of:
>
> (a) you;
> (b) any principal, owner or employee of your firm;
> (c) a family member of any of the above
>
> and the gift is of a significant amount, either in itself or having regard to the size of the client's estate and the reasonable expectations of the prospective beneficiaries, you must advise the client to take independent advice about the gift, unless the client is a member of the beneficiaries' family.[15] If the client refuses, you must stop acting for the client in relation to the gift.[16]

---

[13] See *Bacon v Kennedy* [2000] WTLR 169 for an example of failure to seek timely assistance.
[14] *Barry v Butlin* (1838) 2 Moo PCC 480: 'if a party writes or prepares a will, under which he takes benefit, that is a circumstance that ought generally to excite the suspicion of the court'.
[15] See also comments in *Sinclair v Franks* [2007] WTLR 439 at [85]: 'One of the duties of a solicitor [when taking will instructions] even if he is the son of the testator is to discuss and, if appropriate, question the terms of the will, in order that the testator reaches a fully informed decision. [The son] was incapable of impartial discussion of his mother's instructions.'
[16] See also *Re a Solicitor* [1975] 3 All ER 853.

5.14 The current guidance in the SRA Code of Conduct 2011, Chapter 3 does not deal specifically with wills, but it does contain an absolute prohibition on acting where there is a conflict of this nature: 'You can never act where there is a conflict, or a significant risk of conflict, between you and your client.' On the face of this instruction, will preparation where the draftsman takes any benefit of substance could not be authorized by the client.

C. Training

5.15 Ongoing training is now required by most professional bodies' CPD schemes, and making use of the relevant training to meet CPD requirements is vital. Training of staff is a requirement of Chapter 7 of the SRA Code of Conduct 2011.[17] The framework of the statute law relating to wills does not change often, but new developments in case law and practice make it necessary to undertake continuing development of skills.

5.16 A number of firms involved in will drafting provide in-house training and this is generally to be welcomed. A cautionary note, however, comes from *Esterhuizen*: avoid silly names in the training exercises. The names used in exercises do not in themselves detract from the usefulness of the training, but comments in court about such an exercise involving 'the will of a gentleman called Mr Mickey Mouse'[18] can undo years of partnership or corporate image and reputation building. The validity of the training exercise is not affected by the choice of names, but people's perception of it is.

5.17 With the advent of CPD schemes, there has been a rise in commercial conferences and seminars. There is plenty of theoretical training available and most firms make good use of it. However, attendance at CPD events is no guide to future performance and there is a continuing need to monitor individual development by review of work standards and assessment of capabilities. In other words, do not assume that simply because someone has done the course that they can safely carry out the work.

D. Codes of Practice

5.18 After consultation, the government decided in 2013 that they would not put forward proposals for formal regulation of will preparation and estate administration, and also rejected the option of making these areas reserved legal activities.

5.19 Therefore, wills will still be delivered through diverse companies and members of different professions. Some will providers, though not all, have codes of practice specifically relating to the preparation of wills and the administration of estates.

5.20 Reference will be found in various parts of this work to the SRA's Code of Practice. In addition to this mandatory code for all solicitors, members of the Law Society have the benefit of Practice and Guidance notes directed at wills, estates, and trusts. The Law Society also has a Wills and Inheritance Scheme 'designed for SRA-regulated firms that specialise in will

---

[17] Outcome 7.6: 'you train individuals working in the firm to maintain a level of competence appropriate to their work and level of responsibility'.

[18] *Esterhuizen v Allied Dunbar* [1998] 2 FLR 668 at 670E.

writing, probate and estate administration work'.[19] The Protocol on wills and estate administration that is part of this is compulsory for firms that choose to become accredited under this scheme.

Other providers, for example, the Society of Will Writers and the Institute of Professional **5.21** Willwriters, have mandatory codes of practice for their members although it should be noted that these codes do not necessarily cover the same ground as the Law Society's optional scheme.

While codes and quality schemes serve an excellent aim of improving standards and safe- **5.22** guarding clients' interests, there are still those who prepare wills outside these codes. It is therefore in the clients' interests to ensure that that they are dealing with a provider who is obliged to deliver acceptable standards of practice.

---

[19] Law Society website <www.lawsociety.org.uk> accessed July 2013.

6

INSTRUCTIONS, PREPARATION, AND EXECUTION

A. Taking instructions

The process of drafting a will runs the risk of being seriously flawed unless the client's instructions are accurately ascertained and recorded. It is necessary for the draftsman to have asked the right questions[1] (and clarified any answers where necessary) in order to arrive at clear and unambiguous instructions. In addition, there is a significant amount of information relating to **6.01**

- the testator;
- his family and circumstances;
- his previous wills;[2] and
- his wealth

---

[1] 'There are, in most cases, a raft of questions which the draftsman ought to ask before putting pen to paper or, as is now the case, searching through a database of precedents' (Michael Waterworth, *Parker's Modern Wills Precedents*, 7th edition (Bloomsbury, 2011) [1.7]). 'It may be helpful to have a checklist of issues to be addressed and a standard form of questions to ask the client, to ensure that all the necessary information is obtained and that any areas of uncertainty or complexity can be explored further' (*Zurich @risk* newsletter, May 2008).

[2] The absence of consideration given to the dispositions in previous wills was a factor of some significance in *Sifri v Clough & Willis* [2007] WTLR 1453 and the will under consideration in the earlier (unreported) probate action.

that needs to be obtained and then taken into account in evaluating the instructions and advising the client.

6.02   In several reported decisions, the court has been critical of the instruction process where the work of the draftsman has been found to be seriously flawed or even mainly responsible for the subsequent dispute.[3] Although the costs settlements in these cases may not have been made public, there is good reason to think that the draftsman, or his insurers, may have been responsible for part of them. These decisions have served to highlight the risks of sketchy instructions or flawed meetings.

6.03   Where the standard of the instruction interview falls below that which should reasonably be expected of a professional draftsman, the draftsman may well be at risk for any loss that is caused to the testator (or his intended beneficiaries) through his failures.

6.04   Where there is a defect in the instructions that produces a will that does not implement the testator's wishes, rectification of the will under s.20 Administration of Justice Act 1982 must be a possibility. Whilst this may be a less costly solution than a claim for loss of benefit from a beneficiary, there is still the risk that the costs of rectification will be claimed from the draftsman.[4]

6.05   Far too high a percentage of wills that give rise to later problems start to go wrong at this stage of gathering information and taking instructions. Generally these problems arise from inadequacies in the information gathered; often caused by lack of time and attention.

6.06   In order to address these issues it is helpful to examine the will instruction process in some detail. 'Taking will instructions' is in many ways a misleading description as it understates the complexity of the meeting. What happens is that:

> Step [1] The draftsman establishes a wide range of information (family, assets, etc), this is by way of both questioning and listening—rarely will the client provide all the answers needed without questions and follow-up questions based on the first answers. This is because the client will seldom understand the need for the information (or its implications) that the draftsman is seeking from him.
>
> This process will also be part of the draftsman's assessment of testamentary capacity,[5] undue influence, and coercion.
>
> Step [2] The client explains how he wants to dispose of his estate, but the client usually does not have much knowledge about the forms of disposition possible, the taxation consequences of different dispositions, features of ownership of assets, Inheritance (Provision for Family and Dependants) Act 1975 (I(PFD)A 1975), etc.
>
> Step [3] The draftsman forms an understanding of the wishes in Step [2] and what the client is trying to achieve, in the light of the information in Step [1] and then offers his

---

[3] *Sprackling v Sprackling* [2009] WTLR 897; *Martin v Triggs Turner Barton* [2009] WTLR 1339; *Re Key, Key v Key* [2010] WTLR 623 are examples.

[4] *Zurich @risk* newsletter (n 1): 'Where the "clerical error" or "failure to understand the testator's instructions" is caused by the solicitor, it is likely that the solicitor will have failed in his or her duty of care to the testator and the costs of rectification will be recoverable against the solicitor. Similarly, where the terms used are so obscure or ambiguous that they give rise to a construction action, the solicitor runs the risk of being liable for the costs of that action.' See also Chapter 7.

[5] Understanding of assets and debts and family and dependents is essential to the second and third limbs of *Banks v Goodfellow* (1870) LR 5 QB 549.

advice on the options available to the client. The advice will include the relative advantages and disadvantages of the choices available.

Step [4] The client then has to understand and evaluate what he is told in Step [3] and either reject it or modify his dispositions previously given in Step [2]—and this frequently involves questions and discussion as to the relative practicality of several options and the client then decides and communicates his decision after the advice.

Step [5] The draftsman then communicates to the client his understanding of what the client has told him (in order to remove any misunderstanding) and then explains how that will be achieved and what the next steps are. This recapitulation should involve different words to ensure that there is full understanding on the part of both client and draftsman of what is intended.[6]

This is a complex structure for a meeting with changing roles for the participants. It may involve wholly new information and concepts being understood by the client and at the same time complex relationships or assets being understood by the draftsman. It also places great importance on the draftsman's ability to ask questions in an appropriate manner, listen to answers, frame follow-up questions when the testator's replies so require, and then produce relevant and practical advice. **6.07**

In order to have a sound basis of knowledge of the client and his affairs, there is no substitute for a thorough checklist of questions being built into the form used for recording instructions (see Appendix 3 for an example of a will instruction form).[7] **6.08**

A standardized instruction form is important because **6.09**

- it acts as a prompt for the draftsman's memory for all the areas that must be covered;
- it acts also as a vital support if the circumstances of the meeting are difficult, emotional, or confused;
- it allows for clearer recording of information alongside the question that elicited the information or the question that it is relevant to;
- it represents a standardized approach and thus helps to control risk within a firm;[8]
- it allows for easier control and checking of the work of others;
- the reminders and sign-off built into the form control completion of the work.

It is sometimes the case that the draftsman asks the client to sign the will instruction form to indicate that his will instructions have been correctly recorded. The extent to which the draftsman can rely on that signature in the event of a later dispute must be questionable. **6.10**

---

[6] 'On a matter such as this there is plainly scope for misunderstanding. It is a commonplace experience to find that, in the course of a conversation or meeting, people do not express themselves as fully as if they were writing letters or reports. It is entirely possible that in a discussion which must have involved reference to a limit or restriction of £100,000 for someone whose attention was not entirely focused to pick up that it was a restriction on what could be advanced when what was meant was a restriction on what should be left. Usually, as a conversation or meeting progresses such misunderstandings are ironed out—but not always' (*Martin v Triggs Turner Barton* (n 3)).

[7] *Bates v Wheildon* [2008] WTLR 1705: 'did not ask the testator all the questions that one might have expected him to have asked in those circumstances. He had no wills check list with him'. Also *Pollard Estate v Falconer* [2008] BCSC 516; 10 ITELR 992 where Macaulay J observed of the solicitor that 'his notes reveal gaps in the extent of the inquiries I would expect him to have made'.

[8] Provided, that is, that all draftsmen within the same firm use the same questionnaire. If different questionnaires are used, or some choose not to use questionnaires, the risk-management value of a standardized questionnaire is wholly or largely absent.

Much will depend upon the manner in which the questions and answers have been explained again to the client before signature. It is unlikely that the court would accept that a client has understood the implications of, for example, conditions attached to gifts, without those having been carefully explained.[9]

6.11 When considering the information required from the testator, questions should be asked in language that the testator can understand with appropriate explanations of the question subject and the significance of the question. The testator is less likely to provide full and accurate answers if he does not understand the question or its implications.[10] A straightforward question 'What is your domicile?' is most unlikely to elicit anything informative. This process is assisted by the will instruction form having questions in a logical order, which reduces the possibility of confusing the testator.[11]

Attendance notes

6.12 Full attendance notes are required for the will instruction meeting. The use of standard questionnaires simplifies this recording process for factual information, but where there is information that is not, or cannot be, recorded on the will instruction form, additional attendance notes on all relevant matters should be prepared. Such notes should be contemporaneous with the events recorded.[12] The failure to record adequately the instruction meeting can attract the considerable ire of the court.[13] While it is acknowledged that full attendance notes can be time consuming to prepare, from the point of view of managing risk and delivering good client care there is no alternative. The costs involved should therefore be reflected in the fee.

Reviewing the terms of previous wills

6.13 It is good practice when preparing a new will to examine the previous will (and any codicils to it) whenever these can be obtained within a suitable time. Good practice is argued for, because it is this examination that ought to disclose, for example:

- any mutual will agreement where this was recited in the will;
- a power of appointment that has been exercised by will;
- exclusion of property in certain geographic areas from the terms of the previous will (or similar limitations on revocation);
- significant inconsistencies in beneficiaries or property that have not been explained so far by the testator's instructions.

---

[9] *Lines v Porter* [2012] WTLR 629; the signature was of no significance where the will instruction form was not easily intelligible and a limitation against cohabitation was not explained.

[10] For example, with virtually all testators a question about 'dependants' will almost certainly not elicit any meaningful answer without the importance of dependants being explained in language that the client can understand.

[11] For problems caused by questions that are not understood see the will instruction form examined in *Lines v Porter* (n 9).

[12] In *Killick v Poutney* [2000] WTLR 41 (an undue influence matter) there is a warning on the relatively weak value of non-contemporaneous notes (no matter how apparently thorough) especially if they were written up after the writer had notice of the claim being made. See also *Borman v Lel* [2002] WTLR 237 for the court's lack of credit for, and criticism of, notes that not only appear to be prepared after the event but which were also only produced at trial. *Zurich @risk* newsletter, October 2003: 'Make contemporaneous notes. Notes prepared some time after the event will have negligible or no evidential value.'

[13] *Sprackling v Sprackling* (n 3); *Martin v Triggs Turner Barton* (n 3); *Re Key, Key v Key* (n 3).

This is especially true where any of the instructions for the will are expressed at the will **6.14** interview by the testator with reference to a previous will or codicil. To proceed with the new document without seeing the originals or good copies of the executed originals would be fraught with danger.

The safe approach would seem to be that such less obvious matters as mutual will agreements **6.15** or powers of appointment should always be part of the will instructions check list, in case the testator cannot provide a copy of the previous will in sufficient time for the new will to be prepared within acceptable time limits. This approach should then avoid the possibility of later claims and deliver a better standard of client care.

Where instructions have been taken for a codicil it is imperative to see the earlier will in order **6.16** to determine how the codicil should be drafted. To draft a codicil without seeing the earlier will creates unacceptable risks in terms of the effectiveness of the codicil and the continued safe operation of the remainder of the will.

Where instructions are being taken for a will which must be prepared immediately (such as **6.17** a deathbed will), the draftsman is under much greater time pressure and the testator may be unable, or unwilling, to participate in a lengthy interview. It is for the draftsman in those cir-cumstances to concentrate on ensuring that the most vital information is obtained as quickly as possible, as he may not have time to conduct a more thorough interview.

Mutual wills

Where mutual wills have previously been prepared, and a will-preparer is instructed later to **6.18** vary the terms of just one will, there is a very real risk that any litigation costs occasioned by this breach of the mutual agreement[14] will be claimed against the will-preparer, unless he can show that he warned the testator of the consequences of departing from the agreement and that the testator wished to proceed despite the warning. The difficulty comes when a differ-ent will-preparer is instructed for a subsequent will and he has no knowledge of the earlier agreement; hence the need to always enquire about any previous wills having been mutual wills in order to reduce risk.

If testators want new wills to be mutual wills, clear and careful advice is required to ensure **6.19** they understand the agreement that they are about to enter into and have been warned of its disadvantages.[15] The draftsman should proceed with caution, particularly with regard to the agreement between the parties. If mutual wills are intended, both parties must understand

- that the agreement is to be legally binding;
- that there cannot be revocation without the consent of the other—it is not simply suf-ficient that they understand that they want to benefit each other;[16] and

---

[14] For consideration of the nature of the mutual agreement and the enforcement of its terms, see *Re Cleaver* [1981] 2 All ER 1018; *Re Dale* [1993] 4 All ER 129; *Goodchild v Goodchild* [1997] 3 All ER 63; *Birch v Curtis* [2002] WTLR 965; and *Healey v Brown* [2002] WTLR 849.

[15] See *Re Walters, Olins v Walters* [2008] WTLR 339 at [43]. This was approved in the Court of Appeal, [2008] EWCA Civ 782, where Mummery LJ observed: 'As recent cases have shown this equitable doctrine dat-ing from the 18th century . . . continues to be a source of contention for the families of those who have invoked it. The likelihood is that in future even fewer people will opt for such an arrangement and even more will be warned against the risks involved.'

[16] *Birch v Curtis* (n 14).

- if one of them dies without having revoked the will, the other will be bound by the terms of the mutual will and therefore any changes in the future (such as remarriage) cannot be catered for.

6.20 The agreement need not be in writing, but clearly it is foolish to allow clients to rely on such an agreement without clear and explicit evidence of the terms.[17]

6.21 There is no substitute for an express declaration of mutuality in both wills where applicable. By reciting this in the will, any draftsman in the future is given a better chance of realizing that they are mutual wills and not simply mirror image ones (with a separate agreement behind them). It also means that on death recognition of the agreement is much easier. This declaration might take the form of a simple statement or, alternatively, could recite the full terms of the agreement.

6.22 If the mutual wills are to contain specific bequests[18] of interests in land, the contract that underlies the mutual wills is considered to be a contract for the disposition of an interest in land[19] and as such must be made in writing and signed by both parties.[20] This was the result in *Healey v Brown*,[21] where the court would not enforce the terms of the wills on the second death as regards the devolution of the formerly owned joint property. The signed wills did form a contract, but neither will bore both signatures. Therefore, if mutual wills dealing with interests in land are needed the draftsman must ensure that there is separate agreement in writing, signed by both parties, in order for the agreement to take effect over the land.

6.23 In order to avoid allegations that wills are mutual, there is a discernible modern trend to use declarations of non-mutuality in wills. While this should make matters clear, it is of course necessary to explain what such a declaration is to the client.

6.24 Clients can find a superficial attraction in mutual wills, considering them to be a cheap alternative to the use of trusts. However, while a mutual will agreement will prevent the survivor from disposing of his estate by will contrary to the agreement it will not necessarily prevent

- the survivor from spending wealth on health or nursing care;
- wealth being dissipated by a high standard of living.[22]

Foreign wills

6.25 Foreign wills are, generally speaking, outside of the area of competence of an English draftsman. There are therefore substantial risks in drafting them under any circumstances. A foreign element can come into the picture in a number of ways:

---

[17] For difficulties where there was no written agreement, see *Walters v Olins* [2008] WTLR 1449; *Charles v Fraser* [2010] WTLR 1489; and *Fry v Densham-Smith* [2011] WTLR 387.
[18] See *Re Walters, Olins v Walters* (n 15) at [31] where it was held that *Healey v Brown* (n 14) is restricted to specific gifts of land. This was confirmed by the Court of Appeal in *Walters v Olins* (n 17).
[19] Section 2 Law of Property (Miscellaneous Provisions) Act 1989.
[20] This same point will also apply to contracts to make a will which require land to be disposed of.
[21] [2002] WTLR 849.
[22] The nature of the constructive trust that arises after the first death would, on the face of it, prevent these assets from being within reach of an I(PFD)A 1975 claimant (s.25 for the definition of free estate). There is as yet no reported case on any attempt to make such a claim. However, it does seem unusual that capital that is freely disposable in support of the survivor and his dependants while he is alive is apparently beyond the reach of dependants on his death.

1. A draftsman may be consulted by a testator who is domiciled or resident outside England and Wales. An overseas domicile (applying the domicile test under the law of England and Wales) may indicate that another body of law will apply to much of the estate affecting testamentary freedom; dispositions in the will; and devolution of property, particularly that outside of England and Wales. But, even where the draftsman is satisfied that the testator's domicile is that of England and Wales,[23] he must be alert for other indicators (eg citizenship or residence) that might give another jurisdiction an equal or better claim to govern the disposition of the estate.

2. There may be property situated outside England and Wales, and the draftsman can give no assurance, implied or expressed, that the terms of the English will apply to foreign property, particularly realty.

Below is a summary of the rules, so that the draftsman can be alert to problems. A full study **6.26** of the way in which conflicts of laws apply to this area is beyond this work, but certain key concepts do have to be borne in mind by the practitioner.

Preliminary points

The concept of the domicile of the testator is crucial and is dealt with in more detail below. **6.27** The first point is that a distinction has to be drawn between movable and immovable property.[24] In general, land and all interests in it, including those under a trust, are immovables; whereas debts and other choses in action are movables.

The next fundamental point is that, in general, the law of succession in relation to movables **6.28** is governed by the law of the domicile of the testator. The law of succession in relation to immovables, on the other hand, is governed by where they are situated.[25]

A distinction then has to be drawn between the testator's capacity to make a will,[26] the for- **6.29** malities which govern the making of the will,[27] and finally the essential validity of the will.[28] The question of revocation of wills also needs to be looked at separately.

Domicile

This work is not the place for a close analysis of the law of domicile which involves an often **6.30** complex application of the rules to very detailed facts. However, the fact remains that the draftsman may often have to ascertain the domicile of a client and needs to be alive to the importance of exploring the matter as far as he or she is able with a client who has links with

---

[23] Bearing in mind the difficulties in determining this conclusively during a person's lifetime; see *Cyganik v Agulian* [2006] WTLR 565: 'the question under the 1975 Act is whether Andreas was domiciled in England and Wales at the date of his death. Although it is helpful to trace Andreas's life events chronologically and to halt on the journey from time to time to take stock, this question cannot be decided in stages. Positioned at the date of death in February 2003 the court must look back at the whole of the deceased's life, at what he had done with his life, at what life had done to him and at what were his inferred intentions in order to decide whether he had acquired a domicile of choice in England by the date of his death. Soren Kierkegaard's aphorism that 'Life must be lived forwards, but can only be understood backwards' resonates in the biographical data of domicile disputes' (per Mummery LJ).

[24] The distinction is not the same as the difference between real and personal property. The real question is whether the property can be moved or not. Therefore leaseholds and mortgages, while strictly personalty, are nevertheless immovable.

[25] Or their *situs*, but the authors note the current ban on the use of Latin terminology in any form.

[26] ie whether the testator is under age or lacking mental capacity.

[27] ie how many witnesses etc.

[28] eg whether there are any rules of succession which prevent the will being made in particular terms.

other jurisdictions. In some cases sophisticated testators may be keen to give instructions that they remain domiciled outside England and Wales and there is no reason why such specific instructions cannot be relied upon by the will draftsman. On the other hand, in cases where it is clear that the testator was born outside England and Wales or is the citizen of or resides in another jurisdiction, it is vitally important that at least some inquiries are made to try to ascertain whether he is domiciled in England and Wales. The draftsman must consider the practicalities of making enquiries about a client's domicile. The simple question 'What is your domicile?' will not yield any meaningful reply given that it is the very rare client who has any knowledge of what the legal concept of domicile is.

6.31 It may well be good practice to recite the domicile of the testator in the will although any such declaration is neither binding nor conclusive on the issue.[29] Not only is domicile important for the various reasons set out below, but also in relation to claims under the I(PFD)A 1975 and the imposition of inheritance tax.[30]

6.32 All persons have a domicile, which is conferred on them at birth and which is known as their domicile of origin.[31] However, they may change their domicile by acquiring a domicile of choice.[32] The classic statement of the nature of a domicile is that of Lord Chelmsford in *Udny v Udny*:[33] 'Domicile of choice is a conclusion or inference which the law derives from the fact of a man fixing voluntarily his sole or chief residence in a particular place, with an intention of continuing to reside there for an unlimited time.' It is essential to show not only that the testator resided in that country, but intended to do so as his permanent home.[34] A testator can only be domiciled in a territory which is legally recognized and distinct, for example England and Wales, rather than the United Kingdom, or New South Wales rather than Australia.

6.33 In complex cases, the will draftsman will only be able to do his best to establish what conclusions might be reached concerning domicile. However, it is important that he is aware of the issues which may arise if a testator is domiciled elsewhere.

---

[29] While domicile cannot be established in this way as such, it can be a useful indication, but bear in mind Romer LJ in *A-G v Yule and Mercantile Bank of India* (1931) 145 LT 9 at 17: 'I am not prepared to attach importance to a declaration by a man as to his domicile unless there is evidence to show that the man knew what "domicile" means. A declaration by a man made orally or in writing that he intends to remain in a certain country will, if not inconsistent with the facts, be of assistance in determining the question whether he has become domiciled there. Domicile is however a legal conception on which the views of the layman are not of much assistance.'

[30] Where no claim can be made unless the deceased died domiciled in England and Wales. For criticism of this point see Longmore LJ in *Cyganik v Agulian* (n 23) at [58].

[31] His father's domicile if he is legitimate and born in the lifetime of his father, and his mother's in all other cases. He cannot acquire a domicile of choice until he is 16 or marries under that age.

[32] The authors are delighted to note that since 1974 married women have been able to acquire a domicile of choice like anyone else.

[33] (1869) LR 1 HL 441, 448.

[34] The acquisition of a domicile of choice is a serious matter not lightly to be inferred from slight indications or casual words—Scarman J (as he then was) in *Re Fuld's Estate (No 3)* [1968] P 675. A domicile of origin 'is more enduring, its hold stronger and less easily shaken off' than a domicile of choice (*Winans v Attorney-General* [1904] AC 287); 'All the cases state that a domicile of origin can only be replaced by clear cogent and compelling evidence that the relevant person intended to settle permanently and indefinitely in the alleged domicile of choice' (per Longmore LJ in *Cyganik v Agulian* (n 23) at [53]); and see *Morris v Davies* [2011] WTLR 1643. In *Holliday v Musa* [2010] 2 FLR 702 the Court of Appeal held that the real question was not the one the judge at first instance had asked herself: whether the deceased intended to return to Cyprus, but whether it was right to infer at any stage during his residence in England he had formed the intention to settle in the UK indefinitely.

Capacity

In relation to *movables* this is governed by the law of the domicile of the testator. While ques- **6.34** tions have been raised as to whether this is the domicile of the testator at the date of making the will rather than at the date of death, it seems reasonably clear it is the former. It is capacity at the time of making the will which is important.[35]

In relation to *immovables*, however, the law governing capacity is the law applicable to the **6.35** territory in which the assets are situated.

It can therefore be seen that if a draftsman is presented with a client whose domicile is **6.36** England and Wales, but who owns land in Spain, it will be necessary for the draftsman to be sure (if there is any doubt) that the testator has capacity for the purposes of both English and Spanish law.

Formalities

In relation to formalities, there is no distinction now to be drawn between wills of movables **6.37** or immovables. Both types are governed by s.1 Wills Act 1963, which applies to all deaths taking place after 1 January 1964.

Essentially a will is valid from the point of view of formalities if it complies with the internal law of

- the territory where it was executed;
- the territory where at the time of its execution or the time of his death the testator was domiciled;
- the territory where at the time of its execution or the testator's death he had his habitual residence;
- a state of which at the time of its execution or the testator's death the testator was a national.[36]

There is an additional category in relation to immovables. A will executed in accordance with **6.38** the formalities of the territory in which they are situated will also be formally valid.[37] There are also rules relating to the execution of wills on vessels and aircraft. Unless the draftsman is carrying on a particularly glamorous jet-set practice, these will not frequently require a great deal of consideration.

Essential validity

Essential validity governs such matters as to whether, for example, a spouse inherits certain **6.39** property automatically, or whether a witness to a will can take under it. As far as *movables* are concerned, it is the law of the domicile of the testator at the date of his death that governs the matter.

---

[35] Dicey, Morris, and Collins, *The Conflict of Laws*, 14th edition (Sweet & Maxwell, 2008) 1009–11.

[36] There are provisions in the Act to deal with the situation where the testator is a national of a state where there are two systems of internal law governing the formalities of wills. In such a case, either any rule of the internal law as to which system of law should apply will govern the situation, or the system with which the testator was closely connected at the time of execution will be taken (s.6(2) Wills Act 1963). The Act also allows for the fact that the testator may be a national of more than one state, and for applying the law of both states.

[37] Section 2 Wills Act 1963.

6.40   As far as *immovables* are concerned, it is the law of the territory where they are situated that will govern. Matters such as the law of perpetuities and accumulations, for example, will depend on the law of the country in which the immovables subsist.

Construction

6.41   A will of both movables and immovables is construed in accordance with the system of law which the testator intended. Therefore, if there is a clause in the will saying it is to be construed in accordance with English law, then the position is clear. If, on the other hand, the will is silent on the question,[38] it will be construed in accordance with the law of domicile of the testator at the date when the will was made.[39] In the case of immovables, it must be remembered that the essential validity of the will is governed by the *situs* of the assets concerned. Therefore a gift of immovables in Spain by a testator domiciled in England will be construed in accordance with the law of England, unless there is a clause in the will to suggest otherwise; but if it then turns out that in accordance with the law of Spain the gift is invalid, that rule will prevail.[40]

Revocation

6.42   Knowing whether the testator is revoking an earlier will by making a new one will perhaps not always greatly concern the draftsman; after all if the new will has been properly executed by a testator with capacity it will revoke any earlier wills. The fact that there is a foreign element involved will normally only give rise to some of the problems which are being discussed in this section. Having said that, there follows a very brief summary of the rules relating to revocation so that where there is a foreign element involved the draftsman knows where problems might arise. In cases of real doubt, the leading work on conflicts of laws[41] should be consulted.

6.43   In the case of revocation by a later testamentary instrument, revocation is governed in the case of *movables* by the law of the deceased's domicile at the date of death and in the case of *immovables*, by the law of the territory in which they are situated. This general rule is modified by the Wills Act 1963, so that if the instrument in which the revoking clause appears is executed in accordance with the law of one of the territories mentioned in s.1 of the Act, it will be valid as far as formality goes. It will also be valid if the clause revoking the earlier provision is executed in accordance with any of the laws of the territories under which the will it is revoking would have been valid.[42] In other words, there is a wide selection of laws to ensure that the revocation is valid, although in some cases this will mean that the revocation clause is valid in an instrument that is otherwise invalid to dispose of any property.

6.44   In the case of revocation by any other means, such as subsequent marriage or destruction, *movables* are governed by the law of the domicile of the testator. Unfortunately it has not yet been decided whether that is his domicile at the date of death or the date of the act of revocation. *Immovables* are governed by the law in which they are situated.

---

[38]   And many if not most wills are.

[39]   Section 4 Wills Act 1963 states expressly that a change in the domicile of the testator after execution will not alter the law in accordance with which the will must be construed.

[40]   As the law where the immovable is situated is the law which will apply to its essential validity.

[41]   Dicey, Morris, and Collins (n 35), is the authoritative work.

[42]   Section 2(1)(c) Wills Act 1963.

Powers of appointment

The rules concerning the exercise of powers of appointment where the testator is not domi- **6.45**
ciled in England and Wales, but the instrument creating the power was English, are labyrinthine. Certain basic principles can be discerned, but it will be necessary for the practitioner
to consult works such as that by Dicey, Morris, and Collins on this subject if it is truly raised
in any particular case.

1. If the Testator has capacity to make the will by the law of his domicile, then he will have
    capacity to exercise a power of appointment over movables.
2. A will exercising a power of appointment will be valid as far as formalities are concerned,
    if it is executed in accordance with the Wills Act 1963; or the law of the country governing
    the instrument creating the power.[43]
3. If the appointment is under a special power,[44] the fact that the testator's domicile might
    impose restrictions on the way in which the testator leaves his property will have no
    impact on his ability to exercise the power. The rationale behind this is that he is disposing
    of someone else's property and not his own.[45]
4. On the other hand, if the power is a general one,[46] it depends whether the failure to
    exercise the power will result in the property falling into the estate of the testator or being
    disposed of in default of appointment. In the first case, it will be the domicile of the testa-
    tor that will govern the matter.[47] In the second case, the position is governed by the law
    of the territory in which the instrument creating the power was made.[48]

Conflict of rules

A key idea for those taking instructions to come to terms with is that other jurisdictions may **6.46**
well not use domicile as a test of jurisdiction (only common law jurisdictions are likely to do
so). Foreign jurisdictions are far more likely to use tests based on residence (and their tests
for residence will also vary from state to state) or nationality. Therefore, although you may be
clearly satisfied that your client is domiciled in England and Wales, if he is resident abroad or
is a national of another state, beware and consider further and better advice, for you may well
be attempting to draw a will where there is going to be conflict of jurisdictions.

What is important, from a practical point of view, is for the will draftsman to know when he **6.47**
can act in preparing such a will, and to understand why he might have a problem so that he
can explain the difficulties to the client. There do not appear to be any reported cases where
someone has been found liable for failing to deal adequately with the foreign element in a
will, but as negligence is an ever developing area, no great comfort can be derived from that.

Guidance for the draftsman where there is a foreign element

The labyrinthine nature of the rules relating to wills with a foreign element underlines the **6.48**
need for specialist advice in complex cases. However, the following provide some general
guidelines:

---

[43] Section 2 Wills Act 1963.
[44] ie a power where the appointment can only be made among a specified class.
[45] *Pouey v Hordern* [1900] 1 Ch 492.
[46] In other words, the testator can appoint anyone he wishes.
[47] See *Re Pryce* [1911] Ch 286 (CA) and *Re Khan's Settlement* [1966] Ch 567. The reasoning is that the
property has effectively become the property of the testator.
[48] *Re Pryce* (n 47).

1. Where the testator has a foreign domicile, the English practitioner unversed in anything other than his own law is simply not competent to draft a will relating to anything other than immovables situated in England and Wales. The only exception to this is if the draftsman obtains advice from a lawyer competent in the jurisdiction in which the client is domiciled.[49] Otherwise, if the client wishes to have a separate will dealing with English immovables, it should be stated that it is confined to that, and it is important that the will says that its construction is governed by the laws of England and Wales.[50] It might also be a good idea to include a recital of the domicile of the testator.

2. Where the client is domiciled in England and Wales, but owns foreign movables and immovables, the position is somewhat different. The draftsman is competent to deal with the client's property in this country, and arguably movables abroad, as these will be governed by the law of the client's domicile. However, it should be stressed that this is only in relation to English private international law, and another jurisdiction where the movables were situated might take a different view.

3. In relation, however, to foreign immovables, the English practitioner cannot go ahead without taking advice from a practitioner competent in the jurisdiction in which the immovables are situated.

4. If at all possible a separate will dealing with foreign immovables and movables should be executed. In that case, the practitioner must make sure that it is clear on the face of the will what property is excluded from it. In particular the practitioner needs to ensure that the new English will does not revoke any existing foreign wills by accident.

Existing foreign wills

6.49　The draftsman of a will needs to be aware of any existing foreign will. Although he might intend preparing a will to govern only the English property (or the property not covered by the foreign will) and indeed succeed in doing so, this will require the revocation clause to be amended so as to not revoke the foreign will. (The same point can apply in reverse if a later foreign draftsman is similarly careless of a will after an earlier English will.[51])

6.50　Where the draftsman knows of foreign wills that should not be revoked by the will he is instructed to prepare, and he fails to suitably amend the revocation clause, prima facie he has acted negligently and will be liable for lost benefits and additional costs.[52]

Time taken

6.51　Knowing who the client is, and what his circumstances are, should also give some information to the draftsman as to the urgency of the will. It may appear obvious that the sick and

---

[49] The fact that organizations such as the Society of Estates and Trusts Practitioners are global assists in finding foreign lawyers with the requisite expertise.

[50] Otherwise, the law of the testator's domicile will govern construction with potentially very interesting results.

[51] In *Re Wayland's Estate* [1951] 2 All ER 1041 it was found that such a clause in an English will did not revoke the prior Belgian will on the grounds that there was no intention to revoke. However, this judgment was probably only arrived at because of the lack of clarity in the wording of the revocation clause. There is also *Lamothe v Lamothe* [2006] WTLR 1431, which involved an English will and one from Dominica. The court considered the issue of whether or not the Dominican will was intended to revoke the English will notwithstanding that the usual revocation clause was used. It was decided that it was intended to revoke the English will, but implicit in this is that a court would look at intention.

[52] There are no decided cases on this liability, but it does seem to fall well within the scope of *White v Jones* [1995] 1 All ER 691.

elderly require priority of service, but their needs for wills are not always established at the initial client contact, even though it is essential that this is done.

In terms of assessing the risk of time taken to prepare a will, the time period starts when the client instructs the draftsman to prepare a new will. Where the client makes it known that he wants a new will prepared, which is often when he requests an appointment, that is when the time period will usually be considered to start (see the opening lines of the quotation from *X v Woollcombe Yonge* below). If the client's request is vague as to whether or not he wants a new will it is important to clarify this quickly (see Chapter 4 Part D earlier on retainers). It cannot be safe practice to delay seeing the client unless the client has the risks of delay explained and accepts them. Where the solicitor's diary simply will not allow for an interview within a reasonable time, unacceptable risk should be avoided by arranging for another draftsman within the firm to attend. **6.52**

In the New Zealand case of *Gartside*, a seven-day delay in preparing the will was found excessive for a client, aged eighty-nine, who was in a nursing home and had recently had a fall. It is therefore vital to establish such relevant information at the outset in order to assess what is an acceptable time to complete the instructions. This point matches generally with the need to know the client's circumstances. **6.53**

This aspect of assessing the urgency of a will necessitates some degree of training for other staff, such as secretaries, if they are in charge of a will draftsman's diary. Unless the draftsman is to assess the client and make the appointment himself, the secretary must be sufficiently trained to make an informed assessment of salient issues and thus control ongoing risk. **6.54**

X v Woollcombe Yonge

The following observations from Neuberger J (as he then was) in *X v Woollcombe Yonge* are the most detailed review of time taken in any of the will negligence cases so far reported. It is an important passage in its approach to time taken and sets out clearly that it is part of the will draftsman's duty to assess the likelihood of death, and therefore the urgency of the matter, on a realistic basis on the facts of each individual testator. **6.55**

> It can always be said that, when a client indicates to a solicitor that he or she wants to make a will, or wants to make a substantial change to a previous will, the solicitor should draw up something very quickly for the client to sign then and there as a holding operation. There can always be a risk of death from heart attack, stroke or accident.[53] The question as to whether a solicitor should be concerned about that possibility must, as I have said, be one of fact and degree. Where the client is old or ill, the delay which may be acceptable will obviously be less than in the absence of age or illness. Where there is a plain and substantial risk of the client's imminent death, anything other than a handwritten rough codicil prepared on the spot for signature may be negligent. It is a question of the solicitor's judgment based on his assessment of the client's age and state of health . . .

> So far as preparing the will promptly is concerned, I consider a period of seven days[54] [for a late middle-aged cancer sufferer with no imminent expectation of death], as she appeared [to the solicitor] was not an unreasonable period[55] . . .

---

[53] Although the judge did not say so, loss of testamentary capacity arising from these accidents should also be included in this risk.

[54] This was in fact 7 calendar days.

[55] This finding is contrary to the recommendation contained in the final sentence of a *Law Society Gazette* article on this issue, of 15 November 1991, that 7 days is appropriate where the client 'is elderly or likely to die'.

[the] suggestion that a solicitor should only act urgently when he thought that there was a likelihood, by which I take it to mean a more than 50 per cent risk, of his client dying before he could return with the will, appears to me to be a significantly too generous a test to solicitors. I consider that the right test is whether there was a real prospect of such an eventuality.[56]

6.56 Neuberger J was, in essence, setting out a test to determine the urgency of a will—the draftsman should

- establish the client's age, health, and any other factors affecting the urgency of the will;
- consider how quickly the will must be prepared in the light of the above;
- agree any holding documents with the testator if they are appropriate;
- set a reasonable time limit for the will.

Omitting this assessment will, prima facie, breach the duty of care if loss ensues.

6.57 The importance of age in this test had been highlighted earlier by Chadwick LJ in *Carr-Glynn v Frearsons*[57] where he observed:

it is necessary to bear in mind that the testatrix was 81 years of age when she made her will in 1989. It must have been within the contemplation of a solicitor who was instructed to make a will for a client of that age that the matter ought to be dealt with promptly, lest the client's testamentary intentions be defeated by events beyond his or her control.

6.58 This urgency is not driven solely by the possibility of death, but also by the possibility of medical events, such as strokes, which, while not immediately resulting in death, may deprive the client of testamentary capacity. Other known risk elements such as forthcoming surgery or dangerous occupations and activities need to be taken into account.

6.59 It was suggested that the solicitors should, under the circumstances in *X v Woollcombe Yonge*, have been required to inspect the patient/client's medical notes or consult the hospital staff to determine the client's state of health and life expectancy. In other words, verify with the medical staff the conclusion that the solicitor had reached about his client's lack of imminent expectation of death. The judge rejected this as potentially placing the medical staff in a position of conflict with their duty of confidentiality to their patient.[58]

6.60 The passage on likelihood of death is a little more difficult to implement. Clearly Neuberger J envisaged that approaching urgency only on 50 per cent or greater risk of death was to be too conservative. However, although these remarks indicate that a less than 50 per cent chance should be the threshold, how much less is hard to quantify. Does a 'real prospect' translate to 'within the bounds of real possibility', perhaps, as opposed to a remote possibility? However, despite this difficulty, the safe course for the practitioner must be to err on the side of caution, knowing that it is less than a 50 per cent probability, however he chooses to quantify a 'real prospect'. Some help, as far as the elderly are concerned, can be found in those judgments that express a need for the elderly to be treated as having a greater risk of death.[59]

---

[56] *X v Woollcombe Yonge* [2001] WTLR 301.
[57] [1999] Ch 326 at 331G–H.
[58] This claim also ignored the question of whether or not a solicitor is qualified to make any such judgement based on a hospital file.
[59] *White v Jones* (n 52); *Carr-Glynn v Frearsons* (n 57); *Gartside v Sheffield Young & Ellis* [1983] NZLR 37.

It is quite possible that the solicitor's assessment of the client might conclude that there was **6.61**
not a high degree of urgency attached to the client's circumstances—a view that later proved
to be wrong (as happened in *X v Woollcombe Yonge*). A test of reasonableness will be applied
to the solicitor's judgement in forming his view of the client.[60]

The suggestion by Neuberger J that a solicitor might draw up a will or codicil as 'a holding **6.62**
operation' is not a suggestion that this should be done in all cases, but it is of relevance where
there is a plain risk that the client might not survive the short time taken to have a will prepared in the office. Such a temporary will can also be significant where there is a change of
wishes by the testator, and it is important that the dispositive terms of the will are changed
to reflect this, while more careful planning of the taxation structure of the will is considered
further. This is a point to discuss with the client where significant changes or a substantial
estate planning exercise are contemplated.

Tax planning exercises are not easily fitted into the timescales of will preparation, and it is **6.63**
therefore much safer for the draftsman to discuss the question of time and give advice on
whether or not an interim will is needed, which will be reviewed, and if necessary replaced,
after the estate planning exercise has been completed.

Urgent and non-urgent wills

We have clear examples that where factors of urgency are present then the draftsman must **6.64**
act appropriately. There is no specific time determined by these decisions and each testator
must be assessed on an individual basis.

We know from *X v Woollcombe Yonge* that if illness is present but death is not imminent, then **6.65**
seven days from instructions to execution would not be unreasonable. However, the absence
of urgency factors does not mean that the draftsman is free to take as much time as he likes
with the will. Although the court has not provided any guidance on time for a will where
the urgency factors are absent, there must be a degree of risk involved where any client dies
before his will is prepared and executed. The only way to minimize that risk is to avoid delays
and deliver wills without delay.

Standard or optimum times

Apart from the above passage from *X v Woollcombe Yonge*, in all other reported will negligence **6.66**
cases there has been only limited consideration of how long a will should take from client
request to execution. This may seem surprising, but generally the court has been required
to decide whether any actual period was either too long or appropriate, and not to set out
what it regarded as the optimum period, either in general or particular terms, although
in *X v Woollcombe Yonge*, Neuberger J did observe that 'seven days would seem to me to be
plainly a sufficiently short period in most cases'.[61]

---

[60] 'On the facts of this case, it does appear to me, as I have said, that [the solicitor] took a view which a reasonable solicitor could perfectly well have taken' (per Neuberger J in *X v Woollcombe Yonge* (n 56) at 316C, having
earlier cited with approval Lord Diplock in *Saif Ali v Sydney Mitchell & Co* [1980] AC 198 at 218D–E: 'Those
who hold themselves out as qualified to practise other professions, although they are not liable for damage
caused by what in the event turns out to be an error of judgment on some matter upon which the opinions of
reasonably informed and competent members of the profession might have differed, are nevertheless liable for
damage caused by their advice, acts or omissions in the course of their professional work which no member of
the profession who was reasonably well-informed and competent would have given or done or omitted to do.'
[61] [2001] WTLR 301 at 316F.

6.67 At what point does delay become unreasonable and cause a breach of the solicitor's duty? Clearly, on the issue of what is an acceptable time span, very much will depend upon the individual facts. Translating this into practical advice, it can be dangerous to think in terms of a 'standard' period to prepare any given will, as clearly the court does not think in these terms. Like the court, practitioners must think carefully about the individual circumstances of each set of will instructions in order to assess risk and a suitable preparation time, and this is the antithesis of a standard time. However, having said this, it does make sense to have some 'target' time established as part of a firm's control of will-preparation policy, eg that where special circumstances do not require earlier preparation, all wills should be prepared within seven working days. This enables risk to be controlled by preventing wills with an original low risk assessment from creating risk through unwarranted delay; in other words, using the target time as a default reporting time for any wills not completed within it.

6.68 A consensus among those that were approached by the authors after *White v Jones* seemed to be that ten working days, or fourteen calendar days, was a reasonable outer limit of time available for a will, unless there were circumstances (health, age, travel, etc) that made that length of time dangerous. However, asking such questions today tends to produce shorter estimates, commonly in the order of seven calendar days. If draftsmen are collectively living up to this aim, clients must now be getting a better service and will draftsmen must be becoming more risk aware. It is probable that this aim of a shorter period is driven in part by nervousness produced by increased litigation. Additionally, seven days has now received judicial blessing as being a not unreasonable period in the absence of special factors.[62] However, the presence of special factors will radically change the time-scale.

6.69 The suggestion has been put forward previously that, if there was a delay in preparing the will and the defendant sought to justify the delay, cross-examination in court could involve the will-preparer being taken through each day of the period in question and being asked for each day (or part of the day), 'Why was it not done on this day?' When looked at in this light, even seven calendar days can be difficult to justify.[63]

Delay must be attributable to the will-preparer

6.70 Time delay in itself is not evidence of negligence, as there may be valid reasons for it.[64] The delay in having the will prepared or executed, for which liability could potentially rise, must be delay that is attributable to the will-preparer. There can be no liability for delay where it results solely from the actions or inactions of the testator.[65]

6.71 Delay which is genuinely attributable to the client should not give rise to liability for the draftsman, but danger can lie with unnecessary procedures imposed on the client by the

---

[62] *X v Woollcombe Yonge* (n 56).

[63] A view confirmed by Alastair Norris QC (as he was then) in his article, 'A Sense of Direction' (2001) 151 NLJ, Wills and Probate Supplement, 22 June, 932, with reference to his experience in appearing (successfully) for the defendant in *X v Woollcombe Yonge*.

[64] *Smolinski v Mitchell* [1995] 10 BCLR (3d) 366 where the Court in British Columbia held that the delay was excusable. The testatrix intended that her estate should pass to her attorney and her cousin equally. The attorney advised, quite properly, that the testatrix should take independent advice, but during the time taken to obtain the advice the testatrix died. The court found that the attorney was not culpable for the cousin's loss of benefit as in the circumstances the attorney's duty to his client was paramount.

[65] *Smolinski v Mitchell* (n 64); *Trusted v Clifford Chance* [2000] WTLR 1219; *Atkins v Dunn & Baker* [2004] WTLR 477.

draftsman. It is not, for example, reasonable to attribute delay to the client if the client has had to take time to reply to unnecessary letters. If the process has been delayed by letters that should not have been written, or if all the information/questions should have been dealt with in one letter (or at the stage of instructions), the delay is more likely to be attributable to the draftsman.[66] Any temptation to refer matters unnecessarily to the client in order to get the file temporarily off the draftsman's desk is to be avoided. Simply being able to say that it is with the client cannot excuse in any way past delays or even current delay if the referral is unnecessary.

Deathbed wills

The reference in the judgment in *X v Woollcombe Yonge* to a rough codicil leads to the question of practice with deathbed wills generally. Few areas of will drafting better exemplify the need for awareness of time and process. Taking deathbed instructions is never an easy matter, and the pressure induced by trying to help someone *in extremis* can lead to simple errors.   **6.72**

Generally, advance planning is required to avoid being put into a position where the draftsman is unsure of what to do or how to do it. At its simplest, this may be a binder with appropriate notes, checklists, and precedents in it. Others have designated laptops with similar information. The laptop solution is particularly good as it speeds drafting, and with use of a small portable printer, can produce a professional document quickly. A checklist for the contents of an emergency will pack is in Appendix 5. Anecdotal evidence suggests   **6.73**

- some firms now refuse to undertake this work because of the risks associated with it;
- some firms restrict the work to partners or very experienced practitioners; and
- where such wills are undertaken, fees are adjusted to reflect the risk.[67]

The Cancellation of Contracts made in a Consumer's Home or Place of Work etc Regulations 2008[68]

Leaving matters outstanding with the client for too long without a warning of the dangers should be avoided, at least on the grounds of good client care.   **6.74**

These regulations were clearly not designed to deal with any known or perceived mischief arising from draftsmen taking will instructions from a client away from the draftsman's office. Nonetheless, at first reading they appear to give a client a seven-day period, after concluding the contract, for the supply of goods or services to be cancelled. On the face of it, this could present difficulties if the will draftsman, mindful of his *White v Jones* obligations, has prepared and delivered a will within that period. However, it would seem that this risk is fairly marginal, given that will instructions are not that often cancelled and that there are some safeguards with the regulations.   **6.75**

The regulations envisage a 'cooling-off period' and make provision that, if work on the contract is required to start before the expiry of the seven-day cancellation period (as would almost invariably be the case with a will), the client should request this in writing.[69] It would   **6.76**

---

[66] See *Bacon v Kennedy* [1999] 1PNLR 1 for examples of unnecessary letters of this nature.

[67] See also para 8.26 onwards regarding fees.

[68] SI 2008/1816 which came into force on 1 October 2008; these Regulations revoke the Cancellation of Contracts Concluded away from Business Premises Regulations 1987 and reimplement the requirements of EC Directive 85/5777/EEC. It is not possible to contract out of these regulations—see Regulation 15(1).

[69] Regulation 9(1): without this authority 'the trader' is not required to start work on his contract for seven days after agreement, which, in terms of the will draftsman's duty of care, would be potentially dangerous.

therefore seem sensible that a client should provide a simple written confirmation that he requires work to start straight away.

6.77 Once the work on performance of the contract has started in this way, the client is bound to pay for any work done before cancellation if the contract is cancelled within the seven-day period.[70] The amount to be paid is 'in accordance with the reasonable requirements' of the contract. What might be unreasonable in this context is not set out. If the client cancels the contract, but does not pay the reasonable costs, he must return any 'goods supplied'.[71]

6.78 It would seem that, while it is unfortunate that such regulations appear to impinge upon will preparation practice (as clearly they were not framed with this type of work in mind), their practical effect should be minimal, particularly if the client requests work to start immediately.

The reluctant testator

6.79 There are testators who do not proceed with their wills once the document has been drafted or even engrossed. In such circumstances it is important to establish that the will-preparer has done all that can possibly be required of him, and that the failure to execute the will is attributable only to the testator. In *Atkins v Dunn & Baker*[72] a will was prepared for the client to make provision for the client's new wife and his daughter from his previous marriage. The draft will was sent to the client seeking his approval prior to preparing the engrossment. The client did not reply and there was no further communication from the solicitors about this will. The deceased died intestate some three years later. The Court of Appeal found that the duty of care did not extend to reminders in the circumstances of this case:

> I am unable to accept that invariably and inevitably there is a duty upon a solicitor, who carried out his instructions to prepare a draft will and sent that draft to the client, to follow the matter up. There will often be situations in relation to wills and other documents where there is a duty to send a reminder or further guidance to the client . . . In the circumstances of this case the Recorder was entitled to hold that 'the ball was in the client's court' and that the failure to send a reminder did not constitute such a fall below the standard to be expected of a competent solicitor as to amount to negligence.[73]

6.80 In *Atkins v Dunn & Baker*, the claimant used the argument that the solicitor's retainer continued, and was not concluded after the submission of the draft will. The continuation of the retainer would have meant that there should have been a follow-up letter as clients ought to be entitled to expect that as a minimum level of service. The court rejected this approach as being 'misplaced in the present circumstances',[74] an expression which must leave this line of argument open in other circumstances. The difficulty is identifying the circumstances that the court found had an effect on its conclusion. Furthermore, the court added:

> The evidence was that the instructions were that a draft will should be prepared and submitted to the client. This was done promptly in accordance with instructions. The solicitor had completed the task which he had been asked to perform. It does not follow from the retainer

---

[70] Regulation 9(2).
[71] Regulation 13(2).
[72] [2004] WTLR 477—this particular claim appeared to have most significant problems of causation, as the Court of Appeal also indicated.
[73] [2004] WTLR 477 at 483E–G.
[74] [2004] WTLR 477 at 483B.

rules, which cover a variety of situations, that in this situation there was inevitably a duty on the solicitor to send a reminder.[75]

The difficulty with these remarks is that the court found that the testator had given 'clear and emphatic instructions that [the solicitor] was to provide a new will'.[76] If instructions were given for the preparation of a will what circumstances are not reflected in the findings that persuaded the court that instructions to provide a new will are completed with only the provision of a draft? There is no further comment from the court in the *Atkins* judgment to cast further light on this point. Normally the client engagement letter will refer to 'preparation of a will' rather than 'preparation of a draft will'. **6.81**

It will therefore be prudent, notwithstanding the *Atkins* judgment, to send a letter, or to make a contemporaneous note of a conversation (but a letter is better) in which the testator is asked quite clearly if there is anything further that the testator requires the will draftsman to do to assist with the execution of the will. For example: **6.82**

> I am sorry that you do not want to proceed with your proposed will, but it is important that you must be quite satisfied that you approve of the terms of the will, and intend to give effect to them, before you sign the will. Without the execution of this will, your wishes, as expressed to me, will not take effect. As you are uncertain/do not wish to proceed at the present time, I will take no further action with regard to this will, unless I hear from you to the contrary.
>
> My account for the work to date is attached.

A letter in these, or similar, unequivocal terms should be clear evidence that the draftsman can go no further in default of the client's further instructions regarding execution. Delay at this point is clearly not the fault of the draftsman and his papers can be filed away once the bill is paid. This is far safer than, as so often happens, allowing the matter to peter out with no conclusive evidence of what further was offered by the draftsman or asked for by the testator.[77] **6.83**

The difficult question is: how soon after the will has been prepared does the draftsman send such a letter? Bearing in mind that seven calendar days is a reasonable outer limit for the whole process, it seems that such a letter ought to be sent no later than that, unless the client has expressly asked the draftsman not to contact him earlier. However, in order to send such a letter, it is clear that there should have been a discussion with the client which has ended inconclusively. The possible danger in waiting too long before sending such a letter is that the client dies or loses capacity and the draftsman has failed to establish conclusively that he has done all that he can for the client. **6.84**

It is also a possibility that a client does not reply to the letter sending out the will (or draft) and subsequent telephone calls and letters are unanswered. Under these circumstances there should be evidence on the will draftsman's file to show what has been tried and that he has not received any cooperation. That ought to reduce the risk, as long as it is clearly evidenced, but nonetheless a letter similar to the one above should be sent as soon as possible after **6.85**

---

[75] [2004] WTLR 477 at 483B—if the solicitor had completed the task for which he had been instructed, why was no account submitted at its conclusion?

[76] [2004] WTLR 477 at 479D.

[77] See *Esterhuizen v Allied Dunbar* [1998] 2 FLR 668 for the dangers of an inconclusive ending to a transaction. *Smith v Claremont Haynes* The Times, 3 September 1991 is also a good illustration of this point, with confusion as to what instructions had been given to the solicitor. One cannot help thinking that the solicitor's case would have been immeasurably improved with more accurate and timely notes.

reasonable attempts have been made to contact the client. To delay can add to the risk, especially if attempts to contact the client are not fully evidenced on the file.

6.86   Because a will-preparer is safer from risk with an executed, rather than unexecuted, will, there should obviously be no undue pressure placed on a testator to sign simply to ease the position of the will-preparer. It is most important that the testator cannot say that he only signed the will because the solicitor told him to do it, or that he did not want to disappoint the solicitor and not sign after the solicitor had made a journey especially to see him. Some clients, especially the elderly, can be a little in awe of the legal process, and their solicitor, and they can tend to do as they believe they are told rather than as they want; therefore, outstanding wills for the elderly should be handled sympathetically.

Control of time

6.87   From the first contact with the client, planning and monitoring of the time taken is vital. *Planning* and *monitoring* are two different, but complementary, aspects of the same risk control.

Planning

6.88   Establishing the time requirement for the will at the outset should help to avoid embarrassment. Practically, this is not just the draftsman's assessment of urgency, but also involves the client's plans, such as holidays etc, that could cause delay if not advised to the draftsman at the outset. Predicting a seven-day process is less than helpful if, in three days, the draftsman is going on holiday, or the client is. Planning the time and advising the client of the likely time span provides a better (more informative) service to the client, and gives the client an opportunity to raise issues that will help, eg restrictions on their own time. The key dates and times from the planning must then be backed with diary entries etc.

6.89   Agreeing a time frame with the client (and keeping to it) is good practice and much more likely to produce timely preparation than an open-ended time frame. Apart from focusing the will-preparer's attention on what must be done, it demonstrates what has been agreed with the client. Thus, if death occurs before the new will is completed, it might help refute claims of negligence. This is of course conditional upon a realistic and appropriate time frame having been agreed.

Monitoring

6.90   Control of the process within the will draftsman's office must then allow for identification of how far each will file has progressed against the planned time. The process must be both robust and accurate, with the minimum scope for files or drafts to be delayed, mislaid, or, worst of all, missed off the monitoring system. Far too often, it is this sort of monitoring or control that is absent when delays occur.

Internal audit of time taken

6.91   In order to see if the will-preparer's work (or the whole department's work) is matching the exacting standards that both the law and the firm's own policies require, a periodic internal audit of the time taken to complete the work for recent will files will probably be an illuminating and worthwhile exercise. This is something worth doing on a regular basis, if only to prove that systems are working properly to minimize risk. It is all very well setting target times, but it is just as important knowing that they are being achieved. If they are not being achieved, then there is a risk issue to be addressed.

B. Precedents

There are now substantial volumes of authoritative precedents fairly easily available, and **6.92** there is little excuse for the use of old or outdated precedents. However, blind reliance on precedents is to be avoided. The text should always be examined critically. Using old, or manifestly inadequate, precedents, which give rise to unnecessary expense in administration or fail to give effect to a testator's true intentions, must be a source of risk for the future. Tempting though it is for the individual to draft new precedents or to revise old ones, the risk is now increasing for all but the most accomplished draftsmen, and published precedents are preferred.

Consistent use of precedents within the same firm also leads to easier training and better **6.93** control of risk. A draftsman should not try to draft what he does not understand, or use precedents that he does not understand[78] but which are simply blindly followed—precedents are there to help but they are not a substitute for knowledge. Ensure also that eccentric or odd bequests are properly understood, can be effectively drafted, and are not void for uncertainty.[79] Precedents are also assembled for ease of use into standard templates for frequently used wills (eg estate to spouse with gift over in default to issue). Whilst this may assist speed of production and reduce drafting errors the danger of this approach is the inclusion of provisions that do not get discussed with the testator and lack his consent. *Lines v Porter*[80] provided a bizarre example of what the court found to be a provision included as 'a default setting' for all the company's wills and in that case was included without the testator's understanding or agreement.

It is very convenient for draftsmen to use standard schedules of administrative powers, but **6.94** they can encourage laziness, ie they are automatically included in a will without necessarily considering the appropriateness of all the terms to the individual testator or to the terms of the bequests in the will. This is less dangerous where the schedule is comprised only of true administrative powers (those which solely serve to facilitate the administration of the estate) and omits any other powers, often mislabelled administrative, that in fact could materially affect the distribution. Thus, powers to extend ss.31 and 32 Trustee Act 1925 should be individually considered in each case, with the appropriate client instructions, as should any decisions to exclude s.33 Wills Act 1837 or blanket provisions to provide a stirpital distribution to any named beneficiary who predeceases.

Schedules of administrative powers should not be included without the testator having **6.95** knowledge and approval of them. To obtain knowledge and approval of them the testator should receive an explanation of their terms that provides sufficient detail for him to

---

[78] A example of this was an IHT saving scheme that involved a reversionary lease. The husband and wife concerned had the scheme set aside on the grounds that they were not made aware of all the consequences of the scheme. There was comment in the judgment that the solicitor did not fully understand the scheme and the documentation. *Wolff v Wolff* [2004] WTLR 1349.

[79] In *Anthony v Donges* [1998] 2 FLR 775 there was an attempt to leave to a spouse 'such minimal part of my estate as she may be entitled to for maintenance purposes', which was held to be void for uncertainty; see also *Nathan v Leonard* [2002] WTLR 1061, which involved forfeiture of all gifts if any beneficiary contested their own gift, but the whole scheme failed through the condition being drafted in a way that was void for uncertainty.

[80] [2012] WTLR 629.

understand the essence of them. Where the testator is given bland or meaningless statements that give no useful information, there is a real risk that knowledge and approval will be lacking for this part of the will. The more significant provision is (eg exoneration of liability; powers that may be exercised to vary beneficial interests) the greater the prospect of a court finding a lack of knowledge and approval unless they have been explained and the testator has understood and consented.

6.96 Precedents for trustee exoneration clauses, when used, now require greater care. The Solicitors' Code of Conduct 2007 in the Guidance on Rule 2.07[81] contained a requirement that reasonable steps were taken to ensure that the client was aware of the meaning and effect of the provision.[82] The Society of Trust and Estate Practitioners, in its Code of Professional Conduct, also requires client understanding of such provisions.

6.97 It is worth remembering certain key points about drafting:

1. The purpose of a will is to communicate accurately a testator's wishes. The literary merit in a will is clarity and accuracy. Supposedly literary flourishes, verbosity, or circumlocution have no place in this process. The draftsman's concern is efficiency not literary style.
2. Precision of definition is vital both in definition of property bequeathed, and identifying beneficiaries.
3. Ambiguity is the particular enemy of the draftsman. It is the source of much litigation and at the same time is hard to eradicate. The draftsman knows what he is drafting and understands what he is trying to achieve, and it is simply human nature to then read what has been drafted in that light. The draftsman's skill lies in being able to read not merely what he intended, but to be able to analyse what he has written to identify possible other constructions—a difficult skill but one that must be developed.
4. If time permits, it is best to leave checking a document for twenty-four hours in order that there is a better chance that it is not checked with the same mindset as when it was prepared. Again, if time and resources permit, a check by a second draftsman is preferable.
5. The simplest approach to achieving what the client wishes is very often the best approach.
6. Plain English is generally a virtue, but not at the cost of failing to use terms that are well-known and well-defined technical expressions, as the meaning of such terms is well established.
7. New law means reappraising existing drafting precedents—and new law is more frequent than is sometimes apparent from wills.[83]

Send out drafts or engrossments?

6.98 Is sending a draft to the client always necessary in a straightforward matter, or can an engrossment be sent out straight away? After all, if the draft is right, further time will be taken preparing the engrossment and then sending that out; while, if the first-time engrossment is right, days will be saved. Even if the first-time engrossment is wrong, no more time has been lost when compared with the draft then engrossment route. The chances of getting the first-time engrossment right are immeasurably improved by greater accuracy of notes when instructions

---

[81] [66] and [67].

[82] See now the SRA Code of Conduct 2011 Chapter 1 O(1.8)/IB(1.8).

[83] eg Trust of Land and Appointment of Trustees Act 1996, Trustee Delegation Act 1999, Trustee Act 2000, Gender Recognition Act 2004, Civil Partnership Act 2004, Perpetuities and Accumulations Act 2009, and annual Finance Acts are just a selection of such recent changes.

are taken and informed discussion with the testator as to the effect of his wishes (together with potential difficulties). One problem that can be encountered with drafts is the inability of the client to understand their provisions.[84] It is important to ensure that either an accompanying explanation is given when a draft is sent out or there is a proper explanation given before execution. Providing neither places an unreasonable burden on the understanding of most clients.

C. Execution

Supervision of the execution of the will

Esterhuizen v Allied Dunbar[85] and *Gray v Richards Butler*[86] are the two principal cases relevant to this issue. They are, however, difficult to reconcile fully, and in part this may be due to the court in *Esterhuizen* being unaware of the earlier, and at that time unreported, decision in *Gray*.[87] *Esterhuizen* has undoubtedly received the greater publicity.   **6.99**

The view of the standard of care determined in *Esterhuizen* is reflected in two quotations from the judgment of Longmore J (as he then was), firstly that   **6.100**

> a prudent solicitor regards it as his duty to take reasonable steps to assist his client in and about the execution of his will, rather than merely to inform the client how it is to be signed and attested. This means that once the client has approved the draft of a will a prudent solicitor will *either invite the client to his office so that the will can be executed there or visit him with a member of his staff to execute the will at the client's house*.[88] (authors' emphasis)

Secondly: **6.101**

> Any testator is entitled to expect reasonable assistance *without having to ask expressly for it*. It is in my judgement not enough just to leave written instructions with the testator. *In ordinary circumstances, just to leave written instructions and to do no more will not only be contrary to good practice but also in my opinion negligent*.[89] (authors' emphasis)

Longmore J set a rather rigid and inflexible standard for 'ordinary circumstances' that does not easily lend itself to an interpretation that gives any consideration to the different levels of understanding and different abilities of individual testators, or the greater geographical spread of the modern client base.

In *Gray* some of the same ground was covered as in *Esterhuizen*, with some points of similarity, but ultimately with different conclusions. It was quite clearly common ground in both *Gray* and *Esterhuizen* that a solicitor owes a testator a duty to take proper care in advising the testator as to the formalities of execution.[90] Lloyd J in *Gray* also found that   **6.102**

---

[84] *Lines v Porter* (n 9) at [17]: 'they had checked their names were correctly stated but they did not read the terms, "the legal parts" in detail because they would not understand the terms of the will…And trusted the solicitors to know what they were doing'.

[85] [1998] 2 FLR 668.

[86] [2000] WTLR 143.

[87] The decision in *Gray* pre-dates that in *Esterhuizen*, but we have been unable to discover if it was given in argument in *Esterhuizen*. However, the absence of any reference to *Gray* in the *Esterhuizen* judgment would appear to indicate that it was not cited.

[88] [1998] FLR 668 at 674.

[89] [1998] FLR 668 at 677.

[90] It would of course be surprising if this had not been the view given the decision in *Ross v Caunters* [1979] 3 All ER 580.

a solicitor is under a duty, when the will is returned to him after execution, if he did not supervise its execution, to consider if it appeared on the face of it to be properly executed, and to advise the client if it appeared that it was not. Lloyd J expanded on these duties by observing:

> What steps are appropriate in discharge of these various duties in any given situation may depend on who the client is and the view that the solicitor has formed, or ought to have formed if acting with reasonable competence, as to the ability of the client to understand and follow advice as to the relevant procedures.[91]

6.103 This statement contrasts with the more sweeping comments of Longmore J in *Esterhuizen*, where he observed:

> Allied Dunbar got... [the formalities of execution]... entirely right in their instructions left with the will... Is it enough for a solicitor or a professional will provider to leave it at that? There was some suggestion in argument that this might depend on how competent or intelligent the testator was perceived to be but I cannot believe that this is correct, save only insofar as actual performance of the duty may vary according to a defendant's perception of his client... The fact is that the process of signature and attestation is not completely straightforward and disaster may ensue if it is not correctly done. Any testator is entitled to expect reasonable assistance without having to ask expressly for it. It is in my judgement not enough just to leave written instructions with the testator. *In ordinary circumstances to leave written instructions and to do no more will not only be contrary to good practice but also in my view negligent*.[92] (authors' emphasis)

6.104 In *Esterhuizen* the testator was described as 'elderly', 'reclusive', 'not well educated', and difficult to communicate with. It was, however, observed that he probably understood that two witnesses were needed (after this had been explained to him) but that 'he did not have the intellectual equipment or frame of mind to arrange it for himself'.[93] This description argues that the testator was someone to whom more care should have been given. However, did this view of the testator justify the more general views of the judge, which recommended the same level of attention as the norm for all testators, whatever their 'intellectual equipment'?

6.105 By contrast, Mrs Gray is characterized in the *Gray* judgment as 'a lively amusing and vivacious person' with an approach to life which led her, on occasions, to ignore formalities. A friend of the testatrix gave evidence that in his opinion: 'completing a will would have presented an unclimbable mountain to her without expert help... and she would have paid little or no attention to any written instruction provided to her if she had bothered to read it at all'. Mrs Gray's son provided evidence to similar effect. Lloyd J felt that the solicitor's view, that he saw his client as being capable of understanding and acting on the written instructions, should be preferred. The implication of the way this view was framed was not that neither the son's, nor the friend's, views were wrong, but that it was not to be expected that a solicitor would know the testatrix as well as the family or friends and ought not to be expected to have the same view of her character. That is to say that, from proper contact with the client, it was reasonable for the solicitor to reach the conclusion that he did as to her level of understanding and therefore to act as he did.

---

[91] [2000] WTLR 143 at 157E.
[92] [1998] FLR 668 at 676.
[93] [1998] FLR 668 at 674.

Lloyd J's view of the wording of the attestation clause again provides an interesting contrast: **6.106**

> On the particular point of the vital need for the witnesses to be present together when the testatrix signs the will it is necessary also to bear in mind the *very clear terms of the attestation provision of the will*.[94] (authors' emphasis)

This is a point missing from the judgment in *Esterhuizen*. There is no comment on the word- **6.107** ing of the attestation clause helping the testator's understanding of what is required, but there is a reference to the requirement of 'signature and attestation being if not complex, comparatively strict'. Few would argue with the strictness, but that does not at this point seem particularly relevant to the clarity of the clause.

There is a comment in 1969 from Sir Jocelyn Simon, then President of the now reformed **6.108** Probate, Divorce and Admiralty Division,[95] which runs counter to the view in *Esterhuizen* of the attestation clause. However, it is probably not to be relied upon too heavily on this particular point, especially as non-supervision of the execution of the will was not the real issue under consideration in this case:

> The second plaintiff told the deceased very generally what was the right method of execution; but realising that the deceased was an intelligent man, he relied in the main on the attestation clause to be a guide to the deceased. That was in the usual form, and it seems to me to have been a perfectly reasonable course for the second plaintiff to have taken.[96]

However, this was a case about whether or not the two witnesses were present at the time **6.109** of acknowledgement by the testator of his signature and, as far as we can establish, negligence against the drafting solicitor was not alleged or argued.[97] Therefore these remarks are *obiter* and, despite the eminence of the judge, almost certainly do not carry enough weight to dislodge the consideration given specifically to this point in *Esterhuizen*. However, we should also consider the changes in standard drafting since these remarks and the greater simplicity of the modern attestation clause, for example, 'Signed by the above-named testator in our presence and by us in his' or 'Signed first by the testator in our joint presence and then by each of us in the testator's presence'. Are these so very difficult to understand that they really require a solicitor's presence to explain them and ensure compliance in every case?

The *Esterhuizen* and *Gray* judgments appear to set different standards for the duty to advise **6.110** (or perhaps a duty to assist). Longmore J looks more to a single standard for all testators, although he does concede there might be some variance depending upon the testator's 'degree of perception'—though he did not express this in the wording of his standards of care quoted earlier in this section.

By contrast, Lloyd J readily accepts that different testators require different levels of assist- **6.111** ance and that the test of the testator's ability is not what a court finds that it was, but what the court finds that a competent solicitor should have established it was from normal and proper business dealings. This was a view which, in a different context, the Court of Appeal expressed when Donaldson LJ in *Carradine Properties v Freeman* observed:

---

[94] [2000] WTLR 143 at 158C.
[95] Which was more colourfully and informally known as 'Wills, Wives and Wrecks'.
[96] *Re Groffman* [1969] 2 All ER 108 at 109F.
[97] But being 10 years prior to *Ross v Caunters* this is not wholly surprising.

the precise scope of that duty will depend *inter alia* upon the extent to which the client appears to need advice. An inexperienced client will need and be entitled to expect the solicitor to take a much broader view of the scope of his retainer and his duties than will be the case with an experienced client.[98]

6.112   In other areas of negligence, the defendant has successfully raised the defence that the sophisticated or commercially aware client requires a less wide duty of care than the unsophisticated client.[99] At the present time this area should be approached with some caution, given that there is as yet no further view from a higher court on the intelligent and aware client in the narrow area of wills, but *Gray* does appear to be consistent with the Court of Appeal's approach in *Carradine* and to set out a more reasonable and practical standard of care than *Esterhuizen*.

6.113   Ultimately, it will be left to other courts to decide which of the two approaches to this issue should prevail, but it does seem that *Gray* is potentially more helpful in resisting claims based on *Esterhuizen*, particularly where

- the testator can be shown to have intelligence; and
- the solicitor has acted with the level of care and competence shown by the solicitor in the *Gray* case.

Some support for this view is to be found in the judgment of Mann J in *Humblestone v The Martin Tolhurst Partnership*[100] where the view was expressed, *obiter*, that 'a solicitor instructed in the matter has a duty to the testator to ensure that the formalities are complied with (so far as it is reasonably possible for him to do so)'. The judge also implicitly accepted in his judgment that it was not a breach of duty to the testator for the solicitor not to supervise the execution of the will but to provide instead instructions on how to execute a will. This was notwithstanding the failure of the testator to comply with those instructions.

6.114   It is recognized that the standard set by *Gray* is easier to attain, but the risk of using this as the usual approach is that it may be applied to testators less capable of understanding the required formalities. Operating a dual standard approach:

- not supervising execution, but providing accurate and easily understood written guidance for all testators capable of acting on it; but
- providing supervised execution for all not meeting the first category

would seem to be both practical and reasonable, as well as reflecting better the actual standards used by draftsmen, rather than those set out in *Esterhuizen*.

6.115   The more difficult client for this *Esterhuizen* standard is the client overseas or at some considerable distance from the will-preparer. Is it reasonable or practical to expect the solicitor

---

[98]   (1985) 1 PN 41. Limiting the scope of the retainer or setting contractual limits on what is to be provided under the retainer is an issue that is looked at in more detail at Chapter 4 Part D.

[99]   See, eg *Ata v American Express* The Times, 26 June 1998 (CA), on a highly experienced investor making speculative investments and failing in his action against his adviser for the losses; *Thompson v Hunter* (unreported, 12 December 1990) on the wider duty owed to an unsophisticated investor; *Hornsby v Clark Kenneth Leventhal* [1998] PNLR 635 on the failure of articulate and intelligent investors to take adequate steps to consider fully the risks that they were taking.

[100]   [2004] WTLR 343 when the issue concerned the defective execution of a will that was not supervised by the draftsman, but it was not necessary to decide the case on this issue.

based in London to supervise execution of a will for a non-resident client or one who lives over 100 miles away? It would seem to be both reasonable and necessary to do so, if the client can be reasonably classified as not capable of understanding or following the written notes on execution. Equally it is reasonable for the client to have this explained to him (together with the costs implications) in order that he can consider other options. However, where the client is capable of understanding the issues, it is reasonable to apply the standards of the *Gray* judgment.

Failure to supervise correctly the execution of the will

In the Australian case of *Hill v Van Erp*[101] the solicitor failed to take action to secure proper **6.116** execution of the will when one of the proposed attesting witnesses was known to her to be married to the beneficiary named in the will. The solicitor raised no objection to the witness, despite being asked by the same about the correctness of him witnessing, and his wife successfully claimed that her loss of benefit arose out of the solicitor's breach of his duty to supervise the execution properly.[102] The court did not find that the solicitor should supervise the execution of all wills that she prepared, only that where the solicitor did so, she should carry out the task properly and obtain a valid execution, ie one that did not cause any benefit under the will to fail for reason of a defect in the execution.

Corbett v Newy[103] should also be considered under this heading. The execution of the will **6.117** was not supervised, but that in itself did not attract criticism. The executed and undated will was returned to the solicitor by the testatrix with the instruction that the will was not to be dated and that it was only to take effect once certain *inter vivos* gifts had been completed. When these were completed some time later, the will was dated by the solicitor. The probate action established the invalidity of this will, as the Court of Appeal found that at the time the testatrix executed her will she lacked the requisite *animus testandi* for such conditional execution. Subsequently, the action of the solicitor in failing to ensure the valid execution was conceded by the defendant's insurers as negligent, given that the solicitor knew what the testatrix intended but did not ensure that the terms of the execution and/or its method secured a valid execution.[104]

Another Australian decision, *Summerville v Walsh*,[105] also dealt with a failure to procure effec- **6.118** tive execution. The testator having received burns (which would prove fatal) gave instructions for a deathbed will, but was physically unable to sign it. Instead of following the statutory provision for signing by another at the direction of the testator in his presence, the solicitor merely prepared a statement, signed by himself, of the testator's intention. This fell short of the standard expected of a New South Wales solicitor and the court found him liable to the disappointed beneficiary for her lost interest.

---

[101] (1977) 71 ALJR 487; s.15(1) Succession Act 1981 (Queensland) makes similar provision on this point to s.15 Wills Act 1837.
[102] *Zurich @risk* newsletter, March 2004: 'Despite the passage of time since Ross, failing to prevent the spouses of beneficiaries acting as witnesses, or not noticing that this has occurred, is a particular favourite among our insureds.'
[103] [1996] 2 All ER 914.
[104] This seems a rather harsh concession given that the will was found to be valid at first instance. If the will is found to be invalid only at the stage of the Court of Appeal, was the action of the solicitor really negligent or was it only a matter of professional misjudgement?
[105] [1998] NSWSC 52.

6.119 In *Marley v Rawlings*[106] a married couple executed each other's will in error. The error was not noticed by the supervising solicitor at the time of execution but came to light after the death of Mr Rawlings.[107] The Supreme Court found (reversing the Court of Appeal where it was found that the will could not be rectified as it was not a valid will for the testator did not intend to give effect to that will) that this mistake was capable of being rectified, as a clerical error[108], applying s,20(1)(a) Administration of Justice Act 1982.[109] The rectification ordered was the replacement of the typed parts of the will with the typed parts of the will signed by Mrs Rawlings.[110]

6.120 The consequences of a *Marley* error in execution have led to some firms introducing a simple post-execution checking procedure to ensure that a record is made where the will was executed, who was present (each confirming that s.9 Wills Act 1837 was complied with), and who has checked that the formalities of execution were correctly observed.[111]

Reading over a will

6.121 Where the circumstances of a testator require the will to be read over this must be done in the best manner that will lead to knowledge and approval of the contents.[112] This is not to say that a solicitor is in breach of his duty of care if a testator is later found to lack knowledge and approval of the contents of his will, but the solicitor's position will become difficult if he has failed to take all reasonable steps to ensure understanding. What is sufficient was reviewed in *Franks v Sinclair*.[113] In *Franks* an elderly testatrix, Mrs Franks, had made several wills over a period of time. She had left little or nothing to her son (a solicitor in private client practice) under these wills and she had been on poor terms with him for some time. The 1992 will left the residue of her estate to her daughter's son, J, with whom she had a close relationship.

6.122 In 1994 a new will was prepared by the son, although he had not prepared the previous wills. The son gave evidence that this new will was prepared at his mother's request because of a dispute with her granddaughter. It was claimed that Mrs Franks directed that the new will should bequeath the residue equally between her son and daughter. The son did not ask why there was this change of heart. Mrs Franks said nothing of a new will to J, and later appointed him her enduring attorney.

6.123 The son prepared the new will and took it to his mother. He was accompanied by another solicitor from his firm and a secretary. The will was read over carefully and slowly in front of the two witnesses and Mrs Franks signed it without any significant comment. The residuary

---

[106] [2014] UKSC 2; [2012] EWCA Civ 61; [2011] WTLR 595 Ch D.

[107] Mrs Rawlings had died 3 years prior to her husband, but it is thought that no probate application was necessary and the mistake in the execution was not noticed then.

[108] A "clerical error" is not restricted to the acts of the draftsman, nor is it restricted simply to drafting and engrossment errors, but is any part of the will preparation process that is than can be called "clerical".

[109] The argument that s.20 would only apply to a validly executed will was rejected "it appears to me that the reference to a will in section 20 means any document which is on its face bona fide intended to be a will, and is not limited to a will which complies with the formalities" per Lord Neuberger (para 65).

[110] s.9(b) Wills Act 1837.

[111] While this can seem a little cumbersome, potentially saving the cost of a rectification action more than outweighs the time taken to ensure correctness.

[112] *Morrell v Morrell* [1882] 7 PD 68: 'it seems most unusual not to do one or other of two things viz either read over the whole of the document which the party is about to sign or go through it passage by passage, and say there is a clause to this effect and a clause to that effect and so on'.

[113] [2007] WTLR 439.

clause did not name, but merely described, the residuary legatees. The son took the original will back to his office (he did not leave a copy with his mother) and once the new will was prepared he destroyed his notes of the meeting.

> This is a case in which serious suspicion is aroused as to whether Mrs Franks knew and approved the contents of the 1994 will. In my judgment, Mr Franks has failed to dispel the suspicion. Having regard in particular to the improbability of instructions in 1994 that the residue should be divided between Mr Franks and Mrs Sinclair, and to Mr Franks' lack of credibility as a witness, I am satisfied that Mrs Franks did not give those instructions to Mr Franks. I conclude that she did not know and approve of the contents of the 1994 will.[114]

The judge further observed of the verbatim reading over of the will that the residuary clause was **6.124**

> expressed in the customary language of wills, which most lay people will find impenetrable and many may consider to be gobbledegook—I think it very unlikely that Mrs Franks understood the effect of clause 8 just as a result of it being read out to her.

The judge believed that had Mr Franks' intention been that the will would have been understood then that would have been **6.125**

> more easily and more obviously accomplished by an explanation of the provisions in terms which Mrs Franks could clearly understand . . . In my judgment, the reading of the will cannot be relied on as establishing Mrs Franks' knowledge and approval of its terms.

The judge also observed that **6.126**

> One of the duties of a solicitor in these circumstances,[115] even if he is the son of the testator, is to discuss and, if appropriate, question the proposed terms of the will, in order that the testator reaches an informed decision.

That reading over of itself may not be sufficient was also the subject of judicial comment in *Wharton v Bancroft*:[116] **6.127**

> the fact that a will has been properly executed, after being prepared by a solicitor and read over to the testator, raises a very strong presumption that it represents the testator's intentions at the relevant time. But proof of the reading over of the will does not necessarily establish knowledge and approval. Whether more is required in a particular case depends upon the circumstances in which the vigilance of the Court is aroused and the terms (including complexity) of the will itself.

Failure to inspect an executed will

There is comment above on Lloyd J's views in *Gray*[117] on inspecting a will for apparent conformity with s.9 Wills Act 1837.[118] It was claimed that there were four aspects of the signature and attestation that should have raised doubts as to valid execution: **6.128**

- the delay between delivery of the will and its apparent date of execution;
- the signature of the testatrix and the first witness were slightly unusually placed;

---

[114] In a subsequent costs hearing, costs were awarded against Mr Franks on the indemnity basis, *Sinclair v Franks (costs)* [2007] WTLR 785.
[115] Where he was to receive a very significant bequest and the new will disinherited a member of the family with whom he was not even on speaking terms.
[116] [2012] WTLR 693.
[117] *Gray v Richards Butler* [2000] WTLR 143.
[118] 'No will shall be valid unless—

- the witnesses failed to add their occupations and this showed that the instructions had not been followed; and
- the different geographical addresses ought to have raised doubts as to whether the witnesses could have been present together.

6.129 The court accepted in respect of these four points that

- delays are in themselves not unreasonable as clients frequently take time to think over what they ought to do;
- signatures being placed in slightly odd positions is not unusual;
- failure to add occupations raised no presumption that the rest of the attestation was incorrect; and
- there are quite logical explanations as to why geographically diverse addresses can be given.[119]

6.130 It was not possible to establish what exactly occurred when the testatrix's signature was attested, as the bank official involved had no recollection of the event. It was, however, thought to be reasonable for the solicitor to draw comfort from one of the witnesses having been a 'reasonably senior official' of a bank. In respect of the slightly misplaced signatures, the solicitor said that any concern that he may have had was removed once he noticed that one witness was a bank official. Lloyd J observed of the attestation that

> In my view...[the solicitor]...was entitled to obtain reassurance from the fact that an employee of Coutts was one of the attesting witnesses since it would be extremely unlikely that such a person would fail to insist on the correct procedures being followed.[120]

6.131 Lloyd J considered a solicitor to have a duty to examine a will which was returned to him post-execution. Can one infer from this that a solicitor is under a duty to insist on the return of the document in order to carry out this inspection? We would certainly not like to think so; as surely a testator is entitled to do what he wants with his will and this may well not include returning it to the solicitor or keeping it in safe custody with the solicitor. On the other hand, it would seem a little unreasonable to say that this duty could be avoided simply by not asking to see the will. In *Humblestone v Martin Tolhurst Partnership*,[121] where *Gray* was approved on this point, it was said that

> First, the solicitors were instructed to draft the will and knew that in due course they would be asked to keep it in safe custody. In the course of their functions it became apparent that they would not be supervising its execution. I think that the normal fulfilment of such a retainer

---

    (a) it is in writing and signed by the testator, or some other person in his presence and by his direction; and

    (b) it appears that the testator intended by his signature to give effect to the will; and

    (c) the signature is made or acknowledged by the testator in the presence of two or more witnesses present at the same time; and

    (d) each witness either

        (i) attests and signs the will; or

        (ii) acknowledges his signature,

in the presence of the testator (but not necessarily in the presence of any other witness, but no form of attestation shall be necessary.'

[119] A duty to check the will post-execution was part of the claim in *Ross v Caunters* (n 90), but the judgment did not examine the point.

[120] [2000] WTLR 143 at 160F—despite the fact that manifestly the attestation did fail in this case.

[121] [2004] WTLR 343.

would require the solicitors, when the document was returned to them for safekeeping, to check that, on its face, and on the facts known to them, its execution was ostensibly valid.[122]

However, it does raise the question that this duty to inspect a will, once it has been returned, **6.132** in turn raises the question that negligence could be alleged if a solicitor failed to ask for the return of the will in order to inspect it. Once the will-preparer has asked for the return of the will for examination, and the testator refuses to comply, that must be the end of the issue. But not asking at all must be, at least to an extent, unsafe unless the terms of engagement make it clear that the solicitor's duty will not extend thus far.

No post-execution check can conclusively show that a will is valid. However, it can be **6.133** examined for:

1. *Signature of testator*, not only is it present, but does it look like any others held on file and is the manner of execution consistent with the attestation clause?
2. *Date* (not vital but very useful in avoiding costs of proving when it was executed).
3. *Two witnesses* (with their details in case they need to be traced later).
4. *Signature by the witnesses* as opposed to merely printing their names? (The printed name may in fact be a signature, but it is better to establish this now than be faced with trying to trace a witness some years later after the testator's death.)
5. *Are the witnesses likely to be beneficiaries*? Are there substantial similarities of their names or addresses with beneficiaries?
6. *Are the witnesses likely to be married to beneficiaries* on the face of their information, the details in the will, and the information recorded on your file?
7. *Is the will damaged* (consider an affidavit of plight and condition now while the evidence is available or re-engrossing the will).
8. *Alterations*, obliterations, and interlineations correctly initialled?
9. Is there anything about the manner of execution that requires an affidavit of due execution? (It is better, and easier, to obtain it now rather than after the testator's death.)

If the execution is being checked there should be no presumption that the execution was defect- **6.134** ive in the following instances:

1. Signatures being placed in slightly odd positions is not unusual.
2. Failure to add occupations raises no presumption that the rest of the attestation was incorrect.
3. There are quite logical explanations as to why geographically diverse addresses can be given.

All three of these points were considered in *Gray* and accepted. However, personal experience **6.135** has shown that the first and third of the above points can at times be indicators of problems. Whilst it seems that the decision in *Gray* does give some protection on these three specific points, the better course of action does seem to be to check and save arguments later.

It can be reasonable for the solicitor to draw comfort from one of the witnesses having been **6.136** a 'reasonably senior official' of a bank. In *Gray* it was thought that any concern (because of slightly misplaced signatures) the solicitor may have had was removed once he noticed that one witness was a bank official. Lloyd J observed of the attestation that it would be extremely unlikely that such a person would fail to insist on the correct procedures being followed. It

---

[122] [2004] WTLR 343 at 354H.

would appear that, whilst this view may serve to remove doubts about minor unusual features, it does not appear to remove the duty to check. On a practical level how easy is it to determine the seniority and responsibility of a witness? A safer course must be to check any apparent irregularities and thereby deliver a safer service and better standard of client care.

6.137 Where supervision of execution has been excluded in the will-preparer's terms of engagement, this does not exclude the post-execution duty to check that execution was validly carried out.[123]

Failure to give adequate written directions on how to execute a will

6.138 Where the solicitor will not be supervising the execution of the will, he will be negligent if he does not ensure that the client is provided with accurate and intelligible[124] instructions to ensure that proper execution can be effected.[125]

6.139 If, either of necessity or because of an arrangement with the client, written instructions on the formalities of execution are to be provided, it is recommended that they should be in a standard form.[126] To dictate bespoke letters containing these details each time is to increase the risk of omission of a salient detail.[127]

6.140 It is worth giving some care and thought to the standard text[128] used to ensure that:[129]

1. The signature and attestation process is simply, but correctly, described (it is probably best to concentrate on how to comply with the signature being 'made' and not explain the 'acknowledgement' possibility[130]). Similarly, directing all three parties to sign in the presence of each other is simpler than explaining that the witnesses need not sign in each others' presence.[131]
2. The requirement that witnesses must not be beneficiaries or married to beneficiaries[132] or the civil partner of a beneficiary[133] is clearly included.
3. A witness must not be blind.[134] There is no prohibition on minors acting as witnesses, but for obvious reasons of understanding they are best avoided and the notes should suggest

---

[123] *Humblestone v Martin Tolhurst Partnership* (n 121).

[124] The intelligibility of the instructions has not been expressly considered, but it must be the case that instructions that are of a degree of complexity such as to defeat the lay person run the risk of being deemed inadequate by the courts. Under such circumstances, the standard of care set out in *Esterhuizen v Allied Dunbar* (n 77) would become much more understandable.

[125] *Ross v Caunters* (n 90).

[126] If stored in a database, amendments should be securely controlled to prevent unauthorized changes.

[127] As apparently occurred in *Ross v Caunters* (n 90).

[128] An example of which can be found in Appendix 4.

[129] The warning, often used previously about individual executors who were authorized under the will to charge fees for their work need no longer be used. Previously such provision in a will was regarded as a legacy (*Robinson v Pett* (1734) 3 P Wms 249; *Re Barber* (1886); *Re Orwell's Will Trust, Dixon v Blair* [1982] 3 All ER 177) and an attesting solicitor, for example, would not have the benefit of his charging clause because of s.15 Wills Act 1837 preventing benefit to an attesting witness. Since 1 February 2001 (the commencement of Trustee Act 2000) this is no longer the case. Provision for remuneration in a will, whilst still being made by the testator, is not a legacy: s.28 Trustee Act 2000.

[130] Section 9(c) Wills Act 1837.

[131] Section 9(d) Wills Act 1837.

[132] Section 15 Wills Act 1837.

[133] Paragraph 3 Sch 4 Civil Partnership Act 2004 directs that s.15 Wills Act 1837 be applied to civil partners as well as spouses. (Quite why this way was chosen, rather than the more helpful route of a direct amendment to the text of s.15, remains something of a mystery.)

[134] *In the Estate of Gibson* [1949] 2 All ER 90.

that they are not used. A witness lacking the understanding of what is happening should not be used. Such a witness's attestation is capable of being valid,[135] but for the obvious reason of the possible need to prove what occurred, should not be used.[136]

4. Experience also leads the authors to suggest that the notes can benefit from an example of what the correctly attested will looks like in order to provide further guidance as to where to place signatures, descriptions, addresses, and date.[137]

Usually the notes regarding execution stop at this point, but it is worth looking at further information to assist the testator. From a risk perspective, avoiding possible difficulties is much to be preferred to arguing about duties at a later stage. On the basis that it is sound policy to advise on the correct formalities in order to avoid cost and dispute about liability, should the draftsman also warn about factors which may lead to a challenge to the will, or at least lend support to a challenge? **6.141**

High on any list of such issues must be capacity. Although the draftsman may have satisfied himself as to capacity when instructions were taken, many factors may intervene between then and the execution, and of concern in particular are drugs (whether prescribed or not) and alcohol. Having seen a testator with a drug or alcohol problem when they were sober and lucid could mean that the draftsman has no knowledge of the issue, but does not necessarily help if the testator later executes a will when they do not have capacity.[138] Therefore, a warning such as this may be appropriate: **6.142**

> After the death of a person sometimes a legal challenge is made to their capacity to have made their will. Such challenges can be expensive for an estate and time consuming and distressing for your beneficiaries and can produce a result which was not intended. Although it is up to the individual to decide whether or not to do so, we recommend that your doctor's opinion on your mental capacity to sign your will is obtained if
> *   you are elderly;
> *   you are receiving medical treatment for an illness which could affect your capacity;
> *   you habitually use alcohol or drugs (whether prescribed or not).

Advice

As has been commented earlier, a solicitor, while having a duty to act in accordance with his client's instructions, also has a duty to advise on the legal implications of those instructions in order that the client can proceed with the benefit of proper advice. The client cannot be compelled to accept or follow that advice.[139] The duty does not extend to advising on the commercial prudence of the transaction.[140] **6.143**

---

[135] Section 14 Wills Act 1837.

[136] The authors have also seen it suggested that one should not use as a witness a member of the family who receives nothing under the will, but who could inherit on intestacy, on the grounds they have an interest in the will being invalid and may therefore be unhelpful if the will is challenged. There is some justice in this point, but it is difficult to cover in the type of note in Appendix 4 as testators cannot be relied on to accurately identify such persons.

[137] Descriptions, addresses, and the date are not prescribed by law, but are invaluable if it is necessary to show at a later date when and how the will was executed. See Appendix 4.

[138] *Re Heinke* The Times, 22 January 1959, although it is conceivable that it could be saved under the rule in *Parker v Felgate* (1883) 8 PD 171, but who wants the cost and trouble if it can be avoided?

[139] See above at Chapter 3 Part G.

[140] *Bowdage v Harold Michelmore & Co* (1962) 106 Sol J 512; *Reeves v Thrings & Long* [1996] PNLR 265; *Clarke Boyce v Mouat* [1994] 1 AC 428; *Haigh v Wright Hassall & Co* [1994] EGCS 54.

6.144 Where incorrect advice is given it does not automatically follow that the advice is negligent. Where the law is unclear, complex, or it concerns an obscure or infrequently encountered point, the solicitor is not negligent if the advice that he gives is reasonable in the light of the difficulty,[141] but he would nonetheless be prudent in drawing the difficulty of the matter to the client's attention so that further advice may be taken if the client agrees.[142] The converse applies in that, where the area of law is not complex or is frequently encountered, wrong advice is far more likely to be negligent.[143]

Destruction of previous wills

6.145 When a new will has been executed, the question of the old will frequently arises. A testator will often ask the draftsman to destroy the previous will.[144] Many firms prefer to send the will to the client for the client to destroy it. If the will is returned to the client, it is good practice to advise him in particular that the previous will cannot be revived by destruction of the later will.[145]

---

[141] *Fordgate Wandsworth Ltd v Bernard Neville & Co* [1999] EGCS 98.

[142] While this is clearly a prudent course of action it was held that a solicitor's duty did not extend so far in *Blair v Assets Co* [1896] AC 409.

[143] *Otter v Church Adams Tatham & Co* [1953] 1 All ER 168; *Winston Cooper v Smith Llewellyn Partnership* [1999] PNLR 576.

[144] Valid revocation by actual destruction requires that destruction is either by the testator or by another at his direction and in his presence: s.20 Wills Act 1837; see the remarks of Richards J in *Re Rawlinson, Kayll v Rawlinson* [2010] WTLR 1443 at [17].

[145] Section 21 Wills Act 1837 stipulates that revival is only possible by re-execution or a new codicil.

7

OTHER ISSUES

A. Terms of wills that will give rise to costs and/or litigation

Inheritance (Provision for Family and Dependants) Act 1975

This is dealt with in more detail elsewhere.[1] However, it can generally be observed that it is **7.01** not established that there is a duty to give advice on the potential for claims under this Act when taking will instructions from a client, although there could be an attempt to found a claim on there being such a duty. But, it is good client care to offer to give such advice if it is needed. Where the client declines any advice, a restriction to this effect in the terms of the retainer is a sensible step to safeguard the will-preparer's position against possible later claims from beneficiaries. Alternatively, if the client requires the advice, then it can be given for the appropriate fee. In a sense, asking if the client requires the advice is a win/win situation for the will-preparer—a refusal can reduce the potential for a claim against the will-preparer (if properly recorded) while requiring the advice can produce additional work.

It is necessary, however, to add a note of caution. Advice on the application of the Act, par- **7.02** ticularly as to how the court will apply its provisions, is not necessarily within the capabilities of all will-preparers and care must be taken to ensure that if the advice needed cannot safely be given then additional assistance should be obtained.[2] This can be of particular importance if steps are to be taken which run the risk of infringing the anti-avoidance provisions of the Act. The terms of the Act were substantially amended by the Civil Partnership Act 2004 and it is important to work with an amended version of the Act where giving advice.

---

[1] See Chapter 3 Part F and Chapter 23.
[2] Note the words of caution from the Court of Appeal in *Ilott v Mitson* [2011] WTLR 779: 'It seems to me that the jurisprudence reveals a struggle to articulate, for the benefit of the parties in the particular case and of practitioners, how that value judgment has been, or should be, made on a given set of facts.'

7.03 It is possible for the testator to state either in the will or in a separate letter his reasons for excluding a particular beneficiary and the court can take this into account on any application.[3]

7.04 Provisions in wills which attempt to oust the court's jurisdiction, so as to make the executor the final and binding arbiter[4] of an I(PFD)A 1975 claim, are to be avoided as they will almost certainly be invalid. Attempts to make a benefit conditional upon the beneficiary not exercising his rights to claim under the I(PFD)A 1975 are also likely to fail, as although the will may validly express a condition that the beneficiary should not dispute a will, it will not be valid if it seeks to prevent a beneficiary taking legal proceedings to enforce his rights.[5] It would also be fairly irrelevant as far as I(PFD)A 1975 claims are concerned, as they are not logically a deterrent to someone unless fairly substantial benefit was left to them in the will (and in which case the I(PFD)A 1975 claim is probably of little consequence).

Wills that are poorly or obscurely drawn

7.05 Similar to the question of an I(PFD)A 1975 claim, is the will which is so poorly or obscurely drawn that its terms cannot be safely established without substantial costs, and possibly also litigation, to determine its true effect. This is not to be confused with actions for construction which arise simply out of the everyday risks of drafting. At the opposite end of the spectrum to such everyday risks, there are those wills whose terms are manifestly impossible to apply without counsel's or the court's assistance; and these must carry a risk for the draftsman that the estate will seek recovery of the costs that the claim arose solely out of the negligent, or incompetent, drafting.[6]

7.06 Where the defect in drafting arises out of the draftsman's mistake, which is capable of being rectified by application to the court under s.20(1) Administration of Justice Act 1982 (clerical error or failure to understand instructions), there is a real possibility that the personal representatives will look to the draftsman for reimbursement of costs. There is far less likelihood of this where the clerical error is that of the client.[7] Rectification will not be available where the draftsman is in error but that error arises neither through his failure to understand the testator's wishes nor through a clerical error.[8] Again, see later for more detailed comment on rectification.

---

[3] The court can take the deceased's reasons into account under s.3(1)(g) 1975 Act, and a written statement is rendered admissible as evidence by s.21 of the Act. But the court may also reject the statement: *Gold v Curtis* [2005] WTLR 673. To be avoided is the belief by the testator that a recital of his opinions (of those he is failing to make provision for) will persuade the court of the correctness of the testator's action. A court may pay some attention, but in general, they will be of little weight. Such remarks are best minuted for the file. Extreme expressions, if contained in the will, can be excised from the will by the Probate Court on grounds that they are atrocious, offensive, or libellous (*Re Hall's Estate* [1943] 2 All ER 159; *Re T's Estate* (1961) 105 Sol J 325; *Wartnaby's Goods* [1846] 4 Notes of Cases 476); besides which, if such words were to be published, the will is a public document and an already delicate family problem could be made infinitely worse.

[4] *Re Raven* [1915] 1 Ch 673; *Re Wynn's Will Trusts* [1952] 1 All ER 341.

[5] *Cooke v Turner* [1846] 14 Sim 493; *Rhodes v Muswell Hill Land Co* [1861] 29 Beav 560; *Re Williams* [1912] 1 Ch 399.

[6] *Zurich @risk* newsletter, May 2008: 'Where the "clerical error" or "failure to understand the testator's instructions" is caused by the solicitor, it is likely that the solicitor will have failed in his or her duty of care to the testator and the costs of rectification will be recoverable against the solicitor. Similarly, where the terms used are so obscure or ambiguous that they give rise to a construction action, the solicitor runs the risk of being liable for the costs of that action.'

[7] A clerical error for the purposes of s.20 may be the error of the testator: *Re Martin, Clarke v Brothwood* [2007] WTLR 329; *Re Williams* [1985] 1 All ER 964.

[8] *Kell v Jones* [2013] WTLR 507.

B. Mail order and Internet providers of wills

Contractual limitation of the service provided by both post and Internet appears to be the **7.07** key to the safer operation of these services, the basis being that a contract is entered into, and defined by the service's terms and conditions of service, for only the provision of documents and without responsibility for advice, supervision of execution, etc. The limited service that is then provided is for a fee that reflects the limited nature of what is delivered. Such a limited service is fundamentally different from the traditional approach to will preparation (but a considerable advance on the only other choice previously available to a testator—that of a home-made will).

The limitations contained in the terms and conditions of service must be carefully thought **7.08** through and tailored to the service being offered. Where duty exclusions are involved they should not be excessive and should reflect accurately what is excluded. Matters to be considered include

- the provision of advice on the type of will required, gifts under the will, Inheritance Tax (IHT), I(PFD)A 1975 claims;
- any assessment or advice on the capacity of the testator;
- where supervision of the execution of the will is excluded, the provision of as much material as is feasible to assist in the correct execution;
- issues of identity of the testator;[9]
- post-execution checking of the will.

There appears to be a general assumption that both mail order and Internet provision of wills **7.09** is possible, as there are a number of disparate types of providers of both services currently operating. However, it would seem that the legal position surrounding the duty of care and such providers is not wholly certain, and as yet there has been no litigation about their service. Most prudent organizations that operate these services will have looked most carefully at the risk and structure of their operations.

Both types of provider start from the point that if a service of limited scope is being provided, **7.10** the extent of that service, and importantly its exclusions (particularly from the duty of care), must be clearly described in the contractual terms of business. Furthermore, such terms of business must be explicitly drawn to the attention of the client and accepted by him at the outset of the exercise. Examples of Internet and mail order providers have been found where such terms and limitations are only drawn to the client's attention at the stage that the engrossed will is supplied for signature. In these circumstances, the contract for the preparation of the will must have been concluded well before this stage and this later, unilateral, attempt to impose a variation to its terms must be ineffective unless expressly agreed to by the testator.

There is a wide range of organizations providing wills through the Internet. A number of **7.11** solicitors are exploring this route, but for solicitors there is an additional issue, namely the extent to which a solicitor's obligations to the client under his rules of professional conduct[10] contemplate involvement in Internet business.

---

[9] The preparation of a will is not a regulated transaction for the purposes of AML regulation.
[10] See generally Chapter 1—Client Care SRA Code of Conduct 2011.

7.12 At the heart of this problem is the question of what the will provider is doing.

1. Is he simply providing a competently drawn document reflecting what the testator has instructed him to provide?
2. Is he providing a will in the full sense of the traditional service with all the advice and duty of care that is usually associated with such instructions?

7.13 The writers take the view that a will draftsman should be able to provide a will using whichever service the client requires, provided that

- the client is aware of which of these two types of service he is requesting;
- the terms of what is being provided in (1) above are clearly contracted for by him; and
- the cost of a will prepared under (1) above very clearly reflects the much smaller amount of work involved.

7.14 If, as an alternative, one sets out to say that type (1) cannot be provided either by a solicitor or by another will provider, one must be saying that wills can only be provided by the traditional method, type (2), with all that this entails. In other words, a potential testator cannot select the service and price that he feels is appropriate to his perception of his needs, but must only have his request met in a manner and at a price that is imposed on him by the provider. This would appear to be a negation of the client's personal choice, and more seriously a matter of some considerable cost (if the true extent of the measures to meet the duty of care set out in this book are fully costed and charged) to the client.[11]

7.15 These views on the validity and effectiveness of Internet and mail order provision have not been tested in court[12] and anyone providing such services needs to be aware of this and plan as prudently as possible.

C. Joint property

7.16 The question of negligence and will preparation in this context was considered by the Court of Appeal in *Carr-Glynn v Frearsons*.[13] The testatrix had purchased a home for her sister to live in and had retained the sole ownership of the house until, at the point that one of her sister's two children became an adult, she transferred the property into the joint names of herself and that nephew. The property was then held by them as beneficial joint tenants. Some years later, the testatrix instructed the defendant firm to prepare a will for her which was to leave her share of the property to her niece (the second child of her sister). When taking the will instructions the solicitor for the defendant firm became aware that

---

[11] In *Blackman v Man* [2008] WTLR 389 the validity of a will prepared by the will preparation unit of a trust company was challenged on grounds of capacity. It is implicit in the judgment of Sir Donald Ratee that the testatrix was entitled to use the method of her choice for the provision of a will. The fact that she was capable of filling in the postal service questionnaire was a factor in establishing her capacity. The suggestion from an expert witness that the use of this service, rather than the traditional route of a solicitor, tended to suggest a lack of capacity was rejected. The terms and conditions of the postal will service were not an issue in this case.

[12] See *Blackman v Man* (n 11).

[13] [1998] 4 All ER 225. In this judgment there is reference to the earlier judgment in *Kecskemeti v Rubens Rabin & Co* The Times, 31 December 1992. This case was not reported in full, which is unfortunate as it was very similar to the joint property issues explored in *Carr-Glynn*. On similar facts to *Carr-Glynn* the court held the solicitors to be in breach of their duty of care where the joint ownership of property, of which they were aware, obstructed the terms of the will. Perhaps there was a warning here which was not fully heeded at the time.

- the property was owned jointly;
- her firm had acted in the transfer; and
- her firm no longer had a file on the transfer nor did it hold the deeds.

Although the solicitor was aware that she did not know how the property was held, and **7.17**
hence how it would devolve, the solicitor did draw the testatrix's attention to the problem.
The solicitor understood that the testatrix would obtain the deeds for her so that she could
examine the tenure, but the testatrix did not do this and the solicitor took no further action.
The will was executed and, on the testatrix's death shortly afterwards, the property passed by
survivorship to the nephew and the claimant received no benefit under the will. The claimant
sued the defendant firm for breach of their duty of care and received in compensation the
value of the half share in the property under the failed gift.

The Court of Appeal found that the solicitor's actions had been insufficient and that more **7.18**
should have been done to prevent the terms of the will being frustrated by the terms of
the joint ownership. The Court of Appeal's view on this point does at least have the simplicity of safety in terms of time in resolving the devolution straight away. If the solicitor
had explained, as the court thought that she should, that the notice of severance could be
prepared straight away for the testatrix's signature, any answer but 'yes' from the testatrix
would probably have thrown sufficient doubt on her intentions as to absolve the solicitor
from the risk.

In reaching this decision the court appeared to extend the decision in *White v Jones* further. **7.19**
In contrast to *White*, in *Carr-Glynn* the estate had suffered loss in that the estate was diminished by the severed share of the joint property not being an asset of the post-death estate. If
damages for that loss were recovered by the personal representatives they would be held as
part of the residue of the estate, which would not pass to the disappointed legatee (ie not to
the person who had suffered a loss). There would therefore be no lacuna in the law in terms
of recovery,[14] but arguably a lacuna in allocating the amount recovered to the person who
had suffered loss. The court, nonetheless, were content to find that there was a duty owed to
the disappointed beneficiary.[15]

The judgment contains some important comments on the analysis of a solicitor's duty in the **7.20**
will-making process where joint property is involved.

- 'The lack of care lay in failing to ensure that the asset fell into the estate.'[16]
- 'It is essential to have in mind that, in the circumstances of the present case, the need to
  take care to ensure that the asset fell into the estate was integral to the carrying into effect
  of the testatrix's intention that her share in the property should pass to the appellant under
  her will.'[17]
- 'On proper analysis, the service of a notice of severance was part of the will-making
  process.'[18]

---

[14] Bearing in mind that in *White v Jones*, Lord Goff considered that extending the *Hedley Byrne* principle to
the intended beneficiary should operate only 'in circumstances in which neither the testator nor his estate will
have a remedy against the solicitor' ([1995] 1 All ER 691 at 710).
[15] See Chapter 2 Part C for a more detailed comment on the nature of this duty.
[16] [1998] 4 All ER 225 at 233E.
[17] [1998] 4 All ER 225 at 233G.
[18] [1998] 4 All ER 225 at 233J.

- The duty owed by the solicitors to the testator is a duty to take care that effect is given to his testamentary intentions. The duty in relation to the relevant property is a duty to take care to ensure that that property forms part of the testator's estate so that it can pass to the intended beneficiaries on his death. It is, also, a duty to take care to ensure that effect is given to the testator's testamentary intentions. The duties owed by the solicitors to the testator and to the specific legatee are not inconsistent. They are complementary. To the extent that the duty to the specific legatee is fulfilled, the duty to the testator is fulfilled also.[19]

7.21 There are some further observations to be made on these findings and the position that now arises in respect of the duty of care of the draftsman.

1. The findings in *Carr-Glynn* were in respect of a specific bequest that failed. There is no reason why the court's reasoning should restrict this liability solely to specific bequests. Such a liability could equally arise where all, or more likely, a substantial part, of a residuary gift is frustrated because the property passed by survivorship to another, thus diminishing the residuary gift below the level that the testator intended and based his instructions on. However, in these circumstances, the intention of the testator might be harder to establish. The initial instructions for the will including the assets of the estate ought to clarify this point.
2. Changes to the ownership of an asset after the date of the will are deliberate acts of the testator that may deprive the legatee of his originally intended benefit.[20]
3. The court did not consider what the position would have been in *Carr-Glynn* if the solicitors had not have acted in the earlier transfer, ie that they had no prior knowledge of the property being jointly owned. In *Carr-Glynn* the testatrix clearly pointed out to the solicitor that she only owned a half of the specifically devised property. The solicitor was therefore put on notice of the potential for the legacy to be frustrated by the co-ownership and her prior knowledge of the transfer, or absence of it, probably becomes irrelevant.

7.22 It therefore seems to follow that, where the testator tells the solicitor that property is not jointly owned, when in fact it is, it will be reasonable for the solicitor to rely on that information[21] unless he has information to the contrary or the circumstances are such that the testator's comment cannot reasonably be true. It does not appear that the *Carr-Glynn* judgment places any onus on the solicitor to be proactive and check the testator's view of his ownership of all of his assets as part of the will-making process (unless the testator requests it and the solicitor is to be appropriately authorized and remunerated).

7.23 The remaining possibility is where the solicitor does not ask about the assets or their ownership and as a consequence the testator offers no comment on them. Is the *Carr-Glynn* liability then avoided in this way? The court was silent on this point and it must to some extent be regarded as still undecided. However, it can hardly be considered to be safe to approach will instructions on this basis, and it is easily within the bounds of possibility that a court will in future find that the will-making process should encompass basic questions regarding the nature and extent of the assets (or at least the major assets) in order for the draftsman to meet his duty of care. On this basis it is recommended that safe practice is always to establish such

---

[19] [1998] 4 All ER 225 at 235A–D.
[20] See Chapter 3 Part D.
[21] Evidentially recording accurately what was asked and what was replied becomes very important on this point.

information, unless the client refuses to give it despite an explanation as to the necessity for it. Standard will instructions forms should be adapted to reflect this.

The court in *Carr-Glynn* considered only a written notice of severance as the way to resolve **7.24** this issue.[22] It is suggested that any method of severance appropriate to the circumstances of the testator and his property can be used. Although the Court of Appeal expressly referred to a written notice of severance,[23] this is not the only practical method of complying with their views[24] as the pre-1925 methods of severance also continue to be effective. Primarily, for the will-preparer wanting to resolve the *Carr-Glynn* duties, this could offer methods which do not involve communication with the co-owner (a point which concerned the testatrix in *Carr-Glynn*). Severance could therefore be by 'an act of any one of the persons interested operating upon his own share',[25] which will be any valid act of alienation,[26] such as

- assignment in writing[27] to a third party[28] who could hold under a declaration of trust for the assignor;
- charging,[29] even if for only a nominal amount.

Where there is real urgency, methods which can give immediate severance, without notice **7.25** needing to be served on the co-owner, may be more appropriate than using a written notice, which is not effective until served. Urgency of severance is not only to be judged in the light of particular circumstances, but also in the light of the will-preparer's duty to move swiftly with the will preparation.[30] The will-preparer should bear in mind the decision in *X v Woollcombe Yonge*[31] that ordinarily seven working days is an acceptable length of time to prepare a will, but in particular circumstances a shorter time could be required.[32] It is, of course, possible to prepare the will within this time, and sort out the appropriate method of severance later, but this will not be free from risk and tends to run counter to the Court of Appeal's advocacy of severance being effected immediately to reduce risk.

Although the court in *Carr-Glynn* did not expressly say so, it seems to be implicit in their **7.26** advocacy of severance, without waiting to identify the correct ownership, that the severance is either effective if the property is held under a joint tenancy or ineffective if it is held as

---

[22] 'The ease with which a joint tenancy can be converted into a tenancy in common seems one of the simplest procedures in an area of law where procedures are not always simple. All [the testatrix] had to do was write the requisite letter. The simple letter of severance would have eliminated the risk. In my opinion [the solicitor] was plainly negligent in failing to advise the sending of a letter of severance once she appreciated that she was unable to discover the nature of the existing joint ownership.'

[23] [1998] 4 All ER 225 at 236G and J.

[24] Section 36(2) Law of Property Act 1925 provides that when a joint tenant wishes to sever a beneficial joint tenancy 'he shall give to the other joint tenants a notice in writing of such desire or do such other acts or things as would, in the case of personal estate, have been effectual to sever the tenancy in equity'.

[25] Per Page-Wood V-C in *Williams v Hensman* [1861] 1 J&H 546 at 557.

[26] Given that common law and equity favour alienation against survivorship: '*Alienato rei praefertur juri accrescendi*' (Co Litt 185a, and in equity see *Patriche v Powlett* (1740) 2 Atk 54 at 55).

[27] Required to be in writing by s.53(1)(c) Law of Property Act 1925.

[28] *Williams v Hensman* (n 25).

[29] *First National Securities v Hegerty* [1985] QB 850.

[30] Where an emergency will is being prepared and a notice of severance is to be used, communication is as urgent as the will. Posting a notice is an effective method of communication and it is not necessary that the co-owner receives the notice before death (*Re 88 Berkeley Road NW9* [1971] Ch 648; *Kinch v Bullard* [1998] 4 All ER 650); service is deemed to be made when in the ordinary course of events the letter would have been delivered. Time is best saved with personal delivery if this is possible.

[31] [2001] WTLR 301.

[32] See Chapter 6 para 6.51 onwards.

a tenancy in common. If it is the latter, the attempted act of severance will be of no consequence other than to have been a useful precaution.

7.27   Although there is no decision on the point, where the draftsman has knowledge that other property is owned jointly (or even not owned at all, eg an insurance policy written in trust) *Carr-Glynn* must be a danger.

7.28   Given the Court of Appeal's findings in *Carr-Glynn*,[33] knowledge of circumstances and ownership of assets becomes important during the will instruction process.

1.   What information is already known and held on file? If it is known, or it should have been known, that an asset is owned jointly with another and the client intends or expects the asset to pass as a specific gift under the terms of the will, the will-preparer is on notice that to take no action is unsafe.

2.   What is told to you in the interview that may mean the terms of the will could be frustrated? Apart from the joint asset issue in *Carr-Glynn*, there could be assets owned in trust (life policies are a particular danger) where their passing outside of the terms of the will can alter radically the balance of the benefits under the will. There may not be scope to alter the devolution of the assets themselves, but the testator is likely to adjust the terms of the will if he is aware of the difficulties.

3.   Should you verify ownership of the assets? Probably not, unless the testator indicates doubt or gives you definite information that an asset is co-owned or is not capable of being left by will. It is, however, important to ask whether or not any of the significant assets are in joint ownership and to clearly record the information provided by the client. It does not seem safe to neglect to ask about the ownership of the client's assets as this is part of the normal process of establishing the nature of the estate and the appropriateness of the dispositions. Whilst this point was not dealt with expressly in *Carr-Glynn*, it does seem that not to ask any questions about which assets are jointly owned exposes the will-preparer to risk in the event that a gift under the will fails.

4.   It is not safe to leave it to the client to establish the nature of the joint ownership, as his view is that of a lay person. Nor is it safe to leave it to the client to obtain the title deeds for inspection, unless the will-preparer has confidence that the client will do this without delay. Death during the period before the deeds are produced leaves the will-preparer at risk unless the client was made aware of this risk and agreed that it was acceptable.

5.   Although this problem usually manifests itself in the context of specific gifts under a will, there is no reason why it should not apply where the joint property is expected by the client to pass under the gift of residue. Admittedly, in these circumstances it can be harder to realize what the client's expectations are, but the normal discussion establishing the client's wishes for the will covers their assets as well.

6.   In the absence of any information indicating possible or probable joint ownership there would not seem to be any duty for the will-preparer to verify the ownership.

7.   The 'impossible' legacy is a potential danger where, for example, foreign realty is to be bequeathed to a stranger rather than a family heir. It is difficult to say that an English practitioner should have sufficient knowledge to know how such property will devolve, but not to draw attention to and investigate the point is to invite trouble later if the

---

[33]   [1998] 4 All ER 225.

beneficiary is significantly disappointed. Most practitioners should be aware of the risks of trying to deal with such assets under an English will.

8. If it is not possible to determine the ownership without delay, it is not safe to accept that delay, and a notice of severance should be prepared in order to ensure that the testator's wishes expressed in his will are capable of being carried out. This is said even though the notice of severance may turn out to be superfluous. Consider also if any other form of severance is appropriate.

One professional indemnity (PI) insurer has observed in their newsletter that 'it is disap- **7.29** pointing that claims of this nature still occur when the Court of Appeal made it clear 10 years ago in [*Carr-Glynn*] that a solicitor is under a duty to prepare a notice of severance if there is any doubt about the ownership of the property'. In case the insurer's view might not be understood this observation was prominently placed and highlighted.[34]

It is not too difficult to find from *Carr-Glynn* a more general proposition that it is not only **7.30** frustration of the terms of the will by the rules of devolution of joint property, but also frustration of the devolution of other property, which carries risk. Where the will-preparer has knowledge of the manner of ownership then there must be consideration of how that may or may not meet the testator's wishes expressed in his will.

In the Canadian case of *Earl v Wilhelm*[35] the will instructions dealt with certain specific **7.31** bequests of land, which, whilst in the testator's legal ownership, he held under a declaration of trust as trustee for his farming company.[36] The will-preparer was well aware of this[37] and was found to have failed in his duty to the testator, as his lack of advice on the point did not allow the testator to consider how else his wishes might be effected.[38] The court added:

> To suggest that it is a sufficient discharge of a solicitor's duty to a testator in circumstances such as these to simply inquire of him what he wishes and then to record and thereafter prepare the will without anything further is to relegate a solicitor and his obligations comparable to that of a parts counterman or order taker. The public is entitled to expect more from the legal profession.

It is quite commonly found that a testator attempts to meet his wishes (and obligations) by **7.32** the bequest of pension policies or life policies that have been written in trust. Whilst it is not suggested that there is the need to enquire into ownership of all assets, if the will-preparer does not address the difficulties which he knows of, there is substantial risk of a claim. The professional will-preparer should, of course, be aware of the general inability to bequeath pension interests. Life policies written in trust may be less obvious, but carry risk if the

---

[34] *Zurich @risk* newsletter (n 6).
[35] (2000) 183 DLR (4th) 45; [2001] WTLR 1275.
[36] This was apparently fairly common practice among Saskatchewan farmers to avoid land title fees.
[37] The lawyer dealt with the corporate affairs of the farming company as well.
[38] Citing Madam Justice Blacklock Linn's definition in *Couture v Lamontagne* (1996) 151 Sask R 283 (QB) that a lawyer's obligation to his client was to be skilful and careful; to advise his client in all matters relevant to his retainer, so far as may be reasonably necessary; to protect the interests of his client; to carry out his instructions by all proper means; to consult with his client on all questions of doubt which do not fall within the express or implied discretion left to him; to keep his client informed to such an extent as may be reasonably necessary, according to the same criteria. Also quoting with approval Sherstobitoff JA in *Credit Foncier (Canada) v Grayson* (1987) 61 Sask R 212 in the Saskatchewan Court of Appeal that there is an obligation on a lawyer to explain the nature, effect, and significance of a document to a client.

will-preparer knows that they are owned in this way (and indeed an increased number of such policies have been written in trust for inheritance tax reasons).

D. Office issues

Storage

7.33 Where a solicitor holds wills in safe storage he is obliged to make effective arrangements for safekeeping.[39] A will entrusted to a firm for safekeeping is the property of the testator and remains so until his death when it passes to his estate.

7.34 There is no period prescribed for retention by law, but when looked at from the point of view of ownership it can readily be seen that even after a considerable passage of time (and pressure on storage space), destruction is fraught with risk. If it is known or believed that a later will has been made, destruction is still not advised[40] as retention of the will for examination in the event of establishing a pattern of will making is preferable.

7.35 Any will draftsman should have a central register of the wills that are held in storage. This is essential in order to

- control the safe custody process and to be able to say when wills were released and to whom, as well as when they were deposited or redeposited;
- be able to provide an accurate record of what is held that is capable of being reconciled against what is actually held in order to maintain the integrity of the storage system.

The combined effect of the above points is to ensure that the solicitor can say with certainty whether or not any given will is, or is not, held by him.

7.36 The latter point becomes important in order to minimize the risk of a firm denying that it has a will in safe custody, only for it to come to light after the estate has been administered as an intestacy or under an earlier will. It will also assist in showing where a will may be held for clients long after correspondence files have been destroyed. Consider storage of a duplicate register off-site to ensure that the register is not lost if the rest of the building is.

7.37 In the Australian case of *Hawkins v Clayton*,[41] the solicitors who held a will in safe custody were found to owe a duty to take reasonable steps to locate the executor and disclose the will to him.

> Consider the usual purpose for which a solicitor entrusts custody of his will to his solicitor (or, for that matter, to some other custodian of wills). The usual purpose is for the safekeeping both before and after death so that, after death, the will can be produced in order that it may be made effectual. That is the purpose for which, in the ordinary case, custody is accepted. But if the executor is ignorant of the will, he will not call for production of the will nor will he enter upon the administration of the estate. If the custodian has reasonable grounds for believing that the executor is ignorant of the will, it is foreseeable that non-disclosure of the will to the executor will result in the will not

---

[39] SRA Code of Conduct 2011 O(7.4) and IB(7.1).
[40] Also bear in mind that even where the client might request destruction, s.20 Wills Act 1837 permits revocation by destruction with intention to revoke only where it is by the testator, or by another in his presence and at his direction.
[41] (1988) 164 CLR 539 at [9] of the judgment of Brennan J.

being produced and not being made effectual. Unless some duty of disclosure must be imposed on the custodian that is not to infer a contract or undertaking to disclose from acceptance of custody; it is merely to regard the acceptance of custody for the stated purpose as material to the existence of a duty. The duty of the custodian 'is cast upon him by law, not because he made a contract, but because he entered upon the work', as Windeyer J said of an architect in *Voli v Ingelewood Shire Council* (1963) 110 CLR 74 at p 85 ... it is the nature of the instrument which the custodian accepts which gives the relevant character to the work on which the custodian has entered.

There is no directly comparable view on this issue from the English courts, but there must be a real risk of a similar finding by the English courts.[42] Safer practice must undoubtedly be to act on the basis of a duty existing. **7.38**

A periodic audit of what is held against a firm's will register is important, as this will help to identify any missing wills and enable them to be traced, or replaced, while the testator is still alive and capable. This is much cheaper than leaving the problem until after death or loss of capacity of the testator. **7.39**

Damage or loss

Failing to store a will safely can result either in it being lost completely or it being produced in a damaged form. Neither of these circumstances should give rise to a claim for loss of benefit, as it must be unlikely that there can be proof of the contents of a will that is sufficient to prove loss, but which is insufficient to admit the terms of the missing will to probate. Nevertheless, the additional costs of administration caused by the loss or damage would seem to be a valid claim against the solicitor, bank, or safe custody service that failed to store a will safely. This is of course subject to the terms and conditions of storage, but it is difficult to see a testator accepting terms which disclaimed liability for loss or destruction as that tends to defeat the notion of safe custody. **7.40**

Safe storage facilities, if offered as such, should have basic protection against damage from fire, water, etc. The protection should be reasonably effective against those risks and not in itself cause destruction (such as sprinkler systems). Where wills are stored in premises that contain other risks (airport flight paths, flood plains, high tides) consideration should be given to moving the storage facility or maintaining a store of duplicate documents in a safer location. This should assist with the risk of the complete loss of wills through fire, theft, or incompetence (assuming negligence to be present) when there is otherwise insufficient evidence to prove what the terms of the will were. It is difficult, without the specific circumstances, to offer conclusions, but it can safely be said that such a loss will prove costly and time consuming for whoever had custody. Thus, the importance of the periodic check referred to in the list at paragraph 7.43 below becomes very important. **7.41**

---

[42] In *Cancer Research Campaign v Ernest Brown* [1997] STC 1425 it was held that a solicitor/executor was under no duty to advise the beneficiaries of the death of the testatrix, the terms of the will, and other material facts of the estate. It was found as a matter of law that as executor the solicitor had no duty to notify the beneficiaries and that if the executor had no such duty then the solicitor, as solicitor, had no duty to inform them. However, this is not the same as the solicitor/client duty considered in *Hawkins v Clayton* and the duty to inform the executor.

Conditions of storage

7.42 Safe storage is not merely a question of keeping the will free from fire and theft. Dampness and extremes of temperature can also play their part. Advances in modern technology have added the additional dangers of chemically unstable paper or paper that will not retain print. Modern printers can also increase the risk, as can plastic document covers and envelopes.[43] When deciding on printers and paper, the 'print life' of the document needs to be discussed and must be a factor in what is purchased.

7.43 In general,

1. The adequacy of both printers and paper should be checked with your suppliers.
2. Plastic covers should not be used where the plastic touches the text of the will itself (use another sheet between the text of the will and the cover if such covers must be used).
3. Wills should not be stored in an area where they are exposed to extremes of temperature and humidity.
4. Never store them on the floor or in contact with it; if there is flooding or fire, the floor will be the first place to get wet.
5. Wills should not be stored in a way that subjects them to pressure, eg being stored under piles of other papers or stored in a pile; they are best stored on shelves book fashion.
6. A periodical check should be made of at least a sample of wills held in order to ensure that their condition is acceptable.

7.44 After all, it is easier to put right problems revealed by such checks while the testator is still alive than only discovering them after the testator's death.

7.45 It will usually be quite sobering to calculate the full cost of providing will storage (the physical space and the clerical time to administer it, as well as the insurance and safety precautions) and some charging to the client may be appropriate as the firm providing the storage will normally carry the risk.

7.46 As an alternative to the potential liability for negligent loss or damage and the costs attached to storage, use can be made of the statutory will deposit arrangements.[44] Rules governing such provision are made by regulations prescribed by the President of the Family Division with the concurrence of the Lord Chancellor. The sole prescribed depository under these rules, to date, is the Principal Registry of the Family Division.[45]

7.47 A will may be lodged in safe custody personally by the testator or on his written authority by his agent at the Principal Registry, any district probate registry, or at any sub-registry. Postal deposit is available only through the Principal Registry. The current deposit fee is £20.[46]

7.48 A search on the Internet will yield a number of organizations which offer storage of wills. If use is to be made of them, normal commercial principles must be applied to assessing the worth of the proposition and the long-term security and costs. Storage services must not be

---

[43] See 'Beware of Disappearing Wills!' *STEP Journal*, November 1994, 15.
[44] Introduced by s.126 Senior Courts Act 1981, which required the provision of 'safe and convenient depositories for the custody of wills of living persons' to be made. A detailed commentary on the operation of this procedure can be found in Tristram and Coote's, *Probate Practice*, 30th edition (LexisNexis, 2008) chapter 20.
[45] Regulation 3(1) Wills (Deposit for Safe Custody) Regulations 1978, SI 1978/1724.
[46] Fee 6 Non-Contentious Probate Fees (Amendment) Order 2011, SI 2011/588.

confused with those who simply offer 'will registration', for a price, as a record of where a testator has deposited a will.

There is provision[47] for the United Kingdom to ratify the Council of Europe Convention on the Establishment of a Scheme of Registration of Wills,[48] but no ratification has yet been made. However, a pan-European approach to mandatory registration is still an issue which is aired from time to time in Brussels. **7.49**

A further resource is Certainty.co.uk. Certainty provides a registration service for any will and a complimentary search facility to locate wills that have been entered in the register. **7.50**

Storage by the client

The client may choose to store the will himself. There is nothing to stop a client choosing this option. There is no obligation on the draftsman to advise on the issues that could arise from this, but it would appear to be good client care to deliver some warning as to the risks involved. Later trouble could also be avoided if the provisions of s.21 Wills Act 1837[49] are brought to the client's attention in an attempt to avoid the well-intentioned, but misguided, post-execution alteration. It is also prudent to ensure that a copy of the executed will is held on the solicitor's file. **7.51**

Electronic storage of information

Databases of will information, documents prepared, and storage details, as well as data from Internet services, can pose storage problems. Cases have been seen where, after office system replacement or upgrade, it has proved difficult or even impossible to recover the information from previous storage. It is important that, unless the new system can access old data, some part of the old system is retained in order to have access. **7.52**

Where data is stored on CD, DVD, or floppy disk the conditions of storage are important in order to prevent degradation of the data on the disk. The firm's IT department or outsourced IT manager should be consulted on a suitable storage environment. The security of such data against unauthorized use or copying must also be considered. **7.53**

Files

There appears to be no legal or regulatory requirement for the length of time for which will files must be retained by the draftsman. Guidance prepared by the Law Society's Wills and Equity Committee is helpful on this subject.[50] **7.54**

Examples have been encountered in practice where such files are destroyed quite quickly after a will has been executed. Such a policy, whilst economical with storage space, hardly seems to serve any practical value other than to help frustrate any subsequent enquiries about the will instructions and preparation process. It also goes against the reality of ownership of a will file, which generally speaking belongs to the client. The Law Society guidance on files analyses a will file as containing four broad categories of document: **7.55**

---

[47] Sections 23–26 Administration of Justice Act 1982.
[48] Cmnd 5073.
[49] No alteration in a will after execution, except in certain circumstances, shall have any effect unless executed as a will.
[50] Law Society Practice Note of 6 October 2011.

1. Documents prepared by the solicitor for the client which have been paid for by the client.
2. Documents prepared by third parties for the client which have been paid for by the client.
3. Documents prepared by the firm for its own benefit for which the client has not been charged.
4. Documents written by the client to the firm where ownership passed to the firm on dispatch.

7.56 Categories 1 and 2 belong to the client, while categories 3 and 4 belong to the firm. Where there are contentious or delicate issues of information about the family on the will file, particularly in the papers belonging to the client, it may be suitable to draw the attention of the client to the position post-death when ownership of the client's papers will pass to his executors. If those papers are potentially embarrassing for the testator, he should be made aware of this and decide whether or not he wishes to remove them.

7.57 Good practice might be to retain files until such time as the limitation period ends, but there are issues with establishing when this is.[51] In addition, when it is necessary for either the draftsman, or later the court, to examine the history of the testator's will-making activity, the more comprehensive this is the more useful and informative it is. The difficulties with formulating an appropriate policy include

- clients who cease contact with the firm which prepared a will for them;
- a later will that is invalid leaving an earlier will as valid;
- the potentially lengthy period between the will and death.

7.58 Because of storage costs, editing will files to remove the less important documents is sometimes considered, but in practice it can often be difficult to determine what might prove to be important in the event of a dispute and a *Larke v Nugus*[52] request for information. In addition, if thinning of files is to be considered it should only be undertaken by someone of sufficient experience and skill to understand the importance of the documents being considered. As this can involve utilizing quite expensive practice time, it is often not undertaken.

7.59 The work relating to wills should be kept on a discrete file cross-referenced to other files maintained for that client. If, say, a conveyancing matter is undertaken at the same time as a will is prepared, using a single file is likely to lead to a conveyancing destruction period being applied to the file which is patently unsuitable (if only on limitations grounds) to the will work.

---

[51] See Chapter 21.
[52] [2000] WTLR 1033.

8

RISK

A. Introduction

Risk is the exposure to harm from future events. The harm, in the context of the subject of **8.01** this book, will almost always be financial (it may also be reputational but this ultimately has a financial impact as well). Warren Buffett is reported as having observed that 'risk comes from not knowing what you are doing' and he was without doubt correct. Being aware of risk considerations is essential to the process of assessing the risk of 'what you are doing'. However, it needs to be kept in mind that not all risk is manageable and that any work or process involves the acceptance of some risk.[1]

> Climbers talk of two kinds of danger—subjective and objective. The subjective is the danger that is in the hands of the climber to influence—having the right equipment, maintaining the correct level of fitness or skill, gleaning as much information about a target mountain as possible. Climbers aim to reduce the subjective danger as much as they possibly can. Objective danger is different. This is danger from random storms closing in, or an unpredictable break in a piece of equipment. It is a danger over which climbers have no influence. They accept a certain amount of objective danger when they set about a potentially life threatening route. It is regarded fatalistically. While something can be done about subjective danger, there is nothing that can be done about the second type—it is an occupational hazard.[2]

Whilst this passage is about the risks of climbing, it takes very little effort or imagination to **8.02** read this as applying to any legal work. The risk that has to be controlled is the subjective, and this is the aim of a risk-management policy applying to a firm's own processes. The objective risk from outside factors (such as economic or the limitless variety of human conduct) is one that is mitigated (if at all possible), accepted, and lived with, or it is not accepted and the type of work not then undertaken.

---

[1] It was said of the USA's Saturn 5 rocket that 'you want a valve that doesn't leak and you try everything possible to develop one. But the real world provides you with a leaky valve. You have to determine how much leaking you can tolerate.'

[2] Tim Butcher, *Blood River: A Journey to Africa's Broken Heart* (Vintage Books, 2008).

8.03 The risk to the practitioner in preparing wills has two potential effects:

1. financial
2. reputational.

8.04 The effect on the reputation of a firm will in turn usually have longer-term financial consequences for that firm.

B. Financial risk

8.05 Whilst the risk to the practitioner is one that will, at least to some extent, be covered by professional indemnity insurance, there is additional financial exposure in the sense of the excess provisions of his PI cover[3] and in the extra, and obviously unremunerated, work that always arises in dealing with any allegations of a breach of duty (not to mention the high probability of then losing the administration of the estate and any further legal work from the family involved).

C. Reputational risk

8.06 There is quite clearly a risk to the professional reputation of the will draftsman if a successful claim reveals defects or errors in the will-preparation process of his firm;[4] and the more costly the claim (or the more well known the client) the greater the risk of publicity. Damage to a firm's professional reputation by publicity of a problem (through both local and national press in particular) can take time to repair and can affect levels of business in the interim. The risk is not limited to will preparation but can affect all areas of a firm's business if the public perception of their abilities is affected.

> The last three years of the Solicitors Indemnity Fund's existence saw a steady increase in probate related claims, both in number and value. There is nothing to suggest that this trend has changed over the last year. . . .
>
> The underlying causes are
>
> - Missed time limits
> - Delay
> - Poor communication with clients, third parties and within the firm
> - Ineffective delegation
> - Inadequate supervision
> - Undertakings
> - Poor organisation
> - Lack of knowledge of the law.[5]

8.07 Zurich have indicated[6] in the past that common allegations against their insured solicitors' firms (65 per cent of which prepare wills) include:

---

[3] Or even refusal of future cover if the claims record is bad.

[4] See, eg the remarks regarding competence made by the court in *Bacon v Howard Kennedy* [2000] WTLR 169; *Re Key, Key v Key* [2010] WTLR 623; or *Sprackling v Sprackling* [2009] WTLR 897.

[5] John Verry, Risk Management Practice Leader, St Paul International Insurance in an article, 'Risk Management for Probate Practitioners' in *Elder Law and Finance*, September 2001.

[6] *Zurich @risk* newsletter, April 2003.

1. Failing to prepare the will and have it executed before the death of the testator.
2. The terms of the will being frustrated by failing to address the devolution of property and, more commonly, of joint property.
3. Failing to ensure the will carries out the testator's intentions.
4. Errors in execution—failing to give adequate written instructions on how to execute the will, failing to supervise the execution of the will, or failing to check the attestation of an executed will.
5. The testator lacking testamentary capacity.
6. The will being procured by fraud or undue influence.
7. Failing to revoke a will effectively.

While undoubtedly a number of these allegations failed, this summary gives a good idea of the common allegations and, therefore, the areas of risk to the will-preparer. **8.08**

When the House of Lords was considering the appeal in *White v Jones*, Lord Goff observed that **8.09**

> In the course of the hearing [there was] placed before the Committee a schedule of claims of the character of that in the present case notified to the Solicitors' Indemnity fund following the judgement in the Court of Appeal below. It is striking that, where the amount was known, it was, by today's standards, of a comparatively modest size. This perhaps indicates that it is where a testator instructs a small firm of solicitors that mistakes of this kind are most likely to occur, with the result that it tends to be people of modest means, who need the money so badly, who suffer.[7]

This view, whilst undoubtedly true about the financial effects, may well no longer be an **8.10** entirely accurate view (there are no statistics on the size of settlements in court or out); but we suggest that no one should take any comfort from Lord Goff's thoughts, as clearly

- we have moved into a period of the elderly owning a greater part of the national wealth than ever before;
- bigger reputations and amounts have been involved in will negligence claims since his remarks were made; and
- the increasing call for estate planning in wills makes the advisory and drafting processes more complex and thus increases the scope for error.

D. A risk-management policy

The aim of this section is to prompt the process of review of current procedures in the light of **8.11** the risks examined in this book.[8] This should not be regarded as a one-time exercise, because future law and professional regulatory changes almost certainly will eventually throw a different light on some of the areas of risk (as will changes in volumes of work and staff).

The management of risk is required by Principle 8 SRA Code of Conduct 2011. In addition **8.12** a relevant person for the purposes of the Money Laundering Regulations 2007 is required to also have a risk-management policy 'in order to prevent activities related to money

---

[7] [1995] 1 All ER 691 at 702G.
[8] This book is about one area of practice and therefore concentrates on that. But as a basic principle risk management is an essential tool for practice management and should therefore be an integral part of business management starting at the highest level of that business.

laundering and terrorist financing'. Demonstrating compliance with any risk-management policy without a written policy would be difficult.

8.13 'If a claim comes in from a disappointed beneficiary, ask yourself, "Could the client have complained of the way I handled the retainer?" If the will draftsman can answer that question in the negative then he or she has nothing to fear.'[9] This is a vital question, worth asking at any stage of the whole process, provided that it is answered accurately, honestly, and with up-to-date knowledge of law and practice. However, from the point of view of managing risk it is better to start posing this question well before any claim arises. The best single piece of advice in order to guard against negligent work on wills (or any piece of work) is to be self-critical, and self-critical assessment of a work process will usually start with posing five questions about any part of the process:

1. What is being done?
2. How is it being done?
3. Why is it being done?
4. When is it being done?
5. Who is it being done by?

8.14 When dealing with will instructions, or any other process, simply doing what has always been done in the past may well not be safe enough for the future (or indeed really have been safe enough in the past). It should also be said that a more fundamental question is 'Should I be doing this work?' Staying away from work that cannot be safely or remuneratively carried out is a fundamental principle of risk management. The last question (above) about who is doing the work, will inevitably lead to consideration of a firm's duty under the SRA Code of Conduct 2011.[10] Indicative Behaviour 1.7 is the relevant conduct.[11] Will preparation in this regard is no different from any other specialized area of practice.

Six steps in policy creation

8.15 This book, by highlighting risks and offering some commentary on how they may be controlled, should prompt the process of how a firm develops a risk-management strategy for the control of this work. There are six steps to the creation of such a strategy for any firm, and at each step the earlier five questions forming a self-critical approach can be applied.

1. *Identification of the areas of risks*: these may range from types of business undertaken, to the processes applied and to the staff undertaking the work. Is anything that the firm is doing, or omitting to do, exacerbating the risk inherent in will drafting, particularly, but not exclusively, from the point of view of time? This may also throw up issues of supervision, training, record keeping, drafting practice, etc.[12]

---

[9] Alastair Norris QC (as he then was) in (2001) 151 NLJ, Wills and Probate Supplement, 22 June, 934.

[10] Rule 2.01(b) SRA Code of Conduct 2007 and the requirement or resources and competence to undertake work was the previous regulation.

[11] 'considering whether you should decline to act or cease to act because you cannot act in the client's best interests'.

[12] *Zurich @risk* newsletter, April 2003 contained a claim where a will for an 88-year-old in hospital was not prepared within 17 days because of a 3-week typing backlog. A second example, where over 5 weeks elapsed without a will being prepared for a 93-year-old in a home, was attributed to pressure of work and staff absences on holidays. A third example was of a will not being followed up where the member of staff left the firm and telephone messages and a letter were left on his desk. Systems that produce these errors are not robust enough to control risk. Zurich observe that: 'what is clear is that pressure of work, typing backlogs, or the absence from

2. *Analysis and understanding of those risks*: this is looking at the identified areas of risk in the light of the present law and establishing an understanding of why the risk arises and how significant and probable it is (and also bearing in mind the earlier comments in this section on subjective and objective risk). Probability must not be looked at alone without assessing financial significance of that event occurring. An event of low probability but high impact is harder to deal with in policy terms than a high-probability, low-impact event.

3. *Creation of policies to reduce or eradicate risks*: a continuation of step 2 by developing ways of reducing, controlling, or eradicating the risks that have been identified. This step always requires an element of proportionality in that the remedy for the risk must keep in proportion the risk that has been identified and the potential additional costs burden that it might create. This step is always better informed by the probability/impact assessment of the previous step.

4. *Implementation of those policies*: the whole process so far is pointless unless a firm is prepared to change the way that those in the firm who are involved with the will-preparation process work. Implementation must involve effective communication both to existing staff and future staff (ie communication is a continuing exercise involving those joining later).

5. *Continued monitoring of compliance with these policies*: part of the new risk-management policy requires the development of a routine for sampling and assessing the wills prepared (since the previous check) to establish continuing compliance with policies. Without this the preceding four steps are probably wasted. Monitoring in this way is also a useful management tool to provide knowledge of work standards and practices (and thereby identify training and staffing needs as well). IT solutions for some monitoring issues should not be overlooked, but monitoring of work quality this way is difficult for a complete solution. It can be cost effective in time.

6. *A continual updating of the policies as new areas of risk are identified*: it is not sufficient to treat steps 1 to 4 as a one-time exercise. The policies constructed must be reviewed when changes in law require changes of practice, and the whole process is then re-examined in the light of the new law or practice.[13]

To a large extent, a risk-management policy based on the above steps is the application of **8.16** common sense, but it does require some considerable discipline to keep steps 5 and 6 going. Without those two steps the effectiveness of the policy will wane considerably over time. However, comfort may be found in the welcome that the application of such an exercise ought to receive from a firm's professional indemnity insurers, and also from the reassurance that the firm will get from verifying that its business is conducted on a sound basis.

Consistency of approach

In building a risk-management policy, a key factor is having consistent application of the **8.17** policy by all those who participate in will preparation. This inevitably means putting some guidance on paper to

---

the office of the will drafter or staff to act as witnesses due to illness or holiday will not provide a defence to a professional negligence claim.'

[13] See generally Chapter 7 SRA Code of Conduct 2011.

- inform those it applies to;
- be available as a point of reference for the future; and
- be available to train and inform those who join a firm later.

8.18 Where a firm has produced standard format letters, checklists, questionnaires, etc the aim is to produce consistency and this will be absent where staff are free to use other materials. There will then be no consistent approach to risk management.

8.19 This consistency of approach cannot be achieved and risk cannot be managed where members of a firm work outside of their competency; and in order to control risk this must also be controlled. A good example is the number of firms that prohibit those outside the private client department from preparing wills.

8.20 Consistency of approach is of course essential where there are security aspects to be considered as well.

8.21 Whilst much of the above can appear a little bureaucratic, it will prove of great assistance to those who are confronted with issues covered by the guidance and should avoid the debate that vague or incomplete policies will produce. For example, having available a firm's policy for dealing with deathbed wills can be of great assistance when one is encountered for the first time.

8.22 Failures in the global financial market in recent years have focused attention on the role of risk managers. The role of a risk manager is too often perceived as a brake on profit. When business times are good, few think of the potential for risk management to save losses as the good times invariably start to convince everyone that the bad times will not return. Longevity and experience should start to persuade business managers of the contrary. Risk management in any business should not stop the development of sound projects, but it should put into perspective

1. the true potential for risk;
2. the steps necessary for management of that risk; and
3. the correct pricing to reflect the potential of the risk.

Risk management should be in everyone's job description.

Areas to cover in a policy for risk management in wills

8.23 As well as the analysis of process set out above, there are known areas of difficulty with wills where a risk-management policy can provide assistance. The word assistance is chosen carefully, as the correct policy helps control risk for the firm while also assisting the individual with decision making.

8.24 For example, the area of testamentary capacity is an area of high risk and it seems less than prudent to require members of a firm to make policy on the hoof when faced with an issue. Within the area of testamentary capacity there are issues of

- who may take instructions from the elderly or infirm[14]
- control of time
- recording the interviewer's impression of the client

---

[14] See other references in this book to *Re Parsons, Borman v Lel* [2002] WTLR 237 or to the dangers of practice outside areas of knowledge and expertise, etc.

- when to seek medical advice (and who from and how they are instructed)
- refusal of instructions
- reinterviewing the client
- the interaction of the need for medical advice with *White v Jones*
- execution.

Examples of other areas which readily benefit from policies are   **8.25**

- wills and non-domiciled clients
- deathbed wills
- use of will instruction forms
- checking of wills
- third party instructions
- others present at will instruction meetings and interpreters
- control of time.

E. Fees

The levels of fees charged for will preparation have generally undergone significant increases **8.26**
since *White v Jones*, but it is still questionable if today's fee levels accurately reflect both the
risk involved and the additional skills required today for much of the tax-driven drafting.

Some of the increases in will fees will have been inflation driven and, additionally, **8.27**
many wills are still prepared on a fixed fee, which is generally lower than a time-costed/
responsibility-uprated fee basis. The risks that now attach to will advice and preparation are
such that the traditional (pre-*White v Jones*) approach to fees has become inadequate in terms
of reward when risk is balanced against it. Fee structures and rates for wills were clearly inadequate, and in many cases remain inadequate, to provide a financial return that would realistically compensate not only for the urgency and expertise applied, but also for the financial
and reputational risks that are encountered—after all a risk is only ever worth accepting if
there is commensurate financial reward which justifies it. However, although fees are higher
in amount (and probably in real terms) much of this work still remains as fixed fee rather
than being more tailored to the advice and expertise required to undertake the work properly.

Increasing fees may produce difficulties in managing the clients' expectations (particularly **8.28**
in view of the costs that clients have traditionally expected to be charged in the past and also
most clients' perception of the simplicity of the exercise[15]) but the old fee-charging structures
were, to a large degree, shaped by the previous absence of the modern duty of care, ie the
absence of risk. Without tackling the question of will pricing to accurately reflect the work
and responsibility involved, the risk/reward ratio is still too much against the will-preparer
and very much for the client.

It is often suggested that the unwillingness to charge economic fees is based on the wish **8.29**
not to upset the client and ensure that the more remunerative estate administration will be
undertaken. Given the increased mobility of the UK's population it is questionable how
many testators retain the same solicitor when the client moves after retirement, or whose

---

[15] Much along the lines of the frequently expressed view that 'any fool can buy a will form from the station-
ers'—and many fools do.

executors or heirs want the firm that prepared the will to act in the estate. There is also the question of the number of wills and the length of time between their preparation and any administration of the estate. In the absence of any data being produced it will be impossible to tell if the old reasons still hold true, but there must be a significant doubt that they do or if they really justify the reduced level of charging.

8.30 The first chapter of this book opens with a quotation from the 6th edition of *Cordery on Solicitors*, published in 1968, which states quite clearly that mistakes in will preparation give no cause of action to the disappointed beneficiary. This view held true for a further ten years until *Ross v Caunters* in 1979. In essence, all that this part of this book is about is a mere thirty-five years of legal development (with most of it concentrated in the last twenty years). A whole new area of risk has developed during this period, but the approach to fee charging for the work has in many firms failed to adequately recognize this growth of negligence risk. It is probably also true to say that fee charging has often failed to recognize

- the increasing level of litigation;
- the increasing ingenuity now used to attack wills; as well as
- the increased willingness to complain.

8.31 It remains a mystery why, in this particular area of work, so much of the charging level is driven by the clients' expectation of how much the work should cost. Such expectations do not markedly dominate fee charging in other areas of practice.

PART C

ADMINISTRATION OF ESTATES AND TRUSTS

9

INTRODUCTION AND NEW BUSINESS

A. Introduction

In this part of the book there is a greater emphasis placed on avoidance of the risk of negligence claims and disputes generally regarding an estate or trust. The administration of estates and trusts both offer combinations of law, assets, and personal circumstances that are so infinitely variable in their possibilities as to make it impossible to examine in detail the whole range of possible acts of negligence. But rather than testing the boundaries of negligence, better practice is to avoid those areas completely. **9.01**

This is also not really the book in which to set out a detailed analysis of breaches of trust, devastavit, and their remedies, but these are subjects that must be considered, to a degree, in order to appreciate some of the pitfalls and their consequences in administering estates and trusts. There is a general lack of court decisions regarding negligent actions in the administration of estates and trusts; this chapter therefore looks much more generally at how the personal representative (PR) or trustee can manage his exposure to the risk of negligence claims through his actions, as well as highlighting some common sources of problems. **9.02**

It is important to consider administration in the context of avoiding claims. Even the successfully defended claim is disadvantageous in terms of wasted time and damage to client relations. Therefore, this part also recommends conduct which may well help to avoid disputes arising, even if there might not be a case in negligence against the PR or trustee. **9.03**

Risk management for professional PRs and trustees (and professional advisers to PRs and trustees) should always have been a fundamental part of their businesses. But today's **9.04** business climate requires a more robust process that casts its net wider in looking for potential pitfalls. The risk-management process needs to be proactive in preventing undue risk arising, rather than functioning as a damage limitation exercise after the problem has occurred.

9.05   The risk to PRs and trustees can also be regarded as having three potential effects on the trustees:

- the liability to compensate the trust where their actions have caused loss to the trust;
- the penalties, costs, etc which may attach to them personally and for which they have no recourse to the trust's assets, or the penalties that can arise after they have parted with the assets; and
- the damage to professional reputations and client relations.

9.06   The risk management required for estate and trust business should not be just an estate- or trust-focused exercise, concentrating on the administration in any given estate or trust. Risk management must start with an overview of the business in order to create the risk control framework for the entire business, before starting to assess the risk issues within individual trusts. This can be approached in three stages (below).

1st Tier Risk	*Risks inherent in being in business*
	Requirements of business law and regulation (eg company law, professional bodies, FSA)
	Regulation of professional conduct (eg professional bodies, training, FSA, competition, fraud prevention)
	General obligations of law (eg AML/CTF, Data Protection)
	Disaster (eg fire, fraud, IT failure, acts of terrorism)
	Employment law
	Financial management/business model
2nd Tier Risk	*The risk of asset ownership—the burdens placed on all legal owners of any type of property*
	Legal liability for the safety of others (mixture of regulation and law, eg Health and Safety, Environmental Protection, and tort)
	Law and regulation for sale/purchase of assets (eg insider dealing, Law of Property)
	Asset management (policy and investment risk, company law)
	Requirements of continued ownership (enforcement of title, jurisdictional requirements)
	Landlord and Tenant
	Insurable risks
3rd Tier Risk	*The risk of acting as a PR or trustee*
	Law relating to PRs and trustees
	Family and Property law
	Taxation
	Tort of negligence
	Conduct of litigation

Note 1: These three tiers are not set out in a one to three descending order of importance, but in an order descending from the more general to the more particular. The examples given are illustrative and not exhaustive.

Note 2: Too often PRs' and trustees' risk management, when it occurs, is focused more on Tier 3 issues rather than considering the issues that arise at Tier 2. The issues at Tier 1 are much wider issues involving the business more generally, and often receive better attention than Tier 2.

Policies and structure of control, training, and compliance are the starting point, as without **9.07** these policies and structure, controlling (or even identifying) risk at the individual estate/ trust level is going to be rather hit or miss.[1] The training aspect is not dealt with in any detail in this book as it is assumed that it is common ground with all firms involved in the administration of estates and trusts, as not using professionally trained staff, adequately skilled for their tasks, would be litigation waiting to happen.

The PR or trustee is the legal owner of the assets vested in him and is treated by the law as **9.08** the legal owner. It therefore follows that the risk-management process must start by identifying not merely the risk of taking certain PRs' or trustees' actions with regard to those assets, but the risk inherent in ownership of them. For example, a PR or trustee owning a property should not be concerned just with the risks of distribution, sale, or letting of the property, but also with whether or not ownership of the property poses dangers to others and those dangers may range from environmental risk, to dangerous condition, to onerous covenants.

In some ways a PR's or trustee's exposure to claims and litigation is greater than that of the **9.09** ordinary property-owning citizen. The citizen is at risk of litigation or prosecution in the conduct of his affairs if he conducts them in a way that offends the law. The PR or trustee runs the same risk, but must also conduct his affairs to comply with additional burdens of the law of succession and trusts. Concentrating on the succession and trusts aspects at the expense of the general law, or vice versa, will give risk that is not managed. PRs and trustees are more likely to concentrate on the succession and trusts aspects at the expense of considering how the remainder of the law develops and affects them.

Unfortunately, for trustees in particular, the long-running nature of most trusts means that **9.10** the consequences of actions, or inactions, typically take years to come to light; and this passage of time tends to increase significantly the financial consequences of the action or inaction. This puts much of trustees' risk in a category of risk, hated by most risk managers, that is sometimes known as 'long tail risk'; this is risk that

- is hard to recognize initially, and most frequently only comes to light after some passage of time;
- if seen early, is hard to quantify initially (and hard to predict what the final liability will be if left uncorrected);
- is hard to control without robust checks; and
- has an alarming tendency to grow in money terms with the passage of time before the consequences of the risk can be seen.[2]

The position and role in a business of any risk-management function needs to be thought **9.11** through and understood. Risk management has a limited upside (scope for generating profit) and a near unlimited downside (scope for permitting loss). This inevitably results in risk decision makers either being seen as destructive to the efforts of the 'real workers' or simply as a parasitic body that lives on the profits of the same workers. Understandably the

---

[1] See Chapter 8 on the creation of a risk-management policy for wills. The basic principles outlined there will apply to the creation of a risk-management policy for other business.

[2] A US attorney offered the following definition of a trust to one of the authors: 'A trust is a keg of dynamite with a forty year fuse.' This is a very graphic and memorable way of describing the long-term nature of much of the risk that is found in trust administration.

business line is intent on maximizing the profit and this too always needs to be recognized, but at the same time the threat to a business of profits turning to losses unless there is proper evaluation of the risk needs to be recognized.[3]

New business generally

9.12 For both estates and trusts there is a primary consideration of competence for professionals, either acting as trustees or as trustees' advisers. Accepting new business that is of a size or complexity that a firm has not handled before should involve a careful evaluation of both the skills and systems available in order to determine if a firm is capable of undertaking the work within acceptable risk parameters. Similar considerations will apply if there is a significant increase in the volume of work, even if this does not contain issues of size and complexity. Not judging new business in this light significantly increases the potential for risk.

9.13 The SRA Code of Conduct 2011 in Chapter 1 at Outcomes 1.4 and 1.5 insists that

- 'you have the resources, skills and procedures to carry out your clients' instructions' and
- 'the service you provide to clients is competent, delivered in a timely manner and takes account of you clients' needs and circumstances'.[4]

9.14 It is implicit in these requirements that an assessment of competence and resources must be made in order to comply. Compliance clearly is vital (for control of risk, client service, and professional standing): ensuring compliance requires a clear decision hierarchy for who can commit a firm to what types of business (especially in terms of allocation of resources available). To have uncontrolled acceptance of new business makes it difficult for a firm of solicitors to comply with the Code of Conduct. For other professionals, such as trust companies, failure to control new business risk would be a serious problem for the integrity of corporate risk management and governance, which in turn raises issues as to competence for its regulator.

9.15 Allied to the assessment of competence and resources is the important question of profitability. A major factor involved in this will be whether the quantity of work required can be done within the fixed fee structure (trust companies), or for hourly billing, whether the hours required for the work will be acceptable to the client (and whether the hourly charge will be inflated by the additional time spent on the unfamiliar). Also to be considered is the degree to which assistance will be required to deal with features of the administration and the degree to which that assistance will be chargeable.

Estates

9.16 Competence to deal with a matter can be a question that cannot be answered fully at the outset of an estate administration, as some difficulties with the estate may not become apparent until after some investigation has been made. However, this risk can be reduced by an organized and thorough gathering of information at the outset. A recommended step in this is to

---

[3] 'The business line was more focused on getting a transaction approved than on identifying the risks in what it was proposing. The risk factors were a small part of the presentation and always "mitigated". This made it hard to discourage transactions. If a risk manager said no, he was immediately on a collision course with the business line. The risk thinking therefore leaned towards giving the benefit of the doubt to the risk-takers. Collective common sense suffered as a result' (from 'The Confessions of a Risk Manager' on the credit crunch, *The Economist*, 9 August 2008).

[4] Applying Principles 4 and 5 of the SRA's mandatory ten principles.

use a prepared checklist of key questions that should be asked. This enables a standardized approach to be used across a firm to ensure that the maximum amount of important information is sought as early as possible. Recording the information in a standardized format also allows for easier control and review of subordinates', or trainees', work. Use of a standard questionnaire means, in theory, that no matter who in your firm conducts the interview, all relevant information will be recorded and placed on file in a common format. The downside is that it can give the impression to the client that they are being 'processed'. On balance, the benefits outweigh the concerns.

What questions should be on such a form is really a matter of policy for each firm. Some **9.17** thought should be given to what areas need to be covered and then those areas filled in with more detailed questions. Without a procedure form a firm relies on individual members of staff

- to have sufficient knowledge to cover all the necessary areas;
- to remember all the questions that should be asked on each occasion;
- to record the information accurately in a way that is easily accessible and intelligible to anyone else who may work on the file.

Ideally the interview ought to be conducted by the person who will deal with the adminis- **9.18** tration of the estate. Where this is not possible, the interview should at least be conducted by a colleague with the knowledge to ask all relevant questions and the skill and experience to understand the answers and identify areas that require further questions. This latter point is particularly important given the almost infinite variety of circumstances that can be encountered.

The questions needed to establish the information are wide ranging and generally should **9.19** best be dealt with by way of a pre-drafted questionnaire. Having such a questionnaire has the same advantages as those listed earlier[5] for will instructions.

Careful consideration should be given to the major factors that may impact on the viability **9.20** of the administration as being one that can be undertaken within the available competence.

The deceased
His domicile needs to be established, and if this cannot be done with accuracy then as much **9.21** relevant information as possible needs to be collected. Too often the domicile of the deceased is not looked at critically enough before irrevocable steps are taken in the administration. Identifying the likelihood of a dispute as to UK domicile, particularly with HMRC, is only part of the process, as it should also be determined if any other jurisdiction can claim jurisdiction over devolution and/or taxation. Even where there is only an England and Wales domicile, the jurisdiction in which assets are located is important in assessing whether or not the firm has the skills to deal with substantial cross-border issues, including real property issues and the application of *lex situs*.

His personal details, which will include marital history (including proof of marriage or civil **9.22** partnership, particularly if IHT relief is to be claimed); any trusteeships, receiverships, and powers of attorney (whether acting under or applying to the deceased); executorships or administrations where the deceased was the personal representative, will be required.

---

[5] See Chapter 6 Part A.

9.23 Details of the deceased's family and beneficiaries will be required, eg divorces, issue, adoptions, dependants (identifying any potential claims or inconsistencies of description when compared to the will), deaths of named beneficiaries.

9.24 An early examination of the death certificate should avoid missing factors that may be highly relevant to how the estate must be conducted. Is death as a result of:

- *Accident*—are there going to be claims for and/or against the estate? Is any potential risk to the estate covered by the deceased's insurance?
- *Industrial injury*—is it covered by any national compensation agreement/employer's insurance?
- *Suicide*—if it is, will this negate any life insurance policies?
- *Homicide*—will the issue of forfeiture arise?
- *Illness associated with war service*[6]—such claims arising out of death from injuries incurred during active service in the Second World War still occur and other post-war military engagements can qualify. The wound need only be a cause of death and not the only cause.[7]

9.25 The complexity of the family relationships involved will be a factor, but it is one that can be difficult to assess and is often overlooked as a risk issue. The sheer antagonism (and at times worse) between some family members can make an administration a very unpleasant experience and one that is difficult to manage. Furthermore, such warring families will usually significantly increase the potential for complaint and litigation—again factors that should affect decision making at the outset. If relationships have deteriorated to the extreme that a beneficiary is accused of killing the deceased, then the approach to the administration must be one of great care, particularly as regards the benefit to the accused.

9.26 The terms of divorces or current maintenance for adults and children will enable an initial view of the likelihood of Inheritance (Provision for Family and Dependants) Act 1975 (I(PFD)A 1975) claims (with the consequences for costs, delays, and altered devolution) and certainly prevent planning of early distributions.

9.27 The appropriate certificates to support the claimed relationships are essential, often to simply confirm entitlement. This is true for spouses as well. Anecdotally, 'common law' spouses have

---

[6] Section 154 IHTA 1984

(1) Section 4 above shall not apply in relation to the death of a person in whose case it is certified by the Defence Council or the Secretary of State—
   (a) that he died from a wound inflicted, accident occurring or disease contracted at a time when the conditions specified in subsection (2) below were satisfied, or
   (b) that he died from a disease contracted at some previous time, the death being due to or hastened by the aggravation of the disease during a period when those conditions were satisfied.
(2) The conditions referred to in subsection (1) above are that the deceased was a member of any of the armed forces of the Crown or (not being a member of any of those forces) was subject to the law governing any of those forces by reason of association with or accompanying any body of those forces and (in any case) was either—
   (a) on active service against an enemy, or
   (b) on other service of a warlike nature or which in the opinion of the Treasury involved the same risks as service of a warlike nature.

[7] *Barty-King v Ministry of Defence* [1979] 2 All ER 80; *R v Criminal Injuries Compensation Board, Ex parte Ince* [1973] 1 WLR 1334.

been encountered who were aware of the advantages of purporting to be married (or at least not correcting an erroneous assumption) and relying on the usual indifference to checking marital status.[8] Apart from the need to adequately identify a client or a beneficiary[9] there is no reason why a professional PR or a professional adviser to a PR should set out to claim a substantial IHT relief without correctly identifying that it is correctly available.

Where the deceased was in the process of acting as executor of other estates, and some or all of them are uncompleted, then the effect of the chain of representation needs to be considered. An executor in becoming PR of the other estates by representation needs to consider not only the amount of work required to complete the administrations (and the arrangements for his fees if he is a professional), but also the potential additional work if the standard of work of the deceased in these administrations has fallen below acceptable standards. Where the deceased executor has wrongly or negligently administered the estate(s), the executor by representation would need to consider the extent to which he must apply any unadministered assets to correct the position. The disputes that can arise can be problematic, particularly to the extent that there are funds available to both resolve the issue and to allow reimbursement of the executor's costs.   **9.28**

Assets

The investment risk inherent in any asset is going to make decision making more urgent and often more difficult, particularly where the risk is one that either the PR assesses as inappropriate (as it could threaten to substantially reduce the amount available for distribution) or that is at a level that the beneficiaries are not prepared to accept for their inheritance. As risk is also a major factor in valuation and price volatility, high investment risk can quite foreseeably impact on the ultimate size of the net distributable residue and substantial falls in value are a frequent source of dispute with the beneficiaries.   **9.29**

Physical security of assets is also a risk factor where the deceased owned assets of high theft risk (jewellery, antiques, an art collection). The security risks accepted by the deceased may have been low and simply continuing to accept them may fall below the standard expected of a PR. In addition, the insurance terms and conditions of the valuables need to be considered carefully, particularly with regard to unoccupied premises, and swift action is often needed to comply with the insurance requirements. Generally, failure to take steps to review security and insurances (or implement new policies where necessary) will be a fruitful area for dispute if loss arises after death.   **9.30**

The complexities introduced into an administration by asset risk should give a firm pause for thought as to whether or not they have the experience and skill to deal with the assets or if they know how to obtain and apply advice. The investment risk becomes greater the longer it takes to deal with sale/transfer of the asset, and controlling that time is more difficult if either the risk is not appreciated or the PR is not aware of the steps required.   **9.31**

For land, the possibility of, or extent of, any contamination should not be overlooked. The level of clean-up costs may be a key factor in deciding if the estate is a viable proposition,   **9.32**

---

[8] The attitude is often that as HMRC do not seek proof of marriage to grant this relief, no one else needs to bother.
[9] *Fea v Roberts* [2006] WTLR 255.

as clean-up will present a substantial management challenge[10] and often a substantial cost. This issue can become even more important if, under the terms of the will, the land is to be held in trust.[11]

9.33 Properties that are let nearly always pose challenges in terms of effective management. The issues will include levels of rent, ease and financial advantage/disadvantage of possession, for commercial premises the processes undertaken therein (see para 9.32 above in particular), state of repair and liability to undertake remedial repairs, compliance with insurance and other covenants, and planning consents for use. The identity of the tenant or occupier and compliance with the lease should be checked before rent is accepted.

9.34 The location of the assets and the ability to control them, particularly if they are located out of this jurisdiction or are managed or occupied by others, must be considered. The practical steps necessary to gain both control and title need to be considered early on in order to avoid wasted time after a grant is received.

9.35 The liquidity of the assets is an important factor where cash for outgoings needs to be raised or where the investment risk of the asset makes disposal or reduction an issue. Again, the practical steps necessary to gain both control and title need to be considered early in order to avoid wasted time after a grant is received.

9.36 Any asset where, although the title is in the name of the deceased, the equitable interest is not an asset of the estate and that interest will not devolve under the will or intestacy of the deceased, needs to be identified as early as possible to avoid planning the administration and devolution on a false premise (which could mislead the beneficiaries and misled beneficiaries are understandably apt to argue and look for someone to blame when they are disappointed).[12]

Debts

9.37 The size of the debts is obviously an early assessment as the whole approach to an administration must change if there is either abatement or insolvency.

9.38 The nature of the debts in the context of the deceased also needs to be considered. In the past, high credit card balances for a person bedridden in a nursing home have been found to have been incurred by others using the credit cards improperly.[13]

9.39 Liquidity is an issue for the payment of not only debts but also legacies and administration expenses. Where the greater part of the estate is represented by a single asset (eg land or a private business) consideration needs to be given as to how the debts and expenses will be paid if the single asset is not expected to be disposed of. Avoiding sale may require the beneficiaries to put the estate in funds before the outgoings are paid and before the asset can be transferred.

The will

9.40 It is dangerous to assume that a previously executed will was validly executed without re-examining it. Rechecking the apparent validity of execution is always a worthwhile

---

[10] There are also reputational issues if the contamination is a significant local or national issue, as the public may be slow to appreciate the difference between the estate and firm involved as PR or adviser.

[11] See the facts of *X v A* [2000] WTLR 11.

[12] See Chapter 13 for 'assets' that are not assets.

[13] With this problem also goes use of ATM cards to make regular unauthorized cash withdrawals from bank accounts.

precaution before proceeding. In the light of the information established about the deceased, checking the will against the marriage certificate or date of divorce can also prevent error.

It is also dangerous to assume that the deceased has not made any later wills or codicils, and enquiries starting with the family should be made. Any instructions for a new will or codicil need to be checked for. **9.41**

The existence of a foreign will should be checked for where there is any evidence of sufficient foreign property to make such a will worthwhile. The foreign will needs to be considered carefully in case it revokes the English will. **9.42**

Litigation

Existing litigation, regardless of whether the deceased was claimant or defendant, needs to be reviewed as a PR must consider whether to continue or settle. Not only will the assessment of the prospects of success, and impact of costs, be altered by absence of the deceased's evidence in person, but the PR will need to take into account the wishes of those beneficiaries affected by the costs and the outcome. The PR's reappraisal is also needed as to continue the litigation because the deceased had chosen to fight it could be simply adopting the same personal animosities that may have influenced the deceased's judgement in the first place. The decision making can be difficult where the PRs are also partners of the firm conducting the litigation, as it becomes important for their decision to be transparent and free from the influence of the potential future earnings from continuing the litigation. **9.43**

The potential for future litigation needs to be considered early in this information-gathering process. Potential challenges to the validity of the will can have the potential to cause loss to the PR if not approached correctly (see Chapter 10 regarding neutrality). There is also a threat to earnings where a PR has charged professional fees prior to grant and a grant is not obtained, or where fees were charged after grant but the grant was subsequently revoked. Where there is a non-professional PR, this is still a point on which his professional advisers should advise him as the PR would be personally liable for their fees. **9.44**

Tax

In the early evaluation of the estate an investigation of circumstances which will affect the IHT cannot be overlooked. Lifetime gifts (and available exemptions), aggregable funds, qualification for reliefs, gifts with reservation, etc are all matters that affect the approach to an administration and its planning and should not be put to one side for later consideration in the administration. Failing to look at the impact of tax in this early assessment produces a danger of missing issues such as abatement as well as misleading the residuary legatees as to the extent of residue. **9.45**

The correctness of the deceased's lifetime tax returns also comes into consideration. Whilst it is common (and advisable) to use past tax returns to check assets, disposals, etc, it is also advisable to keep an eye on the accuracy of the disclosures made of major disposals and sources of income to establish if there are potential problems. **9.46**

Although there is no duty on the professional PR to recommend a deed of variation in order to establish a tax saving,[14] it is widely recognized that such a step represents good client care. **9.47**

---

[14] *Cancer Research Campaign v Ernest Brown & Co* [1997] STC 1425.

It is therefore important to establish as early as possible if there is an inheritance that can be used for such a deed (or consider quick succession relief if a deed is not going to be possible).

9.48   Investigation and information gathering on the above basis is usual at the start of an administration. However, it is not unknown for the non-professional PR to instruct solicitors to act on his behalf in the administration of the estate; provide them with what he regards as sufficient information for the matter to be dealt with; and not agree to the cost of further investigations. The solicitor is then faced with the question of whether or not he is prepared to proceed without verifying that there is no significant information missing. It is not impossible to act under these circumstances (although a number of firms are known to have refused), but if the instructions are to be accepted the retainer needs to be carefully drawn and to be quite explicit as to the very narrow nature of the instructions.

B. Trusts

New trusts

9.49   As with any potential business, the professional trustee or professional adviser to a trustee should consider carefully the nature of the proposed trust to test that he has the resources and competence to deliver what will be required. Matters to be considered include the following (and it is of course preferable that these issues are checked *before* accepting the trustee ship).

9.50   **Conflicts of interest**   Are there any conflicts that will prevent a trustee from accepting the trust, or if the settlor requires it, can the conflict be authorized by the trust deed? This will include whether or not the settlor's adviser has advised on how issues of conflict might arise with the terms proposed in order to ensure that any conflict authorization implicit in the deed is understood by the settlor.

9.51   **The nature and extent of the trust property**   It is a truism to observe that there is a great difference between a small will trust and a multi-million pound family settlement, but the different resources and skills needed can too often be under estimated. In addition, the intended assets need to be considered as a factor in the complexity of the trust's administration.

9.52   **The complexity of the trusts**   The number of actual or potential objects that will need to be enquired of and considered. The harmony or disharmony within the family (including their relations with the settlor and previous trustees and any indications of future disharmony). Few trusts seek an appointment as trustee of a settlement where there is major disharmony within the family. The time that is taken up with disputes, challenges and complaints is usually disproportionate to the issues at stake and often leads to an unremunerative appointment. Too often a misguided belief by the trustee in his powers of tact and diplomacy can lead to appointments that are later regretted.

9.53   **Are the remuneration provisions for professional trustees effective and acceptable?**

9.54   **Anti-Money Laundering/Counter Terrorist Financing (AML/CTF)**   Checks to comply with the Money Laundering Regulations 2007[15] will be required on the creation of a trust and, once the trust is in existence, by professional advisers taking on the trustee as a client.

---

[15]   And avoiding possible money laundering offences (Proceeds of Crime Act 2002 and Terrorism Act 2000).

Are there statutory provisions that could cause the trust to be set aside? See later in this chapter on negligence and the creation of trusts. **9.55**

Some settlors may seek to give the impression that they have created a trust while at the same time retaining a high degree of control over the trust property. The danger of this approach is that too much retained control can lead to a finding that no trust was created. In *Rahman v Chase Bank (CI) Trust Co Ltd*[16] the settlor retained such extensive powers of the appointment of funds (including to himself) and the administration of the trust, that the Jersey Court found that he had 'retained dominion *and control over the trustee in the management and administration of the settlement*'. The trust was found to be invalid. Some jurisdictions have enacted legislation that provides for settlements to be valid notwithstanding the retention by the settlor of very wide powers over the trust.[17] Whilst the jurisdictions concerned will recognize a trust as valid where substantial powers are retained, there is the problem that the existence of the trust might well not be recognized in another jurisdiction that takes a more traditional approach. A similar problem exists for so-called asset protection trusts. **9.56**

The intentions and expectations of the settlor is an issue that needs to be explored Where the settlor's first language is not English there can be difficulties in establishing his understanding of **9.57**

- the nature of the transaction that he is entering into;
- the powers and duties of the trustee (and where applicable the protector); and
- the extent of any powers reserved to the settlor.

This can be made even more difficult if the person providing the trust fails to explain it adequately or is misleading.[18] Given that foreign lawmakers and lawyers have such difficulty in understanding trusts, it is a continuing mystery how readily ordinary citizens of other jurisdictions appear to grasp the concepts of trusts and agree to create them.[19] **9.58**

Where a settlor has it in mind at the time of creation of the trust that it should be administered according to his own design, and not in accordance with the terms of the deed, the potential for a sham trust exists. However, the trust will not, as the law stands at present, be a sham unless the 'trustee' shares the intention, or agrees with the intention, of the 'settlor'[20] and there is an intention that the deed will give a false impression[21] to the world.[22] If the trust **9.59**

---

[16] [1991] JLR 103.

[17] eg International Trusts Act 1984 (Cook Islands), Trusts (Amendment No. 4) (Jersey) Law 2006, Trustee Act 1998 (Bahamas), and Trusts (Amendment) (Immediate Effect and Reserved Powers) Law 1998 (Cayman Islands).

[18] See J Wadham, *Willoughby's Misplaced Trust*, 2nd edition (Gostick Hall, 2002) at Appendix 2 for a bizarre series of extracts from brochures issued by trust providers that display little or no understanding of what a trust actually is, and which cannot have informed accurately a prospective settlor of what he would be creating.

[19] J Glasson and G Thomas (eds), *The International Trust*, 2nd edition (Jordan Publishing, 2006) at 596 observes that a finding of no binding trust in the absence of certainty of intention is relevant in the offshore context where 'settlors' from civil law jurisdictions may have been completely misguided as to the nature of a trust and ignorant of the implications of its creation.

[20] *Shalson v Russo* [2005] Ch 281; [2003] WTLR 1165.

[21] *Hitch v Stone* [2001] STC 214.

[22] 'where it appears that an off-shore trust with its professional trustees and associated companies...have been woven together to create a shroud that is designed to bury the husband's resources from view. Should the court respect the legal structure of that screen? Or, if it becomes apparent that the husband himself pierces the

is a sham it has in fact never been a trust and the terms of the trust deed will not apply. If the trustee accepts the terms of trust and later deviates from it in accordance with the design of the settlor, it does not make the trust a sham, but the trustee will instead have breached his trust (with all the consequences that will normally follow).

9.60 **Consequences of shams for trustees** If a trust is found to be a sham, the trustee will need to be prepared for some or all of the following seven areas of risk (and none of them is remotely pleasant or cheap for the trustee). This is not to say that all seven areas *must* arise in each sham, as at the outset of a sham it would not be possible to predict which will actually arise. The areas are:

1. The determination of who the trustee then holds the funds upon *constructive trusts* for.
2. The risk that he cannot recover his *costs* in the sham action, that he may be liable for a share of the claimant's costs in that action and his exposure to costs in subsequent actions, eg tracing actions.
3. The very real prospect of *tracing claims* by those, other than the 'settlor', who may be entitled to the trust funds, and this will include those sums distributed by the trustee before the finding of sham.
4. Possible loss of reimbursement by the trustee of his *fees and disbursements* charged before the finding of sham.
5. Loss of protection from *indemnity/exoneration clauses* for his actions.
6. Regulatory investigation.
7. Revenue *investigation/penalties* for the incorrect tax returns.

9.61 **Constructive trust** Quite clearly, if the trust deed is a sham, the trustee cannot hold the funds upon the terms of the trust, as it does not exist. Therefore, the trustee, not being the beneficial owner of the assets, must hold the assets upon a constructive trust for someone else. If the trustee is lucky this will simply be the settlor, but the problem lies in determining who is actually entitled to the fund. The position will most often be complicated by the motives behind the settlor's creation of a sham trust and whether or not those motives included deception of others.[23] Competing claims are therefore to be expected.

9.62 **Costs** Much of the risk to costs is going to depend upon the type and number of actions in which the trustee becomes involved as a consequence of the sham. In a successful finding of sham it is difficult to envisage circumstances where the trustee would recover his costs in the action because of his participation in the sham (ie because of his conduct in colluding with the shammer). Equally, there must be significant exposure of the trustee to a part of the successful claimant's costs.

9.63 The correct stance of a trustee in such litigation, when a trust is under challenge, ought to be neutrality.[24] But where there is an allegation of sham that touches on the conduct of the trustee, a professional trustee is in a difficult position. The trustee will be tempted

---

veil as and when it suits him, should the trustees and directors be surprised that a court . . . will strain to see through the smoke and will set the structure aside . . .?' (*Minwalla v Minwalla* [2005] 1 FLR 771; [2006] WTLR 311). The court was more than a little surprised to see a manager of the Jersey trust company contradicting his previous instructions to a Jersey bank regarding whether or not the husband was a beneficiary—he was perhaps confused by the fact that he held two letters of wishes, dated the same day, signed by the settlor: one saying his wife was to be a beneficiary and the other the opposite.

[23] The difficulties inherent in this are well illustrated in *Shalson v Russo* [2005] Ch 281; [2003] WTLR 1165.
[24] *Alsop Wilkinson v Neary* [1995] 1 All ER 431.

to defend the deed and protect his position (and possibly his reputation) but this would significantly increase his costs risk. Even a neutral stance will involve the trustee in significant expenditure given the disclosure of documents that will be required in the action and the evidence required as to the conduct of the trustee on matters disputed by the claimants.

Further litigation involving tracing actions, recovery of fees and expenses from the trustee, **9.64** Revenue or regulatory hearings, etc all carry further costs risks.

Tracing claims The true owner of the funds which were 'settled' in the sham trust may not **9.65** be the settlor (consider here the reasons for which shammers wish to create such trusts and their reasons for apparently cloaking considerable assets behind the ownership of another), and others may have good claims against the shammer for all or part of the assets. The claims of others will have to be proved, often against the resistance of the settlor, or there may be two or more competing claims. The position of the trustee will be even more fraught if there have been distributions from the trust, or if the claim includes any losses incurred by the trustee. The recovery of the trustee's costs in such an action will not be certain and will depend upon several issues, such as upon the stance taken by the trustee in the litigation.

Expenses and disbursements There is not, to the best of the authors' knowledge, a detailed **9.66** examination by a court of this particular point. However, given that we know that in the event of revocation of a grant of probate (because of the will subsequently being found to be invalid) the executor's fee authority fails,[25] it is not difficult to see that by analogy a trustee's fee authority in a sham deed will be difficult to sustain. The authority could be good against the settlor's claims, if the settlor is entitled to the trust funds, on the grounds of what he might have contracted with the trustee for, but it must be doubtful that it is effective against a third party's claims.

The trustee is likely to have similar difficulties with disbursements. Those disbursements **9.67** which arose in connection with the safe preservation or essential management of the trust assets may be substantiated, but costs incurred otherwise are difficult and the trustee may find his recovery of them from the 'trust' fund is negated at the claim of the true owner of the trust property.

Exoneration/indemnity clauses The protection given to the trustee by such clauses is con- **9.68** ferred by the settlor in the trust deed. If that deed is a sham it is hard to see that the protection given could be valid against claims other than from the settlor who gave the authority. This matter is not one that we believe has yet been considered by a court, but it must be a matter of real concern for the sham trustee. Such clauses are mainly an issue when losses have occurred within the 'trust'. Whether or not the sham trustee will be liable for losses will depend very much on the individual circumstances and the nature of the claim being made.

Regulatory investigation Financial regulators will be concerned about findings of sham **9.69** which involve a professional trustee. The collusion necessary between trustee and settlor in order to create a sham raises serious questions about the conduct of a professional trustee and his fit and proper status for the purposes of regulation. This regulatory view could become worse depending upon the degree of dishonesty involved in the sham and the possibility that the funds 'settled' are from a criminal source.

---

[25] *Gray v Richards Butler* [2001] WTLR 625.

9.70 The roles of individual trust managers in the acceptance and management of the sham trust may, depending upon local regulation, lead to personal sanctions against them. The position is more serious, however, if the purpose of the sham was to commit a crime or handle the proceeds of crime,[26] in which case further criminal sanctions may be available against either or both the firm and its employees. Once substantial regulatory or criminal offences arise the very continuance in business of the trustee is brought into question, with the possibility of individuals being barred from practice. The future professional indemnity cover for a firm involved in such serious matters may also be more problematic.

9.71 It should also be considered that an adviser, who did not become a trustee of the sham trust, but who was instrumental in advising on its creation as a sham, is also at risk depending upon the Revenue, regulatory, or criminal offences that may arise.

9.72 **Tax investigations/penalties** Depending upon the jurisdiction, the trustee's participation in a sham may well have led to false declarations by the trustee to the Revenue authorities. It is unlikely in these circumstances that the trustee would have any protection against Revenue penalties and interest and would have no recourse to reimbursement from the trust assets. Depending upon the extent of the false declarations/returns, criminal sanctions are also a possibility.

9.73 The Revenue authorities may also have taken the lead in setting out to prove that there was a sham trust. For obvious reasons they have a vested interest in establishing the true basis of the taxation of the assets (after all, few settlors are likely to establish a sham trust in order to increase the taxation of the assets). HMRC in England have followed this course against transactions (in some cases other than trusts) in recent years.[27]

Conclusions

9.74 It seems hardly worth adding, after the above seven areas of the possible consequences of sham, that any professional trustee's risk-management policy must be directed firmly towards the avoidance of sham trusts.

9.75 The consequences of any individual finding of sham can be absurdly expensive when viewed against the potential reward of fee earnings if the sham had not been discovered. On that simple financial basis of risk/reward alone a sham would not be a worthwhile risk. (It is worth also considering the amount of a firm's time that will be involved in sorting these issues out if a claim is made, let alone proved.)

---

[26] Within the UK see generally the Proceeds of Crime Act 2002 and the Money Laundering Regulations 2007.

[27] *Hitch v Stone* [2001] STC 214; *R v Stannard* [2002] EWCA Crim 458; *R v Dimsey; R v Allen* [1999] STC 846.

There is also the US case of *Robert and Colleen Lund v CIR* [2000] TNT 211-8 where the US Tax Court upheld a challenge by the IRS against a trust on the basis of sham. The business, claimed to have been transferred to the trust, remained under the effective management of the settlor, to the exclusion of the trustees.

The relationship between the settlor and his business did not change post settlement.

The trustee had never performed any meaningful work for the trust or attempted to assert its rights over the trust property.

There was no evidence of any economic benefit for the named beneficiaries (two Caribbean companies of uncertain ownership).

The settlor had shown no regard for the terms of the trust.

Reputationally, a finding of sham against a trustee is harmful and the consequent unravel- **9.76**
ling of the issues with Revenue or regulatory authorities is likely to give rise to further reputational damage.

But add to this the fiscal and personal consequences of regulatory, Revenue, or criminal **9.77**
offences and it becomes clear that the work circumstances are capable of destroying a business.

It is further clear that any professional firm needs to structure its new business control policy **9.78**
to avoid marketing or accepting sham trust risks.[28] This will also include making the trustee's
general business policy sufficiently effective to prevent even those shams which could be
taken on by a single rogue member of staff.

Existing trusts

The duties on becoming a new trustee of an existing trust can be summarized as: **9.79**

Require the previous trustees to produce all trust documents   This will cover all of the **9.80**
trust documentation (including any letters of wishes) and files relating to the administration
of the trust. Where a trust company is the retiring trustee, the papers should include internal
memoranda and advice relating to the administration of the trust.[29] Broadly speaking the
papers that should be transferred to the new trustee include all papers that a beneficiary
would normally be able to see (it would be impossible to make adequate disclosure to a
beneficiary in the future if this were not followed); they include legal advice that has been
taken at the expense of the trust. Documents regarding the previous exercise of dispositive
discretions need not be transferred.

An important part of the trust documents will be the trust accounts (and supporting docu- **9.81**
ments such as copy tax returns) as a great deal can be gleaned about the way that the trust has
been administered from these if they have been prepared on a correct basis and disclose the
correct amount of information and detail.[30] Where accounts are missing or are prepared on

---

[28] In this context it is rather worrying to hear some of the quite sizeable estimates that are produced from
time to time as to the extent of sham trusts, particularly offshore (there are no hard statistics for this issue). One
of the authors, after speaking at a conference on this subject, was approached by a trust company representative
from Europe and was told that his approach was 'too hard' on sham trusts as 'they had their uses'!

[29] *Tiger v Barclays Bank Ltd* [1952] 1 All ER 85.

[30] (a) A summary of the terms of the trusts currently applicable (but not giving details of any letter of
   wishes) as this aids the understanding of the accounts themselves.
   (b) Who the current beneficiaries are and if any of those with a vested interest are minors or under
   a disability.
   (c) The period the accounts cover.
   (d) The assets and their acquisition costs. For stocks and shares this should include the number of
   shares or amount of stock. For the period covered by the accounts the dates of acquisition/sale
   for any assets sold/acquired.
   (e) Detail of income received such that individual interest payments or dividends can be checked
   against the assets and what it is believed that each asset should have produced.
   (f) Sufficient detail for the outgoings so the amounts paid out can be considered for their correctness; this includes the payees.
   (g) Dates of distributions and who they were made to.
   (h) Sufficient information to show the trust's solvency, including notes as to relevant issues, particularly anticipated outgoings if a reserve account has not been created for them.
   (i) A sign-off by the trustees to show that they have approved them together with any auditor's
   statement—if they were independently audited.
In the UK guidance can be obtained from the general accounting principles set out in *Financial Accounting
Standard 18* issued by the Accounting Standards Board. Accounts should be:

a seriously inadequate basis, this ought to give the proposed new trustee pause for thought about either the wisdom in proceeding or the need for caution in accepting that the trust has been administered correctly in the past.

9.82   What is reflected in the accounts is of such importance to any decision to act as a new trustee that they should, in the authors' opinion, be disclosed and examined by the proposed new trustee before any decision to act is made.

9.83   **Familiarize themselves with the terms of the trust**   Too often this exercise seems to be limited in practice to reviewing only the current trusts. Close attention needs to be paid to the administrative powers and also any future trusts after the present interests terminate. The practicalities of administration and the complexities of the future trusts will be significant factors in deciding to accept the appointment.

9.84   As for the accounts (above) it is necessary for the deed to be examined prior to accepting the trust. Without this the new trustee cannot even be satisfied that he can be validly appointed as a new trustee in

- ensuring that his appointment is in accordance with deed or law;
- bringing trust property under his control;
- being alert to any prior breaches of trust remedies and seeking rectification of them.

9.85   The last bullet point above can be more problematic in deciding how far any investigations should go.

> What are the duties of persons becoming new trustees of a settlement? Their duties are quite onerous enough, and I am not prepared to increase them. I think that when persons are asked to become new trustees, they are bound to inquire of what the property consists that it is proposed to be handed over to them, and what are the trusts. They ought to look into the trust documents and papers to ascertain what notices appear among them of incumbrances and other matters affecting the trust.[31]

9.86   In 1888 this was a good summary of the position for both existing trusts and new trusts. However, the complexity of trusts, assets, regulation, and negligence law leads to a bit more investigation than was the case in 1888.

9.87   Traditionally the view has been that a new trustee is not required to expend a great deal of time and effort to hunt down breaches of trust.[32] This has perhaps led to underestimating the thoroughness with which, for the proposed trustee's own protection, he should examine the trust deed and accounts. However, in examining the deed and accounts thoroughly it

---

[i]   *Relevant*—in that they provide information about financial performance and position that is useful in assessing the trusteeship and making economic decisions.

[ii]   *Reliable*—in that they
    [a]   represent faithfully that which they purport to represent;
    [b]   are free from error and bias;
    [c]   are complete within the bounds of materiality; and
    [d]   under consideration of the uncertainty, are prudent.

[iii]   *Comparable*—with previous financial statements for the same trust.

[iv]   *Understood*—that they are presented in a way which makes them understood and enables their significance to be appreciated by their users.

[31] Per Kekewich J in *Hallows v Lloyd* [1888] 39 Ch D 686.

[32] *Re Forest of Dean Coal Mining Co* [1878] 10 Ch D 450.

would be most unwise to switch off one's critical faculties and not look carefully at possible breaches.

In considering possible breaches, it is not simply the very obvious risk of distributing trust **9.88** assets to someone who is not a beneficiary that needs to be considered. Other, more frequent, areas of error are in the interpretation of the investment powers, the exercise of (or failure to exercise) the investment powers, delegation collectively by the trustees, and powers of appointment and the charging of professional fees.

Acquiescence in the breach of trust (without the authority of all those who will be affected) **9.89** can leave the new trustee exposed to liability for his predecessor's breach.[33] Even if ultimately the new trustee is not liable for the breaches of his predecessor, such claims are best avoided from the outset.

C. Negligence and the creation of trusts

The standards of work required from a solicitor in advising a settlor on the creation of a trust **9.90** are exactly the same as would be required in any other transaction for a client given the terms of the retainer. There is clear authority for the liability of the advisers where the transaction results in a tax liability for the settlor that he was either not advised of, or was advised would not arise (see also comments on *Estill* case at para 9.179). There is also the possibility that a trust might fail completely through defective drafting of the deed. The Jersey Court was presented with this issue in *Re Double Happiness Trust, Grant Thornton Stonehage Ltd v Ward*.[34]

In England and Wales, the terms of s.22 Solicitors Act 1974 previously restricted the prepar- **9.91** ation of settlement deeds to the legally qualified. This is now covered by Part 3 Legal Services Act 2007. Section 12(1) lists the reserved legal activities, one of which is 'reserved instrument activities'. These are further defined in paragraph 5 of Schedule 2. Paragraph 5(1)(c) refers to 'preparing any instrument relating to real or personal estate for the purposes of the law of England and Wales'.[35]

The problem with this definition is the use of the word 'preparing'. In the traditional **9.92** approach to a trust the draftsman advised, drafted, supervised execution and then charged appropriately for his work. Trust deeds are now delivered in other ways, frequently not by the draftsman of the deed. Examples of this are standard deeds for life policies available from life companies and deeds offered by some non-solicitor will-preparers often designated as asset protection trusts. Often significant fees are charged for providing a standard deed that was prepared originally by an authorized person, but is then sold by an unauthorized person. If that unauthorized person advises, fills in the blanks in the standard deed, and then charges a fee is he 'preparing' a deed? The question would seem to hang on whether or not assisting the settlor by filling in the blanks is preparing a deed. If it is possible for trust deeds to be sold legally in that way there may be a significant lacuna in the Act.

The description of 'any instrument relating to real or personal estate for the purposes of **9.93** the law of England and Wales' appears to cover a notice of severance of a beneficial joint

---

[33] *Harvey v Olliver* [1887] 57 LT 239.
[34] [2003] WTLR 367.
[35] Wills and powers of attorney are excluded from this definition: para 5(3) Sch 2.

tenancy.[36] Similar questions then arise as to what is preparation if such notices are provided for gain when the vendor is simply assisting with completion of a pre-prepared standard letter.

9.94 Reserved legal activities are reserved to exempt or authorized persons.[37] Anyone who carries out a reserved legal activity, but is neither of these, commits an offence[38]—penalties range from a fine to a maximum of two years' imprisonment. There are other offences connected with this.[39]

9.95 As a criminal offence is committed by an unauthorized person preparing a trust deed, fees charged will constitute the proceeds of crime. This has implications for others within the same firm or company who handle those proceeds.[40]

9.96 '[P]reparing any instrument relating to real or personal estate for the purposes of the law of England and Wales' contains the restriction to England and Wales.[41] This can pose problems for a trust deed provided outside this jurisdiction that applies to any property within this jurisdiction. While the words of the Act could be more explicit, the implication of this is that any other deed affecting interests in a trust governed by English law must be drafted by an authorized person.

9.97 Where there is an as yet unresolved issue is if the settlement does not confer the benefits as advised or suffers adverse tax assessments that the adviser either did not advise on or on which he gave incorrect advice. In these circumstances, the loss is not suffered by the settlor (he has parted with the same amount that he intended to settle) but his beneficiaries receive less than he intended. The idea that the settlor has not suffered loss but the beneficiaries have is not that far removed from the problem facing the court in *White v Jones*.[42] It remains to be seen whether or not a court when faced with this issue will follow the reasoning in *White v Jones*. It would seem unsafe when assessing risk to a business not to assume that the court would. An alternative approach by the court would be to allow the trustee to pursue the claim for the benefit of the trust. Although he has not suffered a loss the court could be prepared to treat the trustee as representative of the beneficiaries and capable of pursuing the claim for the benefit of the trust. This was the solution used by Neuberger J in *Chappell v Sommers & Blake*[43] to permit an executor to sue for loss caused to an estate by solicitors negligently failing to act on the executrix's instructions.

9.98 The Canadian case of *Crowe (Committee of) v Bollong*[44] examined the issue of suitability of the particular trust prepared to the requirements of the testator and beneficiary. A will had been prepared with benefit for the daughter being on a bare trust, which was not only

---

[36] Section 36(2) Law of Property Act 1925.
[37] Schedule 4 deals with exempt persons and Schedule 5 with authorized persons. The authorized persons will be those approved by an authorized regulatory body and almost exclusively these are regulators of the legal profession.
[38] Section 14 Legal Services Act 2007.
[39] Sections 15–17 Legal Services Act 2007.
[40] Sections 327–329 Proceeds of Crime Act 2002.
[41] Section 212 further confirms that the Act is restricted to England and Wales.
[42] Some authors already regard this point as more settled in favour of the beneficiaries' claim: see James Kessler QC and Leon Sartin, *Drafting Trusts and Will Trusts*, 11th edition (Sweet & Maxwell, 2012).
[43] [2003] WTLR 1085; a solution described in *Jackson and Powell on Professional Liability*, 6th edition (Sweet & Maxwell, 2007) at [11-053] as 'interesting and ingenious'.
[44] 42 CCLT (2d) 1; 1998 Carswell BC 740 (BCSC, 25 March 1998).

manifestly unsuitable, but because of her right to collapse the trust[45] deprived her of state benefits. The court found that the will, which contained the trust, was not appropriate and did not meet the instructions of the testatrix. The testatrix had suffered no loss, but the beneficiary's position was adversely affected by the loss of benefits and the court held that the preparer in these circumstances owed the beneficiary a duty of care as well.

The Missouri Court of Appeals has produced a decision[46] in this area where an estate plan **9.99** involving partly an *inter vivos* trust was substantially defeated by a spouse claim under relevant family provision legislation. The court found that an attorney had a responsibility when proposing changes to the existing inheritance planning (including the *inter vivos* trust) to ensure that the client fully understood the existing plan before setting out with the changes. And in this case failure to do so resulted in a successful claim from the disappointed beneficiaries of the depleted *inter vivos* trust. Whilst as yet there is no comparable decision by an English court, it is quite easy to see an attempt being made.

The principle of solicitors acting on behalf of the trustees owing a duty of care to the bene- **9.100** ficiaries of an existing trust has been examined and, in the particular circumstances of the case, accepted by an English court.[47] Where a solicitor is advising trustees of an existing trust, it was held in *Yudt v Leonard Ross & Craig*[48] that the solicitor had assumed a responsibility towards the beneficiaries as well as towards the client, the trustees. Ferris J found that the relationship between solicitor and beneficiary was the same as that between solicitor and trustee, and that the solicitor had assumed responsibility under the *Hedley Byrne* principle and that this finding was not an application of *White v Jones*. But, where a person did not have a vested interest, but was merely a potential object of the exercise of a discretion, and the solicitor's negligent acts prevent the trustee from making an appointment (which they had decided to do), then the beneficiary could have a basis of claim by applying *White v Jones*. This view was not put in conclusive terms and it must be said that nothing within the decision in *White v Jones* seemed to anticipate that it had an application beyond that of wills (see Chapter 15 Part G for further comment on this point).

Usually, where a solicitor's negligent advice has caused loss to a trust, the trustee will have **9.101** standing to bring a claim for the benefit of the trust.[49]

Where a solicitor has failed to prepare a trust deed sufficiently expeditiously, and the would-be **9.102** settlor has died, there is little guidance on whether or not a beneficiary might recover such a loss. In *White v Jones* Lord Goff expressed the view that a loss arising out of an imperfect *inter vivos* gift would not be recoverable if the would-be donor was still alive. This view does not seem contentious and was the view reached in *Hemmens v Wilson Browne*.[50] In such a case it would be open to the donor to perfect his gift and prevent the 'loss', but in the absence of him doing so no action would lie against the solicitors, however negligent.[51]

---

[45] Applying *Saunders v Vautier* (1841) 4 Beav 115.
[46] *Johnson v Sandler, Balkin, Hellman & Weinstein* PC 958 SW 2d 42, 48 (Mo App 1997). This decision is interesting in the sense that the earlier decisions considered in *White v Jones* were from North America.
[47] *Yudt v Leonard Ross & Craig* (1998/99) ITELR 53.
[48] *White v Jones* (1998/99) ITELR 531.
[49] *Malkins Nominees Ltd v Société Financière Mirelis SA* [2004] EWHC 2631 (Ch).
[50] [1993] 4 All ER 826.
[51] [1995] 1 All ER 691 at 704G; the circumstances outlined had arisen earlier in *Hemmens v Wilson Browne* (n 50).

9.103 Lord Goff went on to say:

> equity will not perfect an imperfect gift, though there is some authority which suggests that exceptionally it may do so if the donor has died or become incapacitated: see *Lister v Hodgson* (1867) LR 4 Eq 30, 34–35, per Romilly MR. I for my part do not think that the intended donee could in these circumstances have any claim against the solicitor.

9.104 It was observed in *Lister v Hodgson*[52] that 'no amount of evidence…will at all justify the court in compelling [a settlor] to introduce into the deed that which he does not choose to introduce now'.

9.105 In a later consideration of this point, it was observed that if the settlor is dead

> and it is afterwards proved…that beyond all doubt the deed was not prepared in the exact manner that [the settlor] intended, then the deed may be reformed, and those particular provisions necessary to carry his intention into effect may be introduced.[53]

9.106 That these points really apply to rectification of a deed completed before death but rectified after death does not seem too controversial.

9.107 However, compensating for the failure of gift because of the negligence of the draftsman in failing to draft it before the death of the settlor must still be an open point. It is, however, one that as far as possible is to be avoided by timely preparation of trust deeds.[54]

9.108 The settlor's intention in creating a trust is something that the adviser needs to establish. In doing so the adviser must be able to give advice where these intentions could give rise to difficulties. There are a number of grounds on which a trust can be challenged and the adviser needs to be aware of his client's intentions and the true purpose of the creation of the settlement.

Inheritance (Provision for Family and Dependants) Act 1975

9.109 Intending to use a trust to shield assets from potential I(PFD)A 1975 claims has difficulties. There is an anti-avoidance code contained in ss.10–13 of the Act, which deals with disposals within six years of death. Sections 10–13 cannot be used to attack dispositions made more than six years before death. Disposals of property[55] can be recovered by a court in order to increase the financial assets available for claims under this Act. The provisions require

1. an intention to defeat financial provision on death; and
2. that full valuable consideration was not given in exchange for the disposition.

9.110 Up to all of the value disposed of can be recovered, but not any later appreciation on the amount(s) settled. Where distributions have been made from the trust, recovery can be ordered from the beneficiary in possession of the property.[56]

9.111 Section 11 of the Act contains similar anti-avoidance provisions attaching to contracts to leave property by will with the intention of defeating claims. It applies to such contracts where the other party has not paid full valuable consideration. Unlike s.10 there is no time limit on when the contract was entered into (other than the commencement of the Act).

---

[52] At the pages cited by Lord Goff.
[53] *Van der Linde v Van der Linde* [1947] Ch 306.
[54] See *Underhill and Hayton: Law of Trusts and Trustees*, 18th edition (Butterworths, 2010) at [15.27].
[55] The provisions cover both absolute gifts and gifts into trust.
[56] Section 10(2)(b) I(PFD)A 1975.

Creditors

Section 423 Insolvency Act 1986 allows the court to set aside transactions entered into at an **9.112** undervalue (this includes gifts) with the intention of defrauding the settlor's creditors. Any trust attacked in this way is treated as voidable, ie it is valid until a successful application is made.

There is no requirement to prove dishonesty or improper conduct on the part of the settlor, **9.113** merely that there was an intention to prejudice creditors. This intention will be established from the facts. That the settlor acted on professional advice is not evidence that he lacked the requisite intention.[57] The intention to prejudice creditors can be one among several factors. It need not be the dominant factor,[58] but it must not be a minor factor.[59]

Creditors that did not exist at the time of settlement are able to use this section[60] to attack **9.114** a disposal. Creating a settlement as a precaution against unforeseen problems arising with future creditors from a new business venture can be within the scope of this section.[61] Where the aim of the settlement was to avoid tax it is caught by this section, even though at the time of the settlement there was no prejudice to the Revenue.[62]

For the adviser it is important that once a case has been shown that this section is applicable, **9.115** no legal professional privilege attaches to any documents relating to the creation of the settlement as between settlor and adviser.[63]

Time limits for claims is a complex area. **9.116**

1. Where this section is being used to recover a sum of money the limitation period is six years from the transfer.[64]
2. Where this section is being used to recover a specialty the limitation period is twelve years (this would cover an action to set aside a trust).[65]
3. Claims out of time can be successful if advantage can be taken of s.32(1) Limitation Act 1980. This provides that where the action is based on
   (a) the fraud of the settlor; or
   (b) a fact relevant to the claimant's right of action has been deliberately concealed from him
   the limitation period shall not begin to run until the fraud or concealment could with reasonable diligence have been discovered.

A further difficulty is when does the limitation period start to run? There is the possibility that it starts with the creation of the settlement, but this is considered to be unlikely by at least one leading work.[66] It is more likely to start at a later date such as the date of insolvency. A full discussion of the possibilities around this time issue is not within the scope of this work.

---

[57] *National Westminster Bank v Jones* [2001] EWCA Civ 1541.
[58] *IRC v Hashmi* [2002] WTLR 1027.
[59] *Hill v Spread Trustee Co Ltd* [2006] WTLR 1009.
[60] *Midland Bank plc v Wyatt* [1997] 1 BCLC 242.
[61] *Re Butterworth* (1882) 19 Ch D 588.
[62] *Hill v Spread Trustee Co Ltd* (n 59).
[63] *Barclays Bank plc v Eustace* [1995] 1 WLR 1238.
[64] Section 9(1) Limitation Act 1980.
[65] *Hill v Spread Trustee Co Ltd* (n 59) and s.8(1) Limitation Act 1980.
[66] G Thomas and A Hudson, *The Law of Trusts*, 2nd edition (Oxford University Press, 2010).

9.117 Sections 339–342 Insolvency Act 1986 can apply where a transaction was made at an undervalue and

- there was no consideration; or
- the transaction was in consideration of marriage or a civil partnership; or
- it was at a significant undervalue; and
- the application is made by the trustee in bankruptcy.

If a bankruptcy petition is brought within two years after property was put into the settlement, the settlement can be set aside

- without any proof that the settlor was insolvent when the settlement was made; or
- without requiring any proof of intention to defraud creditors.

If a bankruptcy petition is brought within five years after property was put into the settlement, the settlement can be set aside only if

- the trustee in bankruptcy can show the settlor was insolvent when the settlement was made (or he became insolvent as a consequence of the settlement);
- but the burden of proof is reversed if the payment was to an associate[67] of the bankrupt.[68]

9.118 Section 357 Insolvency Act 1986 provides for a criminal offence to be committed where a settlor becomes bankrupt within five years after creating the settlement, unless he can prove he had no intention to defraud or to conceal.[69] The burden of proving there was no such intention is on the settlor.[70] The standard punishment on conviction will be a custodial sentence.[71] As a crime can be committed in this manner, professional advisers who are involved in the creation of such a settlement could have aided, abetted, or conspired with the settlor to commit the crime.[72]

9.119 Section 342A Insolvency Act 1986 provides that excess contributions to both approved and unapproved pension schemes can be recovered for a bankrupt's estate on the application of the trustee in bankruptcy.

9.120 Section 412A Insolvency Act 1986[73] now reverses the result achieved in *Re Palmer*,[74] where it was held that joint property owned as beneficial joint tenants was not available to the administrator of the insolvent estate of the first co-owner to die. This now provides, in certain circumstances, for joint property owned as a beneficial joint tenant, which has already passed to the surviving co-owner, to be made available to meet creditors' claims against the estate of the first co-owner to die. This has potential concerns for any legal personal representative (LPR) where he administers the estate of someone who has previously inherited joint property by survivorship, but also for a trustee where the surviving joint owner has placed the property in trust within five years of the death of the insolvent co-owner.

---

[67] 'Associate' is widely defined in s.425.
[68] Section 341 Insolvency Act 1986.
[69] Section 352 Insolvency Act 1986.
[70] *A-G's Reference (No 1 of 2004)* [2004] EWCA Crim 1025.
[71] *R v Mungroo* (1997) 25 LS Gaz R 33.
[72] Under the general aiding and abetting offence in s.8 Accessories and Abettors Act 1861 (as amended).
[73] As inserted by s.12 Insolvency Act 2000.
[74] [1994] 3 All ER 835.

Section 412A applies where **9.121**

1. an insolvency order has been made in respect of the estate of a deceased person; and
2. the petition for the order was made after the commencement of this section and within five years of the date of the insolvent's death; and
3. immediately before his death the insolvent was beneficially entitled to an interest in any property as joint tenant;
4. the survivor, who inherited by survivorship on the death of the insolvent is alive, or, if he is dead, died after the making of the insolvency administration order against the first co-owner.

Settlement by a settlor on himself

A person can create a settlement on himself until his bankruptcy with alternative provisions **9.122** on that event. However, although such a settlement would be valid until his bankruptcy, then his limited interest in the trust would be treated as an absolute interest in the entire trust property, which therefore becomes available towards his debts. The determining trust provisions relating to bankruptcy are void and his interest vests in his trustee in bankruptcy.[75] Thus, a protective trust (either express or under s.33 Trustee Act 1925) created by the settlor, settling income on himself, will not offer protection against the settlor's creditors. In *Tasarruf Mevdati Sigorta Fonu v Merrill Lynch Bank and Trust Co (Cayman) Ltd*[76] the Privy Council found that where a settlor had an unfettered non-fiduciary power of revocation (which would result in the trust funds revesting in him), that power was capable of being treated as property. Accordingly it found that it was an asset available to creditors and the court could order the delegation of the power by the settlor to a creditor (who had undertaken to apply the funds for the benefit of all creditors).

In terms of legal capacity a settlement cannot be made by a bankrupt, as the ownership of his **9.123** property does not lie with him.

Personal chattels

For the avoidance of fraud against creditors, the Bills of Sale Acts 1878–82 provided for a public **9.124** registration of bills of sale of chattels as a measure to prevent fraud on creditors. Therefore if A makes a declaration of trust over some or all of his chattels and retains possession of them, A cannot use the trust to shield the chattels from his creditors unless the transfer of ownership is evidenced by a duly registered bill of sale in the form required in the schedule to the 1882 Act.

Divorce

The jurisdiction of the Family Division is far more extensive than trust practitioners and **9.125** their clients are often aware. The ability of the court to take trusts into account in determining ancillary relief poses a number of issues for the adviser.

Section 37 Matrimonial Causes Act 1973[77] (MCA 1973) contains powers[78] which enable **9.126** a court to restrain a disposition from being made with the intention of defeating provision on divorce (and provision in this context is not limited to a spouse but includes children).

---

[75] *Re Burroughs-Fowler* [1916] 2 Ch 251.
[76] [2011] WTLR 1249.
[77] Schedule 5 paras 74–75 Civil Partnership Act 2004 contain similar powers in respect of the dissolution of civil partnerships.
[78] Section 37(2)(a).

9.127   Section 37 also gives the court powers to set aside existing dispositions that were made with a similar purpose.[79] There is effectively no time limit on how far a court may go back in the exercise of this power,[80] but the greater the passage of time, the greater the difficulty there will usually be in proving intention. However, for dispositions made within three years before any application there is a rebuttable presumption[81] that the disposition was made with the intention of defeating provision. This presumption would not apply if the disposition did not reduce the resources available for provision. Where a settlement is made during the three-year period before an application, with a motive other than defeating provision on divorce, there will still be the distinct possibility of challenge if it was the inevitable consequence of the disposition that provision on divorce would be reduced.

Ante- and post-nuptial settlements

9.128   A court in England and Wales has powers to make the following orders for financial provision on divorce:

- An order varying for the benefit of the parties to the marriage and of the children of the family or either or any of them any ante-nuptial or post-nuptial settlement[82] made on the parties to the marriage, other than one in the form of a pension arrangement.[83]
- An order extinguishing or reducing the interest of either of the parties to the marriage under any such settlement.[84]

9.129   These powers apply to any settlement ante-nuptial or post-nuptial. They are a substantial weapon in preventing the misuse of trusts that any adviser or trustee needs to be familiar with. Advisers need to be aware of

- the status of any trust where they advise on its creation so that they can correctly advise the client on the availability of the trust as a resource on divorce;
- the potential for negligence claims against the adviser, in the area of planning and wealth preservation using trusts, if he gives any assurance, express or implied, that a nuptial settlement is not vulnerable to attacks on divorce.

9.130   Further, trustees need to be aware of

- the court's powers to make orders against trusts that the trustees must comply with;
- the importance of their neutrality in disputes regarding the trusts interest on divorce.

9.131   What then is an ante- or post-nuptial settlement? This is not a classification that is usually used in relation to trusts by trustees and their advisers, but it is also a classification that is not easily set out. The court will

- take a broad approach to this definition, and
- take this approach in the interest of financial justice for the parties involved.

---

[79]   Section 37(2)(b) and (c).
[80]   Apart from the limitation in the s.37(7) of 1st January 1968.
[81]   Section 37(5).
[82]   Including such a settlement made by will or codicil: s.24(1)(c) MCA 1973; see for example *F v F* [2012] EWHC 438 (Fam).
[83]   Section 25D MCA 1973.
[84]   Section 24(1)(d) MCA 1973 other than one in the form of a pension arrangement (s.25D MCA 1973).

In *Brooks v Brooks*[85] such a trust was defined as, 'broadly stated...one which makes some form of continuing provision for both or either of the parties to a marriage, with or without provision for their children'.

Trustees and their advisers have traditionally thought of 'nuptial settlement' as being a mar-   **9.132**
riage settlement. While this may have been true once, today it is wrong. It will be a settlement with some connection to a marriage made on either or both parties with some reference to the marriage or their married state. Where the settlement contains no reference to a spouse and is not a nuptial settlement, but a spouse of a beneficiary is later added to the class of beneficiaries as that person's spouse, then that will add the nuptial element to bring it within s.24. Even where there is no mention of marriage or spouse, a settlement for the benefit of a person who is married at the time the settlement is made will be a nuptial settlement. This definition is very broad and capable of including most trusts regularly used by private client advisers.

The Family Division has approached trusts in a way which could be described as a broad brush   **9.133**
approach. In seeking to do justice to all parties affected by a divorce, the Family Division is more likely to include rather than exclude arrangements that may not look like a trust to the trust adviser, but are less conventional arrangements containing benefit for at least one of the parties (by adopting 'a robust questioning and, where appropriate, sceptical approach'[86]).

Advisers when recommending the use of trusts should heed the following advice: **9.134**

> I would suggest that it is only a small number of cases in which there is scope for any per-
> ceived conflict between the approach to trusts taken by family lawyers and trust lawyers.
> Furthermore, such cases will often, if not usually, be those in which wealth protection turns
> into wealth denial. If those engaged with trusts are to ensure the legitimate benefits provided
> by trusts, I would also suggest that they should seek to ensure that wealth denial is not seen as
> part of this protection.[87]

It is inherent in the nature of discretionary trusts that until the trustees exercise their discre-   **9.135**
tion a beneficiary has no interest of value[88] and until the trustees exercise their discretion in his favour an object of a power of appointment is not a beneficiary.

Reliance on this position to deny that the trust can be a nuptial asset is misplaced as it is   **9.136**
highly likely that a spouse will challenge it. Currently, a possible interest in a discretionary trust is regarded as potentially being capital for divorce purposes and it can be considered as a resource[89] if a trustee would be likely to advance capital or pay income immediately or in the foreseeable future.[90] The court will take into account, when assessing such interests, the likelihood of the beneficiary receiving a distribution ('the reasonable expectation of the beneficiary'[91]). This concept was reviewed by the Court of Appeal in *Charman v Charman*.[92] Having noted that it was easy to characterize such an interest as a resource, Wilson LJ went on to consider what a resource should be in this context:

---

[85] [1995] 3 All ER 257.
[86] *A v A* [2007] 2 FLR 467 (per Munby J).
[87] Moylan LJ in his paper to the Trust Law Committee Conference, April 2012.
[88] 'As I have said, a discretionary beneficiary has no proprietary interest in the fund. But under s.25 the court looks at resources; not just at ownership...The question is not one of control of resources; it is one of access to them' (per Lewison J in *Whaley v Whaley* [2011] EWCA Civ 617).
[89] Section 25(2)(a) MCA 1973.
[90] *Whaley v Whaley* (n 88).
[91] *B v B (Financial Provision)* [1982] 3 FLR 298.
[92] [2006] WTLR 1.

> In my view, when properly focused, that central question is simply whether, if the husband were to request it to advance the whole (or part) of the capital of the trust to him, the trustee would be likely to do so.
>
> In other cases the question has been formulated in terms of whether the spouse has real or effective control over the trust...But, unless...there is ground for doubting whether the trustee is properly discharging its duties or would be likely to do so, it seems to me on reflection that such a formulation is not entirely apposite...in most cases there seems no reason to doubt that the duties of the trustees are being, and will continue to be, discharged properly...
>
> A trustee—in proper 'control' of the trust—will usually be acting entirely properly if, after careful consideration of all relevant circumstances, he resolves in good faith to accede to a request by the settlor for the exercise of his power of advancement of capital, whether back to the settlor or to any other beneficiary.

9.137 The judge continued to distinguish his conclusion in one small regard from that reached in *Browne v Browne*[93] where this question had been addressed as one of 'immediate access to the funds' rather than 'effective control'. Rather than 'immediate', Wilson LJ preferred the test to be whether or not the trustee would be likely to advance the capital 'immediately or in the foreseeable future'.

9.138 In determining whether or not trust funds are available in this way, the history of the trust will be examined in order to establish how the trustees have exercised their discretion.[94] In *Charman*,[95] the argument was put forward that the Dragon Trust in Bermuda (value £68m) was a dynastic trust established for future generations. In rejecting this argument the court noted the lack of any such references in any of the letters of wishes. More importantly, even if the dynastic intention could have been shown to exist, the court would have been incorrect if it found that the assets were not available as a resource. The terms of the trust clearly encompassed that funds could be advance to the husband and the court confirmed that in this regard it is the terms of the trust and not any letters of wishes which determine the availability of funds.

9.139 Finding that an interest in a discretionary trust is a resource does not, of itself, determine that provision can be made from it. Unless the trust is caught by s.37 or s.24 it is not open to a court to make an order forcing the trustee to distribute the trust. Instead, the court can take the resource into account when establishing the overall value available, which then encourages the trustee to advance assets from the trust to one party. Although such an order can be said to encourage the trustee, it is a fine line between encouraging and placing improper pressure on the trustee.[96] An example of improper pressure would be where the terms of the order would leave the trustees with little alternative but to comply (unless they were to ignore the urgent needs of a member of their discretionary class, which in all probability put them in breach of trust).

9.140 To put this in context, the relevant considerations for a trustee's powers are that he[97]

- must consider the exercise of his powers from time to time;
- must consciously exercise his own discretion in good faith and not blindly follow the wishes of the settlor his co-trustees;

---

[93] [1989] 1 FLR 291 (the judgment of Butler-Sloss LJ).
[94] *Browne v Browne* [1989] 1 FLR 291; *B v B (Financial Provision)* (n 91).
[95] [2006] WTLR 1.
[96] *Howard v Howard* [1945] P 1; *B v B (Financial Provision)* (n 91).
[97] See generally *Underhill and Hayton: Law of Trusts and Trustees* (n 54), Article 61.

- must exercise his discretions, within the scope of the power, for the purpose for which they were conferred on him;
- must not exercise his discretions perversely to any sensible expectation of the settlor;
- must act fairly between the beneficiaries;
- must exercise his distributive discretions responsibly in an informed fashion, taking account of relevant matters and ignoring relevant matters.

It would be unusual circumstances where a trustee, if considering the powers he has in the light of the above, would be disinclined to distribute at least part of the trust to those left in need. But, nonetheless, there are trusts where value, in particular, will make for more difficult decision making. **9.141**

The trustee must of course have regard to the interests of other trust beneficiaries, as must the court when considering the terms of any judicial encouragement to the trustees. In particular the court must have regard to the interests of any beneficiary when a request from them could be expected to result in some provision. In *Thomas v Thomas*[98] it was said that **9.142**

> If on the balance of probability the evidence shows that, if trustees exercised their discretion to release more capital or income to a husband, the interests of the trust or of other beneficiaries would not be appreciably damaged, the court can assume that a genuine request for the exercise of such a discretion would probably be met by a favourable response.
>
> In that situation if the court decides that it would be reasonable for a husband to seek to persuade trustees to release more capital or income to him to enable him to make proper financial provision for his children and former wife, the court would not in so deciding be putting improper pressure on the trustees.

Judicial encouragement is still an area being developed. The court has already recognized the problem that would arise were it to be able to make orders that could only be met if the trustee advanced funds.[99] **9.143**

Local authorities

It is outside the scope of this work to examine all of the issues surrounding financing of care for the elderly, particularly given the inconsistencies of approach between different local authorities. However, given the determination of some clients to preserve wealth from financing their care in old age, many clients either want to use trusts for this purpose or receive advice to use them. The danger for advisers is that with escalating costs, changes to local authorities' approaches are likely, as indeed are changes to the current law. **9.144**

Where there is deliberate deprivation of capital[100] that occurs within six months before the person first approached the local authority for funding assistance, s.21 Health and Social Services and Social Security Adjudications Act 1983 (HASSASSA) gives a local authority the power to **9.145**

---

[98] [1995] 2 FLR 668.
[99] 'What happens if the person being encouraged says very politely "Thank you for your encouragement, but I have decided not to assist"? Or as here "I am only prepared to assist to such and such an extent"...Is the court supposed to ignore that stance and simply make an award on the basis that the assistance will be given?...What happens if and when it is not?...How is the court supposed to enforce its order?...It could hardly be said that the payer is in wilful default justifying a penalty under the Debtors Act 1869. It is for this reason that I expressed the view during argument that often the so-called "judicial" encouragement can turn out to be no more than empty rhetoric' (per Mostyn J in *TL v ML* [2006] 1 FLR 1263 at [85]).
[100] In order to treat transfers as deliberate deprivation, *Charging for Residential Accommodation Guide* (April 2011 at [6.070]) offers the advice:

recover care costs from the person to whom the asset was transferred. This section cannot apply to deliberate deprivation of capital more than six months before the first approach.

9.146 Where there is deliberate deprivation of capital that occurs more than six months before the person first approached the local authority for funding assistance, the HASSASSA power (above) is not available to a local authority. However, it can seek to recover sums owed in care fees by using the Insolvency Act 1986 powers (see the above section on creditors' rights).

Proper law

9.147 Where it is advised that a trust be created in this jurisdiction, by a settlor with a connection to another jurisdiction, careful consideration must be given to the question of which body of law applies to the settlor, ie his personal law (the body of law that applies to his personal estate), which arises through his connection with that other jurisdiction. This may be a body of law that attaches by virtue of his nationality, his habitual residence, or for common law countries, his domicile. If he is connected to another jurisdiction that has rules of forced or mandatory inheritance, the danger is that, if there is insufficient wealth at his death to meet the forced heirship provision, then the heirs under those provisions will seek to claw back all, or sufficient, of the settled funds to provide for their inheritance.[101] The tests for the extent to which property can be recovered are complex and outside the scope of this work (as are the difficult areas that arise when more than one jurisdiction claims competence).[102]

Defective formalities

9.148 The validity of a trust may be absent where

- the formalities have not been complied with;
- in the case of a trust of land, generally, it is not evidenced in writing;[103]
- the three certainties are absent (*Knight v Knight*[104]);
- execution of the deed is defective;
- the trust offends the rule against perpetuities;[105]
- the deed is void for uncertainty;[106]
- the trust was not completely constituted. An express trust is said to be completely constituted when the trust property has been transferred to the trustees. Thus, for a voluntary settlement where the subject matter is not transferred the trust will not have come into existence;[107]

'The timing of the disposal should be taken into account when considering the purpose of the disposal. It would be unreasonable to decide that a resident had disposed of an asset in order to reduce his charge for accommodation when the disposal took place at a time when he was fit and healthy and could not have foreseen the need for a move to residential accommodation.'

[101] *Re Annesley* [1926] Ch 692.

[102] See, eg *Lewin on Trusts*, 18th edition (Sweet & Maxwell, 2009) section 11 on this question and on the application of *The Recognition of Trusts Act 1987* and the *Hague Convention on the Law Applicable to Trusts and on Their Recognition*.

[103] Section 53(1) Law of Property Act 1925. Although generally a trust need not be in writing, from the point of view of evidential value of its existence and terms (and clarity of knowledge and approval of its terms by the settlor) a written trust deed is much the preferred solution.

[104] (1840) 3 Beav 148.

[105] eg attempting to create a perpetual trust for an unincorporated association or a trust for the maintenance of a pet exceeding 21 years.

[106] eg *Re Double Happiness Trust, Grant Thornton Stonehage Ltd v Ward* (n 34).

[107] Not overlooking the possibility of perfection of the gift under the rule in *Strong v Bird* (1874) LR 18 Eq 315.

- the trust is for an invalid purpose;[108]
- the settlor was not the owner of the property settled.

The settlor must intend to create a trust, ie it will not be valid if the settlor executes   **9.149**
the deed

- as a result of fraud or duress. If a trust has been obtained by deception, fraud, or by deliberately obtaining a settlement from someone who manifestly lacks capacity, the trust will not be valid. There is the realistic prospect that there may be criminal acts on the part of the person procuring the invalid settlement and that brings into play the Proceeds of Crime Act 2002 as well;
- in ignorance or by mistake;
- by misrepresentation or undue influence.

A minor can create a trust that is beneficial to him, but it is voidable. Whether or not a minor   **9.150**
could create a trust that is not beneficial to him is much less clear.

Capacity

A settlor must have the requisite mental capacity to make the disposition and enter into the   **9.151**
trust deed. For a person not subject to an order under s.16 and s.18 Mental Capacity Act
2005, the test is whether or not the settlor has the capacity to understand the transaction
when it is explained to him. The level of comprehension required is relative to the complexity, size, and circumstances of the transaction.[109] The test of capacity is specific to the individual and to the act in question.[110] The greater the proportion of the estate being gifted, the
greater the understanding required:

> In the circumstances, it seems to me that the law is this. The degree or extent of understanding required in respect of any instrument is relative to the particular transaction which it is to effect. In the case of a will the degree required is always high. In the case of a contract, a deed made for consideration or a gift inter vivos, whether by deed or otherwise, the degree required varies with the circumstances of the transaction. Thus, at one extreme, if the subject matter and value of a gift are trivial in relation to the donor's other assets a low degree of understanding will suffice. But, at the other extreme, if its effect is to dispose of the donor's only asset of value and thus, for practical purposes, to pre-empt the devolution of his estate under his will or on his intestacy, then the degree of understanding required is as high as that required for a will, and the donor understands the claims of all potential donees and the extent of the property to be disposed of.[111]

If a person creates an *inter vivos* settlement while subject to a subsisting order under s.16 and   **9.152**
s.18 Mental Capacity Act 2005, the settlement will not be valid, even if it was made during
what was clearly a lucid interval. For such a disposition to be valid it would conflict with the
court's control over that person's affairs. An attorney acting under a lasting power of attorney
has no power to make gifts in excess of those permitted by statute[112] and cannot therefore
create a settlement on behalf of a donor without the direction of the court. Similarly with

---

[108] eg immoral (*Blodwell v Edwards* (1596) Cro Eliz 509) or criminal purposes or is contrary to public policy (*A-G v Pearson* (1817) 3 Mer 353).
[109] *Re Beaney* [1978] 1 WLR 770; *Hammond v Osborne* [2002] WTLR 1125.
[110] *Masterman-Lister v Brutton* [2003] WTLR 259.
[111] *Re Beaney* (n 109).
[112] Section 12 Mental Capacity Act 2005.

an enduring power of attorney, once registered, the power does not permit gifts of any substance[113] except by direction of the court.

9.153 Where a settlor has the mental capacity to create the settlement when the instructions are given, but by the time of execution he lacks sufficient capacity, the settlement may still be validly executed. If the settlor gave the instructions when he had capacity and when he executes the deed he has sufficient capacity to recollect that he previously gave such instructions (and the deed embodies his instructions) the execution is saved by application of the rule in *Parker v Felgate*.[114]

9.154 Where there is doubt as to the mental capacity of a settlor, or he is elderly or ill, the guidance given by Templeman J in *Re Simpson*,[115] which has since become known as the Golden Rule, is relevant. Although the Golden Rule was put forward to guide will draftsmen it is a good guide to trust draftsmen as well:

> In the case of an aged testator or a testator who has suffered a serious illness, there is one golden rule which should always be observed, however straightforward matters may appear and however difficult or tactless it may be to suggest that precautions be taken: the making of a will by such a testator ought to be witnessed or approved by a medical practitioner who satisfied himself of the capacity and understanding of the testator, and records and preserves his examination and finding.

> There are other precautions which should be taken. If the testator has made an earlier will this should be considered by the legal and medical advisers of the testator, and if appropriate, discussed with the testator. The instructions of the testator should be taken in the absence of anyone who may stand to benefit, or who may have influence over the testator. These are not counsels of perfection. If proper precautions are not taken injustice may result or be imagined and great expense and misery may be unnecessarily caused.

Anti-money laundering/counter terrorist financing

9.155 There are powers in Part 5 Proceeds of Crime Act 2002 (POCA 2002) for the Serious Organised Crime Agency (SOCA) to recover property obtained through unlawful conduct. Recovery is effected through High Court civil proceedings against anyone who holds the proceeds of crime property or, where the nature of the property has changed, the property that now represents it. It is not necessary for there to have been a criminal conviction concerning the acquisition of the property.[116]

9.156 There are, in addition, powers for confiscation orders to be made.[117] Such an order may be made for a sum of money equal to the proceeds of crime. This is not an order for the confiscation of the specific criminal property, but for a sum equal to the value of the criminal property. Pending such an order, an interim restraining order prohibiting a specified person from dealing with property held by him can be obtained.[118] Such orders can be made against trustees.

9.157 These powers can be used to recover the proceeds of crime from *inter vivos* and testamentary trusts.

---

[113] Schedule 4 para 3(3) Mental Capacity Act 2005.
[114] (1883) LR 8PD 171, extended to *inter vivos* deeds in *Re Singellos* [2011] WTLR 327.
[115] (1977) 127 NLJ 487.
[116] *Director of the Assets Recovery Agency v Taher* [2006] EWHC 3406.
[117] Section 6 POCA 2002.
[118] Section 41 POCA 2002.

There are powers to recover terrorist property following a conviction for terrorist offences **9.158** connected with terrorist finances and money laundering.[119]

Joint property

The settlement of property where the settlor is the sole legal owner is not free from challenge. **9.159** Where joint property exists, either as a beneficial joint tenancy or a tenancy in common, the legal title is always held in the form of a joint tenancy. Therefore, after the death of one co-owner the property will have the outward appearance of sole ownership, unless another co-owner is appointed as trustee of the title. The surviving co-owner will have the outward appearance of being able to settle such property as the sole legal owner.

The position will be more straightforward for land given the greater ease, even with unreg- **9.160** istered land, of identifying the existence of equitable interests in it. Of more difficulty will be the position where land is in the sole legal ownership of one person and a second person has acquired an equitable interest in the property, eg where land is acquired in one name and a second has contributed part of the acquisition cost but no gift was made or intended, or where there are equitable rights of cohabitants who no longer reside in the property. The purported settlement of property will be ineffective, at least to the extent of that other person's interest. This highlights the need for the adviser to check on the nature of ownership of assets proposed for settlement.

Similar issues could arise where there are claims of proprietary estoppel against the property **9.161** that is intended to be settled, as there is no obvious reason why a settlement of such property cannot be challenged if the settlement is used as a shield against the claim and there are insufficient other assets to meet the award.[120]

Settlor is a constructive trustee for another

Where a person holds property as a constructive trustee for another he cannot validly settle **9.162** it upon trust for his own purposes. This has relevance in particular where a fiduciary may be seeking to conceal unauthorized profits in an *inter vivos* settlement.

Where a trustee has made an unauthorized profit from his trusteeship he will have personal **9.163** liability for his breach of trust,[121] but also have a proprietary obligation to account to the trust beneficiaries as a constructive trustee for any profit he may have made.[122] Typically this will arise with those traditionally treated as fiduciaries: trustees, company directors, partners, and agents. However, the categories that can be considered to be fiduciaries are not closed. Constructive trusts will, for example, be imposed on those in public office who accept bribes. In *A-G for Hong Kong v Reid*[123] Lord Templeman observed that

> bribery is an evil practice which threatens the foundations of any civilised society. In particular bribery by policemen and prosecutors brings the administration of justice into disrepute. Where bribes are accepted by a trustee, servant, agent or other fiduciary, loss and damage are caused to the beneficiaries, master or principal whose interests have been betrayed.

---

[119] Section 23 Terrorism Act 2000.
[120] The minimum equity to do justice to the claim: *Crabb v Arun DC* [1976] Ch 179.
[121] *Target Holdings v Redferns* [1996] 1 AC 421.
[122] *Boardman v Phipps* [1967] 2 AC 46.
[123] [1994] 1 AC 324.

Although this is put in the context of bribes, secret commissions and unauthorized profits are also within the ambit of this principle.

9.164 The use of a trust to conceal and attempt to retain these profits will not be effective and the property can be recovered by the beneficiaries of the constructive trust. The difficulty for the adviser when the trust is being created is that ignoring any suspicions of the true provenance of the property potentially exposes the adviser to having committed a money-laundering offence where the breach of the fiduciary duty was also a crime.

9.165 **Setting aside a settlement for mistake** A trust may be set aside in its entirety on the grounds of mistake. This area has been the subject of review by the Supreme Court in *Pitt v Holt; Futter v Futter*.[124]

9.166 In *Pitt v Holt* the late husband of the claimant had been very badly injured in a road accident. His personal injury claim was compromised by way of (amongst other things) a lump sum and an annuity. His wife, who had been appointed his receiver, sought professional advice and placed the damages into a discretionary trust for the husband's benefit with the authorization of the Court of Protection. The transfer into the settlement incurred an immediate charge to inheritance tax as well as ten-yearly charges that could have been avoided if the trust had been drafted so as to fall within the definition of a disabled trust.[125]

9.167 Based on the previous principles which had developed with regard to voluntary mistake the judge at first instance and the Court of Appeal refused to set aside the trust.

9.168 The Supreme Court held that to set aside on the grounds of mistake 'the true requirement is simply for there to be a causative mistake of sufficient gravity' and that 'the test will normally be satisfied only when there is a mistake as to the legal character or nature of the transaction, or as to some matter of fact or law that is basic to the transaction'. Lord Walker emphasized that a mistake had to be distinguished from mere ignorance or inadvertence and what academics call misprediction.[126] However, he made clear that ignorance or inadvertence could give rise to a false belief or assumption and urged courts of first instance not to shrink from drawing the inference of conscious belief or tacit assumption from the fact. He also emphasized that the court had to consider whether it would be unconscionable not to set aside the transaction on the grounds of mistake. He drew interesting parallels with the law of proprietary estoppel.

9.169 As far as mistake as to the taxation consequences of the disposition are concerned, they will be relevant to the gravity of the transaction. But there were words of warning that artificial tax avoidance schemes may lead to a court refusing relief on grounds of mistake—'either on the ground that such claimants, acting on supposedly expert advice, must be taken to have accepted the risk that the scheme would prove ineffective, or on the ground that discretionary relief should be refused on grounds of public policy' (*WT Ramsay Ltd v IRC*,[127] in which Lord Walker observed 'an increasingly strong and general recognition that artificial tax avoidance is a social evil which puts an unfair burden on the shoulders of those who do not adopt such measures').

---

[124] [2013] UKSC 26; and as a consequence of this decision the previous test in *Gibbon v Mitchell* [1990] 3 All ER 338 with its distinction between effect and consequence is no longer to be applied.
[125] Section 89 Inheritance Tax Act 1984.
[126] At [104].
[127] [1982] AC 300.

While it is not entirely clear what impact this last principle will have on the law of volun- **9.170**
tary mistake, there is clearly scope for trusts to be set aside if they have unfortunate tax
consequences.

The court will also be prepared to set aside a settlement where the deed was executed as **9.171**
a consequence of fraud and misrepresentation.[128] An adviser or draftsman needs to be as
alert for this in connection with trusts as he would be for the issue in connection with will
preparation.

Rectification   Trust deeds that through an error of drafting do not correctly reflect the **9.172**
settlor's intention can be rectified by the court.

The settlor in *Allnutt v Wilding*[129] was eighty-two in 1995 and he relied on his son-in-law **9.173**
(the first claimant) in business matters. The first claimant consulted the defendant solicitor
as the settlor wished to give away £550,000 in a manner that would save IHT if he survived
the gift by seven years. A settlement was drafted which the settlor signed without reading.
The settlement was a discretionary trust for children or remoter issue born in the eighty-year
trust period.

When the settlor died in 2004, the Inland Revenue pointed out that the settlement was not **9.174**
a potentially exempt transfer (PET) and that there was therefore a chargeable transfer on its
creation. The executors of the estate (the two claimants) issued proceedings against themselves as trustees and others seeking rectification as the settlement was not what was intended
by the settlor.[130]

The court held that rectification was a discretionary remedy to correct mistakes in the **9.175**
way that a transaction was recorded. It was not part of the remedy to change the whole
substance of the transaction. Further, the court found that the settlor's instructions were
quite general in nature and that he intended to execute that which was put in front of him.
He was not labouring under any mistake as to language, meaning, terms, or effect. His
mistake was relying on defective advice and the court had no jurisdiction to remedy that
sort of mistake.

The Court of Appeal upheld these views on appeal:[131] **9.176**

> I am unable to accept the trustees' submission on the availability of rectification in this case.
> The position is that the settlor intended to execute the settlement which he in fact executed,
> conferring benefits on his three children. The settlement correctly records his intention to
> benefit them through the medium of a trust rather than the alternative of making direct gifts
> in their favour. I am unable to see any mistake by the settlor in the recording of his intentions
> in the settlement. The mistake of the settlor and his advisers was in believing that the nature
> of the trusts declared in the settlement . . . created a situation in which the subsequent transfer
> of funds by him to the trustees would qualify as a PET and could, if he survived long enough,
> result in the saving of inheritance tax. That sort of mistake about the potential fiscal effects of a
> payment following the execution of the settlement does not . . . satisfy the necessary conditions
> for grant of rectification.

---

[128] *Lady Hood of Avalon v McKinnon* [1909] 1 Ch 354; *Bullock v Lloyds Bank* [1954] 3 All ER 338; *Gibbon v Mitchell* (n 124).

[129] [2006] WTLR 1317 (Ch); see also *Gibbon v Mitchell* (n 124).

[130] Suing oneself (even in a different capacity) was an incorrect step and they were struck out as defendants.

[131] *Allnutt v Wilding* [2007] EWCA Civ 412.

Chapter 9: Introduction and New Business

9.177 **Taxation advice and the settlor** There is little doubt that there is a duty of care owed to the settlor in respect of the taxation advice given to him to support a recommendation to create a trust. If the taxation consequences for the settlor are such as to create an unwanted liability for him or to leave him without the advised tax saving, the potential for a claim exists. There equally seems little doubt that a similar duty of care is owed in advising a settlor on the appropriate form of trust to be used. This is not to say that a liability must arise as much will depend upon

- the standard of care appropriate to the client and the transaction;
- the foreseeability of the taxation liability; and
- the terms of the retainer.

9.178 In *Estill v Cowling Swift & Kitchen*[132] Mrs Estill, who was in her eighties, was the controlling shareholder of a substantial private company. She owned 1,100 of the 1,120 issued shares. She had no issue and was intending to give each of her five nephews and nieces 100 shares from her shareholding; however, she did not want any of the five involved in the management of the company as long as she and the existing directors were alive.

9.179 In 1988 Mrs Estill sought the advice of a partner of the defendant solicitors' firm on the matter, making it quite clear that while she was not worried about tax liabilities on her death, she did not want to pay any significant tax on any lifetime gifts. Although the partner (of some forty years' experience) was familiar with wills and trusts, it was estimated that this was no more than 15 per cent of his work. He sought the advice of counsel (the second defendant) on her wishes. The advice was that a discretionary settlement was appropriate and one was drafted by counsel and executed in 1988.

9.180 The discretionary settlement, as executed, did not meet Mrs Estill's requirements in two significant ways. First, the beneficiaries did not have fixed interests and second, the class was not limited to the nephews and nieces. However, counsel had not advised that this settlement would trigger an immediate IHT charge and the solicitor was not aware that this was the case and thought that the transfer was a PET. In 1990 Mrs Estill received, and paid, a £185,000 IHT bill. The settlor was shocked at the size of the bill and was adamant that had she been advised that an assessment of this size would become payable then she would not have created the settlement.

The court found that:

9.181 (1) **There was a duty of care owed by both the solicitor and counsel to both the settlor and the trustees** The duty was to both the settlor and trustees because both would be affected by it (immediate charge and ten-year charge). This was so even though when the advice was given the individual identity of the trustees was not known.

9.182 (2) **That the solicitor owed a duty of care to the settlor** Mrs Estill was elderly and lacked detailed knowledge of trusts and tax. The advice he was called upon to give was within the knowledge expected of a reasonably competent solicitor and it was reasonable to expect such a solicitor to have taken steps to obtain the knowledge if he was unsure. His instructions were not merely to relay Mrs Estill's instructions to counsel and to argue that they would have required him to show express terms to that effect. Further, the

---

[132] [2000] WTLR 417.

solicitor's act of negligence was not exonerated by the subsequent act of negligence by counsel.[133]

(3) That counsel owed a duty of care to the solicitor Although the court did not set the **9.183**
standard of care to be that of a tax specialist, it was found that the tax knowledge required
for the particular issue was within that to be reasonably expected of a barrister in general
Chancery practice.

In a failed rectification case, *Bartlam v Coutts*,[134] the defendant bank had advised the claim- **9.184**
ant to set up an accumulation and maintenance settlement for his children in order to mitigate tax. A standard-form trust deed was prepared and executed. It was discovered that
instead of age twenty-five for attainment, thirty had been inserted into the deed. There was
no apparent reason for this, but as long as it remained there the settlement did not qualify
under s.71 Inheritance Tax Act 1984.

The bank's file did not explain matters nor was it possible to identify how, or why, or by **9.185**
whom, this age was inserted into the deed. There was sufficient evidence to show the settlor's
clear intention and that he was mistaken in his belief that he was executing a deed which
qualified for tax benefits under s.71, and rectification was ordered:[135]

> whether or not Coutts & Co had been negligent or not, and I have to say that this [evidence]
> confirms my instinctive view of Coutts & Co's inadequate performance in the services that
> they provided to their client, should not have any impact on whether or not the trust ought to
> be rectified. It was probably in that light that I was told that Coutts & Co were paying for the
> entirety of this application. I can well understand their concerns in that regard.

These words, although *obiter*, clearly indicate the judge's view that if negligence had been **9.186**
a point which he was required to decide on, he would have found Coutts to have been
negligent. Coutts' decision to pay for the whole rectification action appears to indicate an
acknowledgement of a degree of culpability and a sensible economic approach to resolution.

There is another Canadian case worthy of comment here and that is *Rosenberg Estate v* **9.187**
Black,[136] which, although it also involved a claim of negligence for the delay in preparing
a will, also involved delay in implementing an estate plan which had been prepared by the
defendant. (There is clear English authority that delay in such matters, where the settlor cannot decide how to proceed, does not lead to liability for the solicitor.[137]) The defendants were
found not liable on the facts, but the judgment does seem to tacitly accept that tardiness in
carrying out this work could have produced a liability.

---

[133] In this case the court quoted with approval Sir Thomas Bingham MR in *Ridehalgh v Horsefield* [1994]
3 All ER 848: 'We endorse the guidance given on the subject in *Locke v Camberwell Health Authority* [1991] 2
Med LR 249. A solicitor does not abdicate his professional responsibility when he seeks the advice of counsel.
He must apply his mind to the advice received. But the more specialist the nature of the advice, the more reasonable is it likely to be for a solicitor to accept and act on it.'

[134] [2006] WTLR 1165.

[135] The judge was following his own decision in *Martin v Nicholson* [2005] WTLR 175.

[136] 2001 Carswell Ont 4504 (Ont SCL, 19 December 2001).

[137] *Trusted v Clifford Chance* [2000] WTLR 1219.

10

NEUTRALITY OF PRs AND TRUSTEES

A. Neutrality

Both PRs and trustees are fiduciaries. A fiduciary is someone who has undertaken to act for **10.01** or on behalf of another in a particular matter, in circumstances which give rise to a relationship of trust and confidence. The key obligation of a fiduciary is the obligation of loyalty. It follows from this that

- the fiduciary must act in good faith;
- he must not make a profit out of his trust;
- he must not place himself in a position where his duty and interest may conflict; and
- he may not act for his own benefit or the benefit of a third party without the informed consent of his principal.

The non-professional PR or trustee will usually be unaware of these principles, and the constraints **10.02** that they place on him in acting as PR or trustee, and he will therefore need guidance on them from his professional advisers. However, there are many areas of conflict that can have implications for the unaware professional as well and some more common examples are commented on below.

A PR's role in Inheritance (Provision for Family and Dependants) Act 1975 claims

I(PFD)A 1975 claims made on the basis that a will or intestacy makes inadequate provision[1] **10.03** should not be lodged until after a grant of representation has been issued[2] and then within

---

[1] For someone within the classes set out in s.1(1) I(PFD)A 1975.
[2] *Re McBroom (deceased)* [1992] 2 FLR 49. A grant for these purposes does not include a limited grant which does not permit the distribution of the estate such as an *ad colligenda* grant or an *ad litem* grant.

a six-month window after the grant.[3] Given that a grant has been issued a PR will then be a party to the action, but to what extent?

10.04   The role of the PR in such a matter is to assist the court with the provision of information.[4] After (1) returning the acknowledgement of service, the PR must (2) file a witness statement with the court, within twenty-one days of the service of the claim form on him. The witness statement should

- give full particulars of the net estate;[5]
- set out details of the beneficial interests in the estate, giving names and addresses of all living beneficiaries and the value of their interests if known;
- state if a beneficiary is known to be a minor or a patient;[6] and
- give any information that the PR has which might affect the exercise of the court's discretion.[7]

10.05   All of the above information should be given to the best of the PR's belief and ability. The PR is not bound to expend money in making further researches into information not yet known to him, or in further verification of what he already knows. It is, however, reasonable and helpful for the PR to continue any existing enquiries that will produce information in time or to make such enquiries as can easily establish helpful information. There is no cost risk to the PR in complying with these requirements.

10.06   PRs will sometime rush to defend the terms of the will that they have proved, on the basis that their duty to execute the terms of the will extends to defending the beneficial interests in it from attack. It does not; and taking such a partisan role in the litigation can expose the PR to having a substantial part of his costs disallowed. A solicitor may be instructed by some, or all, of the beneficiaries under a will and will then seek to bring pressure to bear on the PR to take an active role in defending the will or will offer to jointly represent the beneficiaries and the PR. Both approaches seem confused as to where the cost burden should correctly fall and therefore also have very real costs risks for the PR.

10.07   It is therefore far safer for the PR's legal representation to be independent of that of the parties with beneficial interests or claims and for the PR's solicitors to represent only that interest.[8] The solicitors will have an important further role to play in advising the PR of the practicality of any compromise agreement and ensuring that the terms of any order are capable of being put into effect by the PR.[9] Also, if the contending parties accept the PR's solicitors in the role, they may act as facilitator or broker between the parties, provided that it is acknowledged that the additional costs will be accepted and not be challenged.

---

[3] Section 4 I(PFD)A 1975; but late applications will be permitted at the court's discretion: see *Re Salmon* [1981] Ch 167 for the factors that will be considered in a late application.

[4] Rule 57.16(5) CPR as supplemented by para 16 PD 57.

[5] The definition of the net estate is to be found at s.25(1) I(PFD)A 1975.

[6] Within the meaning of r.21.1(2) CPR.

[7] This can cover a wide diversity of information: information about domicile that might prevent the claim, statements made by the testator about the dispositions in the will, lifetime dispositions, and information about the standing of the claimant to make a claim.

[8] This need not be the case where the PR is the sole beneficiary of the estate.

[9] Also they should ensure that the proposals make correct and adequate provision for the PR's costs. The practicality point is worth stressing as negotiations can easily overlook the practical consequences of the agreed

Where the PR also has a beneficial interest in the estate, care should be taken to keep the two **10.08** interests separate (unless the PR is entitled to the entire estate).[10]

There may also be cases where the estate is held wholly or partly on discretionary trusts and it **10.09** is the trustees of those trusts who, far from being able to take the neutral stance which executors can take, have to defend an action and decide on what basis to compromise it. None of the beneficiaries of the trust has any guarantee of benefit under the will and they may have conflicts with other beneficiaries. Like all trustees they can seek the directions of the court under the *Beddoe* jurisdiction[11] in an appropriate case. As an alternative the court may sometimes appoint a beneficiary to represent the class and defend the claim.

The use of caveats[12] to gain time in matters where an I(PFD)A 1975 claim is intended has **10.10** been criticized. In *Re Parnall*[13] the court commented:

> [The claimant's solicitors] had entered a caveat against the estate. Given that the intention of [the claimant's solicitors] was to mount a claim under the Inheritance Act, this was wholly inappropriate. It is elementary that the only proper object of a caveat is to prevent the issue of a grant in respect of a testamentary paper which, on the caveator's case, is not the valid will of the deceased. To enter a caveat where the caveator's intention is to make an Inheritance Act claim is wholly wrong: first because, ex hypothesi, the validity of the will is admitted; second, because a delay in the grant of probate entails a corresponding delay in getting the caveator's claim on foot.

The routine use of caveats in matters where an I(PFD)A 1975 claim is intended is an abuse of **10.11** process that can readily lead to a worsening of relations between the parties. It also appears, on the face of it, contrary to r.1.1(2)(b) CPR on saving expense and r.1.1(2)(d) CPR on ensuring that a matter is dealt with expeditiously.

Where different interests in the estate are opposed

Potential litigation in an administration can place the PR in a difficult position if two dif- **10.12** ferent interests in the estate have two different interests in the litigation. In *Re Clough*[14] the testatrix had specifically bequeathed a chattel to the defendant, with the residue of her estate then bequeathed to seven charities. After the death of the testatrix, the chattel was removed from the house by a third party who alleged that the testatrix had given the chattel to him during her lifetime.

The specific legatee claimed that it was the duty of the executor to resolve the dispute,[15] **10.13** recover the chattel, and deliver it to her as the legatee entitled to it under the will (the terms of which the executor was obliged to carry out). The residuary legatees maintained that the

---

points. For this see *Stephanides v Cohen* [2002] WTLR 1373 where the incidence of tax led to a failure in the compromise agreement when in the final analysis no IHT was payable. Costs finally reached £250,000.

[10] See *Re Rochelle (deceased) (costs)* [2003] WTLR 1483 for the general risk in costs matters of confusing the relative positions of PRs with a material interest and PRs with a neutral position.

[11] In accordance with the procedure set out in Part 64 of the Civil Procedure Rules.

[12] 'A caveat is a notice in writing lodged in the Principle Registry of the Family Division, or in any district probate registry or sub-registry, by a person wishing to show cause against the sealing of a grant, that no grant is to be sealed in the estate of the deceased named therein without notice to the person who has entered the caveat (NCPR 44)' (*Tristram and Coote's Probate Practice*, 30th edition (LexisNexis, 2008) 676).

[13] *Re Parnall, Parnall v Hurst* [2003] WTLR 997.

[14] *Re Clough Taylor, Coutts v Banks* [2003] WTLR 15.

[15] Section 25 Administration of Estates Act 1925.

executor should not resolve the dispute at the expense of the estate, effectively their expense, as the costs of litigation would fall against the residue of the estate (ie in a part of the estate in which the specific legatee had no financial interest). As the charities had no interest in the outcome of the dispute, but would be risking any irrecoverable litigation costs, they argued that it was against their interests for the dispute to be resolved in this way. They sought to have the executor assign what rights the estate had in the chattel to the specific legatee and then the legatee could enforce them (or compromise them) on whatever terms he was prepared to accept and at whatever costs he was prepared to risk.

10.14 The court held that the executor, in carrying out its obligations under statute and the will (collect in the estate and administer it according to law), was not required to take anything other than normal or routine steps to collect and deliver assets. The executor was not bound to issue proceedings for recovery unless this was at the legatee's expense. It would therefore be proper for the executor to assent the asset in favour of the legatee and assign the cause of action so that she could enforce title at her own financial risk. This decision appears to be both just and useful to the PR.

10.15 The same issue in trust litigation can be found in *Breadner v Granville-Grossman (costs)*.[16] In earlier litigation[17] the trustees adopted a partisan role, siding with one group of beneficiaries against the interest of the others.[18] The trustees lost the litigation. The burden of the costs was awarded against the trustees—who therefore bore the costs personally.[19] The trustees should undoubtedly have sought protection from the court before the action by way of a *Beddoe*[20] application, which would almost certainly have failed to gain them protection, thus giving a clue of the potentially dangerous course that they were following.

Assignment of a right of action

10.16 A PR can assign other rights of action, for example to a sole residuary legatee, where it may be more expedient for the legatee to pursue the matter with his own advisers—or simply where this may be the most cost-effective method of taking the litigation forward.[21] Similarly, where there is a choice as to who might make the claim, it will generally be financially more advantageous for the beneficial interests to make it.

10.17 An example of this is a claim under the Fatal Accident Act 1976 arising out of the death of the testator. The PR has a right to bring a claim for the benefit of spouse, former spouse, parent or child of the deceased, sibling, aunt, or uncle, including their issue both adopted and illegitimate,[22] but are they the most appropriate persons to do so?

10.18 The PR has no beneficial interest in the claim and if he does not bring the claim within six months then the person for whose benefit it might be brought can bring the claim. There

---

[16] [2006] WTLR 411.

[17] *Breadner v Granville-Grossman* [2000] WTLR 829.

[18] Ignoring the risks of such a course: see *Alsop Wilkinson v Neary* [1996] 1 WLR 1220 at 1225.

[19] And the total costs of the action were into six figures. See also *Shovelar v Lane* [2011] WTLR 1411.

[20] *Re Beddoe* [1893] 1 Ch 547. See also *Shovelar v Lane* (n 19) for the severe costs risk of the partisan involvement of PRs.

[21] See *Green v Astor* [2013] EWHC 1857 (Ch) where this proved a solution when one beneficiary wanted certain causes of action pursued which the PR had been advised had no prospect of success.

[22] Section 83 Civil Partnership Act 2004 has now extended this category to include civil partner, former civil partner, a child treated as a child of a civil partnership to which the deceased was a party. *Ghaidan v Mendoza* [2004] 3 All ER 411 also extends the class of claimants to include same-sex and opposite sex cohabitants.

is a strong case to be made for the PR not choosing to pursue the claim and allowing the beneficiary (or, for a patient or minor, their representative) to bring the claim, in order to reduce the costs and allow the decisions on costs and tactics to be taken by the person who has suffered the loss.

Challenges to the validity of the will

A similar approach underlies the PR's neutral role where there is a challenge to the valid-   **10.19**
ity of the will, for example where a caveat is lodged, or in an ensuing probate action. The PR who attempts and fails to prove a will is exposed to his costs being disallowed and left with him personally (unless those potentially benefiting under the will have indem-nified the PR against this risk and it is possible to enforce the terms of the indemnity economically).[23]

The PR is on far safer ground leaving the negotiation as to possible compromise to those   **10.20**
parties with a beneficial interest in the estate and furnishing those interested parties with all relevant information in his possession that is relevant to the dispute.[24] The cost risk then lies with those who have, or are attempting to have, a beneficial interest in the estate.

Variations to the will

The PR has no duty to promote a deed of variation to the will or intestacy,[25] although it is   **10.21**
recognized that bringing it to the attention of those interested may well represent good client care. The implementation of such a deed is, however, a matter where there can be dangers for the overzealous PR. *Jemma Trust Company Ltd v Kippax Beaumont Lewis*[26] concerned in part the actions of the PR in promoting a deed of variation, including an application to the Court of Protection to implement it.

The PRs were criticized by the court for their proactive, and central, role in procuring the   **10.22**
deed of variation. Whilst it was quite clear that the terms of the deed provided benefit to an interest in remainder after a life interest, it was far from clear that the life tenant obtained any benefit from the surrender of her interest in exchange for a capital payment. The executors in pushing through the deed of variation were following the advice of the defendant firm (one of the executors was a partner of the firm). The court observed:

> 89. I agree with the Claimant that the role adopted by the executors, on the advice of KBL, in formulating and promoting the Deed of Variation, and prosecuting the Application [in the Court of Protection] was inappropriate and improper.

> 90. The role adopted by the executors inevitably placed them in an impossible position of conflict of duties. As executors, and as trustees, they owed fiduciary duties to all those bene-ficially interested in the [trust].

---

[23] The PR in this position should note as well that his costs incurred generally in the administration to date will not necessarily be recoverable if the will is not proved: see *Gray v Richards Butler* [2001] WTLR 625.

[24] The PR should also bear in mind the requirement that he assist in answering questions regarding the execution of the will and circumstances surrounding it: *Larke v Nugus* [2000] WTLR 1033. To fail to deliver a *Larke v Nugus* letter not only is a breach of professional duty, but raises the possibility of a wasted costs order against him. No better incentive to timely and full recording of attendance notes exists than the possibility that at some stage the will-drafter might be called upon to deliver a *Larke v Nugus* letter.

[25] *Cancer Research Campaign v Ernest Brown* [1997] STC 1425.

[26] [2004] EWHC 703 (Ch).

92. ... the duty of the executors and the trustees was to uphold and to enforce the trusts of the will and not to drive forward proposals for their change.[27]

10.23 The same principle guides the PR in other matters of dispute, such as construction actions.

Trustee's duty to act fairly between beneficiaries

10.24 In *Edge v Pensions Ombudsman*[28] the question of the trustee's need to act fairly between beneficial interests was considered. A trustee is sometimes said to be required to act 'equally' or 'impartially' between beneficiaries, but these words can lead to error. What is required is that a trustee considers his discretion properly and fairly and, if then the exercise of that discretion benefits one interest over another, that is no more than the proper outcome of the exercise of the trustee's discretion. There is no mathematical balance between interests, and trying to balance the exercise of discretions in order to arrive at equality for equality's sake is likely to give rise to improper exercise of the discretion.[29]

> Properly understood, the so called duty to act impartially is no more than the ordinary duty which the law imposes on a person who is entrusted with the exercise of a discretionary power: that he exercises the power for the purpose for which it is given, giving proper consideration to the matters which are relevant and excluding from consideration matters which are irrelevant. If trustees do that, they cannot be criticised if they reach a decision which appears to prefer the claims of one interest over others. The preference will be the result of a proper exercise of the discretionary power.[30]

10.25 The concept of fairness is not limited to distributive powers, but can also be found in administrative powers such as investment powers, which are also to be exercised fairly as between interests.[31]

B. Balance when investing

10.26 A trustee has a duty, when investing, to maintain fairness and act impartially, between the different classes of beneficiaries,[32] unless

- the deed expressly directs the trustee not to do so;
- where the beneficiaries, all being *sui juris*, have collectively agreed to hold the trustee free from any liability arising from not holding such a balance; or
- where the circumstances of the beneficiary, who could be considered to be the primary object, requires it.

---

[27] Notwithstanding all of the above, it was found that no loss had arisen and that the claim regarding the deed of variation was dismissed.

[28] [2000] Ch 602.

[29] eg a practice sometimes encountered is of advances to beneficiaries (under s.32 Trustee Act 1925 or an express power) being made without any real reason other than to equalize the amounts that the remaindermen have each received. There is nothing in s.32 to suggest that this by itself is a proper purpose.

[30] *Edge v Pensions Ombudsman* [2000] Ch 602 at 627.

[31] *Nestle v National Westminster Bank plc* [2000] WTLR 795.

[32] *Cowan v Scargill* [1985] 2 All ER 750 at 760F; *Re Mulligan, Hampton v PGG Trust* [1998] 1 NZLR 481 at 501; *Nestle v National Westminster Bank plc* (n 31) at 803.

This duty was expressed by Hoffmann J, as he then was, in an often quoted passage from his **10.27** first instance decision in *Nestle*:

the trustee must act fairly in making investment decisions which may have different consequences for different classes of beneficiaries. There are two reasons why I prefer this formulation to the traditional image of holding the scales equally between tenant for life and remainderman. The first is the image of the scales suggests a weighing of known quantities whereas investment decisions are concerned with predictions of the future. Investments will carry current expectations of their future income yield and capital appreciation and these expectations will be reflected in their current market price, but there is always a greater or lesser risk that the outcome will deviate from those expectations. A judgement on the fairness of the choices made by the trustees must have regard to these imponderables. The second reason is that the image of the scales suggests a more mechanistic process than I believe the law requires. The trustees have in my judgement a wide discretion. They are for example entitled to take into account the income needs of the tenant for life or the fact that the tenant for life was a person known to the settlor and a primary object of the trust whereas the remainderman is a remote relative or a stranger. Of course these cannot be allowed to become the overriding considerations, but the concept of fairness between the classes of beneficiaries does not require them to be excluded. It would be an inhuman law which required trustees to adhere to some mechanical rule for preserving the real value of the capital when the tenant for life was the testator's widow who had fallen upon hard times and the remainderman was young and well-off.[33]

On appeal this view was endorsed by Staughton LJ in the following terms: **10.28**

A life tenant may be anxious to receive the highest possible income while the remainderman will wish the real value of the fund to be preserved. If the life tenant is living in penury and the remainderman already has ample wealth common sense suggests that a trustee should be able to take that into account, not necessarily by seeking the highest possible income at the expense of capital but by inclining in that direction. However, before adopting that course a trustee should require some verification of the facts.... Similarly I would not regard it as a breach of trust for the trustees to pay some regard to the relationship between [the life tenant] and [the remainderman]. [The life tenant] was merely [the remainderman's] uncle and she would have received nothing from his share of the fund if he fathered a child who survived him. The trustees would be entitled to incline towards income during his life tenancy... I do not think it would be a breach of the duty to act fairly or impartially.[34]

From the above passages it is possible to formulate the following propositions to guide a **10.29** trustee when investing:

1. There is a need to act fairly between the different interests in a trust fund when investing, but the differing nature of interests in capital and income prevent an exact balance being maintained.
2. Circumstances can exist to justify favouring one set of interests over another, although rarely could this be to the total exclusion of one set of interests, unless those interests, with their free and fully informed consent, have agreed to the policy which excluded consideration of their interests.
3. The factors which may justify favouring one set of interests over another set can only be assessed on a case-by-case basis and, once established to the trustee's satisfaction, must

---

[33] *Nestle v National Westminster Bank plc* (n 31) at 803C–F.
[34] *Nestle v National Westminster Bank plc* [1994] 1 All ER 118 at 137.

be kept under review to see if circumstances change sufficiently for the trustees to change their policy.

4. The relationship between the settlor and the different sets of interests can be a factor that could influence the policy towards the different interests and this may in practice be directed expressly by the terms of the deed.

5. A trustee must ascertain the circumstances of all the interested beneficiaries if the circumstances of one are to be a factor in favouring that interest over another.

6. The decision of the trustee will be easier for him to justify (assuming his decision was reasonable) if he can show that the information from the preceding points has been regularly and formally assessed and recorded, and that the trustee's process for verifying it was, in the circumstances, reasonable.

7. The decision to favour one set of interests over another must, in the light of all of the above, be reasonable.

10.30 The above summary will only be relevant where there are competing interests to be balanced, and the primary example of this will be where there are different interests in capital and income, such as in the life interest trust.

10.31 In most other types of trust where the interests in capital and income are the same (such as many discretionary trusts) the overall return from the investment is the important issue (subject to the taxation considerations of the relative desirability of capital or income return). Whether or not there are competing interests will depend upon an exact reading of the terms of the trust.

C. Other issues

Manipulation of administrative powers

10.32 In *Wendt v Orr*[35] the trustee decided that profits on actively traded investments were income and distributed them as such.[36] When challenged he relied upon the power in the will to determine whether receipts or outgoings were capital or income (or partly from both). The court disagreed, and observed that the provision in the will was merely an administrative provision and not a dispositive one, and that the words capital and income bore their usual meanings.

10.33 The trustee's defence was that he had no liability because of the provision in the will which relieved liability for loss not attributable to his dishonesty or wilful commission of any act known to be a breach of trust. The trustee was found to have acted dishonestly on the basis of both of two definitions from *Walker v Stones*.[37] The court also observed that at the very least the trustee was completely indifferent to the capital beneficiaries' interests.[38]

---

[35] [2005] WTLR 223—an Australian case.
[36] The life tenant was the sister-in-law of the executor.
[37] [2000] WTLR 875; [2000] 4 All ER 412—that a trustee acts dishonestly if: (1) he commits an act either knowing that it is contrary to the interests of the beneficiaries or being recklessly indifferent as to whether or not it is contrary to their interests; or (2) according to an objective standard the belief that he is acting in the interests of the beneficiaries is so unreasonable that no trustee could have held it.
[38] Costs were awarded against the trustee without indemnity from the estate.

Purchase of estate property by the PR or trustee[39]

The purchase of an estate or trust asset may offend any one of three rules developed to control **10.34**
this aspect of conflict of interest:

1. The two party rule—two parties are required to form a valid contract, and thus a PR or
   trustee cannot validly contract with himself to purchase estate property.
2. The genuine transaction rule—prevents the two party rule being circumvented by a sale
   to the PR's, or trustee's, nominee.
3. The self-dealing rule—based on a wider principle than the two above rules that the PR or
   trustee must not place himself in a position of conflict in dealing with estate property on
   his own account.[40]

An example of the self-dealing rule, which poses a danger to PRs, and their advisers, arises
out of s.41(3) Administration of Estates Act 1925, which gives a PR the power to appropriate
assets (see Chapter 14 for further comment on appropriations issues).

This becomes more complicated where a PR is a beneficiary as well and he is making the **10.35**
appropriation to himself. There are no problems where the PR is the sole beneficiary, as no
one else can be affected by the value that is used, but where there is at least one more beneficiary, whose interest is affected by the appropriation value used, difficulties can arise. There
is, however, no prohibition against such appropriations in s.41 itself.

Where the asset to be appropriated is cash or securities (with a readily accessible independent **10.36**
value, eg publicly quoted securities or unit trusts) there is little difficulty in establishing the
value. It is one that should not be open to question and one which does not involve judgement as to value being exercised by the PR. However, land, chattels, unquoted shares, etc
are more difficult for the PR to appropriate to himself as he must form an opinion as to the
value to be used.

In *Kane v Radley-Kane*[41] the court applied the self-dealing rule to such transactions (ie where **10.37**
the asset is not cash, near cash, or quoted investments) and found that any appropriation by
the PR was voidable in these circumstances unless either sanctioned by

* the court;[42] or
* the beneficiaries whose interests are affected.[43]

---

[39] See *Lewin on Trusts*, 18th edition (Sweet & Maxwell, 2008) chapter 20 for a more detailed commentary
on this subject; and also *Williams, Mortimer and Sunnucks—Executors, Administrators and Probate*, 20th edition
(Sweet & Maxwell, 2013) chapter 57.
[40] *Tito v Waddel (No 2)* [1977] 3 All ER 129 at 240–1: 'the self-dealing rule is (to put it very shortly) that if
a trustee sells the trust property to himself, the sale is voidable by any beneficiary ex debito justitiae* however
fair the transaction'; *Re Thompson's Settlement* [1985] 2 All ER 720 at 730: 'it is clear that the self-dealing rule
is an application of the wider principle that a man must not put himself in a position where duty and interest
conflict or where his duty to one conflicts with another'; *Aberdeen Railway Co v Blaikie Brothers* (1854) 1 Macq
461; *Bray v Ford* [1896] AC 44; *Brudenell-Bruce v Moore & Cotton* [2012] WTLR 931.
* A remedy which the applicant gets as of right.
[41] [1998] 3 All ER 753. The widow appropriated private company shares in part satisfaction of her statutory
legacy using a value of £50,000. £50,000 was the value claimed at death in May 1994 and appropriation probably took place in September 1995. She subsequently sold them for £1,131,438 in January 1997. Her step-sons
objected to the value used.
[42] For an example of the strict compliance with the formalities required by the court in sanctioning
self-dealing, and the consequences of non-compliance see *Re Peck, Hall v Peck* [2011] WTLR 605.
[43] The same rule applies to appropriation in testate estates as in intestate estates.

10.38 Where relations between the person entitled to act as PR (either under the will or the intestacy) and the other beneficiaries are known to be poor:

1. Consider, when preparing the will, if the problem could be eased by expressly giving the PR the power to make such an appropriation and safeguarding the interests of the other beneficiaries by appointing a co-executor.
2. Consider, when preparing the will, if the testator should be advised to appoint an independent PR.
3. At the outset of an intestacy, consider recommending another administrator being appointed[44] together with the person entitled to apply for letters of administration.
4. In an intestacy the appropriation of the matrimonial home will not offend the self-dealing rule if two administrators act.[45]

10.39 A sale to the spouse of the trustee does not automatically come within this rule, but the circumstances of the sale and the nature of the relationship will be examined to see if it is realistic to treat the spouse as the trustee's alter ego.[46]

10.40 Although trustee mortgages are less common than they have been, trustees granting a mortgage to themselves will cause self-interest problems. The difficulty is the impartial assessment of the adequacy of the security that is required and which the borrowing trustee is not capable of making.[47] The reverse position of a trust lending to his trust has the approval of the court in this country, but the disapproval of the court in Canada.[48] It seems to be a practice more safely avoided.

Incidental profits

10.41 A PR or trustee is not entitled to profit from his position and is accountable to the estate for any incidental profits received. This can be an area of concern for the professional PR or trustee who provides other services to the estate from which he derives a profit.[49]

10.42 A simple illustration of this used to be the inability of a bank, which acts as a PR or trustee, to place estate monies in an account with itself from which it will have derived a profit as banker. This specific issue of acting as banker has now been rectified by s.29 Trustee Act 2000.[50] However, s.29 does not authorize any other types of incidental profit (other than those derived from the provision of banking services[51]) and care is needed by the PR or trustee who provides the additional services commented on below.

---

[44] The spouse of the administrator is to be avoided for obvious reasons.

[45] Where the surviving spouse is 'one of two or more personal representatives, the rule that a trustee may not be a purchaser of trust property shall not prevent the surviving spouse or civil partner from purchasing out of the estate of the intestate an interest in the dwelling house in which the surviving spouse or civil partner was resident at the time of the intestate's death' (para 5(1) Sch 2 Intestate's Estates Act 1952).

[46] *Tito v Waddel (No2)* [1977] 3 All ER 129.

[47] *Stickney v Sewell* (1835) 1 Myl & Cr 8; *Re Waterman's Will Trusts* [1952] 2 All ER 1054.

[48] *Re Mason's Orphanage and London and North Western Railway* [1896] 1 Ch 54; *Re Lerner* (1952) 6 WWR (NS) 187.

[49] The fees of the PR for acting as such will normally be expressly authorized in the will or authorized under ss.28–29 Trustee Act 2000.

[50] Prior to this, bank PRs relied upon the will to authorize their standard terms and conditions of business, which contained provision for them to act as banker.

[51] By an authorized institution under the Banking Act 1987.

Stock exchange dealing   Where a trust company owns a stockbroking business and places **10.43** estate and trust sales and purchases through that business, are alternative brokers cheaper or can the service, despite the higher cost, be justified on operational grounds? With the simplified dealing brought about by electronic dealing this can be a factor in saving substantial paperwork handling by the PR or trustee.

Valuation services and in-house investment products   There can be a significant risk for **10.44** the trustee who invests trust monies with a company associated with the trustee, unless any additional profits earned by this are authorized under the trust deed (usually, for a trust company, by authorization of their standard terms and conditions of business).[52]

The risk to the trustee has several aspects. First, where such an investment policy is fol- **10.45** lowed as a result of corporate policy (eg that all trust portfolios administered will contain a certain percentage of in-house investment funds; or that foreign investment exposure must be through a particular in-house vehicle) there is the risk that the exercise of the investment discretion itself will be impugned. This is on the basis that (1) it was not considered and exercised specifically in the light of the circumstances and requirements of each individual trust and (2) if it can be shown that it was exercised on the basis of corporate policy rather than trust investment requirements.[53] Corporate policy in this context could also be an indicator of a conflict of interest if the investment decision is one from which the trustee will increase his earnings. Second, although the use of in-house investment funds has been accepted by a court,[54] there appears to have been an acceptance by the court in this case that the investment was a market leader. Clearly, not all in-house funds could make such a claim. Does it use those investment products in trusts it administers because they are competitive and suitable, or simply because the trustee would earn more? The level of fees and commissions earned may well be a factor unless these cannot also be shown to be competitive with usual market charges. Third, if the investment in an in-house investment fund was facilitated by the sale of authorized investments, any capital gains tax (CGT) paid on that sale could be repayable by the trustee if the investment is successfully challenged.[55] Regarding trust funds as a captive market for in-house investment vehicles is potentially dangerous.

Foreign currency transactions   Trust companies always have to be vigilant for conflicts of **10.46** interest given their commercial aims of profiting from their work as PR and trustee.[56] The trustee owes a duty of undivided loyalty to his trust,[57] but a trust company also owes a duty to its shareholders to manage its affairs in the interests of the shareholders. That is, unless managed correctly, a fundamental conflict lies at the heart of every trust company's work. It is a conflict that is manageable, but it needs a constant awareness of it in order to approach the issue fairly. It is, however, strongly arguable that the interests of the shareholders are only properly met by placing the interests of the beneficiary first, ie that the interests of the shareholders are properly served by conducting the business of the company in compliance with the legal requirements that apply to that business.

---

[52] *Marley v Mutual Security Merchant Bank and Trust Company Ltd* [2001] WTLR 483 where the court refused to approve incidental earnings from bank deposits that were not authorized by the trust deed.
[53] And thus argued that such an exercise is for an improper purpose: *Balls v Strutt* (1841) 1 Hare 146.
[54] *Jones v AMP Perpetual Trustee Co NZ Ltd* [1994] 1 NZLR 690.
[55] Together with any shared brokerage received or investment charged.
[56] This is of course not restricted to trust companies as professional PRs and trustees are, almost by definition, looking to profit from their work.
[57] 'undivided loyalty to the beneficiaries': *Cowan v Scargill* (n 32).

10.47   Examples of conflicts:

1.   If a trust company discovers that its standard fee authorities are defective, it should of course voluntarily reimburse the trusts involved, but that action can have severe repercussions for the trust company profits.

2.   If a problem arises in the investment policy followed by one trust, does the trustee then check to see if the same problem also exists in other trusts where no complaint about the investment has been made? This particular question arises for any professional trustee who has the conduct of several trusts.

3.   Providing one's own investment management service to a trust, should a range of investment advisers be beauty-paraded instead and the most suitable selected? (This does have an apparent commercial problem as, to the uninitiated, the use of outside advisers would give the appearance of the trust company's investment arm not being good enough.) Does the trust company provide its own service because it is competitive and suitable, or simply because it would make more money rather than employing a different investment manager with lower fees or a more competitive record? Posing this question is not another way of saying that a trust company cannot use its own in-house investment expertise; however, the underlying reasons for doing so are where the problems might lie.

4.   Delegation of investment management to an investment adviser removes from the trust company the responsibility for the investment work (but not the supervision of the manager). An adjustment in the usual fee would be necessary (to reflect the decrease in work and responsibility) if the delegation were not to become tainted by the increased profit for the trust company. This is particularly so where the actual fee scale applicable is an old and currently uneconomic fee that cannot be increased.

5.   Commercial advantage can be obtained by negotiating better rates for the supply of services to the trust company (such as estate agency services for valuation and sale of properties). The benefit of such agreements should work for the benefit of the individual trusts and not the trustee.

10.48   A custodian trust also cannot profit from his trust and is prevented, without the sanction of the court, from contracting with the managing trustee to provide services additional to his custodianship, from which he would profit.[58]

D.   Applications by trustees and PRs

Introduction

10.49   Advisers to trustees and PRs may sometimes find themselves presented with a problem where they simply do not know the answer or where they have doubt as to whether they should advise a trustee or executor to take a particular course of action. Sometimes there may be litigation threatened against a trustee or executor or they may themselves wish to take action.

10.50   In these circumstances the adviser should consider whether it is appropriate for his client to make an application to the court for directions. Trustees and PRs can always seek the directions of the court in the event of doubt as to a particular course of action, or where they cannot agree or where they want the protection of the court in respect of a decision which

---

[58]   *Re Brooke Bond & Co Ltd's Trust Deed* [1963] 1 All ER 454.

might be open to attack from the beneficiaries. Probably the first course in a difficult case is to seek the advice of counsel. It may be that the advice is sufficiently certain that an application proves to be unnecessary. In any event, many applications require the advice of counsel to be exhibited and so it is worth obtaining at the outset.

However, if there are cases of doubt the safe course is to advise the trustees or PRs to obtain **10.51** the guidance of the court. The thought of making a court application can be daunting to the private client lawyer whose *raison d'être* is to avoid anything ever going near the courtroom. Wise objective as this is, an application for the directions of the court need not be either time consuming or costly and it has the virtue that if the trustees/PRs act in accordance with the guidance of the court, they will not expose themselves to liability to a disgruntled beneficiary. That in turn will provide protection for the adviser.

Part of the jurisdiction of the court to provide guidance to trustees and PRs comprises **10.52** *Beddoe* relief, which is simply the trustees or PRs seeking the directions of the court as to whether to bring or defend proceedings so that they can guarantee their indemnity from the fund.

Applications generally: the principles

In *Public Trustee v Cooper*[59] Robert Walker J, as he then was, identified three types of appli- **10.53** cations which the court has jurisdiction to deal with:

1. Decision on questions of construction as to the ambit of trustees' powers.
2. 'Blessing' a particular transaction proposed by the trustees in relation to which they are not surrendering their discretion to the court.
3. Where trustees/PRs surrender their discretion to the court.

The last sort of application is very rare. Often trustees or PRs will ask the court to answer questions under both (1)and (2).[60] The role of the court in dealing with issues under (2) was set out by Millett J in *Richard v Mackay*[61] where he said that the role of the court was

> to ensure that the proposed exercise of the trustees' powers is lawful and within the power and that it does not infringe the trustees' duty to act as ordinary, reasonable and prudent trustees might act, but it requires only to be satisfied that the trustees can properly form the view that the proposed transaction is for the benefit of beneficiaries or the trust estate.

What the court does not do is to decide how it would exercise the discretion. This type of **10.54** application is a powerful tool in the trustee's armoury. Once the court has blessed a proposed application, the beneficiaries are prevented from bringing a breach of trust allegation or indeed making any complaint against the trustees.

So, for example, in *X v A*[62] trustees applied to the court for guidance as to whether they had **10.55** power to advance trust monies to charitable causes and for the court to bless the transaction. The court refused to do so. Had the trustees gone ahead without the court's guidance they may have been subject to a claim by the beneficiaries of the trust; and of course their advisers might have borne the ultimate liability.

---

[59] [2001] WTLR 901, 922–4.
[60] For an example see the case of *X v A* [2006] 1 WLR 741.
[61] (1987) 11 Tru LI 23, 24.
[62] *X v A* (n 60).

10.56   Care has to be taken as to how PRs and trustees use this jurisdiction. In *Green v Astor*[63] a court-appointed administrator was subjected to constant criticism from one of the beneficiaries and sought retrospective approval of a Tomlin Order into which she had entered to which he had alleged she had obtained the consent of the beneficiaries by fraud. The court held that she was seeking the approval of the court (which it would not give) for her own benefit and she had to pay the costs of that part of the application (15 per cent of the total) personally.

Applications for directions: procedure

10.57   Proceedings must be started by way of a Part 8 claim form.[64] Part 8 requires that the claim form states that Part 8 applies to the claim and must include a statement of truth.

10.58   All the trustees/PRs must be joined,[65] which means if they do not all bring the application (perhaps because they disagree) any dissenters have to be joined as defendants. It is then a question of which of the beneficiaries to join.[66] If the trustees consider that the court can give them directions without joining any beneficiaries, they can apply using the procedure in r.8.2A CPR, which requires them to apply for permission to the court before issue of the claim exhibiting a copy of the proposed claim.[67] That course might also be appropriate where it is clear that some beneficiaries will need to be joined but it is not clear who[68] and the initial application to the court can be coupled with an application to give notice to certain classes of beneficiary under CPR r.19.8A. Sometimes if it is clear that one of the joined beneficiaries will advance one argument and the trustees/PRs can present the other, there is no need to join any further beneficiaries.[69]

10.59   Evidence should be contained in a witness statement and must make full disclosure of all material facts if the trustees wish to be protected.[70] The evidence should contain the value of the trust/estate assets, the proposed transaction or litigation in respect of which directions are sought, and why directions are needed.[71] It should set out what consultations there have been with adult beneficiaries.[72] If there is a child beneficiary joined, he should be represented and the instructions and opinion of a properly qualified lawyer should be exhibited before the court.[73]

10.60   The claim will initially be referred to a Master for case management.[74] Sometimes the directions can be dealt with on paper. There are provisions for the directions hearing to be held in private.[75] The CPR do not deal with entitlement to costs, which are still dealt with on established principles.[76] In friendly litigation in general all parties' costs will come out of the trust fund but trustees' costs are assessed in general on an indemnity basis.[77] However, trustees

---

63 [2013] EWHC 1857 (Ch).
64 Rule 64.3 CPR.
65 Rule 64.4(1)(b) CPR.
66 Rule 64.4(1)(c) CPR.
67 Paragraph 4.2 of the Practice Direction 64b to Part 64.
68 Paragraph 4.3 of the Practice Direction 64b to Part 64.
69 Paragraph 4.1 of the Practice Direction 64b to Part 64.
70 Paragraph 7.1 of the Practice Direction 64b to Part 64.
71 Paragraph 7.5 of the Practice Direction 64b to Part 64.
72 Paragraph 7.7 of the Practice Direction 64b to Part 64.
73 Paragraph 7.10 of the Practice Direction 64b to Part 64.
74 Paragraph 5.1 of the Practice Direction 64b to Part 64.
75 Rule 39.2 CPR and the Practice Direction in relation to Part 39.
76 *Re Buckton* [1907] 2 Ch 406.
77 Rule 48.4 CPR.

must beware of taking the side of one class of beneficiaries or they may find a costs order being made against them.[78] Further it is by no means a foregone conclusion that beneficiaries will be entitled to their costs out of the fund. If the application is only brought because they have been unreasonable and the application becomes akin to hostile litigation they may be ordered to pay some or all of the costs, which was the outcome in *Green v Astor.*[79]

Beddoe applications

This is the most frequent use of this jurisdiction.[80] It is trustees or PRs simply asking the **10.61** court to approve in advance costs which they intend to incur on behalf of the trust fund in litigating. It is important that *Beddoe* applications are used in the right circumstances and they should never be made in the litigation itself. What is more, consideration should always be given as to whether it is necessary to go to court at all. If all the beneficiaries are adult and capable, then the trustee/PR should first of all consult them and see if they are prepared to offer an indemnity. Alternatively, in an appropriate case it might be preferable for the adult beneficiaries themselves to pursue or defend any litigation.[81]

The best exposition of this jurisdiction can be found in the judgment of Lightman J in *Alsop* **10.62** *Wilkinson v Neary*[82] where he set out the categories of litigation in which trustees/PRs might be involved:

(1) The first (which I shall call 'a trust dispute') is a dispute as to the trusts on which they hold the subject matter of the settlement. This may be 'friendly' litigation involving eg the true construction of the trust instrument or some other question arising in the course of the administration of the trust; or 'hostile' litigation eg a challenge in whole or in part to the validity of the settlement by the settlor on grounds of undue influence or by a trustee in bankruptcy or a defrauded creditor of the settlor, in which case the claim is that the trustees hold the trust funds as trustees for the settlor, the trustee in bankruptcy or creditor in place of or in addition to the beneficiaries specified in the settlement. The line between friendly and hostile litigation, which is relevant as to the incidence of costs, is not always easy to draw: see *In re Buckton; Buckton v. Buckton.*[83]

(2) The second (which I shall call 'a beneficiaries dispute') is a dispute with one or more of the beneficiaries as to the propriety of any action which the trustees have taken or omitted to take or may or may not take in the future. This may take the form of proceedings by a beneficiary alleging breach of trust by the trustees and seeking removal of the trustees and/or damages for breach of trust.

(3) The third (which I shall call 'a third party dispute') is a dispute with persons, otherwise than in the capacity of beneficiaries, in respect of rights and liabilities eg in contract or tort assumed by the trustees as such in the course of administration of the trust.

It is in respect of this latter type of dispute that the trustees/PRs will apply to the court under **10.63** this jurisdiction—sometimes referred to as hostile litigation. Trustees are of course entitled to an indemnity from the fund for their costs but the objective in obtaining *Beddoe* relief is to ensure that no beneficiary can complain that their costs were incurred unnecessarily. The

---

[78] *Breadner v Granville-Grossman* [2001] WTLR 377.

[79] [2013] EWHC 1857 (Ch).

[80] And not without occasional drama: see *Howell v Millais* [2007] EWCA Civ 720 for a *Beddoe* application where the Court of Appeal held that the judge should have recused himself as a result of bias against the firm of which the applicant trustee was a partner.

[81] *Re Evans* [1986] 1 WLR 101.

[82] [1996] 1 WLR 1220 at 1223.

[83] [1907] 2 Ch 406.

application should always be brought in separate proceedings from the hostile litigation. The failure to apply for such an order, although perhaps unwise, has recently been held not to be a breach of trust.[84]

10.64 Sometimes guidance of the court might be sought as to whether it is right for the trustees/PRs to take no action in respect of possible proceedings.[85]

Procedure

10.65 The procedure is in general as above with certain specific points to take into account:

1. The evidence needs to exhibit the advice of a properly qualified lawyer as to the merits of the claim.[86]
2. It should also set out a costs estimate for the litigation, what is known about the other party, and a draft statement of case.[87]
3. Further it should set out whether any pre-action protocol has been followed and the position in relation to alternative dispute resolution and mediation.[88]

If the litigation involves one of the beneficiaries then the claim form can be expressed in general terms[89] and any privileged material should be exhibited to the statement of the claimants and not served on him.[90] The beneficiary can be excluded from all or any part of the hearing.[91] In some cases the court will be prepared to deal with the matter on paper.

10.66 It is important that such applications are kept within sensible bounds. In *Howell v Lees-Millais*[92] Lord Neuberger MR (as he then was) said:

> In *Re Beddoe, Downes v Cottam* [1893] 1 Ch 547, a trustee was refused permission to take his costs out of the trust in relation to certain proceedings in which he had taken part on behalf of the trust and had been unsuccessful. In justifying that refusal, Lindley LJ referred at [1893] 1 Ch 547, 558 to 'the ease and comparatively small expense with which trustees can obtain the opinion of a Judge of the Chancery Division on the question of whether an action should be brought or defended at the expense of the trust estate'. To the same effect, Bowen LJ mentioned at [1893] 1 Ch 547, 562 the 'inexpensive method' available to a trustee who 'is doubtful as to the wisdom of pursuing or defending a lawsuit'.
>
> The possibility that an application of that type would involve well over twelve days of court time, would require more than 3,000 pages of evidence, would take some five years (or more than eighteen months if one ignores the costs issue) to resolve, and would incur the parties in costs exceeding the equivalent of £1m in present day value, would have seemed inconceivable to those two experienced judges. This should never happen again. In expressing this view, I am not seeking to suggest any particular person is to blame. The Judge may have thought that the trustees carried a large proportion of the blame, but it would be unfair and inappropriate for us to express any view on the point.

---

[84] *Bonham v Blake Lapthorn Linnell* [2006] EWHC 2513 (Ch).

[85] The guidance provided by the court in *Graham v Turthill* (unreported, 11 February 2000).

[86] Paragraph 7.2 of the Practice Direction 64b to Part 64—a properly qualified lawyer will normally mean counsel or a partner with the conduct of the litigation.

[87] Paragraph 7.3 of the Practice Direction 64b to Part 64.

[88] Paragraph 7.5 of the Practice Direction 64b to Part 64.

[89] Paragraph 2 of the Practice Direction 64b to Part 64.

[90] Paragraph 7.6 of the Practice Direction 64b to Part 64 reflecting the previous practice in *Re Moritz* [1960] Ch 251.

[91] Paragraph 7.6. of the Practice Direction 64b to Part 64.

[92] [2011] EWCA Civ 786.

11

PROCESSES

A. Fraud and security of estate and trust assets

11.01 All of the processes used for information; management; control; and safe custody of assets, distributions, and receipts

- must be constructed with a view to efficient operation;
- must also be sufficiently robust to deter fraud (both internal and external) during the administration; and
- in the case of estates help detect any pre-death fraud against the deceased.

11.02 It is a truism to say that no system is completely fraud proof and that the determined fraudster will always find possible weaknesses in it. However, that truism is no excuse for not building systems that are robust enough to deter and detect most attempts. There have, regrettably, been too many probate and trust frauds reported in the press, and many others have become common knowledge within the profession. Fraud on the elderly, which is often not detected until after death, is believed to be widespread in this country, but unless the estate administration is conducted with proper regard to lifetime transactions, even less fraud will be detected.

11.03 Failure to take even basic precautions against fraud during an administration leaves a firm vulnerable and also at risk of substantial liability if their anti-fraud precautions were below those which can reasonably be expected of competent practitioners handling assets as a fiduciary or agent. Whilst security is often thought of in terms of cash and payments, control over the transfer of assets and sales of investments and property is also required. Similarly, robust checks on the identity of beneficiaries and pre-death transactions will reduce risk.

Estates

11.04 The efficient administration of an estate is based, in part, on the systematic acquisition and processing of information. Without an organized approach, the gathering of information becomes a random exercise with random results. Far too often an administration goes wrong

- because too little is found out too late; and
- that which is found is not understood or overlooked through either inadequate recording or analysis.

11.05 There is less risk in starting quickly and making the fullest practical enquiries than there is in undue delay in gathering information. Obtaining information is the key to the start of the process as it enables a view to be formed of

- what is involved; and
- any risk factors involved.

11.06 Obtaining information is of itself not intermeddling. But when requesting information it is prudent to indicate the basis on which the information is sought, such as 'making the usual preliminary enquiries in the assets and liabilities of the estate' rather than indicating that the office of executor has been accepted—'we are the executors of' or 'we are acting as executors' (see also the comments in Chapter 9 on the commencement of an estate administration).

Who is the client?

11.07 The first meeting is, commonly, with the deceased's immediate family where a professional PR is involved, or with the PR where the professional is to act as adviser to the PR. Whilst the family may well benefit from the estate as a result of the death, that does not necessarily mean they can give the solicitor instructions to act in the administration of the estate. It is the deceased's PR who is responsible for the administration, and thus instructions will be required from him for the solicitor to act. It is with the PR that the solicitor/client relationship will be established. Often the PR, family, and beneficiaries will be the same individual(s), but it must be remembered that a PR, and not the beneficiaries, has particular duties and responsibilities towards the estate generally. It is important, therefore, not to lose sight of who the client is and who is entitled to administer the estate, especially where useful information may be provided by other members of the family. It is not infrequently the case that the PRs and one or several beneficiaries will have differences of opinion as to the way forward in the administration, and it is important to be very clear as to who can validly instruct the adviser. At the same time the adviser needs to keep in mind the information that can be supplied to the PR and to the beneficiaries, as frequently this will not be the same information at the same time. The PR may well decide to consult with and share information with the beneficiaries who might be affected by the contemplated action, but this is a decision for the PR, whether as the result of professional advice or not.

11.08 The lay PR may well be unfamiliar with the different roles of PR and adviser and the duties placed on both. Much misunderstanding can be avoided by discussing this with the PR at an early opportunity to help ensure that both understand each other's roles.[1]

---

[1] See in particular Chapter 10 on the fiduciary nature of PRs.

Modification of duties

Where the PR requires the role of his adviser or agent to be limited, or there are aspects of **11.09** the administration that the adviser cannot, or does not, wish to undertake, modification of the retainer to reflect this is highly advisable.[2] This will then require the adviser to fulfil the limited retainer provided they have not inadvertently undertaken the excluded work.

Where a professional PR is appointed, any modification of the PR's duties will be by express **11.10** direction in the will or with the post-death agreement of all beneficiaries. With corporate trustees, some standard modifications to duties may be found in the standard terms and conditions of business published by them.[3]

Enquiries

In Chapter 9 it was suggested that the initial investigations into the various aspects of the **11.11** estate should be undertaken with both diligence and speed. Factors to be taken into account in determining how quickly and how thorough this initial process should be include

- that interest starts running on IHT six months after death;
- that time wasted before statutory notices to creditors[4] start running in turn can delay the first distributions;
- possible loss of interest through failure to collect and bank income and capital in interest-bearing accounts;
- property lease expiry dates and loss of rent through failure to let vacant property;
- possible interest on unpaid debts (especially tax liabilities and overdrawn accounts);
- risk to beneficiaries of market falls (these are not necessarily the fault of the PR or the adviser, but beneficiaries will usually think otherwise);
- time limit for any variation of this estate;
- time limit for variation of any interest inherited before death;
- time-critical events of any litigation involving the estate.

Relationship with beneficiaries

Whilst not in quite the same category, there are also substantial issues attached to the needs **11.12** and expectations of the beneficiaries which should not be ignored, particularly regarding the time taken for administration and to make interim distributions. Managing the beneficiaries' expectations (whilst not a legal duty of a PR) is a practical business skill that generally repays the effort expended and leads to a more harmonious administration. It is also not an exaggeration to say that this should also produce, because of the reduced chance of disputes, a more profitable administration. Obviously it is primarily part of the role of the PR to deal with his beneficiaries, but where much of the administration will be dealt with by the PR's advisers then it should be clearly agreed who will take the responsibility for this task. Some firms have explanatory leaflets that outline in layman's terms what will need to be done in an administration. These can be very useful when used in conjunction with reasonable estimates of time.

---

[2] See Chapter 4 Part D regarding retainers and wills as the same general considerations will apply.
[3] Ensuring, of course, that the standard terms and conditions of business consulted are the ones authorized by will and not a later publication which may not be authorized.
[4] Section 27 Trustee Act 1925.

11.13 The expectations of charities, who are probably the only real professional beneficiaries that will be encountered by PRs and their advisers, also need careful consideration. Importantly, from the charities' point of view, their work is heavily dependent upon both the legacies they receive and the timely administration of the estate. Charities have a collective wealth of experience of both good and bad administration[5] and quite realistically expect more of the former. Acknowledging this and attempting to meet it, whilst at the same time ensuring that the realities of the administration are understood, should prevent unrealistic expectations on either side. This dialogue should be a constructive exercise on both sides, as a better understanding of each other's position helps.

B. Information management

11.14 Inadequate information or worse, wrong information, is a perennial complaint of beneficiaries; and an accurate and managed flow of information is key to resolving this problem. However, getting this process right requires management of information in the estate and trust files and records.

Files

11.15 Probate work can generate a great deal of paper and having a systematic approach to filing and storage is invaluable. Trust files may generate less paper less quickly, but covering, as they do, longer periods of time, the quantity of filing still requires a systematic approach. Any realistic approach also requires accurate filing.

11.16 As with all files, estate and trust files should always be maintained carefully in chronological order: wrong decisions, or repeated actions, are too often caused by information not being filed correctly. Date order is often crucial to understanding the actions that are needed. Even when items filed out of date order do not cause such a problem, too much time can be wasted locating the information needed—and when looked at objectively such time should not really be a burden on the client if it is incurred by reason of inadequate office management.

11.17 However, accurately filing correspondence is only part of the issue. Whilst one needs correspondence to go onto the file as soon as possible,[6] the use of a diary (or a centralized correspondence diary, or an IT correspondence system) in conjunction with accurate filing, to ensure that letters are correctly followed up, is just as important.

11.18 As estate correspondence tends to generate a lot of paper, the use of subsidiary files rather than one comprehensive file can make the different issues easier to control and easier to cost. However, where this is done,

- be prepared to copy correspondence on to more than one file if it covers more than one topic—otherwise files can become misleading;
- too much division of correspondence files can lead to a loss of the overall picture or confusion as to where things should be filed.

---

[5] And this includes fraud committed against them by both lay and professional PRs.
[6] Correspondence kept off the file because it is 'waiting to be dealt with' is a real menace as, apart from the possibility of losing it or overlooking it, the file is incomplete and will mislead anyone who looks at the file in the fee earner's absence. Paperwork kept off a file also prevents adequate supervision of a fee earner and is insecure from a fraud perspective.

There is also a regrettable tendency with the growth of email correspondence for emails not **11.19** to make it into estate and trust files, and this is a recipe for wrong or uninformed decision making. Leaving key emails in a personal mail system away from the main file makes little sense.[7] Alongside this problem is also the inherent lack of safety in email correspondence. Email, after all, offers no guarantee of who the sender of an email actually is, it is merely indicative of whose computer or account it was sent from (and even this is hard to take for granted given the ease with which paper copies of emails can be altered or even completely fabricated). Just like the use of fax, email has such risk that using it without some express agreement dealing with liability for acting on email instructions with the PR or beneficiary is ill advised. Some firms will not accept correspondence in either format, except at the risk of the correspondent. Clearly, the more important the information or instruction, the greater the risk in using fax or email.

Estate and trust minutes

'There is no law that I am acquainted with which enables the majority of trustees to bind the **11.20** minority. The only power to bind is the act of [them all]'.[8]

Notwithstanding that this is a statement from 1879 it remains a true statement of the law **11.21** today. Trustees' majority voting, ie the majority binding the minority, is only possible where the trust deed expressly authorizes it. Given this general principle, it is obvious that trustees' decisions should be taken as clearly and unambiguously as possible—and recorded in that way so that there is limited later scope to argue either over what was decided or that there was any lack of unanimity for the decision. PRs' decisions should be similarly recorded.

Trustees' or PRs' minutes are a useful tool for this policy. Minutes may be used for recording **11.22** decisions taken at meetings of the trustees or PRs (either physical meetings or telephone meetings), or they may record one-off decisions taken, for example, as the result of correspondence.

The recording process should include all trustees and PRs having signed the minute to sig- **11.23** nify their agreement to the minute's contents, and it should be dated after the last signature.[9] Signature by some of the trustees or PRs, or merely the draftsman of the minute, is far less satisfactory and of far less value, unless it is clear that all those present have expressly agreed the actual contents of the minute and authorized one of their number to sign it on behalf of all.[10]

It also needs to be noted that any minute should record clearly and unambiguously what **11.24** was decided. Ambiguity or omitting relevant points can be fatal to the value of the minute. Where a decision is being minuted, it is also useful to record any features of how that decision is to be carried—when and who by—if that has also been decided.

There is no legal requirement that minutes are used in this way, but clearly explicit recording **11.25** of agreements does reduce the scope for any later dispute as to what exactly was decided and whether all trustees agreed to the course of action.

---

[7] Experience also shows that emails have a regrettable tendency to be poorly written and expressed in loose terms. At times one is tempted to conclude that email correspondents do not think that what is written is part of the estate record or is disclosable in litigation.

[8] *Luke v South Kensington Hotel Co* [1879] 11 Ch D 121.

[9] The minute should show separately the date of the actual meeting (which may well be different to the date that the minute was signed).

[10] But if the minute is dealt with in this way, make sure that the supporting evidence is retained.

11.26 Trustees' minutes are prima facie trust documents that will be available for inspection by a beneficiary.[11] The trustees' decision itself, whilst it may represent the exercise of a discretion, is available for inspection by beneficiaries as the decision is simply a question of fact. The reasons for taking the decision are a different matter, and it is suggested that the reasons for a decision should not be recorded in the minute, but if they need to be recorded[12] then this should be done by way of a separate file note.

Trustees' and PRs' meetings

11.27 Whilst it is possible that business may be conducted by letter,[13] periodic meetings enable greater and easier debate of issues and decisions. However, the same points as above for minutes apply to the recording of discussions. Unlike the minuting of other meetings, where decisions have been taken and are to be acted on straight away, approval of the decision should be signed off by the trustees or PRs either at the meeting or soon afterwards and not left as a matter in the general minutes of the meeting, which may not be approved until much later.

11.28 As with all meetings, agendas help to give the discussion and decision making more focus and structure. The advance circulation of papers that are to be considered should, as with all meetings, also lead to more informed and focused debate.

11.29 Trustees' meetings are particularly helpful for

1. The consideration and approval of accounts.
2. Reviews of investment policy and portfolio performance (including the review of the investment policy statement where there has been delegation of asset management[14]). It may be appropriate for the investment manager/adviser to be present to deal with questions arising out of the delegated management.
3. Reviews of property policy—new investment, sales and retention, letting and repairs. If there is a property portfolio, particularly one where management has been delegated, then the previous point applies as well.
4. Reviews of delegation of functions and appointments of professional advisers and agents together with their terms of engagement and fee charging.
5. Reviews of policy regarding exercise of distributive discretions and the exercise of those discretions.
6. Advance planning for future events, eg coming of age, ten-year IHT charge, vesting of interests.
7. Reports and advice on litigation and discussion of future options.

11.30 The discussions should be summarized in conventional meeting minutes, which are then available at the next meeting in order to remind the trustees of their previously decided policies or the matters that they wished to defer for future consideration.

11.31 For PRs, there is similar value in meetings for

- planning an administration;

---

[11] Within the meaning of 'trust documents' in *Re Londonderry's Settlement* [1964] 3 All ER 855.
[12] Particularly if the reasons for exercising a discretion are a factor in future exercise of the discretion: *Re Pauling's Settlement Trusts* [1963] 3 All ER 1.
[13] In theory email is possible, but it is fundamentally insecure and lacks the key ingredient of signatures.
[14] Section 15 Trustee Act 2000.

- decisions on IHT payment;
- sale/transfer of assets;
- distributions; and
- litigation.

Estate progress summaries

A large number of complaints made about solicitors have in the past related to probate files, **11.32** and these complaints mainly concerned delay in administration and failure to communicate with PRs and/or beneficiaries. Such complaints always involve additional time and cost (some of which will not be recoverable). It is therefore sensible to avoid confusion as to progress and to keep progress summaries for each estate. Relying on individual memory for what has been done and what needs to be done in each estate

- is usually unworkable;
- leads to mistakes; and
- confuses others who need to cover work during absences, assess training, or control business progress generally.

It is therefore recommended to develop a standard progress sheet (which will include **11.33** all key progress points) and a suggested form is in Appendix 6. Many firms already use software that provides a similar function and such IT systems can provide sophisticated control functions. Standardization of progress information using paper or computers also saves much wasted time in reviewing and re-reviewing files to check progress—again time which may well not be properly chargeable if it can be avoided by simple information recording.

Such controls also have a useful role for those responsible for the work and training of others. **11.34** They provide clear summaries of what has been achieved and when. This can highlight areas of weakness and focus attention on what needs to be done. If used sensibly, focusing on what needs to be done can also be used to drive forward a firm's earnings, by achieving completion of work more quickly. These forms can be particularly useful where partners in a firm are the PRs and the administrative work is handled by others within the firm. As well as responsibility for the conduct of members of their firm, those partners have precise personal legal responsibilities for the administration of the estate being, as they are, the PRs. It is suggested that this dual responsibility makes it necessary to be able to show conduct and control of the administration.

C. Trust records

Know the deed

The foundation of a trust is its trust deed. This means that the process of administration must **11.35** start with what the contents of that deed are, ie

- What are the beneficial interests?
- What are the trustees' powers and discretions?
- Who are the trustees?
- What administrative powers are there?

11.36 This knowledge is then informed by the law applicable, eg

1. The deed may show a life interest.
2. That may be qualified, eg by a protective trust.
3. The trust may have wide investment powers.
4. These may be qualified with a consent.
5. The manner of application will then be in accordance with (a) the general law on trust investments and (b) the specific requirements of the Trustee Act 2000.

11.37 What constitutes the trust deed?

- original settlement document;[15]
- any supplementary documents, such as deeds of appointment, assignment, or variation, etc;
- documents incorporated by reference, such as the STEP standard provisions;
- court orders varying the terms or construing the terms;
- but *not* the letter of wishes.[16]

11.38 Supplemental to these are those documents that help to make sense of the deed:

- death certificates—confirm the death of interests specified in the deeds and therefore the current trusts applicable;
- marriage certificates—explain changes of names;
- other certificates establishing members of classes, and also genealogists' reports etc of family trees;
- counsels' opinions on construction of the trust;
- letter of wishes.

11.39 In the light of this, there may well be a considerable amount of information that may have to be assimilated in order to understand how any given trust should be administered. Two key points come out of this:

1. Those documents necessary to understand the trust need to be preserved and stored securely together in order that *at any stage the correctness of the administration can be checked from the full and original sources.*
2. *It is not economic in time to have to repeat this exercise too often* and needing to repeat it a number of times increases the chances of error (and the chances of mislaying deeds).

11.40 It is therefore helpful, the first time this exercise is done, to summarize the salient points of the trust on a standard information sheet,[17] typically containing

- details of the current trust, including names of beneficiaries of the current trusts;
- income arrangements—what is currently done with it, any limitations on accumulation, methods of payment, etc;
- the events that will terminate current trusts, eg death of life tenant, coming of age, alienation of interest;

---

[15] There is no deed where a trust arises on intestacy. For this purpose it is replaced with Part IV Administration of Estates Act 1925.

[16] This may be of use to the trustee in the exercise of his powers, but it is wrong to elevate it to the status of the documents listed here as it is not binding on the trustee.

[17] Creating a standard template for this not only leads to consistency, but the template itself acts as a reminder of points to be checked.

- applicable perpetuity period;
- investment powers—in some detail as to what they are, any consents required, etc;
- other powers such as advancement/maintenance,[18] together with any additional consents or prescribed methods of exercise;
- any conditions attached to retirement of trustees and the power to appoint new trustees;
- whether or not equitable or statutory apportionments apply;[19]
- predetermined tax events, eg ten-yearly charges;
- a summary of the administrative powers also helps—eg STEP express provisions or statutory provisions only apply.

However, there is one huge caveat attaching to this process—the preparation of this information should *always* be checked by a second fee earner, as should any subsequent alterations for changing events or circumstances. This should also be done if the trust terms have to be re-analysed, say on the death of a life tenant. This should both ensure correctness of analysis and also assist security. Obviously, carrying out this exercise requires a careful and thorough analysis of the documentation. Time spent on this exercise at the start repays itself in the control of risk and the subsequent time saving of having an accurate guide. **11.41**

The trust administration process again requires accurate record keeping. The accessibility of records that reflect the history and current state of the administration makes the administration easier and less time consuming, and increases immeasurably the chances of accurate decision making. In addition control, training, and supervision are made more feasible, as, without some verifiable record of what was required, what has been done and what is outstanding, supervision becomes haphazard to the degree that it is often neglected entirely. **11.42**

D. Diaries

The creation of trust diaries, or more usually a combined perpetual diary for all trusts in a particular office, is an essential control on future management of those trusts. Such diaries are card or computer based. The key purpose of such a diary is to avoid reliance on memory and to ensure accurate and timely actions. A central diary also enables central administration of it, which in turn acts as a control over the progress of actions across the trusts. Each item of information in such a diary should be trust specific, unless it is for a global action regarding all trusts. **11.43**

The diary entries for any trust can be broken down into three types: **11.44**

1. trust events;
2. administrative actions; and
3. asset actions.

Examples of these are shown below.

---

[18] Or where there is nothing in the deed, a note that the statutory powers apply.
[19] The Trusts (Capital and Income) Act 2013 (commencement 1 October 2013) disapplies the Apportionment Act 1870 from new trusts arising on or after 1 October 2013, together with the equitable rules of apportionment known as *Howe v Earl of Dartmouth*, *Re Earl of Chesterfield's Trusts* and *Allhusen v Whittell*. These apportionment rules will continue to apply to trusts created before that date, subject to the provisions of the trust deed (in this context it should be remembered that the Administration of Estates Act 1925 makes no provision to disapply apportionments to trusts arising on intestacy).

11.45 *Trust events*:

1. Dates of coming of age and other dates of vesting of interests (or more helpfully warning a year ahead as well as on the expiry date).
2. Income distributions (where interests are limited to income).
3. Ends of perpetuity and accumulation periods (or more helpfully warning a year ahead as well as the expiry date).
4. Expiry of trust period, where a fixed period has been used (or more helpfully warning a year ahead as well as the expiry date).
5. Confirmation of perpetuity period continuing when non-beneficiary lives (eg royal lives) clauses have been used.
6. Expiry of trustees' powers (such as powers of appointment).
7. Review of circumstances of beneficiaries where the exercise of trustees' discretion is involved (eg ss.31 and 32 Trustee Act 1925).

11.46 *Administrative actions*:

1. IHT ten-year charges.
2. IHT instalment payments and other tax deadlines.
3. Fee assessment and charging.
4. Review meetings for trustees (see earlier section on meetings).
5. Investment reviews and meetings.
6. Preparation of accounts for whatever frequency has been agreed with the trustees.

11.47 *Asset actions*:

1. Rent reviews/lease renewals/insurance payment/property reviews for performance of tenants' obligations, and work required under landlords' obligations.
2. Rent collection/ground rent payment.
3. Health and Safety issues for trust properties (eg gas installations require mandatory inspections with criminal sanctions for breaches. Commercial premises also require regular inspections for Legionnaire's Disease contamination in water systems).
4. Encashment periods for loan notes and repayment dates for other fixed interest stocks.
5. Conversion dates for convertible stocks and similar stock option dates.
6. Checks on receipt of private company accounts and information and dates of AGMs and receipt of dividends.
7. Confirmation of reversionary interests not yet falling into possession.

11.48 Similar diaries can be maintained for estate events, but given the generally shorter-term nature of estates, the diary will not be as useful. However, as it is wrong to assume that all estates are completed quickly, an initial assessment of the more complex and potentially long-running estates, particularly those with complex assets, will usually show that there are critical dates that need to be carefully diarized.

E. Accounts

Estates

11.49 Part of the information that beneficiaries and PRs require during an administration is provided by the estate accounts (see also below on trust accounts as many of the general issues highlighted there apply also to estate accounts). The books of account (or corresponding IT-based accounting) must be both accurate and sufficiently detailed to permit financial analysis of progress during an administration. Mere cash records are not sufficient. The practice, sometimes encountered, of cash accounts only during an administration (from which an accountant will eventually be expected to construct estate accounts) represents poor financial control of an estate with many possibilities for error. For safe interim distributions during the administration, a trial balance of the estate together with the recalculation of outstanding expenses is essential.

On a similar basis, for long-running, or more complex, estates the preparation of interim **11.50** accounts can be invaluable for both the beneficiaries' information and the guidance of the PRs and their advisers. Interim accounts consolidate actions that have taken place, while at the same time enabling a focus on what is outstanding.

The purpose of trust accounts

Trust accounts should **11.51**

1. Present an accurate picture of the trustees' management of the trust fund.
2. Enable the beneficiaries, and/or their advisers, to assess the management of the trust fund including the level of taxation, fees, and expenses.
3. Enable the beneficiaries, or their advisers, to assess that all sums due to the trust for the period in question have been correctly received and all liabilities similarly dealt with.
4. Allow the beneficiaries to establish that any distributions of income and capital have conformed to the terms of the trust (or in the event of a breach of trust, to enable the enforcement of the trust through the court).
5. Assist the trustees to manage the trust by presenting an accurate picture of the financial position of the trusts.
6. In jurisdictions that require it, be lodged with the court and/or internal Revenue.

On this basis the preparation of trusts accounts **11.52**

• *should not be* a mechanical exercise of simply consolidating transaction figures into a set of accounts; but
• *should be* a final check that the information that will be presented in the accounts gives the correct picture.

Preparation on this basis entails reviewing **11.53**

1. The correctness of transactions (eg if an investment has been acquired which is not authorized, what proper remedial action can be taken?).
2. The way the transaction has been treated in the accounts (eg is the transaction allocated correctly to capital or income?).
3. The tax liabilities of any transactions (eg if CGT arose on a disposal has the correct amount been paid or reserved for?).

It must not be overlooked that the checks that should be inherent in preparing accounts **11.54** properly also have security aspects to them in order to prevent or detect fraud.

For a more detailed schedule of actions and information regarding the preparation of **11.55** accounts see Appendix 7.

Reviews

11.56 Where accounts are not prepared annually[20] then there will not be the thorough review of transactions in the accounting period that should be part of the accounts preparation. In these circumstances it is strongly advisable that there is a periodic review of the past transactions (since the last review or accounts preparation) against a pre-prepared checklist to ensure that the administration is on track. Such reviews can be time consuming (depending upon how wide ranging), but they have the great virtue of generally finding errors and omissions before too much damage has been done. The key lies in developing a good checklist that acts as a prompt for the matters to be checked and the documents that should be inspected.

11.57 Areas of review should include

1. The current trusts: are those currently applicable being applied correctly?
2. Income: paid to the beneficiary entitled to it? (with reserves for anticipated expenses payable from income?)
3. Power of accumulation: not expired; can new accumulations be made?
4. Investments: powers correctly applied, existing investments reviewed, reports considered by trustees, actions agreed implemented, private company reports and balance sheets received, current Memorandum and Articles of Association held?
5. Cash: invested where appropriate, cash requirements for next year planned and reserves created, adequate interest rate on cash held on deposit?
6. Chattels: if held by beneficiary, confirmation of existence and insurance; if in store or with other third party, costs settled and safe condition confirmed?
7. Delegation of management: power complied with, statutory requirements complied with, actions of delegate reviewed satisfactory/remedial action, investment policy statement still as required or should changes be made?
8. Tax returns: all those due submitted on time, assessments agreed, tax due paid (or reserve held for payment), conditions of any conditional tax relief complied with?
9. Rent: correct amounts received, action taken for any arrears?
10. Dividends: correctly received (care with XD and cum div investment changes), accrued interest scheme liabilities cleared?
11. Property: leases current and renewals completed, rent reviews due initiated, insurances paid and any premiums borne by correct party, all Health and Safety and environmental or planning issues dealt with, taxes on empty properties correct, insurance requirements for empty properties met?
12. Fees, disbursements, and other outgoings: fees charged on correct basis, co-trustees fees and/or expenses?
13. Preparation of accounts considered: if not issued have any changes in investment been advised to life tenant, if not issued have cash movements been reviewed for correctness?
14. Discretions considered?
15. Trustees' meetings: records complete?

---

[20] There is no legal requirement that trust accounts should be published annually and many trustees, where there are few transactions during a year, do not prepare annual accounts. However, they must be prepared to issue accounts when requested, even if that request is retrospective.

12

TIMING

A. Timing

Delays in taking action both by a PR and a trustee are a frequent source of complaint. Even where the complaint is not justified, these complaints can sour relations with the beneficiaries. Postponement of actions that are required can have genuine reasons behind them and it is good practice to explain this when a beneficiary may not readily see the justification. If time management is looked at, in terms of justification to a beneficiary, most delays would not occur. **12.01**

Delays in locating the executor

In the Australian case of *Hawkins v Clayton*[1] the solicitors prepared a will and after execution stored the executed will for the testator.[2] The residuary beneficiary/executor was unaware of the will or its terms. The testator died and six years elapsed during which the solicitors, who had been notified of the death, made little effort to trace the executor and, during this period, the estate suffered avoidable loss. The High Court found that there was no implied term in the contract between the solicitor and the client that they would be obliged to trace the executor or any of the beneficiaries after the testator's death. However, the court found that the solicitor owed a tortious duty of care to the testator, and thereby to the executor: **12.02**

> The law imposes the duty on the custodian of the deceased's testator's will for the protection of the executor and, derivatively, for the protection of the beneficiaries. It is not a duty owed to the deceased testator. The damage suffered in consequence of the breach of duty is not the loss of title to the assets in the estate nor a loss of the executor's right to possession of the assets... The loss is the loss of the exercise or enjoyment of the rights of ownership by an

---

[1] (1988) 78 ALR 69.

[2] 'The usual purpose is for safekeeping both before and after death so that, after death, the will can be produced in order that it may be made effectual. That is the purpose for which, in the ordinary case, custody is accepted' ((1988) 78 ALR 69 judgment of Brennan J at [9]).

executor who does not know of his entitlement. As such a loss increases with the passing of time, the duty to disclose is a duty to disclose promptly.[3]

In my opinion, a duty of disclosure arises from custody of the will after the death of the testator, the nature of the will, and the purpose for which custody is accepted as well as from the foreseeable consequences of non-disclosure.[4]

12.03   It must be said that there is no guarantee that were such an issue to come before the English court that a duty would be found or would be found in these terms. However, the absence of an English authority on this point does not remove the real risk that the court could find in favour of one. It is suggested, therefore, that where the solicitor who holds a will becomes aware of the death of the testator, it is safer to take reasonable steps to locate the executor, or principal beneficiaries, to establish if the will is still valid, and if it is, on being satisfied as to the identity of the person contacted, advise him of the will's existence.

Delays in notifying a beneficiary of his interest

12.04   A PR has been found not to be under any duty to inform a beneficiary of his interest where that beneficiary's legacy was subject to a condition in default of which the executor took personally.[5] The justification for this was the proposition that a will once admitted to probate was a public document. This reason, which was criticized in *Hawkesley v May*,[6] seems artificial and unrealistic and it may be unwise to rely on it today. Additionally, a PR has been found to have no duty to notify a beneficiary of his entitlement in sufficient time to allow that beneficiary to save IHT by way of a deed of variation;[7] and in that case the point was reiterated that as a PR has no duty to inform a beneficiary of his entitlement, the PR's adviser cannot be in a worse position.

12.05   In *Hawkesley v May*[8] the court found that a trustee has a duty to notify a beneficiary of an *inter vivos* settlement of the existence of the trust and his interest in possession in it. Where a beneficiary has a future interest it is not possible to say if the same duty exists. Where the future interest is so remote that it is unlikely to ever arise, it is difficult to see that any loss could arise from a failure to notify. Where, however, the interest is far more likely to arise, it does seem safer for the trustee to notify the beneficiary. In addition to making the beneficiary aware, contact with the beneficiary should mean that the trustee is better informed for the exercise of his discretion when the interest and needs of that beneficiary can be taken into account.

12.06   The last point in the paragraph above applies also in the case of a discretionary trust, where there is also no duty to disclose the existence of the trust to members of the class.[9] However, it is difficult to see how, in practice, a trustee can give proper consideration to his powers if he does not allow a beneficiary to make representations to the trustee for the discretion to be exercised in his favour. Without the trust beneficiary being aware of the interest he cannot

---

[3] (1988) 78 ALR 69 judgment of Brennan J at [12].

[4] (1988) 78 ALR 69 judgment of Brennan J at [10].

[5] *Re Lewis* [1904] 2 Ch 656.

[6] [1956] 1 QB 304; where at 311 Havers J stated 'Trustees have a duty to inform a beneficiary not only of the existence of the trust but his rights under it'.

[7] *Cancer Research Campaign v Ernest Brown & Co* [1977] STC 1425 where the judgment has not been without criticism, particularly in its view that the use of deeds in this way was less than widespread among probate practitioners.

[8] [1956] 1 QB 304.

[9] *Re Manisty's Settlement Trusts* [1974] Ch 17.

exercise his rights to enforce accounting and proper administration—rights that are normally zealously protected by the court.[10]

Although the duty to disclose an interest arises when the beneficiary reaches his majority, it **12.07** is not safe to assume that no disclosure is needed in respect of minority interests. Although there are no reported cases on it, disclosure to the parents of a minor (unless the terms of the trust prevent it) seems to be required as

- the trustee cannot safely consider the exercise of powers of advancement and maintenance;
- the trustee cannot safely consider investment of accumulated income without some consideration of future cash requirements for future maintenance; and
- the minor's interest in the trust is capable of enforcement by his parents acting in litigation for him.

Delays in obtaining a grant

In *Chappel v Somers & Blake*,[11] the executrix instructed the defendant firm to act on her **12.08** behalf in the administration of an estate. The executrix claimed that the solicitors had done 'absolutely nothing' for five years after she terminated the retainer. It was claimed that the solicitors' inaction meant that two properties in the estate had remained empty for almost five years.

The executrix obtained probate, through another firm, and proceeded to administer the **12.09** estate. She claimed for the loss of income during the five-year period. At first instance, the judge found that the executrix had not suffered loss, but that the loss was suffered by the charity beneficiary. On appeal it was found that:

> Considering this issue by reference to general policy, as opposed to legal principle, I am of the view that there are two main points. The first is that it would be wrong if the solicitors escaped any liability for damages in a case such as this, merely because they could identify a dichotomy between the person who can claim against them for a breach of duty, namely the executrix, and the person who can be said to have suffered the damage, namely the beneficiary. I believe that this principle, 'which is identified as the impulse to do practical justice' is supported by *White v Jones*... to the effect that it would be 'unacceptable' if a solicitor escaped liability in that case.
>
> The second principle appears to me that, given that any damages would ultimately come to the beneficiary, irrespective of who has the right to sue, the *question of whether it is the executrix or the beneficiary who can bring the proceedings is not of great significance.*
>
> It seems to me... that it is appropriate to treat the executrix as representing the interest of the owner of the property.[12]

Neuberger J, as he then was, refers to considering this issue by reference to 'general prin- **12.10** ciples' and also quoting *White v Jones* on 'the impulse to do practical justice'. This is a warning that should be heeded: that where there are areas of potential liability the court has not necessarily felt excessively constrained by rigid legal principles when arriving at just decisions. In an area such as delays in the administration, where we are not overburdened with decision, it is as well to be cautious with questions of liability as the court may

---

[10] See *Underhill and Hayton: Law of Trusts and Trustees*, 18th edition (LexisNexis, 2010) at [1.1(7)].
[11] [2003] EWHC 1644 (Ch); [2003] WTLR 1085.
[12] See earlier at Chapter 2 para 2.40 for a fuller quotation from this judgment.

be inclined to push the boundaries of liability a little further in order to reach justice for the complainant.

12.11 There is, from the above passage, a clear duty when instructed to act on behalf of a PR to act with a reasonable degree of urgency and that excessive delay, attributable to the adviser, that causes loss, will involve liability for the adviser. This approach is a matter of professional negligence of the adviser in dealing with his client and does not create a precedent for finding a PR liable for delays in obtaining a grant. Indeed one of the interesting points that emerges from this case is that, as a matter of law, a person who is appointed executor under a will cannot be held liable for any losses which accrue to the estate or to the beneficiaries under the will, as a result of a prolonged delay before the will is proved.[13]

12.12 As there is no duty to accept the office of executor[14] the person named is free to renounce. It is of course proper that any executor should make reasonable enquiries into the nature of the estate and assess the burden that would be placed on him if he accepted the appointment. It is because of this that it is difficult to formulate a principle of liability for delay in obtaining a grant. In *Re Morris*[15] it was concluded that there was no liability and in *Re Stevens*[16] it was not necessary to answer the question, but in *Chappell v Somers & Blake*,[17] Neuberger J appears to have accepted the argument that *Re Stevens* supported that proposition. These are both old decisions and the view of the court today must be to some degree uncertain if it had to specifically address the issue.

12.13 Loss caused by delay was one aspect of a negligence claim in *Sifri v Clough & Willis*.[18] The claim for loss concerned liability for delay which arose out a failure to prepare a will correctly; and it did not succeed. However, the judgment did accept that an action might be successful where a probate dispute delayed the administration of the estate and there was a failure to advise on the advantages of an administrator *pendent lite* to protect the assets, and loss thereby ensued.[19]

12.14 However, the question of liability for loss arising from delay may be approached differently where the PR has clearly accepted the office, but then delays unreasonably the administration, thus causing loss. There are several difficulties in assessing this given that identifying when an executor is committed to accepting the office can be difficult. The exact date on which intermeddling would prevent the executor from withdrawing can be difficult to pin down. Where professional executors are involved and accounts for professional fees have been prepared, then it may not only be difficult to argue that the executor was not committed to acting, but further the court is likely to take into account the underlying professional standards expected (and these may well have a bearing on the liability for delay). However, this area clearly remains one where there is no modern determination of risk and caution is urged when relying upon the old authorities.

---

[13] Court of Appeal in *Re Stevens* [1898] 1 Ch 162.
[14] *Re Stevens* (n 13).
[15] [1908] 124 LT 315.
[16] [1898] 1 Ch 162.
[17] [2003] EWHC 1644 (Ch); [2003] WTLR 1085.
[18] [2007] WTLR 1453.
[19] [2007] WTLR 1453 at 1459B.

Delays in collecting assets

Where loss arises out of the PR's delay in collecting or realizing assets it is suggested that the reasonableness of the PR's actions will be judged against the standard of Lindley LJ's 'prudent man' test.[20] **12.15**

Delays in settling debts

Where debts are left unsettled when the PR has either the cash to settle them, or assets from which sufficient cash can be raised reasonably easily, the PR will be at risk if any interest incurred on the debt exceeds the benefit that has accrued to the estate from the funds or asset that should have been used to settle the debt. This is illustrated relatively simply where the deceased has an overdrawn current account and cash on a deposit account. The interest paid on a deposit account will rarely ever exceed the interest charged on an overdrawn account. Elsewhere in this book we have commented on the advisability of planning an administration. **12.16**

Delays in tax payments and HMRC penalties

Where there is IHT to pay on delivery of an HMRC account, the PRs must arrange for the appropriate amount of money to be sent to HMRC with the account. Until this tax is paid, the grant cannot issue. Funding the tax bill may be problematic as most of the deceased's assets vesting in the PRs will be 'frozen', and therefore untouchable, until the grant issues giving the proof of title to the PRs. The following options may be available to raise the IHT: **12.17**

Assets realizable without production of the grant

By applying the Administration of Estates (Small Payments) Act 1965 some assets may be realized without production of the grant, although this is generally of little practical application. The maximum value of any one asset that may be realized is £5,000. The assets that can be collected in this way fall into two general classes: funds associated with the deceased's employment and assets in a defined class of funds. The principal assets in the second class are small holdings of gilts and savings bonds. However, where the estate is of sufficient value to require a grant, these institutions will usually require a sight of a grant. Further, where IHT is payable, the assets that could be realized would fund a very small part of the tax bill. For details reference should be made to the schedules to the Act. **12.18**

Outside of this statutory provision, it is common practice for financial institutions to allow for the release of accounts in exchange for the PR's or residuary beneficiaries' indemnity. Release of account balances in this way without grant is accepted by the institutions as a simple commercial risk, justified by ease of dealing and simplicity for beneficiaries. There is plenty of anecdotal evidence of this method being abused with incorrect disclosure of the other assets or size of the estate. **12.19**

Loans from beneficiaries

Wealthy beneficiaries may be prepared to fund the IHT from their own resources,[21] on condition that they will be repaid from the deceased's estate once the grant issues. Alternatively, **12.20**

---

[20] 'The duty of a trustee is not to take such care only as a prudent man would take if he had only himself to consider; the duty is rather to take such care as an ordinary prudent man would take if he were minded to make an investment for the benefit of other people for whom he felt morally bound to provide' (per Lindley LJ, *Re Whiteley, Learoyd v Whiteley* [1886] 33 ChD 347 at 355).

[21] eg where they receive the benefits from life assurance payable to them on the death of the deceased, payment of which may well require only registration of a death certificate and not a grant.

beneficiaries may already have received assets as a result of the death which they are prepared to use to pay the tax, such as money from a jointly held bank account. However, it is likely that the deceased arranged for such assets to provide financial assistance for that beneficiary while his estate was being administered, and the beneficiary may not be able to afford to make a loan.

Banks

12.21 **Borrowing**   Banks will usually lend against an undertaking by the PRs. A bank may also require an undertaking from the solicitor to repay the loan from the proceeds of the estate. Where the solicitor is not a PR, any undertaking should be limited to 'such proceeds as come into the solicitor's control'.

12.22 While it is often the only viable option, bank borrowing is expensive, because the bank will charge an arrangement fee and interest on the amount borrowed. Money borrowed should be repaid at the earliest opportunity so as to honour any undertaking and to stop interest running. Income tax relief is available on interest paid on a separate loan account in respect of IHT payable on personalty vesting in the PRs.

12.23 **Early release of funds**   Most banks will consider making a payment from the deceased's banking accounts directly to the Revenue at the application of the PRs or their solicitors. The mechanics of such payments were the subject of a tripartite discussion between the Law Society, the British Bankers' Association, and HMRC several years ago.

National Savings

12.24 Payment of tax may also be made from National Savings Bank accounts or from the proceeds of National Savings Certificates, any government stock held on the National Savings register, or any other National Savings investment. Full details of the investments and the procedure are given at <http://www.hmrc.gov.uk/payinghmrc/inheritance.htm#9>.

Investment management accounts

12.25 Where the deceased had securities managed by a broker or investment manager in an account where the securities were held by the manager's nominee, it may be possible to agree with the manager that money can be raised towards the IHT due. Managers are usually very reluctant to sell equities to do this, but fixed interests stocks (which tend to have less volatile prices) are more likely to be sold.

HMRC postponement of payment

12.26 In exceptional circumstances HMRC will permit a grant application to be made without payment of the IHT due if the PR 'can demonstrate that it is impossible to raise the money before obtaining the grant'.[22] Undertakings will be required and where necessary HMRC will protect their position with land charges.

12.27 All of the above might need to be considered; there are advantages to be obtained for the estate, but these generally depend upon planning as early as possible which sources will need to be used, rather than delaying the grant application because none of them has been looked at early enough.

---

[22] *HMRC IHT Manual* at IHTM05071.

With the Excepted Estates limit now quite high, and the advent of the transferable nil rate **12.28** band, there will often be no need to obtain detailed valuations of the assets and liabilities before applying for probate. In addition, where the conditions to submit a reduced account are satisfied, reasonable estimates can be used, provided the estimate is sufficiently accurate to be sure that the Excepted Estate procedure is applicable.

However, in other cases, all assets and liabilities must be valued and those figures disclosed in **12.29** IHT 200. Where a valuation is later shown to be incorrect, an IHT corrective account can be filed subsequently.

In considering the valuation of assets and liabilities it is also necessary to be aware of **12.30**

- HMRC's ability to assess penalties where figures are fraudulently or negligently submitted;[23] and
- the requirement that the PR make the fullest enquiries that are reasonably practicable in the circumstances.[24]

If values cannot be established with reasonable accuracy, it is acceptable to disclose good **12.31** estimates, clearly indicating that they are such, and even giving brief details to HMRC of the nature of the problem preventing valuation. HMRC can, and will, raise penalties if they think that the PR has not acted in accordance with the statutory requirements.

In *Robertson v CIR*,[25] R, a solicitor, was one of the executors of a Scottish estate. He compiled **12.32** an inventory of the estate and submitted the CAP 200 with a cheque. Estimated values were used for some of the items and this was expressly stated. Subsequent professional valuations showed that personal chattels valued at £5,000 were worth £24,845 and a cottage in Hertfordshire estimated at £50,000 was valued at £315,000. A corrective account was sent promptly and the additional IHT due was also paid.

The Revenue sought to impose penalties under s.247(1) Inheritance Tax Act 1984 (IHTA **12.33** 1984) on the grounds that R had failed to make the fullest inquiries that were reasonably practicable in the circumstances, as required by s.216(3A), to ascertain the exact values of the particular items, and as a consequence had negligently submitted an incorrect return. It was held by the Special Commissioner that R had acted reasonably. His reason for submitting the inventory as quickly as he did was that he wanted to sell another property comprised in the estate and, if he had waited for the professional valuations, there might have been considerable delay. Even if he had been in breach of his strict duty, he had followed accepted practice and had not been negligent.[26]

See also **12.34**

- *Cairns v HMRC*[27]—not describing a figure as an estimate was not fatal to the defence although said to be 'careless' but nonetheless a minor and inconsequential error. The original valuation of £400,000 (the figure disclosed) was said by the valuer to be 'an arbitrary figure pending investigations as to costs involved in upgrading'.[28] Despite difficulties with

---

[23] See generally ss.245–253 IHTA 1984.
[24] Section 216(3A) IHTA 1984.
[25] [2002] WTLR 885.
[26] See also [2002] WTLR 907 where the Revenue had the costs of the action awarded against them.
[27] [2009] UKFTT 0008 (TC).
[28] The property was a dilapidated wreck although the deceased still lived in it.

the sale it was sold for £660k. IHT was paid immediately on the increase. HMRC argued that it was negligent not to have obtained another valuation, despite the lack of evidence that a second valuation would have achieved anything. The Special Commissioner found against HMRC observing: 'Negligent conduct amounts to more that just being wrong or taking a different view from HMRC'.

- *Adams v Revenue & Customs*[29]—'the fact that the Revenue disagreed with [the taxpayers professional advisers] does not mean that they were guilty of negligent conduct'.
- *Sokoya v Revenue & Customs*[30]—a penalty notice was defective and unenforceable because the time limit was stated incorrectly.
- *Howard Barnett v HMRC*[31]—complaints that HMRC have treated an appellant unreasonably or unfairly are not within the jurisdiction of the Tribunal.

12.35 Where a penalty for the submission of an incomplete return is correctly assessed against the PR, he should carefully consider how it arose and if it is due to any failing on the part of either the PR or the solicitors advising/acting for him, in having failed to make reasonable enquiries or having overlooked information. Then he should consider whether or not it is correct that the estate bears the cost of the penalty. It does not automatically follow that such penalties are the burden of the estate. When such penalties have been assessed, a PR should take legal advice on the burden of the penalties. A solicitor who may be acting in the administration on behalf of the PR must consider if he has a conflict of interest in advising the PR if there is a possibility that the penalty could be attributed to the action or inaction of the solicitor.

12.36 Similar considerations apply to the assessment of interest on outstanding tax. Tax which is overdue will attract an interest assessment. Such interest is quite properly a liability of the estate where it was in the interests of the estate that tax payment be delayed or where there are insufficient liquid assets to pay the tax. However, where interest is incurred through avoidable delay on the part of the PR or his advisers (usually in paying the tax, submitting figures for assessment, or raising funds to settle a liability) it is questionable whether that burden should fall on the estate. Clearly, if interest has been earned in the estate during this period, and that interest exceeds the interest charged, the estate has not suffered loss; but where there is a net loss that was avoidable the question of *devastavit* can arise.

Delays in taking legal advice

12.37 It is perhaps part of human nature to tend to put off those issues which are not understood or perceived to be rather difficult. The issues that frequently arise in trust and estate administration which require legal advice can, and do, fall into this category. There is danger for the PR or trustee, and their professional advisers, in leaving unresolved matters on which legal advice should be taken.

1. In the interim how can the administration proceed safely without knowing that it is on the correct basis?
2. Will a failure to investigate lead to inadvertent acceptance of a position that cannot later be changed?
3. Prompt consideration of limitation issues will not take place (and a similar comment applies to other time-sensitive issues—see Part B below).

---

[29] [2009] UKFTT 048 (TC).
[30] [2009] UKFTT 163 (TC).
[31] [2010] UKFTT 39 (TC).

4. Trustees and PRs often have to make decisions in relation to tax which are time-sensitive.
5. There is the risk, particularly with construction of a gift under the terms of a will or trust, that the beneficiary's views of what he is entitled to will become settled in his own mind and lead to a greater confrontation if he is mistaken.
6. There is the risk that where work is dealt with by others, in the absence of the person with conduct of the file, that they will be unaware of the issue and act in ignorance of the problem.
7. Postponing consideration of the issue has the potential to delay further an administration.

All of these issues (with the possible exception of 5) carry risk for the PR or trustee in that **12.38** they can cause loss to the estate or trust. While the PR or trustee may not be liable for the loss, there is equally the possibility that they may be, and the greater the loss the more likely claims become. It is simply not efficient management of risk to leave issues unaddressed or unquantified.

B. Consequences of delay

Delay in administering an estate is a frequent ingredient in practice in applications to remove **12.39** PRs,[32] and it has been established in the Court of Appeal that there is no limitation period for bringing such a claim.[33] Advisers to PRs who fail to act in the administration of an estate timeously may find that their clients face a removal application or indeed proceedings for the due administration of the estate, and that the costs bill is laid at their door.

It should not be forgotten that PRs have a year in which to administer an estate after the **12.40** death, at the end of which they must pay interest on legacies, and that interest can build up substantially if there is significant delay.

It is also the case that exposure to claims by beneficiaries to be paid their legacies does not **12.41** go away quickly. In *Green v Gaul*[34] the Court of Appeal held (albeit as it happens *obiter*) that the twelve-year limitation period applicable to a claim by a beneficiary against a PR could not begin before the date of the grant of letters of administration; or, if there were successive grants, the date of the first grant and in fact not until administration was complete and the PR was in a position to pay the legacy. Therefore, if the PR delays in administering, the exposure to a claim by a beneficiary will last for a substantial period of time. A claim that *laches* barred relief in that case also failed.

---

[32] For recent court decisions on applying the test in *Letterstedt v Broers* (1884) 9 App Cas 371 when considering applications to remove PRs (s.50 Administration of Justice Act 1985) see *Thomas and Agnes Carvel Foundation v Carvel* [2007] WTLR 1297; *Alkin v Raymond* [2010] WTLR 1117; *Angus v Emmott* [2010] EWHC 154 (Ch).
[33] See *Green v Gaul* [2007] 1 WLR 591.
[34] [2007] 1 WLR 591.

13

ASSETS

A. Introduction

Personal representatives have a duty to collect the assets of the estate.[1] While this may not always require the PR to take physical control, or have all assets transferred into his name (eg the use of nominees), it is essential for him to ensure that he establishes effective control over the assets. **13.01**

A trustee similarly has a duty to gain control of trust property. Leaving property in the control of a stranger is insufficient unless he is a properly authorized agent, nominee, or custodian. Trust property should additionally be under the joint control of the trustees where there is more than one (again subject to properly authorized delegation). A trustee will not avoid responsibility for losses by simply leaving trust assets under the control of another trustee.[2] **13.02**

B. General investment duties of a PR

When considering the investments owned by the deceased, the PR must have regard to his duty to consider the suitability of the investments and diversification[3] in so far as is necessary **13.03**

---

[1] Section 25 Administration of Estates Act 1925.
[2] *Lewis v Nobbs* [1878] 8 Ch D 591; *Underwood v Stevens* [1816] 1 Mer 712.
[3] The Standard Investment Criteria s.4 and s.35 Trustee Act 2000.

in the context of the estate. This will entail setting to one side the assets that are specifically bequeathed (unless there is an abatement) and considering the remainder in the light of any sales that will be needed to meet the cash requirements of the estate.

13.04 Establishing what investments are owned by the deceased can involve the same amount of collection of information as with other assets. Obtaining reasonably prompt valuations of investments puts the individual holdings into context, in terms of value, structure of portfolio, and degree of diversification present. However, this process can be flawed without some reconciliation of what the PR understands was owned by the deceased with

- pre-death dividend counterfoils;
- pre-death disclosure in tax returns;
- scrip held;
- for more complex holdings, confirmation of the holding by the registrar;
- for 'old' scrip for companies taken over, a check for the cash proceeds in the bank account, scrip in the new company and checks on dissenting share registers of the old company.[4]

13.05 It is helpful to also identify any shareholding from outside the UK where additional probate formalities (or other processes in lieu of probate) will be needed. This can avoid errors in trying to sell or redeem holdings backed only by an English grant, which is insufficient to show good title.

13.06 For funds already invested at the time of death, the PR, with a power to postpone and retain (common in most wills), will not as a general principle be at risk for retaining authorized investments. However, the PR should look critically at what investments he holds and whether or not he should continue to hold them, including recognizing that

1. The statutory investment criteria, of suitability and diversification, apply to a PR just as they do to a trustee.[5]
2. The statutory duty to review investments from time to time also applies to a PR.[6]
3. The level of risk in, and suitability of, the individual investments that may have been acceptable to the testator are not necessarily acceptable to a PR in the light of his general duties, the need for realizable value, and the wishes and circumstances of the beneficiaries.[7]

13.07 At a very early stage in the administration the assets and liabilities should be reviewed in order that the overall outgoings of the estate can be calculated (with sufficient allowance for contingencies etc); and specifically what they are likely to be in terms of

- debts;
- taxes and other testamentary expenses;
- legacies;
- professional fees.

---

[4] Also a check for outstanding dividends on such holdings.
[5] Section 4(3)(a) and (b) and s.35 Trustee Act 2000.
[6] Section 4(2) and s.35 Trustee Act 2000.
[7] Often an elderly person's portfolio can become fairly static where large gains make dealing prohibitive and the potential CGT charge is the main reason for accepting the risk of a large holding. Rebasing of values for CGT on death will free the portfolio from this restriction and may well mean that undue exposure to one share can be rectified in order to minimize risk.

Similarly, estimating the expected realization values of assets will then reveal any issues of

- insolvency;
- abatement;

and, if there is a sufficiency of assets, give an estimate of the expected size of residue. This will then enable the PR to consider how money to meet the outgoings of the estate can be raised and from which assets, bearing in mind in particular liquidity of the assets and the ease or difficulty of realization.

This in turn allows the PR to   **13.08**

1. Warn beneficiaries of insolvency or abatement at a sufficiently early stage to prevent misunderstandings developing.
2. Determine the priority of sales (which may have implications for the order of registration of grant).
3. Consult with residuary legatees about preferences for sales and appropriations of investments.
4. Plan for early interim distributions (with appropriate safety margins for contingencies).

This later point is important as often it   **13.09**

1. Enables the PR to distribute assets of high investment or management risk that the beneficiaries want to retain, but which the PR, acting prudently, might otherwise want to sell.
2. Can negate the need for the PR to consider issues of investment diversification by passing investments quickly to either beneficiaries or the trustee of any trust interests arising under the will at an early opportunity. This point is of considerable practical importance as retaining large undiversified holdings, where either it is not necessary to retain them, or as reserves against liabilities, will often bring out difficult claims of a failure to diversify if the share concerned suffers a significant price fall before realization. Avoiding such issues is far easier than dealing with the dispute.

The risks of the deceased holding large lines of stock needs to be looked at early on. This **13.10** review will include advice on the company itself and methods of disposal where the holding may require unusual approaches, for example, placement or private tender. This early research is particularly important where the PR is unfamiliar with the share and the methods of disposal and is anxious to control risk.

Falls in the value of investments post-probate may not necessarily be the fault of the executor, **13.11** but beneficiaries are usually slow to see this. Often, much of the usefulness in moving speedily is in removing the potential for disputes through not holding investments any longer than necessary.

Investment management accounts

Where the deceased had arranged for his investments to be managed under an investment **13.12** management agreement, this will usually have involved the assets being placed in the name of the manager's nominee. The PR must contact the investment manager, without delay, in order to ensure that the manager is aware that his agreement with the deceased has terminated by his death.

13.13 Clearly if the manager has not been advised of the death he will continue to manage the portfolio under the original mandate with changes being made in accordance with the policy agreed with the deceased. Importantly, the terms and conditions of the agreement are likely to specifically address management after death, where notice of death has not been received, providing for no liability arising out of that management period other than through the negligence of the manager (eg if a specifically devised holding has been sold before the manager has become aware of death, the burden of correcting this will fall on the estate).

13.14 Where the manager is aware of death, but has no instructions from the PR, continued management under the agreement (and the charging of management fees) appears to be impossible in practical terms, for

1. The 'Know Your Customer' exercise (for the purposes of financial regulation) previously done on the client will no longer be valid.
2. The Customer Due Diligence (for the purposes of anti-money laundering) originally performed on the deceased is no longer valid and the exercise would need to be repeated on the PR.[8]
3. The risk profile created in the light of the client's wishes and instructions regarding, for example, restrictions or speculative transactions will no longer be valid.
4. There is an argument that the contractual authority given by the client for management will cease on advice of death.
5. Any new agreement requires the PR to comply generally with Part IV Trustee Act 2000 on delegation to an agent.

13.15 If the PR is tempted to agree to any continuation of management (whether or not this is wise) the PR, in delegating any discretion over the management, must have regard to

- any authority in the will; and
- the statutory requirements for delegation.[9]

A new investment management agreement would be required from the PR and difficulties then arise in defining investment aims, risk profile, or appetite for CGT, etc on behalf of the underlying beneficial interests. It would also be important to inform the manager of any investments that are not to be sold (eg specifically bequeathed holdings).

13.16 The most practical approach to this issue is probably to agree with the manager to what extent he may manage or refer suggested changes to the PR and what basis of charging will be agreed for this more limited service and for how long—usually until a grant is issued. In practice, some investment managers have found long delays between notification of death and instructions for realization or closure of the investment account. This can be dangerous for the PR as little or no effective management can take place.[10]

13.17 Although a trustee needs to be wary of failing to invest the trust fund,[11] the PR has no such corresponding burden. The PR has no duty to invest the funds of the estate.[12] This does not excuse the PR from taking adequate steps to ensure that the manner in which cash balances

---

[8] See generally the Money Laundering Regulations 2007, SI 2007/2157.
[9] Part IV Trustee Act 2000.
[10] See Chapter 12 generally on issues of timing regarding delays.
[11] See below at para 13.28.
[12] *Perotti v Collyer-Bristow* [2003] WTLR 1473.

are placed on deposit to secure a reasonable return for the estate are commensurate with the security of the deposit-taking institution.

C. General investment duties of a trustee[13]

The duty of a trustee in relation to the investment of trust funds, and the performance of the **13.18** investments selected, together comprise one of the most vexed areas of trustee/beneficiary relations.[14] It is therefore one of the areas of risk that requires a clear understanding of what the trustee's duties are and careful monitoring for compliance with them. It is an area where

1. Keeping the basic principles firmly in view is essential.
2. Consultation with the beneficiaries can avoid misunderstandings, but all parties should understand that the key decision-making role of the trustee should never be abdicated.
3. Taking advice is not restricted to investment reviews, and those who do not understand their duties, or what products are suitable to meet them, must obtain properly qualified and instructed assistance.[15]
4. The investment policy must always be determined in light of the individual requirements of a trust, and the trust should not be shoehorned into a standard investment policy (unless this is drawn as very high-level guidelines).
5. Common sense must never be thrown overboard, as things that are too good to be true nearly always are.
6. Investments that are not understood should be approached cautiously as, without enquiries to establish an understanding of their nature, it is difficult to understand their risk.[16]
7. Mistakes can be very expensive, which should make this area one of greater vigilance for risk control. There is nothing routine about a trust investment policy.

Duty to invest

It is the duty of a trustee to invest the trust property in such investments as are authorized **13.19** by law, or by the trust deed, so as to obtain the best return by way of income and capital

---

[13] See also Chapter 10 para 10.24 onwards for commentary on impartiality of application of the investment policy.

[14] In light of this it is rather surprising that so few of the disputes end in court, but this is thought to be an area where there is a general reluctance for matters to progress to court and therefore there is a much higher likelihood of a negotiated settlement.

[15] Not the policy once described to the authors as 'dump and run'—leaving the certificates with the broker and then leaving him to it.

[16] Warren Buffett's famous description of credit derivatives as being 'weapons of mass financial destruction' (March 2003) was clearly ahead of most investment views on the subject, but it had beneath it a warning that their complexity was not understood and that therefore their risk was not understood (or priced)—a view that was proved to be very prescient when 2007 rolled around. The authors are also tempted to warn trustees to be wary of fashion in investments until the risks of new products are properly understood, evaluated, and priced, the opaqueness of some hedge fund strategies being a case in point.

Historically, the Dutch investment bubble based on the value of rare tulips (1637), the South Sea Bubble (1720), and the French Mississippi scheme (1720) are too often forgotten.

For other examples, see also when railway mania arrived (Britain, 1840s) or Internet shares toppled (2000). The lack of transparency of some investment schemes involved should have been remembered later when investments in Barlow Clowes or Madoff Investment Securities Inc came around. Both of these more recent criminal schemes had features that were clear indicators of danger that were ignored in the stampede for anticipated market-out-performing profits. Non-criminal dangers, such as the size of the Iceland banking industry, were also ignored despite clear press warnings that the country could not guarantee safety of its banking deposits.

appreciation, judged in relation to the risks involved.[17] This duty may be modified, or indeed removed, by the terms of the trust deed but, in the absence of such provisions, the duty to invest remains one of the primary duties of a trustee.

13.20 This principle refers to a trustee investing in accordance with his powers and it is important that all trustees are aware of what the full extent of their investment powers are. It is not necessary for trustees to use such investment powers to the fullest extent that they are available, unless that is appropriate for the needs of the trust. Failure to understand the full extent of the power available does not of itself cause the trustees to have breached their trust as the resulting investment policy might nonetheless be acceptable.[18] However, failing to understand the investment powers might just as easily cause an investment policy that is in breach of trust and therefore have the potential to cause loss to the trust, and liability for the trustee.

13.21 If there is any doubt as to the nature and extent of the investment power of a trust, a trustee must take legal advice on the power before exercising it.

13.22 The trustee needs to bear in mind, when considering the investment powers available to him, that the fact that an investment that is authorized within those powers does not absolve him from considering that investment's suitability to his particular trust. There are many investments that fall within the ambit of a wide investment power that can be quite unsuitable for particular trusts.

13.23 In recent years, there has been a clear trend towards the settlor seeking influence over the investment policy. Where a settlor would like the trustees to follow a particular course of investment, or apply particular policies, the appropriate place to define the powers or restrictions is within the deed itself.

Investment restrictions in letters of wishes

13.24 Some settlors are known to have expressed investment powers or restrictions in letters of wishes for the trustees. This is acceptable where the power, or its restriction, is clearly drawn and the letter is one that is a legally binding document accepted as being part of the trust document and thus open to inspection by the beneficiaries.[19] Such legally binding letters are unusual, as being accessible by the beneficiaries tends to negate the point of letters of wishes. Including investment powers or restrictions in letters that are not legally binding is wholly inappropriate, unless the settlor and the trustees both understand that the letter of wishes is merely a non-binding expression of the settlors' wishes and that the trustee, while being permitted to take into consideration the settlor's views, is not bound to follow them. It therefore follows that attempts to restrict the trustees' investment powers through letters of wishes are fraught with danger for the trustees as ultimately they are accountable to the beneficiaries according to the terms of their deed and not according to the settlor's informal wishes.

Personal or fiduciary power?

13.25 The power under which the trust investment is made is generally characterized as a fiduciary power.[20] It is possible that where the investment power is exercisable by a beneficiary (who

---

[17] *Harries v Church Commissioners* [1993] 2 All ER 300, citing *Cowan v Scargill* [1985] Ch 270 at 286, 287.

[18] *Nestle v National Westminster Bank plc* [1994] 1 All ER 118.

[19] *Re Londonderry's Settlement* [1965] Ch 918 and the subsequent development of this principle up to *Schmidt v Rosewood Trust Ltd* [2003] 3 All ER 76.

[20] *Lord Vestey's Executors v IRC* [1949] 1 All ER 1108.

can direct the trustees as to the investment that he requires to be made) the power could be a personal one. However, to make such a power personal rather than fiduciary would require very clear and express wording[21] and it is questionable as to whether or not such an important power ought to be drafted so as to be non-fiduciary given the effect that it can have upon the value of the trust.

Meaning of investment by trustees

'To invest' or 'investment' have no statutory definitions within this context[22] and when the Law Commission presented their proposals, which resulted in the Trustee Act 2000,[23] they considered that it was not appropriate to provide a definition, considering instead that 'the notion of what constitutes an investment is an evolving concept to be interpreted by the courts'.[24] Examples of current dictionary definitions of 'to invest' are

13.26

- 'to employ money in the purchase of anything from which interest or profit is expected';[25]
- 'to lay out for profit as by buying property, shares, etc'.[26]

An investment has been judicially defined in the past as 'property... purchased in order to be held for the sake of the income which it will yield',[27] but this definition is no longer acceptable in that investment solely for an income yield is unrealistic and outdated in the modern investment market[28] as the sole means of investing (in itself a good illustration of the Law Commission's point about investment being an evolving concept). A trustee must now consider the capital return from an investment portfolio as well as its income yield.[29]

13.27

1. The power of investment 'must be exercised so as to yield the best return for the beneficiaries, judged in relation to the risks of the investments in question; the prospects of the yield of income and of capital appreciation both have to be considered in judging the return from the investment'.[30]
2. Trustees should invest for 'the maximum return whether by income or capital growth, which is consistent with commercial prudence... having due regard to the need to diversify, the need to balance income against capital growth and the need to balance risk against return'.[31]

---

[21] *Underhill and Hayton: Law of Trusts and Trustees*, 18th edition (LexisNexis, 2010) 49–56 fn 1.
[22] The definition provided by the Financial Services and Markets Act 2000 is not sufficient in that it is a definition for regulated investments only.
[23] Law Comm 260.
[24] See Law Comm 260 [2.28] at fn 56, but, as Hoffmann J commented in reviewing the conduct of trustees, 'one must be careful not to endow the prudent trustee with prophetic vision or expect him to have ignored the received wisdom of his time' (*Nestle v National Westminster Bank* [2000] WTLR 795 at 802). Also to be avoided, if possible, is the human trait that 'as we travel through time, we peer through the front window with nearsighted glasses, yet we glance through the rear-view mirror with rose-colored glasses' (Todd Buchholz, *New Ideas from Dead Economists* (Penguin, 1999)).
[25] *Shorter Oxford English Dictionary.*
[26] *Chambers English Dictionary.*
[27] *Re Wragg* [1919] 2 Ch 58 at 64 per Lawrence J; see also *Re Somerset* [1894] 1 Ch 231. Also considered to be of no modern relevance is *Bethell v Abraham* (1873) LR17 Eq 24 where it was held that 'invest' meant to lend at interest, not take part in a trading speculation.
[28] 'Investing is laying out money today to receive more money tomorrow' (Warren Buffett, chairman of Berkshire Hathaway, *Fortune* magazine, 10 December 2001).
[29] See *Cowan v Scargill* (n 17) and *Re Mulligan, Hampton v PGG Trust* [1998] 1 NZLR 481.
[30] *Cowan v Scargill* [1984] 2 All ER 750 at 760G.
[31] *Harries v Church Commissioners for England* (n 17) at 304C.

3. '[I]nvestment is laying out of money in anticipation of a profitable capital or income return'.[32]

4. '[T]he term investment was not a term of art but has to be interpreted in a popular sense'.[33]

5. '[I]n my judgment in 1986 it is not any longer self-evident that unless land is producing income it cannot be an investment—new approaches to investment have emerged putting the emphasis in investment on the making of a capital profit at the expense of income yield'.[34]

To what extent to invest?

13.28 This is, for any trustee, a question of some considerable importance and risk. There is old authority for the proposition that a trustee should be fully invested.[35] This is not an unreasonable proposition in that, apart from liquidity that is required for administrative or distribution purposes, to be fully invested could be considered to have met the trustee's duty to invest and to have served the interests of the beneficiaries (by having the funds invested for profit). The Trustee Investments Act 1961 referred to investment being made 'as soon as may be'[36] and contemporary comment regards this as being 'as soon as possible' or 'within a reasonable time'.[37] Many modern portfolio managers would dispute that this is appropriate and would instead advocate the role of liquidity within a modern portfolio, particularly as a hedge against short-term market falls.

13.29 Halsbury's *Laws of England*[38] states the law as follows:

> Unless a trustee is expressly otherwise authorised or required under the terms of his trust, he must duly and promptly invest all capital trust money coming into his hands...and he is liable for any loss which may result from its...being left uninvested for any unreasonable length of time, and for interest during the period of its being so left.

The main case cited in support of this statement[39] involved a period of fourteen months where cash was held pending a suitable investment. This period ended with the failure of the bank where the funds were deposited. More recently a Jersey pension case[40] contained the issue of the failure to invest a substantial sum, because of a misunderstanding of the law during the period of transfer of the fund to new trustees. The period was short (two months), but during that time the stock market rose substantially. The breach of trust was admitted. However, the circumstances of both of these cases do not amount to an authority for a general proposition that part of a trust fund may not be held in the form of cash deposits as part of an investment strategy where it is reasonable and prudent to do so.

---

[32] *Cook v Medway Housing Society* [1997] STC 90.
[33] *IRC v Desoutter Brothers* [1946] 1 All ER 58.
[34] *Marson v Morton* [1986] 1 WLR 1343 at 1350B–C.
[35] *Cann v Cann* (1884) 51 LT 770.
[36] Section 2(2).
[37] Commentary on s.2(2) Trustee Investments Act 1961 in *Current Law Statutes* for 1961; with the additional view that what was reasonable would be a question of fact in each case.
[38] 4th edition (reissue), vol 48, [843].
[39] *Cann v Cann* (n 35).
[40] *Midland Bank Trustee (Jersey) Ltd v Federated Pension Services Ltd* [1994] JLR 276 in the Jersey Court of Appeal.

The point is not fully resolved in English law and it is therefore suggested that a trustee **13.30** should consider carefully the reasons and uses of liquidity within the investment portfolio and decide upon the appropriate approach, before accepting a significant liquid position. The following factors need to be taken into account:

1. *Long-term liquidity* will leave a trustee vulnerable to claims, by beneficiaries, of a failure to invest, particularly if the stock market has risen during the same period, unless perhaps the yield that was obtained on the cash was greater than that which could be obtained from fixed interest investment.

2. *Highly liquid positions* (as a percentage of the overall trust portfolio) carry the same risk, even for a short period, unless the liquid funds are being held for some administrative purpose, such as a beneficiary being entitled in the near future, or anticipated trustee expenditure.

3. *The reason why liquidity is being advocated.* Speculation against short-term market movements is in all probability a risky course for a trustee to follow. If the manoeuvre fails, it is likely that claims that the trustee was speculating, and so was in breach of his duty of care, will arise. In other words that he was not following a prudent investor course.[41]

4. *The liquidity needs will vary* between larger trusts and smaller trusts as their ability to diversify risk is increased.

5. *Did the liquidity arise simply because of delay or was it caused by mistake or error?* If it did arise out of error, it may be difficult to show that the investment arose out of a prudent investment policy.

6. *Did the liquidity arise out of a policy of favouring the income interest in the estate at the expense of the capital return?* If so, there may well be a breach of the trustee's duty to maintain a balance between interests in the investment policy, depending upon the extent to which this has been done.

7. *The liquidity needs of charities* must be viewed in the light of their cash requirements for funding their charitable activities.

8. *In times of market turmoil* it is not unreasonable to withhold trust monies from an unstable or plummeting market, but there is still danger in this if the trustee fails to be alert to stabilization and recovery and omits to commit funds to the market. The extent of the market difficulties in the mid-1970s caused many trustees to withhold funds from the market but they then failed for some years to switch from this policy back to the stock market and many claims resulted.

This issue is very much one of

- degree;
- circumstance;
- amount;
- reason; and
- length of time.

---

[41] If a trustee has invested the trust fund after appropriate advice, in general, that will not result in a liability for loss because of a simple fall in the market. Holding funds out of the market in anticipation of a fall in the market may earn an advantage for the trust, but this is potentially at the risk of the trustee, should the anticipated fall not happen. Investment seems the safer course.

Investment and speculation

13.31 It is a truism to say that all investment involves speculating about future market performance. Trustees' conduct towards what is generally accepted as speculation is one of degree:

> The duty of a trustee is not to take such care only as a prudent man would take if he had only himself to consider; the duty is rather to take such care as an ordinary prudent man would take if he were minded to make an investment for the benefit of other people for whom he felt morally bound to provide.[42]

It is impossible to approach a definition of speculation by reference to specific types of investment or circumstances beyond this general statement of trustees' duty of care.[43] Speculation is much like the 'elephant test', that is that an elephant is impossible to describe, but anyone would know one when they saw one. The guidance needed really lies in applying Lindley LJ's prudence test (above) to any unusual investment proposition or circumstance. The final part of Lindley J's guidance ('for the benefit of other people for whom he felt morally bound to provide') is one of the keys to distinguishing between the attitude to risk of trustees, when compared to an individual investor's view of risk when investing on his own behalf alone. The individual, lacking the restriction of being morally bound to provide for another, may find acceptable risks and potential returns on his own behalf that a trustee cannot. From this point of view a trustee's investment policy will generally be more risk averse than that which a private investor would choose.

13.32 The Scottish courts were faced with a speculative investment in *Lutea Trustees Ltd v Orbis Trustees Guernsey Ltd*.[44] The trustees, at the request of the settlor, lent $914,000 to a third party on the basis that the principal would be repaid in twenty-two days together with a further $914,000. Company shares were offered as security. The loan was not repaid and predictably the security was worthless.

> On the face of it, a loan of such a sum, even at the behest of the truster, to an individual on such terms was an investment that was 'too good to be true'. A borrower who could promise to repay the loan plus a further sum equal in amount to the loan within a matter of weeks must have been a borrower in an extraordinary position. Had he not been in an extraordinary position he could surely have borrowed at commercial rates. Thus it was manifest that the defenders as trustees were being called on to lend a large sum from the trust funds to a man in desperate straits who could not obtain borrowing facilities in the ordinary market. The cases quoted showed that the duties, even upon gratuitous trustees, were heavy and a high standard of care was demanded. That was because the underlying principle was that it was their duty not to throw away the estate ... It was not helpful to look at the individual facts of each different [case cited] in order to make comparisons of degrees of negligence in different sets of circumstances but the general run of the cases illustrated that the standard of care demanded was a high one ...[45] No doubt there might be circumstances in which trustees acting under this trust deed could lend without security: for example to a highly reputable bank. But a loan of the character condescended upon, and admitted,

---

[42] Per Lindley LJ, *Re Whiteley, Learoyd v Whiteley* (1886) 33 Ch D 347 at 355.

[43] *Chambers English Dictionary* provides several definitions including 'a more or less risky investment of money for the sake of unusually large profits'.

[44] (1998/99) 2 OFLR 227.

[45] Here the judge drew attention to three Scottish cases, *Henderson v Henderson's Trustees* (1900) 2 F 1295; *Knox v Mackinnon* (1888) 15 R (HL) 83; and *Alexander v Johnstone* (1889) 1 F 639.

cried out for an explanation and demanded very reliable security if it was to be made at all.[46]

Within this topic also lies the question of 'gearing' a trust portfolio. This is the practice of using express powers within a trust to borrow funds, on the security of part, or all, of the existing portfolio, in order to invest the borrowed funds in further securities. The underlying rationale for the transaction being the belief that the portfolio acquired with the borrowed funds can be managed in such a way so that it will provide an overall return (net of the cost of borrowing) that will be sufficient to justify the risk. The risk in the transaction is that the performance of the portfolio acquired with the borrowed funds is less than is required to repay the borrowing (and interest) and then part of the original trust portfolio is needed to repay the loan; thus resulting in an overall loss. **13.33**

It is possible to envisage circumstances where such a policy produces a return and where, in relation to the overall size of the portfolio, the risk might be acceptable. However, the risk of such transactions will probably only be acceptable to a trustee as a small part of a fairly large scheme of management, which has clearly established limits/policies to stop losses becoming excessive. **13.34**

A balance between competing interests

A trustee has a duty when investing to maintain fairness, impartially, between the different classes of beneficiaries,[47] unless the deed expressly directs the trustee not to do so, where the beneficiaries, all being *sui juris*, have collectively agreed to hold the trustee free from any liability arising from not holding such a balance, or where the circumstances of the bene-ficiary—who could be considered to be the primary object—requires it. **13.35**

This duty was expressed by Hoffmann J, as he then was, in an often quoted passage from his first-instance decision in *Nestle*: **13.36**

> the trustee must act fairly in making investment decisions which may have different con-sequences for different classes of beneficiaries. There are two reasons why I prefer this for-mulation to the traditional image of holding the scales equally between tenant for life and remainderman. The first is the image of the scales suggests a weighing of known quantities whereas investment decisions are concerned with predictions of the future. Investments will carry current expectations of their future income yield and capital appreciation and these expectations will be reflected in their current market price, but there is always a greater or lesser risk that the outcome will deviate from those expectations. A judgement on the fairness of the choices made by the trustees must have regard to these imponderables. The second reason is that the image of the scales suggests a more mechanistic process than I believe the law requires. The trustees have in my judgement a wide discretion. They are for example entitled to take into account the income needs of the tenant for life or the fact that the tenant for life was a person known to the settlor and a primary object of the trust whereas the remainderman is a remote relative or a stranger. Of course these cannot be allowed to become the overrid-ing considerations, but the concept of fairness between the classes of beneficiaries does not require them to be excluded. It would be an inhuman law which required trustees to adhere

---

[46] Per Lord McCluskey (1998/99) 2 OFLR 227 at 240–1. His colleague Cullen LJ-C also added that 'the duties of the trustees are independent of the interests or wishes of any particular beneficiary or class of ben-eficiary or, for that matter, the truster himself. The trustees are under an overriding duty to preserve the trust estate.'

[47] *Cowan v Scargill* (n 30) at 760F; *Re Mulligan, Hampton v PGG Trust* (n 29) at 501; *Nestle v National Westminster Bank plc* (n 24) at 803.

to some mechanical rule for preserving the real value of the capital when the tenant for life was the testator's widow who had fallen upon hard times and the remainderman was young and well-off.[48]

13.37 On appeal, this view was endorsed by Staughton LJ in the following terms:

A life tenant may be anxious to receive the highest possible income while the remainderman will wish the real value of the fund to be preserved. If the life tenant is living in penury and the remainderman already has ample wealth common sense suggests that a trustee should be able to take that into account, not necessarily by seeking the highest possible income at the expense of capital but by inclining in that direction. However, before adopting that course a trustee should require some verification of the facts.... Similarly I would not regard it as a breach of trust for the trustees to pay some regard to the relationship between [the life tenant] and [the remainderman]. [The life tenant] was merely [the remainderman's] uncle and she would have received nothing from his share of the fund if he fathered a child who survived him. The trustees would be entitled to incline towards income during his life tenancy...I do not think it would be a breach of the duty to act fairly or impartially.[49]

13.38 From the above passages it is possible to formulate the following propositions to guide a trustee when investing:

1. There is a need to act fairly between the different interests in a trust fund when investing, but the differing nature of interests in capital and income prevent an exact balance being maintained.
2. Circumstances can exist to justify favouring one set of interests over another, although rarely could this be to the total exclusion of one set of interests, unless those interests, with their free and fully informed consent, have agreed to the policy which excluded consideration of their interests.
3. The factors which may justify favouring one set of interests over another set can only be assessed on a case-by-case basis and, once established to the trustee's satisfaction, must be kept under review to see if circumstances change sufficiently for the trustees to change their policy.
4. The relationship between the settlor and the different sets of interests can be a factor that could influence the policy towards the different interests and this may in practice be directed expressly by the terms of the deed.
5. A trustee must ascertain the circumstances of all the interested beneficiaries if the circumstances of one are to be a factor in favouring that interest over another.
6. The decision of the trustee will be easier for him to justify (assuming his decision was reasonable) if he can show that the information from the preceding three points has been regularly and formally assessed and recorded, and that the trustee's process for verifying it was, in the circumstances, reasonable.
7. The decision to favour one set of interests over another must, in the light of all of the above, be reasonable.

13.39 The above summary will only be relevant where there are competing interests to be balanced, and the primary example of this will be where there are different interests in capital and income, such as in the life interest trust.

---

[48] *Nestle v National Westminster Bank plc* (n 24) at 803C–F.
[49] *Nestle v National Westminster Bank plc* (n 18) at 137.

In most other types of trust where the interests in capital and income are the same (such **13.40** as many discretionary trusts) the overall return from the investment is the important issue (subject to the taxation considerations of the relative desirability of capital or income return). Whether or not there are competing interests will depend upon an exact reading of the terms of the trust.

The social and political views of a trustee

The social or political views of a trustee should not be a factor in the investment decision **13.41** making of the trustees. This issue was examined in some detail in *Cowan v Scargill*.[50] This case concerned a dispute regarding the management of the National Coal Board Pension Fund and the desire of some of the trustees (in particular the trustees appointed by the National Union of Mineworkers) to invest according to their own ethical or political beliefs, and also the NUM representatives' perception of what types of investment would benefit, at that time, the existing employees of the National Coal Board.[51] The judgment of Megarry V-C is regarded as the most significant judicial statement of a trustee's duty to invest in this context.[52] Although the case involved pension fund trustees, it is quite clear from the judgment that the points made apply generally to trustees.[53]

The judgment contained the four following general principles: **13.42**

1. It is the duty of a trustee to exercise his investment power in the best interests of the present and future beneficiaries of the fund.
2. The best interests of the beneficiaries will normally be their best financial interests and the power of investment must therefore be exercised so as to provide the best financial return, judged in relation to the risks of the investments and the prospects of income yield and capital appreciation.[54]
3. Only if two investments are of equal financial merit can moral, ethical, or political factors influence the selection of an investment, otherwise the individual views of the trustee on these factors must be put to one side.
4. Where trusts are set up to provide financial benefits (and this will be nearly all trusts) the financial considerations are paramount unless the beneficiaries are all *sui juris* and between them absolutely entitled to the trust fund. In this case, should the beneficiaries all agree, they are capable of indemnifying the trustee against liability should he invest according to their moral, ethical, or political preferences. There is also the question of incidental benefit which might meet the political considerations of the beneficiaries. Such benefit is immaterial if the financial criteria for the investment were paramount.[55]

---

[50] [1984] 2 All ER 750; but reconsidered and approved in *Martin v City of Edinburgh District Council* [1988] 1 Pensions LR 9 and *Harries v Church Commissioners for England* (n 17).

[51] In the case of a coal industry pension fund, would investment in the oil and gas industry be to the detriment of the future employment of the existing employed members of the pension fund?

[52] In this country, but see *Blankenship v Boyle* 329 F Supp 1089 (DDC, 1971) from the USA, which was examined in the *Cowan v Scargill* judgment (n 30) at 760J onwards, and which came to a similar conclusion.

[53] [1984] 2 All ER 750 at 763C.

[54] See also *Buttle v Saunders* [1950] 2 All ER 193 for this principle. In the case of charities: 'Most charities need money; and the more of it there is available, the more the trustees can seek to accomplish' (per Nicholls V-C in *Harries v Church Commissioners* (n 17) at 304D.

[55] *Cowan v Scargill* (n 30) at 764B approving the US decision of *Withers v Teachers Retirement System of the City of New York* 447 F Supp 1248 (SDNY, 1978).

13.43 Having made these points about the underlying principles, it should be noted that an ethical investment policy can be entirely consistent with these aims.[56] There is evidence to suggest that companies which conduct their activities in a socially responsible manner may flourish (and avoid risk from regulatory fines, restrictions on trading, etc) and offer sound long-term prospects. If a policy which embraces these companies in all regards meets a trustee's duty with regard to investment, such a policy should safely discharge a trustee's duty.

13.44 A fifth principle can be added to the above four from the subsequent re-examination of this issue in *Martin v City of Edinburgh District Council*.[57] This is, that where charities are concerned, the trustees are not expected to conform to the preceding four principles to the extent that the investment being considered would be fundamentally at odds with the charity's specific aims.[58] A charity would nonetheless still be expected to meet the other standards of trust investment.[59]

13.45 In *Harries v Church Commissioners*, the court envisaged three possible examples where a charity could avoid certain investments:[60]

1. '[W]hen the objects of the charity are such that investments of a particular type would *conflict* with the aims of the charity'.
2. '[W]hen trustees' holdings of particular investments might *hamper a charity's work* either by making potential recipients of aid unwilling to be helped because of the source of the charity's money or by alienating some of those who support the charity financially'.
3. 'Trustees may, if they wish, accommodate the views of those who consider that on *moral grounds* a particular investment would be in conflict with the objects of a charity, so long as the trustees are satisfied that course would not involve a risk of significant financial detriment'.[61] (authors' emphasis)

13.46 Nothing in these general principles prevents a settlor from limiting or framing the investment power according to his own moral, ethical, or political requirements and the trustee would then be bound to follow them (even though these principles may not accord with the beneficiaries' preferences). If settlors do wish to create investment powers framed in this way, draftsmen are well advised to consider very carefully the definitions used to make sure that

---

[56] *Harries v Church Commissioners* (n 17) at 307H: 'It will be seen therefore that the commissioners do have an "ethical" investment policy. They have followed such a policy for many years. Indeed, they have done so ever since they were constituted in 1948. Let me say at once that I can see nothing in [their policy statement] which is inconsistent with the general principles I have sought to expound.'
[57] [1988] 1 Pensions LR 9.
[58] Ethical investment means investing in a way that reflects a charity's values and ethos and does not run counter to its aims. However, a charity's trustees must be able to justify why it is in the charity's best interests to invest in this way. The law permits the following reasons:
  • a particular investment conflicts with the aims of the charity;
  • the charity might loose supporters or beneficiaries if it does not invest ethically; or
  • there is no significant financial detriment.
Charities and Investment Matters: A Guide for Trustees (Charity Commission, 2011).
[59] Per Nicholls V-C in *Harries v Church Commissioners* (n 17) at 304E.
[60] *Harries v Church Commissioners* (n 17) at 304–5.
[61] Qualified by the Charity Commission in *Legal Underpinning: Charities and Investment Matters (CC14) (October 2011)* at [4.10]: 'But trustees are not free to use their investment powers to make moral statements at the expense of their charity.'

they are in terms sufficiently clear and certain that trustees can follow them without risk to themselves or possibly making recourse to the court for clarification necessary.

The application of these principles may also be modified if *all* of those entitled to the trust **13.47** fund are *sui juris* and agree between themselves and with the trustee that a particular investment policy is to be applied.

Standard investment criteria

This concept, now contained within the Trustee Act 2000, is not new, although the label **13.48** was: the wording was largely taken from the Trustee Investments Act 1961. The Trustee Act 2000 provides:

(1) In exercising any power of investment whether arising under this Part or otherwise, a trustee must have regard to the standard investment criteria.
(2) A trustee must from time to time review the investments of the trust and consider whether, having regard to the standard investment criteria, they should be varied.
(3) The standard investment criteria, in relation to a trust, are—
  (a) the suitability to the trust of investments of the same kind as any particular investment proposed to be made or retained and of that particular investment as an investment of that kind, and
  (b) the need for diversification of the trust, in so far as is appropriate to the circumstances of the trust.

These criteria **13.49**

• cannot be subject to a contrary intention in the trust instrument or modified or excluded by the trust instrument;
• are to be applied to all trust powers of investment whatever the date when they were created; and
• apply to the purchase of new investments as well as to the process of reviewing existing investments.

Trustees excluded from the application of the standard investment criteria are **13.50**

• trustees of occupational pension schemes;[62]
• trustees of authorized unit trusts;[63]
• trustees managing a common investment scheme;[64]
• trustees managing a common deposit scheme.[65]

Suitability and diversification go very much hand in hand and it is difficult sometimes in **13.51** practice to separate one from the other.

Investment policy is aimed at producing a portfolio of investments which is balanced overall and suited to the needs of the particular trust. Different investments are accompanied by

---

[62] Section 36(5); occupational pension scheme is defined as in the Pension Schemes Act 1993.
[63] Section 37(1); authorized unit trust is defined as a scheme for which an order under s.78 Financial Services Act 1986 is in force.
[64] Section 38(a); a common investment scheme is defined as a scheme made, or having effect as if made, under s.24 Charities Act 1993, other than such a fund the trusts of which provide that property is not to be transferred to the fund except by or on behalf of a charity the trustees of which are the trustees appointed to manage the fund.
[65] Section 38(b); a common deposit scheme is defined as a scheme made, or having effect as if made, under s.25 Charities Act 1993.

different degrees of risk, which are reflected in the expected rate of return. A large fund with a widely diversified portfolio of securities might justifiably include modest holdings of high risk securities which would be imprudent or out of place in a smaller fund. In such a case it would be inappropriate to isolate one particular investment out of a vast portfolio and enquire whether that can be justified as a trust investment. Such a 'line by line' approach is misplaced. The inquiry, rather, should be to look at a particular investment and enquire whether that is justified as a holding in the context of the overall portfolio.[66]

Suitability

13.52 This, in effect, is a two-stage test:

- first, to ascertain if the class or type of investment is suitable to the trust concerned; and
- second, if the general type of investment is suitable, if the individual investment of that type being considered is suitable.

It is quite conceivable, for any given investment being considered, that it can pass the first stage of the test but fail the second. (It is, however, much harder to conceive of one which could fail the first test but pass the second.) The key point, however, is that all investments must pass both tests.

13.53 Suitability must be assessed in the context of the particular trust under consideration. Therefore, the suitability of any given investment will vary from trust to trust. It is also suggested that, in accordance with the views of Hoffmann J, as he then was, in *Nestle v National Westminster Bank*[67] that suitability is tested in the context of the whole portfolio:

> Modern trustees acting within their investment powers are entitled to be judged by the standards of current portfolio theory which emphasises the risk level of the whole portfolio rather than the risk attaching to each investment taken in isolation.[68]

This results in the suitability of an investment being tested in the context of the entire portfolio rather than being tested as a single investment in isolation from the remainder of the portfolio. The latter was an approach more favoured historically.

13.54 As for diversification (below), the words used in the Trustee Act 2000 are essentially the same as for the 1961 Act. It might therefore be considered appropriate to look to decisions regarding that Act (or earlier on points of suitability and diversification generally), but there were words of caution on examining past decisions, from the Court of Appeal in the *Nestle* appeal:

> What the prudent man should do at any time depends upon the economic and financial conditions of that time not on what judges of the past, however eminent, have held to be the prudent course in the conditions of 50 or 100 years before...when investment conditions were very different.[69]

This does tend to lead one to the view that, subject to the duty of care, the suitability of an investment will depend to a degree upon the market conditions and types of investment available at the time.

---

[66] Lord Nicholls in an article on trust investment ((1995) 9 *Trust Law International* 71).
[67] [2000] WTLR 795.
[68] [2000] WTLR 795, 802.
[69] *Nestle v National Westminster Bank plc* (n 18) at 126.

Diversification

As observed above, generally suitability and diversification are interrelated issues, but diversification is qualified by the phrase 'in so far as is appropriate to the circumstances of the trust'. Circumstances will vary, but clearly **13.55**

1. The size of a trust will limit both the amount and the methods of diversification.
2. The purpose of a trust may clearly indicate that diversification is not required (eg the devise of a house for a beneficiary for life).
3. A trust deed may contain clear expressions hampering the trustee's ability to dispose of particular investments.
4. The trust deed may attempt to negate the statutory duty to diversify and, whilst this is ineffective in its literal terms, it could well amount to a circumstance of the trust[70] which the trustee can take into account, subject to his statutory duty of care, when deciding upon diversification, particularly if the deed contains provisions exonerating the trustee from any failure to diversify.
5. Potential capital gains tax on the sales needed to create the diversification is a factor to be taken into account when deciding if diversification is appropriate, which may decrease the amount of diversification possible.
6. Where a single holding is settled, and it is the settlor's intention that no diversification should take place, the deed, and the appropriate exoneration provisions/trust powers, should reflect this. Simply relying upon what the settlor's wishes were perceived to be may well be insufficient to protect the trustee.
7. Diversification becomes more difficult when a single investment's size gives control (either absolute or in practical terms) and reducing the holding becomes impractical, leaving the choice as sale of the whole or retention of the whole.

The wording of s.4 begins with 'In exercising any power of investment'. In *Gregson v HAE Trustees Ltd*[71] it was suggested that these words control the duty to consider diversification and that therefore this duty would not arise when shares were settled. Although it was not necessary to decide this point,[72] the point had been fully argued and the court was asked to rule on the point. The view of the court was that the duty to consider diversification applied to shares that were settled. **13.56**

Reviews

As well as setting out the standard investment criteria, the Trustee Act 2000 also sets out an express statutory duty to review investments and to apply the standard investment criteria to such reviews.[73] In requiring reviews to be carried out, the statutory provision repeats the previous position at common law.[74] **13.57**

Prior to the Trustee Act 2000, the Trustee Investments Act 1961 contained a duty to decide how often advice should be taken on retaining investments which were either in a narrower **13.58**

---

[70] '[I]n so far as is appropriate to the circumstances of the trust' (s.4(3)(b)).
[71] [2008] WTLR 999.
[72] This was because the primary claim that directors of a trust company are liable personally to the beneficiaries, if the company lacks the funds to meet the claim, failed.
[73] Section 4(2).
[74] *Nestle v National Westminster Bank* (n 24).

range requiring advice or wider-range securities.[75] This duty required the trustees to take into account the circumstances of the trust and the types of investment in making this decision. Trustees were required to take, and consider, that advice. This statutory duty did not extend beyond these two investment issues.

The frequency of reviews

13.59　The Act does not specify the frequency of reviews or the information to be taken into account when considering the investments. However, as a review will involve the exercise of the investment power, whether statutory or express, it will be subject to the statutory duty of care. Therefore, the information required to carry out a review should reflect this, as should the frequency of the reviews.

13.60　The correct frequency of reviews will be dictated by

- portfolio value; and
- nature of assets (unit trusts and particularly index trackers may not require the same frequency of consideration as, say, a bespoke portfolio of individual investments. On the other hand, some individual equities, because of the nature of their market or activities, may require closer attention than others).

It could be suggested that a reasonable guide to how frequent the reviews should be is probably to apply the same frequency as a private client asset manager would to a personal portfolio of that size, constituent investments, and complexity. However, increasingly, reviews at set time intervals are regarded by professional investment managers as being inappropriate and are being replaced with a constant monitoring process. The reasons behind this are twofold. First, in today's market, with today's flow of investment information, reviewing portfolios at set time intervals can miss crucial information which should be considered and possibly applied to the portfolio.[76] Second, and quite correctly, financial regulation has affected this review process. If information regarding a particular investment is known, it should be applied to all holdings held at that time by a manager, not merely to those portfolios that are being reviewed at that time through some quirk of the calendar. It is therefore suggested that if a trustee is not knowledgeable or skilled enough to monitor investments in a trust on this basis, then delegation of the investment management becomes imperative for the safe management of the portfolio. However, it still remains suitable that at reasonable intervals the trustees stand back from the detail of the investment and look at the overall investment position of the trust to assess whether it needs change in the light of the current circumstances of the trust. Where investment is delegated, this type of review should be ahead of review meetings with the delegated manager.

13.61　Examples of trust-specific information to be taken into account when considering the investments are:

1.　Any information expressly specified by financial or other regulation (eg the investment policy statement of the trustees if the management has been delegated to managers. Also the correctness of the agreement under which the funds' management is delegated).

---

[75] Section 6(3) Trustee Investments Act 1961.

[76] The speed with which share prices can move is generally a factor in this, but in particular a price may fall rapidly on bad news or adverse market sentiment and not reviewing a holding because the portfolio review date is not yet due makes little sense.

2. The expected duration of the trust. For example, the age of a life tenant (including state of health where known), or the ages of other beneficiaries whose existence is relevant to the continuation of the trust, or the period until the beneficiaries will attain vested interests.
3. The current yield in relation to the future income requirements of the trust.
4. The administrative requirements of the trust for capital expenditure.[77]
5. Capital gains tax: from the point of view of the pros and cons of realizing particular investments, the nature of the investments made (are they exempt or relieved from CGT or is it more appropriate to use investments which are?), the availability and safety of investment structures which might avoid the tax, the expected tax-free uplift on the death of a beneficiary, the possibility of roll-over/hold-over relief being available, etc. Will the reinvestment of the proceeds of sale after the deduction for the tax charge out-perform the original investment if it was retained?
6. Income tax: both the tax position of the beneficiaries and also the taxation advantages of specific types of investments.
7. The current degree of diversification and that which is desirable in a trust of the particular type, although other factors listed here may limit what can realistically be achieved.
8. The suitability of the current investments; not only in the context of the statutory criteria[78] but also from the standpoint of the other factors listed here and the general circumstances of the trust (together, of course, with the same suitability issues being assessed in relation to any replacement investments).
9. Currency risk of the investments in relation to the spending requirements of the beneficiaries.
10. The investment powers available either from the deed or from statute, together with any applicable limitations or consents that may apply, or if any duty in relation to the powers is placed with someone other than the trustee.
11. The domicile and residence of the trust, the trustees, and the beneficiaries, for the effect that these may have on the taxation of the trust.
12. The performance history for the guidance that this will give to the past performance of the individual investments and the collective portfolio.

The general power of investment

Part II Trustee Act 2000 deals with investment issues and introduced a new statutory power **13.62** of investment, known as 'the general power of investment':

> Subject to the provisions of this Part, a trustee may make any kind of investment that he could make if he were absolutely entitled to the assets of the trust.[79]

The form used for this gives wide powers to the trustee—generally the same type of power as has been favoured by modern trust draftsmen. However, the general power of investment is subject to the restrictions in the remaining provisions of Part II of the Act and these are:

- the power can only be exercised with regard to the standard investment criteria;[80]
- the use of the power is required to be regularly reviewed;[81]

---

[77] For both this point and the previous, a degree of budgetary planning is required ahead of investment reviews to make the process more efficient.
[78] Section 4 Trustee Act 2000.
[79] Section 3(1) of the 2000 Act and the wording used follows that previously used in s.34(1) Pensions Act 1995.
[80] Section 4.
[81] Section 4(2).

- the exercise of the power is subject to certain requirements regarding advice;[82]
- the power does not give any power to invest in land, other than loans secured on land[83] (but there are express powers relating to land elsewhere in the Act);[84] and
- the power can be restricted by the terms of the trust instrument.[85]

In addition, the exercise of the statutory investment power is subject to a new statutory duty of care.[86]

Investment in land

13.63   Land has been a feature of the purpose of creating trusts for far longer than stocks and shares, although it is now of much less importance[87] than these investments. At the time when land was so important in trust investment, there was little statutory authority for its purchase, but today there are significant statutory powers available to trustees to purchase land.

13.64   Trust deeds which pre-date the Trustee Act 2000 usually contained express powers to acquire land, particularly for a beneficiary's occupation, as somewhat surprisingly neither the Trustee Act 1925 nor the Trustee Investments Act 1961 conferred any statutory power on trustees to purchase freehold or leasehold land.[88]

13.65   The new general power of investment in s.3 Trustee Act 2000 expressly excludes the acquisition of interests in land (other than loans secured on land), but the Act contains a new statutory power to acquire land in Part III.[89]

13.66   Land for the purpose of this power is not defined in the Act and is presumed to be defined in s.5 and Schedule 1 Interpretation Act 1978 and, therefore, subject to any contrary intention in the trust deed, land will be 'Buildings and other structures, land covered with water, and any estate, interest, easement, servitude or right in or over land'.[90]

Buildings will not include chattels, however well connected in terms of association with the building they may be. It is thought that if there are chattels that are being considered for acquisition with the building, they could only be purchased under the investment power (express or statutory) where their acquisition can be justified on investment grounds.

13.67   The statutory power[91] provides:

> (1) A trustee may acquire freehold or leasehold land in the United Kingdom—
>   (a) as an investment
>   (b) for occupation by a beneficiary, or
>   (c) for any other reason.
> (2) 'Freehold or leasehold land' means—
>   (a) in relation to England and Wales, a legal estate in land,
>   (b) in relation to Scotland—

---

[82] Section 5.
[83] Section 3(3).
[84] Section 8.
[85] Section 6.
[86] Contained in s.1 and applied to the investment power by para 1 Sch 1.
[87] Assuming that in this context the trusts of joint property are not included.
[88] Although there were powers to lend money on mortgages secured on land.
[89] Which replaced the previous powers of s.6 Trusts of Land and Appointment of Trustees Act 1996.
[90] NB not the definition provided by s.205(1)(ix) Law of Property Act 1925.
[91] Section 8.

    (i) the estate or interest of the proprietor of the dominium utile or, in the case of land not held on feudal tenure, the estate or interest of the owner, or

    (ii) a tenancy, and

  (c) in relation to northern Ireland, a legal estate in land, including land held under a fee farm grant.

(3) For the purposes of exercising his functions as trustee, a trustee who acquires land under this section has all the powers of an absolute owner in relation to the land.[92]

- Only land within the United Kingdom may be acquired under this power;
- only freehold or leasehold land may be acquired; and
- within England and Wales, only legal estates in land may be acquired.

Application of s.8

The power contained in s.8 is not available to trustees of the following trusts: **13.68**

- a trust which contains settled land;[93]
- a trust to which the Universities and Colleges Estate Act 1925 applies;[94]
- any pension scheme;[95]
- authorized unit trusts;[96] and
- common investment schemes for charities.[97]

Mortgages

The statutory power of trustees to lend money on the security of land (mortgage) is now to   **13.69** be found in the statutory general investment power.[98] Prior to this, the statutory authority for mortgages was to be found in s.8 Trustee Act 1925 and the Trustee Investments Act 1961. Although now repealed by the Trustee Act 2000, the terms of the earlier authorities are still relevant when considering the validity of mortgages made under them, which may still be trust investments.

Although the Trustee Act 2000 repealed the previous provisions, the changes are not particu-   **13.70** larly significant. As has been noted earlier, the new statutory general power of investment will include acquiring a loan secured on land[99] (lending on mortgage). However, without the specified lending limits of *s.8 Trustee Act 1925*, it becomes even more important that the amount of lending is considered carefully. Whilst there is now no statutory definition of

---

[92] An oddity of the amendments made by the Trustee Act 2000 is that s.6(3) Trusts of Land and Appointment of Trustees Act 1996 is amended to read: 'The trustees of land have power to acquire land under the power conferred by section 8 of the Trustee Act 2000'. Given the extent of the new statutory power found in s.8 it is difficult to see the reason for amending s.6(3).

[93] Section 10(1)(a).

[94] Section 10(1)(b).

[95] Section 36(3); pension scheme is defined in s.36(1) as an occupational pension scheme within the meaning of the Pension Schemes Act 1993, established under a trust and subject to the law of England and Wales.

[96] Section 37(1); an authorized unit trust means a unit trust scheme in the case of which an order under s.78 Financial Services Act 1986 is in force.

[97] Section 38(a); a common investment scheme is defined as one under s.24 Charities Act 1993; by s.38(b) this power also does not apply to common deposit schemes under s.25 Charities Act 1993.

[98] Section 3(3) excludes the general power from applying to investments in land 'other than in loans secured on land'.

[99] 'Land' is as defined in s.5 and Sch 1 Interpretation Act 1978 and, subject to any contrary intention, will be 'Buildings and other structures, land covered with water, and any estate, interest, easement, servitude or right in or over land'. (NB not the definition provided by s.205(1)(ix) Law of Property Act 1925.)

the report that should be obtained, it is suggested that, with the exception of the two-thirds limit, the report procedure used previously by the Trustee Act 1925 should now form the basis of good practice for future trustee lending.

13.71 The provisions of the 1925 Act did not expressly provide that the report, or the instructions to the valuer, should be in writing. However, with such an issue it is unquestionably sound practice to ensure that both are in writing and to continue this practice for the future. The instructions should

1. Explain that it is a trustee mortgage that is being considered.
2. Give details of the property, its location, tenure, etc, together with any other relevant information about boundaries, rights of way, covenants, etc that are known to the trustee.
3. Make it clear that the remuneration of the surveyor is not dependent upon his recommendation or the mortgage proceeding.[100]
4. Require that the report be prepared in writing and cover the following issues:
   (a) the agent's professional standing, experience, and any other factors that qualify him to write the report;
   (b) the agent's understanding of the nature and extent of the property that he has surveyed (to ensure that there is no confusion or misunderstanding of the nature of the property);
   (c) any particular factors that it has been necessary to take into account in the valuation;
   (d) the current market value of the property and the amount that in his opinion can be safely advanced; and
   (e) the surveyor's recommendation that such an advance is suitable in the particular instance as a mortgage from a trust.[101]

13.72 Because the lending on mortgage under the statutory power is an application of the general power of investment, all of the other characteristics of this power apply:

- the duty of care;
- the standard investment criteria; and
- the duty to review.

Any sum lent should have been on a first legal mortgage only, unless the trust deed authorized otherwise, but even then a power to lend otherwise would need very careful consideration on the point that a mortgage less than a first legal mortgage was a suitable trust investment. A first mortgage is required in order to prevent the trustee from having the security threatened by the actions of the first mortgagee.[102] The mortgage is required to be a legal mortgage because of the protection given to the mortgagee.[103]

13.73 The solicitor instructed by the trustee to act in the matter should be satisfied as to the adequacy of the title for the trustee's purpose. Because of this duty to the trustee, it is not recommended that the trustee should agree to instruct the mortgagor's solicitor for this work. Generally speaking, trustee mortgages are bespoke deeds and a solicitor in such

---

[100] *Smith v Stoneham* [1866] WN 178; *Marquis of Salisbury v Keymer* [1909] WN 31.
[101] The particular significance of this point lies in a trustee's general aversion to hazard. The risk attached to the mortgage granted by a trustee is less than that which could be accepted by a non-trustee investor. The surveyor should therefore be aware of this.
[102] *Norris v Wright* (1851) 14 Beav 291.
[103] *Swaffield v Nelson* [1876] WN 255.

circumstances would in all probability find the conflict of representing both sides to be too great.

Who can trustees lend to?

Trustees are not able to lend to themselves, or to some of their number, unless the trust deed **13.74** makes express provision for this. Trustees are otherwise required to exercise unanimous and impartial judgement as to the sufficiency of the security that is being offered, and if a trustee is offering the security that impartial assessment is not possible.[104] An open question is the lending of money on mortgage to the spouse of a trustee. Where the spouse is likely to have an interest in the loan being made (such as occupying it with his spouse), prudence seems to suggest that the same objection to impartial judgement could arise.

Lending to beneficiaries of a trust has tended to be the most common trustee lending in the **13.75** last half century. Before this, loans to strangers were a much more common form of investment. There is no restriction on the class of beneficiary that may borrow in this way (unless the beneficiary is a trustee). Trustees must be aware of the need to justify the loan on investment grounds rather than on grounds of simple convenience for the beneficiary. Selling interest-yielding stock, such as gilts, in order to lend it on similar terms to a beneficiary produces no advantage to the trust.[105]

However, trustees do need to consider carefully the suitability of a mortgage in the con- **13.76** text of the entire trustee investment policy, and whether or not advancing funds in this way unduly benefits one beneficiary ahead of the others. The following can be aspects for consideration:

1. The risk/diversification issues: is too much of the trust fund being committed to one asset?
2. What is the advantage to the trust of making the loan, or is the benefit mainly for the mortgagor?
3. Unless the mortgage makes provision for the capital sum lent to be index/inflation linked, or for the lender to participate in the future capital appreciation of the property, is the trust to be committed to an excessive amount being invested in a non-appreciating asset?
4. Is the income produced adequate to compensate the investment beneficiary (if that is not the mortgagee)?
5. Does the income produced excessively advantage the income beneficiary?
6. If the loan is to one of several capital beneficiaries, is that beneficiary excessively benefited through having the mortgage, even on full commercial terms, unless some capital appreciation is produced for the benefit of the other capital beneficiaries?

These questions need to be considered in respect of mortgages in the present circum- **13.77** stances. Historically, (and especially in times of very low inflation or deflation) the capital appreciation aspect of investment was not an issue,[106] but in an age when capital appreciation is an integral part of investment, is a conventional mortgage still a suitable asset? Undoubtedly it may be, but it is probably rarer today that it is suitable within the needs of the whole trust.

---

[104] *Stickney v Sewell* (1835) 1 My & C 8; *Fletcher v Green* (1864) 33 Beav 426.
[105] *Whitney v Smith* (1869) 4 Ch App 513.
[106] See *Re Wragg* [1919] 2 Ch 58 at 64 per Lawrence J: an investment being defined as 'property ... purchased in order to be held for the sake of the income which it will yield'.

D. Agents, nominees, custodians, and bearer securities

Agents

13.78 Prior to the commencement of the Trustee Act 2000 there was no statutory power of delegation of management to an agent. Delegation of ministerial actions was permitted after 1925;[107] ministerial acts being the carrying out of the trustee's decisions. In practice this was of limited value for the management of assets as the decision making could not be delegated to the investment manager. Delegation was, in more modern trust deeds, often expressly authorized in order to allow the employment of professional investment managers. This area of the law was reformed by Part IV Trustee Act 2000.

13.79 The statutory power

- applies to trusts whenever created;[108]
- is addition to any powers otherwise conferred on the trustees; and[109]
- is subject to any restriction or inclusion imposed by the trust instrument or any provision of subordinate legislation.[110]

13.80 The new statutory power to employ agents has much wider application than merely the use of investment or asset managers. But for the purpose of this work it will be examined mainly in the context of asset management.[111] It is of prime importance to note that the appointment of agents is subject to the new statutory duty of care imposed by this Act.[112]

13.81 Trustees are given a general power of delegation.[113] Those functions that may be delegated are defined as *any function* other than

- any function relating to whether or in what way any assets are distributed;
- the power to decide whether fees or other payments are made from capital or income;
- any power to appoint a trustee; and
- any power to delegate functions or appoint a nominee or custodian.

13.82 The trustees of charitable trusts are also given a power to delegate,[114] but this is framed differently, with the delegable functions being defined positively as

- any function consisting of carrying out a decision that the trustees have taken;
- any function relating to the investment of assets subject to the trust (including, in the case of land held as an investment, managing the land and creating or disposing of an interest in the land);

---

[107] Section 23 Trustee Act 1925.
[108] Section 27.
[109] Section 26(a).
[110] Section 26(b).
[111] 'Asset management functions' are defined in s.15(5) as '(a) the investment of assets subject to the trust, (b) the acquisition of property which is to be subject to the trust, and (c) managing property which is subject to the trust and disposing of, or creating or disposing of an interest in, such property'. Asset management is where the management of all of the assets of the trust and management may, quite reasonably, be divided between different managers or between managers and the trustees themselves.
[112] Section 1 and para 3 Sch 1.
[113] Section 11(2) and (3).
[114] Section 11(3).

- any function relating to the raising of funds for the trust otherwise than by means of profits of a trade which is an integral part of carrying out the trust's charitable purpose; and
- any other function prescribed by an order of the Secretary of State.

Section 11 does not permit the decision to delegate and the appointment of agents to be delegated and it remains a function that the trustees must exercise themselves. **13.83**

Delegation of investment management for both non-charitable and charitable trusts is authorized; the former because it is not excluded from delegation and the latter because it is expressly permitted. The power to delegate the management of investment in s.11 does include delegation by PRs,[115] but does not extend to **13.84**

- trustees of occupational pension schemes;[116]
- trustees of authorized unit trusts;[117]
- trustees managing a common investment scheme; and[118]
- trustees managing a common deposit scheme.[119]

A failure by the trustees to act within the limits of the statutory power in authorizing an agent to exercise a trustee function does not invalidate the authorization.[120] Trustees should clearly record their decision to delegate; preferably by trustees' minute. **13.85**

Who may act as an agent?

The Act defines those who may act as agents.[121] Significantly a beneficiary of the trust may not act as the trustees' agent,[122] but one of several trustees may act in this way.[123] Where a beneficiary is both a trustee and a beneficiary he is expressly barred from acting as agent.[124] **13.86**

Where the trustee appoints more than one person to exercise the same trustee function the trustee must appoint them jointly.[125] The agent can, if the trustees see fit, also act as nominee or custodian.[126] The Act refers to a 'person' being appointed as an agent, and in this context person also includes a corporation.

Terms of appointment

An agent may be appointed under the statutory power on such terms and with such remuneration as the trustee may determine,[127] but unless it is 'reasonably necessary for them to do **13.87**

---

[115] Section 35(1).

[116] Section 36(5); occupational pension scheme is defined in the Pension Schemes Act 1993.

[117] Section 37(1); authorized unit trust is defined as a scheme for which an order under s.78 Financial Services Act 1986 is in force.

[118] Section 38(a); a common investment scheme is defined as a scheme made, or having effect as if made, under s.24 Charities Act 1993 other than such a fund the trusts of which provide that property is not to be transferred to the fund except by or on behalf of a charity the trustees of which are the trustees appointed to manage the fund.

[119] Section 38(b); a common deposit scheme is defined as a scheme made, or having effect as if made, under s.25 Charities Act 1993.

[120] Section 24(a).

[121] Section 12.

[122] Section 12(3).

[123] Section 12(1).

[124] Section 12(3).

[125] Section 12(2).

[126] Section 12(4).

[127] Section 14(1).

so' they should not authorize the agent to appoint a substitute, cap his liability for his actions, or act in a position of conflict of interest.[128]

13.88   The acceptance by the trustee of the agent's terms and remuneration is subject to the trustee's statutory duty of care.[129]

13.89   For any appointment of an agent, whether under the statutory power or otherwise,[130] the agent may be remunerated by the trustees out of the trust funds if they were engaged on terms that permitted remuneration and the level of remuneration is 'reasonable'.[131] The trustee may also reimburse the agent for any expenses reasonably incurred by them.[132] Neither provision authorizes the charging of remuneration or expenses for work incurred prior to the commencement of the Trustee Act 2000.[133]

13.90   What terms are reasonable may possibly be judged by what terms and conditions of business and provision for remuneration are routinely quoted by professional investment managers for the type of trustee work being considered. It is suggested that it would be good practice for the trustees to record the factors that they took into account at the time the appointment is made.

Issues relating to investment management

13.91   Anyone who acts as an agent for the purpose of investment management, under the statutory authority, is subject, whatever the terms of his appointment, to any specific duties or restrictions that attach to that function.[134] The words used in the Act appear to make this duty of the agent incapable of modification by the trust instrument, unless the trust instrument, instead of modifying the statutory power, creates an express power of delegation. This point is expressly illustrated in s.13(1) by the example that the agent authorized to exercise the general power of investment, under this Act, is to be subject to the standard investment criteria of s.4. As the standard investment criteria apply to all trustees,[135] the standard investment criteria will be bound to apply to them even if the delegation under this Act is of an express investment power.

13.92   The agent is relieved from the necessity to obtain advice on investments if he is the kind of person from whom advice would otherwise be obtained.[136]

13.93   Delegation of authority in respect of asset management also has further specific conditions attached by s.15. The 'asset management functions of trustees' are defined in this section as

- the investment of assets subject to the trust;
- the acquisition of property which is to be subject to the trust; and
- managing property which is subject to the trust and disposing of, or creating, or disposing of an interest in, such property.[137]

---

[128] Section 14(2) and (3).
[129] Paragraph 3(1)(a) Sch 1.
[130] Section 32(1).
[131] Section 32(2).
[132] Section 32(3).
[133] Section 33(1).
[134] Section 13(1).
[135] Section 4(1).
[136] Section 13(2).
[137] Section 15(5).

The specific conditions set out in s.15 are: **13.94**

1. There must be a written agreement for the delegation or the agreement must be evidenced in writing.[138]
2. No delegation is permissible unless the trustee has prepared a written[139] policy statement as to how the investment policy is to be run[140] and this must be with a view to ensuring that management will be in the best interests of the trust.[141]
3. The written agreement must contain an express undertaking from the agent to comply with the policy statement or any amended or substituted statement.[142]

The conditions in s.15 appear to be mandatory and not capable of being modified or excluded   **13.95**
by the trust instrument. Whether or not s.15 applies to the delegation of asset management
functions under the power in the Trustee Act 2000 only, or to all investment delegation
under whatever power, has been the subject of some debate, although the authors consider
that it does apply to all asset management delegation.[143] If it is eventually found that s.15
does not apply to non-statutory delegation, the authors submit that it would be best practice for trustees to follow s.15. The preparation of the written policy statement remains the
responsibility of the trustee and it cannot be delegated to the investment manager, although
of course he will be consulted. The trustee is, however, entitled (indeed advised) to take
advice on the content of this statement.

Delegation under s.15 must be on an individual trust basis and cannot be in respect of a   **13.96**
number of trusts. For each trust the factors for and against delegation must be weighed
together with the suitability of the agent to the individual trusts. This obviously requires that
individual policy statements are also required. Delegation is therefore a matter to be measured
against the individual trust and its needs and benefits and not the need of the trustee in relation
to a portion of his business.

The position of trusts subject to the Settled Land Act 1925 is still anomalous. Notwithstanding   **13.97**
the transfer of the tenant for life's investment powers to the trustee (from the commencement of the new Act),[144] the trustee is bound to consult the tenant for life regarding changes
and, as far as is consistent with the general interests of the trust, give effect to those wishes.[145]
This will prevent the trustee of such a trust from delegating investment on a fully discretionary basis to an agent.

Supervision of agents

The Act creates a framework of supervision of the agent by the trustee where the statutory   **13.98**
power has been used to delegate. Furthermore, these supervisory requirements will apply
to any delegation under an express power or the enactment or provision of subordinated

---

[138] Section 15(1).
[139] Section 15(4).
[140] Section 15(2)(a).
[141] Section 15(3).
[142] Section 15(2)(b).
[143] The Charity Commission: *Investment of Charitable Funds: Detailed Guidance* (February 2003) also considered that for charities a written agreement is required whatever power delegation is made under, and the current edition of CC14 (*Charities and Investment Matters: A Guide for Trustees* (October 2011)) simply says that there must be a written contract and that this must require the manager to follow the investment policy of the charity (section F6).
[144] Paragraph 10 Part II Sch 2 amending s.75(2) Settled Land Act 1925.
[145] Paragraph 10 Part II Sch 2 amending s.75(4) Settled Land Act 1925.

legislation to the extent that they are not inconsistent with the terms of the express power.[146] The review is subject to the statutory duty of care.[147]

13.99 While powers are delegated to any agent, the trustee must keep under review 'the arrangements under which' the agent acts and how 'those arrangements are being put into effect'.[148] The trustee must consider, if circumstances are appropriate, whether he needs to intervene[149] and if he considers that there is a need to intervene he should do so.[150] The Act gives no guidance as to the frequency of this review or the factors that the trustee should take into account. It is suggested that allowing the arrangements to run for longer than twelve months without a review might be excessive. It is also suggested that whatever fixed period might be determined for future reviews, the trustee should review the arrangement earlier if he becomes aware that matters are not as he would reasonably expect.

13.100 However, there are additional requirements where the delegated functions are asset management functions. The trustee's duty to consider the arrangements with the agent must also include reviewing whether or not there is any need to revise or replace the investment policy statement.[151] If the trustee considers that there is a need to revise or replace the policy statement then he has a duty to do so.[152] If the trustee concludes that the policy statement should be amended or replaced, the new or amended policy statement must be prepared in the best interests of the trust and be in writing, or evidenced in writing.[153]

13.101 The trustee also has a duty in considering the arrangements with the agent to consider if the policy statement is being complied with.[154]

Some practical considerations concerning the appointment of agents

13.102 There will usually be several stages involved in any delegation of investment management:

1. decision in principle to delegate;
2. selection of a manager;
3. appointment of a manager; and
4. monitoring and review.

13.103 The new statutory duty of care will apply to stages 2, 3, and 4.

13.104 **Stage 1. The decision in principle to delegate** The decision to delegate needs to be taken with particular regard to

- the type of assets currently held;
- the type of assets which are likely to be purchased;
- the value of the trust; and
- the particular professional skills and knowledge of the trustees.

---

[146] Section 21(2) and (3).
[147] Sections 1 and 2 and para 3(1)(e) Sch 1.
[148] Section 22(1)(a).
[149] Under the statutory power to intervene in s.22 or the terms of any express power.
[150] Section 22(1)(c).
[151] Section 22(2)(a).
[152] Section 22(2)(b).
[153] Section 22(3) applying s.15(3) and (4).
[154] Section 22(2)(c).

This must be a unanimous act of the trustees, unless the trust deed makes a special provision otherwise. Unanimity is a potential source of difficulty where there are several trustees, as it is not too far fetched to foresee trusts where a lay co-trustee does not want to delegate, but a professional co-trustee does. The professional trustee has potentially greater risks involved through a greater awareness of the diligence required of a trustee, and therefore needs to assist the lay trustee's understanding and persuade the trustee to follow rational and defensible policies.

Stage 2. The selection of an agent   The type of agent and the knowledge that he should   **13.105** have will vary according to the needs of the trust. A tendering process involving written proposals and beauty parades will no doubt be right for major trusts (and this almost certainly happens at present), but such a process may well not be appropriate for smaller trusts. But this should not mean employment of

- the first agent approached by the trustee; or
- the first agent that approaches the trustee; or
- the agent that has always been used by the trustee in the past for other trusts.

Some greater awareness is needed of the features of the individual investment managers and   **13.106** the products they offer. These should include the following:

Costs   **13.107**

- Are they reasonable in the context of the particular trust?
- How do they compare to similar managers?
- Are they clear, understandable, and predictable?

Terms and conditions of management   **13.108**

- Are they reasonable?
- Do they attempt to impose any exclusions of liability that are unreasonable in the context of the assets, the trust, and the service required?
- Do they permit dealings where there is a conflict of interest?
- Were the terms and conditions drawn up with trustees in mind, or are they simply standard private client conditions?
- Do the terms of the agreement include an undertaking to observe the trustee's investment policy statement?

Performance and reporting   **13.109**

- What will be the frequency of the reporting of performance? Is what is proposed appropriate or are different arrangements more suitable?
- Is the format in which reports and performance statistics will be presented sufficiently clear and appropriate to the needs of the trustees in monitoring the arrangements?
- Will the manager's reports contain all that the trustee requires to monitor the delegation?
- Is the basis on which performance is to be calculated appropriate for the trust?
- What benchmarking of the portfolio performance is available as it is to be based on adequate comparisons?

Regulatory standing   **13.110**

- Is the manager regulated and appropriately registered?

- Are there professional indemnity insurance schemes/compensation schemes/ombudsman arrangements available?

13.111 *Products or investment policies that the manager offers*

- Is what is being offered suitable for a trust portfolio?
- Does the manager have experience of running trust portfolios?
- Is the manager conversant with trustee attitudes to risk and how they may differ from those of a private individual?

13.112 **Stage 3. Appointment of an agent** The Act requires a written statement of policy from the trustees and this should be considered very carefully and discussed with the agent. Some very competent investment advisers may not be as conversant with trustee standards of investment and risk as trustees, but equally even a professional trustee may not be as conversant with the investment market as the professional investment manager. A dialogue is essential. Investment managers who are properly conversant with trustee investment may well have available standard trust policy statements.

13.113 A crucial issue is what should be in an investment policy statement. It should contain quite specific directions defining the policy that is to be followed in order to meet the trustees' duties. This will almost certainly mean that it will set out different standards from those which would usually be applied by managers to private client portfolios. It must be a document agreed by all of the trustees (it cannot be delegated to just one of the trustees) and it must be acceptable to the investment manager. The preparation of the investment policy document cannot be delegated to the proposed agent, although a trustee is able to take independent advice on its contents.[155]

13.114 Examples of some policy issues that need to be considered include

13.115 **Liquidity**[156] This can be a very vexed area within trusts. There can obviously be valid administrative reasons for requiring cash reserves, but should liquidity be a substantial feature of the investment policy? Long-term liquidity can bring complaints of a breach of the trustee's duty to invest. Big short-term liquidity positions can be a result of taking short-term speculative views of the market. Whatever the trustee's own views on the desirability or otherwise of liquidity, it is a policy issue that needs to be faced from the perspective of trustee risk as well as investment policy and then clearly defined in the policy statement.

13.116 **Capital and income issues** Allocations between capital and income need to be covered. Some problems in demergers still exist for trustees, albeit not to the same extent. The Trusts (Capital and Income) Act 2013 commenced on 1 October 2013[157] and from that date demerged shares, referred to as 'a tax-exempt corporate distribution', are treated as a capital receipt in the hands of trustees.[158] Where the trustees receive a distribution that is treated as capital by this provision and they are satisfied that it is likely, but for this provision, that there

---

[155] Section 15 Trustee Act 2000. The Charity Commission's *Charity and Investment Matters: A Guide for Trustees* (n 58) at 22: 'Preparing the policy statement cannot be delegated to the investment manager...Trustees might find it helpful to prepare it in consultation with the proposed investment manager to ensure its terms are workable and achievable.'

[156] See earlier at para 13.28 regarding trustee liquidity.

[157] Before that date *Sinclair v Lee* [1993] 3 WLR 498 and the analysis of direct and indirect demergers applied.

[158] Section 2 Trusts (Capital and Income) Act 2013—this applies to all trusts whenever created.

would have been an income distribution from the company they can compensate the income beneficiary.[159] The compensation, in the form of cash or property, should be for the amount that the trustee considers would have been distributed as income but for the demerger.[160] This compensatory payment is to be treated as a payment of capital.[161] While the trustee may well take advice on the size of a capital payment, the decision as to payment and the amount of the payment remains that of the trustee.[162]

There are, for example, still issues of special dividends and redeemable preference shares in lieu of dividends. The correct allocation of these distributions between income and capital will affect both performance and correct payment of benefits from the trust (as indeed will any decision to sell a holding prior to a direct demerger in order to protect capital value). The investment manager is not the correct party to make these decisions, and reporting and responsibility for them needs to be defined. **13.117**

Similarly, a policy on stock dividends needs to be covered by the statement. Many issues come into this subject, particularly the type of trust. For example, accepting stock dividends would not only deprive the life tenant of income, but it would apparently boost capital performance. Even where the type of trust makes this an option, a policy still needs to be determined by the trustee in the light of the power to accumulate and the income/cash requirements of the trust. **13.118**

Taxation   If the trustees have particular income tax issues these should be clearly defined in the policy statement. The trustee's attitude to capital gains tax is an important tax issue which must be defined in the policy statement. The anticipated future duration of the trust is relevant to the trustee's appetite for incurring gains. The future duration of the trust may well limit the ability of the portfolio to recover value lost through the payment of large amounts of tax on gains. Life interest trusts are likely to have a tax-free uplift on distribution on the death of a life tenant. Realizing substantial taxable gains for very elderly life tenants may therefore not be the wisest course, unless the investment grounds for sale are imperative. **13.119**

Generally, a policy on the amount of realized gain should be agreed, together with some mechanics for exchange of information if there are potential gains on other assets (such as investment property) that may be outside the investment manager's knowledge (or securities gains that may be outside the property manager's knowledge). However, to formulate a sensible capital gains tax policy does require the investment manager being made aware of the trustees' policy on realization of chargeable gains. **13.120**

Investment for the elderly   If a current life tenant is aged ninety, will the investment manager apply the same investment policy as he would for a fifty-year-old life tenant, or should the trustee expect the investment manager to alter the policy in these circumstances? Will the portfolio have the same fixed interest proportions? Will the same view of equity investment be taken, bearing in mind the reduced life expectancy? **13.121**

---

[159] Defined as a 'person entitled to income arising under a trust, or for whose benefit such income may be applied' (s.3(4) Trusts (Capital and Income) Act 2013).
[160] Section 3(2) and (3) Trusts (Capital and Income) Act 2013.
[161] Section 3(2) Trusts (Capital and Income) Act 2013.
[162] Section 11(2)(a) Trustee Act 2000.

There are no easy answers to these points, but they are questions that need to be faced in discussion with the investment manager to arrive at an understanding that is appropriate to the trust.

13.122 **Returns** The level of income return in life interest trusts needs to be defined. Defining what is being looked for in terms of capital and income return enables the investment manager to know the extent that his policy can accommodate, say, zero-income-yield stocks within his policy. Overall return on investment is not, by itself, a good enough measure for life interest trusts when it is feasible to acquire capital return at the expense of the level of the life tenant's income. The reverse of this coin can be some discretionary or accumulation trusts where income return may be secondary to securing capital return. Before delegation you need to know what sort of policy you want and then discover if the manager can deliver it.

13.123 **Risk definitions** This is something that is potentially a difficult issue. The trustee will, however, need to address the point with the investment manager. Trustees will not be able to take the same level of risk as some private clients can accept. In practice, the bottom line is that losses which arise from the trustee taking unacceptable investment risks involving a breach of his duty of care are potentially the liability of the trustee, whereas profits from similar investments will go to the credit of the trusts.

13.124 **Currency issues** To what extent is it acceptable to have foreign currency risks (eg overseas stocks whose return may be affected by foreign exchange movements) in a trust for UK beneficiaries? A very difficult question to address and much will depend upon the circumstances of each trust. Nevertheless, the level of foreign currency risk is an issue and it is one where there needs to be an informed dialogue at the outset.

13.125 **'Know your customer'** This is compliance and money laundering terminology for the principle behind the investment manager's need to establish relevant information to identify his client's needs and then aim his management towards meeting those needs. This will inevitably mean that the trustee will have to be prepared to disclose details of the trust and the trust's requirements.

13.126 **Stage 4. Monitoring and review** This is inescapable, as quite reasonably, the Trustee Act 2000 imposed a duty on the trustees to carry out some monitoring of the agent. How this is achieved is, however, a vexed question. Benchmarking against a chosen index or performance factor is the usually accepted route.

13.127 Published performance figures are often quoted showing that a substantial part of the active (as opposed to passive or tracking) UK unit trusts failed to meet their chosen benchmark. Are they poor performers, or is the benchmark chosen too high? Quite possibly a benchmark can be too high, but trustees at least have the chance to set their own target rather than have an industry one imposed on them. Whatever benchmark is chosen it should be one that reflects an appropriate trustee policy.

13.128 Trusts have smaller annual CGT allowances than do individuals and this can produce a degree of investment paralysis as the gains get bigger and the life tenant gets older (and thus nearer the CGT free uplift on death). This is important from the point of view of benchmarking as the paralysis can produce a degree of underperformance against the benchmark.

On the other hand the CGT liabilities, if sales are made, can produce even worse net performance.

Failure to meet a benchmark is not proof of negligence, nor is failure to dismiss an invest- **13.129** ment manager who fails to meet a benchmark. Failure to meet a benchmark is an indicator of *what has happened* and it therefore requires interpretation to establish *why it happened*. This applies to both good and bad performance. The analysis of why a better than benchmark performance was obtained can reveal that unacceptable risks were taken in order to boost performance.

Nominees

A nominee is someone appointed by the trustee who is to hold the title to specified trust **13.130** assets in his name. The nominee is no more than a bare trustee who holds the title to the order of the trustee and acts according to the trustee's instructions.[163] The trustee's relationship with the nominee is contractual and the trustee retains his fiduciary duty towards the trust and its beneficiaries.

Typically nominees are used to facilitate discretionary investment management. By using **13.131** their own nominee company the investment manager can deal expeditiously and without the necessity to revert to the trustees for transfers to be signed. The appointment of the fund manager's nominee will often be covered within the investment management agreement. A second type of nominee arrangement that a trustee might use is where a nominee service (usually provided by the stockbroker) allows for easier dealing by the trustee. Of growing importance is the use of nominees within electronic systems of stock and share holding such as Euroclear. The inability to enter the world of 'paperless' securities that this offers, without committing a breach of trust, was an important issue for trustees, prior to the Trustee Act 2000, when a significant number of trusts did not contain express nominee powers.

A nominee may be appointed under an express power in the trust deed or under the statu- **13.132** tory authority of s.16 Trustee Act 2000. The statutory authority provides that the trustees of a trust may appoint a person to act as their nominee in respect of any trust asset (other than settled land) and that they may take such steps as are necessary to vest the title to the assets in the nominee.[164] An appointment of a nominee under this power is required to be in writing, or evidenced in writing.[165]

The statutory power does not apply **13.133**

• to any trust which has a custodian trustee;
• in respect of any assets which are vested in the Official Custodian for Charities;[166]
• to any pension scheme;[167]
• to any authorized unit trusts;[168]

---

[163] The nominee is not obliged to follow the instructions where they are unlawful or where they could involve them in personal liability (*Ingram v IRC* [1977] 4 All ER 395).
[164] Section 16(1).
[165] Section 16(2).
[166] Section 16(3).
[167] Section 36(8); occupational pension scheme is defined as in the Pension Schemes Act 1993.
[168] Section 37(1); authorized unit trust is defined as a scheme for which an order under s.78 Financial Services Act 1986 is in force.

- trustees managing a common investment scheme;[169] or
- trustees managing a common deposit scheme.[170]

13.134 The new statutory power

- applies to trusts whenever created;[171]
- is in addition to any powers otherwise conferred on the trustees;[172]
- is subject to any restriction or inclusion imposed by the trust instrument or any provision of subordinate legislation.[173]

13.135 **Who may be appointed a nominee?** The trustees may only appoint a nominee who satisfies one of the following three conditions:[174]

- carries on a business which consists of or includes acting as a nominee; or
- is a body corporate controlled by the trustees;[175] or
- is a body corporate recognized under s.9 Administration of Justice Act 1985.[176]

13.136 Unlike the appointment of an agent, there is no bar on a suitably qualified beneficiary being appointed to act as a nominee. The nominee can, if the trustees see fit, also act as agent or custodian.[177]

13.137 Additionally, unless a charity is exempt from the supervision of the Charity Commission, the trustees of the charity are required to 'act in accordance with any guidance' given by the Charity Commission in selecting a nominee.[178]

13.138 The trustees may appoint one of their number as a nominee if they are a trust corporation[179] or two or more of their number to act as joint nominees.[180] The Act refers to a 'person' being appointed as a nominee, and in this context 'person' also includes a corporation.

13.139 A failure by the trustees to act within the limits imposed by the Act when exercising their power under the Act to appoint a nominee will not invalidate the appointment.[181]

13.140 **Terms of appointment** A nominee may be appointed on such terms and with such remuneration as the trustees may determine,[182] but unless it is 'reasonably necessary for them to do so' they should not authorize the agent to appoint a substitute, cap his liability for his

---

[169] Section 38(a); a common investment scheme is defined as a scheme made, or having effect as if made, under s.24 Charities Act 1993 other than such a fund the trusts of which provide that property is not to be transferred to the fund except by or on behalf of a charity the trustees of which are the trustees appointed to manage the fund.

[170] Section 38(b); a common deposit scheme is defined as a scheme made, or having effect as if made, under s.25 Charities Act 1993.

[171] Section 27.

[172] Section 26(a).

[173] Section 26(b).

[174] Section 19(1) and (2).

[175] 'Control' is determined in accordance with s.840 Income and Corporation Taxes Act 1988.

[176] This recognition is provided by the Law Society for companies (owned by solicitors and incorporated in England and Wales) which can then operate within the Solicitors' Incorporated Practice Rule. The companies provide professional services such as nominee and custodian services.

[177] Section 12(4).

[178] Section 19(4).

[179] Section 19(5)(a).

[180] Section 19(5)(b).

[181] Section 24.

[182] Section 20(1).

actions, or act in a position of conflict of interest.[183] The acceptance by the trustees of the nominee's terms and remuneration is subject to the trustees' statutory duty of care.[184]

For any appointment of a nominee, whether under the statutory power or otherwise,[185] the nominee may be remunerated by the trustees out of the trust funds if he was engaged on terms that permitted remuneration and the level of remuneration is 'reasonable'.[186] The trustees may also reimburse the nominee for any expenses reasonably incurred by him.[187] Neither provision authorizes the charging of remuneration or expenses for work incurred prior to the commencement of the Trustee Act 2000.[188] **13.141**

What terms are reasonable may possibly be judged by what terms and conditions of business and provision for remuneration are routinely quoted by nominees for the type of trustee work being considered. **13.142**

Supervision of nominees The Act creates a framework of supervision of the nominee by the trustee where the statutory power has been used to appoint one. Furthermore, these supervisory requirements will apply to any appointment under an express power or the enactment or provision of subordinated legislation to the extent that they are not inconsistent with the terms of the express power.[189] The review is subject to the statutory duty of care.[190] **13.143**

While any nominee is appointed, the trustees must keep under review 'the arrangements under which' the nominee acts and how 'those arrangements are being put into effect'.[191] The trustees must consider, if circumstances are appropriate, whether they need to intervene[192] and if they consider that there is a need to intervene they should do so.[193] The Act gives no guidance as to the frequency of this review or the factors that the trustee should take into account. It is suggested that allowing the arrangements to run for longer than twelve months without a review might be excessive. It is also suggested that whatever fixed period might be determined for future reviews that the trustee should review the arrangement earlier if he becomes aware that matters are not as he would reasonably expect. **13.144**

Custodians

A custodian is someone appointed by the trustees who is to undertake safe custody of specified trust assets, documents, or records.[194] It is not necessary to do this for the custodian to take the title to the assets into his name, although that may be the case if it is suitable for him to do so. The custodian is no more than a bare trustee who holds the asset at the order of the trustees and acts according to the trustees' instructions. The trustees' relationship with the custodian is contractual and the trustees retains their fiduciary duty towards the trust and its beneficiaries. **13.145**

---

183 Section 20(2) and (3).
184 Paragraph 3(1)(a) Sch 1.
185 Section 32(1).
186 Section 32(2).
187 Section 32(3).
188 Section 33(1).
189 Section 21(2) and (3).
190 Sections 1 and 2 and para 3(1)(e) Sch 1.
191 Section 22(1)(a).
192 Under the statutory power to intervene in s.22 or the terms of any express power.
193 Section 22(1)(c).
194 Section 17(2); the office and function of a custodian is not to be confused with a custodian trustee.

13.146 The power to use a custodian for the custody of documents replaces s.21 Trustee Act 1925,[195] which permitted trustees to place trust documents in safe custody with a bank or any other company carrying on safe custody business. The costs of such deposit, if any, were to be paid out of trust income.

13.147 A custodian may be appointed under an express power in the trust deed or under the statutory authority of s.17 Trustee Act 2000. The statutory authority provides that the trustees of a trust may appoint a person to act as their custodian in respect of any trust asset (or documents or records). An appointment of a custodian under this power is required to be in writing, or evidenced in writing.[196]

13.148 The statutory power does not apply

- to any trust which has a custodian trustee;
- in respect of any assets which are vested in the Official Custodian for Charities;[197]
- to any pension scheme;[198]
- to any authorized unit trusts;[199]
- trustees managing a common investment scheme;[200] or
- trustees managing a common deposit scheme.[201]

13.149 The new statutory power

- applies to trusts whenever created;[202]
- is in addition to any powers otherwise conferred on the trustees;[203]
- is subject to any restriction or inclusion imposed by the trust instrument or any provision of subordinate legislation.[204]

13.150 **Who may be appointed a custodian?** The trustees may only appoint a custodian who satisfies one of the following three conditions:[205]

- carries on a business which consists of or includes acting as a custodian; or
- is a body corporate controlled by the trustees;[206] or
- is a body corporate recognized under s.9 Administration of Justice Act 1985.[207]

---

[195] Repealed by the Trustee Act 2000.

[196] Section 17(3).

[197] Section 17(4).

[198] Section 36(8); occupational pension scheme is defined as in the Pension Schemes Act 1993.

[199] Section 37(1); authorized unit trust is defined as a scheme for which an order under s.78 Financial Services Act 1986 is in force.

[200] Section 38(a); a common investment scheme is defined as a scheme made, or having effect as if made, under s.24 Charities Act 1993 other than such a fund the trusts of which provide that property is not to be transferred to the fund except by or on behalf of a charity the trustees of which are the trustees appointed to manage the fund.

[201] Section 38(b); a common deposit scheme is defined as a scheme made, or having effect as if made, under s.25 Charities Act 1993.

[202] Section 27.

[203] Section 26(a).

[204] Section 26(b).

[205] Section 19(1) and (2).

[206] 'Control' is determined in accordance with s.840 Income and Corporation Taxes Act 1988.

[207] This recognition is provided by the Law Society for companies (owned by solicitors and incorporated in England and Wales) which can then operate within the Solicitors' Incorporated Practice Rule. The companies provide professional services such as nominee and custodian services.

Unlike the appointment of an agent, there is no bar on a suitably qualified beneficiary being appointed to act as a custodian. The custodian can, if the trustees see fit, also act as agent or nominee.[208] **13.151**

Additionally, unless a charity is exempt from the supervision of the Charity Commission, the trustees of the charity are required to 'act in accordance with any guidance' given by the Charity Commission in selecting a custodian.[209] **13.152**

The trustee may appoint one of their number as a custodian if that trustee is a trust corporation[210] or two or more of their number to act as joint custodians.[211] The Act refers to a 'person' being appointed as a custodian, and in this context 'person' also includes a corporation. **13.153**

A failure by the trustees to act within the limits imposed by the Act when exercising their power under the Act to appoint a nominee will not invalidate the appointment.[212] **13.154**

Terms of appointment   A custodian may be appointed on such terms and with such remuneration as the trustees may determine,[213] but unless it is 'reasonably necessary for them to do so' they should not authorize the agent to appoint a substitute, cap his liability for his actions, or act in a position of conflict of interest.[214] The acceptance by the trustee of the custodian's terms and remuneration is subject to the trustee's statutory duty of care.[215] **13.155**

For any appointment of a custodian, whether under the statutory power or otherwise,[216] the custodian may be remunerated by the trustees out of the trust funds if he was engaged on terms that permitted remuneration and the level of remuneration is 'reasonable'.[217] The trustees may also reimburse the custodian for any expenses reasonably incurred by him.[218] Neither provision authorizes the charging of remuneration or expenses for work incurred prior to the commencement of the Trustee Act 2000.[219] **13.156**

What terms are reasonable may possibly be judged by what terms and conditions of business and provision for remuneration are routinely quoted by custodians for the type of trustee work being considered. **13.157**

Supervision of custodians   The Act creates a framework of supervision of the custodian by the trustees where the statutory power has been used to appoint one. Furthermore, these supervisory requirements will apply to any appointment under an express power or the enactment or provision of subordinated legislation to the extent that they are not inconsistent with the terms of the express power.[220] The review is subject to the statutory duty of care.[221] **13.158**

---

[208] Section 12(4).
[209] Section 19(4).
[210] Section 19(5)(a).
[211] Section 19(5)(b).
[212] Section 24.
[213] Section 20(1).
[214] Section 20(2) and (3).
[215] Paragraph 3(1)(a) Sch 1.
[216] Section 32(1).
[217] Section 32(2).
[218] Section 32(3).
[219] Section 33(1).
[220] Section 21(2) and (3).
[221] Sections 1 and 2 and para 3(1)(e) Sch 1.

13.159 While any custodian is appointed, the trustee must keep under review 'the arrangements under which' the custodian acts and how 'those arrangements are being put into effect'.[222] The trustees must consider, if circumstances are appropriate, whether they need to intervene[223] and if they consider that there is a need to intervene they should do so.[224] The Act gives no guidance as to the frequency of this review or the factors that the trustee should take into account. It is suggested that allowing the arrangements to run for longer than twelve months without a review might be excessive. It is also suggested that, whatever fixed period might be determined for future reviews, the trustees should review the arrangement earlier if they become aware that matters are not as they would reasonably expect.

Bearer securities

13.160 Where trustees retain or invest in bearer securities they must appoint a custodian to hold those securities.[225]

13.161 This statutory requirement does not apply

- to a sole trustee that is a trust corporation;[226]
- to any trust which has a custodian trustee;
- in respect of any assets which are vested in the Official Custodian for Charities;[227]
- to any pension scheme;[228]
- to any authorized unit trusts;[229]
- trustees managing a common investment scheme;[230]
- trustees managing a common deposit scheme.[231]

13.162 The new statutory requirement

- applies to trusts whenever created;[232]
- is in addition to any powers otherwise conferred on the trustees;[233]
- is subject to any restriction or inclusion imposed by the trust instrument or any provision of subordinate legislation.[234]

13.163 The appointment of a custodian for bearer securities is then to be made in accordance with the previous section of this book dealing with custodians.

---

[222] Section 22(1)(a).
[223] Under the statutory power to intervene in s.22 or the terms of any express power.
[224] Section 22(1)(c).
[225] Section 18(1).
[226] Section 25(2).
[227] Section 18(4).
[228] Section 36(8); occupational pension scheme is defined as in the Pension Schemes Act 1993.
[229] Section 37(1); authorized unit trust is defined as a scheme for which an order under s.78 Financial Services Act 1986 is in force.
[230] Section 38(a); a common investment scheme is defined as a scheme made, or having effect as if made, under s.24 Charities Act 1993 other than such a fund the trusts of which provide that property is not to be transferred to the fund except by or on behalf of a charity the trustees of which are the trustees appointed to manage the fund.
[231] Section 38(b); a common deposit scheme is defined as a scheme made, or having effect as if made, under s.25 Charities Act 1993.
[232] Section 27.
[233] Section 26(a).
[234] Section 26(b).

The appointment of a custodian to hold bearer securities under this section should be in writing or evidenced in writing.[235]   **13.164**

These provisions of the Trustee Act 2000 replaced s.7 Trustee Act 1925, which required any trustee, other than a trust corporation, to deposit bearer securities with a bank. Where a trustee has deposited bearer securities with a bank, under the power in s.7 Trustee Act 1925, the bank is now deemed to be a custodian appointed under s.18 Trustee Act 2000.[236]   **13.165**

E. Miscellaneous

Special dividends   One area where the trustee will still have difficulty is that of the special dividend declared *in specie*. Where a company resolves to return surplus capital to its shareholders by way of a special dividend, usually of abnormal size, if the exercise is to be of practical value, *Re Lee* is of no application and the previously held views of such a distribution will prevail,[237] making it income in a trustee's hands. This can in consequence place a considerable part of the capital value of the shareholding in the income beneficiary's hands.[238]   **13.166**

The position for the trustee where a special dividend is announced is difficult. The trustee may well have expended trust capital in the purchase of the holding only to then be faced with a return of capital to shareholders that would place part of the value of that holding in an income beneficiary's hands. If a trustee deliberately purchased such a holding as a way of getting trust capital into the hands of an income beneficiary there seems little doubt that the trustee would be accountable to the capital beneficiaries for his actions.   **13.167**

It is more difficult to state the duty of a trustee when a special dividend is announced, but given a trustee's duty to act fairly between competing interests,[239] sale of the investment prior to the ex-special dividend date and reinvestment in an alternative investment seems to be a balanced approach. However, the reality of this proposition is that in practice the CGT consequences of sale may make a sale impractical, giving the trustee little option but to retain the investment and accept the consequences of the special dividend. A similar analysis will apply to the demerger where the demerged shares would be income in the hands of a trustee.   **13.168**

Trust portfolio in holding company   The contrast between a trustee's view of capital and income and a company's view, highlighted by Nicholls V-C in *Re Lee*, has also been examined in *JW v Morgan Trust Company of the Bahamas Ltd*.[240] Here the trustee did not directly own the portfolio of investments, they were held in a private company which in turn was owned and controlled by the trustee. The issue involved what the income of the trust was from the company. The accounts of the private company treated both profits and investment gains as the income of the company, whereas the court found that the trustee was correct in looking   **13.169**

---

[235] Section 18(3).
[236] The transitional provisions of para 1(2) Sch 3 Trustee Act 2000. Under s.7 it was necessary to have a written agreement and these transitional provisions will operate even though there may not be a written agreement as now required by s.18(3). It is suggested, however, that it would be good practice to have the agreements meet the requirements of s.18(3) as soon as is practical.
[237] *Hill v Permanent Trustee Company of New South Wales Ltd* [1930] AC 720.
[238] In one example, an exercise of returning surplus capital by way of a special dividend resulted in Unilever plc paying a dividend of approximately 10 per cent of its market capitalization.
[239] *Nestle v National Westminster Bank plc* (nn 18 and 24).
[240] A decision of Hayton AJ in the Supreme Court of the Bahamas ((2002) 4 ITELR 541).

through the company accounts and treating the company investments as trust investments, thus only treating the trust income as being the income from the investment, with the gains on sales as being trust capital.[241]

13.170   **Scrip issues**   The practice of companies making scrip, or bonus, issues of shares is a way of the company concerned capitalizing its reserves. There is no change in the substance of the holding and because of this no reason for a change in the overall value of the shareholding. The shares issued in this way are additions to a trust's holding with no change in the book value of the holding. The shares received are capital.

Private company shares

13.171   A PR will have to collect the base information needed for the valuation of such shares—the memorandum and articles of association of the company and the published accounts for a minimum of three years preceding the death of the shareholder. Particular attention needs to be paid to any restrictions on who may hold the shares and also any mechanism within the memorandum and articles of association for the sale of a deceased shareholder's holding to the other company members. There will often be a method of valuation prescribed for these circumstances together with a timetable. Great care should be taken not to start any such timetable until the PR is satisfied as to its operation, the fairness of the valuation process, and that a sale of the shares is what is required.

13.172   The investigation process for a private company shareholding becomes more complex with greater size of the shareholding. Holdings that represent control of the company will require greater diligence[242] from both PRs and trustees. There is no duty for a PR or a trustee, having a controlling interest in a company, to sit on that company's board or to place his nominee on the board. These are, however, two of the possibilities that he should consider in order to take reasonable steps to protect and manage that trust asset.

13.173   In *Re Lucking's Will Trusts*,[243] Cross J considered this issue:

> What steps, if any, does a reasonably prudent man who finds himself a majority shareholder in a private company take with regard to the management of the company's affairs? He does not content himself with such information as to the management of the company's affairs as he is entitled to as a shareholder, but ensures that he is represented on the board. He may be prepared to run the business himself as managing director or, at least, to become a non-executive director while having the business managed by someone else. Alternatively he may find someone who will act as his nominee on the board and report to him from time to time as to the company's affairs. In the same way trustees holding a controlling interest ought to ensure so far as they can that they have such information as to the progress of the company's affairs as directors would have. If they sit back and allow the company to be run by the minority shareholder and receive no more information than shareholders are entitled to, they do so at the risk of things going wrong.

13.174   Important though this above passage is, it has not been read subsequently as imposing a duty on the PR (or trustee) to sit on the board or appoint a nominee director;[244] it is more that this

---

[241] Somewhat surprisingly expert evidence was given to the effect that trust accounting principles do not exist; a proposition flatly rejected by the court.

[242] *Bartlett v Barclays Bank Trust Company* [1980] 1 All ER 139; *Re Lucking's Will Trusts* [1967] 3 All ER 726.

[243] [1967] 3 All ER 726.

[244] *Re Miller's Deed Trusts* [1978] LS Gaz R 454 where it was accepted that it was not necessary for a nominee director to be appointed where one of the trustees (an accountant) was the company auditor.

step might be one of several steps to consider. This was commented on further by Brightman J in *Bartlett v Barclays Bank Trust Company Ltd*:[245]

> [Cross J] was merely outlining convenient methods by which a prudent man of business (as also a trustee) with a controlling interest in a private company can place himself in a position to make an informed decision whether any action is appropriate to be taken for the protection of his asset…Alternatives which spring to mind are the receipts of copies of the agenda and minutes of board meetings, the receipt of monthly management accounts in the case of a trading concern or quarterly reports.

> Every case will depend on its own facts…The purpose to be achieved is not that of monitoring every move of the directors, but of making it reasonably probable…that the trustees or one of them will receive an adequate flow of information in time to enable the trustees to make use of their controlling shareholding should this be necessary for the protection of their trust asset, namely the shareholding.

The appropriate solution for controlling interests will not always be the same and the full facts will require carefully consideration by the PR on each occasion.

Both important decisions referred to above considered the need for a 'nominee' director to be appointed on behalf of the estate or trust, but have not offered guidance on exactly what such a director is[246] or indeed what his duties would be. Clearly the PR or trustee using their shareholding to place a director who is nominated by them on the board is a legally permissible action but, once appointed as a director of the company, that nominee and all the other directors, are subject to the predominant and overriding duty to serve the interest of the board (and not those who may have appointed them).[247] Any attempt by the PRs to contractually curtail this duty by way of the terms on which they appoint a director is to be avoided.[248] **13.175**

The duty of a director towards the company may not give rise to tension, or even conflict, where the company's shares are owned solely by the trust. However, where there are other shareholders, the nominated director cannot be precluded from considering their interests. The tension between these interests becomes greater where the commercial activities of the company require commercial judgement and assessment of reasonable commercial risk for commercial enterprises. Quite clearly a company director's role in the management of commercial activity encompasses a greater acceptance of commercial risks than would normally be the case with a PR (or trustee) in his management of an estate or trust.[249] In effect two different standards are involved and may conflict; the shareholding may be the property of the estate and subject to the duty of care of a PR, but the nominee director's duties towards the management of the company assets are of a different standard and purpose. The trustee and his nominee must understand this issue and be prepared to manage it. **13.176**

---

[245] [1980] 1 All ER 139.

[246] For a fuller exploration of this issue see Christopher Cant, 'Trusts Controlling Interests and Nominee Directors' (2002) 1 *The TACT Review* 18 and revised and republished as 'Breaches of Trusts, Controlling Interests in Companies and Nominee Directors' (2003) 1(1) *Trust Quarterly Review* 24.

[247] *Bennetts v Board of Fire Commissioners* (1967) 87 NSWWN 307.

[248] *Boulting v ACTAT* [1963] 2 QB 606.

[249] 'The duty of a trustee is not to take such care only as a prudent man would take if he had only himself to consider; the duty is rather to take such care as an ordinary prudent man would take if he were minded to make an investment for the benefit of other people for whom he felt morally bound to provide' (per Lindley LJ in *Re Whiteley, Learoyd v Whiteley* at 355 (n 42)).

Ademption

13.177 The general subject of ademption is beyond the scope of this work. However, specific bequests of investments have a particular difficulty where the named shareholding no longer exists—a not uncommon position in the current financial world.

13.178 A specific gift in a will of an investment will fail if the investment is no longer held at the date of death. Of more difficulty is the investment that has changed through takeover or amalgamation: does it still exist for the purposes of the gift? All such cases will depend very much on the facts of the particular investment. Where there is merely a change of name ademption will not arise.

13.179 The test which was put forward in *Re Slater, Slater v Slater*[250] was that there should be

1. a 'unity' of company issuing the securities, that is to say that it is identifiable as being substantially the same company or a company newly formed merely to take over the old;
2. a similarity in the two securities, that is to say that the old and new securities were of a similar class;
3. a similarity in the quantity of the holding.

13.180 None of these tests is particularly satisfactory or easy to apply. The financial markets of the age in which the test was formulated are very different to those of today.[251] Does the modern application of the test give a fair result?

Reserves against contingencies

13.181 The PR will usually need to retain reserves against outstanding liabilities until their settlement, or where the PR is certain the liability will not materialize. Similarly a trustee may hold reserves against anticipated liabilities or expenditure. However, the form of the reserve needs to be considered carefully. A reserve needs to offer

- a margin of safety over the estimated value of the liability;
- reasonable stability of value; and
- ease of realization.

All this tends to point towards highly liquid reserves such as cash, bank deposits, and fixed interest stock (gilts usually being better than corporate loan stocks in terms of investment risk). Equities in times of calm markets can suffice, but by their nature will have greater price volatility. There is of course a risk of problems for that company affecting the price further, but the greater risk lies in market turmoil.[252]

13.182 The ease or difficulty of realizing an asset needs to be considered very early in the administration. It is of no real use to earmark an asset for sale to meet liabilities or to keep it as a reserve to meet possible liabilities, if it cannot be realized easily when it is

---

[250] [1907] 1 Ch 665.

[251] National Westminster Bank was taken over by the smaller Royal Bank of Scotland. A gift of RBS shares remains valid after the takeover, but a gift of NatWest shares does not. The subject matter of both is in reality the same, only the nominal form of the RBS gift has not changed.

[252] Such as occurred in the mid-1970s or 2008.

needed.[253] For a trustee, similar considerations arise once he knows of the liability or expenditure required.

Private company shares, AIM shares, or even quoted shares with a very thin market make **13.183** unsuitable reserves—they cannot be realized easily and lack price stability (and hence are difficult to rely on to meet the full value for which they are reserved). Even fairly major quoted investments make dubious reserves—many PRs in 1974–75 will have been very uncomfortable after a major stock market fall.[254]

Reserves can be an even more important issue where the administration or distribution of a **13.184** trust is going to be delayed, for example by difficulties in tracing beneficiaries. There is much to be said for safeguarding the value of the estate by realizing the assets which lack price stability and holding greater liquidity on higher-interest-bearing accounts. This tends to meet the beneficiaries' expectations better than retaining investments that may fall adversely affecting the value received when the beneficiary is identified. Retaining shares in these circumstances tends to be an unmanaged process—that is no managers are appointed—as what are the investment aims or risk profile of the beneficial owners?

Where reserves are retained there can be conflict between the investment aims of the benefi- **13.185** ciaries and the PRs', or trustees', need for price stability and liquidity. Where this is the case the PRs', or trustees', needs in relation to the exercise of the investment power can be taken into account and preferred over the needs of the beneficiaries, but this power must always be exercised as far as possible in a fair manner towards the needs of the beneficiaries.[255] A PR has no general duty to invest liquid assets in an estate pending distribution of them.[256]

Sales

Dealing prices for PRs and trustees

PRs and trustees have a duty to do the best they can financially, within the context of what **13.186** may reasonably be expected of them. The price at which they might decide to realize an investment was considered in *Buttle v Saunders*,[257] where Wynn-Parry J observed:

> It is true that persons who are not in the position of trustees are entitled, if they so desire, to accept a lesser price than that which they might obtain on the sale of property, and not infrequently a vendor, who has gone to some lengths in negotiating with a prospective purchaser, decides to close the deal with that purchaser, notwithstanding that he is presented with a higher offer. It redounds to the credit of a man who acts like that in such circumstances. *Trustees, however, are not vested with such complete freedom. They have an overriding duty to obtain the best price which they can for their beneficiaries.*[258] (authors' emphasis)

---

[253] Generally properties have frequently been earmarked to raise cash needed in the administration. This is because of the general bull market in properties over the past 40 years. However, the short but nonetheless difficult, bear markets of the early 1970s and 1990s should not be dismissed, as they caused major difficulties in selling properties.

[254] Similarly for Black Monday 1987, 9/11, or 2008.

[255] *X v A* [2000] 1 All ER 490; [2000] WTLR 11.

[256] *Perotti v Collyer Bristow* [2003] EWHC 25 (Ch); [2003] WTLR 1473.

[257] [1950] 2 All ER 193.

[258] [1950] 2 All ER 193 at 195; this has been vividly described as a trustee's 'dishonourable duty to gazump', *Underhill and Hayton: Law of Trusts and Trustees* (n 21) at [48.25]. See also Nicholls V-C in *Harries v Church Commissioners* (n 17) at 309D: 'it is not a proper function for the commissioners to sell their land at an undervalue in order to further a social object...If the commissioners' land is to be disposed of at an undervalue, they need an express power to do so.'

Although this decision was in the context of a property sale, it is clearly applicable to any sale of an asset by a PR or trustee that when selling an asset they have a duty to obtain the best price that they can. Best price in this context will usually, but not always, mean the highest price. It must also follow that the duty when purchasing or exchanging an investment is similar.

13.187 As a general proposition, a PR or trustee should take reasonable steps to make themselves aware of the value of the property in order that any dealing in the property can be at the best price reasonably attainable. Similarly, with purchases, the PR or trustee should take reasonable steps to make themselves aware of the value of the asset they are purchasing and that the price being paid reflects this value. Reasonable steps in this context will include obtaining advice and dealing through accepted agents and markets (such as recognized stock markets).[259]

13.188 Where the price that can be obtained for an estate or trust asset is capable of being increased by cooperation with the owners of adjoining property (or blocks of shares) a trustee ought to consider if the price he can obtain can be maximized through cooperation with others. What the trustee must beware of in these circumstances is any agreement that would cause a loss of control of the trust property or even having the value of the trust's property tainted through defects in the property or title of those that he cooperates with.[260]

13.189 A trustee has a general duty to take the documents of title to trust property into his name.[261] Where the documents of title are imperfect to the extent that the defect may affect the price for which the asset could be sold, a trustee should take such steps as are reasonable and cost effective to ensure that the defects are rectified and the trust property is then fully marketable.

Timing

13.190 Sales of assets before agreement of their values at the date of death with HMRC is not of great significance for the disposal of quoted stock exchange assets or unit trusts and open-ended investment companies (OIECs). Where there can be difficulties in the sale of land or private company shares, even in arm's-length transactions, is that it does not necessarily follow that HMRC will be prepared to accept that the sale value negotiated matches their value at the date of death. Disposals that are not at arm's length are even less likely to be accepted and will not qualify for IHT relief for loss on sale. It is important where assets are being sold ahead of agreement with HMRC to consider if HMRC seeking a higher value at the date of death will create problems and the extent to which such problems can be managed.

Jointly owned assets

13.191 A PR's duty to collect (or at least control) estate assets makes it vital for him to address the nature of the deceased's interest in any jointly owned property. This work should be undertaken as quickly as possible after death, in order to determine the devolution of the joint

---

[259] *Oliver v Court* (1820) 8 Price 127; *Campbell v Walker* (1800) 5 Ves 678; *Re Cooper and Allen's Contract for sale to Harlech* (1876) 4 Ch D 802.

[260] *Re Cooper and Allen's Contract for sale to Harlech* (n 259): 'suppose there were a house belonging to trustees, and a garden and forecourt belonging to somebody else; it must be obvious that those two properties would fetch more if sold together than if sold separately. You might have a divided portion of a house belonging to trustees and another divided portion belonging to somebody else. It would be equally obvious, if these two portions were sold together, that a more beneficial result would thereby take place... But in those cases where it is not manifest on a mere inspection of the properties that it is more beneficial to sell them together, then you ought to have reasonable evidence... [t]hat it is a prudent and right thing to do, and that evidence, as we know by experience, is obtained from surveyors and other persons who are competent judges.'

[261] See *Underwood and Hayton: Law of Trusts and Trustees* (n 21) at 42–30.

property, and consequently, whether or not any interest in it is an asset of the estate. Speed is an element in this, particularly where the joint asset is readily disposable by the surviving owner (eg joint bank accounts or investments).

These investigations can be straightforward if the exact nature of the ownership is clearly **13.192** recorded (and matches the way that the asset was treated by the co-owners) and the title deeds were in the deceased's possession. But it is more difficult if the title does not properly or fully reflect the manner of holding the property or if the documents of title were not in the possession of the deceased at the time of his death.

There may be jointly owned assets in which the deceased was interested in the following **13.193** circumstances:

1. The documents of title were not in the deceased's possession (and therefore there is a lack of information immediately available to the PR).
2. Where acts of severance have occurred.
3. During the deceased's lifetime, the asset may have been managed by the co-owner(s) (and therefore there is very little information about the history of the assets in the deceased's possession, eg its current insurance).
4. Where (3) above applies, the joint interest in the asset may only be revealed by a careful review of cash movements through the deceased's bank accounts.
5. If the joint asset produced income, the previous year's tax returns might assist (but if the asset was not net income producing this will not help).
6. The deceased's papers might reveal some information, but care is needed as a layman's description of the property or its title should not be relied upon without further investigation.

Experience has shown that all too often PRs, including professional PRs, have made inad- **13.194** equate enquiries into the title to jointly owned assets. It is an easy, but frequently erroneous, assumption that joint ownership must have been by beneficial joint tenancy and that the deceased's interest must therefore pass by survivorship on his death. Any assertion by the co-owner that this is indeed the case should, of course, be treated with caution, because of his interest in asserting this.

Failure to take all reasonable steps to identify correctly the nature of the deceased's interest in **13.195** joint property will in all likelihood be an act of negligence on the part of a PR. An interest in a tenancy in common is an asset which does not pass by survivorship and is therefore an asset of the deceased's estate. In addition, there is also the possibility that property where the legal title is in joint names may not be jointly owned in equity but is held by the surviving co-owner on a resulting trust for the deceased's estate,[262] in which case it is an asset of the deceased's estate.

A PR is substantially at risk for the loss that he may have caused to an estate where he neg- **13.196** ligently or carelessly addressed these questions. His liability can include the loss of value to the estate (in both capital and income), to the extent that it cannot be recovered from the co-owner. The costs of recovery, if the PR has been in error, will most likely be a burden on the PR personally. This necessity for identifying the true nature of the interest in any joint property can be broken down into the following four factors:

---

[262] *Sillars v IRC* [2004] WTLR 591.

1. The estate receives that to which it is entitled (and does not suffer loss of capital or income) and this then results in the correct devolution of the interest in the property under the terms of the will.
2. The valuation, disclosure, incidence, and accountability for IHT is correct. Correct disclosure means that the free estate is not inflated by the inclusion of joint property nor undisclosed by not including a tenancy in common interests.
3. The income of the estate is correctly identified and disclosed in the PR's income tax return.
4. Gifts that might have been involved in the creation of the joint property are identified and then all of the taxation consequences that flow from the gifts are understood and the tax liabilities settled.

13.197 In order to carry out the process of identification, the PR must verify the nature of the joint ownership by reviewing all relevant documentation himself or, if he is not sufficiently knowledgeable, by employing a solicitor, at the expense of the estate, to do so. Too often, the PR's enquiries go no further than a simple exchange of correspondence with the surviving co-owners. Equally often, the PR apparently accepts without further investigation the position as set out by the co-owner (usually to the co-owner's advantage). Often, he can be seen taking false comfort from the advice having come from the co-owner's solicitor (failing to understand that he is not the solicitor's client and is therefore owed no duty by that solicitor). This is an inadequate approach to the duty of a PR to impartially investigate the assets and liabilities of an estate and render a true account of them.

13.198 That there can be substantial difficulties in ascertaining the nature of the ownership is clear from the long succession of property cases in this area that have progressed to the courts.[263] The ownership of land, or interests in land, at least in theory, should be easier to establish than personalty. Land nonetheless in practice offers many problems, but the even greater likelihood of inadequate documentation makes personalty a potentially harder area to resolve.

13.199 The PR usually has difficulty with identifying the co-ownership of chattels. Contrary to what is so often seen in estate records, it should be observed that very rarely are all chattels in a marriage jointly owned, and assuming that they are when taking valuations or distributing an estate (or indeed taking will instructions) is a mistake. It is also worth noting that those chattels within a marriage that are jointly owned are rarely owned as tenants in common and simply showing a half share of the joint chattels as an asset of the estate is wrong (and probably only serves to inflate administration charges) unless there is clear evidence of a tenancy in common.

13.200 As the interest of a deceased joint tenant devolves by survivorship to the surviving co-owner(s), the interest is not part of the deceased's free estate and nothing is required of his PR in order

---

[263] And the exasperation of judges being faced with a continuing flow of these issues is clear from the judgment in the Court of Appeal of Ward LJ in *Goodman v Carlton* [2002] FLR 259, which closed with the memorable passage: 'I ask in despair how often this Court has to remind conveyancers that they would save their clients a great deal of later difficulty if only they would sit the purchasers down, explain the difference between a joint tenancy and a tenancy in common, ascertain what they want and then expressly declare in the conveyance or transfer how the beneficial interest is to be held because that will be conclusive and save all argument. When are conveyancers going to do this as a matter of invariable standard practice? This Court has urged that time after time. Perhaps conveyancers do not read the law reports. I will try this one more time: ALWAYS TRY TO AGREE ON AND THEN RECORD HOW THE BENEFICIAL INTEREST IS TO BE HELD. It is not very difficult to do' (the part in capitals is as it appears in the original judgment). The implications of this passage raise interesting questions of negligence for conveyancers, but happily that is beyond the scope of this book.

to complete the devolution of the property. The surviving co-owner can apply to be registered as the sole owner on production of proof of death.[264]

Control of tenancies in common

The general principle is that the surviving co-owner in a tenancy in common will have **13.201**
the legal title to the asset vested in him (evidence of death being sufficient to remove the
deceased's name from the legal title). But the PR of the first co-owner to die will need to
consider carefully how he intends to safeguard the estate's interest in the joint property.

Land

After the death of a testator owing an interest in a tenancy in common, the surviving **13.202**
co-owner(s) of the legal estate will hold that title to the entire property upon a trust of
land for themselves and the estate of the deceased co-owner. Where there is more than one
surviving co-owner (or the single surviving co-owner is a trust corporation) the surviving
co-owners will be competent to convey the legal title to the property on any later sale and
give a valid receipt for the proceeds of sale or mortgage. The sale proceeds of the asset are
received by the trustees of the legal title who are responsible for its distribution. They have
the trustee's statutory duty of care in respect of their dealings with the land. They also have a
statutory duty to consult with beneficiaries when exercising their power.[265] The trustees will
be accountable for dealings that give rise to avoidable losses.

It follows in these circumstances that the PR of the deceased tenant in common needs to **13.203**
contact the trustees of the land as the PR will expect to be consulted about the exercise of
the trustees' powers in relation to the land[266] as that exercise may well impact upon the value
of the PR's interest. Usually the relationship between PR and the trustee of the legal title
will not present any difficulties, but it would be unwise to assume this at the outset without
discussion. In the event of dispute between the PR and the trustees, ultimately consideration
may need to be given to the powers of the court to make orders[267] regarding the exercise of
the trustees' functions.

Where there is only one surviving trustee of land, who is not a trust corporation, the posi- **13.204**
tion can become more difficult if a satisfactory level of cooperation cannot be achieved. The
power to appoint a further trustee rests with the sole surviving co-owner (trustee) and he is
not obliged to appoint any other trustees as long as there is no need for him to give a receipt
for capital monies[268] arising out of the land. However, more than one trustee is required to
give a receipt for capital monies and the sole trustee may, if he chooses, only appoint another
trustee, solely for this purpose, at the time of sale. The additional trustee need not be, and
indeed frequently is not, the PR of the deceased co-owner.

The PR of the deceased co-owner might be content for the legal title to be held by one trustee, **13.205**
particularly if that individual will inherit the estate's interest in the property. But generally,
the PR should be reluctant to let the title rest with only one trustee of the trust of land.

---

[264] Quite commonly this is not done, but the co-owner instead merely places a copy death certificate with
the property deeds for production later (NB the death certificate used should be a registrar's copy death certificate and not a photocopy of such a certificate. Apart from the copyright breach if photocopying is done without
a licence, the photocopy is not sufficient for this purpose).

[265] Section 11 Trusts of Land and Appointment of Trustees Act 1996.

[266] As provided for in s.11.

[267] Under ss.14 and 15 Trusts of Land and Appointment of Trustees Act 1996.

[268] Arising out of sale or mortgage of the property.

1. The PRs will have no control over any sale, including the choice of agent, methods of marketing, asking price, costs, and timing.
2. Management of the property, including any sale, may be hampered by the loss of capacity of the co-owner, his idiosyncrasies of management, or his absences from the country.
3. The PR will not be able to ensure that the property is fully insured and also loses the ability to deal with any insurance claim or the proceeds of sale. This latter point is important as the sole surviving legal owner would be able to give a receipt for insurance claim proceeds.
4. Delays to management or sale can be caused by the death of the co-owner, particularly if there are any disputes surrounding his estate which prevent or delay a grant of representation.
5. If the co-owner dies, the right to appoint new trustees of the land will rest with the PRs of his estate.

13.206 For what may well be a valuable asset, these are all potentially substantial problems and they could be minimized if the surviving co-owner would agree to the PRs of the first co-owner to die being added to the title. This is especially true where the interest in the tenancy in common must be disposed of to raise cash required in the administration of the estate. These problems also point towards the difficulties inherent in retaining interests in tenancy in common properties as reserves for future liabilities in an administration—realization of the assets can be beyond the PRs' control.

13.207 Consideration also needs to be given to circumstances of the surviving trustee. Are they

- hampered in business management by age, illness, or declining mental capacity;
- inexperienced in practical business matters; or
- susceptible to the influence of others?

In these circumstances the PR's concerns about the security of his asset will become greater.

13.208 However, the PR should have some concerns about his appointment as co-trustee of the legal title, if there is to be longer-term retention of the estate's interest in the property. Where the terms of the will create a trust, the trustee (who in all likelihood will also be the PR) is faced with the same issues set out above for PRs, but with a far longer time period and hence a greater degree of risk. The choices for trustees are really the same as those for the PRs.

13.209 A factor in deciding whether or not the PR or trustee should seek to persuade the surviving trustee(s) of the legal title of the advantages in appointing them as an additional trustee, will be the possibility that they will become involved in substantial additional work in relation to the whole property rather than just the interest that they hold. For trust corporations this can be a fairly major issue as their fee-charging authority derives from the will and only covers their work in acting as trustee of the will, and this would not usually extend to the work involved in acting as trustee of the trust of land in respect of the other interests.[269] Other professionals will have to consider where their remuneration would come from and what authorities will be needed from those also interested in the property.

13.210 Where the interest in the tenancy in common can, and will, be transferred to a beneficiary absolutely entitled, it makes sense for that beneficiary to be appointed as a trustee of the

---

[269] Their fee is usually value based relating to the assets held in their trust.

legal title if the existing trustee agrees. This would then give the beneficiary a degree of comfort in participation in the management of the property. Such an appointment can have risks if made prior to the PR being able to vest the equitable interest in the property in that beneficiary.

The other side of this particular issue is where the deceased was the sole surviving trustee of **13.211** the tenancy in common property. Identifying correctly the nature of the beneficial interests remains a key issue for the PR who obviously should not assume a joint tenancy without adequately investigating the issues. However, there are three sets of other circumstances that the PR will need to consider:

1. *Where the estate has no equitable interest in the land.* The PR will look to exercise his statutory power as the PR of the last surviving trustee to appoint new trustees.[270] Before that power is exercised, the PR's powers of management, sale, remuneration, etc under the will do not extend to the trust of land in relation to the joint property and, as a consequence, apart from the costs of exercising the power under s.36 Trustee Act 1925, the PR will have to look to his statutory powers in relation to the trust of land for its management. The PR will not be remunerated under the will for the trusteeship of the land, although it might be possible to argue that a professional acting as the trustee of land could charge in accordance with Part IV Trustee Act 2000. The appointment of new trustees would normally be made after the PR has obtained a grant, but this power can also be exercised by those intending to renounce their appointment before they do so.[271]

2. *Where the estate, which is absolutely distributable, has an equitable interest in the property.* The appointment of new trustees of the legal title to the joint property would seem to be the most practical course, provided that the equitable interest owned by the estate can be appropriated to the beneficiary entitled and is not needed to meet the outgoings of the estate. Under these circumstances, appointing the beneficiary as a trustee is appropriate together with at least one further trustee, preferably one of the others with an equitable interest in the property.

    Where a sale of the property is required the position of the estate is safeguarded in that the PR can exercise the powers of the deceased trustee and therefore sale is under his control.

3. *Where the estate, which is to be retained in trust, has an equitable interest in the property.* The PR's decision on whether to appoint new trustees, or to remain as a trustee, of the trust of land is likely to be determined by several factors:
    - the size and complexity of the property;
    - the extent of the estate's interest; and
    - the extent to which the other equitable owners have been involved in the deceased trustee's decision making.

Assets other than land

Where the joint asset is other than land, many of the above difficulties are reduced because of **13.212** the ability, usually, to divide the asset or its proceeds (eg bank and building society accounts

---

[270] Section 36(1)(b) Trustee Act 1925.
[271] Section 36(5).

and quoted investments). However, the need to identify correctly the original interest of the deceased remains a key issue.

13.213 For less liquid assets, particularly chattels, problems more akin to those of land arise. This is particularly so with insurance, safe custody, and preservation where it is very important to ensure the adequate arrangements are in place.

Forfeiture and safeguarding interests in joint assets

13.214 It is a general rule of public policy that a killer should not profit from his crime.[272] The rule applies to all cases of deliberate killing.

13.215 The common law forfeiture rule was modified by the Forfeiture Act 1982, which gave the court a discretion[273] to relieve the killer of forfeiture, wholly or partly,[274] in all circumstances bar those of a conviction for murder.[275] Proceedings for relief under this Act must be brought within three months of conviction.[276] However, exercise of the discretion of the court requires the court to consider all material circumstances, including the conduct of the deceased and the killer.[277] It should be stressed that unless the court does exercise its discretion the full rigour of the rule applies.

13.216 Where the deceased and the killer were jointly interested in assets, either as beneficial joint tenants or as tenants in common, the benefit of inheriting the property by the right of survivorship is forfeit. The difficulty with the forfeiture rule for the practitioner is that there will then be periods of uncertainty during which it is necessary to safeguard the position of those potentially interested in the joint property if forfeiture occurs.

13.217 Once the killer is identified as the joint owner, there will be some time that will elapse before

- trial;
- conviction (or acquittal);
- commencement of a Forfeiture Act 1982 application; and
- completion of the criminal conviction appeals process.

During this time, the accused will be the legal owner of the joint property and the PR should look to reach agreement with him (or his legal representative) on the way that the joint property will be retained and managed. If sale is agreed on in respect of an asset, how the proceeds will be held pending resolution of the forfeiture issue is important. Voluntary agreement on a new trustee for sale may help to safeguard matters. However, in the event that there is no

---

[272] *Cleaver v Mutual Reserve Fund Life Association* [1892] 1 QB 147; *In the Estate of Crippen* [1911] P 108; *Re Callaway* [1956] Ch 559; *Re Royce (deceased)* [1985] Ch 22.

[273] 'The court shall not make an order under this section...unless it is satisfied that, having regard to the conduct of the offender and of the deceased and to such other circumstances as appear to the court to be material, the justice of the case requires the effect of the rule to be modified' (s.2(2)).
  Clearly the court need not make any order at all if it is not satisfied that there is reason to do so (*Re Murphy deceased, Dalton v Latham* [2003] WTLR 687).

[274] Particular assets, interests in property, or a percentage of the estate (*Re Forfeiture Act 1982 (Manslaughter: Forfeiture of Widow's Pension)* [1999] Pens LR 1).

[275] Section 5; this does not prejudice the individual's right to apply for provision under the I(PFD)A 1975; also *Land v Land* [2006] WTLR 1447.

[276] Section 2(3); see *Land v Land* (n 275) where it was considered that the court has no discretion to consider late applications.

[277] Section 2(2); *Dunbar v Plant* [1998] Ch 412; see also *Re Murphy (deceased), Dalton v Latham* [2003] WTLR 687.

cooperation from the accused it may be necessary to lodge a caution on the title or, in the case of personalty, where there might exist a real risk of the asset being disposed of or dissipated, to seek an order restraining disposal. It is not sufficient for the PR to simply sit back and await the outcome of a Forfeiture Act application as the estate's share of the joint property may have been dissipated by the survivor.

Valuations

In practice too many problems arise with the valuation of assets because of ill-thought-through or incomplete instructions to the valuer. It is of course the more complex valuations such as of land or private companies where this can cause particular problems. **13.218**

1. The person or firm to be instructed should be selected on the basis of their suitability for the asset and valuation in question. It is not simply a question of using someone who has been instructed before. Their qualification, professional insurance, experience, and reputation are all issues. Experience in this context is not merely length of time in the profession, but experience in the location, type of market, or asset in question.
2. The basis of charge for the valuation should be established and agreed before work commences. This should include establishing how negotiations of the valuation with HMRC or the District Valuer, if needed, will be charged for. This should also clearly indicate that responsibility for acceptance of any negotiated valuation lies with the PR as will the decision making regarding appeals etc.
3. Instructions to an agent for valuation should always be in writing. There is far too much scope for error and argument if verbal instructions are given. Even where there have been preliminary discussions with the agent these should always be subject to written confirmation. The written confirmation should then deal with all issues already discussed with the agent.
4. The purpose for which the valuation is required should always be specified. The purpose will inform the agent as to the basis on which his valuation should be prepared. If it is intended to use the valuation for more than one purpose, again it is helpful to advise the agent. Care should be taken where there is more than one aspect to the valuation to ensure that all elements are covered. For example, instructions to value a farm have been known to omit instructions for valuation of the live- and deadstock.
5. The property to be valued should be clearly identified. This is particularly important where real property is concerned. Farms in particular may be covered by several different titles (and be referred to by a variety of names). Difficulties with identifying boundaries, or existing boundary disputes, should be drawn to the valuer's attention.
6. For land, tenure is important and where the property is leasehold full details of the salient features of the lease (duration, rent, rent review, repairing obligations, insurance, maintenance charges, etc.) should be set out. The same applies where the property is tenanted—full details of the tenant and tenancy agreement should be given. It also assists, if it is a business tenancy, for the agent to be advised of the nature of the business understood to be being conducted at the premises.
7. For any land it is important to ask for an assessment of any development value or increase in value by change of use.
8. Testamentary options to purchase land are notoriously difficult to construe and where a valuation is required for this purpose it should not be left to the valuer to construe the terms of the option, but the basis of the valuation should be explicitly set out in the instructions.

9. Where private company shares are concerned, copy documentation required by the agent will include the company's memorandum and articles of association, trading accounts, and any other information about the company (profits warnings, assets sales, etc) that has been issued to shareholders; not forgetting the details of the deceased's shareholding, information regarding any recent share sales (date, price, amount, and whether or not it was at arm's length), the nature of the company's activities, and whether or not the holding is to be valued with reference to any other holdings.

10. Where the asset is to be sold, the valuation agent's advice on the method of sale is useful, as is any agreement that can be negotiated that the valuation could be offset against the selling commission where the agent will be instructed to carry out the sale.

11. Chattels valuations should be considered carefully in the light of what might be described as the 'Antiques Roadshow' approach. Probate valuations of chattels are not, as is often suggested, an artificially low value below the open market sale value. Where a sale of the chattels is being considered, advice should be taken on the type of auction that is suitable. Where the chattel is of particular quality a specialist or national sale may be a much better prospect. Again, agreements to merge valuation fees into selling commissions can help.

12. Valuation reports must be looked at critically. Whilst the agent instructed should have been chosen because of his experience of the work required (see (1) above), it is not safe to suspend one's critical faculties simply because of his expertise. Obvious errors in calculation, inconsistency of views, or a mismatch between what was concluded by the valuer and what is known to the PR should be challenged or clarified. It is not unknown for PRs to have been defrauded in asset disposals and, when this occurs, it can often start at the valuation stage with the suppression of advantageous features of the property such as planning potential.

Insurances

13.219 It is good practice[278] to review the insurance of all assets owned by the deceased that either are, or should with normal prudence, be insured. It is not sufficient to assume that assets either are insured or are insured for sufficient value, as there is potential liability for the PR or trustee who neglects insurance when common prudence suggests that it is called for.

13.220 Experience shows that few testators have sufficient insurance cover at the time of death. It should therefore be an issue that is approached with urgency when commencing investigations into a new estate.

13.221 Particular attention should be paid to the insurance policy's requirement for empty property insurance. Commonly issues arise with a failure to consider the length of time for which contents will be insured in empty properties or the requirements for draining water systems when the property is unoccupied.

---

[278] The exact position in terms of legal duty to insure is unsatisfactory, but it can be strongly argued that insuring property falls within the general duty to use such diligence and care as an ordinary prudent man would use in the conduct of his own business affairs—see *Lewin on Trusts*, 18th edition (Sweet & Maxwell, 2008) at [34-61] and [34-02].

Assets that may not be assets

There can be several different circumstances where the PR, having identified assets as being **13.222**
owned by the testator, may have to conclude that they are not assets of the estate:

1. Property held by the testator as a sole trustee.
2. Property held by the testator on a resulting or constructive trust for others.
3. Property disposed of by the testator under a pre-death contract where the transaction was not completed as at death.
4. Property owned by the testator but disposed of under a foreign will.
5. Property owned by the testator in another jurisdiction where the devolution of the property is directed, outside of the terms of the will, by the law of that jurisdiction.

These are all potential issues that could result in assets being unavailable to the PR in the administration of the estate. Therefore, whilst these circumstances certainly do not arise in every estate, the prudent PR will be alert when investigating assets for any indicators that they might apply.

Of similar effect, but not identical, in removing at least beneficial ownership from the PR, **13.223**
or making the asset unavailable for distribution under the will being administered, are questions of

- property that is subject to a proprietary estoppel claim;
- mutual wills;
- doctrine of election;
- charges on assets to secure debts of others.

The key with all of the issues above is being aware of the possibilities and therefore being alert **13.224**
to any potential indicators. Being alert to them is far preferable to ignoring the possibilities as then this can lead to much unnecessary work and at worst incorrect distributions.

Impact of regulation on asset ownership

Regulation is now far wider than just financial regulation. Increasingly trustees need to look **13.225**
beyond the narrow limits of trust law and understand where they, their settlors and beneficiaries, and the assets they administer, fit within this ever more complex skein of public law. Risk management should embrace sufficient knowledge to cover regulatory risk from the trust assets and also from transactions regarding those assets.

It is also too easy to overlook the effect of diversity of regulatory provisions in different **13.226**
jurisdictions. It is a quick, but erroneous assumption that everyone else's regulations mirror those that we are used to in our own jurisdictions. This is not only an obviously wrong path to follow, but it exposes the trustee to undue risk.

To approach a matter correctly the trustee in any jurisdiction has a substantial task in **13.227**

- obtaining;
- understanding; and
- applying

advice on the requirements of any other jurisdiction, apart from that where he is resident, in assessing risk in the jurisdictions

- from which the settled funds derive; or
- where the settlor is resident; or
- where the funds will be invested; or
- where the beneficiaries will be resident; or
- where the trustee's parent company (if the trustee is corporate) may be based.

13.228 Obviously not all of these points will be applicable in every case, but each point will need to be at least considered when assessing risk. Somewhat uncomfortably, some jurisdictions' regulations will be significantly inconsistent with others. It therefore must form part of the risk management culture of any professional trustee that staff should find it second nature to analyse a transaction to establish which regulatory regimes need to be complied with before participating in the transaction.

13.229 In a sense, the risk of committing a criminal offence is not new as trustees have always been subject to criminal sanctions for their criminal acts. The issue now is recognizing those acts which may not be easily recognizable as carrying criminal sanctions.

13.230 One area where the change of risk has not been so quickly recognized is that of trust investment. Property investment in particular has become an area of expanded risk given the statutory regulations which now deal with an owner's liability for some premises affected by, or containing, the following:

- gas supply and appliances;[279]
- asbestos;[280]
- water systems;[281] and
- electricity supply and equipment.[282]

Breaches of these regulations carry criminal penalties and in serious cases breach has resulted in imprisonment.

13.231 Environmental issues and the contamination of land have also come to the fore in recent years. Potential liabilities are there and trustees must have the same environmental risk management attitude and programmes as any commercial landlord. Taking contaminated property into a trust is something trustees should guard against given the potential costs/expense of clean-up and the enforcement penalties (without considering the civil liability).

13.232 Investment issues are more normally considered under civil liability, but here there are also criminal offences, mainly involving insider dealing and restrictions on directors' dealings[283] and the overall problem of financial regulatory compliance.

13.233 Trustees have long been used to the perils of civil liability for their actions, or inactions, but the variety of the risks that can give rise to civil actions is becoming greater.

---

[279] The Gas Safety (Installations and Use) Regulations 1998 (as amended); a prosecution in May 2006, where breaches led to a tenant's death, resulted in a landlord being fined £42,000 with £18,000 of costs.

[280] Control of Asbestos at Work Regulations 2002.

[281] Approved Code of Practice and Guidance 2000—Legionnaire's Disease (made under the Health and Safety at Work Act 1974) for the possibility of charges of manslaughter (see Barrow-in-Furness legionellosis outbreak where charges were brought unsuccessfully).

[282] The Electrical Equipment (Safety) Regulations 1994.

[283] Which were present in *Wight v Olswang* [2001] WTLR 291.

It is interesting to note that during the latter half of the nineteenth century, and the early **13.234** part of the twentieth, the courts' strict view of trustee liability was seen as being a deterrent to honest individuals acting as trustees.[284] This view almost certainly would be as relevant today, but because of the significant number of professionals, both corporate and personal, offering trustee services, there are not the same risks to trusts through failing to find trustees. Nevertheless, a side effect of increased risk is bound to be higher charges to the trust.

---

[284] 'There existed, however, an inherent and very real tension. It was accepted that the object of the law should be to recompense the trust for the loss it suffered through a breach. Moreover, no one doubted that fraudulent trustees should be harshly dealt with: a deliberate abuse of trust could not be tolerated and beneficiaries should certainly not be permitted to suffer loss because of it. But it was equally clear that a good supply of honest and able men willing to take on the office of trustee and perform a task of such importance to English life was absolutely necessary to the survival of the institution' (Chantal Stebbings, *The Private Trustee in Victorian England* (CUP, 2002) at 173).

14

DISTRIBUTIONS

A. Introduction

The obvious risks in making distributions are that either they are for too great an amount or **14.01** that they are to the wrong beneficiary. The former can be guarded against by accuracy of the estate or trust accounts and the careful calculation of outstanding liabilities. Comment is made later on the identification of beneficiaries. There are, however, other aspects of policy and planning concerning distributions that should be considered in order to control risk.

B. Timing

Comment is made elsewhere (see Chapter 13 at para 13.09) on the value of interim distri- **14.02** butions in estate administration. Much of that comment is also valid for early distributions from trusts when they become distributable, for example after the death of a life tenant. Quite clearly, no distributions should be made until the PR has a grant and is satisfied that it is safe to distribute in terms of the solvency of the estate or abatement of gifts. There are, however, two other time factors to consider. Section 27 Trustee Act 1925 notices to creditors are dealt with below, but the question of possible claims under the Inheritance (Provision for Family and Dependants) Act 1975 may be an issue. Any application under s.2 of the Act must be made ('made' is issued not served[1]) within six months of the date on which a grant of representation is first issued (unless the court gives leave for a later application to be made[2]). This has the effect that a PR, when considering a distribution from an estate, must consider both the statutory six-months period in s.2, as well as a four-month period available for service of the claim form (s.20 of the Act does not affect this point[3]). Distributions cannot be

---

[1] *Re Chittenden* [1970] 1 WLR 1618.
[2] Section 4.
[3] It is applicable only to late claims, ie those originating, with the consent of the court, after the 6-month period has expired.

made safely under ten months from the date of grant where there is a possibility of a claim under this Act. In practical terms there will be many estates where it is safe to distribute earlier than this because there is no possibility of a claim. However, to reach this conclusion requires the PR to have made adequate enquiries and reached a reasonable conclusion.

14.03 A grant is taken out for these purposes on the date on which it is issued by the Probate Registry (the date on the face of it). A grant limited to settled land or to trust property is left out of account. Other limited grants such as *pendente lite* (pending litigation, such as to determine the validity of the will) or *ad colligenda bona* (for the preservation of assets) are also left out of account as they are essentially neutral administrative provisions enabling the estate to be protected, but not distributed, and are not determinative of beneficial interests. Similarly an *ad litem* grant issued for the purposes of pursuing a negligence claim concerning an accident in which the deceased was killed is not a grant for the purposes of the time limits for applications. Where a grant has been issued and then revoked, time does not start running until a grant which was effective and valid is issued.[4]

14.04 An application should not be made before the grant is taken out: *Re McBroom*.[5] *Re Searle*[6] decided the contrary for time limits under an earlier Act, but *McBroom* is the decision now followed. Making such claims after the issue of a grant is in practical terms preferred as that enables the defendants to be identified. For consideration of the factors that the court will take into account for late applications see *Re Salmon*.[7]

Section 27 Trustee Act 1925 statutory notices to creditors

14.05 A PR may appropriate assets to a beneficiary at any time after he has proved title to them, that is obtained a grant of representation. Appropriation before then is thought not to be possible, given that the PR cannot transfer title to the legatee in the absence of the grant and has not proved his own title. A PR would also be unwise to appropriate assets after the issue of grant but before such time as his statutory notices to creditors have expired without claims having been made under them.

14.06 Section 27 Trustee Act 1925 sets out the basis of protection against debts of which the PR has no notice before distribution of the estate. By placing a notice in the *London Gazette* and also a notice in a local paper circulating in the area where any land is held (if any land is held[8]) the PR gives notice to creditors to bring forward any claims that have not either been notified to him or that he does not have knowledge of.

14.07 The approach to these notices in a testate estate is to place the notices as soon as possible in order that the two-month period for claims can start running soon and thus allow for interim distributions as early as possible. A further reason for early notices is that the protection that they give to a PR is not valid in respect of any assets distributed prior to the notices, even if the debt is notified after the two-months period has expired.[9]

---

[4] *Re Freeman, Freeman v Weston* [1984] 1 WLR 1419.
[5] [1992] 2 FLR 49.
[6] [1949] Ch 73.
[7] [1981] Ch 167.
[8] It is an unresolved point if an interest in jointly owned land requires such a local press notice. Generally executors and administrators place such notices out of caution.
[9] *Re Kay* [1897] 2 Ch 518.

Such notices are valid, even if placed before the grant is issued, as the property vests in the **14.08** executor at death.[10] Where notice of a debt is not given to the PR until after the two-months period has expired, the creditor's debt can only be enforced against the PR to the extent that he holds assets of the estate. For the balance of any debt the creditor can only recover the amount by following the assets to the beneficiaries.

However, in an intestate estate it is not thought safe to place these notices until the admin- **14.09** istrator's position is confirmed by the issue of a grant. This is on the basis that the applicant has no standing or authority to give notice to creditors prior to his appointment by the court, confirmed by the issue of the letters of administration. The effect of the notices, once validly placed, is the same in both testate and intestate estates.

There is an additional insolvency aspect to be considered. The wording of s.27(2)(b) is too **14.10** often overlooked:

> nothing in this section—
> ...
> (b) frees the trustees or personal representatives from any obligation to make searches or obtain official certificates of search *similar to those which an intending purchaser would be advised to obtain.* (authors' emphasis)

Although the correct placing of advertisements will deal with potential creditors' claims, the notices will not give protection against a claim from a trustee in bankruptcy where the PR has made a distribution to a bankrupt beneficiary without bankruptcy searches having been made. Searching the Land Charges Register for notice of the bankruptcy of a beneficiary is the only way safely to ascertain bankruptcy, as the statute, by its wording, does not operate to make s.27 notices by themselves effective against claims from trustees in bankruptcy.[11]

The implications of this restriction on the operation of s.27 are considerable. PRs and **14.11** trustees may normally carry out searches when distributing land or interests in land, but the restriction in s.27(2)(b) applies to all distributions including those of personalty.

The practical difficulty with the PR making bankruptcy searches against the beneficiaries is **14.12** the duration of the validity of the searches. There is much more familiarity with the protec- tion that a search provides for a purchaser of property, if a purchase is completed within fifteen days of the date on the certificate of search[12] but this fifteen-day protection period is clearly expressly limited only to purchasers. For a PR (or trustee) distributing assets, there is no continuing validity of such a search; the certificate only gives the information as at the date of search and does not protect against an order in bankruptcy being registered, say, the day after.[13] It is therefore suggested that where bankruptcy searches are thought appropriate that risk is reduced by distributions being made straight away on receipt of the search results, or making fax or telephone searches on the day of distribution. Consideration should also be given to the position of a beneficiary at the death of the testator. At that time his interest in

---

[10] Grant acting as confirmation of the title.
[11] This particular point was the subject of two letters in the *Law Society Gazette* in 2001, which drew atten- tion to these risks.
[12] Section 11(5) Land Charges Act 1972.
[13] This is an annoying inconsistency of approach that could be tidied up if a trustee was given the same protection as a purchaser.

the estate will vest in the trustee in bankruptcy[14] and searches should identify that fact and ensure that any future dealings with regard to the inheritance are with the correct party. This will not remove the need for later searches as, of course, a beneficiary may become bankrupt during the course of the administration.

14.13   Conventionally s.27 notices are used during the administration of estates, but the position of trustees should not be overlooked. Notices are not generally placed by trustees when making distributions probably because they consider themselves to be fully acquainted with the trust property and aware if there are any claims against it. This view, while perfectly valid, does not address the issue of the potential claim from a beneficiary's trustee in bankruptcy and usually knowledge of this will only come from bankruptcy searches. From this it follows that all trustees should have a policy to consider bankruptcy searches when making trust property distributions.

Capacity in which a distribution is made

14.14   Where a will contains provisions which create trust interests, the division of functions between the PR and the trustee is of some considerable importance. However, the boundary can become blurred in practice, particularly where both PRs and trustees are the same persons and where particular attention is not paid to what is being done and the capacity in which it is being done.

1. The CGT position of the two offices is different both in terms of annual allowances and, as far as the PR's gains are concerned, in the ability to offset administration losses against trust gains. However, where the trust fund has been properly, if partially, created by interim distributions, it is possible for the two offices to co-exist and for each to have the appropriate CGT allowance.
2. The powers and duties of both offices are different and they should be clearly exercised in the right capacity.
3. The income tax returns are made in different capacities and, depending upon the nature of the trust interests, the taxation of the income may be on a different basis.
4. For anti-money laundering purposes, the positions of trustee and PR are treated differently by those conducting business with them.[15]

14.15   In order to maintain the correct approach to the above issues, interim distributions should be made and separate estate and trust accounts should be maintained for those distributions. This not only presents an accurate picture to the beneficiaries of what has taken place, but assists the management of either fund and reduces the risk of actions being taken in the wrong capacity. The proper management of the trust investments can also be put in hand earlier in the administration (see Chapter 13 on investments).

Appropriations of assets in satisfaction of interests

14.16   Section 41(3) Administration of Estates Act 1925 gives a PR[16] the power to ascertain the value of property that is to be appropriated and to employ a valuer for this purpose where

---

[14]   *Re Hemming, Saul v Holden* [2008] WTLR 1833.
[15]   See Part 2 of the Money Laundering Regulations 2007; the provisions relating to beneficial owners in Regulation 5 are applied in a significantly different way for PRs of estates in the UK by Regulation 6(8).
[16]   Applies to PRs of both testate and intestate estates: s.41(9)—but it does not apply to trustees.

necessary. The value for appropriation is to be determined at the time of appropriation[17] (not the date of death) applying normal valuation principles.[18] The purpose of revaluation on appropriation is to achieve fairness of distribution, by applying current values as opposed to historic, and, whilst this may be understood by the PR, beneficiaries will be more ready to challenge it if appropriations are made of part of the same asset to different beneficiaries at different dates. Thus, dividing a holding of shares among the residuary legatees will require different appropriation values if made on different dates and for the appearance of fairness to the beneficiaries, this is to be avoided if possible.

The date of appropriation is a question of fact and a more suitable date cannot be chosen **14.17** or retrospectively allocated. This means that appropriations to beneficiaries should be accurately recorded in the books of account when they are made and not dealt with retrospectively when administration accounts are being prepared. Where there are taxation consequences in dividing sales of investments between sales in the administration and sales on behalf of the beneficiary (or trustee) there should be careful planning as the division between the capacities in which sales are made is one of fact and cannot be retrospectively allocated.

When an asset has been appropriated, the PR ceases to hold the asset in the capacity of PR. **14.18** If the asset is not immediately transferred into the name of the beneficiary (or trustee if the legacy is settled) the PR holds the appropriated asset as trustee for the beneficiary and not as an asset of the estate. This means that the PR must be aware of the consequences of the appropriation and should not make it without satisfying himself that the reserves held for estate liabilities are sufficient. Once appropriated an asset is not then available to meet the general liabilities and expenses of the estate.[19]

Section 41 requires a PR to consider the interests of all present and future beneficiaries **14.19** when making an appropriation. This can be characterized as a duty to act fairly between all the interests, although acting fairly does not require the PR to hold an even balance between all of the competing interests.[20] Fairness in appropriations was considered in *Lloyds Bank v Duker*[21] in the context of an estate holding a 99.9 per cent shareholding in a private company. If appropriated to the beneficiaries, one beneficiary would have received a 57.44 per cent interest in the company. The remaining 42.46 per cent would have been divided equally between the five other beneficiaries absolutely entitled. After appropriation the 57.44 per cent holding would have been worth significantly more per share than the other holdings (arising from the disparity in values between majority and minority holdings). The minority holdings would, post-appropriation, have had a value far below that at which they were appropriated (ie as part of a majority holding at appropriation) and this would have placed the beneficiary taking the majority share at a manifest advantage in being able to acquire the minority shareholdings by purchase. The court ordered an open-market sale

---

[17] *Re Charteris* [1917] 2 Ch 379; *Robinson v Collins* [1975] 1 All ER 321.

[18] An appropriation of qualifying investments made in satisfaction of a pecuniary legacy, made with the consent of the legatee under s.41 (and not under a special power not requiring consent), can be a sale for the purposes of IHT relief for loss on sales (ss.178–89 IHTA 1984).

[19] The recovery of sums distributed in error by a PR is possible, *Ministry of Health v Simpson* [1951] AC 251 and *Kleinwort Benson v Lincoln CC* [1998] 3 WLR 1095, but this process is unlikely to be an easy, cheap, or ready remedy for the PR.

[20] *Edge v Pensions Ombudsman* [1999] 4 All ER 546; *Re Charteris* (n 17); *Re Hayes* [1971] 1 WLR 758.

[21] [1987] 1 WLR 1324.

(at which any of the beneficiaries could bid) with the proceeds then to be distributed proportionally among the interests.

14.20 Care is needed for minors' legacies which do not carry intermediate income.[22] Not only can the power under s.42 not be used to appoint new trustees, but it is in practice difficult to segregate funds from the residue of the estate, for future payment of the legacies, by appropriation.[23] As such legacies do not carry the intermediate income and that income therefore is payable to others (usually the interests in residue) during the minority, there is a risk of an IHT charge should a beneficiary die while still entitled to that income. This means that in practice, this type of minors' legacy is reserved for in residue, without appropriation, and the amount reserved should make an allowance for the potential tax charge. The PR who distributes residue without a reserve for potential IHT charges runs the risk of having the tax assessed upon him while not having the assets to settle it.

14.21 In an intestate estate, a surviving spouse or civil partner has a statutory right,[24] should they elect to exercise it within twelve months of the grant of letters of administration, to have the deceased's interest in the matrimonial or civil partnership home appropriated 'in or towards satisfaction of any absolute interest'[25] the spouse or civil partner has in the estate. Although this right[26] is usually considered in the context of the spouse's, or civil partner's, other rights in the estate, the cash part of the statutory legacy is often an important part of the value of their interest. If that value exceeds the total value of the spouse's, or civil partner's, absolute interests in the intestate estate, they can introduce the balance of funds needed from their own resources.[27] In the Intestates' Estates Act 1952 the matrimonial home is defined as 'a dwelling-house in which the surviving husband or wife was resident at the time of the intestate's death'. It is to be noted that this definition may not necessarily accord with how a matrimonial home is usually defined and indeed may allow an interest in a property which was not the usually accepted matrimonial home to be appropriated.

14.22 If the surviving spouse or civil partner makes this election, the value of the interest in the property is, in accordance with usual practice, to be determined at the date of appropriation, not the date of death.[28] This has significant practical implications for the adviser to the spouse or civil partner. During the past forty years there have been generally (but not always) high, and at times quite rapid, rates of property appreciation.[29] Undue delay, or a failure to understand the effect of a rising property market on the value of the election, and a

---

[22] eg minors' legacies that are contingent and where the legatee is not a child of the deceased or a child in respect of which the deceased stands *in loco parentis*.

[23] *Re Hall* [1903] 1 Ch 226.

[24] Schedule 2 Intestates' Estates Act 1952 as amended by para 13 Sch 4 Civil Partnership Act 2004.

[25] Paragraph 1(1) Sch 2 Intestates' Estates Act 1952 as amended by para 13 Sch 4 Civil Partnership Act 2004.

[26] It is not at the discretion of the PR and it does not require his consent, and solvency permitting, he cannot refuse it.

[27] *Re Phelps* [1979] 3 All ER 373 and these resources will include those other capital interests that the spouse, or civil partner, might have in the intestate estate.

[28] *Re Collins, Robinson v Collins* [1975] 1 WLR 309.

[29] In 2008 the very opposite conditions prevailed in the property market and in theory a beneficiary could have benefited in terms of property value from the adviser dragging his feet. It is suggested if there is to be deliberate delay in seeking an appropriation for this reason then the risks of short-term speculation should be very carefully weighed up and the beneficiary should be fully aware of them.

failure to explain that to the client, can leave the adviser exposed to a claim from the widow or surviving civil partner.[30]

The determination of the value, where the spouse or civil partner is the PR, will be subject **14.23** to the self-dealing rule.[31] If that value exceeds the total value of the spouse's or civil partner's absolute interests in the intestate estate, the spouse or civil partner can introduce the balance of funds needed from their own resources. The valuation will be subject to the surviving spouse's or civil partner's rights of occupation and, where it applies, co-ownership.

There could have been further difficulty with this right to acquire the dwelling-house if **14.24** the rule against a trustee purchasing trust property had not been expressly barred where there is more than one PR[32] acting. However, where the spouse or civil partner is the sole PR he is prevented from exercising this power. The practical implication of this is that where there is a matrimonial home to be appropriated under this power the spouse or civil partner should not act by themselves as PR and that this problem should be tackled at the outset.

Section 36 Charities Act 1993 is relevant to charities and appropriations. Where there are **14.25** one or more charity residuary legatees[33] the charity/charities will rightly be concerned that all reasonable steps should be taken to avoid CGT being paid on disposals of land (in England and Wales) by the PR. Therefore charities will often request that

- the PR appropriates an asset that is full of gain;
- the PR holds the asset under a simple declaration of trust for the charity;
- the PR sells the asset in the capacity of trustee of the declaration of trust (and presumably only with the consent of the charity to the terms of the selling contract); and
- the PR accounts for the net proceeds to the charity/charities.

Appropriation, declaration of trust, and then sale in this way is accepted by the HMRC as **14.26** being an effective way of ensuring that the sale of the asset is not a sale by the PR (in that capacity) and is a sale on behalf of the charity/charities.

The difficulty, however, is in identifying where the responsibility for applying s.36 **14.27** Charities Act 1993[34] lies—with the PR or the charity/charities? The Institute of Legacy Management have obtained an opinion from senior counsel who advised that a PR who sells land in this way on behalf of charities is the trustee for the purpose of s.36 and the

---

[30] This will also be linked to advice on the spouse's, or civil partner's, right to a capital payment in lieu of his life interest in the estate (s.47A Administration of Estates Act 1925 as amended by para 9 Sch 4 Civil Partnership Act 2004) and the amount to be obtained from this may well also be affected by the passage of time.

[31] *Kane v Radley-Kane* [1998] 3 All ER 753 (see Chapter 10 para 10.37); see also *Re Peck* [2011] WTLR 604 on the strictness of applicable procedures where self-dealing is permitted by court order.

[32] Paragraph 5(1) Sch 2 Intestates' Estates Act 1952.

[33] But only charity residuary legatees; this section does not apply where there is a mixture of charitable and non-charitable legatees.

[34] Disposal of land can only be made without an order of the court or Charity Commission if
(1) it is not to a connected person, their trustee, or nominee (see Schedule 5);
(2) *before* agreeing to the sale the trustee:
- obtains and considers a written report from a qualified surveyor acting exclusively for the trustees that contains all the information in the prescribed regulations;
- advertises the property as recommended by the surveyor;
- decides that they are satisfied that in the light of the report the terms they are minded to accept are the best that can reasonably be obtained.

responsibility for complying with the duties of s.36 rests with him. This has considerable costs implications for the PR given the onerous nature of s.36. It is not thought that a sale in this way is any part of the PR's duties and he is at liberty to refuse to sell and transfer the property to the charity/charities unless appropriate arrangements for instruction and remuneration can be made.

14.28 For CGT purposes a legatee who receives assets by appropriation is deemed to have acquired them not at the appropriation value, but at the value at the date of death.[35] Where stocks and shares are appropriated to a beneficiary and sold on his behalf there can be significant CGT advantages for a beneficiary in terms of the availability of his own reliefs and allowances. However, the position of HMRC is that sales made before residue are prima facie sales of the PR in the administration and for them to be considered otherwise there should be evidence of compliance with s.41 (where it applies and particularly the prior consent) before sale.[36] See para 14.25 (above) regarding charities as HMRC take a similar view of the requirements for a sale of land to be made on behalf of a non-charity legatee.

14.29 Some modern wills contain provisions purporting to permit the PR to make a choice of value at which property is appropriated (usually allowing either probate value or date of appropriation to be selected).

1. Such a provision is of course not binding on HMRC—the law is that the value for appropriation is the value at the date of appropriation.[37] Using a value less than the actual value at the date of appropriation will inflate the amount of the property that can be appropriated in satisfaction of an interest and HMRC will be concerned about that effect (eg the amount of property transferred in satisfaction of a nil-rate band legacy).[38]
2. If the executor is given a choice of value, in whose interest does he select a value: the interest of the residuary beneficiary or the legatee (as benefiting one will disadvantage the other) and what factors should he take into account?

14.30 It is now fairly standard practice to amend the statutory power of appropriation to permit appropriation without consent[39] and to extend such a power to a trustee (as s.41 does apply to trustees).

Receipts for distributions

14.31 A PR or trustee is entitled to ask for, and receive, a receipt for each payment or asset transfer made in satisfaction of a beneficiary's interest in an estate or trust. The payment or transfer should not be withheld until the receipt is signed and returned.[40] A PR has no general right to obtain a formal discharge by deed or a beneficiary's indemnity as to the PR's administration of the estate unless this has been an agreed term of the settlement of a dispute.

---

[35] Section 64(2) Taxation of Chargeable Gains Act 1992.
[36] *HMRC CGT Manual* at CG30750: 'have taken specific steps to vest those assets sold in legatees ... If personal representatives are involved in such a sale it can only be as bare trustee for the legatees'.
[37] *Re Charteris* (n 17) and *Re Collins* [1975] 1 WLR 309.
[38] The converse would be that the beneficiary would not get full value for his legacy.
[39] Section 41(1) Administration of Estates Act 1925; see s.41(1)(ii)(a) for consent requirement.
[40] *Law Society Gazette*, 14 October 1992.

The approval of and receipt to the estate accounts signed by residuary beneficiaries is a reasonable step for the PR to require. However, the PR is not entitled to seek more than that. The occasional practice of withholding settlement of the estate until a beneficiary executes an indemnity is to be deprecated. **14.32**

Money Laundering Regulations 2007

The administration of an estate or assisting a client with the administration is not within the list of activities excluded from the work of 'an independent legal professional' unless, in the case of assistance to a client, the work is limited solely to legal advice.[41] **14.33**

For the PR or the PR's advisers there are in addition significant issues to be considered relating to offences under the Proceeds of Crime Act 2002 and the Terrorism Act 2000 for money laundering.[42] The concerns arise in two different areas: (a) the deceased and his assets and (b) actions surrounding the deceased's will. **14.34**

Deceased's estate

Concerns may arise where **14.35**

- the deceased has unusually large amounts of cash, precious metals, or illegal substances at the time of his death;
- the deceased's wealth or lifestyle is inconsistent with his employment or position in life;
- there are unusual bank account transactions or unusual patterns of cash movement involving his bank accounts;
- the deceased failed to disclose taxable income or chargeable gains;
- the deceased had made fraudulent social security claims or fraudulent insurance claims.

These issues cannot be ignored because of the real suspicions that the deceased held the proceeds of crime at his death. Any attempt to ignore these issues will potentially expose the PR to money laundering offences when distributing the estate. The correct route will be a suspicious activity report for one in the regulated sector or a disclosure under s.330 for others.

The will of the deceased

Given the curious activities that can sometimes surround the making of wills, it should not be overlooked that criminal activity can be involved, for example: **14.36**

- impersonating the testator to procure an apparent will for him;
- forging a testator signature;
- destroying a will with the aim of inheriting on intestacy;
- obtaining a will in one's favour through fear, force, or coercion;
- obtaining a will from someone who obviously lacks testamentary capacity.

These and other fraudulent activities surrounding wills should be recognized as potential crimes[43] and not simply dismissed as the games that families play over wills.

---

[41] The Law Society of England and Wales Anti-Money Laundering Practice Note, 22 February 2008 [1.4.5].

[42] Reference should be made to one of the standard works on money laundering for the structure and detail of the UK regime.

[43] Potential offences are under the Theft Act 1968, Fraud Act 2006, and the Forgery and Counterfeiting Act 1981.

14.37 In addition, payments to beneficiaries need to be considered in the light of HM Treasury's Consolidated List of Financial Sanctions Targets within the UK.

C. Identification

14.38 Although PRs and trustees are well used to checks on identification for the purposes of the Money Laundering Regulations 2007, there are other issues that ought to be considered.

    1. *Photocopy documents*: Photocopy documents can be the fraudsters' weapon of choice. Photocopying amended or fake documents is a way of hiding imperfections or alterations. The use of photocopy certificates is governed by Crown copyright of registrars' copy certificates. Without a licence no one is permitted to photocopy these certificates other than as a record of what has been exhibited to them.[44] Therefore production of a photocopy certificate by a beneficiary is not acceptable proof of information as it is not in a form that can be used.

    Allied to this is the use of scanners to scan documents into computer systems for the information to be manipulated and reprinted. Flaws in the paper, absence of watermarks, inexact trimming of the paper, or inaccurate colours can give these away, but care is needed.

    2. *Short form birth certificates*: These are generally not acceptable in establishing entitlements which relate to descent (eg on intestacy) as they give no details of parentage.

    3. *Foreign certificates*: These present other problems of verification that they are authentic and also translation of information. Depending upon country and document, verification can be by notary or by embassy legalization. The legalization process certifies the validity of the document but does not certify the accuracy of the information that it contains. Translation will be a separate process in order to establish the information in the document.

14.39 The PR's and trustee's duties to distribute the estate or trust correctly by implication must extend to identifying the beneficiaries correctly. This does not merely require the correct construction of the gift under the will,[45] but also establishing the identity of the individuals to whom payment is made.

Recovery of payments to those not entitled

14.40 As a general rule money paid away under a mistake[46] can be recovered and a PR or trustee prima facie can recover sums distributed to the wrong persons. The negligence of the PR or trustee in the manner of the distribution is not a bar to the action (see commentary on *Fea v Roberts* below). However, a more substantial defence can be provided by the recipient's change of position based on his receipt of the payment.[47]

---

[44] The government guidance on this point was updated in May 2005 and can be found at <http://www.nationalarchives.gov.uk/documents/information-management/copying-bmd-certificates.pdf>.

[45] It is beyond the scope of this book to set out a detailed consideration of the rules of construction, and reference should be made to one of the standard works on wills.

[46] The old distinctions between mistake of fact and mistake of law are not needed following *Kleinwort Benson Ltd v Lincoln City Council* [1998] 4 All ER 513.

[47] *Lipkin Gorman v Karpnale Ltd* [1992] 4 All ER 512.

Where there is a failure to correctly identify the right beneficiary, recovery of the wrongly **14.41**
paid sum may be possible where the conduct of the person who received the distribution
exhibits a lack of good faith. In *Fea v Roberts*,[48] after the death of the life tenant of a will trust
the estate was to be divided between a nephew, a niece, and four godsons. Enquiries of the
testator's bankers revealed that one godson, William Edward Roberts, banked with them.
However, the Mr Roberts then contacted by the bank, to tell him that he should contact the
solicitor-trustees, was not the same person, although he had the same name. The considerable correspondence that followed was clearly marked with the name of the estate and Mr
Roberts was supplied with a copy will that contained the reference to godson and the name
of the deceased.

The distribution of the estate was completed in July 1998 and Mr Roberts received a mix- **14.42**
ture of investments[49] and cash. In October 2003 a claim was received from the correct Mr
Roberts.[50] Mr Roberts had spent the inheritance.

A defence against recovery on limitation grounds was rejected.[51] Other defences were **14.43**
founded on estoppel and change of position. The trouble was the apparent absence of good
faith in the actions of Mr Roberts.

> I do not think that it is desirable to attempt to define the limits of good faith; it is a broad con-
> cept, the definition of which, in so far as it is capable of definition at all, will have to be worked
> out through the cases. In my view it is capable of embracing a failure to act in a commercially
> acceptable way and sharp practice of a kind that falls short of outright dishonesty itself. The
> factors which will determine whether it is inequitable to allow the claimant to obtain restitu-
> tion in a case of mistaken payment will vary from case to case, but where the payee has volun-
> tarily parted with the money much is likely to depend on the circumstances in which he did
> so and the extent of his knowledge about how the payment came to be made. Where he knows
> the payment he has received was made by mistake, the position is quite straight-forward: he
> must return it. This applies as much to a banker who receives payment for the account of his
> customer as to any other person … Greater difficulty may arise however, in cases, where the
> payee has grounds for believing that the payment has been made by mistake, but cannot be
> sure. In such cases good faith may well dictate that an inquiry be made of the payer. The nature
> and extent of the inquiry called for will, of course, depend on the circumstances of the case,
> but I do not think that a person who has, or thinks he has, good reason to believe that the pay-
> ment was made by mistake will often be found to have acted in good faith if he pays the money
> away without first making enquiries of the person from whom he received it…
>
> [I]t is a matter to be viewed in terms of a duty of good faith which a person, who has received
> a payment that he has good reason to think was made under a mistake, owes to the person
> who made it. If under those circumstances the payee fails to make inquiry of the payer before
> disposing of the money he can properly be described as failing to act in good faith because he
> acts in the knowledge that he may be infringing the rights of another despite having the means
> of avoiding that consequence.[52]

---

[48] [2006] WTLR 255.

[49] Mr Roberts' professional adviser had charged £13,000 commission for selling £115,000 of investments.

[50] It was accepted that the solicitor-trustees had been 'careless' in not making adequate checks into the
identity of Mr Roberts.

[51] Section 32(2)(c) Limitation Act 1980 started the limitation period running from when it was reasonable
to have discovered the mistake. Note: 'when it was reasonable to have discovered', so not when the mistake was
made but when it was reasonable to have discovered it.

[52] *Niru Battery Manufacturing Ltd v Milestone Trading Ltd* [2002] 2 All ER (Comm) 705 at [135] and [138],
approved by the Court of Appeal [2004] 1 All ER 193.

While the judge pointed out that Mr Roberts did not act dishonestly, he did find a lack of good faith.[53] Mr Roberts was ordered to repay in excess of £114,000.

Tracing beneficiaries

14.44 There are two aspects of this issue: establishing those entitled (eg on intestacy or members of a class) and then having established identities there is the question of physically locating them.

14.45 In an intestacy, a fundamental question for the administrator is establishing the detail of the family tree[54] and thus who is entitled to what interest in the distribution. An administrator who is a family member may well have sufficient detailed knowledge to hand already. This can be a possible source of error if he was not told about all of the family secrets and in truth there is really no substitute for full research involving production of full birth certificates and relevant marriage and death certificates. Indeed, even where the PR is reasonably satisfied as to the identity of the person he is dealing with identities should be proved.

14.46 The professional PR is faced with either researching the family tree himself[55] or instructing a genealogist. There appear to be two different approaches by genealogists to this work:

1. Those that quote an hourly fee rate plus expenses and generally try to estimate the likely number of hours involved.
2. Those that operate on the basis of a percentage fee being charged to the beneficiary when they are traced—often referred to, probably incorrectly, as contingency fees.

Category 1 will usually quote a rate for the work, although it is common for the fee arrangement to include further charging if work outside the usual sources is needed. The genealogist's report will then be the property of the administrator who will then use it to determine the basis of the distribution. The genealogist's fee is a disbursement of the estate as would be the cost of any missing beneficiary insurance.[56] Depending upon the instructions, the genealogist's report is likely to cover locating those identified.

14.47 Those in category 2 receive no fee from the estate,[57] but they are given all relevant information that the PR has from his estate file. The genealogist then carries out the tracing work at his own cost/risk expecting to recoup his percentage fee in due course from the beneficiaries, once located. The beneficiary, when traced, is given no information about his inheritance, but he is required to sign an agreement whereby his inheritance passes to him through the hands of the genealogist who deducts a sum of usually 25–35 per cent[58] before paying the

---

[53] And also rejected a significant part of his evidence.

[54] 'Family tree' in this context is a diagram displaying relationships and it is useful for understanding the family structure, but without the support evidence of birth, death, and marriage certificates it can only guide further research.

[55] Although often they will lack the skills and it may not be sufficiently remunerative work for the time involved. Additionally, from a risk management perspective, undertaking such work may well not be advisable.

[56] *Evans v Westcombe* [1999] 2 All ER 777.

[57] There appear to be some of these contracts that are entered into by PRs directly with the genealogist with the fee being payable by the PR by deduction from the missing legatee's interest when he is located. For a PR to sign such a contract without competitive quotations for alternative methods would appear to be commercially highly imprudent.

[58] Where the missing beneficiary's interest is substantial, such as that of a residuary legatee such a fee could dwarf the entire charges for administration of the estate.

balance to the beneficiary. It is difficult to see that a fee that is not directly related to the work involved in the individual estate can be justified.

There are concerns that the practice of using genealogists in this second category can be con- **14.48** trary to the interests of the beneficiary,[59] although so far this matter has not been considered by an English court. It can of course also be against the interests of the PR as he will not discover the beneficiary if he does not sign the genealogists' agreement. Some of the issues surrounding this practice are set out below.

1. The PR has a duty to distribute to the correct beneficiary. Instructing a stranger to the estate in the knowledge that this will deprive the beneficiary of something approaching one-third of the inheritance, when there may well be cheaper ways of locating him, could be judged to be failing in the duty to the beneficiary.
2. If the PR is unable to take advantage of the information on his file to make a similar agreement with the beneficiary,[60] how can his agent[61] be authorized to do so?
3. Breach of confidence by the administrator in providing information regarding the estate for a stranger to make a profit at the expense of the beneficiary is a major concern. The information on the administrator's file has been obtained by him when acting in a fiduciary capacity and there must be an argument that there must be a duty of confidentiality.
4. The contract that the beneficiary is expected to enter into may be champertous and unenforceable.[62]
5. The contract entered into is an unconscionable bargain because of the weak position of the beneficiary in lacking the information that is known to the genealogist.[63]
6. The costs of location of a beneficiary have been held to be *not* attributable to his share alone and should generally be charged against the residue before division.[64] However, there is a degree of doubt as to whether a modern court would follow these authorities, but there are no modern cases on the point.

The position must be that there is, at best, substantial uncertainty as to the ability of the PR **14.49** (or trustee) to enter into arrangements with the genealogist if the remuneration is on the so-called 'contingency fee' basis, rather than the fee payable from the estate. Further, there must be doubt as to the enforceability of the contract that the genealogist enters into with the beneficiary.

It is suggested therefore that professional PRs and trustees, and professional advisers to **14.50** trustees, should consider carefully the policy they wish to follow in this regard. PR and trustee

---

[59] Title Research (a firm of genealogists that does not operate on the contingency fee basis in locating heirs) have widely circulated a counsel's opinion which was obtained on their instructions and which raises serious objections to such contingency fee instructions.

[60] *Keech v Sandford* [1726] 2 AC 46.

[61] It is of course arguable that the genealogist is not the PR's agent in this, but if he is not, how can he be put in possession of information from the estate file?

[62] *McElroy v Flynn* [1991] IRLM 294; *Fraser v Buckle* [1996] 2 IRLM 34; [2003] WTLR 1389 (both Irish decisions, but both were on agreements governed by English law).

[63] The authors have been unable to trace any reported case of these contracts being litigated in English courts. The absence of a contract being successfully enforced is worrying given that these contracts are not rare and can involve substantial values.

[64] *Sharp v Lush* [1879] 10 Ch D 468 in which it was held that the estate generally should bear the expenses 'incidental to the proper performance of the duties of personal representatives as personal representatives'.

need to consider their duties towards the beneficiaries and the consequences if they breach those duties in instructing a genealogist.

Gender Recognition Act 2004

14.51 Section 9 contains what is the core principle of this Act, that once a full gender recognition certificate is issued a person's gender becomes for all purposes in the future the acquired gender.

14.52 Once a full gender recognition certificate is issued after a change of gender, the Registrar General must be supplied with a copy.[65] Schedule 3 sets out the procedure[66] for the Registrar General to create a Gender Recognition Register[67] to contain amended birth entries.

14.53 On receipt of a full gender recognition certificate the original entry for birth will then be annotated and a link created between the original entry and the amended birth entry in the new Gender Recognition Register. This link between the entries will not be apparent on the face of a certificate, nor will it be apparent in any search or inspection of the Register. The notes to the Act add that if a search is made

1. In the name on the original birth certificate then a copy of the original unamended birth certificate will be produced.
2. In the name after change of gender then this will produce an amended birth certificate.

14.54 Neither certificate will have any notation on its face that will link it to the other. It is difficult to know how easily genealogical researchers will be able to deal with this, as effectively there will be two distinct persons on the face of the publicly available register and this could provide difficulties in future tracing.

Statutory declarations

14.55 Traditionally evidence of birth, death, and marriage has been collated into statutory declarations setting out the family tree (or part of it) and confirming the truth of the information. This was often done where a professional genealogist was not used, but the documentation was provided by the family. They have also been seen as ways of dealing with 'negative' information, such as a person dying without issue, which cannot be proved from registry information. Where this is a preferred course some points should be borne in mind.

1. A statutory declaration is not in itself protection for the PR: it provides no guarantee or indemnity. It is, however, evidence that he has acted reasonably and not negligently in the way that he has made a distribution. It is self-evident therefore that distributions should not be made before any necessary statutory declarations have been completed. As the declaration is sworn to under the Statutory Declarations Act 1835 it can be given as evidence in court by the PR.[68]
2. The statutory declaration is worthless if the deponent has a material interest in the distribution and the information he gives affects the size of that entitlement. Declarations should, whenever possible, be taken from an uninterested party.

---

[65] Section 10.
[66] See also the Gender Recognition Register Regulations 2005, SI 912/2005.
[67] Which is not open to public inspection or search.
[68] Knowingly swearing to incorrect information in a statutory declaration is a criminal offence (but unfortunately this has not stopped relatives swearing to wrong information).

3. The statutory declaration is worthless if it is based largely on information provided to the deponent by the PR and the deponent does not have all the information within his personal knowledge.

4. It is not necessary to attach all relevant certificates as exhibits to the declaration (this substantially increases the swear fee) but whoever drafts the declaration should see all the certificates.

5. Rather than simply reciting the facts of a marriage, it is better for the declaration to recite that the person was married 'once only' or 'twice', thus establishing clearly the number of times that they were married and therefore the number of possible lines of descent that need to be covered.

6. Describing someone as having died 'unmarried' should be avoided as a widower or widow dies unmarried.

7. There is also a degree of ambiguity about 'died without issue' and 'died without having had any issue' is to be preferred.

8. Probates and letters of administration are not acceptable as proof of death and death certificates must be seen.

9. Where the Adoption Acts 1958/76 (as amended) are applicable and would affect any distribution, but there are no persons adopted, the declaration should state 'to the best of my knowledge and belief none of the persons mentioned in this affidavit has at any time either alone or jointly with any other person adopted any infant child within the meaning of the Adoption Acts 1958 and 1976 [nor have they themselves whilst infants been adopted by any other persons within the meaning of the said Acts prior to the date of death of the deceased]'. The latter part in square brackets could usefully be used in all statutory declarations of this type.

10. Section 15 Family Law Reform Act 1969 applies to deaths post-1 January 1970, but pre-4 April 1988 so as to entitle illegitimate persons, or those claiming through them, to share in the distribution. Therefore the declaration should state that to the best of the deponent's knowledge either there are no such persons, or that there are; then giving details. For deaths after 3 April 1988 the illegitimacy is not a bar to inheritance whatever the degree of relationship to the intestate. Declarations in respect of deaths after that date should refer to s.19 Family Law Reform Act 1987 and not s.15 Family Law Reform Act 1969.

11. For post-3 April 1988 intestacies it is recommended that all declarations should contain a statement to the effect that to the best of the deponent's knowledge there are no persons entitled to claim by virtue of s.18 Family Reform Act 1987 (obviously if there are any such persons the statement is omitted and details of the persons concerned are recited).

12. For intestacies post-5 December 2005 references to 'marriages' and whether or not a person had entered into one will have to be extended to also recite whether or not a civil partnership had been entered into.

13. In building a family tree in order to determine who is entitled, it is never necessary, in an intestate estate, to go back further than the grandparents as they define first, the most senior level that can benefit and second, the point of common descent.

Missing beneficiary insurances

There are companies that will supply such insurance, but the subject needs to be approached **14.56** with a degree of caution.

1. Such insurance is not a substitute for research. Approach an insurer for cover without adequate research and a refusal is likely to follow.[69]
2. Consider carefully the amount of cover that the policy should provide. Missing beneficiary claims can surface many years after a distribution and can involve substantial interest claims. Cover can sometimes be obtained which contains an escalator provision that can assist with the interest part of any claim.
3. Such insurance will almost certainly contain an agreement not to undertake any further research into the family tree or to disclose the insurance outside of the beneficiaries and professional advisers. Make sure that the beneficiaries are aware of this and agree to it before any distribution is made.
4. Insurance is only needed in a minority of intestacies as good research usually finds those entitled. There can be a case made for insurance being used more widely in order to cover the risk of children from relationships not known to the family. However, this should be examined carefully on a case-by-case basis.
5. The PR or trustee should always be clear what it is they are looking for cover for. Insurance should not provide cover for the entire intestate distribution, but only cover that part which is attributable to the missing beneficiary.

D. *Benjamin* orders

14.57   The jurisdiction to make a *Benjamin* order[70] can be very useful when leave can be given by the court to distribute the estate on a certain footing, for example, on the basis that a person died without issue, that all debts and liabilities have been ascertained, that a person is presumed dead,[71] or on the basis that a claim will not be made on the estate.[72]

14.58   The purpose behind a *Benjamin* order is to protect the PR from being personally liable for distributing to the wrong beneficiaries. It does not destroy any beneficial interests in the estate. So, if the PR does obtain a *Benjamin* order to distribute on the footing that a particular set of facts obtains, which later turns out to be false, he would be protected from a personal action against himself. However, if, for example, it was on the footing that a missing beneficiary had predeceased the testator, and he later turns up after distribution of the estate, nothing would prevent him pursuing the overpaid beneficiaries.

14.59   The court does of course need to be satisfied that the proposal is a reasonable basis upon which to proceed and therefore it is never wise to make an application until fairly exhaustive enquires have been made. Our experience suggests that often the Master will ask for further advertisements to be placed or avenues to be explored and it is only when a dead end is reached that an order will be made. In all cases it is worth exploring alternatives—insurance, or obtaining indemnities from beneficiaries to whom the executors are distributing—before exploring this course of action.

---

[69] Arguably what is being asked for in this instance is not cover for a missing beneficiary but insurance for not doing any more work.

[70] See *Re Benjamin* [1902] 1 Ch 723.

[71] For declarations that someone is presumed dead see the Presumption of Death Act 2013, which applies to those domiciled or habitually resident in England and Wales.

[72] *Re Gess* [1942] Ch 37.

15

POWERS AND DUTY OF CARE

A. Trustees' exercise of powers

When trustees are considering the exercise of their powers, whether administrative or dispositive, they need to take various considerations into account. Failure to do so will be a breach of trust.[1] Advisers to trustees also need to be able to provide confident advice to their clients as to the width of the powers and the restrictions on them and as to the considerations which they should take into account when exercising them. It is not, of course, the role of the adviser to tell the trustees how to exercise their powers, but to caution them if they appear to be exercising them in a manner which is inappropriate.   **15.01**

The first and most obvious point is to construe the power in question. What does it enable   **15.02**
the trustees to do? In most cases no difficulty will arise. Clauses in modern trusts tend to follow fairly tried and tested precedents. In cases of doubt an application to the court may be necessary and far better than waiting for the beneficiaries to challenge what has been done as being outside the powers of the trustees.

The second issue is to consider whether the proposed exercise of the power is compliant with   **15.03**
the duties which the trustees have under the general common law or statute. So, for example, trustees who are investing trust property need to have regard to their common law duties to take 'such care as an ordinary prudent man would take if he were minded to make an investment for the benefit of other people for whom he felt morally bound to provide'.[2] They must also have regard to their duties under the Trustee Act 2000,[3] which impose on them the duty to have regard to the standard investment criteria which require the trustees to have regard to the suitability of the investments and the need for diversification.[4] Before exercising any power

---

[1] See further on the subject of the exercise of trustees' powers and the rules following the decision of the Supreme Court in *Futter v HMRCC; Pitt v HMRCC* [2013] UKSC 26 in Chapter 23.
[2] See, eg *Cowan v Scargill* [1985] Ch 270.
[3] For further discussion of this see P Reed and W Wilson, *The Trustee Act 2000: A Practical Guide* (Jordan, 2001).
[4] Section 4 Trustee Act 2000.

of investment, or reviewing investments, there is a duty to obtain and consider proper advice[5] about the way in which, in accordance with the standard investment criteria, the powers should be exercised, unless the trustee reasonably concludes that in all the circumstances it is unreasonable for him to do so.[6]

15.04 The exercise of other powers also gives rise to the obligation to comply with the statutory duty of care contained in s.1 Trustee Act 2000.[7]

15.05 In relation to the exercise of powers of appointment, the trustees must also be aware of the obligations on them not to commit a fraud on a power. This does not necessarily mean fraud in any pejorative sense.[8] Traditionally fraud on a power has been divided into three categories:

1. Where the power is exercised for a corrupt purpose.
2. Where there is a bargain with the appointor to benefit a non-object of the power which precedes the exercise of that power.
3. Where the power is exercised for a purpose foreign to the power.

15.06 The trustees and their advisers therefore need to consider whether the purpose for which the power is being exercised is a proper one, and whether it has an improper ulterior motive such as to benefit someone who is not a beneficiary of the trust.

15.07 Powers of advancement often give rise to issues as to what constitutes a benefit for the beneficiary in whose favour they are being exercised. Trustees and their advisers need to be alert to this and need to look carefully at the power to see how wide it is. The statutory power contained in s.32 Trustee Act 1925 is in wide terms and many trust instruments simply extend that power to cover the whole of the presumptive share of a beneficiary rather than one half, and to dispense with the consent of those who have prior interests.

15.08 As a matter of general principle, the statutory power of advancement can be used to vary or resettle funds if that is for the benefit of the beneficiary in whose favour it is being exercised.[9] There was a view[10] that the power of advancement could not be used to settle on discretionary trusts (and equally not include wide dispositive powers) as this would be improper delegation of the discretions of the trustees. However, that view has been doubted by the authors of *Lewin on Trusts*[11] and it is widely accepted to be incorrect.

15.09 'Benefit' has been given a very wide meaning but trustees do need to be aware of some limitations. In *Re Clore's Settlement Trusts*[12] an advance to charity was regarded as of benefit to a very wealthy beneficiary as it discharged his moral obligations to be philanthropic. On the other hand in *X v A*,[13] Hart J refused to sanction the use of a power to apply capital to the life tenant to make a substantial advance to charity. He did not consider objectively that the proposed

---

[5] Section 5(1) Trustee Act 2000.
[6] For more discussion of investment matters see Chapter 13.
[7] See later at para 15.17.
[8] *Vatcher v Paull* [1915] AC 372 at 378.
[9] *Pilkington v IRC* [1964] AC 612 HL.
[10] *Underhill and Hayton: Law of Trusts and Trustees*, 15th edition (Butterworths, 1995) at 704 relying on *Re Wills' Will Trusts* [1959] Ch 1.
[11] 18th edition (Sweet & Maxwell, 2012) at [32-20], based on a proper reading of *Pilkington*.
[12] [1966] 1 WLR 955.
[13] [2006] 1 WTLR 741.

advance was relieving the beneficiary of an obligation she would otherwise have to discharge out of her own resources, if only because the amount proposed to be advanced exceeded her own resources. The remaindermen who were interested in capital opposed the advance.

An exercise of the power to advance which is not for the benefit of the beneficiary will be void.[14] **15.10**

To summarize, trustees and their advisers need to ask themselves the following questions: **15.11**

1. Is there any power, statutory or express, to enable the trustees to do what they propose?
2. Is the power one which is subject to the statutory duty of care?
3. What are the common law duties on the trustees in exercising the powers?
4. Is the power being exercised for a proper purpose?
5. In the case of a proposed advance, is it for the benefit of the beneficiary?

As a matter of practical administration it should never be assumed either that statutory powers are always extended in application by modern deeds or that all deeds will have standard additional powers. The very fact that these two assumptions could often be correct can lead to a failure to ascertain precisely what powers are available in each individual trust. The precise nature of the powers must always be checked whenever it is intended to exercise them, as assumptions will eventually lead to error. If the powers contained in the deed are insufficient it can be possible to seek their enlargement under s.57 Trustee Act 1925.[15] **15.12**

B. Retirement of trustees

There are many different circumstances in which trustees may wish to retire. Sometimes it will be because they are faced with an application for removal by the beneficiaries, and good advice will generally be to retire unless there is some compelling reason not to. To fight an application for removal by hostile beneficiaries is often pointless and gives rise to the risk of a costs order being made against the trustee if opposition has been unnecessary. It is far better for the trustee to negotiate an exit with the benefit of an indemnity and release from liability, which the court will not order if the trustee is removed. **15.13**

Indeed, trustees are usually concerned to ensure that they are indemnified in respect of any liabilities and released from any claims. There is a tendency to push for the widest possible indemnities but it can be instructive to consider the position of a trustee as a matter of general law on retirement. Trustees have the right to indemnify themselves from the trust fund and that right consists of the right of reimbursement, exoneration, retention, and realization.[16] When he retires a trustee loses control of the trust fund and cannot retain assets from which to indemnify himself. However, it seems clear that he does not lose his right to be indemnified from the trust fund.[17] It is also reasonably clear that a trustee's right over the trust fund is a proprietary equitable charge or interest over the trust assets[18] and the better view seems **15.14**

---

[14] The true *ratio* of *Re Hastings-Bass* [1975] Ch 25 as explained in the Supreme Court in *Futter v HMRCC; Pitt v HMRCC* (n 1).

[15] *Anker-Petersen v Anker-Petersen* [2000] WTLR 581 is an example of modern application of this section.

[16] See *Lewin on Trusts*, 18th edition (Sweet & Maxwell, 2008) at [14-58].

[17] *Rothmore Farms Pty Ltd v Belgravia Farms Pty Ltd* [1999] 2 ITELR 159.

[18] *Stott v Milne* (1884) 25 Ch D 710; *Jennings v Mather* [1901] 1 KB 108.

to be that it is not lost when he retires as trustee and new trustees are appointed in his stead. However, that right will cease to exist on the distribution to a beneficiary.

15.15 Hence many indemnities provide for what should happen if the fund is distributed to a beneficiary and maintain the indemnity not just out of funds in the new trustees' hands, but also up to the value of any amounts distributed.

15.16 An adviser to a trustee who is retiring needs to give careful thought to the indemnities available at common law and what additional ones might be negotiated. If beneficiaries have threatened claims against a trustee, or there are concerns they might be made, it might well be wise to negotiate a release. Continuing trustees have to examine their powers carefully. They will not always have the power to provide extended indemnities to retiring trustees and this is something which is often forgotten.

C. Duty of care

15.17 In considering both the standards of work that PRs and trustees should attain, and their position after any claims have been made against them, regard must be given to the duty of care applicable to their conduct. Non-professional PRs and trustees will usually be unaware of these standards and their advisers should explain the basic issues involved in order that they may be better aware of both their position and the basis on which future advice will be given.

D. Statutory duty of care

15.18 PRs and trustees have two duties of care to consider. The statutory duty of care comes from the Trustee Act 2000.[19] These provisions, notwithstanding the title to the Act, apply to PRs as well as trustees.[20] The statutory duty of care did not replace the previously existing duty of care under general law[21]—the duties continue to co-exist.

15.19 In considering the application of the statutory duty of care it is essential to refer to Schedule 1 and the categories of actions to which the duty applies. These are:

1. When exercising any power of investment (not merely the general power of investment at s.2).
2. When acquiring land under any power (not merely that in s.8) or exercising any power in relation to land.
3. When appointing agents, nominees, or custodians under any power (not merely those of ss.11–18) and when carrying out the statutory requirement to review delegation arrangements.[22]
4. When compounding liabilities under s.15 Trustee Act 1925 or any other power.
5. When insuring property under any power (not merely that of s.19 Trustee Act 1925).
6. When taking any actions regarding reversionary interests under s.22 Trustee Act 1925 or any corresponding power.

---

[19] Part I Trustee Act 2000 and Sch 1.
[20] Section 35 Trustee Act 2000.
[21] Sometimes referred to as the common law duty of care.
[22] Section 22, which also applies to any power of delegation unless s.22 is inconsistent with the terms of that power.

Much of Schedule 1 applies the duty of care 'when exercising' a power; the use of this phrase **15.20** restricts the duty of care to positive action and it does not apply when refraining from exercising the power. However, the duty of care under general law would apply to such failures to act instead.

The statutory duty requires the exercise of 'such skill and care as is reasonable in the circumstances'. In establishing this regard must be had to

1. any special knowledge or experience that the trustee has or holds himself out as having and,
2. if he acts as a trustee in the course of a business or a profession, to any special knowledge or experience that it is reasonable to expect of a person acting in the course of that kind of business or profession.

In considering the application of these two tests, note should be taken of the differences **15.21** between them. The first considers the individual trustee in question and the knowledge that he has or claims to have. In this it is a subjective test of the trustee. The second test is then a test that will only apply to a trustee acting in the course of business. The test is then of what is to be expected of a member of that profession. This then is an objective test of what should be expected of, say, a lawyer acting as trustee.

The objective test is applied to all trustees and the second test is only applied to those acting **15.22** in the course of business.

E. Duty of care under the general law

This duty of care will apply to the exercise, or failure to exercise, of all powers outside of the **15.23** exercise of the powers that the statutory duty of care applies to. The classic definition of the duty of care under the general law is that found in *Speight v Gaunt*: '[as] a general rule a trustee sufficiently discharges his duty if he takes in managing trust affairs all those precautions which an ordinary prudent man of business would take in managing similar affairs of his own'.[23] This formulation is constructed with reference to an 'ordinary prudent man of business' and this is again an objective test and is not determined with reference to what might reasonably be expected of the actual trustee. However, since originally formulated, the court has tended to apply a higher standard to remunerated trustees[24] or those such as a trust company which holds itself out as particularly well qualified against its competitors.[25] Brightman J in *Bartlett v Barclays Bank Trust Company Ltd*[26] held 'that a higher duty of care is plainly due from someone like a trust corporation which carries on a specialised business of trust management'. This opinion has always been viewed as a standard that set the bar higher for a trust company than all of its competitors. However, this is a view that ought to be tempered with a dose of reality. Is it to be argued that a trust company has a higher standard applied to it than any other competitor who also offers a specialist service in relation to estates and trusts? It is perhaps more likely that Brightman J's view would apply to all those who carry

---

[23] [1883] 9 App Cas 1 (HL) at 19, per Lord Blackburn approving Jessel MR in the decision below [1882] 22 Ch D 727.

[24] '[A] paid trustee is expected to exercise a higher standard of diligence and knowledge than an unpaid trustee' (per Harman J in *Re Waterman's Will Trusts* [1952] 2 All ER 1054).

[25] *Bartlett v Barclays Bank Trust Company Ltd* [1980] 1 All ER 139 at 152C.

[26] [1980] 1 All ER 139.

on, or claim to carry on, a specialized business of trust (or estate) management. This makes it important that brochures and advertising (including websites) are reviewed carefully to ensure that descriptions and claims are described accurately and superlatives are avoided. It would be unsafe to assume that in this context a court would treat such statements as mere advertising puffery.[27]

F. Modification or exclusion of the duty of care

15.24 Both the statutory duty of care and the duty of care under general law are capable of being restricted or excluded[28] by the terms of the deed. The statutory duty of care applies to estates and trusts created before the Act and, although any exclusion or modification in such deeds cannot expressly refer to the statutory duty, it is capable of being excluded if the wording of the exclusion or modification is wide enough.

15.25 Although the use of exclusion provisions is said to be widespread, there is a lack of statistical evidence to show how widespread.[29] They are effective to protect the PR or trustee from claims, but there still remains the question of the extent to which they are really required. In practice, do they operate to provide some benefit to the trust or estate and reduce professional fees by relieving the professional PR or trustee of a large area of risk, or do they just operate to protect the PR or trustee from the consequences of lazy or negligent work? It does seem curious that members of the public who would not dream of accepting exclusions of liability from other professions and other areas of work are apparently so ready to accept provisions that give so little protection against grave losses.[30]

15.26 The extent to which such clauses can be relied on where a breach of duty is deliberate has been approached differently,[31] but the position now is possibly that a clause which relieves liability for all breaches other than those which are dishonest will only extend to a deliberate breach where the trustee had a genuine, and reasonable, belief that his action, or inaction, was in the interests of the beneficiaries as a whole. There is nothing to prevent an exclusion clause extending to acts of negligence and gross negligence.[32]

15.27 See the Law Society and STEP requirements regarding the use of exoneration clauses.

G. Duty of care of the adviser to a PR or trustee

15.28 The duty of care of the professional adviser to a PR or trustee is that of the usual duty of care applied to a reasonable member of his profession towards a client, subject to the restraints

---

[27] '[A] term frequently used to denote the exaggerations reasonably to be expected of a seller as to the degree of quality of his product, the truth or falsity of which cannot be precisely determined' (US Federal Trade Commission 54 FTC 648 (1957)) the dangers of which go back to *Carlill v Carbolic Smoke Ball Company* [1893] 1 QB 256.

[28] Paragraph 7 Sch 1 Trustee Act 2000 and *Armitage v Nurse* [1997] 2 All ER 705.

[29] One major work, G Thomas and A Hudson, *The Law of Trusts* (OUP, 2010) at [21.41] refers to modern deeds as 'invariably' including them, to the extent that it 'seems appropriate' to consider them 'as one of the rights of trustees'.

[30] *Bogg v Raper* [1998/99] 1 ITELR 267.

[31] *Royal Brunei Airlines v Tan* [1995] 2 AC 378; *Armitage v Nurse* [1997] 2 All ER 705; *Three Rivers DC v Governor of the Bank of England (No 3)* [2003] EWHC 118(Comm); *Walker v Stones* [2000] 4 All ER 412.

[32] *Spread Trustee Co Ltd v Hutcheson* [2011] UKPC 13; [2012] 2 AC 194.

of his retainer. It is therefore an important consideration to be taken into account that a different duty of care applies when acting as a PR or trustee compared with when acting as an adviser to a PR or trustee.

It is, of course, important for the professional adviser to a PR or trustee to advise his client as to the duties to which they are subject and to advise them if a particular course of action would breach that duty or be an improper exercise of a power, or indeed be beyond the powers vested in the PR or trustee. Failure to do so which exposes the trustee or PR to liability may result in the adviser being sued for negligence. Following the decision of the Supreme Court in *Futter*[33] there is very limited scope for trustees and PRs to escape the exercise of powers which have unfortunate consequences, fiscal or otherwise, and so the liability may well be substantial. **15.29**

The question of a solicitor, when advising an estate or trust, having a duty of care towards the beneficiaries is an interesting point. In general terms beneficiaries cannot sue the trustees' legal advisers because they are not owed a duty of care.[34] However, it may be that this is a rule that applies in cases where the solicitors acting for the trustees have been negligent and that negligence has caused loss to the trust fund (which the trustees can recover). If the loss that has been caused is not to the trust fund but to one of the beneficiaries, the position ought to be different. **15.30**

The point was considered in *Yudt v Leonard Ross & Craig*[35] (where a duty of care towards trust beneficiaries was found). In that case it was argued that the beneficiaries did not fall within the ambit of the decision in *White v Jones* and therefore had no claim. The judge found that, in fact, as they were already beneficiaries under a disposition which had been completed and had a proprietary interest in the trust, they were in sufficiently close proximity to the solicitors to the trust that a duty of care was owed to them.[36] The court drew a distinction between such a case and one where the trust had not been set up or where the beneficiaries were the mere objects of a fiduciary power, which owing to the negligence of advisers had not been exercised in their favour. In the latter case, the judge held that any duty to the beneficiaries would have to be on a *White v Jones* basis. A better view of the nature of the relationship between trust advisers and the trust beneficiaries can be found in *Royal Brunei Airlines Sdn Bhd v Tan* where Lord Nicholls view was that **15.31**

> for the most part [professionals[37]] will owe to the trustees a duty to exercise reasonable skill and care. When that is so, the rights flowing from that duty form part of the trust property. As such they can be enforced by the beneficiaries in a suitable case if the trustees are unable or unwilling to do so. That being so, it is difficult to identify a compelling reason why, in addition to the duty of skill and care vis-à-vis the trustees which the third parties have accepted, or which the law has imposed on them, third parties should also owe a duty of care directly to the

---

[33] *Futter v HMRCC; Pitt v HMRCC* (n 1).

[34] *Roberts v Gill & Co* [2011] 1 AC 240.

[35] (1998/99) ITELR 53. The British Columbia Supreme Court also found a duty of care towards the beneficiary in *Linsley v Kirstiuk* [1986] 28 DLR (4th) 495. This judgment is a little short on reasoning for the finding of liability, but is interesting for a finding of negligence which arises out of a failure of the law firm to advise that the trustees' course of action was inconsistent with their duties under the will. They were well aware of what the trustees intended (one of them was the senior partner of the law firm) although they were not asked for advice on the property development policy in question.

[36] On the basis of *Hedley Byrne & Co Ltd v Heller & Partners Ltd* [1963] 2 All ER 575.

[37] '[T]he hosts of people who act for trustees in various ways: as advisers, consultants, bankers and agents of many kinds'.

beneficiaries. They have undertaken the work for the trustees. They must carry out that work properly. If they fail to do so, they will be liable to make good the loss suffered by the trustees in consequence. This will include, where appropriate, the loss suffered by the trustees being exposed to claims for breach of trust.[38]

15.32   It is possible that a finding of a duty of care towards the beneficiaries of an estate is implicit in the decision of Neuberger J, as he then was, in *Chappel v Somers & Blake*.[39] However, the case can also be explained on the basis that the duty was owed to the executor who could recover any loss and hold it on behalf of the beneficiary.

15.33   *Yudt* suggests that there is a duty of care on the part of advisers to a trust to the beneficiaries who have a proprietary interest in it and it is clear will suffer loss from their negligence. However, in the case of a discretionary trust, it must still be the case that the duty is owed to the trustees.

---

[38] [1995] 2 AC 378 at 391; these observations were made *obiter*.
[39] [2003] EWHC 1644 (Ch); [2003] WTLR 1085. See also n 35.

PART D

TAXATION

16

WILLS AND TAX ADVICE

A. Introduction

Whereas litigation over negligent will drafting seems to abound, there are few reported **16.01** cases of claims against solicitors for negligence in tax advice. This may be because the non-testamentary transactions in which solicitors are instructed largely fall into one of three categories:

1. It is a transaction that cannot attract a tax liability, so there can be no question of negligence in this respect.
2. The transaction is simple and the tax liability clear and well known, so the solicitor is competent to advise upon it.
3. The transaction is complicated and the lay parties' minds are already turned to minimizing the tax liability, so that the solicitor is a tax specialist or is one of a range of professionals engaged, one of which is a 'specialist' tax adviser.

While this categorization can be fairly comfortably applied to the lifetime transactions in **16.02** which a probate or private client lawyer is likely to be instructed (the danger lying in a transaction that falls somewhere between categories (2) and (3)), instructions to prepare a will (which are really instructions to effect a transaction that will take place after the client's death, or more accurately for IHT purposes 'immediately before' it) cannot be so neatly categorized. One would expect this to be reflected by a greater body of reported cases concerning tax advice in respect of will preparation, but that has not been the case.

B. The case law as it stands

Given that the will-preparer has had to live with the impact of taxation on a testator's death **16.03** for a little over a hundred years, and income tax on the benefits under the will for a lot longer, it is quite surprising that there is no major authority on the possible duty to give tax advice in the context of preparing a will. It is, after all, only in the case of the simplest wills affecting the smallest estates[1] that the testamentary disposition of a dead person's estate will not attract tax consequences. In order to determine the will-preparer's duty in respect of tax advice then, we must ask whether the will-preparer is required to

- inform the client of such a consequence; and
- advise the client how to reduce or remove such a consequence.

16.04 One could perhaps have expected the subject to have been thoroughly examined in at least one of the cases in the recent spate of negligence claims regarding will preparation. Quite clearly, with the greater attention being paid to questions of negligence, this area is increasingly likely to be the source of a dispute. While there is a dearth of case law precisely on point, there are some useful authorities on negligence in tax advice (or the lack thereof) in respect of lifetime transactions from which guidelines as to good practice can be extracted. The application to testamentary matters of the case law on lifetime matters is much aided by considering the act of preparing a will as effecting a transaction, albeit a transaction that will occur in the future.

C. Duty or best practice?

16.05 When considering the will-preparer's duty to give tax advice, it is important to distinguish between what a competent and conscientious solicitor may offer to undertake as part of his client care and what he has a duty to deliver. Offering taxation advice may be good client care for which a particular client is willing to pay, but this is not the same as saying that there is a duty to give taxation advice when preparing any will.

16.06 The case that comes closest to considering this is *Cancer Research Campaign v Ernest Brown & Co (a firm)*.[2] The claimants were the residuary beneficiaries of the estate of P, who herself had been the sole beneficiary of N. L was employed by the defendants and an executor of the estates of both N and P. After N's death P had instructed L to draft her will. The claimants claimed L was negligent in not advising first P, then her residuary beneficiaries, of the chance to vary N's estate to effect an IHT saving. Harman J in his judgment said:

> I do not doubt the solicitor, in considering the will, must consider what inheritance tax complications that testator will cause by the bequests for which he is given instructions. But I refuse to hold, extending the duty to advise by, it was said, analogy, that there arises a duty to inform the intended testator, who has come in to instruct a solicitor about his or her will, about tax avoidance schemes in connection with some quite other estate.[3]

16.07 Although the decision is not directed at the point, there is thus an express judicial statement (as part of a description of the duties of the will-preparer in relation to drawing the will and overseeing its execution) that there is a duty to consider the tax consequences of the instructions given by a would-be testator; as a duty to consider would be meaningless without a duty to advise it must be likely that a court would answer the first question posed at paragraph

---

[1] ie estates the taxable value of which can be expected with some certainty to fall comfortably within the IHT nil rate band and are not to be subject to any trusts. To this can be added larger estates where any complicated dispositions are exempt transfers or are transfers to exempt beneficiaries.
[2] [1997] STC 1425; [1998] PNLR 592.
[3] [1997] STC 1425 at 4133H–J.

16.03 above in the affirmative. Before concluding that the duty does not extend to answering the second question in the affirmative, it is necessary to bear in mind both that the case has quite particular facts, and that

1. The decision does not consider that given the information the will-preparer will gather to advise on IHT, a reasonably competent solicitor may see a tax-reducing opportunity.
2. There is difficulty and artificiality in advising on the tax consequences of the proposed dispositions, without highlighting alternative, more tax-efficient arrangements.
3. The decision appears limited to IHT and does not propose that other taxation advice should be given (although the case did not concern any other tax).

Clearly, the position is different if the client—or any other person to whom the professional **16.08** has accepted responsibility—specifically seeks tax advice in respect of an estate of which they are a beneficiary. In *Martin v Triggs Turner Barton*[4] a beneficiary of her husband's estate sought advice from the solicitor-executor as to the tax treatment of national savings certificates forming part of the estate. The court readily accepted the general principle that in the normal course of events an executor does not owe any duty of care to a beneficiary, but was clear that that general principle was subject to the law of assumption of responsibility and reasonable reliance.[5] Thus, where a beneficiary seeks from a professional executor not only advice as to his entitlement under the will but also advice as to the tax consequences for him of that entitlement, and the professional executor purports to give that advice (even if as 'a favour'[6]) he assumes responsibility to the beneficiary in respect of that advice, and so a duty of care to put himself in a position to give, and to give accurate, advice, notwithstanding they were not previously in a solicitor–client relationship.

D. The extent of the duty

The starting point in determining the will-preparer's duty is their retainer. If the will-preparer **16.09** and client have entered into a detailed written contract for the purpose of preparing the client's will, the terms of the retainer should be (in theory) determinative of whether there is or is not a duty to give tax advice. In practice, there may be no written retainer at all, or the engagement letter may not spell out in any detail precisely what the will-preparer has agreed to undertake for the client and what is excluded from the retainer.

In such circumstances, guidance can be derived from the decision in *Carradine Properties* **16.10** *Limited v DJ Freeman & Co*,[7] which confirmed that in the absence of express terms of engagement the scope of a solicitor's duty will depend upon the extent to which the client appears to need advice: the less sophisticated the client, the wider the solicitor's duty is likely to be. Where, for example, the client is 'a high profile, successful, commercial entity with considerable in-house expertise in taxation matters and [is] properly equipped to consider and take appropriate action to deal with the tax implications of their property

---

[4] [2009] EWHC 1920 (Ch); [2010] PNLR 3; [2009] WTLR 1339.
[5] [2009] EWHC 1920 (Ch) at [94].
[6] [2009] EWHC 1920 (Ch) at [97].
[7] [1999] Lloyd's Rep PN 483; [1955–95] PNLR 219; (1989) 5 Const LJ 267; [1982] 1 PN 41; (1982) 126 Sol J 157.

transaction'[8] the solicitor's duty is unlikely to encompass giving tax advice. In the context of will preparation, the client clearly will not be a 'commercial entity' and is much more likely to be an unsophisticated individual unfamiliar with either the mechanics and legal requirements of making a will or with any potential tax consequences, and this places a greater duty on the will-preparer.

16.11 This duty requires, as does good practice, that the will-preparer ensures that his client understands fully the extent of the retainer between them. Though it is not a case concerned with tax advice, this general proposition is illustrated by *Gray v Buss Morton*.[9] There, even though the client gave his instructions imprecisely and in lay terms, so that the (trainee) solicitor was not clear upon what they were being asked to advise, it was held that there was a duty on the solicitor to clarify the terms of the retainer and resolve any confusion. In addition, where there is a dispute between client and solicitor as to the terms of the retainer the client's account is prima facie to prevail. However, that approach does not leave it open to the client to retrospectively seek to widen the retainer simply because a certain matter (eg tax advice) has not been expressly excluded if the facts are not consistent with that matter being within the scope of the retainer: in *Swain Mason v Mills & Reeve*[10] it was made clear on appeal that in construing the scope of the retainer, great weight is to be attached to the fact that the client informed his solicitor of a relevant fact, but did not then ask for advice about it, indicating advice on that fact was neither sought nor proffered and so not within the retainer.[11]

16.12 The extent of the duty to give tax advice when instructed to prepare a will is particularly important given the widely used approach of providing will preparation for a fixed fee, and so the real risk of the service becoming uneconomic: in some cases, usually when offered by solicitors, the will preparation will be done as a 'loss leader' in the hope of obtaining the more lucrative probate work, but often, especially in the case of will-writers, the relatively low fixed fee is intended to allow for a profit margin.

16.13 Another non-tax case, *Inventors Friend Ltd v Leathes Prior*,[12] presents a cautionary tale, and confirms the importance of expressly excluding a duty to give tax advice. In that case, concerned with advising on the terms of a commercial agreement for the marketing of a new invention, the solicitor agreed a fixed fee of £500 to 'look over' the draft agreement and 'discuss key areas', making clear the retainer did not extend to drafting or making detailed enquiries; instead providing brief comments. Notwithstanding that the court construed the retainer in such narrow terms,[13] and the client was commercially experienced in bringing new products to market, once there arose a possible cause of detriment to the client to which the solicitor ought to have been alive (in this case the fact the draft agreement failed to confer on the client sufficient intellectual property rights), it was held that the solicitor's duty was to complete the work necessary to bring that risk to the client's attention and advise him on avoiding it, even though to do so would render the fixed fee unremunerative.

---

[8] *Virgin Management Ltd v De Morgan Group plc* [1996] EG 16 (CS); [1996] NPC 8, where it was held the solicitor did not owe a duty to give tax advice in relation to property matters.

[9] [1999] PNLR 882.

[10] [2012] EWCA Civ 498; [2012] STC 1760; [2012] 4 Costs LO 511.

[11] [2012] EWCA Civ 498 at [50].

[12] [2011] EWHC 711 (QB); [2011] PNLR 20. In addition, the court applied the approach to determining the terms of an unwritten retainer set out in *Carradine Properties*.

[13] Clearly, the solicitor had discharged the obligation on him per *Gray v Buss Morton* to make clear to the client the scope of the retainer.

E. Excluding the duty

There is strong authority in the shape of *Hurlingham Estates Ltd v Wilde & Partners*[14] that in **16.14** practice that to avoid a duty to give tax advice, a will-preparer must expressly exclude from the retainer the giving of such advice with the client's clear, unambiguous, and informed consent.[15] This is because although the preparation of a will is a transaction not directed primarily at tax matters, it is one from which tax consequences naturally flow,[16] and so tax advice falls within the professional's 'ordinary duty'. This 'ordinary duty' is a duty to advise on how the transaction in respect of which the professional is instructed should be structured and, where the client already has a structure in mind, first, to advise of any liability to tax they would incur as a result of that structure, and second, to advise of any alteration to the form (rather than the substance of the transaction) that would result in the avoidance or reduction of that liability.

A client giving instructions to prepare a will will almost certainly have a structure or scheme **16.15** of distribution in mind, but the taxation consequences may be considered unlikely to deter a client giving instructions for a will from conferring his bounty on his chosen objects. Further, how far the form of the scheme of distribution intended can be altered without altering its substance must be limited.

Unless the will-preparer has taken care to exclude tax advice from his retainer then the **16.16** answers to the two questions raised at paragraph 16.03 above are

1. Yes, the will-preparer is required to inform the client of the tax consequences of the will he is instructed to prepare.
2. Yes, he is probably required to advise the client on any alternative *form* of disposition that would reduce any such tax, but is not required to advise of any changes to the *substance* of the disposition that might reduce such tax: this duty seems necessarily a limited one.

Given that the first answer above is 'yes', the will-preparer will need to turn his mind to the **16.17** question of valuation of the would-be testator's estate, as the value of certain items (which may attract property-specific exemptions) and the estate as a whole will inform the advice on the tax consequences. Specialist property, such as land (particularly agricultural land) and shares in private companies require specialist valuations. Ideally, these should be arranged as part of the will preparation process by the client, rather than the will-preparer (so that the valuer is in a direct legal relationship with the client). If the client insists on using their own valuations though, care should be taken to exclude liability for acting on such figures.

Given that the second answer above is probably 'yes', two things should be noted. First, the **16.18** will-preparer cannot contract out of his duty to give tax advice by instructing counsel. That is unless, of course, the will-preparer has limited his retainer (with the client's express consent) to merely obtaining counsel's tax advice, rather than giving tax advice, as would a reasonably competent solicitor.[17] It is not that reliance on counsel's advice is never a defence to a claim

---

[14] [1997] 1 Lloyd's Rep 525.
[15] Though it may be that in the case of instructions to prepare a will, excluding tax advice from the retainer can be done more easily than by the protracted process envisaged by Lightman J in that case.
[16] Except in the very limited cases described at n 1 above.
[17] *Estill v Cowling Swift and Kitchen (a firm)* [2000] WTLR 417.

against a solicitor for negligent advice, but rather it is never enough on its own to constitute a defence: rather, the solicitor must turn his own independent eye to counsel's advice to satisfy himself counsel is not obviously or glaringly wrong, and accordingly he must put himself in a position to be able to do so by acquiring sufficient knowledge himself. Paradoxically perhaps, it appears that the harder it is for the solicitor to discharge that duty—because of the highly specialized nature of the advice—the more reliance he is entitled to place on counsel.[18] In a practical tax context, while a solicitor would be expected to scrutinize the accuracy of an opinion on a relatively straightforward tax matter, he may be excused for not doing so (or not being able to do so) in a highly complex matter. If so, this leads to the slightly surprising result that the practice of obtaining counsel's opinion 'for comfort' (ie where the solicitor thinks he knows the answer and seeks confirmation) offers no increased protection to the solicitor (although would, of course, give him a contribution claim against the barrister). Second, the will-preparer will need to honestly appraise his own tax knowledge and therefore the standard of advice he can give: unless he can genuinely offer a comprehensive tax advice service himself (or within his firm) best practice demands that the will-preparer has in place a policy or procedure as to the retention of an external tax expert, or else ensures the exclusion of taxation advice from his retainer as the default position.

F. Conclusions as to duty

16.19 Taking the cases together then, and bearing in mind that none of them is directed precisely at the special case of preparing a will, it can fairly safely be concluded that

1. Courts are slower to impose wider duties if the client is knowledgeable and reasonably supposed to be astute (particularly if it is a commercial entity).
2. Courts are slower to find a duty to give taxation advice if the taxation questions are not central to the transaction undertaken.
3. Courts will be more ready to help the inexperienced or unaware client.
4. Courts will look carefully for evidence of informed client consent to any attempt by a solicitor to impose a contractual limitation on the solicitor's duty and for the reasonableness of that limitation.

16.20 Therefore, to avoid the risk of a claim in negligence relating to the failure to give tax advice, the wise will-preparer ought to exclude liability for such advice (both in contract and in tort) from the scope of the retainer in clear written contractual terms establishing that the modest cost quoted for the will preparation would not extend to advice on tax issues, but that the tax advice could be accommodated with a separate and additional fee for the work. Viewed positively, this is a win-win situation for the will-preparer: bringing the question of tax advice to the attention of the would-be testator acts as both the first step in excluding liability and a piece of marketing, possibly leading to additional work and a source of further fees.

16.21 Practically then, adopting this practice will allow the will-preparer to continue to offer will preparation at a modest price and within a reasonable time frame. It does not prevent the provision of tax advice in relation to the devolution of the client's estate under a separate, more remunerative, retainer, possibly setting a longer time scale for the preparation of the will. The question of delay in drafting a will, though, will need to be viewed in the light

---

[18] *D Morgan plc v Mace & Jones* [2010] EWHC 3375 (TCC) at [323–5].

of the would-be testator's instructions and all their circumstances, as it is unlikely that an argument that *White v Jones*[19] does not apply where the delay is due to tax planning would succeed. On giving the client a time scale for the completion of a 'tax-efficient' will, it should be made plain to the client that until the will is in place his dispositive intentions will not be met. Therefore, either the client's consent to such a delay should be secured, or instructions should be taken on which, if any, of the planned dispositions the testator views as vital, and if necessary a 'holding will', meeting the dispositive intent, can be put in place pending the preparation and execution of a will that meets both the dispositive intent and the taxation imperatives.

G. Impact of the Finance Act 2008

In fact, the testamentary tax-planning landscape will have been radically altered for many **16.22** would-be testators, and therefore for many will-preparers, by the provisions first announced in the Pre-Budget Report of October 2007 and introduced into the Inheritance Tax Act 1984 by the Finance Act 2008 for the transfer between the estates of spouses of the 'unused' portion of their respective nil rate band (NRB).

Briefly, where the first spouse of a couple dies and by reason of the spousal (or some other) **16.23** exemption, their chargeable death estate falls below the NRB, so that a proportion of that NRB is left unused, such proportion will be available to the surviving spouse at their death as an additional proportion of their own NRB. Thus, for a large number of would-be testators, whose primary concern in will making and tax planning is to provide adequately for their widow or widower whilst protecting their children's inheritance from IHT, virtually no tax planning is required as unless their estates together exceed £650,000[20] in value, there is now no IHT detriment to their estate passing through that of their spouse.

This is likely to impact on the duty to give tax advice to a client who is making a will in two **16.24** ways. First, the need for and thus the use of tax-planning tools such as NRB discretionary trusts[21] are very likely to significantly decrease. Second, the number of clients who will need tax-planning advice, in the sense of advising of alternative structures for bequests so as to reduce the overall IHT burden, will be much reduced. Thus, to discharge the duty in relation to tax advice to a would-be testator who is married and intends to leave all his estate to his spouse (probably on the assumption the spouse will leave it to their children) which, when taken with the spouse's, will fall below the value of double the NRB, it is now almost certainly sufficient simply to explain to them the current rules and how they will apply in their case.

H. Some common tax considerations in will drafting

Although we do not by any means intend to set out an exhaustive list, there are some drafting **16.25** errors often found in wills that have such a profound impact on the estate's tax burden that

---

[19] [1995] 2 AC 207; [1995] 2 All ER 691.
[20] The NRB has been £325,000 since 6 April 2009, and has been fixed at that figure until 5 April 2015.
[21] Discussed more fully below at paras 16.32 to 16.34.

they are worthy of special mention. Whether the particular provision is aimed at avoiding tax in respect of the particular gift altogether, reducing or avoiding the estate's overall IHT, or apportioning the IHT due on the estate amongst particular property or beneficiaries, if it is defective the result certainly will be an unintended tax consequence, usually a higher IHT bill. This obviously creates the risk of a claim against the will-preparer by either the PR or a disappointed beneficiary.

Gifts to charities and for charitable purposes, and to Community Amateur Sports Clubs

16.26 A gift to a charity or on trust for charitable purposes does not attract the IHT charity exemption[22] merely by virtue of that simple fact: if the property gifted may become applicable for non-charitable purposes the exemption does not apply. There is thus a further requirement that the use to which the charity or trustees may put the subject matter of the gift is limited to charitable purposes.[23] Since 14 March 2012, the meaning of 'charitable purpose' has found its definition in the Charities Act 2011.[24]

16.27 Due to the limitation placed on the IHT exemption then, a gift on trust for 'charitable or benevolent purposes'[25] or to a body that is not solely charitable, such as a particular diocese of a church for its general purposes, will not attract the exemption, as the subject matter of the gift could be applied for non-charitable purposes. We have actually seen in practice the latter example where the gift was to a Roman Catholic diocese, and it was necessary for the Vatican to approve the deed of variation that was executed to remedy the drafting error!

16.28 In the case of a gift to a registered or established charity, the will-preparer should ensure the precise name of the organization the client intends to benefit (as many have similar names, or are known by colloquialisms) and need only direct the gift to that named charity for the exemption to apply, and no further words are necessary for the gift to be for charitable purposes.[26] Where the client intends by his will to create a trust for charitable purposes, no purpose that could be non-charitable as a matter of law should be included, and this includes purposes that are, for example, 'benevolent' and 'philanthropic': a general proviso that the subject matter is to be applied for the defined purposes so far as they are charitable will ensure the gift is charitable and the exemption applies.

16.29 Previously, the exemption was limited to UK-established bodies, so that gifts to foreign charities or trusts for charitable purposes resident abroad were liable for IHT. That restriction, long considered likely to be a breach of EU law, has been declared to be such by the ECJ,[27] and accordingly was removed by the Finance Act 2010.[28] From 1 April 2012 the IHT exemption will apply to gifts to charities established in the EU, Iceland, and Norway

---

[22] Section 23(1) Inheritance Tax Act 1984.

[23] Section 23(5).

[24] Section 2.

[25] *Chichester Diocesan Fund and Board of Finance Inc v Simpson* [1944] AC 341; [1944] 2 All ER 60.

[26] *Re Finger's Will Trusts, Turner v Ministry of Health* [1972] Ch 286; [1971] 3 All ER 1050. Although it is possible that a gift in such terms is more likely to be construed as conditional on the actual institution being in existence at death, such that if that is not the case it cannot be applied *cy-pres*: *Kings v Bultitude* [2010] EWHC 1795 (Ch); [2010] WTLR 1571; [2010] 13 ITELR 391; [2010] PTSR (CS) 29.

[27] *Porsche v Finanzant Ludenscheid* [209] STC 586 (ECJ).

[28] Section 30 and Sch 6 Part 1 Finance Act 2010.

('relevant territories'); in addition, by way of concession HMRC will entertain claims from 27 June 2009 on a case-by-case basis.[29] However, in addition to extending the territorial scope of the exemption, the changes have narrowed its scope otherwise: in order for the exemption to reply, the donee trust or corporate body must now satisfy three conditions:

1. The donee must be subject to the jurisdiction of the High Court (in England and Wales, or in Northern Ireland) or the Court of Session (in Scotland), or a court of corresponding jurisdiction in the relevant territory.
2. The donee must satisfy any requirement of registration under the law by which it is governed (although note that not all charities in England and Wales are required to be registered with the Charity Commission, so that the fact of non-registration does not necessarily bar the application of the exemption).
3. The 'managers' of the donee must be fit and proper persons for that role.

Gifts to 'Community Amateur Sports Clubs' will qualify for the exemption if they come **16.30** within the provisions of the Corporation Tax Act 2010, Part 13, Chapter 9. Those provisions require that the club be registered, and HMRC keeps a list of those that are:[30] as at 3 April 2013, there were 6,342 clubs on the list. As in the case of charities, clubs in relevant territories are also within the exemption if they would be eligible for registration if established in the UK, but with the limitation that the facilities they provide for eligible sports must all be within a single relevant territory.

IHT at the lower rate of 36 per cent

In the case of deaths after 6 April 2012, an IHT saving is available in respect of gifts to **16.31** non-exempt beneficiaries if at least 10 per cent of the transfer of value made on death that would otherwise be taxed to IHT at 40 per cent qualifies for the charitable exemption: instead of IHT being applied at the rate of 40 per cent to the remaining 90 per cent, it is applied at 36 per cent.[31] The calculations are not entirely straightforward and are outside the scope of this book (instead reference should be made to the specialist IHT works), but if it is intended to benefit from these provisions they will need to be understood at the point of drafting. As in the case of NRB trusts and the possibility of changes to the size of the NRB (see below), to ensure the relief will apply whatever the size of the estate on death, it will be preferable to use a form of words that will guarantee the 10 per cent threshold is met by using a calculation rather than a fixed sum.[32]

Nil rate band trusts

Although one of the major motivations for including an NRB trust in the will—utilizing the **16.32** NRB of the first spouse to die—has been removed by the provisions for transferring unused NRBs from spouse to spouse brought in by the Finance Act 2008, other motivations remain. Most notably, there may be a desire to keep valuable assets out of the second spouse's estate, so that they are not brought into account on assessment for contribution to nursing home fees and the like.

---

[29] 27 June 2009 is the date of the decision in the *Porsche* case. See *HMRC Inheritance Tax Manual* at IHTM11112.

[30] <www.hmrc.gov.uk/casc/clubs.htm>.

[31] Schedule 1A Inheritance Tax Act 1984 (added by para 1 Sch 13 Finance Act 2012).

[32] See, eg the form of wording suggested by J Kessler and L Sartin in *Drafting Trusts and Will Trusts: A Modern Approach*, 11th edition (Sweet & Maxwell, 2012) at [18.25].

16.33 Often these are drafted as a gift to trustees on discretionary trusts of such sum as equals the NRB in force at the testator's death,[33] with the rest passing under the spouse exemption,[34] but if the estate consists of large amounts of business property or agricultural property that will pass IHT exempt anyway, this leads to the possibility of property that would otherwise avoid IHT being unnecessarily tied up in trust. If the reason for the NRB is merely tax avoidance, then it is preferable that specific gifts of exempt property are made to non-exempt beneficiaries. The preferred wording to constitute an NRB trust is: 'the maximum sum that can at my death be given without any liability being incurred for the payment of inheritance tax on or by reason of my death'. Notwithstanding a contrary view at first instance, this formulation will ensure that the aim of avoiding IHT on all non-residuary gifts is achieved, because the value of any other such gift is taken into account in determining the sum to pass into the trust (regardless of the order of the clauses, as the will must be read as a whole, though doubtless the task will be easier if the NRB trust is declared in the last non-residuary clause).[35] Given the difficulties with even this form of wording, now there is Court of Appeal authority on its effect, there seems little to be achieved by risking the use of an alternative form.

16.34 In the first edition of this book, it was speculated that the NRB had become a political issue, such that it would be likely that significant increases would be put in place year on year, particularly after a change of government. Since then, the world economic outlook has changed and the pressures on the public purse have dictated that the NRB has been frozen at £325,000 since 6 April 2009, and is set to remain at that level until 5 April 2015 at the earliest. Although the spouse is always likely to be a beneficiary of an NRB discretionary trust, it should always be considered whether such a trust would leave free sufficient property to pass to the spouse under the clause of residue. This particularly should be borne in mind where it is expected that a severed interest in a half share of the matrimonial home is to be included in the trust, given the possible unavailability of principal private residence relief from CGT on the gain made on that share.

Providing for the incidence of IHT[36]

16.35 So far as the IHT payable on death in respect of the client's UK free estate (ie property in the UK that vests in his PRs, therefore excluding property passing by *donationes mortis causa*, under nomination, or by survivorship) is concerned, the default position is that it is payable out of residue as a general testamentary and administration expense.[37] Therefore, unless they are to be paid from or charged on a fund consisting wholly or in part of property to which the default position does not apply, it is unnecessary to bequeath pecuniary or general legacies 'free of tax'. Conversely, should the client wish such legacies to bear their own IHT, this will need to be allowed for by words such as 'subject to inheritance tax'.

16.36 It is possible then to simply rely on the default statutory provision in drafting a will if it can safely be assumed the client will not own any property that will not be covered by

---

[33] Section 7 and Sch 1 Inheritance Tax Act 1984. The NRB stands at £325,000 until the end of the tax year 2014–15.

[34] Section 18(1).

[35] *RSPCA v Sharp* [2011] 1 WLR 980.

[36] For a full discussion of this issue and precedents, see *Williams on Wills*, 9th edition (LexisNexis Butterworths, 2008), Vol 2 [214.55]–[214.82].

[37] Section 211(1).

the provision. Otherwise, to achieve the same result in respect of all property, either each non-residuary legacy is best expressed to be 'free of tax and foreign duties', or a general direction as to the incidence of IHT should be included. It is important though that the client understands both the options and their effects. It is all very well asking a client if they wish a legacy to be free of tax, but all too often they do not consider and are not advised of the effect of this. The fact that IHT is likely to be borne from residue (particularly where residue will be partially exempt) will impact on a client's calculations as to who will get what under their will.

17

TAX IN THE ADMINISTRATION OF ESTATES

A. The PR's personal liability

As we have seen in the chapter dealing with tax advice in the course of drafting a will, it is a **17.01** rare estate that on its devolution on the PR does not have any tax consequences. Indeed, if completion of the reduced account due in respect of an excluded estate (ie one the value of which falls within the excepted estate limit at the date of the deceased's death) is included within the definition of a 'tax consequence' then no estate will be tax consequence free.

Liability under the tax legislation

While it is necessary to consider the cases in some detail in order to discern the duties of **17.02** the tax adviser, those of the PR in respect of matters of taxation are, for the most part, codified in the tax legislation. Most notably and most importantly, PRs are liable for the IHT on the value transferred by a chargeable transfer made on death (except where the tax is attributable to settled property).[1] Each PR is thus personally liable[2] for the whole of the tax due on non-settled property passing on the occasion of the deceased's death until it is paid,[3] to the extent of the assets they receive as PR or would have received but for neglect or

---

[1] Section 200(1)(a) Inheritance Tax Act 1984 (IHTA 1984).
[2] *IRC v Stannard* [1984] STC 245. The liability to HMRC is personal, but of course the PR is entitled to be indemnified from the estate for tax properly payable.
[3] Section 205. This includes not just the deceased's free estate (including property held on a joint tenancy), but also *donationes mortis causa*, nominated property, and property passing by survivorship. It does not, however, include property over which the deceased had a general power of appointment unless such property is land in the UK devolving upon or vesting in the PR: s.200(1)(b).

default.[4] This is clearly a most burdensome potential liability which serves to underline the importance to the PR of getting the tax right.[5] It is particularly important for PRs who elect to take advantage of the instalment option to pay IHT to remember that their personal liability for the IHT payable continues throughout the ten-year payment period, so that if instalment property is assented to a beneficiary, and that beneficiary ceases paying the instalments as they fall due, HMRC are entitled to seek the outstanding tax, penalties, and interest from the PRs. This is precisely what happened in *Howarth's Executors v IRC*,[6] where the PRs met with little sympathy from the Special Commissioners, who held that by making the election and consenting to the transfer to the beneficiaries (one of whom had been declared bankrupt) they took an obvious risk. The sensible PR will therefore ensure he has sufficient security for any such future personal liability before transferring property to a beneficiary.

Statutory duty

17.03 In addition to their duties in the tax legislation, PRs are under the statutory duty contained in s.1(1) Trustee Act 2000, as this is expressly extended to them.[7] Thus, they owe the statutory duty of care to those interested in the administration of the estate: they must exercise such care and skill as is reasonable in the circumstances. In the taxation realm, the duty of care is most likely to apply to lay PRs when they employ an agent (most usually a solicitor) to act in the practicalities of administering the estate, including discharging the tax liability: the duty of care applies both in the selection of the agent, and in determining the terms on which they are engaged.[8] In the case of a professional acting as PR himself, the statutory duty is a heightened one, taking into account (a) any special knowledge or experience that he has or holds himself out as having, and (b) any special knowledge or experience that it is reasonable to expect of a person acting in the course of the business or profession in the course of which the PR is acting.

Professional negligence claims

17.04 The lay PR's personal liability exposes the professional agent/adviser to a risk of being brought into a dispute or litigation between an estate beneficiary and the PR. Where the estate beneficiary claims against the lay PR for an act or default of the professional agent/adviser (for which the PR remains personally liable), it is highly likely the PR will look to the professional agent/adviser to recover. When agreeing to act for a lay PR then (rather than as a PR) it is essential that the retainer is limited so far as possible to exclude or limit liability for loss to the estate.

B. Delivering the account

17.05 The PR's first duty is to deliver an IHT account,[9] without which he cannot obtain a grant of probate or letters of administration. This must be done within one year of the end of the month in which the deceased died, or within three months of first acting as PR if this period

---

[4] Section 204(1)(a). An executor *de son tort* is liable to the extent of the assets that have come into his hands: *IRC v Stype Investments (Jersey) Ltd* [1982] Ch 456.
[5] See, eg *Howarth (deceased) (Exors of) v IRC* (1997) STC (SCD) 162.
[6] (1997) *Simon's Weekly Tax Intelligence* 640; *Howarth (deceased) (Exors of) v IRC* (n 5).
[7] Section 35 Trustee Act 2000, see Chapter 15.
[8] Section 11 and para 3 Sch 1 Trustee Act 2000. Thus, the lay PR cannot assume any solicitor will do, but must make sufficient enquiries of them to ensure they have the requisite knowledge and experience to act in the estate on behalf of the PRs.
[9] Section 216(1).

would expire later.[10] This is done by completing and sending to the relevant office of HMRC the form IHT400 (replacing form IHT200): failing to do so exposes the PRs to the risk of a penalty of at least £100, and an additional £60 per day after the failure is declared by a court or the Special Commissioners.[11] It should be noted, however, that for so long as the PR has 'a reasonable excuse' for failing to deliver an account, they are not liable for any penalty.[12]

Failure to deliver the account on time

There is no definition of 'a reasonable excuse' in the statute; HMRC have instead issued guid- **17.06** ance on the question. The circumstances that HMRC will accept as giving rise to a reasonable excuse are limited though, and although they acknowledge that the standard of reasonableness can vary from case to case, their starting point is that 'the law gives ample time for taxpayers to complete and deliver an IHT account in most circumstances' and that it is 'the responsibility of taxpayers to gather all the necessary information, ensure that the account is completed, and send the account in by the deadline'.[13] HMRC will accept as 'a reasonable excuse' the following:

1. An unforeseen interruption to the postal service, such as by fire or flood at the relevant sorting office, or prolonged industrial action.
2. The loss of financial records or papers necessary for the completion of the account, and which could not be replaced in time, by fire, flood, or theft (evidence of which may be required).
3. A serious illness (eg heart attack, coma, or stroke) which prevented the PR from dealing with IHT affairs before the deadline and until the account is submitted.
4. A serious illness of the PR's close relative or partner that took up a significant amount of the PR's time during the period from the deadline to the date the account was submitted (or their death shortly before the deadline), provided steps had already been taken to have the account in on time.

There are certain matters that HMRC will never regard as 'a reasonable excuse': **17.07**

1. Ignorance of the need to submit an account: HMRC take the view the period for submitting an account is long enough for PRs to discover the need and to act on it.
2. The complexity of the account: HMRC expect PRs to seek their help or professional advice at an early date.
3. Pressure of work: again, HMRC view the period for submitting the account as long enough to exclude this excuse being reasonable, and consider that if the PR anticipates difficulty, he should seek professional assistance.
4. Failure by an agent: notwithstanding the PR has engaged a professional to act in the estate on his behalf, and the professional is to blame, the late account, the duty to submit the account on time, and the liability for a late account is personal to the PR.
5. The unavailability of necessary information: HMRC take the view that the reasonableness of this excuse is excluded either by the length of the period for submitting an account, or by the availability of s.216(3A), which permits the use of estimated values (see paras 17.10–17.15).

---

[10] Section 216(6)(a). This provides some relief to those who only become PRs some time after the death, eg someone appointed by the Court under s.50 Administration of Justice Act 1985.
[11] Section 245(2).
[12] Section 245(7).
[13] *HMRC Inheritance Tax Manual* at IHTM36061. For the guidance as to what is and is not accepted as 'a reasonable excuse', see the Manual chapter on 'Penalties', IHTM 36061–71.

6. Waiting for a certified copy of a foreign grant where the deceased dies domiciled outside the UK: although the Probate Registry will not make a grant of probate in respect of UK taxable assets without this, HMRC did not consider it a reason to delay the submission of the account, as the IHT400 can be submitted before and separate from an application for probate in the UK.

17.08 Taking HMRC's guidance as to what they will and will not accept to be 'a reasonable excuse' for the late submission of an account with the PR's personal liability under tax law and their statutory duty of care, then the steps a PR should take to discharge his duties as regards submitting the IHT account can be quite easily divined. Most importantly, the PR should act early to gather in all the necessary information and documents. If the PR is not clear as to his duties and the deadlines for complying with them, then he should seek the advice of either HMRC[14] or a professional. Acting early to gather information will help the PR to meet the deadline, even if problems are encountered: it will, for example, give time to obtain duplicates of any lost or damaged documents and, if necessary, for arranging accurate valuations (whether successfully or unsuccessfully, so that if the latter, the PR can say they have made the fullest reasonable enquiries and thus submit estimated values). Further, if later on before the deadline an event occurs which ultimately prevents the timely submission of the account (eg the PR's partner falls seriously ill), the PR can say they have already taken steps to get the account in on time, and HMRC are thus more likely to accept the excuse as reasonable.

Acting early

17.09 Acting early to gather information should also give an indication both of the complexity of the account, and of the time it is likely to take to complete. As neither of these factors gives a reasonable excuse for a late account, if the PR takes the view that either of them may cause a late submission of the account, the proper step is to engage a professional. Even if the PR himself is a professional (eg a solicitor), if the account is likely to be of such complexity that more specialist input is required (such as from an accountant or chartered tax adviser), the advice of such a specialist should be sought. As we have seen, though, late submission through the fault of an agent is not 'a reasonable excuse', so once the professional is engaged, it is incumbent upon the PR to monitor them so that the deadline is met. Where penalties for late submissions, or penalties and/or interest for late payment, are incurred due to the PR's own fault, it is unlikely they can be considered a testamentary expense for which the PR can claim reimbursement from the estate. Thus, they will fall to be borne by the PR personally. If the PR is a layman and the extra cost has been incurred due to the fault of his professional agent, it is very likely the PR will instead seek reimbursement from the professional.

C. Estimated values

17.10 The PR's potential liability in respect of the IHT400 is not discharged simply by submitting it, though: it is not sufficient for the PR to complete the form with rough 'guestimate' valuations so that he can get it in on time and avoid the penalty. This is because the form includes a declaration by the PR that the information and statements therein are correct and complete. The PR thus faces an element of conflict between his duty to get the account in on

---

[14] HMRC's probate and inheritance tax helpline number, open 9am to 5pm Monday to Friday, is 0845 302 0900.

time (which may be too short a period within which to obtain accurate valuations of estate property), and the binding effect of the declaration he makes on submitting the account (stating the values included therein to be accurate).

Statutory provision for estimates

This is solved to a degree by s.216(3A), which applies to deaths after 8 March 1999 and **17.11** permits a PR who has made 'the fullest enquiries that are reasonably practicable in the circumstances' as to the value of property to give a provisional estimate of the value. Where the PR requires a grant quickly—or at least before he can undertake what may be prolonged and expensive valuation exercises—he can thus submit what is in effect a provisional account and get the probate ball rolling, returning to give a more precise figure once time is more forgiving. This option may be particularly useful where, for example, the major asset is real property and the market is in a downturn, or where the PR needs urgently to access estate assets (eg to prevent deterioration or to protect them in some other way), but cannot without the authority of a grant.

Statements regarding estimates

Although s.216(3A) requires any PR availing himself of that section to include in the **17.12** account a statement that the requirements of the section have been met and an undertaking to deliver a further account once the value is ascertained, it was decided in *Robertson v IRC*[15] that this requirement is met so long as the relevant values are stated to be estimates and the PR has signed the declaration of completion. While the form IHT400 now incorporates an appropriate declaration, it remains best practice when submitting an account that contains estimated values to mark this on the IHT400 itself, and in the covering letter or on some suitable supplementary page to draw attention to them and confirm the undertaking to file the further account. However, although it would be careless to omit to indicate that an estimated valuation is just that (and so is best avoided), it is not necessarily negligent, even if the valuation needs to be revised at a later date.[16]

'Fullest enquiries'

It is not entirely clear what will constitute 'the fullest enquiries that are reasonably practicable **17.13** in the circumstances'. In *Robertson v IRC* the PR followed accepted practice and the Special Commissioners held he had therefore met the test. HMRC have not issued much in the way of guidance, except recommending that the PR contact the professional who will ultimately value the property to check the estimate is realistic.[17] Given the PR is estimating the open market value of the property, it would seem reasonable to base his estimate on the price asked for similar property offered on the open market (obviously, this is most easily done in the case of real property).

However, it appears the duty to make the 'fullest enquiries' may not be as onerous as HMRC **17.14** perhaps would wish. In *Cairns v HMRC*[18] the tribunal held that the solicitor-PR did not

---

[15] [2002] STC (SCD) 182. Interestingly, at a later hearing the Special Commissioners decided the Revenue acted so unreasonably in pursuing the PR they were ordered to pay the PR's expenses of, and incidental to, the hearing: *Robertson v IRC (No 2)* [2002] STC (SCD) 242.
[16] *Cairns v HMRC* [2009] UKFTT 67 (TC).
[17] *IHT Newsletter*, May 2002, Special Edition.
[18] [2009] UKFTT 67 (TC).

act negligently (or fraudulently) in relying on a nine-month-old valuation of real property when completing the IHT return:[19] there was no duty on him to seek a more up-to-date valuation before submission. That was so notwithstanding that the valuation was in the sum of £400,000, but the PR later marketed the property inviting offers 'in excess of £500,000' and sold it for £600,000. On the facts, the tribunal considered that no prudent solicitor-PR could have foreseen, at the time he signed the return, that the property would achieve that price: the property had significant flaws and defects, and there was no evidence a second updated valuation would have been any higher.

17.15 Of course in offering estimates and valuations, it will be necessary to take into account valid debts affecting particular property within the estate (such as an outstanding mortgage debt) and the fullest enquiry into the validity, enforceability, and value of these debts should be made. Relevant to this are two considerations: first, debts charged on assets are borne primarily by the asset, rather than residue, reducing their net value; second, a PR is entitled to pay statute-barred debts, and so the PR should consider whether he intends to exercise this discretion before settling the return. Other than that advice, HMRC have confirmed that in most circumstances they will expect the exact value to be given, but accept that there may be a proven need for an urgent grant, requiring PRs to submit estimated values.[20]

D. A duty to minimize the tax burden

17.16 The potential exposure to penalties and interest in the course of accounting to HMRC for tax due from the estate should provide the PR with all the motivation necessary, if any were needed, to submit accurate and complete accounts on time. PRs are bound to pay all the tax for which they are liable on the delivery of the account,[21] though of course if PRs are choosing to use the instalment option (to pay the tax due on any land, unquoted shares, or interest in a business)[22] it is only the first of the ten equal yearly instalments that is due (provided the election to pay by instalments has been made). It should be noted by PRs that interest is charged by HMRC on any tax due from six months after the end of the month in which the deceased died,[23] so that PRs delivering an account after this time but within the one-year limit will still be liable to pay interest on the tax owed, though there will be no penalty due. Best practice is then to submit the IHT400 within six months of death if at all possible.

17.17 While the PR's duty to HMRC in respect of IHT is to discharge the liability to them, his duty to the estate is to minimize such liability. He is, therefore, under a duty to consider all debts enforceable against the estate, and to claim all exemptions and reliefs available. Failure to do so will cause loss to the estate in the shape of an unnecessary IHT bill, or at least a

---

[19] In fact, HMRC's case was dismissed on a technicality, but the tribunal went on to consider the substantive merits.

[20] In *Robertson v IRC* the PR was under pressure from a beneficiary to secure an early sale of a cottage, so as to avoid deterioration over the winter, and it was his usual practice to advertise estate property for sale only after obtaining a grant, so as to ensure he had full title to complete a sale.

[21] Section 226(2).

[22] Section 227(2).

[23] Section 233(1)(b).

penalty on the submission of a corrective account. In addition, the PR's duty to HMRC arising by virtue of his declaration on the IHT400 requires him to claim only those exemptions
to which the estate is actually entitled. Thus, the PR must tread a fine line between fulfilling
his duty to the estate to minimize the IHT payable, and fulfilling his duty to HMRC to file
a complete and accurate account, and discharge the tax payable as a result, within time (so as
not to cause loss to the estate in the shape of penalties or interest).

There follow the most common exemptions available, and best practice as regards ensuring **17.18**
they can be claimed, so that these dual duties may be discharged.

Exemptions available on death

Exemption for death on active service[24]

1. Where the deceased was a member of the armed forces of the Crown or subject to the
   law governing them by association with or accompanying them, and dies from wounds
   received or a disease contracted while on active service against the enemy or on other
   service of a warlike nature which in the opinion of the Treasury carries the same risks, or
   dies from a previously contracted illness due to or hastened by aggravation during such
   a period, his entire estate is exempt provided those facts are certified by the Defence
   Council or the Secretary of State. This is by disapplication of s.4, so that death is not a
   chargeable event. It should be noted that the wound need only contribute to the death,
   and this is interpreted widely.[25]
2. HMRC will not allow the relief without a certificate. In simple cases the MoD will
   send a letter to the next of kin and this is the necessary certificate. In other cases
   the PRs should apply to Service Personnel and Veterans Agency, Joint Casualty and
   Compassionate Centre (Attn SO3 Deceased Estates), Imjin Barracks, Innsworth,
   Gloucester, GL3 1HW.

Spouse or civil partner exemption[26]

1. Transfers between spouses and civil partners do not incur IHT, so that any property
   becoming comprised immediately in the estate of the deceased's surviving spouse or civil
   partner can be discounted for IHT purposes. Where the property is settled on trusts
   which give the spouse a life interest, the exemption is available as the property is treated
   as forming part of the receiving spouse's estate.[27] A conditional gift (eg one conditional
   upon a period of survivorship) where the condition is satisfied within twelve months
   meets the requirement of immediacy. The exemption is not available to sexual cohabitees,
   nor those in platonic cohabitation relationships,[28] and this position is compatible with
   the European Convention on Human Rights.[29] If the receiving spouse is non-UK domiciled this exemption is limited to £55,000.[30]
2. In practice, it is extremely rare for a PR to ask to see proof of the marriage or civil partnership, but best practice demands this, since the PR on the IHT400 declares the exemption

---

[24] Section 154.
[25] *Barty-King v Ministry of Defence* [1979] STC 218; [1979] 2 All ER 80.
[26] Section 18.
[27] Because it will be an Immediate Post-Death Interest: ss.49 and 49A.
[28] *Holland v IRC* [2003] STC (SCD) 43; [2003] WTLR 207.
[29] *Burden v UK* [2007] STC 252; [2007] 1 FCR 69.
[30] Section 18(2). Where the spouse is domiciled in another EU member state, there must be a question
whether such an exemption is in breach of EU law: see n 41.

available; if it later transpires it was not, the PR will be liable for a penalty and interest. Always ask to see a marriage certificate or certificate of civil partnership. Even in the case of a solicitor who is not the PR (so that he will not be making the declaration himself), he should at least ask the PR to confirm he has seen the certificate, although it is even better to ask the PR to show it to him—otherwise, if the PR is not advised to obtain proof, he may allege negligence against the solicitor for this omission in order to recover the losses he bears.

Gifts to charities[31]

1. The essence of this exemption is that the property gifted must be given to a charity or become held indefeasibly (or defeasible within one year but in the event the gift is not defeated) on trust for charitable purposes only. Since 14 March 2012 'charity' and 'charitable purposes' have been defined by ss.1 and 2 Charities Act 2011, generally considered a broadening of the definition.
2. The exemption is now available in respect of charities in any EU member state (as well as Iceland and Norway) and Community Amateur Sports Clubs.[32] To claim the exemption the PR obviously must ensure the donee qualifies. If the donee is listed in the Charity Commission register it will qualify, but non-registered bodies can qualify too: HMRC give guidance as to those usually accepted, and those usually not accepted, as qualifying.[33] Community Amateur Sports Clubs must be registered under the Corporation Tax Act 2010 to qualify.

Gifts to political parties and housing associations, and gifts for national purposes and historic buildings[34]

1. These exemptions are all available if the donee meets the statutory description contained in each section.
2. As with apparent gifts to charity, the PR must ensure the donee meets the statutory criteria.

Transfers of relevant business property, agricultural property, and woodland property[35]

1. Whereas the exemptions described immediately above depend on the status of the donee, these reliefs depend on the status of the property and the length of ownership. In the case of business property and agricultural property, the relief may be 50 per cent or 100 per cent of the IHT burden.
2. Again, if the PR is to claim the relief, it is incumbent upon him to ensure the property qualifies, and the quality of the deceased's ownership or occupation of that property was as required for the relief to apply. Particularly, it should be noted that agricultural relief is limited to land in the UK, Channel Islands, or Isle of Man,[36] and will apply to farmhouses only so far as they are of a character appropriate to the property.

---

[31] Section 23.
[32] See paras 16.29 and 16.30 above.
[33] *HMRC Inheritance Tax Manual* at IHTM 11134–5.
[34] Sections 24, 24A, 25, and 27.
[35] Part V, Chapters I, II, and III.
[36] Such limitation may also be in breach of EU law.

Exemptions available only during lifetime

Annual exemption[37]

1. Although not available on death, this exemption is to be taken into account when PRs aggregate lifetime transfers for the last seven years. The exemption stands at £3,000 and must be applied to the first chargeable transfer in each tax year (this includes Potentially Exempt Transfers (PETs)—so that where the exemption is allocated to a PET which does prove to be exempt, its benefit is lost). Any unused exemption can be carried forward, but for one year only: thus, a person who has not made any chargeable transfers the previous year will have £6,000 of exemption available, but if he makes a transfer of only £2,000 he will only have £1,000 to carry forward to the following year.
2. Claiming this exemption is really a case of performing an historical accounting exercise, and for this purpose the PR will need to examine the deceased's bank statements and tax returns, and rely on information from any recipients or potential recipients. He should of course do this as a matter of course anyway in order to identify those lifetime transfers that should be aggregated.

Small gifts[38]

1. Gifts below £250 are IHT exempt and these are not limited in number provided each gift is to a different person. The value of the gift must be below £250: the exemption does not apply to the first £250 of gifts of a value exceeding £250.
2. Whether this exemption is available should become apparent upon an examination of the deceased's financial records as above.

Normal expenditure out of income[39]

1. There is no IHT on transfers made from a person's income as part of their normal expenditure after meeting their usual standard of living, whatever the size of the transfer. The gifts must be from income rather than capital, should be of an income nature (ie regular), and must be from surplus income only, so that making the gifts does not impinge on the donor's standard of living (ie he cannot free up income to gift by economizing in his lifestyle).
2. As this is another lifetime-only exemption, in order to claim it the PRs will need to consider the deceased's financial records. It is notoriously difficult to convince HMRC that such gifts fall within this provision though (they otherwise will be PETs): absent a memorandum from the deceased contemporaneous with the commencement of the payments in respect of which the exemption is to be sought, it is very unlikely to be done. Any such memorandum will ideally set out the donor's income, the costs of his usual standard of living, the excess this leaves, and his intention to use this excess to make gifts that would fall within this exemption.

Gifts in consideration of marriage or civil partnership[40]

1. In respect of any one ceremony a gift to a party to the ceremony is exempt up to £5,000 where the donee is the donor's child, up to £2,500 where the donor is an ancestor of one

---

[37] Section 19.
[38] Section 20.
[39] Section 21.
[40] Section 22.

323

party or is one party and the donee is the other party, and up to £1,000 in any other case. Child includes illegitimate, adopted, and step children, and 'ancestor' is to be considered accordingly.

2. Only one exemption per ceremony can be claimed. The ceremony must be valid according to the laws of England, Scotland, or Northern Ireland. HMRC will be sceptical that the exemption should apply if the gift is made other than at the time of or shortly before the marriage concerned. If the gift is after the ceremony it will only qualify if it is made in fulfilment of a binding promise, or the donor has informed the donee of an intention to make the gift and taken steps to put it in place.

E. A duty to save tax?

17.19 The PRs' clear duty to minimize the estate's IHT liability in respect of claiming exemptions and reliefs raises the question whether the duty extends to the chance to save tax by varying the will or intestacy. Admittedly, the commonest reason for doing this—using the nil rate band of the first spouse to die—has now been negated by the provisions of the Finance Act 2008,[41] but a tax saving may still be available; in which case, is the solicitor bound to advise of the fact and of the steps necessary to secure it?

Case law

17.20 This issue was considered in part in the case of *Cancer Research Campaign v Ernest Brown & Co*,[42] though there the claimants were the beneficiaries of P, who was the deceased residuary beneficiary of the estate of N in which the tax saving was available. Upon instructing solicitors (who employed the legal executive L who was an executor of N's estate and subsequently of P's estate) to prepare her will, P was not advised of the possibility of saving tax by varying N's estate. P then died within the time limit for varying N's estate, but the claimants were not advised that as they were absolutely entitled to P's estate they could vary N's estate in her stead. It was held that L and the solicitors had acted properly towards P, as the retainer was limited to the preparation of her will, and had not acted improperly in not advising the claimants of their interests, because a PR is under no such duty.

17.21 It was further pointed out that even if a duty was established, it would be necessary to show that P if so informed would have varied N's estate, which was by no means proven.

Application to the normal case

17.22 It is submitted that by virtue of the fact the IHT liability arises not as a result of an act of the PR administering the estate (except so far as they act to carry out the dispositions of the will or intestacy), but as a result of the will executed by the deceased or the intestacy rules, the duty on the PR does not extend to making any possible IHT saving that could be achieved by a variation.[43] While the PR is under a duty to minimize the IHT due on the transactions

---

[41] Section 10 Finance Act 2008. First announced in the Pre-Budget Report presented on 9 October 2007 and entitled 'Meeting the Aspirations of the British People'. Online at <http://www.official-documents.gov.uk/document/cm72/7227/7227.pdf>.

[42] [1998] PNLR 592.

[43] Indeed, to seek to impose this on the beneficiaries would appear to be a breach of duty: *Jemma Trust Co v Kippax Beaumont Lewis* [2004] EWHC 703 (Ch) [89]–[92].

with which he is presented, he is not under a duty to reorder those transactions so as to reduce the IHT liability further still.

Such a variation would alter the substance of the transaction (the scheme of distribution), **17.23** rather than merely its form, and the duty as described in *Hurlingham Estates* does not extend to advising of alternative transactions of a differing substance. It would follow that a professional adviser is under no duty to advise a PR client of the possibility of varying the estate. The position surely would be different if the client raises the question of minimizing tax, although of course any variation will require the consent of the beneficiaries. Until there is a reported decision on this point though, the distinction argued for here is mere conjecture.

Beneficiaries' desire to save tax

In the first edition of this book, it was submitted that the situation would be different **17.24** though, if the beneficiaries themselves raised the possibility of varying the estate. In that instance the transaction contemplated (an alternative distribution according to the wishes of those entitled), which has a range of possible tax consequences, is different in substance to the transaction that took place immediately prior to the deceased's death, which has only one, so that the professional PR, or the professional agent/adviser to a lay PR, would be then under a duty to advise fully on the tax consequences of the proposed variation, and to suggest alterations in the form of the variation that may bring greater tax benefits. As with the duty in relation to will preparation described in the previous chapter then, the professional would need to consider his own competence in matters of tax and act accordingly, considering consulting an external tax expert or otherwise advising the client (lay PR or beneficiary) to engage a different professional in this respect.

Such a duty would no doubt extend to advising fully on the requirements for securing the **17.25** special tax treatment of certain instruments of variation and following through fully on the transaction. Traps for the unwary here include the two-year time limit, ensuring the instrument includes the necessary statements as to the application of the IHT and CGT provisions,[44] the need for all those whose interest will be affected by the variation to be party to the instrument (and so if there are minor or unascertained beneficiaries, there can be no variation without an application to the court for approval on their behalf),[45] the variation being for external consideration (which will prevent the IHT and CGT provisions applying),[46] and overlooking the fact that there is no provision giving retrospective effect to the variation for income tax purposes. One particular point that is often overlooked is where the instrument creates a settlement of property that was not settled by the will: in such a case the retrospective CGT effect does not extend to identifying the deceased as the settlor of the settlement; rather the person who would have been entitled to the property as legatee, but for the variation, will be the settlor for all CGT purposes.[47]

That view has been all but confirmed as correct by the decision in *Martin v Triggs Turner* **17.26** *Barton*,[48] discussed at paragraph 16.08 above. Given the general principles that can be

---

[44] Section 142(2) IHTA 1984; s.62(7) Taxation of Chargeable Gains Act 1992 (TCGA 1992).
[45] Often under the Variation of Trusts Act 1958.
[46] This could include the payment of the professional fees in respect of the variation by those who gain under the variation.
[47] Section 68C.
[48] [2009] EWHC 1920 (Ch); [2010] PNLR 3; [2009] WTLR 1339.

adduced from *Hurlingham Estates Ltd v Wilde & Partners*,[49] it is likely that the duty that would arise by reason of an assumption of responsibility, described in *Martin v Triggs Turner Barton*, would extend to advising the beneficiary of the possibility of achieving a tax saving by varying the devolution of the estate. Likewise, if the possibility of varying the estate for some other, non-tax, reason arose, the PR would be under a duty (unless expressly excluded) to advise of the tax consequences of doing so.

F. Selling estate assets

17.27 Given that, after a PR has put aside enough cash to meet pecuniary legacies there is often not enough left in residue to meet the IHT liability in respect of the estate, there is a good chance that they will have to sell estate property in order to raise the tax money. It is therefore important for PRs to be aware that special rules apply to the sale within a certain period by the appropriate person of securities[50] and land[51] where a loss is made (ie the value realized is less than the probate value), so that in effect the value of the property for the purposes of calculating the IHT payable in respect of it is treated as being the sale value, rather than the probate value: obviously, this presents the possibility of reducing the IHT burden on the estate, but it is not necessarily always the most beneficial route, as alternative tax savings may be available if the relief is not claimed. The PR will have to consider whether it is preferable for the estate to reduce its IHT burden by claiming the relief, or to benefit from an allowable loss for CGT purposes by not claiming the relief:[52] ie which route will give the greater tax saving to the estate?

17.28 For the purposes of the relief in respect of securities, a 'qualifying investment' includes quoted shares and securities, holdings in an authorized unit trust, shares in an open-ended investment company, and shares in a common investment fund which are comprised in the deceased's estate immediately before his death.[53] Included, therefore, are securities that would otherwise be qualifying investments that are held in a settlement in which the deceased had an interest in possession within the meaning of s.49. There are numerous traps for the unwary. First, the sale must take place within twelve months of the deceased's death.[54] Second, in order for the relief to be claimed that sale must be by 'the appropriate person', that is the person who is responsible for paying the IHT or, if there is more than one such person, the person actually paying the IHT; generally this is the PR, though if an asset has been appropriated to a beneficiary's interest (albeit not transferred to the beneficiary) this is more properly the beneficiary himself. Third, if at any time within two months of the last sale in respect of which the relief is claimed, the appropriate person acting in the same capacity (ie as a PR) uses the proceeds to purchase other qualifying investments, the relief is lost.[55] The relief therefore cannot be used to realize, and then reinvest.

---

[49] [1997] 1 Lloyd's Rep 525. Discussed at Chapter 16 paras 16.14 to 16.18.
[50] Part VI, Chapter III IHTA 1984.
[51] Part VI, Chapter IV.
[52] Because the value as ascertained for IHT purposes will be the market value at the date of death for CGT purposes: s.274 TCGA 1992.
[53] Section 178(1).
[54] Section 179(1)(a).
[55] Section 180(1).

In the case of an interest in land,[56] the period for making a sale at a loss is longer, at four years **17.29** from death[57] (for the purposes of the relief, the sale is made at the time the contract is entered into[58]). If the land is acquired under compulsory acquisition, there is no time limit in claiming the relief.[59] Again, the sale must be by the appropriate person, which usually will be the PR. The relief is not available where the loss is less than the lesser of £1,000 or 5 per cent of the value on death,[60] or where the sale is to someone who between the death and the sale has been beneficially entitled to, or to an interest in possession in, the relevant interest, or to their spouse or civil partner, or their issue, or to the trustees of a settlement in which any of those people have an interest in possession.[61] The relief will also be lost if within four months of the last sale in respect of which the relief is claimed, the appropriate person (acting in the same capacity as he acted in selling the land) buys any interest in land. As with the securities relief, this prevents realization and quick reinvestment. As with the sale of securities, the PR will have to consider the IHT benefits in the context of possible CGT disadvantages.

G. A note on capital gains tax

As a death does not trigger a disposal for CGT purposes as it triggers a transfer of value for **17.30** IHT purposes, a PR may think he will need to concern himself less with CGT than with IHT. As with IHT though, the PR is personally liable for the CGT due from him as PR, and this includes an outstanding CGT liability of the deceased at his death.[62] As the PR can set allowable losses of the deceased against the deceased's chargeable gains in the year of assessment of the death, and so far as they are not exhausted against chargeable gains in the three years of assessment preceding the year of assessment in which the death occurs, there is a possibility for the PR to claim a CGT rebate that will swell the estate, and needless to say he is under a duty to do so where available.

PR's acquisition

Most importantly for the PR is the fact he acquires chargeable assets of the deceased at their **17.31** open market value at the date of the death:[63] as mentioned above, if the value is ascertained for IHT purposes, this will be determinative. This value is the PR's acquisition cost for the purpose of future disposals. Of course, if the estate does not attract IHT (because the beneficiary is exempt, or because there is an applicable 100 per cent relief) the value is not ascertained, and so the acquisition costs of the PR are still 'up for grabs'. Generally, the PR would like a high valuation for CGT purposes, but a low one for IHT purposes, but of course he does not have the luxury of two separate valuations of the same property. Usually, the IHT burden will be higher than the CGT burden (as the former is at a higher rate and applies to total value, while the latter is at a lower rate and only applies to increase in value), so that the lower valuation will be preferred.

---

[56] Except by way of mortgage or other security, which are excluded from these provisions: s.190(1).
[57] Sections 191(1) and 197A(1).
[58] Section 198(1).
[59] Section 197(1).
[60] Section 191(2).
[61] Section 191(4).
[62] Section 65(2) TCGA 1992.
[63] Section 62(1) TCGA 1992.

Sale or transfer of assets

17.32   The PR will thus be charged CGT on the gain made on the sale of estate assets at a rate of 28 per cent[64] over his annual exemption.[65] This is irrespective of the CGT status of the ultimate beneficiaries of the proceeds of sale, so that if proceeds are to be held for CGT-exempt beneficiaries, such as charities[66] or non-UK residents,[67] it is preferable for the asset to be sold to be assented to the legatee for him to make the sale.

17.33   On such transfer the PR makes no loss/no gain, and the legatee[68] acquires the property with an acquisition cost equal to the PR's acquisition cost plus the costs of the transfer. Whether or not the recipient of the property takes *qua* legatee (and so whether or not there will be a CGT charge on the transfer) depends on the individual facts of the case. So far as a beneficiary agrees with the PR to receive more than his strict entitlement, whether by receiving a different asset than that to which he is entitled, or by receiving greater value from the estate than that to which he is entitled, whether for consideration or not, he does not take *qua* legatee.

17.34   Similarly, if the beneficiary receives assets under a trust arising under the will or the intestacy rules, the beneficiary does not take *qua* legatee, but *qua* beneficiary of the trust, so that he becomes absolutely entitled as against the trustee and there is a deemed disposal and a CGT charge on the trustee.[69] The question will be, by the time of the transfer, has the administration been completed, or has the PR assented the property to himself as trustee, such as to constitute the PR a trustee? It should be noted though, that there is no CGT charge where the PR stands only as bare trustee, as the property so held, and the acts of the bare trustee in relation to it, are treated as those of the beneficiary.[70]

Exemptions and reliefs

17.35   Finally, as is the case with IHT and as partly alluded to above, there is a range of exemptions and reliefs available in respect of CGT: the PR is of course under a duty to minimize the estate's CGT burden by claiming these where they apply to or are available in respect of the property, gain, or legatee (as the case may be). Sterling, for example, is not a chargeable asset,[71] nor are national savings[72] or cars.[73] Perhaps the one notable relief worthy of special mention is that applicable to the gain to a PR on the sale of the deceased's former principal private residence: such gain may not be a chargeable gain if a beneficiary of the sale proceeds has lived there before and after the death.[74]

---

[64] Section 4(3) TCGA 1992.

[65] Section 3(1) TCGA 1992. In 2013–14, this stands at £10,900. For CGT purposes, the PRs are treated as one person (s.62(3)), and have available to them the personal allowance in respect of the year of the deceased's death, and each of the following two years.

[66] Section 256 TCGA 1992.

[67] Only persons resident or ordinarily resident in the UK are chargeable to CGT: s.2(1) TCGA 1992.

[68] Anyone taking under a testamentary disposition or on intestacy or partial intestacy: s.64(2) TCGA 1992.

[69] Section 71(1) TCGA 1992.

[70] Section 60(1) TCGA 1992.

[71] Section 21 TCGA 1992.

[72] Section 121 TCGA 1992.

[73] Section 263 TCGA 1992.

[74] Section 225A TCGA 1992.

H. Reserving the estate for contingent legacies

Although the will or the intestacy rules may provide for a specific or residuary testamentary **17.36** gift to vest in the beneficiary immediately upon death, the PR has one year from the date of death to administer the estate, during which time the beneficiary cannot call for payment of his legacy.[75] It follows that the beneficiary is not entitled to interest on the gift until the year expires (or until the expiry of such other period for payment of the gift as stipulated by the will). Although interest does not begin to accrue until this time, such immediate gifts do carry with them from the date of death the income and accretions[76] attributable thereto: thus the property to which a beneficiary will ultimately become entitled is (i) the subject matter of the gift, (ii) the income it generates from the date of death, and (iii) interest from one year (or such other period for payment) after the date of death (paid gross by the PR and taxed on the beneficiary).[77]

Income tax

The beneficiary does not become entitled to that property until the administration of the **17.37** estate (ie the ascertainment of residue,[78] so that it is ready for distribution) is complete though, and is thus not assessable to income tax on the income generated by the estate until such time (when he is assessed on the grossed up value, with credit given for income tax paid by the PR). In the interim then (ie during the administration of the estate), the PR is liable in his representative capacity for income tax on the estate income. Some types of income, such as bank interest or dividend income, will come into the PR's hands net of income tax, while other types, such as rental income, royalties, national savings interest, and income from a business carried on by the PR, will be received gross and the PR will be assessed on it. Thus, in addition to settling the income tax outstanding at the deceased's death by completing a return for the period from the 6 April immediately prior to the deceased's death to the date of the death (as well as for any complete tax years for which the deceased had failed to make a return),[79] the PR will need to make returns in respect of estate income during the administration period.

Income tax becomes a bigger issue for a PR when gifts are given contingently or are deferred; **17.38** the former being dependent on the happening of an event that may or may not occur (eg on some person achieving a certain age), the latter on an event that certainly will occur (eg on the death of some person). In either case, the PR will have to reserve estate property to meet the future liability of the estate to pay out the gift. Unless the will provides otherwise, all such gifts except deferred residuary (rather than specific or pecuniary) gifts of personalty, carry with them the immediate interest which must be accrued and paid over with the capital; the income in respect of deferred residuary gifts of personalty falls into residue. It is possible then that the PR may be required to file income tax returns for some considerable period until the contingency is satisfied and the gift vests.

---

[75] Section 44 Administration of Estates Act 1925.
[76] *Re Buxton* [1930] 1 Ch 648.
[77] Sections 369 and 371 Income Tax (Trading and Other Income) Act 2005.
[78] This is generally when HMRC will consider the administration to be complete: *HMRC Capital Gains Manual* at CG30783.
[79] The PR is accountable for all income tax owed by the deceased: s.74(1) Taxes Management Act 1970.

Contingent gifts held for children

17.39 Most gifts of a contingent nature will be gifts to children contingent on them achieving a certain age. The PR will thus have the statutory power to apply the income for the beneficiary's benefit or maintenance during his minority, and thereafter to him directly.[80] During the beneficiary's minority then, the PR will be required to pay income tax on such income as comes into his hands as it arises, whether that is accumulated or applied, but the beneficiary will only be assessed on that income for the tax year he receives it. So much of the income that is accumulated then will not be received by the beneficiary until it vests with the capital upon the contingency, and he will be assessed to income tax on the entirety of that accumulated income in that tax year. There is obviously a danger this may push the beneficiary into the higher rate of tax for that year, and the PR should give thought to using his power to apply the income in preceding years to guard against this.

17.40 Of course, upon the beneficiary reaching his majority the PR's discretion as to dealing with the income ends and he is required henceforth to pay the income from the property to the beneficiary. Thus, the PR will pay basic rate tax on behalf of the beneficiary on the income as it arises (and after the PR has deducted any legitimate administration expenses) and pay the net amount to the beneficiary: the beneficiary then will be assessed on the grossed up value with a credit for the tax paid by the PR.

I. Conclusions

17.41 The PR may often feel that his dual duties are dragging him in opposite directions: on the one hand he must submit a complete and accurate account to HMRC and pay the tax burden assessed therein by the deadline, and on the other he must consider the type and contents of the estate in order to minimize the tax burden on the estate and maximize the value to be received by the estate beneficiaries. The one calls for promptness, while the other calls for consideration.

17.42 The PR's task, though, is not impossible. While sooner or later every deadline seems unrealistically close, it is possible both to give considered thought to how to deal with the estate in the most tax-efficient manner, and still to meet HMRC requirements. So far as tax is concerned then, the PR's best practice can be summarized thus:

1. Act early to get in the estate and get it valued.
2. If in doubt as to your duties or as to the proper tax treatment, seek professional advice.
3. If a professional is engaged, disclose to them all the information you have on the deceased, the estate, and the beneficiaries, and monitor their progress.
4. Keep HMRC informed as to any expected delays and the reasons for them.
5. If mistakes are made, a prompt corrective account will minimize the damage so far as possible.

---

[80] Section 31 Trustee Act 1925.

18

TAX AND TRUSTS

A. Introduction

The subject of the taxation of trusts is a notoriously complex one. This chapter does not seek **18.01** to give a step-by-step guide to the subject, for which reference should be made to specialist works,[1] but rather seeks to set out the duty of the professional trustee, or the professional adviser to the lay trustee, as well as to give a broad overview of the functioning of the three most important taxation regimes—inheritance, capital gains, and income—and to point out common pitfalls in their application and how to avoid them.

B. A trust or settlement

For IHT and CGT purposes, trusts are subject to special tax provisions so far as they are a **18.02** 'settlement' or 'settled property'. For IHT purposes, a 'settlement' is

> any disposition or dispositions of property ... whereby the property is for the time being—
>
> (a) held in trust for persons in succession or for any person subject to a contingency, or
> (b) held by trustees on trust to accumulate the whole or part of any income of the property or with power to make payments out of that income at the discretion of the trustees or some other person, with or without power to accumulate surplus income, or

---

[1] For a concise review of the taxation of trusts and the matters most frequently of concern to trustees, see E Chamberlain and C Whitehouse, *Trust Taxation*, 3rd edition (Sweet & Maxwell, 2011).

    (c) charged or burdened (otherwise than for full consideration in money or money's worth paid for his own use or benefit to the person making the disposition) with the payment of any annuity or other periodical payment payable for a life or any other limited or terminable period.[2]

18.03 The definition under the Taxation of Chargeable Gains Act 1992 is much simpler. For CGT purposes, 'settled property' is,

> unless the context otherwise requires, ... any property held in trust other than property to which section 60 applies (and references, however expressed, to property comprised in a settlement are references to settled property).[3]

18.04 Section 60 of that Act addresses the relationships of bare trust and nomineeship, which although considered a trust or a fiduciary relationship for the purposes of the general law, for tax purposes are not treated in the same way as 'settlements': rather, the tax legislation 'pierces the veil' of such relationships:

> (1) In relation to the property held by a person as nominee for another person, or as trustee for another person absolutely entitled as against the trustee, or for any person who would be so entitled but for being an infant or other person under disability (or for two or more persons who are or would be jointly so entitled), this Act shall apply as if the property were vested in, and the acts of the nominee or trustee in relation to the property were the acts of, the person or persons for whom he is the nominee or trustee (acquisitions from or disposals to him by that person or persons being disregarded accordingly).[4]

C. Tax a relevant consideration to exercising discretion

18.05 Trustees are under a duty to exercise all their powers under the terms of the trust in a fiduciary manner, for the benefit of the beneficiary or beneficiaries, and they can only do this if they ensure that they take into account all considerations relevant to the exercise of the power, and do not take into account any considerations that are irrelevant. The taxation consequences of the exercise of a power clearly will affect the degree of benefit felt by the beneficiaries of the trust, so that there can be no doubt that tax is a relevant consideration for trustees when making decisions as to the exercise of their powers, and they are thus bound before acting both to take competent tax advice, and to consider it.

Hastings-Bass after *Pitt v Holt; Futter v Futter*

18.06 Thus, the *Hastings-Bass*[5] principle applies to the tax realm, and will make void an exercise by trustees of a discretionary power on the basis of detrimental tax consequences in two distinct circumstances:

- when the trustees fail to take tax advice; or
- when the trustees take tax advice and fail to act upon it.

18.07 Until the Supreme Court decision in *Pitt v Holt, Futter v Futter*[6] the principle had come to be erroneously applied in a third set of circumstances, namely when trustees had taken tax

---

[2] Section 43(2) Inheritance Tax Act 1984 (IHTA 1984).
[3] Section 68 Taxation of Chargeable Gains Act 1992 (TCGA 1992).
[4] This wording is effectively repeated for the purposes of income tax in s.466 Income Tax Act 2007.
[5] So named after the decision in *Re Hastings-Bass* [1975] Ch 25 at 41. See paras 23.42–23.51 for a fuller discussion of the principle.
[6] [2013] UKSC 26.

advice and relied upon it, that advice had proven to be wrong. That previous extended formulation of the principle in *Hastings-Bass* had been expressed most fully by Lloyd LJ in the case of *Sieff v Fox*.[7] For the principle to apply it was necessary that the trustees had exercised their power (rather than decided not to), and that such exercise had had unintended tax consequences. For the relief to be available, it was necessary to show that had the trustees had proper tax advice and taken it into account they *would* not have exercised the power in the way they did (unless the beneficiary can require the trustees to act, in which case it is sufficient that they *might* not have so exercised it).[8]

As a result of *Pitt v Holt; Futter v Futter*, the application of the principle has been narrowed in recognition that the court's jurisdiction to set aside an exercise by trustees of a discretionary power is limited to exercises (i) in breach of fiduciary duty, and (ii) which amount to voluntary dispositions founded on a mistake. Failing to take or failing to act on competent tax advice may amount to a breach of duty within the first limb of jurisdiction, rendering the exercise voidable (not void), but it was confirmed that such a claim should be brought by the affected beneficiaries, not by the trustees in reliance on their own failings. Similarly, while the court declined to lay down any strict rules as to when a mistake would be sufficient for the court to exercise its jurisdiction under the second limb, it was confirmed that relief would be granted on the basis of the gravity of the mistake, including the circumstances in which it was made and its consequences for the person making the disposition, following an objective evaluation of the injustice (or unfairness or unconscionability) of leaving the mistaken disposition uncorrected: a mistake as to the tax consequences could be sufficiently serious. **18.08**

Utility to trustees and advisers

Thus, the utility of the principle in *Hastings-Bass* to trustees and their advisers who make mistakes about the tax consequences of dispositions is now limited, first because it is unlikely to be easy (if possible at all) to establish a breach of fiduciary duty where the tax consequences have been actively considered, and the trustees have sought and acted upon advice, and second because the courts are unlikely to receive well an application by the trustees themselves. **18.09**

In contrast, the doctrine of mistake may now offer increased utility in those circumstances. However, while it is clear that it will be possible for a mistake as to tax consequences to be sufficiently serious for the court to set aside the disposition, this cannot be relied upon, and further there are suggestions in the judgment of Lord Walker that leaving uncorrected dispositions that were aimed at achieving beneficial tax consequences but in fact incur detrimental consequences may not be sufficiently unjust as to justify the intervention of the court. **18.10**

D. The trustee's liability

Trustees (as defined by the tax legislation) are in some ways in a similar position to that of PRs so far as their duties with regard to tax are concerned. Trustees are, of course, under the statutory duty of care under s.1(1) Trustee Act 2000 in respect of all their acts as trustees, and as with PRs this will be particularly relevant in the taxation realm to the employment of specialist tax advisers or practitioners as agents.[9] **18.11**

---

[7] [2005] EWHC 1312 (Ch); [2005] WTLR 891.
[8] *Sieff v Fox* (n 7) at [77].
[9] Section 11 and para 3 Sch 1 Trustee Act 2000.

18.12 So far as his liability to pay CGT is concerned, a trustee is in an identical position to a PR in that he is the sole person liable for the CGT chargeable on or in the name of the trustee (though for this purpose he is not regarded as an individual).[10] As with a PR too, there is a limitation on the extent of a trustee's liability for IHT, so that he is only liable in relation to property he has actually received and disposed of, or become liable to account for to the beneficiaries, and property available in his hands as trustee for the payment of tax, or which would have been so in their hands but for their own neglect or default.[11]

18.13 Otherwise though, when one considers that during the administration of a trust the beneficiaries of the trust have an equitable interest in the trust property, whereas during the administration of a deceased person's estate the beneficiaries have only a chose in action to enforce the due administration, it becomes apparent that in each case the beneficiaries have markedly different property in respect of the fund concerned, and that the trustee–beneficiary relationship is therefore a different type of relationship to that of PR–beneficiary. This is reflected in the tax liabilities of the trustee.

18.14 As already intimated though, because the tax legislation discounts a bare trust from the provisions aimed at trusts and settlements, the trustees' liabilities and duties are much reduced under such a trust. As a matter of general law though, they remain the legal owners of the trust property, and thus the trust income (and capital money) will be paid to them. In the case of dividend and savings income, this is likely to come to the trustees with tax deducted. The trustees may, therefore, elect to make self-assessment returns or payments on account, notwithstanding their bare trusteeship. This will not affect the bare beneficiary's duty to make returns though. Absent an election by the trustees, there will be no liability on the trustees to make returns, this responsibility being solely that of the beneficiary.[12]

E. Inheritance tax

18.15 The differences between PRs and trustees are reflected to a large degree in the IHT legislation: s.201 of the 1984 Act makes the following provision as to the liability for payment of tax (each person named being liable for all the tax[13]):

> (1) The persons liable for the tax on the value transferred by a chargeable transfer made under Part III of this Act are—
> (a) the trustees of the settlement;
> (b) any person entitled (whether beneficially of not) to an interest in possession in the settled property;
> (c) any person for whose benefit any of the settled property or income from it is applied at or after the time of the transfer;
> (d) where the transfer is made during the life of the settlor and the trustees are not for the time being resident in the United Kingdom, the settlor.

---

[10] Section 65(2) TCGA 1992.
[11] Section 204(2) IHTA 1984.
[12] See HMRC press release dated 20 January 1997, and *Tax Bulletin*, Issues 27 and 32, February and December 1997.
[13] Section 205 IHTA 1984.

Finance Act 2006

So far as new settlements are concerned, taxation has been much simplified for trustees by **18.16** the provisions of the Finance Act 2006, whereby all existing trusts without interests in possession and all new settlements whether or not there is an interest in possession (bar some limited examples) are trusts of 'relevant property' and taxed as only discretionary trusts were previously. So far as a trustee fulfilling his duty in respect of properly accounting for all the IHT for which they are liable is concerned, it will be necessary for him to consider whether the modern main regime or previous regime applies.

In the private sphere, the main regime applies to all newly settled property except **18.17**

- property held for charitable purposes;[14] and
- property held in a trust for bereaved minors, a pre-1978 protective trust, a pre-1981 trust for disabled persons, or most trusts for the benefit of employees.[15]

Under the main regime, IHT is essentially chargeable on the occasion of any of three **18.18** events: the property going into the trust,[16] each ten-year anniversary of the trust,[17] and on property exiting the trust.[18] Trustees must make a return on the occasion of any of these (even if no IHT is payable) within twelve months of the end of the month in which the transaction occurred, or (if later) within three months of becoming liable for the tax.[19]

There is one potential danger in the realm of discretionary will trusts of which trustees **18.19** ought to be particularly wary. Just as s.142 Inheritance Tax Act 1984 allows for the dispositions under post-death variations of a deceased's estate within two years of the death to be treated as dispositions under the will, so where property is settled by will and there is a chargeable event (eg a distribution giving rise to an exit charge) within two years of the death, IHT is not charged, but rather the Act will have effect as if the will directed it to be held as it is held after the event.[20] Any of the trustees seeking to take advantage of this provision within three months of death though will be disappointed, as there is no charge against which the provision can bite.[21] If, therefore, this is done with the aim of securing an exemption for that property distributed, which is available only during the deceased's life or on their death (eg spouse exemption), the requirements for it will not be met.[22]

Cases outside the relevant property regime

The previous regime, whereby trusts with interest in possession were treated differently **18.20** for inheritance tax purposes, continues to apply to the trusts in which there subsists an interest in possession that arose before 22 March 2006, and on or after 22 March 2006 and is[23]

---

[14] Section 58(1)(a).
[15] Section 58(1)(b).
[16] Section 3A(1A); a transfer to a trust, unless it is a disabled or bereaved minor's trust, is no longer a PET.
[17] Section 64.
[18] Section 65(1).
[19] Sections 216(1)(b) and (6)(c).
[20] Section 144(2).
[21] Section 65(4) disapplying s.65(1).
[22] *Frankland v IRC* [1997] STC 1450 (CA).
[23] Section 49(1A).

- an immediate post-death interest;
- a disabled person's interest;[24] or
- a transitional serial interest.

18.21 An immediate post-death interest is an interest in possession to which the beneficiary became entitled in a settlement established by a will (on the death of a testator), or under the law relating to intestacy (on the death of an intestate), that is not a trust for bereaved minors or a disabled person's trust.[25]

18.22 A transitional serial interest is an interest in possession either: first, in a settlement commenced before 22 March 2006, in which immediately before that date there was an interest in possession which came to an end on or after 22 March 2006 but before 6 October 2008, upon the occasion of which the beneficiary became entitled to an interest in possession;[26] or second, the same conditions are met, except that the prior interest in possession came to an end on or after 6 October 2008 on the death of the person beneficially entitled to that interest.[27]

18.23 Under the old regime, the person beneficially entitled to the interest in possession is treated as being beneficially entitled to the property in which that interest subsists.[28] Thus, on the termination of that interest, either during the lifetime of the beneficiary or on their death, they are charged to IHT. There are, therefore, no ten-year anniversary charges.

Risks and opportunities

18.24 The two regimes being so divergent it is paramount that no mistake is made as to which is to apply to a particular trust. In the past there was a raft of tax-planning strategies that involved short-lived interests in possession, but the attraction of these is much reduced now that the range of 'qualifying' interests in possession (ie those where the beneficiary in possession is treated as owning the property) is so limited. In particular, for a transfer to be potentially exempt (unless it is into a disabled trust or into a bereaved minor's trust on the occasion of an immediate post-death interest coming to an end) it must be to an individual, and in the context of transfers into a trust in which an interest in possession to which the beneficiary became entitled on or after 22 March 2006, that requirement will only be satisfied if there exists in that trust an immediate post-death interest, a disabled person's interest, or a transitional serial interest.

F. Capital gains tax

18.25 UK resident trustees are taxed on any gain they make over and above their annual exemption, which usually will be half that to which an individual is entitled.[29] Aside from this and the application of principal private residence relief to a beneficiary occupying the residence under the terms of the trust, trustees are taxed on actual disposals just as individuals

---

[24] Defined at s.89B.

[25] Section 49A.

[26] Section 49C, as amended by s.141(1) Finance Act 2008.

[27] Section 49D.

[28] Section 49(1).

[29] Section 3(1) and (8), and para 2(2) Sch 1 TCGA 1992: eg for the tax year 2013–14 they are entitled to an annual exemption of £5,540.

are.[30] It should be noted that the transfer of trust property from trustee to trustee on a change of trustees is not a disposal for CGT purposes.[31]

Deemed disposals

Trustees are also taxed on the gain deemed to arise by the 'deemed' disposal that occurs on **18.26** a beneficiary under the trust becoming absolutely entitled to any settled property as against the trustees (ie the trustees become bare trustees because the beneficiary can direct them as to how to deal with the property). On this event, the trustees are deemed to have disposed of the property and immediately reacquired it at market value.[32] While the trustees are taxed on any gain that arises from that deemed disposal, any loss accrues to the beneficiary who becomes so entitled so far as it cannot be deducted from the trustees' pre-entitlement gains (ie when the trustees do not have any gains in the same year against which to set the loss).

It is often overlooked, but should be noted, that even if there is no IHT charge by virtue **18.27** of the fact that the person whose interest comes to an end becomes on the same occasion beneficially entitled to the property,[33] there will still be a deemed disposal for CGT charges, and thus a potential CGT charge, if the beneficiary has become absolutely entitled as against the trustees. There will be a deemed disposal then, when trustees advance assets to a beneficiary, when a beneficiary satisfies a contingency, or when a life tenant dies and the remainderman is absolutely entitled to the capital (although in this latter case no chargeable gain accrues[34]).

Crowe v Appleby *cases*

Whether and when a beneficiary becomes absolutely entitled as against the trustees will need **18.28** to be considered in the light of the particular settlement concerned, and thus the question of whether a deemed disposal has occurred will be a question of fact to be determined in the circumstances of each individual case. A beneficiary can only direct the trustees as to how they should deal with the trust property if they have the right to end the trust of their share by demanding it be transferred to them.[35] To answer the question of absolute entitlement then, it is necessary to consider both the terms of the settlement and the type of property held.

Contingencies and instances where there are multiple beneficiaries can cause particular dif- **18.29** ficulties. If, for example, the trustees have an express power of appropriation, even if any contingency is satisfied and there is no interest prior to that of the beneficiary, the beneficiary will not be absolutely entitled as against the trustees to their share because the property to which they are entitled cannot be ascertained until the power of appropriation is exercised (thus they cannot direct the trustees as to how to deal with that property).[36] Similarly, if distribution of a share to a bare beneficiary would damage the trust fund because the type of

---

[30] Section 225. This includes beneficiaries with an interest in possession, and those occupying under the trustee's power to permit them to occupy: *Samson v Peay (Inspector of Taxes)* [1976] 1 WLR 1073. Exempt assets in an individual's hands are of course exempt assets in a trustee's hands.

[31] Because they are treated as a single person: s.69(1) TCGA 1992.

[32] Section 71(1) TCGA 1992.

[33] Section 53(2) IHTA 1984.

[34] Section 73(1)(a) TCGA 1992.

[35] This is what is meant in the TCGA 1992 by a beneficiary being absolutely entitled as against a trustee: s.60(2).

[36] A corollary of that, of course, is that HMRC cannot know on which property any gain is to be assessed until the appropriation.

property held is not amenable to division without loss of value, the trustees are not bound to act on a beneficiary's direction to so divide, as to do so would breach their fiduciary duties to the other beneficiaries. Thus, on this basis there is no deemed disposal of land until all beneficiaries meet the contingency.[37] HMRC accept this principle extends to other indivisible assets, such as 'an Old Master painting or valuable antique, or indeed a single share in a company'.[38] If the trust property is of such a nature then the trustees should not file a return declaring a deemed disposal until the last contingency is satisfied and *all* the beneficiaries can direct the trustees as to how to deal with their share.

18.30 A warning, though: if the trustees are not restricted in how they deal with the trust property, they may sell such an indivisible asset and because the cash which is then held on the trusts in the place of that asset is divisible, if one of a number of beneficiaries has satisfied his contingency upon sale he will become absolutely entitled to their share of the proceeds, and a deemed disposal will occur. Thus, a deemed disposal is only avoided for so long as the trust property in respect of which a beneficiary has satisfied his contingency is not divisible, so that his interest in a share when it vests remains of an indivisible nature.

The person becoming absolutely entitled as against the trustees

18.31 Finally, it should be noted that the persons who become absolutely entitled to property as against the trustees can include trustees of a different settlement, and this can include the trustees themselves, if they become absolutely entitled to the property in one capacity (eg as trustees of one trust) as against themselves in another capacity (eg as trustees of a separate trust). There is a risk therefore that in exercising a power of appointment or advancement the trustees will unwittingly create a new settlement and make a deemed disposal, giving rise to a CGT charge. The question of whether a new settlement has been created will be approached in a practical common sense way:[39] how wide the power exercised is will be relevant,[40] but so too will the way in which it is exercised.[41] If there is a deemed disposal for CGT purposes, there is also very likely to be an exit charge for IHT purposes.[42]

G. Income tax

18.32 For income tax purposes, the trustees of a settlement are treated as a single person distinct from the trustees for the time being.[43] Generally, trustees are taxed at the basic rate (but at the dividend ordinary rate on dividend income).[44] That general position though, is subject to the special rate of income tax at which trustees are charged on income that must be accumulated or is payable at the discretion of the trustees, or some other person.[45] The rate is 50 per cent.

---

[37] *Crowe v Appleby* [1976] 2 All ER 914; [1976] STC 301.

[38] *HMRC Capital Gains Manual* at CG37560. See *Stephenson v Barclays Bank Ltd* [1975] 1 All ER 625; [1975] STC 151 where it was accepted that otherwise bare beneficiaries of a share in certain property may have to wait until sale of the property to claim distribution.

[39] *Roome v Edwards* [1982] AC 279. See HMRC's *Statement of Practice* 7/84 for their approach.

[40] *Bond v Pickford* [1983] STC 517.

[41] *Swires v Penton* [1991] STC 490.

[42] Section 65(1) IHTA 1984.

[43] Section 474 Income Tax Act 2007.

[44] Section 11(1) Income Tax Act 2007.

[45] Sections 479 and 480 Income Tax Act 2007. There are also other limited types of amounts of income on which trustees are charged at the special rate for trustees: ss. 481 and 482.

Thus, the special trust rate does not apply where there is a beneficiary with a right to the trust income (ie a beneficiary with an interest in possession in the trust fund). The trustees may deduct from their pre-tax income any allowable expenses for income tax purposes, but not trust management expenses, which are paid from net income.

When the special rate for trustees applies

It should be noted that where the trust is a will trust, the special rates for trustees' income do not apply until the trust is properly constituted and this is at the end of the administration period. The income arising from the trust property during the administration period will be properly payable to the trustees at the end of the administration period though, so that any such income received by the trustees must be included in the trustees' first return. The PRs will have paid income tax on such income during the administration period, for which the trustees should claim credit. **18.33**

Identifying the income interest

Where the beneficiary's entitlement to income depends on some contingency or on the trustees exercising their discretion, the beneficiary is taxed only on income they actually receive. Income which is accumulated does not lose its identity as income by virtue of its accumulation though, so that if trustees have a power to advance both accumulated income and capital to a beneficiary, it is necessary, because of the different taxation consequences for both trustees and beneficiary, for them to consider which it is that they are advancing: this is most conveniently done by keeping separate capital and income accounts. As a result of the permanent distinction for tax purposes between capital and income then, and the fact that a beneficiary with no right to income is taxed only on trust income received, the trustees' duty when exercising a discretion over the distribution of the trust fund extends to considering the beneficiary's tax position and the type and timing of any distribution so as to maximize the benefit to the intended recipient. **18.34**

Where the beneficiary has a vested right in income though, they are taxed on the net income as it arises less expenses properly chargeable to income. Statute provides for the incidence of trust management expenses properly chargeable to income (either as a matter of general trust law, or under the trust instrument)[46] to be borne by the different classes of income in a strict order, so that they are deducted first from dividend income, then from savings income, and then from other income.[47] The net income is then grossed up (to reflect tax paid at source, before the income comes in to the trustees' hands, such as on credit interest and dividends) and the beneficiary is taxed on it, receiving a credit for the tax already paid by the trustees, which may result in him 'topping up' the tax, or receiving a repayment. As a result of the statutory provisions as to the allocation of trust management expenses of an income nature to the various types of income, it is necessary to consider the nature of the beneficiary's interest giving rise to a right to income where the right is to less than the whole income. **18.35**

Income of one half or one half of income?

If, for example, there are two beneficiaries each with an interest in half the income the trustees can properly deal with the trust fund as one complete fund. The trustees should submit a **18.36**

---

[46] Section 500(2) Income Tax Act 2007.
[47] Section 503(2) Income Tax Act 2007.

return and meet the tax burden as normal, deduct the trust management expenses properly chargeable to income from it, and then pay half the net amount to each beneficiary. Each beneficiary will be taxed on the grossed up value of the income, but so far as the incidence of the trust management expenses is concerned, they will be deemed to have received half of each type of income received by the trustees.

18.37 In contrast, if a beneficiary's interest is to the income of half the capital, the income of the whole trust fund cannot be taken together and divided for distribution, but rather it must be considered what types of income are created by the specific half of capital in which the interest subsists as this is relevant both to considering which expenses should be borne by the beneficiary's half of income, and how those expenses are allocated. As different tax rates do (or may) apply to different types of income, it cannot be assumed that each of the capital assets of the whole trust fund has been divided equally between the two beneficiaries, such that each beneficiary may receive different types of income.

H. Trustee's position on retiring from the trust

18.38 As a matter of general law, a retiring trustee is not released from his liabilities in respect of his office simply by the fact of his retirement, as the only persons who can give a trustee a discharge are the beneficiaries upon the trust being wound up.[48] Thus, any tax assessed on a trustee during any tax year during which he was trustee will continue to be his liability even after he has retired, and as a matter of tax law, this liability is personal.

18.39 Although the tax legislation makes trustees personally liable for the tax due in respect of the trust property, as a matter of trust law no trustee is expected to bear personally the costs of his office, and a trustee is thus entitled to be paid back from the trust fund all that he has had to pay out:[49] this is now codified at s.31(1) Trustee Act 2000. This right only extends, of course, to expenses properly incurred, but this covers the trustee's proper tax liability as a trustee. Where, however, a tax liability, penalty, or interest was incurred as a result of that trustee's breach of duty, the right to recover will not extend to such payments. To give effect to the trustee's right to repayment, the trustee has a beneficial interest in the trust in the shape of a non-possessory equitable lien to cover the trustee's present and future liabilities in respect of his office.

18.40 This lien takes priority over the claims of the beneficiaries, and ensures the trustee is not left out of pocket by administering the trust according to the instrument creating it. On the trustee's retirement, his lien binds the new and/or continuing trustees, and the retiring trustee is entitled to refuse to transfer trust property to the new trustees until his lien is satisfied. As the retiring trustee's lien also takes priority to the interests of the beneficiaries, a retiring trustee can also refuse to transfer trust property to a beneficiary absolutely entitled to it as against them, until the lien is satisfied.[50] It should be noted though, that on any distribution of trust property to a beneficiary, the trustee must expressly preserve his lien.

---

[48] *Tiger v Barclays Bank Ltd* [1951] 2 KB 556.
[49] *Re Grimthorpe* [1958] Ch 615 at 623 per Danckwerts J.
[50] *X v A* [2000] 1 All ER 490.

I. Trustee's position on retiring and trust migrating abroad

Where a settlement becomes non-UK resident, by virtue of the trustees becoming neither **18.41** resident nor ordinarily resident in the UK, the trustees are deemed to make a disposal of the settled property immediately before such time, reacquiring the settled property at market value. Therefore, there may arise a CGT liability, but the persons liable for it, the trustees, have ceased to be UK resident. If such liability is not discharged within six months of it becoming payable,[51] HMRC may within three years of the time when the tax is finally determined serve a notice requiring payment within thirty days of the tax and interest thereon[52] on anyone who was a trustee within the twelve months preceding the migration of the trust.[53] While such person may recover any such tax from the migrating trustees, any person on whom a notice is served is liable as if the tax was due and duly demanded of them.[54]

Such a notice may be served on someone who ceased to be a trustee during that twelve-month **18.42** period, though only if he cannot show that when he retired as a trustee there was no proposal that the trust would migrate.[55] Given that a decision in respect of the trust as fundamental as its residence is unlikely to be taken in a short time frame, it seems unlikely that such a former trustee would be able to meet this requirement. A retiring trustee must appreciate, therefore, that where it has been proposed that the trust may migrate and they retire from their trusteeship, they are exposed for twelve months to the risk of being assessed to the CGT charge arising on such migration.

J. Trustees' residence and deemed residence

The CGT provisions are, of course, aimed at keeping the settlement, or a taxable party, **18.43** onshore. The rules for determining the residence of a settlement for CGT purposes have thus become stricter, and it is therefore more likely that trustees may unintentionally cause an offshore settlement to come onshore.

Since the tax year 2007–08, a settlement will be onshore for CGT purposes if just one of its **18.44** trustees is resident and the settlor was UK resident, ordinarily resident, or domiciled at the creation of the settlement.[56] Thus, just one trustee who becomes UK resident could bring the entire settlement onshore. The risk is greater in the case of a professional trustee, for he will be treated as UK resident simply by virtue of acting as a trustee in the course of his business carried on through a branch, agency, or permanent establishment in the UK.[57] Any such trustee who thus brings a settlement onshore clearly risks personal liability for the CGT incurred as a result.[58]

---

[51] Section 82(1)(b) TCGA 1992.
[52] Section 82(2).
[53] Sections 82(3) and (6)(b).
[54] Section 82(4).
[55] Section 82(3)(b).
[56] Section 69(2B).
[57] Section 69(2D).
[58] *Green v Cobham* [2002] STC 820.

K. Foreign tax liabilities

18.45   Traditionally, foreign tax assessments are not enforceable against UK trustees in the English courts, though they are of course enforceable against trust property in the relevant jurisdiction. Strictly then, it would not be in the interests of the beneficiaries to pay such tax, and doing so could expose the trustees to a breach of trust claim. However, where the trustees' liability under foreign law is joint and several with the beneficiaries (as with UK IHT) similarly it may be a breach of duty not to pay such tax.

18.46   If all the beneficiaries are adult and *sui juris*, then the trustees can obviously seek their approval. Otherwise though, the dilemma is real. The trustees' position will be much clarified if they are authorized to pay from the trust fund all taxes. Absent this though, it seems the trustees must conduct the normal balancing act of taking into account all the relevant considerations in deciding whether or not to exercise their discretion. Paramount amongst these is the best interests of the beneficiaries, so that if the beneficiaries may be assessed to the tax if it is not met by the trustees, they would appear justified in paying it from the trust fund.

18.47   This traditional position as to non-enforceability no longer applies in relation to tax assessments by the tax authorities of other EC states, so that such assessments can now be enforced in the UK, with the exception only of inheritance/succession taxes,[59] and it must be that the trustees are therefore entitled to discharge the liability from the tax fund without a claim for breach of trust accruing.

18.48   A further concern for trustees will be their potential exposure under the Proceeds of Crime Act 2002 to criminal liability for money laundering. The offences under that Act are so broad as to effectively entail all holding, using, dealings with, and arrangement of 'criminal property', except where done for the purpose of making an authorized disclosure under the Act.[60] 'Criminal property' is defined as property that constitutes a person's benefit from criminal conduct or represents such a benefit (in whole or part and whether directly or indirectly), and the alleged offender knows or suspects that to be the case.[61] Tax evasion being a criminal offence, trustees that know they are holding property that, in breach of the criminal law (whether by them, the beneficiaries, or the settlor), ought to have been used to discharge a tax liability, are brought within the scope of liability under the 2002 Act. On summary conviction the maximum sentence is six months' imprisonment and/or a fine up to the statutory maximum; on conviction on an indictment it is fourteen years' imprisonment and/or an unlimited fine.

L. Conclusions

18.49   It is clear then that tax should be at the forefront of trustees' minds. Not only are there annual returns to make as to income and capital gains, but also returns in respect of capital dealings, whether or not a tax liability arises. Further, while trustees are most certainly under a duty to pay all tax assessments on the trust enforceable in the UK, they may well be under a duty

---

[59] Section 134 Finance Act 2002.
[60] Sections 327–329 Proceeds of Crime Act 2002.
[61] Section 340(3) Proceeds of Crime Act 2002.

not to pay assessments not so enforceable, but cannot rely on this being so, and thus on such an assessment will need to consider carefully the terms of the trust and the position of the beneficiaries.

These twin considerations, amongst others, will also need to be considered when the trust- **18.50** ees are deciding whether or not to exercise their discretion to enter into the transaction or to make the distribution that will lead to the assessment. There can be no doubt the tax consequences, both for the trust and for the beneficiaries, are a proper consideration to be taken into account, and the trustees are very likely to have acted in breach of duty if they exercise their discretion without acting in accordance with, or at least taking into account, tax advice. While the principle in *Hastings-Bass* (as it survives in more restricted form) and/or the doctrine of mistake may in some way relieve the trustees of the effects of such an exercise in breach, achieving such relief is by no means cost free, and absent anything in the trust instrument to the contrary those costs will have to be borne by someone other than the trust fund, be it the trustees or their professional advisers.

19

TAX ADVICE DURING THE LIFETIME OF THE CLIENT

A. Explaining the risk

Where a solicitor's retainer is squarely within the tax planning realm, that is the instructions **19.01** are centred on minimizing a present or future tax liability so that the transactions carried out will be incidental to that aim, the solicitor's duty in relation to tax advice is clear: the provision of such advice is the purpose for which he has been instructed. The duty is less clear though, when a solicitor is instructed in a transaction that is not primarily directed at tax, but that has tax consequences.

As was noted in Chapter 16 in the context of tax advice in the preparation of wills, there is **19.02** a dearth of case law on the solicitor's duty to advise on the tax issues associated with, or tax consequences of, the proposed transaction in which he is instructed. As was begun to be suggested in that chapter, this may be because tax law is notoriously complex. That being the case, where the proposed transaction is not directed primarily at tax matters (so that tax advice is not at the core of the retainer) it is to be hoped that there will be relatively few solicitors who will fall between the two stools of, on the one hand, being competent to deal with the relevant tax issues and, on the other, recognizing that they are out of their depth as far as the tax is concerned, and seeking tax advice from a third party (or not accepting the retainer in the first place).

The risk of acting negligently in relation to tax advice will thus arise in one of two **19.03** situations: either (i) when the solicitor fails to recognize the potential tax consequences at all, or (ii) when the solicitor thinks he recognizes them and mistakenly believes himself capable to deal with them alone. In effect, negligence in tax matters is borne from a little knowledge being a dangerous thing.

B. Defining the duty

19.04 The case law on tax negligence, such as it is, is at least directed at advice and acts in relation to the tax consequences of *inter vivos* transactions, so that it is not necessary to perform the same exercise in extrapolation as in Chapter 16, which considers tax in will preparation. The leading case on the duty of care of a solicitor is *Hurlingham Estates Ltd v Wilde & Partners*.[1]

19.05 The solicitor, the conveyancing and commercial partner in his firm, was instructed by a number of related parties (which relationships were known to the solicitor) in a chain of transactions, in which, as the solicitor realized, Hurlingham was to be an intermediate profit/loss neutral personality. In fact, the transaction attracted a charge to tax of £69,455.36 levied on Hurlingham by virtue of s.34(1) Taxes Act 1988, of which the solicitor did not advise Hurlingham. It is important to note that it would have been possible to structure the transaction in another way, without altering its substance, thereby avoiding any charge to tax.

19.06 The judge, Lightman J, was withering in his criticism of what he no doubt saw as both the solicitor's rank incompetence, and his exaggerated defence that he had limited the scope of his retainer to exclude tax advice. He is described in the judgment as having 'next to no knowledge of tax law', and being 'quite unqualified to give tax advice or to appreciate, or give any warning as to the existence of any risk of any adverse tax consequences of any transaction'. Lightman J said:

> I find it difficult to comprehend how a solicitor possessed of no real knowledge of tax law can be allowed to occupy [the position of conveyancing and commercial partner] ... certainly it must be questionable whether he should be allowed to do so if any regard is to be paid to the safety of the public.

Hurlingham Estates then, is a case within the first of the two situations described above.

19.07 Whichever of the two situation risks giving rise to negligence though, the *Hurlingham Estates* construction of the ordinary duty owed to the client in respect of tax advice in a transaction not primarily directed at tax matters is the same. It can be easily summarized as a two-part duty, thus:

1. Where the client does not have a structure for the transaction in mind, it is a duty to advise on the most tax-efficient form to achieve the end in respect of which he instructed (the 'substance' of the instructions).
2. Where the client already has a structure in mind, it is a duty to advise of any liability to tax he would incur as a result of that structure, and to advise of any alteration to the form rather than the substance of the transaction that would result in the avoidance or reduction of that liability.

19.08 An example of instructions invoking the first part of the duty would be 'I want my son to have £100,000 of mine'. Here, the client knows that in substance he wishes his son to have the benefit of £100,000, but he does not express any particular form for the transaction by which he intends to achieve his wish. It is therefore for the solicitor to fill this gap by suggesting the form that attracts least tax. A similar instruction that would invoke the second part of the duty would be 'I want to place £100,000 into trust for my son upon him reaching

---

[1] [1997] 1 Lloyd's Rep 525.

twenty-five years of age'. Here, the client has in advance of instructing the solicitor a clear idea of the form as well as the substance of the transaction. It is therefore for the solicitor to make the client aware of the tax consequences of that proposed form, and to suggest the most tax-efficient alternative while still achieving the substance.

In the above examples it is relatively easy to distinguish between the form and the substance **19.09** of the transaction. But what is the solicitor's duty when it is not so easy? Take, for example, the instruction 'I want to place £100,000 into trust for my son': is the substance of the transaction that the son has the benefit of the money (so that there is a broad choice as to the form), or is it that the management of the money be out of his hands (so that the choice as to form is more limited)? The end being paramount, it is clear that in the case of lifetime advice (as in the case of will preparation) for a solicitor to understand and discharge his duty to give tax advice in relation to a particular transaction or retainer it is vital that he understands his client's desires, motivations, and reasoning. Once these are identified, the forms of transaction available to achieve the substance may have been reduced. To choose the most tax efficient amongst them, the solicitor will then (as he would in will preparation) need to understand the client's financial and tax circumstances.

To summarize, in all cases the solicitor's duty in relation to tax advice, in transactions not directed **19.10** primarily at tax, is to recognize, advise the client of, and suggest alternative methods of avoiding or minimizing the tax implications that flow naturally from the transactions that the solicitor is instructed to effect or that are necessary to the ends he is instructed to achieve. On a practical level then (as with taking instructions to prepare a will), this will require an interview taking in the client's circumstances, the motivation for the instructions, and the desired outcome.

This raises one final question: does this mean there is a duty to save tax? When one con- **19.11** siders that the duty as formulated above includes a duty to minimize tax, and a duty to suggest alternative forms of transaction to do this, the answer is yes. However, when one considers that the duty does not extend to altering the substance of the proposed transaction it is clear that to state 'there is a duty to save tax' is too broad. The duty is to advise of the most tax-efficient method of achieving the substance of the proposed transaction, and does not extend to advising of other transactions of a different substance that would result in even less tax. The duty is to minimize, not save.

C. Limiting the duty

The duty that emerges from *Hurlingham Estates* as described above was referred to as the **19.12** 'ordinary duty'. When, then, can an extraordinary duty arise, and how does it differ from the ordinary duty?

It is clear from *Hurlingham Estates* that the ordinary duty can be limited by expressly exclud- **19.13** ing from the scope of the retainer from the outset the provision of tax advice.[2] This, however, is an onerous task and requires the fully informed consent of the client, which necessarily requires the solicitor to inform the client of the lacuna in his legal knowledge.[3] A clear and

---

[2] After all, 'A man cannot be said voluntarily to be undertaking a responsibility if at the very moment when he is said to be accepting it he declares that in fact he is not' (per Lord Pearce in *Hedley-Byrne & Co Ltd v Heller & Partners Ltd* [1964] AC 465 at 533).
[3] *Hurlingham Estates* (n 1) at 529.

unambiguous agreement to exclude tax advice from the retainer should be evidenced by first, an attendance note of the meeting at which the agreement was made, and second a letter subsequently sent to the client confirming the agreement. The letter allows the client to consider his position and its implications away from any constraints imposed by the presence of the solicitor.[4] Asking for a written reply to this letter, confirming the truth of its contents and signed by the client, would be wise: this could be achieved by enclosing an acknowledgement slip.

19.14 Of course, waiting for a reply from the client delays the solicitor starting work on the client's instructions: there is then a tension between the duty to act in good time, and the best practice requirements for clarifying and limiting the retainer, and there is no easy answer as to how to strike the proper balance. Obviously, the client should be chased for their reply to the letter setting out the scope of the retainer, and if there is no urgency to the transaction the solicitor can afford to wait longer for this. Where time becomes pressing though, the solicitor must be best advised to press ahead with the work: after all, the limitations on the retainer have already been discussed and agreed with the client, and at the core of the retainer must be effecting the proposed transaction in the form instructed or in the most common form.

19.15 There is of course a risk that by the solicitor seeking the fully informed consent of the client to exclude from their retainer the provision of advice in relation to the tax consequences of the contemplated transaction, the client will go elsewhere to find an adviser competent in all the matters relevant to the transaction. In the private client field though, this is by no means always the case: there will be those clients who do not wish to meet the extra fees likely to be associated with tax advice (perhaps because they do not consider their estate large enough, or the dispositions of it they propose complicated enough, to warrant it) and those 'who consider that tax avoidance is something rather unattractive'.[5]

19.16 If the client is amenable, the steps a solicitor must follow to conclude an agreement to limit the retainer as divined from *Hurlingham Estates* are:

1. Make clear to the client there is a lacuna in his legal knowledge relating to the law of tax.
2. Make clear to the client that this is not a lacuna that is to be expected of a solicitor having the conduct of a transaction such as that contemplated.
3. Make clear that the client's interests might require him to instruct another solicitor who is competent and does not need to insist on such a limitation on his services and duties.
4. If the client is still in the room and agrees to such a limitation, record the terms of the agreement in the attendance note of that meeting.
5. After the meeting write to the client recording the terms of the agreement as concluded at the meeting and inviting him to consider his position and its implications.
6. (Probably) ask him to reply to that letter in writing confirming he understands the limitations of the solicitor's retainer as set out and agrees to them.

---

[4] *Hurlingham Estates* (n 1) at 526.
[5] '[T]o be indulged in by sharp people with connections in the City of London who use various arcane devices to get out of their proper obligations to the Crown' (*Cancer Research Campaign v Ernest Brown & Co* [1997] STC 1425 at 1430E; [1998] PNLR 592 at 597 per Harman J).

The solicitor is not under such a burden, of course, when he is certain that advice as to the **19.17**
tax consequences of the transaction contemplated and advice as to how the form of the
transaction may be altered to improve the tax position is to be taken from a source other than
himself. This may be from another member of his own firm, or from another professional
engaged by the client.[6] This cannot be assumed, but must be reasonably apparent with regard
to all the circumstances which are known or should reasonably be known.[7] Clearly in such
circumstances best practice is to follow the guideline advice at 4, 5, and 6 above, with respect
to recording the understanding as to the division of advice.

Otherwise, a solicitor is likely to be excused from the ordinary duty only if it was reasonable **19.18**
for him to assume that the client either had the requisite tax knowledge himself, or would be
obtaining tax advice from another source. It seems very unlikely that it would be reasonable
to assume this if the client is a private individual. It is likely to be reasonable though, if the
client is 'a high profile, successful commercial entity with considerable in-house expertise in
taxation matters and was properly equipped to consider and take appropriate action to deal
with the tax implications of their property transactions'.[8]

D. Discharging the duty

There is, then, some practical guidance that can be discerned from *Hurlingham Estates* in the **19.19**
form of questions for the solicitor to consider:

1. Could a tax burden arise from the substance of the transaction he is instructed to carry
   out or suggested, or is he not sure that one will not?
2. If so, has the client already taken tax advice?
3. If he has not, is the solicitor competent to advise on the avoidance or minimization of tax
   issues naturally arising from the transaction?
4. If he is not, is there support in the shape of sufficient knowledge available from elsewhere
   within his firm?
5. If the answers to questions 2, 3, and 4 are 'no', does the client understand
   (i)   the extent of the solicitor's tax knowledge;
   (ii) that he needs fuller tax advice than the solicitor can provide;
   (iii) that other solicitors may have better tax knowledge;
   (iv) that his interests might be best served by instructing a more competent solicitor?
6. If the answers to questions 2, 3, and 4 are 'no', are the matters referred to under question 5
   recorded in the attendance note of the meeting at which they were discussed and agreed,
   and have they been recorded in a letter subsequently sent to the client?
7. If the answer to any of questions 2, 3, or 4 is 'yes', has the person giving the tax advice
   considered whether the form of the transaction could be changed, without changing its
   substance, so as to avoid or minimize the consequential tax liability?
8. If the tax adviser has suggested an alternative structure for the transaction, does this
   alternative structure bring with it any other risks or pros/cons from a (non-tax) legal
   perspective?

---

[6] *Cancer Research Campaign v Ernest Brown & Co* (n 5) at 530.
[7] This will include the type of client.
[8] *Virgin Management Ltd v De Morgan Group plc* [1996] NPC 8.

E. The client's circumstances

19.20 Necessary to discharging the solicitor's duty and giving the client proper tax advice is under-standing his circumstances, financial and personal, past, present, and planned for the future. The proper taking of instructions will thus encompass a wide-ranging enquiry into the cli-ent's financial position (business, personal, capital, debts, income, and expenditure) in order to build up a detailed picture of his personal wealth 'portfolio'. It will also encompass a full investigation into the client's relationships (business, platonic, familial—dependent and otherwise—marital, and extra-marital) in order to construct a corresponding picture of what may be termed his 'social portfolio'. Given the impact that can be made on tax planning by the nature and value of assets, and the nature of relationships (both in the sense of exemp-tions and reliefs that attach to these, and in the sense of the scope they may afford in imple-menting tax-planning schemes), it is only by placing these two pictures side by side that a solicitor will be able to fully discharge any duty he is under to give tax advice.

19.21 Two particular personal factors that will impact upon a client's tax position and/or the scope for tax planning at the most fundamental level—whether he is, or his property is, caught by the legislation at all—should be at the top of the list of questions for an initial consult-ation: residence and domicile.

Residence

19.22 A person is only liable to CGT or income tax if he is resident or ordinarily resident.[9] If he is UK resident, or ordinarily resident, and UK domiciled (as to which, see paras 19.26–19.29 below) he will be liable for CGT on his worldwide gains. Thus, if the client is neither resident nor ordinarily resident in the UK, CGT will not be a relevant consideration when giving tax advice. Similarly, if the client is on the cusp of becoming resident or ordinarily resident, he can be advised how to avoid this and about the tax benefits it will bring.

19.23 Residence for tax purposes is strictly defined, and thus, on the positive side, is relatively easy to advise on. On the negative side though, this strictness means it is easy to fall foul of the rules. Briefly, any person who spends more than 183 days in the UK in the tax year is UK resident for that tax year. Any person who has left the UK and is now resident abroad but who spends on average more than ninety-one days in the UK per tax year will continue to be treated as UK resident; anyone who over a four-year period spends on average more than ninety-one days in the UK per tax year will also be considered UK resident. Any person coming to the UK with an intention to settle permanently is UK resident from his day of arrival.

19.24 The question of ordinary residence is more fluid, and requires a consideration of whether the person has established a settled pattern whereby his presence in the UK has been voluntar-ily adopted as part of the order of his life.[10] The usefulness of that test has been doubted, though, and may depend on the circumstances in which it is to be applied: it was applied in the context of the Education Act 1962, but was rejected in the context of the Mental Health Act 1983.

---

[9] Section 2(1) Taxation of Chargeable Gains Act 1992 (TCGA 1992).
[10] *Shah v Barnet London Borough Council* [1983] 2 AC 309; [1983] 2 WLR 216; [1983] 1 All ER 226.

At the time of writing, the Finance (No. 2) Bill 2013 is yet to receive Royal Assent and **19.25** accordingly the statutory residence test ('SRT') included in it is yet to become law. The test is quite straightforward, albeit rather 'wordy', and by HMRC's own admission, is designed to 'replicate as far as possible the residency outcomes delivered by the current rules'. In essence, the SRT will provide a more structured approach to determining residence, by applying a three-stage test. First, if the person in question meets any one of three criteria in a tax year, then he is 'automatically' non-resident for that tax year. Second, if not, then if the person meets any one of three other criteria in a tax year, then he is 'automatically' resident for that tax year. Finally, if he meets none of those criteria, the question of residency is determined by a 'sufficient ties' test, which is based on number of days in the UK and number of UK 'ties'.

Domicile

The client's domicile will affect his liability to pay both capital and income taxes. Even if he **19.26** is UK resident or ordinarily resident, a non-UK domiciled person will pay CGT and income tax only on income or gains remitted to the UK.[11] Further, property outside the UK to which he is beneficially entitled will not be caught by the IHT legislation.[12] In contrast to residence, there is not a separate body of law (statutory or common) defining domicile for tax purposes; rather domicile is determined under the general law. It is not to be equated with residence or nationality: these are separate from, and will not determine, domicile, but may affect it.

If the question of ordinary residence is fluid, considering the question of domicile is like **19.27** catching butterflies. Every person is born with a domicile of origin, namely the domicile of their father if born legitimately, or their mother if illegitimately. This may be displaced by a domicile of choice. A domicile of choice is established by physical presence in a territory, and an intention to permanently remain there: nothing less will do. Evidence of the intention element of domicile requires a retrospective appraisal of the client's life;[13] every detail is capable of contributing to the overall picture, and even elements that are insignificant to the client may prove to be of great weight.[14] What must be considered is whether the client intends in the normal course of events to stay where he is.[15] Links retained with the territory of his previous domicile may inform this. Presence for a limited time, or for a particular purpose (which purpose may cease), prevents the necessary intention, as does an intention to leave on the happening of a reasonably likely event (ie diagnosis with a terminal illness, but not a lottery win).

It is, it must be said, an exceptionally foolish adviser who purports to give a certain view of a **19.28** client's domicile while he is still alive: it is a question that cannot be answered in stages, but is best considered after death, when it is possible to

> look back at the whole of the deceased's life, at what he had done with his life, at what life had done to him and at what were his inferred intentions in order to decide whether he had acquired a domicile of choice in England by the date of his death. Soren Kierkegaard's aphorism that 'Life must be lived forwards, but can only be understood backwards' resonates in the biographical data of domicile disputes.[16]

---

[11] Section 12(1) TCGA 1992, ss.831 and 832 Income Tax (Trading and Other Income) Act 2005.
[12] Section 6(1) Inheritance Tax Act 1984 (IHTA 1984).
[13] *Agulian v Cyganik* [2006] WTLR 565 at 575F–G per Mummery LJ.
[14] *Drevon v Drevon* (1864) 34 LJ Ch 129 at 133.
[15] *Bell v Bell* [1922] 2 IR 152.
[16] *Agulian v Cyganik* (n 13).

19.29   The question takes in such varied and multiple considerations that the best that can be given is an indication of likely domicile at the moment in time it is given, and nothing more: anything approaching certainty is possible only after the person has died. This uncertainty is demonstrated by two contrasting cases. In *Morris v Davies*[17] the fact that the deceased had not adopted Belgian culture or learnt the language led to the inference that he would cease to live there at weekends (after weeks spent living and working in France) if it became inconvenient—notwithstanding he had purchased a house there that he was renovating with his Belgian fiancée. By contrast, in *Holliday v Musa*[18] the evidence of the deceased's sentiments of feeling a part of the UK outweighed his expressed intentions to return to Cyprus eventually, such that he had acquired an English domicile of choice in place of his Cypriot domicile of origin. Thus, for the purposes of lifetime advice, the professional should limit himself to advising of the factors that will be taken into account by anyone wishing to determine the client's domicile, and the particular relative weight each is likely to be given. So far as possible, conclusions are best avoided.

F. Inheritance tax

19.30   The bulk of lifetime tax advisory work not directed at the tax implications of a particular transaction that the client wishes to achieve for its own sake will be directed at the client's ultimate IHT bill on his death; at passing on as much of his accumulated wealth to his chosen beneficiaries as possible, with the minimum amount diverted to the Treasury coffers. This will go hand in hand with will preparation. Generally, the aim will be to reduce the client's estate for IHT purposes by making pre-death transfers that do not attract an IHT charge so that the IHT payable on the death estate is minimized.

19.31   For IHT purposes, it ought to be borne in mind that a person's estate includes all the property to which he is beneficially entitled, less his liabilities.[19] Note, if he is domiciled in the UK, it is irrelevant whether the property is in the UK or elsewhere (although if it is in another jurisdiction and is liable to tax there, there may be a double taxation treaty relieving one of the taxes). Property to which the client is 'beneficially entitled' includes pre-22 March 2006 interests in possession and post-21 March 2006 interests in possession that are immediate post-death interests (IPDI), disabled person's interests, or transitional serial interests (TSI).[20] It also includes non-settled property over which the client has a general power of appointment.

19.32   By way of definition, an IPDI is an interest in possession in a settlement created by will that came into being after 21 March 2006 on the death of the testator/intestate;[21] a disabled person's interest is an interest in possession in a trust for disabled persons;[22] and a TSI is an interest in possession in a settlement (that commenced before 22 March 2006) that either (i) came into being between 22 March 2006 and 6 October 2008 (on the coming to an end of a prior interest in possession that had subsisted immediately before 22 March 2006),[23] or

---

[17] [2011] EWHC 1773 (Ch).
[18] [2010] EWCA Civ 335.
[19] Section 5(1), (3), (4), and (5) IHTA 1984.
[20] Section 5(1A).
[21] Section 49A.
[22] Section 89B.
[23] Section 49C.

(ii) came into being after 6 October 2008 if the previous interest came to an end on the death of the spouse or civil partner of the person now entitled to the TSI.[24]

Potentially exempt transfers

Although the donor, of course, has available his annual exemption,[25] and a nil-rate band,[26] **19.33** it is possible to take advantage of these provisions only to a limited degree, so that once the financial cap is exceeded, IHT may be chargeable. The simplest way to reduce the estate to an unlimited degree is by making outright lifetime gifts to those the client would wish to benefit by their will anyway. Essentially, so long as these gifts are to an individual (or are gifts into a disabled trust, or are gifts on the occasion of an IPDI coming to an end into a bereaved minor's trust)[27] or are of property that becomes comprised in the estate of another individual,[28] they will not be a transfer of value giving rise to an immediate IHT charge, but rather will be potentially exempt from IHT. Thus, a PET may be to an individual outright, or into a trust in which there subsists an IPDI, disabled person's interest, or TSI.

A transfer will not be potentially exempt, though, if it is into a trust that falls within the rele- **19.34** vant property regime of entry, exit, and ten-yearly charges. These are most commonly discretionary trusts, but post 21 March 2006 include trusts with interest in possession, unless that interest came into possession pre 22 March 2006 or is an IPDI, disabled person's interest, or TSI. Where a transfer into a settlement is considered, then, it is therefore crucial to understand the nature of the interest that exists in that settlement, and to determine whether or not it falls within the relevant property regime. Failure to advise the client that a proposed transfer into a settlement in the relevant property regime will be an immediately chargeable transfer, rather than a PET, and to advise of the type of settlement into which a gift would be a PET, will result in an immediate charge to tax that was almost certainly avoidable, and for which the negligent adviser will thus be liable.[29]

A PET will only become entirely exempt from IHT if the donor survives for seven years **19.35** from the date of the gift.[30] However, on failure of the PET by reason of the death of the donor within seven years of the gift, an IHT saving will still be made if the donor survived three years from the date of the gift, by operation of taper relief (with the saving increasing with every subsequent year of survival).[31] It will be seen, then, that PETs are not an effective tax-planning tool for those whose deaths are relatively imminent (ie likely to be within three years) as there is no saving over a transfer on death, and the deceased will not have had the benefit of the property in the meantime.

PETs are most effective when made by healthy, relatively young clients who do not need the **19.36** property to meet their own needs. They are inappropriate for aged or seriously ill clients, or those of limited means. It should be noted that it is possible to insure against the IHT arising on the failure of a PET, and this of course will be most cost effective when the potential IHT liability is high, but the likelihood of failure low.

---

[24] Section 49D.
[25] Section 19(1).
[26] Section 7 and Sch 1.
[27] Section 3A(1A).
[28] Section 3A(2).
[29] See *Estill v Cowling Swift & Kitchin (a firm)* [2000] WTLR 417.
[30] Section 3A(4).
[31] Section 7(4).

Gifts with reservation

19.37 The tension between the desire to reduce the estate for IHT purposes so as to minimize the bill on death, and the need to have the property in the estate available during the client's lifetime for his maintenance has historically led to a variety of schemes which sought to divest the donor of the ownership of property for the purposes of calculating IHT without denying them the use of it for the rest of their life.

19.38 Not surprisingly, legislation was enacted directed at keeping such 'artificial' disposals within the IHT net, and such provisions now provide traps for the unwary, who may make dispositions not aimed primarily at 'cheating' HMRC, but who will still be caught by their effect.

Application

19.39 The gifts with reservation (GWR) provisions apply where a donor makes a gift but the donee does not take up possession and enjoyment to the exclusion of the donor of the property gifted at the date of the gift, or at the latest seven years before the donor's death.[32] If the provisions apply, the donor is at his death treated as being beneficially entitled to the property,[33] and it will thus form part of his estate; for example, if a parent makes a gift of his house to his child, who may even move in, but continues to live in the house himself.

Exclusion

19.40 The GWR provisions are best avoided by ensuring any continued use, occupation, or enjoyment of the gifted property by the donor is either excluded or is for full consideration. Thus, if the parent mentioned above gifted his house to his child, but continued to live in the house, the GWR provisions could be excluded by the parent paying a full market rent of the house to the child.[34] The payment of full consideration must continue for the entire period of occupation or enjoyment, and thus regular reviews (possibly with provision for determination by an expert, or certainly with provision for reference to a property prices or rent index) should be held. If the parent did not wish to pay rent, the GWR provisions could be avoided only by his ceasing to occupy the house.

Special case of land

19.41 Special provision is made by the legislation in the case of gifts of an undivided share of an interest in land. Although there is prima facie a reservation of benefit in respect of the gifted share, this is not the case if (as above) the donor ceases to occupy the land, or occupies to the exclusion of the donee for full consideration.[35] There is a further exception from the GWR provisions though, if the donee occupies the land with the donor. If that is the case, then so long as the donor does not receive any non-negligible benefit provided by or at the expense of the donee, for some reason connected with the gift, there will be no GWR problem.[36] To avoid such a benefit it will be necessary then for the donor and donee to contribute to the running costs of the house according to the actual incidence of those costs: so if the donor gives away 75 per cent of his interest to the donee, who moves in with him, the donor should

---

[32] Section 102(1) and (2) Finance Act 1986.
[33] Section 102(3) Finance Act 1986. Note though, that the provisions do not apply if the gift is an exempt transfer (eg between spouses): s.102(5).
[34] Paragraph 6(1)(a) Sch 20 Finance Act 1986. See *HMRC Inheritance Tax Manual* IHTM14341 as to the requirements for 'full consideration' so far as HMRC are concerned.
[35] Section 102B(3) Finance Act 1986.
[36] Section 102B(4) Finance Act 1986.

pay 50 per cent of the running costs, as these are connected to his occupation, rather than his interest. Indeed, if the donee can still be said to occupy the land, but does so less than the donor (perhaps he is in the armed forces, and so away for long periods), it will be necessary for the donor to pay for more than 50 per cent of the running costs, as more than 50 per cent of them are attributable to his occupation.

Practical considerations

Before the client makes a gift then, consider: 19.42

1. Is the transfer one of the exempt transfers listed at s.102(5) Finance Act 1986?
2. If not, does the donor intend to give up all his possession or enjoyment of the property?
3. If not, does he intend to pay full consideration for his possession and enjoyment, and is there a process in place whereby the market value is determined and kept under review?
4. If not, is the property intended to be gifted an undivided share in an interest in land?
5. If it is, is it intended the donee will take up occupation with the donor?
6. If so, the donor must ensure he contributes fully to the running costs of the property according to their incidence, so that he does not receive any benefit from the donee's occupation at his expense: err on the side of caution and pay too much.

Pre-owned assets tax (POAT)

So far as property escapes the IHT regime, including the GWR provisions, it may be subject   19.43
to POAT, which is an income tax charge on the benefits enjoyed by a person ('the Chargeable Person') in land, chattels, or settled intangible property he has owned since 17 March 1986. Note though, that if the GWR provisions prima facie apply, but it is not considered that the property is subject to a reserved benefit (eg because the gift is an exempt transfer, or because full consideration is paid, or because the gift was of an undivided share in land and the donor and donee occupy that land together without a non-negligible benefit accruing to the donor at the donee's expense), the gift is still within the IHT/GWR regime so as to exclude the operation of the POAT regime.

Application

Briefly, a charge to POAT will arise where property is occupied by the chargeable person and   19.44
the chargeable person satisfies either the disposal or contribution condition.[37] The disposal condition is satisfied if either (i) the chargeable person has since 17 March 1986 owned or owned an interest in the property, or (ii) another person acquired the property by the application (directly or indirectly) of the proceeds of sale of property owned by the chargeable person since 17 March 1986, and the chargeable person disposed of all or part of his interest in the property otherwise than by an excluded transaction.[38] The contribution condition is met if the chargeable person after 17 March 1986 directly or indirectly other than by an excluded transaction provides another person with any of the consideration that person gives for an interest in the property occupied, or any other property the proceeds of which are used by that person to acquire the property or an interest in it.[39]

---

[37] Paragraphs 3(1) (in respect of land) and 6(1) (in respect of chattels) Sch 15 Finance Act 2004.
[38] Paragraphs 3(2) (in respect of land) and 6(2) (in respect of chattels). See para 10(1) for the excluded transactions, which include some of the IHT-exempt transfers.
[39] Paragraphs 3(3) (land) and 6(3) (chattels). See para 10(2) for excluded transactions for these purposes.

19.45 It will be noted, then, that the POAT provisions go beyond the GWR provisions, in that they trace gifts of cash and property which are used, or the proceeds of which are used, to acquire property for the occupation, whether alone or with other persons, of the originator of that cash or property. The charge is of income tax on 'the chargeable amount'; in the case of land, this is the appropriate rental value (less any actual payments the chargeable person is obliged to pay to the owner of the land in respect of his occupation),[40] and in the case of chattels it is the interest it is deemed would be payable on a cash value of the asset (less any actual payments the chargeable person is obliged to pay to the owner of the chattel in respect of his occupation).[41]

Intention irrelevant

19.46 Where gifts of cash or property are made to individuals in the course of tax planning, then, even where there is no intention to occupy them or property acquired with the proceeds of them, there remains a risk of a future POAT charge. This is because the POAT regime does not operate on intention. Take, for example, the late middle-aged donor who in 1997 makes a PET of £100,000 to his adult child, who uses the money to buy a house; ten years later the donor is too old and frail to live alone and moves in with his child. The donor is exposed to a POAT charge on his occupation of his child's home.

G. Capital gains tax

19.47 Although it is generally IHT avoidance at which tax planning is directed, the transfers necessary to put in place such planning and avoidance are likely to have an effect for the other capital tax, CGT. This is because while IHT broadly taxes diminutions in a person's estate, CGT broadly taxes increases to a person's estate; CGT achieves this by taxing the gain that arises on the disposal of assets. To this end, it is largely irrelevant whether the disposal has actually led to a gain, as the CGT makes provision for calculating the gain that would have been made, and deems such a gain to have been made. This CGT effect therefore must be taken into account not only in those transactions where it would be a natural consideration (ie sales), but also in those transactions which might be considered more properly the realm of IHT (ie gifts).

19.48 In addition to being a PET, a gift to an individual or a sale at undervalue, so far as it is not of an excluded asset (most notably cash),[42] will be a deemed disposal at market value for CGT purposes even though the donor receives no consideration for his disposal of the assets.[43] Thus, while IHT may be avoided, CGT will be charged at 18 per cent (or possibly 28 per cent) on any deemed gain,[44] unless the property or the donee attracts an exemption or relief.

19.49 For CGT purposes then, the most attractive property for tax planning by way of outright gifts is cash or the donor's principal private residence. In the case of cash, this is because it is not a chargeable asset. In the case of the principal private residence, this is because any gain

---

[40] Paragraph 4(1).
[41] Paragraph 7(1).
[42] Section 21(1)(b) TCGA 1992.
[43] Section 17(1).
[44] Section 4.

made on the market value of the residence at the time of gift over the acquisition cost will not be a chargeable gain,[45] but the market value at the time of the gift will be the acquisition cost for the donee. Thus, neither the donor on the occasion of the gift, nor the donee on the occasion of his later disposal of the residence, will be taxed to CGT on the proportion of the gain during the donor's period of ownership.

After the principal private residence and cash, business property will be the most attract- **19.50** ive property (in CGT terms) of which to make a gift. This is because on an election by the donor and donee on a gift of business property, the gain made on the deemed disposal can be held over, so that the donor's disposal cost and the donee's acquisition is treated as being the market value, less the gain.[46] Further, although the donee's chargeable gain on an actual disposal will be higher than if the hold-over relief election was not made, he can of course elect to receive further hold-over relief if he instead makes a gift of the property, and the increased gain will anyway be wiped out by the death uplift if he still owns the property at his death.[47]

Business property includes any asset used for the purposes of a trade, profession, or voca- **19.51** tion carried on by the donor of the property or his personal company (or a subsidiary thereof) and shares or securities of the donor's personal company or that are not listed.[48] It is important to note that listed shares are not business property. Business property does expressly include property that would attract the IHT agricultural property exemption, though.[49]

Of course, a client's business or agricultural property may be required to provide him with **19.52** an income during his lifetime, and may anyway enjoy IHT exemption or relief on his death, so that there is little to be gained from a lifetime transfer. As with IHT considerations above, there is little sense in a client divesting himself of property in the course of tax planning if there is a chance he may need it himself in the future.

H. Conclusions

The professional's duty in relation to advising on matters of taxation is clearer in the case **19.53** of lifetime transactions than in the preparation of a will. For the private client professional, taxation advice will very often be at the core of his retainer, as he will be instructed in trans- actions expressly directed at tax planning, so that the duty he owes to the client will clearly encompass advising both on the tax consequences of any transaction proposed by the client and on alternative transactions that may be even more tax efficient.

If the transaction is not so expressly directed, the private client professional is likely to be **19.54** well versed in tax law, so that the tax consequences and alternatives of his instructions are well understood by him. Even here though, there lies a risk in the professional taking too narrow a view of the retainer, and too broad a view of his own tax knowledge. The risk is of course even greater for the more general practitioner, who may have limited exposure to

---

[45] Section 223(1).
[46] Section 165(4).
[47] Section 62(1).
[48] Section 165(2).
[49] Section 165(5).

the type of tax planning the client wants, and the tax consequences of the transactions it requires, that a more experienced or specialist practitioner may more readily identify. Here the risk is more that the professional fails to identify tax risks, or else begins to identify them but is persuaded by the threat of losing the business to tackle them despite lacking sufficient expertise. In both cases, best practice demands the same response: if in doubt as to the tax consequences of the proposed transaction (or even if it seems there are none) and/or as to your own competence in matters of tax law, limit the retainer to exclude tax advice, and/or bring in a tax expert. Tax is a minefield into which the unprotected should not venture.

Part E

LITIGATION

20

INTRODUCTION AND PROCEDURE

A. Introduction

The first Part of this book concentrates on the practitioner avoiding a negligence claim. **20.01** However, the fact of the matter is that negligence actions still abound and while the last few years have seen fewer cases in this area, particularly *White v Jones* cases, that is not because claims are not made, but because there have been fewer points of principle to fight over.

The nature of the claim may vary considerably. It may be a claim by a disappointed beneficiary **20.02** where a will-drafter failed to draft a will in time; it may be a claim that the will was badly drafted. There may be a claim that a practitioner has failed to give tax advice or has drafted a document, such as a deed of variation, incorrectly so that the tax advantage is lost. There may be a claim arising out of the advice given during the administration of an estate, although it is always important to distinguish between a claim made against a solicitor acting for lay PRs, which will clearly be a claim based on negligence, and a claim made against a professional who has himself taken the grant. The latter will usually take the form of an administration action where the procedures are different. The same distinction applies in relation to actions concerning trusts and it is important to identify from the outset precisely the nature of the action against the professional: is it a claim against him for breach of trust or negligence in the advice he has given trustees?

This chapter deals with claims in negligence, whether they are claims based on tort or con- **20.03** tract. Administration and breach of trust claims are dealt with elsewhere. The object of the chapter is to take the reader first through the course of an action and then to deal with the specific subjects of limitation, assessment of damages, and mitigation, which are often to the forefront of this sort of claim.

B. Ascertaining the claim

The earlier parts of this book deal of course in detail with the nature of the claim that the **20.04** estate, disappointed beneficiary, trustee, or PR may bring against the negligent draftsman.

To summarize, the estate will be able to sue in contract[1] if it has suffered loss as well as in tort. Trustees and PRs suing their advisers are also able to sue both in contract and tort. After some judicial comment to the contrary it is clear that the duties owed in tort and contract are concomitant.[2] For disappointed beneficiaries who were never in a contractual relationship with the will-drafter, the cause of action is clearly in tort alone.[3] The issue as to whether beneficiaries can sue the advisers of trustees and PRs directly in tort is not yet clear.[4]

20.05   It is important at the outset to identify who has a claim and the basis on which it is to be brought. One of the crucial questions to ask is: who has suffered a loss and on what basis they are entitled to claim? While cases such as *White v Jones* have attempted to remedy the injustice where the obvious person to sue is not the person who has suffered loss, there may still be circumstances which are explored below where there is a lacuna.

Pre-action period

Pre-action protocol

20.06   There is a pre-action protocol[5] designed specifically for professional negligence claims which will apply to claims made against professionals in the private client field. The idea behind pre-action protocols under the civil procedure reforms, which came into effect on 26 April 1999, was to ensure the maximum amount of exchange of information prior to the commencement of actions. The stated objects of the professional negligence protocol are to ensure

> that the parties are on an equal footing ... saving expense ... dealing with the dispute in ways which are proportionate: ... to the amount of money involved ... to the importance of the case ... to the complexity of the issues ... to the financial position of each party ... ensuring that it is dealt with expeditiously and fairly.

20.07   These are clearly all laudable aims and insofar as it is possible to do so the practitioner must have regard to the terms of the protocol in every case. The penalty for failure to do so includes the ability of the court to take into account non-compliance on the making of costs orders and either depriving a party who obtains damages or interest, or awarding additional interest.[6] The court will also take into account compliance with the protocols in exercising all its case management functions. Therefore a party who launches proceedings without regard to the protocol will start off very much on the wrong foot.

20.08   The timetable for pre-action steps set down by the protocol is as follows:

20.09   **Preliminary notice**   As soon as the claimant decides there is a reasonable chance that he will bring a claim against a professional, the claimant is encouraged to notify the professional in writing. This letter should contain the following information:

- the identity of the claimant and any other parties;
- a brief outline of the claimant's grievance against the professional; and
- if possible, a general indication of the financial value of the potential claim.

---

[1] On the basis of having inherited the rights of the deceased.
[2] *Henderson v Merrett Syndicates Ltd* [1994] 3 All ER 826.
[3] See Part A (Chapters 1–3) of this work.
[4] See Chapter 15.
[5] The Professional Negligence Pre-Action Protocol, which was published in 2007, merged the protocols which had been produced by SIF (the Solicitors' Indemnity Fund) and CAP (Claims against Professionals).
[6] Section II Practice Direction—Pre-Action Conduct.

This letter should be addressed to the professional and should ask the professional to inform his professional indemnity insurers, if any, immediately. The professional should acknowledge receipt of the claimant's letter within twenty-one days of receiving it. Other than this acknowledgement, the protocol places no obligation upon either party to take any further action.

Letter of claim   As soon as the claimant decides there are grounds for a claim against the professional, the claimant should write a detailed letter of claim to the professional.   **20.10**

The letter of claim will normally be an open letter (as opposed to being 'without prejudice') and should include the following: **20.11**

1. The identity of any other parties involved in the dispute or a related dispute.
2. A clear chronological summary (including key dates) of the facts on which the claim is based. Key documents should be identified, copied, and enclosed.
3. The allegations against the professional. What has he done wrong? What has he failed to do?
4. An explanation of how the alleged error has caused the loss claimed.
5. An estimate of the financial loss suffered by the claimant and how it is calculated. Supporting documents should be identified, copied, and enclosed. If details of the financial loss cannot be supplied, the claimant should explain why and should state when he will be in a position to provide the details. This information should be sent to the professional as soon as reasonably possible.
6. If the claimant is seeking some form of non-financial redress, this should be made clear. This will be rare in cases such as this although an indemnity might be claimed.
7. Confirmation of whether or not an expert has been appointed;[7] if so, providing the identity and discipline of the expert, together with the date upon which the expert was appointed.
8. A request that a copy of the letter of claim be forwarded immediately to the professional's insurers, if any.

The letter of claim is not intended to have the same formal status as a statement of case.[8] If, however, the letter of claim differs materially from the statement of case in subsequent proceedings, the court may decide, in its discretion, to impose sanctions. If the claimant has sent other letters of claim (or equivalent) to any other party in relation to the dispute or related dispute, those letters should be copied to the professional. (If the claimant is claiming against someone else to whom the protocol does not apply.)   **20.12**

The letter of acknowledgement   The professional should acknowledge receipt of the letter of claim within twenty-one days of receiving it.   **20.13**

Investigations   The professional will have three months from the date of the letter of acknowledgement to investigate. If the professional is in difficulty in complying with the three-month time period, the problem should be explained to the claimant as soon as possible. The professional should explain what is being done to resolve the problem and when   **20.14**

---

[7] See also the section on expert evidence at para 20.65. If it is considered that the case will warrant expert evidence, care should be taken about involving an expert at an early stage and incurring cost, as the tendency of the courts is to direct that a single joint expert should be appointed rather than each side having their own.

[8] As to which see para 20.43.

the professional expects to complete the investigations. The claimant should agree to any reasonable request for an extension of the three-month period. The parties should supply promptly, at this stage and throughout, whatever relevant information or documentation is reasonably requested.

20.15 **Letter of response and letter of settlement**   As soon as the professional has completed his investigations, the professional should send to the claimant

- a letter of response; or
- a letter of settlement; or
- both.

20.16 The protocol then goes on to deal with the contents of the letters of response and settlement which can be contained in a single document. In essence the letter of response should be an open letter, and provide reasoned answers to the allegations set out in the letter of claim, including what part if any of the claim the practitioner admits, which facts are disputed and if the quantum of the claim is disputed, the basis for that. If the professional disputes the estimate of the claimant's financial loss, he should set out his own estimate. The letter should also identify any further information which is required and enclose any documents relied upon.[9] The letter of response is not intended to have the same formal status as a defence. If, however, the letter of response differs materially from the defence in subsequent proceedings, the court may decide, in its discretion, to impose sanctions.

20.17 The letter of settlement, assuming that one is appropriate, will normally be without prejudice either generally or save as to costs, and should identify the outstanding issues between the parties (insofar as these have not been dealt with by way of letter of response) and provide the prospective defendant's views on them before setting out a proposal for settlement, or asking for any further information which is required before an offer can be made. The letter should enclose any document relied upon.

20.18 **Effect of letter of response and/or letter of settlement**   If the letter of response denies the claim in its entirety *and* there is no letter of settlement, it is open to the claimant to commence proceedings. However, he should give fourteen days' written notice to the professional indicating the court in which the proceedings are to be brought and proceedings should be served on the professional unless he has indicated that he has instructed solicitors to accept service on his behalf. Indeed the latter is the norm. At any early stage in the pre-action protocol procedure the professional will normally hand over matters to his insurers and the protocol procedure will be conducted by them.

20.19 In any other circumstance, the professional and the claimant should commence negotiations with the aim of concluding those negotiations within six months of the date of the letter of acknowledgement.[10]

20.20 If the claim cannot be resolved within this period

- the parties should agree within fourteen days of the end of the period whether the period should be extended and, if so, by how long;

---

[9] For the details see para B.5.2 Professional Negligence Pre-Action Protocol.
[10] *NOT* from the date of the letter of response.

- the parties should seek to identify those issues which are still in dispute and those which can be agreed; and
- if an extension of time is not agreed it will then be open to the claimant to commence proceedings.

Experts   The protocol makes provision for the use of experts. It provides for the parties   **20.21** to regulate their own use of experts, providing that if the claimant has instructed an expert before sending a letter of claim, the defendant can also obtain expert evidence before sending the letter of response. Otherwise the instruction of a joint expert is encouraged. The use of experts in the sort of claims dealt with in this book is rare.[11]

Impact of the protocols   The protocol encourages the use of alternative dispute resolution   **20.22** at any stage of the proceedings. The protocol encourages parties to seek alternative dispute resolution while acknowledging that they cannot be forced to do so. Many cases are now resolved out of court by mediation. Refusal to mediate can have serious costs consequences unless the party refusing can provide a good justification such as having a watertight case.[12]

It can be seen that the aim of the pre-action protocol is to prevent the all too frequent prac-   **20.23** tice which obtained before the civil procedure reforms of a writ being fired off, perhaps after a vague letter before action, and then thought being given to the true nature of the claim afterwards. The protocol ensures that if it is followed, the parties know the precise nature of the claim before it starts and have explored ways of settling the litigation. They should have disclosed the most important documents to each other, and the litigation should produce no surprises. In essence there is therefore a 'front-loading' of litigation costs, with some hard work being undertaken at the outset to ensure that the claim is properly formulated and is settled if at all possible.

What should be done if there is simply not time to follow the pre-action protocol? What   **20.24** if the solicitor is instructed late one Friday night and the limitation period expires the next Monday? The result of attempting to follow the protocol rather than issuing a Part 7 claim form as a matter of urgency would simply give rise to yet another professional negligence claim. The point is that the pre-action protocol is good practice and failure to follow it without good reason will result in unfortunate consequences for the client,[13] but it is not so important that a time limit should be missed. Sometimes, if the limitation period is about to expire, there may be no choice but to launch proceedings, but the guidance notes to the protocol suggest that the parties apply for a stay of the proceedings in order to comply with the protocol, which seems eminently sensible advice.

Pre-action disclosure

If all goes according to plan, all important documents should be disclosed at the pre-action   **20.25** stage because the parties will be adhering to the protocol. However, if that does not prove to be the case, the court can order disclosure before the action commences.[14] An application[15]

---

[11] Although see para 20.65 below for when it might be appropriate.
[12] See *Halsey v Milton Keynes General NHS Trust* [2004] EWCA Civ 576; [2004] 1 WLR 3002 and in this arena of professional negligence *Swain Mason v Mills & Reeve* [2012] EWCA Civ 498; [2012] STC 1760.
[13] And perhaps yet another professional negligence claim?
[14] Rule 31.16 CPR.
[15] Made in accordance with Part 23.

must be supported by evidence which can be contained in the application notice itself, or in a written accompanying statement. The court must be satisfied that

(1) the respondent to the application is likely to be a party to subsequent proceedings;
(2) the applicant is also likely to be a party to those proceedings;
(3) the documents sought are those to which the applicant would be entitled to standard disclosure if proceedings had been commenced; and
(4) disclosure at this stage is desirable in order to
    (a) dispose fairly of the anticipated proceedings,
    (b) assist the dispute to be resolved without proceedings; or
    (c) save costs.

20.26 If the court makes an order under this rule it must specify the documents which the respondent must disclose and require them to specify any which are no longer in their control, or in respect of which they claim a right or duty to withhold inspection, and may require them to indicate what has happened to any documents no longer in their control and specify the time and place for disclosure.[16]

20.27 The leading case in this area is *Black v Sumitomo Cpn*[17] where the Court of Appeal formulated the following principles:

(1) Contrary to authorities pre-dating the CPR, there is no need to show that proceedings are likely. It has to be shown that the claimants and the defendant are likely to be parties to the proceedings if brought.[18]
(2) It is necessary not to confuse the jurisdictional and the discretionary aspects of the test of 'desirable' in r.31.16(3)(d) CPR, which involves a two-stage process. For jurisdictional purposes the court is permitted to consider the granting of pre-action disclosure only where there is a real prospect in principle of such an order being fair to the parties if litigation is commenced, or of assisting the parties to avoid litigation, or of saving costs in any event. If there is such a real prospect, then the court should go on to consider the question of discretion, which has to be considered on all the facts and not merely in principle but in detail.[19]
(3) The crossing of the jurisdictional threshold on that basis tells the court nothing about the broader and more particular discretionary aspects of the individual case or the ultimate exercise of discretion.[20]
(4) If the case is a personal injury claim and the request is for medical records, it is easy to conclude that pre-action disclosure ought to be made; but if the action is a speculative commercial action and the disclosure sought is broad, a fortiori if it is ill defined, it might be much harder. In cases such as this an application for the solicitors' file would almost certainly succeed.
(5) Pre-action disclosure will be ordered only where the documents sought are those which will have to be produced at the standard disclosure stage. It follows from this that the court must be clear what the issues in the litigation are likely to be, ie what case the

---

[16] Rule 31.16(4) and (5) CPR.
[17] [2002] 1 WLR 1562.
[18] *Black v Sumitomo Cpn* (n 17) at [71]–[72].
[19] *Black v Sumitomo Cpn* (n 17) at [81] and see also *Bermuda International Securities Ltd v KPMG* [2001] Lloyd's Rep PN 392, 397.
[20] *Black v Sumitomo Cpn* (n 17) at [83].

claimant is likely to be making and what the defence is likely to be, being run so as to make sure the documents being asked for are ones which will adversely affect the case of one side or the other, or support the case of one side or the other.[21]

(6) Unless there is some real evidence of dishonesty or abuse which only early disclosure can properly reveal and which may, in the absence of such disclosure, escape the probing eye of the litigation process and thus possibly all detection, the court should be slow to allow a merely prospective litigant to conduct a review of the documents of another party, replacing focused allegation by a roving inquisition.[22]

(7) The more focused the complaint and the more limited the disclosure sought in that connection, the easier it is for the court to exercise its discretion in favour of pre-action disclosure, even where the complaint might seem somewhat speculative or the request might be argued to constitute a mere fishing exercise. In appropriate circumstances, where the jurisdictional thresholds have been crossed, the court might be entitled to take the view that transparency was what the interests of justice and proportionality most required. The more diffuse the allegations, however, and the wider the disclosure sought, the more sceptical the court is entitled to be about the merit of the exercise.[23]

There are some difficulties which need to be overcome, both at this early stage and later on, in relation to standard disclosure[24] where the claim is in relation to the preparation of a will. The most important documents as far as a will negligence case is concerned will almost always be the will-drafter's file. However, where the will was drawn up by a solicitor, the file will almost certainly be covered by legal professional privilege, which attaches to all documents written to or by a solicitor for the purpose of obtaining legal advice and assistance.[25] The death of the client has no impact as far as privilege is concerned and it passes to his PRs.[26] If the estate is suing, there is no difficulty as the PRs enjoy the legal professional privilege and can waive it. What, however, is the position of the disappointed beneficiary? Certainly the solicitors who prepared the will cannot safely disclose the file without the deceased's PRs first waiving privilege, and if they refuse to waive it, it would seem that the court cannot make any order otherwise.[27] **20.28**

The position is not resolved by the fact that in contentious probate proceedings the solicitor who has drawn up the contested will must provide any interested party who asks him with a statement setting out the circumstances in which the will was executed.[28] That does not resolve one way or another the question of privilege attaching to the documents in the file itself. **20.29**

While there would seem to be no reported English case which deals specifically with the point there has been judicial comment from the Court of Appeal in New Zealand.[29] There **20.30**

---

[21] Per Waller LJ in *Bermuda International Securities Ltd* (n 19) at [26] approved in *Black v Sumitomo* (n 17). For standard disclosure see r.31.6 CPR.

[22] *Black v Sumitomo* (n 17) at [92].

[23] *Black v Sumitomo* (n 17) at [95].

[24] Standard disclosure will not be ordered in every case. The parties to litigation now have a duty to consider what disclosure is appropriate in light of the overriding objective and the court will exercise case management powers rigorously to limit or even dispense with disclosure if appropriate (r.31.5 CPR).

[25] See *O'Shea v Wood* [1891] P 286 (CA).

[26] *Bullivant v A-G for Victoria* [1901] AC 196 (HL).

[27] *Curtis v Beaney* [1911] P 181.

[28] *Larke v Nugus* [2000] WTLR 1033.

[29] *Gartside v Sheffield Young & Ellis* [1983] NZLR 37.

Cooke J (as he then was) held that privilege was there for the benefit of the deceased client and a solicitor accused of negligence could not hide behind it. He made the point that in most cases the PRs, or successor, of the deceased would be content to waive privilege. This, however, left open the question of what would happen if the solicitor was content to disclose the file and was not hiding behind it, but for whatever motives the PRs refused to waive privilege. More compelling perhaps was the reasoning of Richardson J[30] to the effect that it is the duty of the PRs to deal fairly with beneficiaries and claimants to the estate and therefore it would be incumbent upon them to waive privilege. As McMullin J put it, PRs must act neutrally and the court might well therefore direct them to waive the privilege.[31]

20.31 This pragmatic approach is clearly an attractive solution to the problem, but it probably would not provide an answer on a pre-action (or indeed a post-action) claim for disclosure of the file.

20.32 In practice, the estate will normally waive privilege, but there may be cases, for example where a beneficiary is also seeking rectification of the will, where the PRs may not wish to do so. It is perhaps surprising that in practice this causes few problems.

Starting the action and statements of case

Choice of court

20.33 If, in spite of going through the process of the pre-action protocol, there is no agreement between the parties, and an action seems inevitable, the first question must be where to commence it. The County Court has concurrent jurisdiction with the High Court in matters of contract and tort but the claim can be brought in the High Court only if its financial value (that is the value of the damages claim excluding interest and costs[32]) exceeds £25,000. Even if over the High Court financial limit many cases started in the High Court will be transferred to the County Court by the Master as part of the court's case management powers, if not a great deal of money is at stake and if there are no difficult points of law.

20.34 If the case is started in the High Court, it can be commenced in either the Chancery or the Queen's Bench Divisions.[33] However, the natural home for a negligence case involving wills, trusts, estates, or tax is manifestly the Chancery Division, where the judges are experienced in matters relating to these areas, and where it would be appropriate to deal with any other associated matters which might arise such as rectification of the will,[34] or any points of construction. It should not be forgotten that there are district registries of the Chancery Division across the country.[35]

Claim form

20.35 Proceedings are issued by way of a Part 7 claim form. It is usually sensible, unless the claim form has to be issued as a matter of some urgency, because, for example, of a limitation problem, for the particulars of claim to be included with the claim form. If this is not done, they must be served on the defendant within fourteen days of the service of the claim form (and

---

[30] *Gartside v Sheffield Young & Ellis* (n 29) at 49–50.
[31] *Gartside v Sheffield Young & Ellis* (n 29) at 55.
[32] Clause 9 High Court and County Court Jurisdiction Order 1991, SI 1991/724, as amended.
[33] Professional negligence is not specifically assigned to one of the divisions by Schedule 1 to the Senior Courts Act 1981.
[34] As to which see paras 23.13–23.33.
[35] ie in Birmingham, Bristol, Cardiff, Leeds, Liverpool, Manchester, Newcastle upon Tyne, and Preston.

in any event no later than the claim form can be served, which is four months from issue) and a copy together with a certificate of service[36] must be filed with the court within seven days thereafter.[37] The contents of the claim form are specified by rr.16.2 and 16.3 CPR, and as claims for professional negligence are 'money claims' the value of the claim will need to be specified.[38] Every claim form must contain a statement of truth.[39]

Some thought should be given to the parties to be joined to the action. The case of a disap- **20.36** pointed beneficiary suing a firm of solicitors on the basis that a will was not prepared may not present too many difficulties. However, it is possible that the estate may also have a claim, in which case consideration ought to be given to whether it should be joined or not. In *Carr-Glynn v Frearsons*[40] Chadwick LJ said:[41]

> in any case in which it could be suggested that there are, or may be, persons interested in the estate (other than the specific legatee) who have suffered loss by reason of the solicitor's breach of duty to the testator and whose interests personal representatives ought to be concerned to protect it would be appropriate for both personal representatives and the specific legatee to be parties to an action brought by either against the solicitor. That would enable the court to ensure that all matters in dispute are effectively and completely determined and adjudicated upon in the same action.

Chadwick LJ went on to point out that failure to join the PRs or the specific legatee as the **20.37** case may be would not invalidate the action, but clearly his guidance makes a great deal of sense and would perhaps have simplified matters in *Corbett v Bond Pearce*[42] if it had been followed.

The difficulties into which a claimant may fall if proper consideration is not given to the **20.38** appropriate parties at the outset were illustrated by the case of *Roberts v Gill & Co*.[43] There, a beneficiary of his mother's estate brought proceedings against the solicitors who had acted for the PRs of the estate in his personal capacity and did so within the limitation period. It was clearly questionable as to whether the solicitors owed him any duty of care when acting in the administration of the estate. Some years after the proceedings began he applied to amend his claim so that he sued not just in his personal capacity but also on behalf of the estate. By then the limitation period had expired. His application was rejected on the basis that it was not just a question of change of capacity. The Court of Appeal held that when the court gave permission for a personal claim, brought by a beneficiary of an estate in his personal capacity, to be continued as a derivative claim, the PR needed to be joined as a defendant. Otherwise, the solicitors were exposed to the risk of a multiplicity of actions. Therefore the principles applicable to adding parties after the expiry of the limitation period had to be complied with. Mr Roberts could not show that it was necessary to join the PRs to pursue his claim, which was merely a personal one, and it was not right to allow him to amend to change capacity and then consider the issue of necessity.

---

[36] See r.6.10 CPR.
[37] Rule 7.4 CPR. There are special rules for service out of the jurisdiction. That is so rare an occurrence in relation to claims of this kind that the rules are not dealt with here, but reference should be made to rr.6.20 and 6.21 CPR.
[38] Rule 16.3 CPR.
[39] Rule 22.1 CPR.
[40] [1998] 4 All ER 225.
[41] *Carr-Glynn v Frearsons* (n 40) at 35H.
[42] [2001] WTLR 419.
[43] The Times, 18 August 2008; [2009] PNLR 2; [2008] EWCA Civ 803.

20.39 There was a considerable amount of debate in the Court of Appeal as to whether the claimant was entitled to bring a derivative action. In general terms it is only PRs and trustees who can sue third parties on behalf of the trust or the estate. However, there is an exception to that rule if special circumstances can be demonstrated. In *Hayim v Citibank NA*,[44] where a trustee (HK) held the trust property on trust for C, the trustee of another trust of which the appellant (H) was a beneficiary, the Privy Council considered the question whether H could bring a derivative action against HK for breach of trust on account of their failure to sell a house in Hong Kong. The Privy Council held that the terms of the trust enabled C to give directions to HK in respect of the retention of this house in the interests of the elderly residents of the house. Lord Templeman, giving the advice of the Privy Council, held that

> The authorities cited by Mr Nugee only demonstrate that when the trustee commits a breach of trust or is involved in a conflict of interest and duty or in other exceptional circumstances a beneficiary may be allowed to sue a third party in place of the trustee. The beneficiary allowed to take proceedings cannot be in a better position than the trustee carrying out his duty in an improper manner.[45]

20.40 Therefore a beneficiary making a claim has to think carefully about the capacity in which he is suing, whether he falls within the exceptional circumstances which entitle him to make a claim by way of a derivative action, or whether his claim is a truly personal one. Trying to sort out the matter part way through the proceedings is unsatisfactory.

20.41 The best approach in any case where it might appear that both the estate and a beneficiary have a claim would be to ask the other party to join in the claim as claimant and if they do not, to join them as defendant. The court has powers to add beneficiaries as it goes along if to do so would resolve all the matters outstanding in the proceedings.[46]

20.42 An interesting case in this regard was that of *Chappell v Somers & Blake (a firm)*[47] where the claim was brought by the sole executrix of the deceased who had retained solicitors to act on her behalf in the administration of the estate, which included two vacant properties. Over five years later, probate had not been obtained and the two properties remained vacant. The executrix terminated the retainer and, having received alternative advice, obtained probate and distributed the estate in accordance with the will. She brought an action against the solicitors alleging breach of their contractual and tortious duties to her and claiming damages in respect of the loss to the estate resulting from the failure of the properties to produce any income during that time. The solicitors applied to strike out that part of her claim on the basis that any loss of income had been suffered by the residuary legatee and not by the claimant, acting in her capacity as executrix of the estate. The application was refused. The judge at first instance refused to strike out the claim, as did Neuberger J on appeal, who held it would be wrong for solicitors to escape liability for damages because there was a dichotomy between the person who was entitled to claim against them for breach of duty and the person who had suffered the damage. Since the solicitors' breach of their duty to the executrix of the will and owner of the properties throughout the period of breach had caused the person who was, or should have been, the owner of the properties to lose the income attributable to

---

[44] [1987] 1 AC 730.
[45] *Hayim v Citibank NA* (n 44) at 747C.
[46] Rule 19.2 CPR.
[47] [2004] 1 Ch 19.

them, the executrix was competent to bring the claim in respect of that loss on the basis that she would account to the residuary legatee for any damages awarded.

Particulars of claim

Rule 16.4 CPR sets out the contents of the particulars of claim. It should always be remem-   **20.43** bered that a claim for interest on any damages awarded must be sought expressly. Other than this it is a matter of setting out the basis of the claim clearly and concisely. The practice direction accompanying Part 16 sets out certain matters which must be expressly pleaded in the particulars of claim. The only item of any major relevance to professional negligence claims is that any facts relating to mitigation of loss or damage must be pleaded.[48] If the particulars of claim are served separately from the claim form, they must contain a statement of truth.[49]

When served with a claim form the defendant has a choice which is set out in Part 9 of the   **20.44** CPR—he can file an admission[50] (which will be rare if the protocol has been observed), file a defence,[51] or file an acknowledgement of service.[52] If the defendant chooses the latter, he has fourteen days after service of the particulars of claim to file an acknowledgement.[53] If he chooses to make an admission, he can make that by letter or statement of case or in any other form of writing at any time including before proceedings are commenced, up until fourteen days after the particulars of claim are served on him.[54] In most cases the defendant will wish to file a defence. Either he must do that within fourteen days of the service of the particulars of claim on him or, if he has acknowledged service, he has twenty-eight days from the date on which the particulars of claim are served on him. Reference should be made to the CPR for the precise timetabling in unusual cases, such as service out of the jurisdiction or where jurisdiction is disputed. The defendant must take care: failing to observe the time limits imposed may result in the claimant being able to obtain judgment in default, and while the defendant may be able ultimately to get that set aside, he will have to pay the costs.

Defence

Any defence served must deny, admit, or put the claimant to proof of matters set out in the   **20.45** particulars of claim in the usual way.[55] It must also contain a statement of truth.[56] There may be any number of defences relied upon by the defendant (and it is assumed for these purposes that the defendant is the professional defending a claim in negligence—of course in many cases negligence will be raised in a defence or Part 20 claim). He may claim that he did not owe a duty of care to the claimant, or that he was not in breach of duty. However, the defence of limitation of actions is a specific defence which demands a closer look and it is dealt with in more detail in the next chapter. The crucial point to note in relation to the defence is that the expiry of any limitation period relied upon must be set out.[57] Indeed historically the practice was for the claim itself to make no mention of the fact that it was made some time

---

[48] Paragraph 8.2(8) of the Practice Direction supplementing Part 16 on statements of case.
[49] Rule 22.1 CPR.
[50] In accordance with Part 14 CPR.
[51] In accordance with Part 15 CPR.
[52] In accordance with Part 10 CPR.
[53] Rule 10.3 CPR, which means that if the claim form contains the particulars of claim, 14 days from the claim form.
[54] Rule 14.2 CPR.
[55] See r.16.5 CPR.
[56] Rule 22 CPR.
[57] Paragraph 13.1 of the Practice Direction supplementing Part 16 on statements of case.

after the expiry of a relevant limitation period. It was then for the defence to raise the point, and the answer to it would be included in the reply. Increasingly, in cases where the primary limitation period has manifestly expired by the time the claim is brought, the particulars of claim acknowledge that fact and plead matters relied upon such as s.14A Limitation Act 1980.[58] The defence should nevertheless state that the limitation period has expired, both of course the primary period and any period of grace relied upon.

Part 20 claims

20.46 Straightforward claims for professional negligence rarely involve bringing in a third party, now dealt with by Part 20 of the CPR. However, claims against solicitors are frequently made in other litigation by way of a Part 20 claim. So, for example, if there is doubt as to the construction of a poorly drafted will or trust, the solicitors responsible for the drafting may well be brought into the proceedings by way of a Part 20 claim against them. Similarly, if there is a claim to rectify a will or other document, a Part 20 claim against the solicitors who drafted it may well be included in the proceedings. Part 20 proceedings may also be appropriate where a solicitor wishes to claim an indemnity against a co-professional—for example in a case where a solicitor and accountant have advised on setting up a trust together with a view to avoiding tax and it has not worked. Part 20 proceedings may also have a part to play in circumventing some of the difficulties in claiming contributory negligence in a case such as this; as to which see Chapter 22.[59]

The course of the action and some common applications

Allocation

20.47 When a party files a defence, the court will provisionally allocate the claim to a track: the small-claims track, fast track, or multi-track.[60] It is unlikely that a professional negligence case will fall within the financial limits for the small claims track,[61] but not impossible. Whether a claim for such a small sum could really ever be justified is perhaps questionable. More likely perhaps is that claims will fall into the category of the fast track, which is limited to claims of less than £25,000 which are not small claims, and where the court considers that they will last for less than one day, and oral expert evidence will be limited to one expert per party, and expert evidence in only one field.[62] The vast majority of professional negligence cases of this kind will be allocated to the multi-track and their seriousness to the professionals involved means that there are good grounds for them being retained for hearing in the High Court.

Case management

20.48 When a defence is filed the court will provisionally allocate the case to a track and require the parties to file a directions questionnaire to ascertain what case management might be required.[63] The court will give directions for the management of the case or will fix a case management conference or a pre-trial review or both.[64] This is the moment for the parties

---

[58] As to which see Chapter 21.
[59] See Chapter 22 paras 22.35–22.47.
[60] Rule 26.3 CPR.
[61] Currently £10,000.
[62] Rule 26.6 CPR.
[63] Rule 26.3 CPR.
[64] Rule 29.2 CPR.

to look at the way in which the case will be run and to find a suitable timetable and to seek directions. These can be agreed, subject to the approval of the court.[65] Some of the matters to which the parties should be giving thought are expert witnesses, disclosure, the length of the trial, and whether there ought to be any preliminary issues. In most cases the parties will be required to provide a costs budget and the court will make a costs management order.[66] The sanction for failing to file a costs budget ahead of the first case management hearing is that costs will not be recoverable; given the new, stricter approach to relief from sanctions, this is a real risk that litigators must take care to avoid or else face a likely professional negligence claim themselves.

20.49 Since 1 April 2013 and the Review of Civil Litigation Costs by Jackson LJ there has been a more robust approach by the courts to compliance with time limits. Rule 3.9 CPR has been rewritten so that it provides:

> On an application for relief from any sanction imposed for a failure to comply with any rule, practice direction or court order, the court will consider all the circumstances of the case, so as to enable it to deal justly with the application, including the need—
> (a) for litigation to be conducted efficiently and at proportionate cost; and
> (b) to enforce compliance with rules, practice directions and orders.

20.50 Finally to get the case to trial, the parties must complete and file a listing questionnaire unless the court dispenses with it.[67]

Disclosure

20.51 The use which might be made of pre-action disclosure has already been dealt with above.[68] There are few points which arise on standard disclosure which apply specifically to actions in professional negligence, but do note the difficulties in relation to the legal professional privilege attaching to the solicitor's file discussed above in respect of pre-action disclosure.

20.52 It should be noted that there is provision contained in the CPR enabling disclosure to be sought against a non-party to the proceedings.[69] Such an application must be supported by evidence specifying the documents sought and the court must be satisfied that the documents are likely to support the case of the applicant or adversely affect the case of the other side.[70] There may be occasions where there are documents in possession, for example, of the PRs of the deceased, or perhaps another firm of solicitors, where disclosure would support the case of the disappointed beneficiary or adversely affect the solicitors' case or vice versa. The question of legal professional privilege will of course still need to be circumvented. This is a power of the court which it will exercise cautiously.[71]

---

[65] Rule 29.4 CPR.
[66] Except in cases where the claim exceeds £2m the parties must file a costs budget in Form H— para 1 Practice Direction 3E. It must be filed and served by all parties (other than litigants in person) by the date specified in the allocation notice under r.26.3(1) CPR if not filed in time, deemed served but limited to court fees.
[67] Rule 29.6 CPR. See *Mitchell v News Group Newspapers Ltd* [2013] EWCA Civ 1537 for the new approach.
[68] Paragraph 20.25.
[69] Rule 31.17 CPR.
[70] This is looked at strictly—it is not enough that the documents *might* have this effect: see *Re Howglen Ltd* [2001] 1 All ER 576.
[71] *Frankson v Home Office* [2003] 1 WLR 1952.

Summary judgment

20.53 Summary judgment is available not only to the claimant but also to the defendant[72] on the basis that the claimant has no prospect of succeeding on his claim, or an issue on the claim, or the defendant has no real prospect of successfully defending the claim or issue and there is no other compelling reason for a trial. To defeat an application for summary judgment, the respondent to the application must show that he has some chance of success which is not fanciful, even if he cannot show that he is likely to win.

20.54 Therefore a solicitor who is alleged to have failed to prepare a will in time, but in fact it is clear that he did all he could within the ambit of his instructions, could well use this procedure to rid himself of a claim. Similarly a claimant could use this procedure in a case where the solicitor had sat on instructions for such a long period that the testator had died.

20.55 There is also no reason why an application could not be made in respect of actions which are clearly statute barred. As a matter of practice, where a limitation defence is raised, it is often directed that the question be tried by way of a preliminary issue and this is clearly sensible. However, an alternative approach would be to bring a claim for summary judgment on the basis that the limitation issue is clear. This may not work if there are issues as to date of knowledge,[73] which may require evidence to be tested because an application for summary judgment cannot turn into a mini trial.[74]

20.56 It should also be remembered that under this jurisdiction the court can consider points of law, and so where the evidence is not seriously in dispute, it can provide a good way of disposing of the action quickly.[75]

20.57 However, in any case of complexity, it must not be forgotten that this procedure may be inappropriate.

Striking out

20.58 The availability of summary judgment to a defendant is in addition to the ability to apply to strike out the claim,[76] but often the more generous provisions of the summary judgment rules will be the best course of action now that the remedy is available to a defendant. The court can, in an appropriate case, treat an application to strike out as an application for summary judgment.[77] In order to strike out, the applicant has to show that the statement of case either

- discloses no reasonable grounds for bringing or defending the claim; or
- is an abuse of the court's process or is likely to obstruct the disposal of the proceedings; or
- has failed to comply with a rule, practice direction, or court order.[78]

20.59 The first ground involves the court looking at the statement of case itself and seeing whether a cause of action is demonstrated at all. The case must be clear and obvious.[79] So, if, for

---

[72] Rule 24.2 CPR.

[73] As to which see para 21.31 below.

[74] *Swain v Hillman* The Times, 4 November 1999.

[75] See *ICI Chemicals & Polymers Ltd v TTE Training Ltd* [2007] EWCA Civ 725.

[76] Rule 3.4 CPR.

[77] *Taylor v Midland Bank Trust Company Ltd* The Times, 21 July 1999.

[78] Rule 3.4(2) CPR.

[79] Or to strike it out may be a breach of Article 6(1) of the European Convention on Human Rights: see *Osman v United Kingdom* (2000) 29 EHRR 245.

example, the particulars of claim failed to show that there was any duty owed by the defendant to the claimant, or that any instructions were given by the deceased for the preparation
of a will in the claimant's favour, the court might well strike that out.

A case might be an abuse of process and struck out if the claimant is attempting to reliti- **20.60**
gate issues which have been litigated elsewhere. So, for example, in a case where an unsuccessful application to rectify a will was followed by a claim against the solicitor who drafted
the will involving similar issues for the court, the judge was sympathetic to submissions
made by counsel for the defendant that this was an abuse, although they were not in fact
pursued.[80] As is discussed in Chapter 23, these types of negligence cases are often linked
with other causes of action such as applications for rectification of the will and perhaps
even claims under the Inheritance (Provision for Family and Dependants) Act 1975, and
ensuring that the issues before the court are litigated on one occasion alone is extremely
important.[81]

The final ground for striking out is on the basis of breach of the court rules and want of pros- **20.61**
ecution, which may apply to will negligence cases as it does to other litigation. The prejudice
which might be caused by a delay in a will negligence case may be exacerbated if the preparation of the will took place many years before the claim is brought.

Again, the defendant has to feel on very strong ground. For example, in the case of *Hughes v* **20.62**
Richards[82] a strong Court of Appeal upheld the decision of HHJ Norris QC (as he then was)
not to strike out a claim by minor beneficiaries against the accountant who had provided
their parents with advice on the setting up of a trust for their benefit. While recognizing that
the defendant had strong legal grounds for resisting the claim, the court considered that
this was a developing area of the law and the decision needed to be made on the facts found
after a trial and not summarily. The same judge refused to strike out a claim that solicitors
had negligently advised on the availability of business property relief on shares in *Vinton v*
Fladgate Fielder (a firm).[83]

Preliminary issues

If there is a limitation defence raised, it can often be convenient to ask for a direction at **20.63**
the case management conference for it to be tried as a preliminary issue.[84] Often the issues
which will determine whether a case is statue barred are quite different from those which will
be needed to establish the claim. If that be the case, it can prove a considerable cost saving
to have tried the question of whether the claim is too late before looking at the substantive
issues. If the claimant does fall at the hurdle of limitation, then his costs exposure will be
limited. If on the other hand he succeeds, that may be a prompt for the defendant (or perhaps
more appropriately the defendant's insurers) to consider settlement proposals.

Preliminary issues are often used in other circumstances, for example when there is an order **20.64**
that the question of liability be tried before the issue of quantum. This is unlikely to represent
a real time and costs saving in private client negligence cases, as quantum will not usually

---

[80] HHJ Behrens QC in *Grattan v McNaughton* [2001] WTLR 1285.
[81] This is discussed in more detail in Chapter 23.
[82] [2004] EWCA Civ 266.
[83] [2010] EWHC 904 (Ch); [2010] STC 1868.
[84] eg this was done in *Daniels v Thompson* [2004] PNLR 33 and *Boycott v Perrins Guy Williams* [2011]
EWHC 2969 (Ch); [2012] PNLR 25 (a claim by the famous former cricketer held to be statute barred).

require a bevy of experts to analyse what has been lost, and that is usually the best reason for postponing the assessment of damages.

The use of experts

20.65   In general terms the correct approach to the use of expert evidence in negligence cases such as these is that adopted by Oliver J (as he then was) in *Midland Bank v Hett, Stubbs & Kem*.[85] There he said that there is a limit to how useful expert evidence can be in a case where most of the issues on which the judge has to make a finding are legal issues on which he or she is an expert. The strident comments of Neuberger J in *X v Woolcombe Yonge*[86] should be taken into account by a litigator considering hiring a plethora of experts. There he said:[87]

> I question the value, indeed the admissibility of [the experts'] evidence. In many cases of professional negligence, expert evidence is not merely admissible, it may be necessary... [I]n the field in which solicitors and barristers practise the role of the expert witness must be more controversial, for the reason that the issue normally is what a reasonably competent lawyer would have done or advised.

20.66   However, there may be cases where expert evidence is appropriate, in particular in relation to a practice adopted in a profession, and of course there are examples of cases in which reliance has been placed on such evidence.[88] Tax negligence cases often involve experts in the field of tax to say what the prevailing view was at a given time.

20.67   The relevant rules are now contained in Part 35 CPR. Rule 35.1 is instructive in that it states that 'Expert evidence shall be restricted to that which is reasonably required to resolve the proceedings'. In fact, a party cannot adduce expert evidence without the permission of the court, and that will require the applicant to identify the field in which they wish to rely on expert evidence and the expert in that field on whom they wish to rely.[89] The rules further emphasize that the role of the expert is to help the court and that duty overrides any obligation to the person who instructs them or pays them.[90] The days of the hired gun are now long over, and parties should think long and hard about whether expert evidence is really justified in their negligence case, and if it is, how it can be kept to a minimum. Somewhat surprisingly, in *Liverpool Roman Catholic Archdiocesan Trustees Inc v Goldberg*[91] a leading tax counsel, who was the defendant to a claim for negligent advice, sought to rely on a colleague and close personal friend as his expert witness. At an interlocutory stage Neuberger J (as he then was) refused to exclude the evidence and left it as a matter for the trial judge. The case settled before judgment was handed down, but the trial judge rejected the expert evidence on the basis that justice had to be seen to be done.[92]

20.68   The usual practice of the courts is to insist on a single joint expert being appointed in cases where expert evidence is required.[93] Having said that, where the evidence of that expert is crucial, the courts have recognized that in some cases the parties should be allowed their own

---

[85] [1979] Ch 384.
[86] [2001] WTLR 301.
[87] *X v Woolcombe Yonge* (n 86) at 310E.
[88] *Esterhuizen v Allied Dunbar* [1998] 2 FLR 668 (QB) is a striking example.
[89] Rule 35.4 CPR.
[90] Rule 35.3 CPR.
[91] [2001] Lloyd's Rep PN 518.
[92] [2001] 1 WLR 2337.
[93] Rule 35.7 CPR.

experts, albeit not in this particular field.[94] It seems in most negligence cases, where expert evidence is going to be of use, it is unlikely to be so central an issue that the court will be impressed by applications for each side to have their own expert.

If the case is appropriate for an expert there are specific rules for the contents of the report[95] with which most experienced experts are now more than familiar.

Compromise and Part 36 offers

At an early stage a view will need to be taken by both claimant and defendant as to the likely **20.69** quantum of any claim. Indeed the pre-action protocol[96] recognizes the need to give a general idea of the financial value of the claim right at preliminary notice stage. The claim form will also require there to be a financial statement of the claim included, and so by the time the proceedings have started, the parties should have a clear idea of the sort of damages likely to be awarded if the claim proves to be successful.

Once this is ascertained, both parties should consider making an offer pursuant to Part 36 **20.70** CPR. An offer can be made even if proceedings have not commenced,[97] and the procedure is available during appeal proceedings.[98] There is no reason why offers cannot be made in any other way although the costs consequences set out in Part 36 will not follow unless the court so orders.

Both claimant and defendant can make Part 36 offers.[99] As a claim against a negligent pro- **20.71** fessional sounds in damages, this is a money claim, but there is no longer any procedure for payment into court.[100]

There are certain requirements as to the form of the Part 36 offer, which can be found in **20.72** r.36.2 CPR. A Part 36 offer must be in writing, state on its face that it is intended to have the consequences of section 1 of Part 36, and must state whether it relates to the whole of the claim or to part of it or to an issue that arises in it and if so to which part or issue.

In most straightforward cases of professional negligence, the offer will be made by the claim- **20.73** ant or the defendant in respect of the whole claim. It must state whether it takes into account any counterclaim.[101] So, for example, if the solicitors being sued are counterclaiming for their unpaid fees, that should be taken into account in the making of any offer, and then that should be made clear in the written offer.

Where the offer is made more than twenty-one days before the date of trial, a period of not **20.74** less than twenty-one days should be specified within which the defence will be liable for the claimant's costs if any offer is accepted.[102] This embodies the concept of the 'relevant period',[103] which is either the period of not less than twenty-one days specified by the offeror

---

[94] *S (a minor) v Birmingham Health Authority* The Times, 23 November 1999.
[95] Rules 35.5 and 35.10 CPR and paras 1.1–1.6 Practice Direction 35 (Experts and Assessors).
[96] As to which see para 20.06.
[97] Rule 36.3(2) CPR.
[98] Rule 36.3(2)(b) CPR.
[99] In effect these rules replace the old payment into court and *Calderbank* offers.
[100] Part 36 was substantially amended from April 2007, although there are transitional provisions which apply to payments into court made before that date.
[101] Rule 36.2(2)(e) CPR.
[102] Rule 36.2(2)(c) CPR.
[103] Rule 36.3(1)(c) CPR.

or where the trial is less than twenty-one days off, the period up to the end of the trial or such period as the court determines. Until the expiry of the relevant period, the offeror cannot withdraw the offer or change its terms to be less advantageous to the offeree without the permission of the court.[104]

20.75 If the defendant makes an offer, that offer must be for a single sum of money payable within fourteen days of acceptance.[105] A Part 36 offer can be accepted at any time up to withdrawal without the permission of the court except where there are multiple defendants and the offer has been made by only one, and the claimant does not wish to discontinue against the others or the claim is not a several one[106] or where the trial has started.[107]

20.76 When a Part 36 offer is accepted and it relates to the whole of the claim, the claimant will be entitled to his costs of the proceedings up to the date of acceptance.[108] In cases where the offer is in relation to only part of the claim, the claimant will be entitled to his costs if he abandons the rest of the claim unless the court orders otherwise.[109] In the event that the offer was made less than twenty-one days before the start of trial or the offer is accepted after the expiry of the relevant period (when of course the offeror is at liberty to withdraw or change it), the court will decide the liability for costs if the parties cannot do so.[110] The default position after the expiry of the relevant period is that the claimant will get his costs up until the date when the relevant period expired and thereafter he will have to pay the costs of the offeror.[111]

20.77 Timing is therefore crucial for both claimant and defendant. It is clearly a good idea to start thinking about making Part 36 offers with rather more than a twenty-one-day margin before the trial starts. It is also incumbent on the party to whom the offer is made to have regard to the relevant period for acceptance. In the unlikely event in cases of this kind that the offer is unclear, the offeree can seek clarification of the offer.[112]

20.78 Part 36 offers are not just a useful method of attempting to settle the litigation. They are a crucial tactical weapon in relation to costs, and it is often the question of costs which becomes central in these as in many other claims.

20.79 It is, however, the failure to beat an offer that has been made which can prove to be so unfortunate for the party concerned. So, in the case of a disappointed beneficiary who is claiming damages of £100,000 but the defendant solicitors assess the damages at only £50,000 and make a Part 36 payment to reflect that, if the claimant beats that payment, all well and good. If, however, he obtains only £50,000, then unless the court thinks it unjust, he will be ordered to pay the defendant's costs from the expiry of the relevant period with interest on those costs.[113]

---

[104] Rule 36.3(5) and (6) CPR.
[105] Rule 36.4 CPR.
[106] Rule 36.12 CPR.
[107] Rule 36.9(3) CPR. There are other cases where permission is needed but they are not applicable to this sort of claim.
[108] Rule 36.10(1) CPR.
[109] Rule 36.10(2) CPR.
[110] Rule 36.10(4) CPR.
[111] Rule 36.10(5) CPR.
[112] Rule 36.8 CPR.
[113] Rule 36.14(2) CPR.

However, if the claimant in the above example is correct and the defendant has underestimated the damages payable, or the claimant does at least as well as in its offer, the court may (and will unless it thinks it unjust to do so) order interest on the damages at a rate not exceeding 10 per cent above the base rate for some or all of the period from the expiry of the relevant period, indemnity costs against the defendant, and interest on those costs not exceeding 10 per cent above base rate.[114]   **20.80**

This is of course subject to the court deciding that it would be unjust to make such an order. There are certain factors which the court will take into account under r.36.14(4) in ascertaining whether it is unjust: **20.81**

1. The terms of any Part 36 offer.
2. The stage in the proceedings when any Part 36 offer was made, including in particular how long before the trial started the offer was made.
3. The information available to the parties at the time when the Part 36 offer was made.
4. The conduct of the parties with regard to giving or refusing to give information for the purposes of enabling the offer to be made or evaluated.

The timing and size of an offer will be vital from a tactical point of view. The assessment of damages, although it raises a number of interesting points, does not often in practice give rise to difficulty, and therefore deciding on the perfect Part 36 payment or offer to make should not normally give rise to problems.   **20.82**

Even if a Part 36 offer is technically defective the court may still give effect to it.[115]   **20.83**

It is now usual in almost every case to attempt alternative dispute resolution wherever possible and mediation has become a very effective method of compromising disputes where without prejudice correspondence and/or discussions have failed. The refusal to mediate may result in the court awarding costs against the refusing party. The principles were set out in *Halsey v Milton Keynes General NHS Trust*[116] and have been usefully summarized as follows:[117]   **20.84**

1. A party cannot be ordered to submit to mediation as that would be contrary to Article 6 of the European Convention on Human Rights.
2. The burden is on the unsuccessful party to show why the general rule of costs following the event should not apply, and it must be shown that the successful party acted unreasonably in refusing to agree to mediation. It follows that, where that is shown, the court may make an order as to costs which reflects that refusal.
3. A party's reasonable belief that they have a strong case is relevant to the reasonableness of their refusal, for otherwise the fear of cost sanctions may be used to extract unmerited settlements.
4. Where a case is evenly balanced or borderline a party's belief that he would win should be given little or no weight in considering whether a refusal was reasonable: but his belief must not be unreasonable.

---

[114] Rule 36.14(3) CPR. The court will also order an additional sum not exceeding £75,000 based on a calculation of the amount of damages awarded by the court at 10% above £500,000 and below £1,000,000 and at 5% on sums above that. Few claims of the kind dealt with in this work would be caught by this.

[115] *Hertsmere Primary Care Trust v Administrators of Balasubramanium Rabindra-Anandh* [2005] 3 All ER 274.

[116] [2004] 1 WLR 3002.

[117] *Hickman v Blake Lapthorn* [2006] EWHC 12 (QB).

5. The cost of mediation is a relevant factor in considering the reasonableness of a refusal.

6. Whether the mediation had a reasonable prospect of success is relevant to the reasonableness of a refusal to agree to mediation, but not determinative.

7. In considering whether the refusal to agree to mediation was unreasonable it is for the unsuccessful party to show that there was a reasonable prospect that the mediation would have been successful.

8. Where a party refuses to take part in mediation despite encouragement from the court to do so, that is a factor to be taken into account in deciding whether the refusal was unreasonable.

The moral is that a party must think long and hard before refusing to mediate. In cases which are very strong, particularly from a defendant's point of view, an application to strike out before mediation becomes an issue worth considering. However, the courts have acknowledged in this area that where a party considers itself to be on strong ground a refusal to mediate may be justified. In *Swain Mason v Mills & Reeve*[118] the allegation against the solicitors was that they had failed to advise on the impact the client's death would have on a tax scheme when they had not been asked to do so and their refusal to mediate was held to be justified.

Trials

20.85 Most cases of this kind do not get near to a courtroom, but of course in cases where the law is unclear or one or both of the parties refuses to settle, a trial may be inevitable. As stated above[119] the natural home for professional negligence cases in respect of private client work is the Chancery Division and the procedure there is fully set out in the *Chancery Guide 2013*,[120] in particular in chapter 6, which deals with listing, and chapter 7, which deals with preparation for hearings, and chapter 8, which deals with the conduct of trials. Often case management directions will specify time limits for the filing of agreed trial bundles for the court, lists of issues, chronologies, and skeleton arguments. The default position is that bundles and skeletons should be filed at least two clear days before a trial.

20.86 The modern approach, which is set out in the *Chancery Guide*, is for the claimant to make a short opening statement, then other parties to be asked to respond. The judge will almost always have done a great deal of pre-reading and it is common for there to be a reading day for the judge to familiarize himself with the bundles and case law. After the evidence is concluded, and subject to any direction to the contrary by the trial judge, oral closing submissions will be made on behalf of the claimant first, followed by the defendants in the order in which they appear on the claim form, followed by a reply on behalf of the claimant. Written closing submissions are encouraged.

20.87 The parties are often asked to provide a trial timetable and to revise this as the case goes along.

Costs

20.88 In most professional negligence cases, issues of costs are straightforward: the losing party pays them subject to any Part 36 offers (as to which see above) or any unreasonable behaviour on the part of the winning party.

---

[118] [2012] EWCA Civ 498; [2012] STC 1760.
[119] Paragraph 20.34.
[120] Available on HM Courts service website at <www.justice.gov.uk/downloads/courts/chancery-court/chancery-guide.doc>.

The exercise of the court's discretion as to costs is dealt with by Part 44.3 CPR, which pro- **20.89**
vides that the court has discretion as to

- whether costs are payable by one party to another;
- the amount of those costs; and
- when they are to be paid.

If the court decides to make an order about costs, the general rule is that the unsuccessful **20.90**
party will be ordered to pay the costs of the successful party; but the court may make a different order. In considering its discretion the court must have regard to all the circumstances
including

1. The conduct of all the parties. This includes conduct before, as well as during, the proceedings, and in particular the extent to which the parties followed any relevant pre-action
   protocol; whether it was reasonable for a party to raise, pursue, or contest a particular
   allegation or issue; the manner in which a party has pursued or defended his case or a particular allegation or issue; whether a claimant who has succeeded in his claim, in whole
   or in part, exaggerated his claim.[121]
2. Whether a party has succeeded on part of their case, even if they have not been wholly
   successful.
3. Any admissible offer to settle made by a party which is drawn to the court's attention, and
   which is not an offer to which costs consequences under Part 36 apply.

Having taken all the circumstances into account, the court may make various orders includ- **20.91**
ing that a party must pay

1. A proportion of another party's costs.
2. A stated amount in respect of another party's costs.
3. Costs from or until a certain date only.
4. Costs incurred before proceedings have begun.
5. Costs relating to particular steps taken in the proceedings.
6. Costs relating only to a distinct part of the proceedings.
7. Interest on costs from or until a certain date, including a date before judgment.

The court has a very useful power to order an amount to be paid on account of costs pending **20.92**
assessment.[122] From 1 April 2013 new rules were introduced following a review of costs in
civil litigation by Jackson LJ[123] ushering in an era when parties have to provide costs budgets
and where only costs proportionate to the claim in question will be recoverable.

---

[121] See, eg *Earl of Malmesbury v Strutt & Parker* [2008] EWHC 424.
[122] Rule 44.3(8) CPR.
[123] <http://www.judiciary.gov.uk/NR/rdonlyres/8EB9F3F3-9C4A-4139-8A93-56F09672EB6A/0/
jacksonfinalreport140110.pdf>.

21

LIMITATION

A. General comments

One of the most common defences which is raised in professional negligence cases is that the **21.01** claim is statute barred. Limitation has become a thorny issue. The practitioner can no longer (if indeed he was ever justified in doing so) destroy his files after six years and breathe a huge sigh of relief. There is a far longer period during which claims can be made.

This area has of late given rise to considerable problems in ascertaining whether a claim has **21.02** become statute barred and, as explored below, this is particularly the case in tax negligence cases.

The crucial question must be to look at the date when the cause of action accrues before turn- **21.03** ing to circumstances where that period is extended.

B. The starting point: general principles

The limitation period for claims in both contract and tort is six years.[1] If a claim is made **21.04** by the estate on behalf of the deceased, or trustees and PRs against their advisers, there are concomitant claims in tort and contract.[2] If it is a disappointed beneficiary suing, then the claim is one made in tort.

The cause of action for claims in contract accrues at the date of the breach, that is, in profes- **21.05** sional negligence cases, the date when the professional is in breach of his contract by failing to act with reasonable skill and care. That is usually easy to ascertain.

---

[1] Section 2 Limitation Act 1980.
[2] See *Henderson v Merrett Syndicates* [1994] 3 All ER 506.

21.06 Where the claim is based on the tort of negligence, however, the cause of action accrues when damage happens.[3] As Lord Nicholls said in *Nykredit Mortgage Bank plc v Edward Erdman Group Ltd*:[4]

> In case of tort the cause of action arises not when the culpable conduct occurs, but when the plaintiff first sustains damage. Thus the question which has to be addressed is what is meant by damage in the context of claims for loss which is purely financial.

21.07 This question has given rise to considerable difficulty in professional negligence cases. The starting point is the Court of Appeal decision in *Forster v Outred & Co*.[5] The Court of Appeal's reasoning cannot be understood without understanding the facts. In that case Mrs Forster mortgaged her house in 1973 to secure the debts of her son. In 1977 the mortgagee foreclosed and she lost her home. In 1980 she claimed against her solicitors who had advised her in relation to the mortgage in 1973. The solicitors pleaded the Limitation Act and the question was whether the cause of action in tort arose in 1973 when she had signed the mortgage, or in 1977 when the mortgagee foreclosed. The Court of Appeal held that she suffered loss the moment she signed the mortgage in 1973 and therefore her cause of action was statute barred. This decision has been relied upon in many cases and indeed approved by the House of Lords.[6]

21.08 The *Nykredit* case itself appears to adopt a somewhat different approach. There the court was concerned with the date of accrual of a cause of action by a lender against a valuer for a negligent valuation in the context of the award of interest on the damages. The competing dates for accrual of the cause of action were the date when the mortgage monies were advanced and the date when the property was sold at a loss. The latter date won the day.

21.09 *Forster* has been described as a transaction case and the apparent difference between that approach and that in *Nykredit* has been explained in the case of *Law Society v Sephton and Co*.[7] In that case the defendant accountants had on various dates between 1990 and 1995 negligently signed reports certifying that a particular solicitor had complied with the Solicitors' Accounts Rules 1991. The solicitor had in fact misappropriated large sums of client monies during those years. The Law Society intervened in the solicitor's practice in 1996 and clients who had suffered loss claimed compensation from the Solicitors' Compensation Fund maintained by the Law Society. The Law Society sought to recover those sums from the accountants and had issued proceedings just under six years from the date of the intervention. The issue before the House of Lords was whether the Law Society had suffered damage more than six years before the issue of proceedings so that the action had been commenced outside the limitation period. The Law Society argued that it had not suffered actual damage until it resolved to make its first payment out of the compensation fund to one of the solicitor's former clients. The defendants argued that the Law Society had suffered damage each time it had received a negligent report or alternatively, every time monies had been misappropriated after receiving a negligent report. The House of Lords held that the Law Society's liability on receiving a negligent report was a contingent one and no actual damage was suffered until it

---

[3] See *Pirelli General Cable Works v Oscar Faber and Partners* [1983] 2 AC 1.
[4] [1997] 1 WLR 1627 at 1630C.
[5] [1982] 1 WLR 86.
[6] In *Nykredit Mortgage Bank plc v Edward Erdman Group Ltd* (n 4).
[7] [2006] UKHL 22; [2006] 2 AC 543.

had to make a payment. Lord Hoffmann explained the *Nykredit* case in the following way:[8]

> The *Nykredit (No 2) case* [1997] 1 WLR 1627 therefore decides that in a transaction in which there are benefits (covenant for repayment and security) as well as burdens (payment of the loan) and the measure of damages is the extent to which the lender is worse off than he would have been if he had not entered into the transaction, the lender suffers loss and damage only when it is possible to say that he is on balance worse off. It does not discuss the question of a purely contingent liability.

In relation to the transaction cases the House of Lords held that the existence of a contingent liability may depress the value of other property, as in *Forster v Outred*, or it may mean that a party to a bilateral transaction has received less than it should have done, or is worse off than if it had not entered into the transaction. But, standing alone, the contingency is not damage. **21.10**

Therefore the questions have to be asked as to whether the transaction renders the claimant immediately worse off in a financial sense[9] or because the claimant has got something he did not want because, for example, it is riskier[10] or has lost a chance of a better deal,[11] in which case the date of the damage is the date of the transaction. If, on the other hand, the transaction is one where it is not clear whether the claimant is worse off or not (as in the mortgage lender cases) then the date of damage will be when it is possible to say damage has been suffered. Finally the case may be one where the loss is contingent. So, for example, a possible but not inevitable tax liability, in which case it is not until that crystallizes that the damage occurs. **21.11**

What constitutes a contingent liability is not always easy to ascertain. In *Lane v Cullens*[12] the PR of the deceased distributed certain sums out of the estate notwithstanding that he had notice of a claim by a third party who obtained orders for the PR to repay to her the distributions when her claim succeeded. More than six years after the distributions had been made, but less than six years after the making of the orders in favour of the third party, the PR sued the solicitors who had been advising him in the administration for failing to warn him that he ought not to make any distributions when notified of a claim. The solicitors applied to strike the proceedings out as statute barred. The PR argued that the third party claim (whether reliant on proprietary estoppel or a constructive trust) was contingent and therefore the limitation period started to run when the orders were made against the estate in favour of the third party. The solicitors argued that the damage was in fact suffered at the point when the distributions were made. The Court of Appeal held that the solicitors were correct and the damage occurred when the distributions were made because the third party claims were not contingent, thereby distinguishing *Law Society v Sephton and Co*. Lloyd LJ held that the mere fact that a notified claim had not yet been pursued or proved did not render the liability contingent and Lewison LJ put it in the clearest possible terms: **21.12**

> In considering when a cause of action in tort accrues it is necessary to compare the claimant's position as it was and as it would have been if the tort had not been committed. In the present

---

[8] *Law Society v Sephton and Co* (n 7) at [21].
[9] *Forster* itself.
[10] As in a riskier pension investment in *Shore v Sedgewick Financial Services Ltd* The Times, 12 August 2008.
[11] As in *Watkins v Jones Maidment Wilson* [2008] 10 EG 166 (CS); (2008) NPC 27; (2008) PNLR 23.
[12] [2011] EWCA Civ 547; [2012] QB 693.

case the tort was Mr Cullen's failure to advise the claimant not to distribute the estate. Before that failure the claimant, in his capacity as administrator, had £61,000 in hand. After that failure he had £21,000. In his capacity as executor, therefore, he was £40,000 worse off. In my judgment he had altered his legal position for the worse as a result of that distribution. I do not regard the fact that Mrs Hannah had not (yet) proved her claim as amounting to a relevant contingency.

21.13 *Forster v Outred* deals with cases where there is a positive act undertaken as a result of the advice of the solicitor. However, often a solicitor or other will-drafter is guilty of a sin of omission rather than commission. In such a case it may be arguable that the cause of action in tort did not accrue until the latest date when the act could have been done. In *Midland Bank v Hett, Stubbs & Kemp*[13] Oliver J held in a case where the defendant solicitors had failed to register a land charge that the cause of action did not accrue until the last moment when it could have been registered. However, in *Bell v Peter Browne & Co*,[14] which involved a solicitor failing to register a caution in the context of matrimonial proceedings, the Court of Appeal held that the damage was caused in 1978 when the divorce settlement was entered into and not at the last point in time when the caution could have been registered. The distinction was drawn between the solicitor in the *Midland Bank* case who was retained by his client and the solicitor in the *Bell* case who was *functus officio* once he had dealt with the divorce settlement. *Bell* is also one of the 'transaction cases' and can be explained in that way.

21.14 In *Cancer Research Campaign v Ernest Brown & Co*,[15] the question was when the cause of action accrued in respect of the alleged negligent failure of solicitors to advise in favour of the execution of a deed of variation of the dispositions in an estate. The answer (which in the event was academic as the claim failed for other reasons) was that it was the latest point of time at which the deed could have been executed tax efficiently, that is two years after the date of death of the testator.

Will cases

21.15 How do these principles apply in the case of claims by disappointed beneficiaries? While the defence of limitation has not loomed large in cases relating to negligence in will drafting, there is no doubt that it could pose particular problems as envisaged by Nicholls V-C in *White v Jones*[16] where he said:

> Finally it is said there are insurmountable difficulties over periods of limitation. If an intended beneficiary has a cause of action against a negligent solicitor, time would run either from the date when the will was made or ought to have been made or from the date of death. The first of these possibilities would be unsatisfactory; a beneficiary intended to take under a will can hardly be said to suffer loss during the testator's lifetime. The second would be unsatisfactory, because it would mean that time might not begin to run indefinitely, subject only to the 15 year longstop under section 14B of the Limitation Act 1980 (as inserted by the Latent Damage Act 1986, section 1). Again these are points best left to be resolved in a case in which they call for decision. If there are problems here, this would not be the first instance of difficulties over limitation in the field of negligence. Even if there are difficulties, as to which I express

---

[13] [1979] Ch 384.
[14] [1990] 3 All ER 124.
[15] [1997] STC 1425; [1998] PNLR 592, 604.
[16] [1995] 2 AC 208 at 226.

no view, this does not militate significantly against the existence of a liability in negligence in this type of case.

The point has been considered by HHJ Bromley sitting as a deputy of the Chancery Division **21.16** in the case of *Bacon v Howard Kennedy*.[17] There, counsel for the defendants argued that the cause of action accrued in 1986–87 when instructions had been given to the defendant solicitors to prepare a will which were ignored. He argued that it was at that date that damage occurred and he relied on *Forster v Outred & Co*. The plaintiff on the other hand argued that the cause of action did not accrue until the date of death of the testator. The judge held that the damage did not accrue until death on the basis that at any time up until the date of death the testator had the ability to remedy the defect. In other words he adopted the sort of approach that was taken in *Midland Bank v Hett, Stubbs & Kemp*. The judge was not impressed by the argument that if mental incapacity had intervened, the ability of the testator to make a will would have ceased before death. He said: 'While he had some infirmities he was in no sense in extremis or mentally disabled, and he might have corrected the omission of having no will at any time over the 9 years or so before his death.'

This decision makes a great deal of sense on the facts of *Bacon v Howard Kennedy* and in **21.17** *White v Jones*-type cases where no will had been executed at all. In such cases the reasoning can be easily justified and applied, but difficulties arise in cases where the complaint is that the will has not been drafted properly, rather than where it has not been drafted at all.

On a strict application of the *Forster v Outred* principle, it is the date when the badly drafted **21.18** will has been executed which ought to represent the date when the cause of action accrues. It is at this date that the damage has been caused. On the other hand, this makes little sense: the limitation period could well expire while the testator was still alive. Wills are frequently made many years before the death of the testator. The answer would seem to be that unlike many other legal documents such as mortgages, wills are ambulatory: they do not take effect until death and it is at this stage that it can be argued that the damage was done—when it is not possible to remedy the situation.

There remains the question of supervening mental incapacity on the part of the testator— **21.19** does this mean that the cause of action accrues at that date? HHJ Bromley sidestepped the issue as he was entitled to do in *Bacon v Howard Kennedy* and it seems that the answer may be that even if the testator ceases to have mental capacity in his lifetime, there is still the Court of Protection jurisdiction to make statutory wills, which could be invoked in the appropriate case.

Trust and administration cases

Trust cases will frequently fall within the 'transaction' type cases—negligently drafted trusts **21.20** or bad advice in respect of the exercise of powers will normally cause immediate damage even if there are contingent losses (such as tax liabilities) to follow in the future. However, it is worth giving some thought to whether the loss may be a purely contingent one.

In cases which concern negligent advice in relation to the administration of an estate, it will **21.21** be a question of looking at the negligent act complained of and seeing what sort of damage one is dealing with and whether the tort is one of commission or omission.

---

[17] [1999] PNLR 1.

Tax cases

21.22   One of the most troubling cases of recent years has been the decision of the Court of Appeal in *Daniels v Thompson*,[18] which concerned the issue of whether a claim against solicitors who had undoubtedly given negligent tax advice was statute barred. Solicitors had advised Mrs Daniels to transfer her house to her son and that this manoeuvre would save IHT notwithstanding that she would continue to live there. The defendants appear to have forgotten altogether the gift with reservation rules which so many tax lawyers have spent so long attempting to circumvent. Mrs Daniels had transferred her house to her son by way of gift in August 1989 and died in 1998. There was no doubt at the date of her death that the house formed part of her estate because it constituted a gift with reservation within s.102 Finance Act 1986. Mr Daniels was the sole executor and beneficiary of her estate and brought the claim in his representative capacity. Counsel for the defendant submitted that Mrs Daniels first suffered loss when she relied on the defendant's advice and did not take steps which (in the event) would have ensured that the transfer was an exempt transfer and not a chargeable transfer for the purposes of IHT; or alternatively seven years before her death, when it became inevitable that the transfer would be a chargeable transfer.

21.23   The claimant's counsel submitted that the estate did not suffer any loss until the date of Mrs Daniels' death: the liability to tax arose only because at her death Mrs Daniels was still residing at her house for no valuable consideration, and the value of her estate exceeded the nil rate band for IHT.

21.24   The Court of Appeal in essence went along with neither of these arguments. Dyson LJ held that if the claimant's argument was right, no loss was suffered until Mrs Daniels died, then Mrs Daniels had suffered no loss, and her estate could not make a claim. An application to amend the pleadings to enable the claimant to plead as PR (a claim which had been accepted as viable by Park J in *Macaulay and Farley v Premium Life Assurance Co Ltd*[19]) was refused and it was indicated that this was on the basis that the PR did not suffer loss as a result of the extra tax to be paid—it was the estate.

21.25   *Daniels v Thompson*[20] is an important case as far as this area of negligence is concerned because it appears to limit the claims which can be made against the negligent practitioner. It was interestingly accepted by the Court of Appeal that had Mrs Daniels sued during her lifetime, there would have been obvious difficulties in assessing the damages which could be claimed, but she would at the very least have been entitled to claim the costs of seeking advice on the matter and of remedying it. However, undoing gifts with reservation is not always easy. It was recognized by the Court of Appeal in *Daniels v Thompson* that a cause of action in negligence will in general terms run from the date on which the damage occurs, which, in the case where the taxpayer has entered into a particular transaction—for example, a settlement, gift, or deed of variation—will be the date of that transaction.[21]

21.26   What, interestingly, was never argued was that Mr Daniels as a disappointed beneficiary had a claim against the defendant on *White v Jones*[22] principles, on the basis that the estate he was inheriting was rather less than he had anticipated.

---

[18] [2004] WTLR 511.
[19] [2000] WTLR 261.
[20] [2004] EWCA Civ 307; [2004] PNLR 33; [2004] WTLR 511.
[21] *Forster v Outred & Co* (n 5).
[22] [1995] 2 AC 905.

In *Rind v Theodore Goddard*[23] Morgan J refused to strike out a claim brought by a residuary **21.27** beneficiary of an estate where additional IHT had been incurred because of negligent advice in respect of estate-planning steps that had resulted in a transfer which was a gift with reservation. The judge considered that a court might find that the solicitors owed a duty of care to the residuary beneficiaries of the estate and expressed some concern with the decision in *Daniels v Thompson*. He pointed out that the court there had not had before it the question of whether a disappointed beneficiary could sue.

Norris J also refused to strike out the claim in *Vinton v Fladgate Fielder*[24] to the effect that **21.28** solicitors had been negligent in providing advice on the availability of business property relief on shares in a family company. He accepted that the claim could not succeed at first instance in light of *Daniels v Thompson* but said in respect of that case:

> I confess that I do not find the distinction between the testatrix and her estate (upon which the conclusion that the testatrix had not suffered any detriment capable of assessment in money terms depends) at all easy to grasp. The estate has no independent legal existence. It is merely the property of the testatrix being administered by her personal representatives. Nonetheless, the distinction is plainly drawn and underpins the conclusion that the testatrix in that case (and the Widow in this case) had not suffered recoverable loss (and, I think would not have suffered recoverable loss even if during her lifetime she had effected an insurance policy to pay the tax sought to be avoided, so as to secure the practical result intended by her instructions if properly executed).

Like Morgan J before him he refused to strike out the claim on the basis that the argument was a purely legal one and indicated that the Court of Appeal might like to reconsider their decision in *Daniels v Thompson*. There is clearly scope for claims to be brought notwithstanding *Daniels v Thompson* and it is fervently to be wished that the Court of Appeal do decide to revisit the point.

In relation to poor tax advice, which does not fall within this area, careful thought needs to **21.29** be given as to whether the liability to pay additional tax is a contingent liability and therefore damage is not caused until the tax is claimed.

Where there is an omission (eg failure to elect for holdover relief) then the limitation **21.30** period of six years will start to run from the last moment when the act could have been performed.[25]

C. Date of knowledge

The law recognizes that the limitation period can sometimes work unjustly in cases where **21.31** damage has occurred, but the fact of that damage does not become known to the claimant until it is too late. This was dealt with by the Latent Damage Act 1986, which inserted ss.14A and 14B into the Limitation Act 1980. Section 14A applies to actions in tortious negligence and provides for a limitation period to run three years from the date of knowledge. Section 14B provides for a longstop date of fifteen years from the date when the negligent act occurred.

---

[23] [2008] EWHC 459.
[24] [2010] EWHC 904 (Ch); [2010] STC 1868.
[25] *Midland Bank v Hett, Stubbs & Kemp* (n 13).

21.32 The provisions for ascertaining the date of knowledge are in many ways complex and have given rise to difficulties in application by the court. The starting point is s.14A(5), which provides that the date is 'the earliest date on which the plaintiff had both the knowledge required for bringing an action for damages in respect of the relevant damage and a right to bring such an action'.

21.33 The knowledge which is required is then defined in subsection (6) as knowledge 'both of the material facts about the damage in respect of which damages are claimed and of other facts relevant to the current action mentioned in subsection (8) below'.

21.34 The reader then has to go on to subsection (7) to find out what those 'material facts' might be. They are 'such facts about the damage as would lead a reasonable person who had suffered such damage to consider it sufficiently serious to justify his instituting proceedings against a defendant who did not dispute liability and was able to satisfy a judgment'.

21.35 Therefore the claimant has to know everything he needs to know to bring an action—or so it seems before the reader gets to subsection (8), which deals with the other facts that he needs to know. These are

> that the damage was attributable in whole or in part to the act or omission which is alleged to constitute negligence; and . . . the identity of the defendant; and . . . if it is alleged that the act or omission was that of a person other than the defendants, the identity of that person and the additional facts supporting the bringing of an action against the defendant.

21.36 This makes sense because without knowledge of these facts it would be difficult for a claimant to mount an action. However, that is not the end of the matter. The reader of the section then has to go on to subsection (9) which reads:

> Knowledge that any acts or omissions did or did not as a matter of law involve negligence is irrelevant for the purposes of subsection (5).

21.37 This subsection has caused some difficulties, as will be seen below, but it is clear that if the facts are all known but the claimant is unaware that what has happened amounts to negligence as a matter of law, advantage cannot be taken of the section.

21.38 Finally, the reader has to take on board the fact that it is not only actual knowledge which is relevant for the purposes of the section but 'knowledge which he might reasonably have been expected to acquire from facts observable or ascertainable by him; or . . . from facts ascertainable by him with the help of appropriate expert advice which it is reasonable for him to seek'.[26] However, that requirement is softened if it is a fact only ascertainable with expert advice and the plaintiff has taken all reasonable steps to obtain and, where appropriate, to act on that advice. So, in other words, if the claimant seeks the advice of a solicitor and the second solicitor too gets it wrong, the defendant cannot allege that the claimant ought to have known a fact they did not in fact know. On the other hand, it has been said that s.14A(10) requires the court to have regard to the position of the actual claimant, not some wholly hypothetical claimant, and if the claimant should have known of the claim because of seeking advice in respect of another aspect of matters, then they may be regarded as having constructive knowledge of the claim.[27]

---

[26] Section 14A(10) Limitation Act 1980.
[27] *Gravgaard v Aldridge & Brownlee* [2005] PNLR 19.

The Court of Appeal has said that the section must be approached 'in a common sense way'[28] **21.39** but there is no doubt that the cases have analysed the section in a manner that has at times been less than down to earth.

The first point to note is that it is clear that s.14A(8)(a) requires the claimant to have know- **21.40** ledge of the causative process,[29] in other words the claimant must know that an act or omission has caused the loss.

However, the claimant does not need to know that the act or omission was negligent as a **21.41** matter of law. In *Haward v Fawcetts (a firm)*[30] the House of Lords examined the interrelation of s.14A(8) and (9). Mr Haward invested money in a company on the advice of his accountant Mr Austreng. The company failed, and Mr Haward lost his money. The speeches of each of their Lordships put the matter in subtly different terms but the general thrust of the decision was that knowledge that the damage was attributable in whole or in part to acts or omissions of the defendant alleged to constitute negligence within s.14A(8)(a) meant knowledge in broad terms of

(a)   the facts on which the claimant's complaint was based;
(b)   the defendant's acts or omissions; and
(c)   knowing that there was a real possibility that those acts or omissions had been a cause of the damage.

As Lord Nicholls said:[31]   **21.42**

> 12.   Difficulties may sometimes arise over the interaction of these 'knowledge' provisions and the statutory provision rendering 'irrelevant' knowledge that, as a matter of law, an act or omission did, or did not, amount to negligence: section 14A(9). By the latter provision Parliament has drawn a distinction between facts said to constitute negligence and the legal consequence of those facts. Knowledge of the former (the facts) is needed before time begins to run, knowledge of the latter (the legal consequence of the facts) is irrelevant. As Sir Thomas Bingham MR said in the clinical negligence case of *Dobbie*... knowledge of fault or negligence is not necessary to set time running. A claimant need not know he has a worthwhile cause of action.

> 13.   A linguistic point, which can give rise to confusion, should be noted here. Sometimes the essence of a claimant's case may lie in an alleged act or omission by the defendant which cannot easily be described, at least in general terms, without recourse to language suggestive of fault: for instance, that 'something had gone wrong' in the conduct of the claimant's medical operation, or that the accountant's advice was 'flawed'. Use of such language does not mean the facts thus compendiously described have necessarily stepped outside the scope of section 14A(8)(a). In this context there can be no objection to the use of language of this character so long as this does not lead to any blurring of the boundary between the essential and the irrelevant.

The decision of the House of Lords in *Haward* followed the decision of an exceptionally **21.43** strong Court of Appeal in *Hallam-Eames v Merrett Syndicates*,[32] where it was said:

> The plaintiff does not have to know that he has a cause of action or that the defendant's acts can be characterised in law as negligent or as falling short of some standard of professional or other behaviour. But, as Hoffmann LJ said in *Broadley*, the words 'which is alleged to constitute

---

[28]   *Spencer-Ward v Humberts* [1995] 1 EGLR 123.
[29]   *Hallam-Eames v Merrett* [2001] Lloyd's Rep PN 178.
[30]   [2006] UKHL 9; [2006] 1 WLR 682.
[31]   At [12] and [13].
[32]   [2001] 2 Lloyd's Rep 178.

negligence' serve to identify the facts of which the plaintiff must have knowledge. He must have known the facts which can fairly be described as constituting the negligence of which he complains. It may be that knowledge of such facts will also serve to bring home to him the fact that the defendant has been negligent or at fault. But that is not in itself a reason for saying that he need not have known them.

21.44 The test as adumbrated by the House of Lords was applied at first instance in the case of *Boycott v Perrins Guy Williams*.[33] Mr Boycott complained that his solicitors had not advised him when purchasing a property with his former partner as beneficial joint tenants that the joint tenancy could be severed. Vos J held that the primary limitation period started to run from the date on which the property was purchased and that the date of knowledge for the purposes of s.14A was when the joint tenancy was severed. At that point Mr Boycott had the requisite knowledge of all relevant facts even if he did not know as a matter of law that his solicitors had been negligent. Vos J considered that *Hallam-Eames v Merrett Syndicates* survived the decision of the House of Lords in *Haward v Fawcetts*.

21.45 Often in tax cases it is not until the taxpayer seeks advice from new solicitors or accountants that the negligence becomes apparent. By then the primary limitation period may have expired. The question in every case must be when the claimant taxpayer has the knowledge that the damage is attributable to the advice he has received. It does not matter that he may not know that the advice was negligent; but he probably needs to know that something has gone wrong.

21.46 To base an example on a negligence case relating to wills, it can be seen that knowledge on the part of the beneficiary that the failure of the testatrix to sever a joint tenancy prior to making her will had lost him a share in property comprised in the estate would be sufficient knowledge of what had caused the loss to trigger the three-year period. The fact that the beneficiary did not realize that the failure of the solicitor to advise severance was negligent would be irrelevant.

21.47 The claimant placed reliance on s.14A in *Bacon v Howard Kennedy*. There the judge rejected the argument on the basis that 'Mr. Bacon's knowledge under section 14A(10) included knowledge whether or not the will had been made being knowledge which he might reasonably have expected to acquire from facts ascertainable by him'.

21.48 In essence the judge held that having been so closely involved in the correspondence relating to the making of the will,[34] he could have inquired further as to whether the will had been executed or not. There is something distasteful in the idea of courts expecting beneficiaries to make inquiries as to the progress of a will, but in the event the s.14A point does not appear to have attained any great importance in the case in light of the decision by the judge that the cause of action did not accrue until death.

D. The longstop

21.49 It is important to have regard to s.14B Limitation Act 1980, which bars a remedy and provides a complete defence to claims brought more than fifteen years from the date of the negligent act, whether or not a cause of action has accrued. Section 14B reads as follows:

---

[33] [2011] EWHC 2969 (Ch); [2012] PNLR 25; the claimant was the famous former cricketer.
[34] Which notably provoked the argument on behalf of the defendants that the testator was under the undue influence of the claimant—an argument on which the judge poured scorn.

(1) An action for damages for negligence [other than one for personal injury] shall not be brought after the expiration of fifteen years from the date (or, if more than one, from the last of the dates) on which there occurred any act or omission—

    (a) which is alleged to constitute negligence; and

    (b) to which the damage in respect of which damages are claimed is alleged to be attributable (in whole or in part).

(2) This section bars the right of action in a case to which subsection (1) above applies notwithstanding that—

    (a) the cause of action has not yet accrued; or

    (b) where section 14A of this Act applies to the action, the date which is for the purposes of that section the starting date for reckoning the period mentioned in subsection (4)(b) of that section has not yet occurred;

before the end of the period of limitation prescribed by this section.

Therefore if a solicitor advised on a tax scheme in 1992 and was guilty of negligence in doing so, **21.50** it does not matter that no loss is suffered until 2008 and the cause of action has not for the purposes of the claim in tort accrued. More than fifteen years has elapsed and the matter is at an end.

E. Concealment

There was a worrying period for professionals when s.32 Limitation Act, having rather lan- **21.51** guished as a method of prolonging the limitation period, became all the rage. This section provides that if there has been 'deliberate concealment' of the right of action, the limitation period is suspended until the claimant has discovered the concealment or could have done so with reasonable diligence. Section 32(2) provides that deliberate commission of a breach of duty in circumstances when it will not be discovered for some time is deliberate concealment of the facts involved in that breach of duty.

In *Brockesby v Armitage and Guest*[35] the Court of Appeal in an *ex tempore* judgment held that **21.52** the solicitors in question had deliberately carried out the act complained of and the circumstances were such that the claimant was not likely to find out about their failure to obtain a release from a building society. There was as such no deliberate concealment but the deliberate (in the sense of intentional) commission of an act that was a breach of duty.

This approach was perhaps taken even further in the case of *Liverpool Roman Catholic* **21.53** *Archdiocese Trustees v Goldberg*.[36] There Laddie J held that it was not necessary that the concealment was of law and not facts, and that there was no requirement of dishonourable conduct.

The position was fortunately resolved by the House of Lords in *Cave v Robinson Jarvis &* **21.54** *Rolf*[37] where it was held that the clear words of s.32 meant that there had to be a 'deliberate commission of a breach of duty', which meant not an inadvertent, accidental, or unintended breach of duty that the actor was not aware he was committing. Lord Millett stated:[38]

> In my opinion, section 32 deprives a defendant of a limitation defence in two situations: (i) where he takes active steps to conceal his own breach of duty after he has become aware of it; and

---

[35] [2000] PNLR 33; [1999] Lloyd's Rep PN 888.
[36] [2000] Lloyd's Rep PN 836.
[37] [2003] 1 AC 384.
[38] At [27].

(ii) where he is guilty of deliberate wrongdoing and conceals or fails to disclose it in circumstances where it is unlikely to be discovered for some time. But it does not deprive a defendant of a limitation defence where he is charged with negligence if, being unaware of his error or that he has failed to take proper care, there has been nothing for him to disclose.

21.55   It now seems clear that s.32 will apply only in cases where a professional has deliberately concealed a cause of action from a client. In *Denekamp v Denekamp*,[39] which involved a bitter family dispute where conspiracy in relation to a deed of variation was alleged and negligence on the part of the solicitors who advised in relation to it, the judge refused to allow the particulars of claim to be amended to plead s.32 on the basis that the simple act of negligence did not thereby deliberately conceal that act of negligence in order to postpone the commencement of the primary limitation period under s.32 of the 1980 Act. An argument under s.14A Limitation Act was similarly rejected.

F. Other arguments in relation to limitation

21.56   In *Cotterell v Leeds Day & Co*[40] the complaint against the solicitors was that they had failed to send a notice of election to the Inland Revenue in respect of a deed of variation executed pursuant to s.142 Inheritance Tax Act 1984. The solicitors had represented to the client that they would compensate her if she died within seven years and there were any IHT ramifications as a result of their failure. It was held that this amounted to a representation upon which the client and her daughter had acted and therefore the defendants were estopped from relying on a defence of limitation. This is a case which turned very much on its facts, but it should not be forgotten that if the claimant cannot get round the defence of limitation by use of s.14A there may be other ways to circumvent the problem.

---

[39] [2004] EWHC 1378 (Ch).
[40] [2001] WTLR 435.

22

THE ASSESSMENT OF DAMAGES

A. General comments

Sometimes, the assessment of damages will take place separately from the trial of the issue of **22.01** liability, for example where a preliminary issue has been ordered on the question of liability. However, both parties need to undertake an assessment of the likely damages at the outset, not just because the likely value of the claim has to be specified when going through the process of the pre-action protocol, but also so that it is possible to attempt to settle the claim at an early stage, and the parties are clear what they are fighting over. It is also, of course, vitally important to ensure that some loss has actually been suffered by the person bringing the claim.[1]

B. The basic approach

There have been many judicial expressions of the way in which damages should be assessed **22.02** for negligence. The following is probably the one most cited:

> You should as nearly as possible get at that sum of money which will put the party who has been injured, or who has suffered, in the same position as he would have been in if he had not sustained the wrong for which he is now getting his compensation.[2]

The modern approach to the assessment of damages was set out by the House of Lords deci- **22.03** sion in *South Australia Asset Management Corporation v York Montague Ltd*,[3] where Lord Hoffmann said: 'Before one can consider the principle on which one should calculate the damages to which a plaintiff is entitled as compensation for loss, it is necessary to decide for what kind of loss he is entitled to compensation.'

This theme was taken up by Sir Christopher Slade in the Court of Appeal in *Corbett v Bond* **22.04** *Pearce*[4] where he said:

---

[1] See *Daniels v Thompson* [2004] PNLR 33 for an example of a case where the claimant was held not to be the person who had suffered loss.
[2] *Livingstone v Rawyards Coal Co* [1880] 5 App Cas 25, 39 per Lord Blackburn.
[3] [1997] AC 191, invariably referred to as the SAAMCO case.
[4] [2001] WTLR 419 at 433.

in the present case it is necessary to determine the scope of the duty of care owed by the defendants to a testatrix by reference to the kind of damage from which they had to take care to keep her harmless, having regard to the terms of their retainer. Having such regard, I think it clear that this kind of damage was the loss which those who would become interested in the estate, whether as beneficiaries under the September will or as creditors, would suffer if effect were not given to her latest testamentary intentions.

C. Causation and quantification

22.05   It can often be difficult when assessing damages to distinguish between matters of causation and questions of quantification of damage. This is particularly acute in cases which involve an omission on the part of the defendant rather than the commission of a negligent act. Some negligence involving wills, trusts, estates, and tax will of course involve failures to advise or act, rather than advising or acting negligently, and these can give rise to some very difficult questions. The clearest analysis of this troubled area is undoubtedly to be found in the judgment of Stuart-Smith LJ in *Allied Maples Group Ltd v Simmons & Simmons*.[5] That case involved the acquisition of shares in certain companies and the facts are of no great assistance to the sort of cases which this book examines. However, Stuart-Smith LJ set out with clarity the various categories of cases and the processes which had to be gone through in analysing causation and then quantifying damages.

(1)   The first question is whether the negligence consists of some positive act or an omission. So, for example, the failure to draft a will before the death of the testator or to exercise a trust power or to bar an entail would clearly be a case of omission. On the other hand negligent drafting of a will or trust is a positive act of misfeasance.

(2)   When dealing with a positive act, the question of causation is clear and easy (in most cases) to answer: did the negligent drafting (for example) on a balance of probabilities cause the loss suffered by the claimant, for example, the costs of having the court construe the will or trust?

(3)   When the act is one of omission, the question of causation is not one of historical fact, but depends on the answer to the hypothetical question, what would the claimant have done had the correct advice been given? This exercise will be relevant in cases where the estate, rather than a third party, is suing. If the testator had been properly advised what would he have done? This is a matter of causation and it is well established that the claimant must prove on a balance of probabilities that he would have acted to avoid the risk to himself or to have obtained the benefit of which the negligence has deprived him. Stuart-Smith LJ referred to the case of *Otter v Church Adams Tatham & Co*[6] where, owing to the solicitors' failure to advise him to do so, the deceased had not disentailed certain property before he died. His estate sued and Upjohn J held that the deceased had been deprived of the opportunity of disentailing and assessed damages with a 10 per cent discount on the basis that he might not have disentailed even if properly advised. This was considered to be the wrong approach in *Sykes v Midland Bank Executor and Trustee Co Ltd*[7] on the basis that the estate, having established on a balance of probabilities that

---

[5]   [1995] 4 All ER 907; applied more recently in *Dayman v Lawrence Graham* [2008] EWHC 2036 and *Veitch v Avery* [2008] PNLR 7.
[6]   [1953] Ch 280; [1953] 1 All ER 168.
[7]   Per Salmon LJ in [1970] 1 QB 113 at 130, and [1970] 2 All ER 471 at 480.

the deceased would have disentailed, should have been awarded damages without any discount.

(4) Stuart-Smith LJ then outlined a third category of case into which many of the *White v Jones*-type cases will fall. This is where the claimant's loss depends on the hypothetical act of a third party, either in addition to his own act or quite independently of his act. So, for example, the claimant may complain that solicitors failed to prepare a will in time, which, if executed, would have benefited him, but the question may arise as to whether the testator would in fact have executed such a will if prepared. In that class of case, the correct approach is to decide first on the question of causation: has the negligence of the defendant caused the claimant to lose a chance? Stuart-Smith LJ relied on two cases: *Chaplin v Hicks*[8] and *Kitchen v Royal Air Force Association*[9] where the correct approach was to see whether the claimant could show that he had a substantial chance of obtaining a benefit rather than a speculative one. So, for example, in the case of *Jemma Trust Co Ltd v Kippax Beaumont Lewis*[10] both the Court of Appeal and the judge at first instance found that solicitors had been negligent in the handling of an application to the Court of Protection to approve a deed of variation, but held that the Court of Protection would not have approved the deed even if the solicitors had handled it better. In other words the claimant could not show that the negligence of the defendants had caused any loss.

In *Feltham v Freer Bouskell*[11] the defendant solicitors had failed to make a will for a testatrix **22.06** aged ninety and she died having persuaded the major beneficiary to draw up the will, which resulted in it being challenged. The issue arose and was fully argued as to the basis upon which the disappointed beneficiary in a *White v Jones* case has to prove to the court what the testator would have done. Was it on the basis of balance of probabilities or on the basis of loss of a chance—the third category of case referred to by Stuart-Smith LJ in *Allied Maples*? Counsel for the defendants argued that the correct approach was balance of probabilities. In fact the court found the testatrix would have made a will in favour of the beneficiary and so the point became academic but the judge nevertheless expressed the view that the testator's intention had to be assessed on the basis of loss of a chance. It ought not to be treated as a category 2 case because that involved judging the claimant's own conduct.

If loss of a chance can be shown, causation is established. It is then for the court, when **22.07** quantifying damages, to assess the value of that substantial chance and discount damages appropriately.

A case in this area which provides a good illustration of the sort of difficulties faced by the **22.08** courts is the decision of Harman J in *Cancer Research Campaign v Ernest Brown*.[12] This case involved an allegation against a firm of solicitors that they had failed to provide the elderly testatrix with advice about a possible deed of variation to vary the dispositions made under the will of her brother who had predeceased her leaving her his estate. Harman J analysed the matter in this way:

---

[8] [1911] 2 KB 786; [1911–13] All ER 224 where the defendant's breach of contract prevented the plaintiff from entering a beauty contest and therefore deprived her of the opportunity of winning one of the prizes.

[9] [1958] 1 WLR 563; [1958] 2 All ER 241 where solicitors failed to issue a writ against a tortfeasor and the plaintiff lost the chance of getting damages.

[10] [2005] EWCA Civ 248.

[11] [2013] EWHC 1952 (Ch).

[12] [1997] STC 1425; [1998] PNLR 592, 604.

any action founded on the failure to advise the testatrix in this way must, of necessity, be one for loss of a chance. From the (now deceased) testatrix point of view, the chance lost was that of executing a deed of variation. From the point of view of the disgruntled beneficiary, what has been lost is the chance of a more bounteous legacy.

22.09 While recognizing that this was a loss of chance case within the third category of Stuart-Smith LJ's analysis, the judge did not then go on to apply the test with any rigidity. In a sense he did not need to because he was not at all persuaded that the deceased would have executed a deed of variation even had she been advised to do so. Putting it in his own inimitable way he said:

> [the testatrix] may have been one of those (there are not insubstantial in number) who consider that tax avoidance is something rather unattractive, to be indulged in by sharp people with connections in the City of London who use various arcane devices to get out of their proper obligations to the Court. She may not. She may have been a person who thought... that no person was obliged so to arrange their personal affairs as to enable the Revenue to put their largest shovel into them.[13]

22.10 In other words, in that case no light could be thrown on the way in which the testatrix would have acted if she had received advice that she should enter into a deed of variation, and therefore there was no substantial chance established that the beneficiaries would have received the benefit of the extra tax saving.

22.11 In *Bacon v Howard Kennedy*,[14] Judge Bromley QC, sitting as a deputy of the Chancery Division, rejected counsel for the defendants' submission that a discount ought to be applied to the damages there on the basis that there was a prospect that the will could have been challenged on the basis of undue influence. Clearly intensely irritated by this argument put forward on behalf of solicitors whom he described as 'incompetent', the judge refused to take into account the 'prospect of misguided litigation to reduce the damages'.

22.12 The Court of Appeal took a similar line in *Horsfall v Haywards*[15] where it considered that it had too little evidence on which to reduce the damages awarded, on the basis that claims of undue influence and under the Inheritance (Provision for Family and Dependants) Act 1975 would have depleted the estate even if the will had been properly drafted.

22.13 Where a beneficiary would not have been entitled to an interest under the will absolutely, but is the beneficiary under a discretionary trust set up by the will, more difficult considerations apply. This was considered by Jonathan Parker J in *Trusted v Clifford Chance*[16] where he found against the plaintiff's claim, but he did explore the basis on which damages would be assessed in a case where the gift was not an outright gift but would depend on the exercise by trustees of a particular discretion. Counsel had submitted to him that as his client was one of nine in a specified class in respect of whom the trustees could exercise their discretion, his loss amounted to one-ninth of that fund. Having described the submission as 'absurd' he set out the principles thus:

> it is clear that under the principle of *White v Jones* damages are recoverable for loss of expectation, and in my judgment that principle will apply notwithstanding that the expectation which has been lost (ie the 'particular testamentary benefit') itself involves an element of expectation

---

[13] *Cancer Research Campaign v Ernest Brown* (n 12) at 1430.
[14] [1999] PNLR 1; [2000] WTLR 169.
[15] [2000] WTLR 29.
[16] [2001] WTLR 1219.

in the sense that it is dependent on the exercise of a discretion. In such circumstances, the court must do its best to arrive at a figure which fairly represents the value of the expectation which has been lost. That is the task which would have to be undertaken, but I cannot see any basis in logic or common sense for arriving at a figure simply by reference to the number of named individuals in a class of beneficiaries which included their spouses, children and remoter issue, and children, and on the assumption that each of the named individuals will benefit equally and that the benefits will be received immediately.[17]

This analysis must be correct. The case would fall within the third category of cases set out **22.14** by Stuart-Smith LJ in *Allied Maples* and it would be necessary to show that the claimant had a substantial chance of benefit under the will. In most cases where the claimant was the discretionary object of a trust, this hurdle could probably be overcome, although there might be cases where the beneficiary was simply a makeweight in the class and the benefit was so remote that it could not be regarded as substantial. Once that exercise has been undertaken (a question of causation), the court could then perform the exercise set out by Jonathan Parker J and evaluate that chance for the purpose of assessing damages. These cases involve double expectation—an expectation to be included as a beneficiary under the trust in the will, then an expectation that benefit from that trust will be forthcoming.

Those clearly are the principles to be applied, but unless there is a clear letter of wishes mak- **22.15** ing it obvious what the trustees would be likely to do, they may not be so easy to apply in practice. Perhaps it is not entirely improper to suggest that had Jonathan Parker J not been fortified by the knowledge that he had found against the plaintiff on almost every other basis and would not in fact have to assess damages, he would have been less keen to propound this test.

A rather different approach was adopted by Lloyd J in *Gray v Richards Butler*[18] where he **22.16** did not have to assess damages, as he found against the plaintiff on liability, but pondered the point of what would happen if a beneficiary was simply a member of a class entitled under a trust set up in the will, which for whatever reason was not effective. There would be the 'double expectation' point, which was considered by Jonathan Parker J in the *Trusted v Clifford Chance* case. Lloyd J said:[19]

> If there had been an existing trust of some kind under which these beneficial interests were defined and through the negligence of a solicitor that trust failed to become entitled to an asset it would be the trustees who would pursue the claim in damages and their recovery would be added to the trust and would therefore go to enhance the trust fund for the benefit of whoever became entitled under the terms of the trust.

His Lordship then accepted that the position was different when the trust never came into **22.17** being, and unfortunately did not go any further on this point as he decided against the solicitors being in breach of duty.

A related point arose in *Martin v Triggs Turner Bartons*,[20] a claim by a widow against the **22.18** solicitors who had drawn up her husband's will under which she had a life interest followed by a discretionary trust in favour of charities. The principal allegation was that the power of advancement was drafted negligently, as instead of providing that a maximum of £100,000

---

[17] *Trusted v Clifford Chance* (n 16) at 1223F.
[18] [2000] WTLR 143.
[19] [2000] WTLR 143 at 165A–C.
[20] [2009] EWHC 1920 (Ch).

could be advanced by the trustees, it should have provided that everything except £100,000 could be advanced. The widow had applied to have the will rectified and that action had been compromised with the charities on the basis of a partition of the fund. The question arose as to whether the damages should be assessed on the basis of a loss of a chance (because whether advances were made to Mrs Martin was dependent on the decisions of the trustees) or whether she had in fact received an interest under the will less valuable as a result of the negligence of the defendants. The latter argument prevailed. In assessing the damages the judge awarded the difference between the sum she had been able to negotiate on a partition bearing in mind the terms of the negligently drafted will but taking into account the prospect that the court might rectify it compared to the value she could have negotiated on a partition had the will been properly drafted.

D. No loss

22.19   It is perhaps a trite point, but the claimant must be able to show that he or she has suffered loss. In *Gray v Richards Butler*[21] monies had already been distributed from the estate when it was established that the will had not been properly executed. In the event, Lloyd J did not accept that there had been any breach of duty, but he also considered that if he had, he would have awarded damages based on the monies which the beneficiaries had been forced to repay to the executor. In other words, it was possible to evaluate the chance retrospectively. However, in the case of two of the beneficiaries whom he did not consider would be asked to repay the sums distributed to them, he considered that no damages would be payable as they would have suffered no loss.

22.20   Similarly in *Trusted* the disappointed beneficiary was actually better off under the earlier will, which proved just one of the many obstacles in the way of a successful claim in that case.

22.21   How far the ability of beneficiaries to benefit under the estates of persons who benefit under the estate should be taken into account was considered in *Earl v Wilhelm*.[22] That case illustrated how difficult it is to establish such a possibility with enough certainty for the court to conclude that no loss has been suffered by a disappointed beneficiary because they will ultimately inherit from a beneficiary who has benefited.

22.22   A distinction needs to be drawn between claims in tort (eg by disappointed beneficiaries) and claims in contract (eg by the estate, trustees, or PRs) because in the latter proof of loss is not necessary to establish a cause of action. However, if no actual loss can be shown the recoverable damages will be nominal only and hence the victory pyrrhic. In *Chandrasekaran v Deloitte & Touche*[23] this was the result.

E. Disappointed beneficiary cases

22.23   Applying these principles to will negligence cases, the claimant must be put in the position he would have been in had the will been executed in time, or had it been properly drafted. For the disappointed beneficiary deprived of the gifts in a will which, owing to the negligence

---

[21] [2000] WTLR 143.
[22] [2001] WTLR at 1282C and D, 1290F.
[23] [2004] EWHC 1378 (Ch).

of a solicitor, has remained unexecuted at the date of death the measure is 'the full amount which he could have received under the will, this being no greater than the damage for which the solicitor could have been liable to the donor if the loss had occurred during his lifetime'.[24]

Indeed, the intended beneficiary in a case where the will has not been executed will recover **22.24** more than the testator could have recovered during his or her lifetime. In fact the testator would not have had a cause of action against the solicitor in his lifetime because he could, of course, at any time have mitigated any loss he had suffered (and arguably he would have suffered nothing) by executing the will. Therefore the remark cannot be accurate in respect of the *White v Jones* type of case where the will has not been executed. Of course, the whole rationale behind the remedy given to a disappointed beneficiary in *White v Jones* was the fact that there is a gap in the law if the estate of the testator has suffered no loss as a result of the negligence, whereas the disappointed beneficiary has, but is owed no duty of care. The true basis of assessment of damages in these cases is that the beneficiary will be put in the position he would have been in had the will been executed or properly drafted.

In *White v Jones* itself, calculating the damage suffered was the most straightforward part of **22.25** the whole case: the will, which was never executed, would have left a legacy of £9,000 to the disappointed beneficiaries. That was therefore the loss which they suffered. It was, however, a loss of expectation.

In more complex cases, it is not always so easy to see how damages should be assessed. How should they be assessed in a case where instead of an outright interest under the will the disappointed beneficiary was one of the objects of a discretionary trust set up by the will? This was discussed by Jonathan Parker J in *Trusted v Clifford Chance*[25] and by Lloyd J in *Gray v Richards Butler*,[26] both of which cases are looked at in more detail under the heading of 'Causation and quantification' above.

In *Feltham v Freer Bouskell*[27] the claimant, who had settled a challenge to the will at medi- **22.26** ation, successfully claimed the monies she had to pay to the other parties together with her costs. Therefore the court will look at the sums paid by way of compromise of claims if that represents the measure of loss.

F. Damages other than loss of expectation

Not all negligence cases relating to the areas covered in this book fall within the category of **22.27** disappointed beneficiary cases. The claimant may be a trustee or PR of the estate. In such a case, the damages will not be a loss of expectation. An example of such a case in the context of wills is the unusual case of *Hines v Willans*[28] where the question of causation arose. There the damages recovered reflected the amount which the widow had had to pay to settle a probate action she had brought to prove an earlier will. The Court of Appeal was clearly concerned with this award and emphasized that the plaintiff had suffered a loss of expectation of inheriting under the first will. However, ultimately the award was confirmed on the basis

---

[24] *White v Jones*, per Lord Goff of Chieveley at 266.
[25] [2001] WTLR 1219.
[26] [2000] WTLR 143.
[27] [2013] EWHC 1952 (Ch).
[28] [2002] WTLR 299.

that the judge at first instance had made a specific finding that the deceased would not have approached another solicitor to make the will which the defendant solicitor had made for him. In other words the plaintiff had not just lost the chance of inheriting but could establish on a balance of probabilities that she had lost her entitlement under the previous will because of the act of the defendant solicitor. It should be noted that this was not a case based in tort, but a breach of contract case, with the duty owed directly to the plaintiff.

22.28 In *Worby v Rosser*[29] an attempt was made by beneficiaries under an earlier will, which had been admitted to probate after a contested probate action, to recover the substantial costs of that action[30] from the solicitor who had prepared the later, invalid will. The beneficiaries failed on the basis they were not owed a duty of care, but the court recognized that the estate would have a remedy against the solicitor. Therefore if the beneficiaries had recouped their costs from the estate rather than obtaining orders for costs against the other parties, that would have enabled the estate to claim for the loss it had suffered from the solicitors who drew up the invalid will.

22.29 *Worby v Rosser* was distinguished in *Feltham v Freer Bouskell*[31] where the claimant was held entitled to the costs she had paid in defending a challenge to a will because she had to bear them personally.

22.30 The costs of litigation were claimed by the estate in *Corbett v Bond Pearce*.[32] There, a probate action was brought which resulted in the last will of the testatrix being declared invalid on the ground of lack of testamentary intention.[33] It is a tribute to the fact that *White v Jones* has become so well established that the defendant solicitors settled the claim of two disappointed residuary beneficiaries under the invalid will by paying them the value of the residuary estate they had lost without any deduction for the costs of the probate action; which must be the correct approach. The defendants then faced a claim on behalf of the estate for the costs of the probate action which had depleted the residuary estate. At first instance, before Eady J, the plaintiffs were successful and the rationale of that judgment would appear to be that the duties owed in tort to beneficiaries of an estate and in contract to the testator/estate are complementary. There are different duties giving rise to different loss and therefore there is no reason why the disappointed beneficiaries cannot recover damages based on the loss they have suffered as a result of the breach of duty owed to them, and the estate cannot recover for its loss. Thus, the disappointed beneficiaries could recover the value of the residuary estate which they had not inherited and the estate could claim the unnecessary costs to which it had been put by having to undertake the litigation. The reasoning is very attractive but the result was startling. The unintended beneficiaries of the estate were not only entitled to the windfall which resulted from the later will being invalid but one supplemented by the costs of the probate action deducted from it.

22.31 The Court of Appeal came to a different conclusion from Eady J and rejected the claimant's claim. It held[34] that the beneficiaries under the invalid September will had already been

---

[29] [1999] Lloyd's Rep PN 972.
[30] £250,000.
[31] [2013] EWHC 1952 (Ch).
[32] [2000] WTLR 655 QB; [2001] 1 WTLR 419 (CA).
[33] The report of the probate case is well worth reading in this area: see *Corbett v Newey* [1996] 2 All ER 914.
[34] *Corbett v Bond Pearce* [2001] 1 WTLR 419 (CA) at 433.

compensated for their loss, and the sums claimed by the estate had in effect already been paid out to the parties who had suffered loss.

Corbett v Bond Pearce is not authority for the proposition that there can never be success-   **22.32**
ful claims by both beneficiaries and the estate. If the beneficiaries had not been entitled to residue but to legacies and the residue had borne the costs, then none of the compensation payable to the disappointed beneficiaries would have been included in the costs borne by the estate. What is more, in *Corbett* the disappointed beneficiaries' claim was dealt with first—enabling the court to say that the defendants had already paid once over for the loss. What if the estate had sued first? It would be hard to say that the estate did not have a perfectly good claim. After all, if the result of negligence on the part of solicitors is that the claimant has to bear the costs of litigation, that is an actual loss, which he has suffered.[35]

Corbett v Bond Pearce did not end there. The Court of Appeal made an order that the estate   **22.33**
should be entitled to recover damages insofar as the residue was insufficient to pay its cred-itors. The order produced by the Court of Appeal clearly perplexed Rimer J in front of whom the inquiry as to damages came. That hearing[36] involved the question as to whether the costs incurred in the litigation before the Court of Appeal could not be claimed as damages against Bond Pearce. He said:

> More generally, I was shown no authority on whether costs ordered to be paid by C to D in the course of a negligence claim by C against D can in any circumstances be recovered by C from D as part of the damages awarded to C against D in the same claim. Whilst 'never say never' may be a counsel of prudence in approaching such a question, it is obvious that it will only be in an exceptional case that such costs might be so recovered.

In other areas there have been few reported cases as to how damages should be assessed   **22.34**
because few cases involving tax, trusts, and administration of estates have succeeded. In such cases it will be a question of looking at the loss which has been caused by the negligence of the solicitor or other professional advising the trustees or PRs based on the general principles set out above. Frequently it will be tax which might have been avoided or sometimes the costs of putting the mistake right if it has been possible for the claimant to mitigate the loss.[37]

G. Contributory negligence

At one time contributory negligence was a complete defence to a claim of negligence in tort.   **22.35**
That was all changed by the enactment of the Law Reform (Contributory Negligence) Act 1945, s.1(1) of which reads:

(1) Where any person suffers damage as the result partly of his own fault and partly of the fault of any other person or persons, a claim in respect of that damage shall not be defeated by reason of the fault of the person suffering the damage, but the damages recoverable in respect thereof shall be reduced to such extent as the court thinks just and equitable having regard to the claimant's share in the responsibility for the damage.

---

[35] See the discussion at Chapter 3 para 3.18.
[36] [2006] EWHC 909.
[37] As to which see Chapter 23 on mitigation.

22.36   It is always a difficult question as to whether contributory negligence should be dealt with in sections dealing with defences to a claim, or in the section dealing with assessment of damage, but it undoubtedly fits better here, whatever the purists' view might be.

22.37   Contributory negligence in general plays a very small role in professional negligence cases. This has been explained on the basis that there is usually sufficient inequality of knowledge and experience between the solicitor and his client that the client will rarely be guilty of contributory negligence. This is undoubtedly true in many cases, but an argument to the effect that contributory negligence will never have a part to play in cases of this kind because the duty of the defendant is to protect the claimant from the very damages they have suffered has not met with success.[38] In that decision of the High Court of Australia, it was said:[39]

> A finding of contributory negligence turns on a factual investigation of whether the plaintiff contributed to his or her own loss by failing to take reasonable care of his or her person or property. What is reasonable care depends on the circumstances of the case. In many cases it may be proper for a plaintiff to rely on the defendant to perform its duty. But there is no absolute rule.

22.38   It seems clear that the question of whether contributory negligence will reduce the damages in any particular case will depend on the facts.

22.39   The issue has not arisen in any of the English negligence cases involving *White v Jones*-type cases,[40] but it did arise in the Saskatchewan case of *Earl v Wilhelm*.[41] The claim in that case was based on the fact that the lawyer drew the will on the basis that the testator owned certain land beneficially, whereas in fact it had been transferred to a company some years before. The judge recognized that the issue of contributory negligence had not arisen in the cases such as *Ross v Caunters* and *White v Jones* because 'In these cases the wills prepared failed because of non-compliance with statutory or other requirements to which understandably the testators could not properly have been held to contribute'.

22.40   However, he went on to hold that the facts in that case warranted a different conclusion. Mr Thornton, the testator, had been aware that the land was held beneficially by a company and had reviewed financial statements and tax returns with his accountant. The judge considered that the testator had been contributorily negligent. He said:

> While a solicitor is not relieved because of inadequate instructions, from the responsibility to ensure that his instructions are complete and sufficiently accurate in law or otherwise that the work the solicitor undertakes on behalf of a client will be effectual and appropriate in the result, nevertheless, a solicitor is entitled to place an appropriate degree of reliance upon the client and the information he provides having regard to all the circumstances of the engagement.

22.41   The Court of Appeal disagreed with the judge at first instance on the question of contributory negligence. They held that there was no applicable statutory provision that applied to render the testator's negligence something which could be taken into account in respect of a claim brought by a disappointed beneficiary. That being the case, the court had no power

---

[38] *Astley v Austrust* [1999] 161 ALR 155; [1999] Lloyd's Rep PN 758.

[39] *Astley* (n 38) at 765, col 2.

[40] Although it is perhaps interesting that the point was not raised in *Carr-Glynn v Frearsons* [1998] 4 All ER 225 where the testatrix said she would get the deeds of the house but failed to do so.

[41] The first instance decision is at [1998] 2 WWR 524, Saskatchewan Queen's Bench, Zarzeczny J; a case well worth reading not only for its erudite description of the law, but also for the marvellous description of the character of the deceased; and in the Court of Appeal [2001] WTLR 1275.

at common law to reduce damages by attributing the cause of the loss to someone else. The Court of Appeal further held on the facts as found by the judge that there was no room for contributory negligence to play a part.[42] The Court of Appeal rejected any argument that the disappointed beneficiaries could not be in a better position than the testator would have been.

The question is whether this decision would be followed in England. As with the statutory **22.42** provisions in relation to contributory negligence applicable in Saskatchewan, the wording of s.1(1) Law Reform (Contributory Negligence) Act 1945 does not fit easily with the type of cases where the claimant is not the testator but a beneficiary, as it discusses the damage being suffered 'partly of his own fault'. The fault will usually lie with the testator and not the beneficiary.

The point arose but was unfortunately not decided by the Court of Appeal in *Gorham v* **22.43** *British Telecommunications plc*,[43] which was in fact a case about pensions' misselling, but the claimant was not the pensioner, but his widow. The Court of Appeal accepted that the structure of the claim was identical to that in *White v Jones*. There Mr Gorham had been advised by Standard Life, which had sold him a personal pension in circumstances where he would have been better off staying in his occupational scheme. He was later advised that he should rejoin his occupational scheme but he failed to do so. In the end the case was not decided on the basis of contributory negligence but a majority (Stuart-Smith LJ dissenting) held that the chain of causation was broken. However, Stuart-Smith LJ did consider the question of contributory negligence in some detail. He said:

> The case seems to have been argued before the judge on the basis of the Law Reform (Contributory Negligence) Act 1945, namely that Mr. Gorham's fault could be relied upon to reduce Mrs. Gorham's damages. I think the judge was right to reject this submission, since the Act only applies where 'any person suffers damage as a result partly of his own fault and partly of the fault of any other person or persons': section 1. Neither Mrs. Gorham nor the children were at fault. But the result does not seem just. Why, it may be asked, should Standard Life be liable for the full extent to the plaintiffs, when at least part of the loss was due to the fault of Mr. Gorham?
>
> Mr. Palmer was inclined to accept that, if the courts were to fashion a remedy to avoid an injustice to the plaintiffs, it should be so fashioned as not to cause injustice to the defendants. We are in the realm of judge-made law here. In *White v. Jones* [1995] 2 A.C. 207 the House of Lords was unable to apply existing principle to meet the facts of the case, because there was no reliance by the beneficiary on the solicitor, and hence the strict doctrine of *Hedley Byrne & Co. Ltd. v. Heller & Partners Ltd.* [1964] A.C. 465 did not assist the claimant. What the majority of their Lordships did was to fashion a remedy to meet the justice of the case. It may be noted that Lord Goff, at p. 268, stated that the assumption of liability by the solicitor 'will of course be subject to any terms of the contract between the solicitor and the testator which may exclude or restrict the solicitor's liability to the testator under the principle in *Hedley Byrne*'. Although Lord Goff is there expressly referring to contractual terms, I do not see why the same principle should not apply to contributory negligence on the part of the testator, since the beneficiary is not a party to the contract.

In other words, Stuart-Smith LJ advocated the rule of contributory negligence applying to **22.44** an action in tort by a disappointed beneficiary in the same way that it would apply if the

---

[42] This seems to be right as the judge found that the services rendered by the defendant to the testator fell below and breached the standard of care required—in other words it was the solicitor's fault.
[43] [2000] 1 WLR 2129; [2000] 4 All ER 867; [2000] Lloyd's Rep PN 897.

testator were suing on the contract between him and the solicitor. While this is perhaps not easy to justify on strict legal principles, it has a great deal of common sense to recommend it.

22.45 It should be said that, until relatively recently, it was not clear that the defence of contributory negligence could be used in a claim in contract. In cases where it is the estate suing rather than a beneficiary, or where the claim is by trustees or PRs against solicitors retained by them, the claim would be in contract. After a number of conflicting authorities, the position now seems to have been resolved in *Forsikringsaktieselskapet Vesta v Butcher*.[44] There the Court of Appeal adopted the distinction between various categories of case which had been set out by Hobhouse J at first instance and where he held that the defence of contributory negligence was available where the defendant's liability in contract was the same as his liability in the tort of negligence independent of any contract.

22.46 In any case where contributory negligence can be established, it will be a matter for the court to decide to what extent damages should be reduced. The question is what is just and equitable and as there is so little guidance at present, little can be said as to how the courts act in this area. In *Earl v Wilhelm*, Zarzeczny J at first instance assessed the reduction in the damages payable at 25 per cent, the only reasoning seeming to be that the deceased had not been so negligent that the damages should be reduced by 50 per cent.

Application of the principles

22.47 Applying the principles set out above to the type of cases which arise frequently in practice:

1. Failure to prepare a will within acceptable time scale: essentially, this is the *White v Jones*-type case and the measure of damages will be the value of the gift which the disappointed beneficiary would have received if the will had been successfully executed before the death of the testator. Essentially the claimant must establish that there is a substantial chance a will would have been made in his favour and then the court must decide whether a discount should be applied to any damages recoverable on the basis that the testator might not have gone ahead. Note the more difficult situation if the beneficiary is a beneficiary under a discretionary trust set up by the will, where it may be necessary to assess damages on the basis of loss of a chance twice over.

2. Failure to give adequate written directions on how to execute a will: this of course is the *Ross v Caunters*[45] situation. Again the measure of damages will be the value of the gift which the disappointed beneficiary claimant would have received had the will been properly executed, or had the gift not been void as a result of the beneficiary acting as a witness. Again considerations of loss of a chance may come into play.

3. Failure to supervise the execution of the will: this is the *Esterhuizen v Allied Dunbar*[46] -type case. The claimant will be seeking the value of the gift lost to him by reason of the faulty execution, with questions relating to loss of a chance again coming into play.

4. Failure to check execution of the will:[47] assessment of damages will be as in the previous cases. There should perhaps also be added here the question of a will which is not validly made for some other reason such as the lack of testamentary intention in *Corbett v Bond*

---

[44] [1989] AC 852 (CA—the case went to the House of Lords but not on this point).
[45] [1979] 3 All ER 580.
[46] [1998] 2 FLR 668.
[47] See Chapter 6.

Pearce.[48] In such a case it would appear that in some circumstances the estate might be able to claim damages on the basis of the costs burden it has suffered as a result of litigation in relation to the problem with the will, but not if a disappointed beneficiary entitled to residue has been fully compensated with no discount for the costs incurred.

5. Failure to address the question of devolution of joint property: this was the case of *Carr-Glyn v Frearsons*,[49] and the loss will in general be the loss of the value of the half which was to pass under the will with the usual questions of loss of a chance being taken into account. It should be noted that the Court of Appeal recognized in that case that the situation might well give rise to cases where the estate itself had suffered loss—for example, if there were creditors who could have been satisfied out of that half share if it had fallen into the estate. On that basis, loss would have to be calculated on the amount the disappointed beneficiary had lost and the amount the estate had lost. The Court of Appeal was keen to emphasize in that case that there should be no double recovery.

6. Failure to address the question of ownership of property: this arose in *Earl v Wilhelm*[50] and damages were assessed on the basis of the loss of the value of the land owned by the company rather than the testator (with an interesting argument on whether or not it should include the value of standing crops—an argument not very likely to arise on a regular basis perhaps). There, of course, at first instance the judge reduced those damages by 25 per cent on account of the contributory negligence of the deceased but that decision was reversed on appeal. The possibility in such a case as this of contributory negligence cannot be completely ruled out until there is some English authority on the point.

7. Terms of the will do not carry out the intention of the testator: the first point of course is that in a case where the failure is due to a clerical error on the part of the will draftsman or a failure on his part to understand the instructions of the testator, then in order to show that he has taken reasonable steps to mitigate his loss, proceedings for rectification of the will ought to be brought first.[51] If that is done unsuccessfully then, in a clear case, it may well be there is no negligence action against the solicitor. If the action is successful, the measure of the claimant's loss will be the cost of the rectification proceedings. If, on the other hand, the failure is clearly for some other reason, such proceedings may not be necessary. If the difficulty is that the terms of the will are obscure, then the claimant may need to apply to the court for the will to be construed. If the will is construed successfully in favour of the claimant, then the measure of loss may well only be the costs of the construction application (if indeed the claimant has had to bear them). In the event that the point is decided against the claimant, they may well be able to claim the loss of the value of the gift of which they have been deprived plus any costs they have incurred. This of course was the position in *Martin v Triggs Turner Bartons*[52] but the rectification claim was settled and so the damages were assessed on the basis of the deal which could have been negotiated had the will been properly drawn.

8. Failure to explain the terms of a will: although it was not the will preparer who failed in this regard, but a solicitor consulted after the event, *Gray v Buss Merton*[53] is an example of this type of case. This type of case may raise interesting questions with regard to assessing

---

48 [2000] WTLR 655 (QB); [2001] 1 WTLR 419 (CA).
49 [1998] 4 All ER 225.
50 [1998] 2 WWR 524.
51 As in *Walker v Geo H Medlicott & Son (a firm)* [1999] 1 All ER 685.
52 [2009] EWHC 1920 (Ch).
53 [1999] PNLR 882.

the loss of a chance. The court will need to be satisfied that if the testator had appreciated the legal effect of the will, there is a substantial chance he would have changed it in a manner to favour the claimant and then will need to evaluate the chance which the claimant has lost.

9. Negligence in setting up a trust: much depends on what has gone wrong and crucially what can be done to remedy the situation. As explored in the chapter on mitigation, the first line of attack will often be to try to rectify the trust or set it aside. In that case the measure of loss will be the costs of doing so if the exercise proves successful. In other cases where the possibility of remedying the situation is not available, it may be an unexpected tax liability which will be the measure of loss—for example as in *Estill v Cowling Swift Kitchin*,[54] where the transfer into a discretionary trust gave rise to an immediate charge to inheritance tax. More difficult questions may arise where tax is not the issue. In *Stephenson v Stephenson*[55] the settlor wanted to crystallize his claim to retirement relief by transferring shares to a settlement in which he had a life interest. It was crucial to him that there was power to advance capital so the shares could go back to him. There was no such power included but the court was prepared to rectify because, without having formulated precisely the mechanism for capital to be available to him, the settlor clearly intended that the trustees should have that power. Had rectification not been available his loss—that is failure to have access to capital but dependent on the trustees exercising their powers—might have raised difficult questions of assessing his loss of a chance.

10. Negligence in advising trustees: again, if it is possible to undo any mistake, then the measure of damages will be the costs of doing so. If that is not possible then frequently the bad advice will have resulted in a tax liability, which will be the recoverable loss. If loss has been caused to the trust fund, that too may be easy to quantify.

11. Negligence in advising on the administration of the estate: there is very little guidance in the limited number of reported cases in this area as to how damages will be assessed, but the loss to the estate or the additional tax payable will generally be the measure.

12. Tax cases: sometimes in tax cases the assessment of the loss is very clear—it is the additional tax payable. However, there may be cases where tax may become payable in the future if certain events occur. Provided that loss can be shown, there is no reason why such exposure to tax should not be included in any claim, and in practice it is almost always dealt with by an indemnity being provided by the defendants.

H. Interest

22.48 Interest can be claimed on any damages sought by the claim. In the High Court this is by reason of s.35A Senior Courts Act 1981, and in the County Court by reason of s.69 County Courts Act 1984, both of which sections are in similar terms and confer upon the court a discretion as to whether to award interest or not.

22.49 The general principle is that interest is awarded to compensate the claimant for being kept out of his money. It is not awarded to punish the defendant for his wrongdoing.[56] In cases where there has been misconduct on the part of the claimant or delay, the court may refuse

---

[54] [2000] WTLR 417.
[55] Unreported decision of Mr John Jarvis QC (HC, 2 March 2004) (see <http://www.lawtel.com>).
[56] *London, Chatham and Dover Ry Co v Southern Eastern Ry Co* [1893] AC 429 at 437.

to award interest.[57] In general, interest will be awarded to the claimant at either the rate of interest on monies invested in court on special account[58] or at the rate in accordance with s.17 Judgments Act 1838.[59] Interest is normally awarded from the date of the loss or the date the cause of action arose[60] to the date when judgment is awarded[61] or earlier payment.

A claim for interest must be made in the particulars of claim[62] and the enactment under which the interest is claimed pleaded. When a specified sum of money is claimed[63] the interest must be calculated in the particulars of claim.[64] **22.50**

---

[57] *Business Computers Ltd v Anglo-African Leasing Ltd* [1977] 1 WLR 578; [1977] 2 All ER 74.
[58] Currently 7 per cent.
[59] Currently 8 per cent.
[60] *BP Exploration Co (Libya) Ltd v Hunt* [1982] 2 WLR 253; [1982] 1 All ER 925 (HL).
[61] The judgment itself will carry interest under the Judgments Act 1838.
[62] See r.16.4(1) CPR.
[63] eg where the claim is for, say, the costs of a probate action or tax payable as a result of the negligence.
[64] See r.16.4(2) CPR. This will not often apply to the sort of damages claim being dealt with in this book.

23

MITIGATION AND THE INTERRELATION WITH OTHER CLAIMS

A. General principles

The basic rule is that a claimant must mitigate his loss, and this area of the law has attained **23.01** great importance as far as professional negligence cases are concerned. It is often the first thought of insurers to advisers in any of the contexts discussed in this book to see if the problem which has arisen can be undone. A distinction has to be drawn between cases where the claimant has a duty to mitigate and failure to do so will affect the damages which he can claim, and cases where it may be possible to put right what has happened and desirable that that course should be followed, but there is no duty on the claimant to do so.

Many negligence claims in this area are resolved by proceedings to put right what has hap- **23.02** pened. Frequently it is cheaper for the insurer to pay the costs of proceedings to undo what has been done, rather than to bear the loss if matters are left as they are. Claimants will often be prepared to cooperate even if they do not have a duty to mitigate if provided with an indemnity from the insurers.

Mitigation has become particularly important in will negligence cases. The first case to explore **23.03** the matter was that of *Walker v Geo H Medlicott & Son (a firm)*.[1] The facts are important to an understanding of the decision on mitigation. The plaintiff claimed that solicitors who had drawn his aunt's will were negligent in not including an absolute gift to him of her house. The Court of Appeal held that in order to mitigate his loss, the plaintiff ought first to have brought a claim for rectification of the will pursuant to s.20 Administration of Justice Act 1982.[2] Care

---

[1] [1999] 1 All ER 685.
[2] Which provides: 'If a court is satisfied that a will is so expressed that it fails to carry out the testator's intentions, in consequence—(a) of a clerical error; or (b) of a failure to understand his instructions, it may order that the will shall be rectified so as to carry out his intentions.'

must be taken in assuming that this decision has general application. This was a case where, as Sir Christopher Slade put it:[3] 'so far as I can see, the evidence on both sides would have been precisely the same. If Mr. Walker had a valid claim in negligence, then a fortiori he would have had a good claim for rectification of the will.'

23.04 On the facts of that case, where the allegation was that the solicitors had failed to follow the instructions of the deceased, it is perhaps easy to see how the court came to this conclusion. However, the court must also be satisfied that the mistake has arisen because of a clerical error or the failure on the part of the solicitor to understand his instructions. It is fair to say that clerical error has been given a fairly wide interpretation by the courts,[4] but even so indicates some sort of inadvertence.

23.05 It was not long before the Court of Appeal had to consider the matter again in the case of *Horsfall v Haywards*.[5] There, Mummery LJ helpfully set out the approach which should be taken to the question of mitigation,[6] which can be summarized as follows:

(1) Plaintiffs (claimants) are under a duty to take all reasonable steps to mitigate the loss suffered by them consequent on the breach of duty by the solicitor. They are not entitled to claim any part of the damage which is due to their neglect to take such steps.

(2) As a general rule it is not the duty of the injured party to embark upon litigation in order to mitigate the damage suffered, even in the event of a solvent defendant offering an adequate indemnity against the costs of bringing proceedings of complexity and difficulty against a third party: see *Pilkington v Wood*.[7]

(3) Notwithstanding the general rule in *Pilkington v Wood*, the courts can reasonably expect in a case of alleged negligence against a solicitor in the drafting of a will that if available the plaintiff/claimant will exhaust that remedy before considering bringing proceedings against the solicitor.

(4) It is obvious that the application of the standard of reasonableness to steps to be taken in mitigation is capable of producing different results according to the circumstances of a particular case.

23.06 The Court of Appeal held on the facts of this case that the plaintiff had not failed to mitigate her loss by not bringing an action for rectification of the will. First of all the claim would have been outside the six-month time limit for bringing such a claim,[8] and in any event the Court of Appeal was not convinced on the facts that the mistake in drafting could be described either as a clerical error or a failure to understand instructions. In other words, the plaintiff had acted reasonably.

23.07 What can be derived from these two cases is that where the allegation against the solicitors is that they failed to record the instructions of the testator in the will owing either to a clerical error or a failure to understand those instructions, it is vital to the success of the claim that an action for rectification of the will is brought first. On the other hand, if there are doubts as to

---

[3] [1999] 1 All ER 685 at 697E.
[4] See *Re Segelman* [1996] Ch 171.
[5] [2000] WTLR 29.
[6] *Horsfall v Haywards* (n 5) at 35.
[7] [1953] Ch 770.
[8] Although it should be noted that the court does have power to extend time for bringing such an application, although permission will not be given simply as a matter of course.

whether such an action should be brought, and as to its likely success, then the argument on failure to mitigate is unlikely to succeed. Each case has to be looked at individually.

In other cases where there has been negligence, it may be necessary for the claimant to **23.08** consider bringing other proceedings before pursuing the solicitors. For example, if a trust is so badly drafted that a clause requires to be construed and may be construed in favour of the beneficiary, it may well be reasonable to expect them to seek that remedy first and try to reduce their loss to the costs of the application for construction. If a transaction or the exercise by trustees of their powers have unfortunate tax consequences an application might be made for the transaction or the exercise to be set aside.

There is no need for proceedings brought by way of mitigation to be fought to the bitter **23.09** end. In *Martin v Triggs Turner Bartons*[9] a rectification claim was compromised and the claim took into account the sums received on that compromise in assessing the damages. The only difficulty if the claim brought by way of mitigation is settled rather than fought is the risk of the defendants arguing that a better deal could be done. However, such arguments are in the authors' view unattractive and unlikely to find favour with the court, which wants to encourage rather than discourage litigants to settle.

B. Construction applications

If a will or trust has been badly drawn, it may be reasonable to expect the claimant to make an **23.10** application for the court to declare the correct construction. Such applications need not be costly or time consuming.[10] The approach of the court to construction of wills was recently reviewed by the Court of Appeal in *RSPCA v Sharp*[11] where Lord Neuberger said:[12]

> As Patten LJ impliedly acknowledges by his reference to *Investors Compensation Scheme Ltd v West Bromwich Building Society* [1998] 1 WLR 896 the court's approach to the interpretation of wills is, in practice, very similar to its approach to the interpretation of contracts. Of course, in the case of a contract there are at least two parties involved in negotiating its terms, whereas a will is a unilateral document. However, it is clear from a number of cases that the approach to interpretation of unilateral documents, such as a notice or a patent, is effectively the same, as a matter of principle, as the court's approach to the interpretation of a bilateral or multilateral document such as a contract: see *Mannai Investment Co Ltd v Eagle Star Life Assurance Co Ltd* [1997] AC 749 and *Kirin-Amgen Inc v Hoechst Marion Roussel Ltd* [2005] 1 All ER 667.

> One obvious difference between a bilateral document such as a contract and a unilateral document such as a will is that parties negotiating a contract may well be consciously content to include an obscurely drafted provision, on the basis that it represents an acceptable compromise which enables overall agreement to be reached, whereas, save in a most exceptional case which it is hard to conceive, a person making a will has no interest in obscurity.

Indeed in a reasonably clear case s.48 Administration of Justice Act 1985 can be used. This **23.11** provides:

---

[9] [2009] EWHC 1920 (Ch).
[10] The procedure is by way of Part 8 application supported by a statement or if there is little evidence it can be set out in Part C of the claim form.
[11] [2010] EWCA Civ 1474; [2011] 1 WLR 980.
[12] *RSPCA v Sharp* (n 11) at [31] and [32] reiterated by him in the Supreme Court in *Marley v Rawlings* [2014] UKSC 2.

Where—

(1)

    (a) any question of construction has arisen out of the terms of a will or a trust; and

    (b) an opinion in writing given by a [person who has a 10 year High Court qualification, within the meaning of section 71 of the Courts and Legal Services Act 1990,] has been obtained on that question by the personal representatives or trustees under the will or trust,

the High Court may, on the application of the personal representatives or trustees and without hearing argument, make an order authorising those persons to take such steps in reliance on the said opinion as are specified in the order.

(2) The High Court shall not make an order under subsection (1) if it appears to the court that a dispute exists which would make it inappropriate for the court to make the order without hearing argument.

23.12   Such applications are usually dealt with on paper and the procedure under r.8.2A CPR can be adopted by not naming any defendant.[13]

C. Rectification: wills

23.13   As set out above, the duty of a claimant to apply for rectification of a will is clear if he wishes to claim against the solicitor who drew it incorrectly. The ability to rectify wills is of relatively recent invention. It was introduced by the Administration of Justice Act 1982 and the section only applies to wills of testators who die after 1 January 1983. It provides as follows:

20   Rectification.

(1) If a court is satisfied that a will is so expressed that it fails to carry out the testator's intentions, in consequence—

    (a) of a clerical error; or

    (b) of a failure to understand his instructions,

    it may order that the will shall be rectified so as to carry out his intentions.

(2) An application for an order under this section shall not, except with the permission of the court, be made after the end of the period of six months from the date on which representation with respect to the estate of the deceased is first taken out.

(3) The provisions of this section shall not render the personal representatives of a deceased person liable for having distributed any part of the estate of the deceased, after the end of the period of six months from the date on which representation with respect to the estate of the deceased is first taken out, on the ground that they ought to have taken into account the possibility that the court might permit the making of an application for an order under this section after the end of that period; but this subsection shall not prejudice any power to recover, by reason of the making of an order under this section, any part of the estate so distributed.

(4) In considering for the purposes of this section when representation with respect to the estate of a deceased person was first taken out, a grant limited to settled land or to trust property shall be left out of account, and a grant limited to real estate or to personal estate shall be left out of account unless a grant limited to the remainder of the estate has previously been made or is made at the same time.

---

[13] And there is no need in this case to seek permission to use this procedure. Paragraph 5 of the Practice Direction to Part 64.

The general approach to these claims was discussed by Chadwick J (as he then was) in *Re* **23.14**
Segelman[14] as follows:

> The subsection requires the court to examine three questions. First, what were the testator's
> intentions with regard to the dispositions in respect of which rectification is sought. Secondly,
> whether the will is so expressed that it fails to carry out those intentions. Thirdly, whether the
> will is expressed as it is in consequence of either (a) a clerical error or (b) a failure on the part
> of someone to whom the testator has given instructions in connection with his will to under-
> stand those instructions.

A 'clerical error' in subsection (1)(a) has been defined as an inadvertent error in drafting or **23.15**
transcribing the instructions of the testator, as in omitting a clause[15] or where the draftsman
had not applied his mind to the significance or effect of a clause.[16] However, a mistake committed by the draftsman advertently because he believes a clause has an effect which it does
not, is not a clerical error and rectification will not be available.[17]

The second limb is failure to understand the instructions of the testator. There a distinction **23.16**
has to be drawn between a failure to understand the client's instructions and a failure to
understand the legal effect of a clause. The court will rectify in the case of the former but not
the latter.[18] The claim will fail if it cannot be established on a balance of probabilities what
the intention of the testator was.[19] Sometimes this will involve a detailed examination of a
great deal of evidence.[20]

In *Marley v Rawlings*[21] a couple made mirror wills and mistakenly executed the will of the **23.17**
other. The Supreme Court (reversing the decisions of the Courts below) held that a clerical
error should be interpreted very widely and included a mistake arising out of office work of
a routine nature. The Supreme Court further held that a wholesale correction should not be
ruled out as a permissible exercise of the Court's power to rectify.

The application must be made within six months of the grant, although the court does have **23.18**
power to extend time and it appears will do so on similar principles as it applies in extending time for applications under the Inheritance (Provision for Family and Dependants) Act
1975. The leading case is *Re Salmon*[22] which held that

(1) The court's discretion is unfettered and must be exercised judicially, in accordance with
    what is right and proper.
(2) The onus is on the claimant to show sufficient grounds for not applying the time bar.
    The claimant must make out a substantive case for it being just and proper for the court
    to exercise its statutory discretion to extend the time limit.
(3) It is material to consider whether the claimant has acted promptly and the circumstances
    in which he applied for an extension of time after the expiry of the time limit.
(4) It is material whether or not negotiations were begun within the time limit.

---

[14] [1996] Ch 171 at 180.
[15] *Wordingham v Royal Exchange Trust Co Ltd* [1992] Ch 412.
[16] See *Re Segelman* (n 4); *Re Martin* [2006] EWHC 2939; *Price v Craig* [2006] EWHC 2561.
[17] *Kell v Jones* [2013] WTLR 507.
[18] *Lily v Pegram* [2002] All ER (D) 265 and *Goodman v Goodman* [2006] EWHC 1757.
[19] *Bell v Georgiou* [2002] WTLR 1105.
[20] *Sprackling v Sprackling* [2008] EWHC 2696; [2009] WTLR 897 provides a striking example of this.
[21] [2014] UKSC 2.
[22] [1981] Ch 167; endorsed by the Court of Appeal in *Berger v Berger* [2013] EWCA Civ 1305.

(5) It is material whether the estate has been distributed before the claim was notified to the defendants.

(6) It is material whether dismissal would leave the claimant without recourse to anyone—that is without a claim against professional advisers.

23.19 Since *Re Salmon*, courts have tended also to consider the substantive merits of the claimant's claim as a factor to be taken into account.[23] There would seem to be no reason why these principles would not also apply to applications to extend time under s.20.[24]

23.20 If the six-month time limit has expired through no fault of the claimant, or if the facts do not fit happily within the concept of a clerical error or failure to understand the testator's instructions, then it is unlikely that a claimant would be under a duty to make an application to rectify a will, but nevertheless if fully indemnified may be prepared to cooperate in doing so.

23.21 Where both claims are to be brought, timing is crucial. The duty to mitigate means that the claim to rectify must be prosecuted first. If it fails, then the negligence claim may fail as well. If it succeeds, there may still be a claim against the solicitors who drafted the defective will, but only if negligence on their part can be established.

23.22 In *Grattan v McNaughten*[25] the claimant took the unorthodox approach of suing the solicitor for negligence, failing, and then claiming rectification of the will. His Honour Judge Behrens QC, sitting as a deputy of the Chancery Division, was strident in his criticism of this approach. He said:

> In those circumstances it is, to my mind, odd that Mrs Grattan persisted in the professional negligence action against Mr Brydson before the resolution of the rectification proceedings. In particular it is odd that she did not issue these proceedings until 14 days before the trial of the professional negligence proceedings. This is not a large estate and the effect of the decision is that the costs of 2 proceedings have now been incurred.

23.23 Notably the failure to mitigate by not taking and fighting rectification proceedings did not seem to have been raised in the negligence proceedings. Moreover, an application to strike out the rectification proceedings on the basis that they amounted to an abuse of process was not pursued. The judge appears to have been somewhat disappointed about that.

23.24 The moral of all this is that if there is the prospect of rectifying the will, that must be pursued first before any negligence claim is brought against the solicitors who drafted it. The claimant who does not follow this advice risks being met with a defence that they have failed to mitigate their loss, and possibly an application to strike out the subsequent rectification proceedings on the basis that they were an abuse of process.

D. Rectification: other instruments

23.25 The opportunities for professionals to fall into traps when drafting trusts and advising on the exercise of powers connected with established trusts are legion. Furthermore, an area where mistakes seem to crop up on a very regular basis is in the drafting of deeds of variation, probably because they are so widely used.

---

[23] *Re Dennis, Dennis v Lloyd's Bank Ltd* [1981] 2 All ER 140 and *Re C* [1995] 2 FLR 24.
[24] Time was extended in both *Price v Craig* [2006] WTLR 1873 and *Pengelly v Pengelly* [2007] WTLR 1619 on the basis that there was no prejudice and nobody objected.
[25] [2001] WTLR 1305.

Often the mistake which has occurred can be cured by an application to rectify the deed in **23.26** question. Unlike rectifying a will, the doctrine is of much wider application. The basic principles which apply to rectification of documents (and not just the sort of voluntary documents which are the subject matter of this work) can be summarized as follows:

(1) Where by mistake a written instrument does not reflect the true agreement of the parties, the court may rectify the document.[26]
(2) The remedy is discretionary.
(3) The court does not rectify agreements, but the instruments reflecting them.[27]
(4) The court will rectify an instrument notwithstanding the fact that the effect of the rectification is to secure a fiscal advantage.[28]
(5) The evidence in support of a claim in rectification must be 'strong irrefragable evidence'.[29]

It is clear that the court has power to rectify voluntary transactions.[30] The crucial distinction **23.27** is between what the parties intended to achieve (eg tax saving of a particular kind) and the transaction they intended to enter into. It is no good if the parties intended to enter into a deed appointing property to X but did not intend the fiscal consequences: rectification is not available in such circumstances. On the other hand, if they appoint more by way of the deed than was intended, that would be a situation where the court might rectify. It is not a legal requirement for rectification of a voluntary settlement that there is any outward expression or objective communication of the settlor's intention equivalent to the need to show an outward expression of accord for rectification of a contract for mutual mistake.[31]

One of the difficulties of invoking the doctrine of rectification in relation to trusts is that the sett- **23.28** lor may have had a fairly clear idea of the tax consequences they wanted to achieve but will not have formed any clear intention as to the type of trust needed to fulfil that objective. In *Allnutt v Wilding*[32] Mummery LJ dismissed an appeal from the refusal of Rimer J to rectify a discretionary settlement, on an unopposed application to turn it into an interest in possession settlement, to avoid an immediately chargeable transfer when the settlement was established. He said:

> It is not a matter of correcting a mistake made in recording the settlor's intentions by inserting words or deleting words, or putting in different words because the words that are there have the wrong meaning. The claim made by the trustees involves substituting a wholly different settlement, an interest in possession settlement, in the place of the discretionary settlement, on the general ground that the substituted settlement would achieve the tax saving which the settlor intended to achieve, but failed to achieve by the document that he executed.

However, if there is clear evidence of what the maker of the deed intended, then the court will **23.29** rectify.[33] So in *Bartlam v Coutts & Co*[34] where the age of thirty rather than twenty-five had been chosen for an accumulation and maintenance settlement, the court did find that was not what the settlor intended. In *Stephenson v Stephenson*[35] the settlor wanted to crystallize

---

[26] *Snell's Equity*, 31st edition (Sweet & Maxwell, 2005) [14-02].
[27] *Mackenzie v Coulson* (1869) LR 8 Eq 368.
[28] *Re Slocock's WT* [1979] 1 All ER 358 explaining *Whiteside v Whiteside* [1950] 1 WLR 65.
[29] *Lake v Lake* [1979] STC 865.
[30] *Re Butlin's Settled Estates* [1976] Ch 251.
[31] *Day v Day* [2013] EWCA Civ 280.
[32] [2007] EWCA Civ 412.
[33] See *Summers v Kitson & Co* [2006] EWHC 3655.
[34] [2006] EWHC 1502.
[35] Unreported decision of Mr John Jarvis QC (HC, 2 March 2004) (see <http://www.lawtel/com>).

his claim to retirement relief by transferring shares to a settlement in which he had a life interest. It was crucial to him that there was power to advance capital so the shares could go back
to him. There was no such power included but the court was prepared to rectify because,
without having formulated precisely the mechanism for capital to be available to him, the
settlor clearly intended that the trustees should have that power.

23.30 Many applications for rectification concern deeds of variation. Whereas with many other
documents, if the parties are all of full age and capacity, they can execute a deed rectifying
the original document, that is not possible with deeds of variation because the parties cannot execute another deed affecting the same property[36] which would have retroactive effect.
Therefore advantage cannot be taken of s.142 Inheritance Tax Act 1984 and s.62 Taxation of
Chargeable Gains Act 1992. Consequently an order for rectification is required.

23.31 In most cases, the application is more than friendly, and sometimes the defendants (if there
are no minors or other persons under a disability involved) will not appear. There has been
some suggestion based on the decision of *Whiteside v Whiteside*[37] that if the sole motivation
for seeking rectification is a fiscal advantage, the court should not rectify because there is no
issue before the court. That decision was explained by Vinelott J at first instance in *Racal
Group Services Ltd v Ashmore*[38] as meaning that there must as a result of the rectification be
some change in the rights of the parties, even if there is in fact no actual dispute between
them. There now seems little doubt that in appropriate cases the court will be prepared to
rectify deeds of variation.[39] The court will rectify an instrument notwithstanding the fact
that the effect of the rectification is to secure a fiscal advantage.[40]

23.32 HMRC have to be informed of the application and in the past it has been the practice for
them not to get involved save to ask for certain authorities to be put before the court. In a
tax bulletin[41] HMRC have indicated that in appropriate cases they will wish to be joined to
the proceedings and make representations to the court. In any event HMRC always ask for
certain cases to be cited to the court.[42]

23.33 Rectification is a discretionary remedy and can be defeated by defences such as laches—considerable delay coupled with change of position—but it is very difficult to run successfully as a defence.[43]

E. Mistake

23.34 The jurisdiction in this area has really grown up as a result of two quite different strands of
authority. The more recent has its root in the decision of Millett J In *Gibbon v Mitchell*[44]
where he held that a court could set aside a voluntary transaction if the donor was mistaken
as to the effect of what he had done but not if he was mistaken as to the consequences. On

---

[36] *Russell v IRC* [1988] STC 195.
[37] [1950] Ch 65.
[38] [1994] STC 416 at 423B–D; approved by the Court of Appeal [1995] STC 1151 at 1157D–F.
[39] See *Lake v Lake* [1989] STC 865; *Wills v Gibbs* [2007] EWHC 3361 where the declaration of intent
under s.142 Inheritance Tax Act 1984 had been omitted.
[40] *Re Slocock's WT* (n 28) explaining *Whiteside v Whiteside* (n 28).
[41] HMRC's *Tax Bulletin*, Issue 83.
[42] *Allnutt v Wilding* [2007] EWCA Civ 412; *Racal Group Services Ltd v Ashmore* (n 38).
[43] *Sargeant v Reece* [2007] EWHC 2663.
[44] [1990] 1 WLR 1304.

the other hand there was an older line of cases based on the decision of the Court of Appeal in *Ogilvie v Littleboy*[45] to the effect that a transaction could be set aside by a donor 'by showing that he was under some mistake of so serious a character as to render it unjust on the part of the donee to retain the property given to him'.

Before the decision of the Supreme Court in *Pitt v Holt; Futter v Futter*[46] the *Gibbon v Mitchell* test proved difficult to apply and the *Ogilvie v Littleboy* test began to attain some popularity,[47] particularly in offshore jurisdictions.[48] However *Pitt v Holt* has changed the law in this area completely.   **23.35**

In *Pitt v Holt* the late husband of the claimant had been very badly injured in a road accident. **23.36** His personal injury claim was compromised by way of (amongst other things) a lump sum and an annuity. His wife who had been appointed his receiver sought professional advice and placed the damages into a discretionary trust for the husband's benefit with the authorization of the Court of Protection. The transfer into settlement incurred an immediate charge to inheritance tax as well as ten-yearly charges, which could have been avoided if the trust had been drafted so as to fall within the definition of a disabled trust.[49] The judge at first instance, Robert Engelhart QC held that the settlement of the lump sum and the assignment of the annuity should be set aside under the *Hastings-Bass* rule, though he would not have come to the same conclusion on the basis of mistake.[50] The Court of Appeal, applying a rather different mistake test, also refused to set aside the transaction.

However, in the Supreme Court the settlement was set aside and Lord Walker set out a **23.37** new test for setting aside voluntary transactions on the grounds of mistake. The first point which Lord Walker considered is what constitutes a mistake. At first instance the deputy judge considered that as nobody had thought about the tax implications that could not be a mistake. Lord Walker emphasized that a mistake had to be distinguished from mere ignorance or inadvertence and what academics call misprediction.[51] However, he made clear that ignorance or inadvertence could give rise to a false belief or assumption and urged courts of first instance not to shrink from drawing the inference of conscious belief or tacit assumption from the facts. Therefore in *Pitt* the assumption would be that no tax was payable.

Lord Walker then turned his attention to the effect/consequences test set out in *Gibbon v* **23.38** *Mitchell* and found that the test caused uncertainty in the law. This is a conclusion to be welcomed as the distinction seemed to be one lifted arbitrarily from the law of rectification. He set out the test as follows:

> I would provisionally conclude that the true requirement is simply for there to be a causative mistake of sufficient gravity; and, as additional guidance to judges in finding and evaluating the facts of any particular case, that the test will normally be satisfied only when there is a mistake either as to the legal character or nature of a transaction, or as to some matter of fact or law which is basic to the transaction.

---

[45] (1897) 13 TLR 399.
[46] [2013] UKSC 26; [2013] 2 WLR 1200.
[47] eg *Ogden v Trustees of RHS Griffiths 2003 Settlement* [2008] WTLR 685.
[48] *Re the A Trust* [2009] JRC 245.
[49] Section 89 Inheritance Tax Act 1984.
[50] A *Gibbons v Mitchell* argument.
[51] [2013] 2 WLR 1200 at [104].

23.39 He then turned his attention to what he called 'the conscience test' and considered that the court had to consider whether it would be unconscionable not to set aside the transaction on the grounds of mistake. He drew some interesting parallels with the law of proprietary estoppel. He made it clear that there was no reason why a mistake as to the tax effect of a transaction would not justify setting aside the transaction although there were some dark warnings about artificial tax avoidance schemes.

23.40 To summarize, the new test requires that there be

(1) a mistake;
(2) of sufficient gravity because either
    (a) it will be as to the legal character or nature of the transaction, or
    (b) as to some matter of fact or law which is basic to the transaction;
(3) and it would be unconscionable not to set aside the transaction.

23.41 The new test clarifies the law in this area and the abandonment of the distinction between effect and consequences is particularly welcome. It will apply to voluntary transactions and also to the exercise by trustees of their powers. As seen below the demise of the so-called rule in *Hastings-Bass* has left something of a lacuna for trustees and their advisers hoping to avoid the consequences of a mistake made in exercising a power under the settlement, but they may now be able to rely on the doctrine of mistake remodelled by Lord Walker.

F. The impact of *Pitt v Holt; Futter v Futter*

23.42 Before the decision of the Supreme Court in *Pitt v Holt; Futter v Futter*[52] there was something of a growth industry surrounding the principles it was said had been established in the case of *Hastings-Bass*.[53]

23.43 What had became known as the rule in *Hastings-Bass* was formulated by Warner J in *Mettoy Pension Trustees Ltd v Evans* in the positive way in which it was regularly applied thus:

> Where a trustee acts under a discretion given to him by the terms of the trust, the court will interfere with his action if it is clear that he would not have acted as he did had he not failed to take into account considerations which he ought to have taken into account.[54]

In other words, this rule enabled trustees who had failed to take into account relevant considerations (usually the unfortunate tax consequences of the exercise of their powers) or had taken into account irrelevant considerations to apply to the court to set aside the transaction. Numerous cases followed.

23.44 Many of the cases in which the principle was applied involved the exercise by trustees of their powers in a way which resulted in unfortunate tax consequences. HMRC were notified of applications but did not join as a party. Eventually their policy changed and they were joined to the claims in *Pitt v Holt* (the facts of which are set out above) and *Futter v Futter*. *Futter v Futter* is a more classic *Hastings-Bass*-style case than *Pitt v Holt*. This case arose from

---

[52] [2013] UKSC 26; [2013] 2 WLR 1200.
[53] [1975] Ch 25.
[54] [1990] 1 WLR 1587.

the exercise by trustees of powers of advancement under two offshore discretionary trusts. In respect of one trust, a power of enlargement was exercised in such a way that the claimant became absolutely entitled to the fund. In respect of the other trust the trustees exercised their power of advancement under s.32 Trustee Act 1925 to advance £12,000 to each of three beneficiaries. Each trust contained stockpiled gains and the intention in respect of the exercise of both powers was to avoid a capital gains tax charge. This was an error as allowable losses cannot be set off against chargeable gains in these circumstances. The judge, Norris J, held that the advancements should be set aside. He held that the consequence was that the transactions were void. There is, it is fair to say, an air of reluctance in his decision.

HMRC appealed and in an impressive judgment in the Court of Appeal Lloyd LJ held that **23.45** the so-called rule in *Hastings-Bass* was not established by that case at all because it involved an alleged exercise by the trustees of powers beyond their scope. That being the case, decisions by trustees could only be set aside if they were in breach of duty and then it was for the beneficiaries to bring the application. He further held that if trustees took and relied on advice before exercising their powers, then they would not be in breach of duty.

Lord Walker gave the leading speech in the Supreme Court and endorsed the views expressed **23.46** by Lloyd LJ. First of all he accepted that the rule had never been established in *Hastings-Bass*, which was a case of excessive execution, and distinguished it from *Futter* and *Pitt v Holt*, which he categorized as cases involving 'inadequate deliberation'.

He further confirmed that it was necessary for the trustee to be in breach of duty before **23.47** the court could set aside the exercise of the power. In the circumstances, it was undesirable for the trustee to bring the application. He also agreed with Lloyd LJ that a relevant consideration for trustees to take into account in exercising their powers was the fiscal consequences of that exercise, thereby making it clear that a failure to do so would be breach of duty: something practitioners in the field have long assumed but which has never actually been decided.

Interestingly, Lord Walker considered that where the rule did still apply, there was no hard **23.48** and fast rule that the test is whether the trustees would have acted differently if they had taken into account relevant considerations or might have done. It remains to be seen how this test will fare in practice.

Finally, Lord Walker affirmed what Lloyd LJ had said on the void versus voidable debate. **23.49** Trustees who are acting within the scope of their powers but fail to take into account relevant considerations or take into account irrelevant ones are exposed to their decisions being set aside at the instance of the beneficiaries. Their exercise is therefore not void but voidable. This can of course give rise to difficulties in terms of the third party acquisition of rights.

There is limited scope for beneficiaries (rather than trustees) to seek to set aside transac- **23.50** tions where trustees have been in breach of duty by not taking relevant considerations into account or taking into account irrelevant ones. However, if trustees seek competent advice and follow it they will not be in breach of duty and therefore there will be no scope for an application. Such applications will also expose trustees to costs if they are in breach of duty, which was usually not the case under the previous *Hastings-Bass* jurisdiction.

It is difficult to avoid the conclusion that this decision will result in professional advisers **23.51** having to pay damages in negligence to trustees in circumstances where previously that loss could have been avoided. It also puts beneficiaries in a rather difficult position. It is established that solicitors acting for PRs in an estate or trustees of a trust do not owe the beneficiaries a duty of care.[55] The beneficiaries therefore have to rely on the trustees to sue the advisers or have to bring a derivative action with the permission of the court. However, the reformulation of the rules allowing voluntary transactions to be set aside on the grounds of mistake will in some cases provide a way out for the trustees.

G. Other ways out

23.52 All is not lost if a transaction does not fall happily within the above principles, as was proved in the case of *Price v Williams-Wyn*[56] where a power of appointment and revocation was exceeded in four deeds of appointment because those appointments permitted the trustees to revoke the appointments without appointing on further trusts, which meant that they would not necessarily be accumulation and maintenance trusts. The Chancellor considered that in fact what was required was for the offending part of the deed of appointment, which was in excess of what was permitted by the original settlement, to be struck down, leaving the rest of the appointment validly standing. He relied on the principles that if an appointment is made subject to an invalid but separable condition, the condition is bad but the appointment is valid.

H. Contentious probate

23.53 Cases where a will has to be proved in solemn form or where a grant of probate has to be revoked[57] are common and clearly may involve negligence on the part of the solicitor who drafted the will. It will be a question of fact in each case as to whether there is a duty to bring a probate claim, which can be costly and complex, in order to mitigate. However, there is a clear link between probate claims on the one hand and negligence claims arising out of them, and insurers may be keen for the validity of the will to be established, rather than face compensating disappointed beneficiaries for their loss.

23.54 It is important to distinguish between the various ways in which a will may be attacked. The following does not in any way purport to be an exhaustive analysis, but provides some of the common arguments against validity:

(1) Lack of testamentary intention (eg *Corbett v Bond Pearce*), which in practice is quite rare.
(2) Want of due execution (eg *Ross v Caunters*).
(3) Lack of testamentary capacity on the basis that at the time the will was executed the deceased was not of sound mind, memory, and understanding.[58]
(4) That the execution of the will was obtained by undue influence.[59]
(5) That the execution of the will was obtained by fraud.[60]

---

[55] A point accepted in the Supreme Court in *Roberts v Gill & Co* [2011] 1 AC 240.
[56] [2006] WTLR 1633.
[57] For the procedure in relation to such claims, which is very specific, see Part 57 CPR.
[58] The test is set out in *Banks v Goodfellow* (1870) LR 5 QB 549 at 565 and practical points in relation to the mentally disordered client are set out in Chapter 4 para 4.45 onwards.
[59] Testamentary undue influence is in essence coercion and must be distinguished from undue influence in relation to lifetime transactions. There are no categories of person where undue influence will be presumed, and it has to be shown that the will of the deceased has been overcome: see *Hall v Hall* (1868) LR 1 P&D 481.
[60] eg by false representations being made to the deceased to cause a particular will to be made.

(6) That the will was forged.[61]
(7) That the deceased did not know and approve the contents of the will.[62]

A distinction has to be drawn between cases in categories (1) and (2) above, where it may well **23.55** be the responsibility of the solicitor to ensure that the will is properly executed and that the testator intended it to be a will, and the other categories of case. In the first category of case, a claim against the solicitor might well lie, as indeed it did in *Ross v Caunters*, to name but one example. Similarly the solicitors who were responsible for the will for which the testatrix was held not to have testamentary intention in *Corbett v Bond Pearce* admitted their liability in respect of the disappointed beneficiaries under that will.

In the other categories of case, although solicitors frequently come in for criticism by the **23.56** courts in contentious probate claims,[63] and much advice has been dealt out in relation to the precautions which solicitors should take when preparing wills, there is in fact no reported English decision whereby solicitors have been sued successfully for preparing a will which has later proved to be invalid.

As far as capacity, undue influence, and fraud cases are concerned, there is unlikely to be a **23.57** claim by a disappointed beneficiary. However, in *Feltham v Freer Bouskell*,[64] the successful claim was brought on the basis that if the solicitor had complied with his duty to prepare a will for which the testatrix had given him instructions before she died, then the major beneficiary would not have prepared a will on behalf of the testatrix, which was later challenged. If the testator did not have capacity to make a will, then the beneficiary can hardly allege that the solicitor should have done something which would have resulted in benefit to him—after all, a solicitor cannot restore the testator to his or her senses. Similarly a beneficiary under a will obtained by undue influence, even assuming that it is not the person who exerted the influence who has the barefaced cheek to sue as a disappointed beneficiary, can hardly complain that he has failed to benefit under a will which ought never to have been made.

The question arose in *Worby v Rosser*[65] whether beneficiaries under an earlier will can claim **23.58** against solicitors who drew up the later will of a testator who lacked testamentary capacity, which gave rise to extremely expensive probate proceedings.[66] In the Court of Appeal, Chadwick LJ considered the proposition that solicitors drawing up a later will owed a duty to beneficiaries under an earlier will as 'startling'. He said:

> In the present case there is no lacuna to be filled. If the solicitor's breach of duty under his retainer has given rise to the need for expensive probate proceedings, resulting in unrecovered costs, then, prima facie, those costs fall to be borne by the estate for the reasons which I have already sought to explain. If the estate bears the costs thereby and suffers loss then, if there is to be a remedy against the solicitor, it should be the estate's remedy for the loss to the estate. There is no need to fashion an independent remedy for a beneficiary who has been engaged in the probate proceedings. His or her costs, if properly incurred in obtaining probate of the true will, can be provided for out of the estate. If there has been a breach of duty by the solicitor,

[61] See *Supple v Pender* [2007] EWHC 829.
[62] *Fuller v Strum* [2002] 1 WLR 1047.
[63] See, eg the comments of Rimer J in *Re Morris (deceased), Special Trustees for Great Ormond Street Hospital for Children v Rushin* [2001] WTLR 1137 and *Key v Key* [2010] EWHC 408 (Ch); [2010] 1 WLR 2020.
[64] [2013] EWHC 1952 (Ch).
[65] [1999] Lloyd's Rep PN 972.
[66] Rather remarkably the costs incurred amounted to £250,000.

the estate can recover from the solicitor the additional costs (including the costs to which the beneficiary is entitled out of the estate). The practical difficulties which would be likely to arise if solicitors were held to owe duties directly to beneficiaries under earlier wills provide powerful support for the view that it would not be appropriate to provide a remedy in circumstances in which it is not needed. For those reasons I would dismiss this appeal.

23.59   The suggestion therefore in that case was that the estate might well have a remedy against the solicitors, but beneficiaries under an earlier will would not. Therefore in circumstances where a contentious probate claim was on foot, and it could be alleged that the solicitor who had drawn up the challenged will had failed in his duty to the testator, there could well be a claim by the estate for the costs of the probate action. However, in *Feltham v Freer Bouskell*[67] costs which the claimant had paid in defending a challenge to a will, which she clearly had to bear herself as a result of a compromise negotiated in a mediation, were found to be recoverable.

23.60   A similar result to *Worby v Rosser* was obtained by beneficiaries suing in the New Zealand case of *Knox v Till*;[68] although the grounds of the decision are markedly different. That too was a case where the later wills of the testator drawn by the defendant solicitors were held to be invalid on the grounds of his lack of testamentary capacity after an expensive[69] probate action. The court there held that the nature of the duty prevented a successful claim by the beneficiaries. Henry J said:[70]

> The setting is an instruction from a client to a solicitor to prepare a testamentary document which will give effect to his wishes as to the disposal of his estate. The particular duty of care was framed initially as a duty to take reasonable steps to ensure that the Testator had testamentary capacity. The breach of such duty would, however, on its own be insufficient to found the present cause of action in negligence. It must be the appellant's case that a solicitor must not only take steps to ensure there is testamentary capacity, but also having ascertained its absence, to refrain from preparing a will as instructed. Absent that duty, and its breach, there would be no entitlement to the damages claimed. Expressed in conventional terms, the duty here must be to take reasonable care to avoid loss to the appellants. The loss is that resulting from the execution of the two later wills. The duty therefore must be to avoid the execution of the wills.

23.61   If this case is right, then even the estate would not be able to claim for the costs of a probate action if there is in fact no duty imposed on a solicitor not to draft a will for a testator who does not appear to have capacity. It is not clear at all on the basis of this decision what the duty of a solicitor would be who was aware that the testator was being subjected to undue influence.

23.62   The approach of the Court of Appeal in *Worby v Rosser* would seem to be the preferable one: that no duty to beneficiaries of a previous will can exist in such circumstances, but the estate could well have a cause of action.[71]

23.63   In cases where disappointed beneficiaries have been able to claim in full their entitlement under wills which have been declared to be invalid for a reason such as lack of execution, the principles enunciated by the Court of Appeal in *Corbett v Bond Pearce* may prevent a claim by the estate. In most cases where the validity of the will was challenged on grounds other

---

[67] [2013] EWHC 1952 (Ch).
[68] [2000] Lloyd's Rep PN 49.
[69] The costs incurred amounted to £430,000.
[70] [2000] Lloyd's Rep PN 49.
[71] See the decision in *Sifri v Clough Willis* [2007] WTLR 1453 where liability was not disputed.

than want of execution or lack of testamentary intention the objections to the estate making a claim for the costs of the contested probate action, which were raised in *Corbett v Bond Pearce*, would not arise.

I. Claims under the Inheritance (Provision for Family and Dependants) Act 1975

Inheritance Act claims may be connected to claims in negligence in this context in that disappointed beneficiaries may wish to hedge their bets and bring a claim for provision out of the estate in the event that they do not succeed in claiming damages against the will-drafter. This is what happened in the case of *Grattan v McNaughten*[72] where the deceased's spouse failed in her claim for damages against the solicitor for negligence, failed to obtain rectification of the will, and finally was awarded provision out of the estate of the deceased. **23.64**

This will only provide a solution where the disappointed beneficiary falls within one of the categories of person[73] who can make a claim under the Act, that is, the spouse or civil partner of the deceased, the former spouse or civil partner of the deceased, a cohabitant of the deceased (in a relationship akin either to marriage or civil partnership), a child of the deceased, any person (not being a child of the deceased) who, in the case of any marriage to which the deceased was at any time a party, was treated as a child of the family in relation to that marriage, and any person who immediately before the death of the deceased was being maintained, either wholly or in part, by the deceased. **23.65**

This is not the place to deal with the provisions of the Act and that jurisdiction in any detail,[74] but it should be noted that claims must be brought within six months of a grant of probate or letters of administration.[75] Although time can be extended by the courts, it is not a good idea to rely on that indulgence being granted. This means that a disappointed beneficiary may well need to get on and make a claim for family provision when any claim for negligence against the solicitor or perhaps a claim for rectification of the will is still at an early stage. The answer is to issue the family provision proceedings and try to make sure that the case management conference for them comes on at the same time as the case management conference for the other proceedings. Family provision proceedings really do need to be brought separately from the other proceedings as they are governed by a specific procedure, which is unique to them.[76] In any event the objective will be to get the Inheritance Act proceedings adjourned to await the outcome of at the very least the rectification proceedings. The court cannot deal with any claim under the 1975 Act unless and until the terms of the will have been settled. **23.66**

How a claim under the 1975 Act ties in with a negligence claim in terms of mitigation is a difficult one. The jurisdiction under the 1975 Act is an uncertain one and it is an interesting point as to whether defendants to a claim by disappointed beneficiaries who also qualify to claim under the Act can insist that they bring a claim. It is the authors' view that it will only **23.67**

---

[72] [2001] WTLR 1305.
[73] Set out in s.2 of the Act.
[74] The authors recommend T Angus, A Clarke, P Hewitt, and P Reed, *Inheritance Act Claims: A Practical Guide* (The Law Society, 2006) as a good starting point.
[75] Section 4 of the Act.
[76] Now contained in Part 57 CPR.

be in the clearest cases that the court would find such a duty. For example, if a spouse were the disappointed beneficiary, and received no or no substantial benefit under the will, her claim would be an extremely strong one and underpinned by reasonably clear principles.[77] In those circumstances, there is no reason why she might not be expected to mitigate her loss by making a claim under the 1975 Act and that would certainly be the case if she were provided with an indemnity.

23.68 On the other hand, claims by other classes of applicant may not be so clear cut, and in those circumstances it may be hard to establish a duty to mitigate. However, there is no reason why an insurer could not offer an indemnity and ask a proposed claimant in negligence proceedings to make a 1975 Act claim.

23.69 Potential claims under the Act have also been used to argue that damages should be reduced because even had a will been drafted properly the disappointed beneficiaries would have faced successful claims under the 1975 Act. In *Horsfall v Haywards*[78] such an argument was run unsuccessfully before the Court of Appeal where it held that the judge had been right to find that he had too little evidence on which to reduce the damages awarded on the basis that claims in undue influence and under the 1975 Act would have depleted the estate even if the will had been properly drafted.

23.70 The interrelation of the 1975 Act and negligence claims does not stop at the question of mitigation. There has been no judicial decision as far as the authors are aware where a will-drafter has been held liable for failure to consider the possibility of a claim under the 1975 Act. Two possible lines of attack can be seen: one on behalf of beneficiaries disappointed in their entitlement under the will because a claimant under the Act has succeeded in having the provisions of the will varied; the second is a claim on behalf of the estate[79] for the costs incurred in defending proceedings under the Act. The first sort of claim would be doomed to fail on the question of causation: it is the order made under the 1975 Act which has caused any loss to beneficiaries deprived of their entitlement under the will, and not the negligence of the solicitor. The second possibility cannot be dismissed so lightly. At present the possibility of such a claim has to be regarded as an open question. Bearing in mind how many family provision claims are made every year, it is perhaps remarkable that blame for the costs has not been laid at the door of the will-drafter. Notably in the case of *Grattan v McNaughten*[80] where the wife of the deceased unsuccessfully sued the solicitors who had drawn up their wills on the basis he had failed to carry out their instructions, and then successfully sought provision out of the estate of her late husband, there was no claim by the estate against the solicitors. It was in many ways a clear case where each spouse was cutting the other out of their will, but there was no suggestion that the solicitor had been negligent in failing to advise that this was a real possibility.

23.71 There are obvious difficulties in expecting a solicitor who is an experienced draftsman and not a litigator to understand all the ramifications in any given case of the particular manner

---

[77] Spouses and civil partners can apply for provision on the basis of what is reasonable and not just what is reasonable for their maintenance; and what they might have expected to receive on a divorce or the dissolution of the civil partnership is a strong factor which the courts take into account: see *Re Cunliffe* [2006] Ch 36.
[78] [2000] WTLR 29.
[79] Similar to that made in *Corbett v Bond Pearce* [2001] WTLR 419.
[80] [2001] WTLR 1305.

in which the testator wishes to dispose of his estate. What is more, the situation at the death of the deceased may be very different from the situation at the date the will is made. While the will at the date it is made may open the estate to a possible claim under the 1975 Act, that claim might well not lie by the date of death. Take, for example, someone who is dependent on the deceased at the time when he makes the will[81] but by the time he dies is no longer being maintained by the deceased. The answer probably is that in a clear case good practice dictates that the draftsman ought to mention the possibility of a claim to the testator. It is also possible for the testator to state either in the will or in a separate letter his reasons for excluding a particular beneficiary and the court can take that into account on any application.[82]

All this is good practice, but whether a failure to deal with these matters could be character-   **23.72** ized as negligence on the part of the solicitor is another issue altogether.

J. Summary

The first thought of possible defendants to a negligence claim and their insurers ought to be   **23.73** whether what has gone wrong can be put right. It will not always be possible to argue that the claimant has a duty to mitigate and it may be that the costs of putting right the mistake are not justified in the context of the loss which has been suffered. However, even if a duty to mitigate cannot be confidently asserted, the claimant, if provided with an indemnity, may be content to make an application to the court to set aside or rectify what has been done so that the loss amounts to the costs of that exercise rather than the overall loss which might be suffered.

---

[81] And therefore able to claim under s.1(1)(e) of the Inheritance (Provision for Family and Dependants) Act 1975.
[82] The court can take the deceased's reasons into account under s.3(1)(g) of the 1975 Act, and a written statement is rendered admissible as evidence by s.21 of the Act.

PART F

STATUTES AND APPENDICES

APPENDIX 1

Wills Act 1837

1837 CHAPTER 26

An Act for the amendment of the Laws with respect to Wills

[3rd July 1837]

1 Meaning of certain words in this Act

...[1] the words and expressions herein-after mentioned, which in their ordinary signification have a more confined or a different meaning, shall in this Act, except where the nature of the provisions or the context of the Act shall exclude such construction, be interpreted as follows; (that is to say,) the word "will" shall extend to a testament, and to a codicil, and to an appointment by will or by writing in the nature of a will in exercise of a power, [and also to an appointment by will of a guardian of a child[2]], [and also to an appointment by will of a representative under section 4 of the Human Tissue Act 2004,[3]]...[4] and to any other testamentary disposition; and the words "real estate" shall extend to manors, advowsons, messuages, lands, tithes, rents, and hereditaments,...[5] whether corporeal, incorporeal, or personal,...[6] and to any estate, right, or interest (other than a chattel interest) therein; and the words "personal estate" shall extend to leasehold estates and other chattels real, and also to monies, shares of government and other funds, securities for money (not being real estates), debts, choses in action, rights, credits, goods, and all other property whatsoever which by law devolves upon the executor or administrator, and to any share or interest therein; and every word importing the singular number only shall extend and be applied to several persons or things as well as one person or thing; and every word importing the masculine gender only shall extend and be applied to a female as well as a male.[7]

2 ...[8]

3 All property may be disposed of by will

...[9] it shall be lawful for every person to devise, bequeath, or dispose of, by his will executed in manner herein-after required, all real estate and all personal estate which he shall be entitled to, either at law or in equity, at the time of his death, and which, if not so devised, bequeathed, and disposed of, would devolve...[10] upon his executor or administrator; and...[11] the power hereby given shall extend...[12]

---

[1]   First words omitted repealed by the Statute Law Revision Act 1893, s 1, Sch.

[2]   Words from "and also to" to "of a child," in square brackets substituted by the Children Act 1989, s 108(5), (6), Sch 13, para 1, Sch 14, para 1.

[3]   Words from "and also to" to "the Human Tissue Act 2004," in square brackets inserted by the Human Tissue Act 2004, s 56, Sch 6, para 1.

[4]   Words omitted repealed by the Statute Law (Repeals) Act 1969, s 1, Schedule, Pt III.

[5]   Words omitted repealed by the Trusts of Land and Appointment of Trustees 1996, s 25(2), Sch 4; for savings in relation to entailed interests created before the commencement of that Act, and savings consequential upon the abolition of the doctrine of conversion, see s 25(4), (5) thereof.

[6]   Words omitted repealed by the Statute Law (Repeals) Act 1969, s 1, Schedule, Pt III.

[7]   Repealed in part, in relation to Northern Ireland, by the Statute Law Revision (Northern Ireland) Act 1954, the Statute Law Revision (Northern Ireland) Act 1976, and the Wills and Administration Proceedings (NI) Order 1994, SI 1994/1899, art 38, Sch 3.

[8]   Repealed by the Statute Law Revision Act 1874.

[9]   Words omitted repealed by the Statute Law Revision (No 2) Act 1888.

[10]   Words omitted repealed by the Statute Law (Repeals) Act 1969.

[11]   Words omitted repealed by the Statute Law Revision (No 2) Act 1888.

[12]   Words omitted repealed by the Statute Law (Repeals) Act 1969.

to all contingent, executory or other future interests in any real or personal estate, whether the testator may or may not be ascertained as the person or one of the persons in whom the same respectively may become vested, and whether he may be entitled thereto under the instrument by which the same respectively were created, or under any disposition thereof by deed or will; and also to all rights of entry for conditions broken, and other rights of entry; and also to such of the same estates, interests, and rights respectively, and other real and personal estate, as the testator may be entitled to at the time of his death, notwithstanding that he may become entitled to the same subsequently to the execution of his will.[13]

4...[14]

5...[15]

6...[16]

7 No will of a person under age valid

...[17] no will made by any person under the age of [eighteen years][18] shall be valid.[19]

8...[20]

[9 Signing and attestation of wills]

[No will shall be valid unless—

(a) it is in writing, and signed by the testator, or by some other person in his presence and by his direction; and

(b) it appears that the testator intended by his signature to give effect to the will; and

(c) the signature is made or acknowledged by the testator in the presence of two or more witnesses present at the same time; and

(d) each witness either—

    (i) attests and signs the will; or

    (ii) acknowledges his signature,

in the presence of the testator (but not necessarily in the presence of any other witness), but no form of attestation shall be necessary.][21]

Amendment

10 Appointments by will to be executed like other wills, and to be valid, although other required solemnities are not observed

...[22] no appointment made by will, in exercise of any power, shall be valid, unless the same be executed in manner herein-before required; and every will executed in manner herein-before required shall, so far as respects the execution and attestation thereof, be a valid execution of a power of appointment by will,

---

[13] Repealed, in relation to Northern Ireland, by the Wills and Administration Proceedings (NI) Order 1994, SI 1994/1899, art 38, Sch 3.

[14] Repealed by the Statute Law (Repeals) Act 1969.

[15] Repealed by the Statute Law (Repeals) Act 1969.

[16] Repealed by the Statute Law (Repeals) Act 1969.

[17] Words omitted repealed by the Statute Law Revision (No 2) Act 1888.

[18] Words substituted by the Family Law Reform Act 1969, s 3(1)(a).

[19] Repealed, in relation to Northern Ireland, by the Wills and Administration Proceedings (NI) Order 1994, SI 1994/1899, art 38, Sch 3.

[20] Repealed by the Statute Law (Repeals) Act 1969.

[21] Substituted, in relation to England and Wales, by the Administration of Justice Act 1982, s 17. Repealed, in relation to Northern Ireland, by the Wills and Administration Proceedings (NI) Order 1994, SI 1994/1899, art 38, Sch 3.

[22] Words omitted repealed by the Statute Law Revision (No 2) Act 1888.

notwithstanding it shall have been expressly required that a will made in exercise of such power should be executed with some additional or other form of execution or solemnity.[23]

11 Saving as to wills of soldiers and mariners

Provided always,...[24] that any soldier being in actual military service, or any mariner or seaman being at sea, may dispose of his personal estate as he might have done before the making of this Act.

12...[25]

13 Publication of will not requisite

...[26] every will executed in manner herein-before required shall be valid without any other publication thereof.[27]

14 Will not to be void on account of incompetency of attesting witness

...[28] if any person who shall attest the execution of a will shall at the time of the execution thereof or at any time afterwards be incompetent to be admitted a witness to prove the execution thereof, such will shall not on that account be invalid.[29]

15 Gifts to an attesting witness, or his or her wife or husband, to be void

...[30] if any person shall attest the execution of any will to whom or to whose wife or husband any beneficial devise, legacy, estate, interest, gift, or appointment, of or affecting any real or personal estate (other than and except charges and directions for the payment of any debt or debts), shall be thereby given or made, such devise, legacy, estate, interest, gift, or appointment shall, so far only as concerns such person attesting the execution of such will, or the wife or husband of such person, or any person claiming under such person or wife or husband, be utterly null and void, and such person so attesting shall be admitted as a witness to prove the execution of such will, or to prove the validity or invalidity thereof, notwithstanding such devise, legacy, estate, interest, gift, or appointment mentioned in such will.[31]

16 Creditor attesting a will charging estate with debts shall be admitted a witness

...[32] in case by any will any real or personal estate shall be charged with any debt or debts, and any creditor, or the wife or husband [or civil partner][33] of any creditor, whose debt is so charged, shall attest the execution of such will, such creditor notwithstanding such charge shall be admitted a witness to prove the execution of such will, or to prove the validity or invalidity thereof.[34]

17 Executor shall be admitted a witness

...[35] no person shall, on account of his being an executor of a will, be incompetent to be admitted a witness to prove the execution of such will, or a witness to prove the validity or invalidity thereof.[36]

---

[23] Repealed, in relation to Northern Ireland, by the Wills and Administration Proceedings (NI) Order 1994, SI 1994/1899, art 38, Sch 3.

[24] Words omitted repealed by the Statute Law Revision (No 2) Act 1888.

[25] Repealed by the Admiralty, &c Acts Repeal Act 1865, s 1.

[26] Words omitted repealed by the Statute Law Revision (No 2) Act 1888.

[27] Repealed, in relation to Northern Ireland, by the Wills and Administration Proceedings (NI) Order 1994, SI 1994/1899, art 38, Sch 3.

[28] Words omitted repealed by the Statute Law Revision (No 2) Act 1888.

[29] Repealed, in relation to Northern Ireland, by the Wills and Administration Proceedings (NI) Order 1994, SI 1994/1899, art 38, Sch 3.

[30] Words omitted repealed by the Statute Law Revision (No 2) Act 1888.

[31] Repealed, in relation to Northern Ireland, by the Wills and Administration Proceedings (NI) Order 1994, SI 1994/1899, art 38, Sch 3.

[32] Words omitted repealed by the Statute Law Revision (No 2) Act 1888.

[33] Words "or civil partner" inserted by the Civil Partnership Act 2004, s 71, Sch 4, Pt 1, paras 1, 4, 5.

[34] Repealed, in relation to Northern Ireland, by the Wills and Administration Proceedings (NI) Order 1994, SI 1994/1899, art 38, Sch 3.

[35] Words omitted repealed by the Statute Law Revision (No 2) Act 1888.

[36] Repealed, in relation to Northern Ireland, by the Wills and Administration Proceedings (NI) Order 1994, SI 1994/1899, art 38, Sch 3.

[18 Will to be revoked by marriage]

[(1) Subject to subsections (2) to (4) below, a will shall be revoked by the testator's marriage.

(2) A disposition in a will in exercise of a power of appointment shall take effect notwithstanding the testator's subsequent marriage unless the property so appointed would in default of appointment pass to his personal representatives.

(3) Where it appears from a will that at the time it was made the testator was expecting to be married to a particular person and that he intended that the will should not be revoked by the marriage, the will shall not be revoked by his marriage to that person.

(4) Where it appears from a will that at the time it was made the testator was expecting to be married to a particular person and that he intended that a disposition in the will should not be revoked by his marriage to that person,—

(a) that disposition shall take effect notwithstanding the marriage; and

(b) any other disposition in the will shall take effect also, unless it appears from the will that the testator intended the disposition to be revoked by the marriage.][37]

[18A Effect of dissolution or annulment of marriage on wills][38]

[(1) Where, after a testator has made a will, a decree[39] [an order or decree][40] of a court [of civil jurisdiction in England and Wales][41] dissolves or annuls his marriages [or his marriage is dissolved or annulled and the divorce or annulment is entitled to recognition in England and Wales by virtue of Part II of the Family Law Act 1986][42],—

[(a) provisions of the will appointing executors or trustees or conferring a power of appointment, if they appoint or confer the power on the former spouse, shall take effect as if the former spouse had died on the date on which the marriage is dissolved or annulled, and

(b) any property which, or an interest in which, is devised or bequeathed to the former spouse shall pass as if the former spouse had died on that date,][43]

except in so far as a contrary intention appears by the will.

(2) Subsection (1)(b) above is without prejudice to any right of the former spouse to apply for financial provision under the Inheritance (Provision for Family and Dependants) Act 1975.

(3) ...[44]]

[18B Will to be revoked by civil partnership]

[(1) Subject to subsections (2) to (6), a will is revoked by the formation of a civil partnership between the testator and another person.

(2) A disposition in a will in exercise of a power of appointment takes effect despite the formation of a subsequent civil partnership between the testator and another person unless the property so appointed would in default of appointment pass to the testator's personal representatives.

(3) If it appears from a will—

(a) that at the time it was made the testator was expecting to form a civil partnership with a particular person, and

(b) that he intended that the will should not be revoked by the formation of the civil partnership, the will is not revoked by its formation.

(4) Subsections (5) and (6) apply if it appears from a will—

[37] Substituted, in relation to England and Wales, by the Administration of Justice Act 1982, s 18(1); Repealed, in relation to Northern Ireland, by the Wills and Administration Proceedings (NI) Order 1994, SI 1994/1899, art 38, Sch 3.
[38] Inserted, in relation to England and Wales, by the Administration of Justice Act 1982, s 18(2).
[39] Words prospectively repealed with savings by the Family Law Act 1996, s 66(1), Sch 8, para 1, as from a day to be appointed, for savings see s 66(2), Sch 9, para 5 thereof.
[40] Words prospectively substituted with savings by the Family Law Act 1996, s 66(1), Sch 8, para 1, as from a day to be appointed, for savings see s 66(2), Sch 9, para 5 thereof.
[41] Words inserted by the Family Law Act 1986, s 53.
[42] Words substituted by the Family Law Act 1986, s 53.
[43] Substituted by the Law Reform (Succession) Act 1995, s 3.
[44] Repealed by the Law Reform (Succession) Act 1995, s 5, Schedule.

(a) that at the time it was made the testator was expecting to form a civil partnership with a particular person, and

(b) that he intended that a disposition in the will should not be revoked by the formation of the civil partnership.

(5) The disposition takes effect despite the formation of the civil partnership.

(6) Any other disposition in the will also takes effect, unless it appears from the will that the testator intended the disposition to be revoked by the formation of the civil partnership.][45]

[18C Effect of dissolution or annulment of civil partnership on wills]

[(1) This section applies if, after a testator has made a will—

(a) a court of civil jurisdiction in England and Wales dissolves his civil partnership or makes a nullity order in respect of it, or

(b) his civil partnership is dissolved or annulled and the dissolution or annulment is entitled to recognition in England and Wales by virtue of Chapter 3 of Part 5 of the Civil Partnership Act 2004.

(2) Except in so far as a contrary intention appears by the will—

(a) provisions of the will appointing executors or trustees or conferring a power of appointment, if they appoint or confer the power on the former civil partner, take effect as if the former civil partner had died on the date on which the civil partnership is dissolved or annulled, and

(b) any property which, or an interest in which, is devised or bequeathed to the former civil partner shall pass as if the former civil partner had died on that date.

(3) Subsection (2)(b) does not affect any right of the former civil partner to apply for financial provision under the Inheritance (Provision for Family and Dependants) Act 1975.][46]

19 No will to be revoked by presumption from altered circumstances

...[47] no will shall be revoked by any presumption of an intention on the ground of an alteration in circumstances.[48]

20 No will to be revoked otherwise than as aforesaid or by another will or codicil, or by destruction thereof

...[49] no will or codicil, or any part thereof, shall be revoked otherwise than as aforesaid, or by another will or codicil executed in manner herein-before required, or by some writing declaring an intention to revoke the same and executed in the manner in which a will is herein-before required to be executed, or by the burning, tearing, or otherwise destroying the same by the testator, or by some person in his presence and by his direction, with the intention of revoking the same.[50]

21 No alteration in a will after execution except in certain cases, shall have any effect unless executed as a will

...[51] no obliteration, interlineation, or other alteration made in any will after the execution thereof shall be valid or have any effect, except so far as the words or effect of the will before such alteration shall not be apparent, unless such alteration shall be executed in like manner as herein-before is required for the execution of the will; but the will, with such alteration as part thereof, shall be deemed to be duly executed if the signature of the testator and the subscription of the witnesses be made in the margin or on some other

---

[45] Inserted by the Civil Partnership Act 2004, s 71, Sch 4, Pt 1, paras 1, 2, 5.

[46] Inserted by the Civil Partnership Act 2004, s 71, Sch 4, Pt 1, paras 1, 2, 5.

[47] Words omitted repealed by the Statute Law Revision (No 2) Act 1888.

[48] Repealed, in relation to Northern Ireland, by the Wills and Administration Proceedings (NI) Order 1994, SI 1994/1899, art 38, Sch 3.

[49] Words omitted repealed by the Statute Law Revision (No 2) Act 1888.

[50] Repealed, in relation to Northern Ireland, by the Wills and Administration Proceedings (NI) Order 1994, SI 1994/1899, art 38, Sch 3.

[51] Words omitted repealed by the Statute Law Revision (No 2) Act 1888.

part of the will opposite or near to such alteration, or at the foot or end of or opposite to a memorandum referring to such alteration, and written at the end of some other part of the will.[52]

22 No revoked will shall be revived otherwise than by re-execution or a codicil, &c

...[53] no will or codicil, or any part thereof, which shall be in any manner revoked, shall be revived otherwise than by the re-execution thereof or by a codicil executed in manner herein-before required and showing an intention to revive the same; and when any will or codicil which shall be partly revoked, and afterwards wholly revoked, shall be revived, such revival shall not extend to so much thereof as shall have been revoked before the revocation of the whole thereof, unless an intention to the contrary shall be shown.[54]

23 Subsequent conveyance or other act not to prevent operation of will

...[55] no conveyance or other act made or done subsequently to the execution of a will of or relating to any real or personal estate therein comprised, except an act by which such will shall be revoked as aforesaid, shall prevent the operation of the will with respect to such estate or interest in such real or personal estate as the testator shall have power to dispose of by will at the time of his death.[56]

24 Wills shall be construed, as to the estate comprised, to speak from the death of the testator

...[57] every will shall be construed, with reference to the real estate and personal estate comprised in it, to speak and take effect as if it had been executed immediately before the death of the testator, unless a contrary intention shall appear by the will.[58]

25 Residuary devises shall include estates comprised in lapsed and void devises

...[59] unless a contrary intention shall appear by the will, such real estate or interest therein as shall be comprised or intended to be comprised in any devise in such will contained, which shall fail or be void by reason of the death of the devisee in the lifetime of the testator, or by reason of such devise being contrary to law or otherwise incapable of taking effect shall be included in the residuary devise (if any) contained in such will.[60]

26 A general devise of the testator's lands shall include copyhold and leasehold as well as freehold lands, in the absence of a contrary intention

...[61] a devise of the land of the testator, or of the land of the testator in any place or in the occupation of any person mentioned in his will, or otherwise described in a general manner, and any other general devise which would describe a...[62] leasehold estate if the testator had no freehold estate which could be described by it, shall be construed to include the...[63] leasehold estates of the testator, or his...[64] leasehold estates, or any of them, to which such description shall extend, as the case may be, as well as freehold estates, unless a contrary intention shall appear by the will.[65]

---

[52] Repealed, in relation to Northern Ireland, by the Wills and Administration Proceedings (NI) Order 1994, SI 1994/1899, art 38, Sch 3.

[53] Words omitted repealed by the Statute Law Revision (No 2) Act 1888.

[54] Repealed, in relation to Northern Ireland, by the Wills and Administration Proceedings (NI) Order 1994, SI 1994/1899, art 38, Sch 3.

[55] Words omitted repealed by the Statute Law Revision (No 2) Act 1888.

[56] Repealed, in relation to Northern Ireland, by the Wills and Administration Proceedings (NI) Order 1994, SI 1994/1899, art 38, Sch 3.

[57] Words omitted repealed by the Statute Law Revision (No 2) Act 1888.

[58] Repealed, in relation to Northern Ireland, by the Wills and Administration Proceedings (NI) Order 1994, 1994/1899, art 38, Sch 3.

[59] Words omitted repealed by the Statute Law Revision (No 2) Act 1888.

[60] Repealed, in relation to Northern Ireland, by the Wills and Administration Proceedings (NI) Order 1994, SI 1994/1899, art 38, Sch 3.

[61] Words omitted repealed by the Statute Law Revision (No 2) Act 1888.

[62] Words omitted repealed by the Statute Law (Repeals) Act 1969.

[63] Words omitted repealed by the Statute Law (Repeals) Act 1969.

[64] Words omitted repealed by the Statute Law (Repeals) Act 1969.

[65] Repealed, in relation to Northern Ireland, by the Wills and Administration Proceedings (NI) Order 1994, SI 1994/1899, art 38, Sch 3.

27 A general gift of realty or personalty shall include property over which the testator has a general power of appointment

...[66] a general devise of the real estate of the testator, or of the real estate of the testator in any place or in the occupation of any person mentioned in his will, or otherwise described in a general manner, shall be construed to include any real estate, or any real estate to which such description shall extend (as the case may be), which he may have power to appoint in any manner he may think proper, and shall operate as an execution of such power, unless a contrary intention shall appear by the will; and in like manner a bequest of the personal estate of the testator, or any bequest of personal property described in a general manner, shall be construed to include any personal estate, or any personal estate to which such description shall extend (as the case may be), which he may have power to appoint in any manner he may think proper, and shall operate as an execution of such power, unless a contrary intention shall appear by the will.[67]

28 A devise of real estate without any words of limitation shall pass the fee, &c

...[68] where any real estate shall be devised to any person without any words of limitation, such devise shall be construed to pass the fee simple, or other the whole estate or interest which the testator had power to dispose of by will in such real estate, unless a contrary intention shall appear by the will.[69]

29 The words "die without issue," or "die without leaving issue," &c shall mean a want or failure of issue in the lifetime or at the death of the person, except in certain cases

...[70] in any devise or bequest of real or personal estate the words "die without issue" or "die without leaving issue," or "have no issue," or any other words which may import either a want or failure of issue of any person in his lifetime or at the time of his death, or an indefinite failure of his issue, shall be construed to mean a want or failure of issue in the lifetime or at the time of the death of such person, and not an indefinite failure of his issue, unless a contrary intention shall appear by the will, by reason of such person having a prior estate tail, or of a preceding gift, being, without any implication arising from such words, a limitation of an estate tail to such person or issue, or otherwise: Provided, that this Act shall not extend to cases where such words as aforesaid import if no issue described in a preceding gift shall be born, or if there shall be no issue who shall live to attain the age or otherwise answer the description required for obtaining a vested estate by a preceding gift to such issue.[71]

30 Devise of realty to trustees or executors shall pass the fee, &c, except in certain cases

...[72] where any real estate (other than or not being a presentation to a church) shall be devised to any trustee or executor, such devise shall be construed to pass the fee simple or other the whole estate or interest which the testator had power to dispose of by will in such real estate, unless a definite term of years, absolute or determinable, or an estate of freehold, shall thereby be given to him expressly or by implication.[73]

31 Trustees under an unlimited devise, where the trust may endure beyond the life of a person beneficially entitled for life, shall take the fee, &c

...[74] where any real estate shall be devised to a trustee, without any express limitation of the estate to be taken by such trustee, and the beneficial interest in such real estate, or in the surplus rents and profits thereof, shall not be given to any person for life, or such beneficial interest shall be given to any person

---

[66] Words omitted repealed by the Statute Law Revision (No 2) Act 1888.
[67] Repealed, in relation to Northern Ireland, by the Wills and Administration Proceedings (NI) Order 1994, SI 1994/1899, art 38, Sch 3.
[68] Words omitted repealed by the Statute Law Revision (No 2) Act 1888.
[69] Repealed, in relation to Northern Ireland, by the Wills and Administration Proceedings (NI) Order 1994, 1994/1899, art 38, Sch 3.
[70] Words omitted repealed by the Statute Law Revision (No 2) Act 1888.
[71] Repealed, in relation to Northern Ireland, by the Wills and Administration Proceedings (NI) Order 1994, SI 1994/1899, art 38, Sch 3.
[72] Words omitted repealed by the Statute Law Revision (No 2) Act 1888.
[73] Repealed, in relation to Northern Ireland, by the Wills and Administration Proceedings (NI) Order 1994, SI 1994/1899, art 38, Sch 3.
[74] Words omitted repealed by the Statute Law Revision (No 2) Act 1888.

for life, but the purposes of the trust may continue beyond the life of such person, such devise shall be construed to vest in such trustee the fee simple, or other the whole legal estate which the testator had power to dispose of by will in such real estate, and not an estate determinable when the purposes of the trust shall be satisfied.[75]

32 Devises of estates tail shall not lapse where inheritable issue survives, &c...[76]

[33 Gifts to children or other issue who leave issue living at the testator's death shall not lapse]

[(1) Where—
  (a) a will contains a devise or bequest to a child or remoter descendant of the testator; and
  (b) the intended beneficiary dies before the testator, leaving issue; and
  (c) issue of the intended beneficiary are living at the testator's death,
  then, unless a contrary intention appears by the will, the devise or bequest shall take effect as a devise or bequest to the issue living at the testator's death.
(2) Where—
  (a) a will contains a devise or bequest to a class of person consisting of children or remoter descendants of the testator; and
  (b) a member of the class dies before the testator, leaving issue, and
  (c) issue of that member are living at the testator's death,
then, unless a contrary intention appears by the will, the devise or bequest shall take effect as if the class included the issue of its deceased member living at the testator's death.
(3) Issue shall take under this section through all degrees, according to their stock, in equal shares if more than one, any gift or share which their parent would have taken and so that no issue shall take whose parent is living at the testator's death and so capable of taking.
(4) For the purposes of this section—
  (a) the illegitimacy of any person is to be disregarded; and
  (b) a person conceived before the testator's death and born living thereafter is to be taken to have been living at the testator's death.][77]

34 Act not to extend to wills made before 1838, nor to estates pur autre vie of persons who die before 1838

... this Act shall not extend to any will made before the first day of January one thousand eight hundred and thirty-eight; and every will re-executed or republished, or revived by any codicil, shall for the purposes of this Act be deemed to have been made at the time at which the same shall be so re-executed, republished or revived; and this Act shall not extend to any estate pur autre vie of any person who shall die before the first day of January one thousand eight hundred and thirty-eight.

[75] Repealed, in relation to Northern Ireland, by the Wills and Administration Proceedings (NI) Order 1994, SI 1994/1899, art 38, Sch 3.
[76] Repealed, in relation to Northern Ireland, by the Wills and Administration Proceedings (NI) Order 1994, SI 1994/1899, art 38, Sch 3.
Repealed by the Trusts of Land and Appointment of Trustees Act 1996, s 25(2), Sch 4; for savings in relation to entailed interests created before the commencement of that Act, and savings consequential upon the abolition of the doctrine of conversion, see s 25(4), (5) thereof.
[77] Substituted, in relation to England and Wales, by the Administration of Justice Act 1982, s 19; Repealed, in relation to Northern Ireland, by the Wills and Administration Proceedings (NI) Order 1994, SI 1994/1899, art 38, Sch 3.

APPENDIX 2

Trustee Act 2000

2000 CHAPTER 29

An Act to amend the law relating to trustees and persons having the investment powers of trustees; and for connected purposes.

[23rd November 2000]

BE IT ENACTED by the Queen's most Excellent Majesty, by and with the advice and consent of the Lords Spiritual and Temporal, and Commons, in this present Parliament assembled, and by the authority of the same, as follows:—

Part I
The Duty of Care

1 The duty of care

(1) Whenever the duty under this subsection applies to a trustee, he must exercise such care and skill as is reasonable in the circumstances, having regard in particular—

(a) to any special knowledge or experience that he has or holds himself out as having, and

(b) if he acts as trustee in the course of a business or profession, to any special knowledge or experience that it is reasonable to expect of a person acting in the course of that kind of business or profession.

(2) In this Act the duty under subsection (1) is called "the duty of care".

2 Application of duty of care

Schedule 1 makes provision about when the duty of care applies to a trustee.

Part II
Investment

3 General power of investment

(1) Subject to the provisions of this Part, a trustee may make any kind of investment that he could make if he were absolutely entitled to the assets of the trust.

(2) In this Act the power under subsection (1) is called "the general power of investment".

(3) The general power of investment does not permit a trustee to make investments in land other than in loans secured on land (but see also section 8).

(4) A person invests in a loan secured on land if he has rights under any contract under which—

(a) one person provides another with credit, and

(b) the obligation of the borrower to repay is secured on land.

(5) "Credit" includes any cash loan or other financial accommodation.

(6) "Cash" includes money in any form.

4 Standard investment criteria

(1) In exercising any power of investment, whether arising under this Part or otherwise, a trustee must have regard to the standard investment criteria.

(2) A trustee must from time to time review the investments of the trust and consider whether, having regard to the standard investment criteria, they should be varied.

(3) The standard investment criteria, in relation to a trust, are—

(a) the suitability to the trust of investments of the same kind as any particular investment proposed to be made or retained and of that particular investment as an investment of that kind, and

(b) the need for diversification of investments of the trust, in so far as is appropriate to the circumstances of the trust.

5 Advice

(1) Before exercising any power of investment, whether arising under this Part or otherwise, a trustee must (unless the exception applies) obtain and consider proper advice about the way in which, having regard to the standard investment criteria, the power should be exercised.

(2) When reviewing the investments of the trust, a trustee must (unless the exception applies) obtain and consider proper advice about whether, having regard to the standard investment criteria, the investments should be varied.

(3) The exception is that a trustee need not obtain such advice if he reasonably concludes that in all the circumstances it is unnecessary or inappropriate to do so.

(4) Proper advice is the advice of a person who is reasonably believed by the trustee to be qualified to give it by his ability in and practical experience of financial and other matters relating to the proposed investment.

6 Restriction or exclusion of this Part etc

(1) The general power of investment is—

(a) in addition to powers conferred on trustees otherwise than by this Act, but

(b) subject to any restriction or exclusion imposed by the trust instrument or by any enactment or any provision of subordinate legislation.

(2) For the purposes of this Act, an enactment or a provision of subordinate legislation is not to be regarded as being, or as being part of, a trust instrument.

(3) In this Act "subordinate legislation" has the same meaning as in the Interpretation Act 1978.

7 Existing trusts

(1) This Part applies in relation to trusts whether created before or after its commencement.

(2) No provision relating to the powers of a trustee contained in a trust instrument made before 3rd August 1961 is to be treated (for the purposes of section 6(1)(b)) as restricting or excluding the general power of investment.

(3) A provision contained in a trust instrument made before the commencement of this Part which—

(a) has effect under section 3(2) of the Trustee Investments Act 1961 as a power to invest under that Act, or

(b) confers power to invest under that Act,

is to be treated as conferring the general power of investment on a trustee.

Part III
Acquisition of Land

8 Power to acquire freehold and leasehold land

(1) A trustee may acquire freehold or leasehold land in the United Kingdom—

(a) as an investment,

(b) for occupation by a beneficiary, or

(c) for any other reason.

(2) "Freehold or leasehold land" means—

(a) in relation to England and Wales, a legal estate in land,

(b) in relation to Scotland—

(i) the estate or interest of the proprietor of the dominium utile or, in the case of land not held on feudal tenure, the estate or interest of the owner, or

(ii) a tenancy, and

(c) in relation to Northern Ireland, a legal estate in land, including land held under a fee farm grant.

(3) For the purpose of exercising his functions as a trustee, a trustee who acquires land under this section has all the powers of an absolute owner in relation to the land.

9 Restriction or exclusion of this Part etc

The powers conferred by this Part are—

(a) in addition to powers conferred on trustees otherwise than by this Part, but

(b) subject to any restriction or exclusion imposed by the trust instrument or by any enactment or any provision of subordinate legislation.

10 Existing trusts

(1) This Part does not apply in relation to—

(a) a trust of property which consists of or includes land which (despite section 2 of the Trusts of Land and Appointment of Trustees Act 1996) is settled land, or

(b) a trust to which the Universities and College Estates Act 1925 applies.

(2) Subject to subsection (1), this Part applies in relation to trusts whether created before or after its commencement.

Part IV
Agents, nominees and custodians
Agents

11 Power to employ agents

(1) Subject to the provisions of this Part, the trustees of a trust may authorise any person to exercise any or all of their delegable functions as their agent.

(2) In the case of a trust other than a charitable trust, the trustees' delegable functions consist of any function other than—

(a) any function relating to whether or in what way any assets of the trust should be distributed,

(b) any power to decide whether any fees or other payment due to be made out of the trust funds should be made out of income or capital,

(c) any power to appoint a person to be a trustee of the trust, or

(d) any power conferred by any other enactment or the trust instrument which permits the trustees to delegate any of their functions or to appoint a person to act as a nominee or custodian.

(3) In the case of a charitable trust, the trustees' delegable functions are—

(a) any function consisting of carrying out a decision that the trustees have taken;

(b) any function relating to the investment of assets subject to the trust (including, in the case of land held as an investment, managing the land and creating or disposing of an interest in the land);

(c) any function relating to the raising of funds for the trust otherwise than by means of profits of a trade which is an integral part of carrying out the trust's charitable purpose;

(d) any other function prescribed by an order made by the Secretary of State.

(4) For the purposes of subsection (3)(c) a trade is an integral part of carrying out a trust's charitable purpose if, whether carried on in the United Kingdom or elsewhere, the profits are applied solely to the purposes of the trust and either—

(a) the trade is exercised in the course of the actual carrying out of a primary purpose of the trust, or

(b) the work in connection with the trade is mainly carried out by beneficiaries of the trust.

(5) The power to make an order under subsection (3)(d) is exercisable by statutory instrument which shall be subject to annulment in pursuance of a resolution of either House of Parliament.

12 Persons who may act as agents

(1) Subject to subsection (2), the persons whom the trustees may under section 11 authorise to exercise functions as their agent include one or more of their number.

(2) The trustees may not authorise two (or more) persons to exercise the same function unless they are to exercise the function jointly.

(3) The trustees may not under section 11 authorise a beneficiary to exercise any function as their agent (even if the beneficiary is also a trustee).

(4) The trustees may under section 11 authorise a person to exercise functions as their agent even though he is also appointed to act as their nominee or custodian (whether under section 16, 17 or 18 or any other power).

13 Linked functions etc

(1) Subject to subsections (2) and (5), a person who is authorised under section 11 to exercise a function is (whatever the terms of the agency) subject to any specific duties or restrictions attached to the function.

For example, a person who is authorised under section 11 to exercise the general power of investment is subject to the duties under section 4 in relation to that power.

(2) A person who is authorised under section 11 to exercise a power which is subject to a requirement to obtain advice is not subject to the requirement if he is the kind of person from whom it would have been proper for the trustees, in compliance with the requirement, to obtain advice.

(3) Subsections (4) and (5) apply to a trust to which section 11(1) of the Trusts of Land and Appointment of Trustees Act 1996 (duties to consult beneficiaries and give effect to their wishes) applies.

(4) The trustees may not under section 11 authorise a person to exercise any of their functions on terms that prevent them from complying with section 11(1) of the 1996 Act.

(5) A person who is authorised under section 11 to exercise any function relating to land subject to the trust is not subject to section 11(1) of the 1996 Act.

14 Terms of agency

(1) Subject to subsection (2) and sections 15(2) and 29 to 32, the trustees may authorise a person to exercise functions as their agent on such terms as to remuneration and other matters as they may determine.

(2) The trustees may not authorise a person to exercise functions as their agent on any of the terms mentioned in subsection (3) unless it is reasonably necessary for them to do so.

(3) The terms are—

    (a) a term permitting the agent to appoint a substitute;

    (b) a term restricting the liability of the agent or his substitute to the trustees or any beneficiary;

    (c) a term permitting the agent to act in circumstances capable of giving rise to a conflict of interest.

15 Asset management: special restrictions

(1) The trustees may not authorise a person to exercise any of their asset management functions as their agent except by an agreement which is in or evidenced in writing.

(2) The trustees may not authorise a person to exercise any of their asset management functions as their agent unless—

    (a) they have prepared a statement that gives guidance as to how the functions should be exercised ("a policy statement"), and

    (b) the agreement under which the agent is to act includes a term to the effect that he will secure compliance with—

        (i) the policy statement, or

        (ii) if the policy statement is revised or replaced under section 22, the revised or replacement policy statement.

(3) The trustees must formulate any guidance given in the policy statement with a view to ensuring that the functions will be exercised in the best interests of the trust.

(4) The policy statement must be in or evidenced in writing.

(5) The asset management functions of trustees are their functions relating to—

    (a) the investment of assets subject to the trust,

    (b) the acquisition of property which is to be subject to the trust, and

    (c) managing property which is subject to the trust and disposing of, or creating or disposing of an interest in, such property.

Nominees and custodians

16 Power to appoint nominees

(1) Subject to the provisions of this Part, the trustees of a trust may—

    (a) appoint a person to act as their nominee in relation to such of the assets of the trust as they determine (other than settled land), and

    (b) take such steps as are necessary to secure that those assets are vested in a person so appointed.

(2) An appointment under this section must be in or evidenced in writing.

(3) This section does not apply to any trust having a custodian trustee or in relation to any assets vested in the official custodian for charities.

17 Power to appoint custodians

(1) Subject to the provisions of this Part, the trustees of a trust may appoint a person to act as a custodian in relation to such of the assets of the trust as they may determine.

(2) For the purposes of this Act a person is a custodian in relation to assets if he undertakes the safe custody of the assets or of any documents or records concerning the assets.

(3) An appointment under this section must be in or evidenced in writing.

(4) This section does not apply to any trust having a custodian trustee or in relation to any assets vested in the official custodian for charities.

18 Investment in bearer securities

(1) If trustees retain or invest in securities payable to bearer, they must appoint a person to act as a custodian of the securities.

(2) Subsection (1) does not apply if the trust instrument or any enactment or provision of subordinate legislation contains provision which (however expressed) permits the trustees to retain or invest in securities payable to bearer without appointing a person to act as a custodian.

(3) An appointment under this section must be in or evidenced in writing.

(4) This section does not apply to any trust having a custodian trustee or in relation to any securities vested in the official custodian for charities.

19 Persons who may be appointed as nominees or custodians

(1) A person may not be appointed under section 16, 17 or 18 as a nominee or custodian unless one of the relevant conditions is satisfied.

(2) The relevant conditions are that—

    (a) the person carries on a business which consists of or includes acting as a nominee or custodian;

    (b) the person is a body corporate which is controlled by the trustees;

    (c) the person is a body corporate recognised under section 9 of the Administration of Justice Act 1985.

(3) The question whether a body corporate is controlled by trustees is to be determined in accordance with section 840 of the Income and Corporation Taxes Act 1988.

(4) The trustees of a charitable trust which is not an exempt charity must act in accordance with any guidance given by the [Charity Commission][1] concerning the selection of a person for appointment as a nominee or custodian under section 16, 17 or 18.

(5) Subject to subsections (1) and (4), the persons whom the trustees may under section 16, 17 or 18 appoint as a nominee or custodian include—

    (a) one of their number, if that one is a trust corporation, or

    (b) two (or more) of their number, if they are to act as joint nominees or joint custodians.

(6) The trustees may under section 16 appoint a person to act as their nominee even though he is also—

    (a) appointed to act as their custodian (whether under section 17 or 18 or any other power), or

    (b) authorised to exercise functions as their agent (whether under section 11 or any other power).

(7) Likewise, the trustees may under section 17 or 18 appoint a person to act as their custodian even though he is also—

    (a) appointed to act as their nominee (whether under section 16 or any other power), or

    (b) authorised to exercise functions as their agent (whether under section 11 or any other power).

20 Terms of appointment of nominees and custodians

(1) Subject to subsection (2) and sections 29 to 32, the trustees may under section 16, 17 or 18 appoint a person to act as a nominee or custodian on such terms as to remuneration and other matters as they may determine.

---

[1] Words substituted by the Charities Act 2006, s 75(1), Sch 8, para 197.

(2) The trustees may not under section 16, 17 or 18 appoint a person to act as a nominee or custodian on any of the terms mentioned in subsection (3) unless it is reasonably necessary for them to do so.

(3) The terms are—

(a) a term permitting the nominee or custodian to appoint a substitute;

(b) a term restricting the liability of the nominee or custodian or his substitute to the trustees or to any beneficiary;

(c) a term permitting the nominee or custodian to act in circumstances capable of giving rise to a conflict of interest.

Review of and liability for agents, nominees and custodians etc

21 Application of sections 22 and 23

(1) Sections 22 and 23 apply in a case where trustees have, under section 11, 16, 17 or 18—

(a) authorised a person to exercise functions as their agent, or

(b) appointed a person to act as a nominee or custodian.

(2) Subject to subsection (3), sections 22 and 23 also apply in a case where trustees have, under any power conferred on them by the trust instrument or by any enactment or any provision of subordinate legislation—

(a) authorised a person to exercise functions as their agent, or

(b) appointed a person to act as a nominee or custodian.

(3) If the application of section 22 or 23 is inconsistent with the terms of the trust instrument or the enactment or provision of subordinate legislation, the section in question does not apply.

22 Review of agents, nominees and custodians etc

(1) While the agent, nominee or custodian continues to act for the trust, the trustees—

(a) must keep under review the arrangements under which the agent, nominee or custodian acts and how those arrangements are being put into effect,

(b) if circumstances make it appropriate to do so, must consider whether there is a need to exercise any power of intervention that they have, and

(c) if they consider that there is a need to exercise such a power, must do so.

(2) If the agent has been authorised to exercise asset management functions, the duty under subsection (1) includes, in particular—

(a) a duty to consider whether there is any need to revise or replace the policy statement made for the purposes of section 15,

(b) if they consider that there is a need to revise or replace the policy statement, a duty to do so, and

(c) a duty to assess whether the policy statement (as it has effect for the time being) is being complied with.

(3) Subsections (3) and (4) of section 15 apply to the revision or replacement of a policy statement under this section as they apply to the making of a policy statement under that section.

(4) "Power of intervention" includes—

(a) a power to give directions to the agent, nominee or custodian;

(b) a power to revoke the authorisation or appointment.

23 Liability for agents, nominees and custodians etc

(1) A trustee is not liable for any act or default of the agent, nominee or custodian unless he has failed to comply with the duty of care applicable to him, under paragraph 3 of Schedule 1—

(a) when entering into the arrangements under which the person acts as agent, nominee or custodian, or

(b) when carrying out his duties under section 22.

(2) If a trustee has agreed a term under which the agent, nominee or custodian is permitted to appoint a substitute, the trustee is not liable for any act or default of the substitute unless he has failed to comply with the duty of care applicable to him, under paragraph 3 of Schedule 1—

(a) when agreeing that term, or

(b) when carrying out his duties under section 22 in so far as they relate to the use of the substitute.

Supplementary

24 Effect of trustees exceeding their powers

A failure by the trustees to act within the limits of the powers conferred by this Part—
-   (a) in authorising a person to exercise a function of theirs as an agent, or
-   (b) in appointing a person to act as a nominee or custodian,

does not invalidate the authorisation or appointment.

25 Sole trustees

(1) Subject to subsection (2), this Part applies in relation to a trust having a sole trustee as it applies in relation to other trusts (and references in this Part to trustees—except in sections 12(1) and (3) and 19(5)—are to be read accordingly).

(2) Section 18 does not impose a duty on a sole trustee if that trustee is a trust corporation.

26 Restriction or exclusion of this Part etc

The powers conferred by this Part are—
-   (a) in addition to powers conferred on trustees otherwise than by this Act, but
-   (b) subject to any restriction or exclusion imposed by the trust instrument or by any enactment or any provision of subordinate legislation.

27 Existing trusts

This Part applies in relation to trusts whether created before or after its commencement.

Part V
Remuneration

28 Trustee's entitlement to payment under trust instrument

(1) Except to the extent (if any) to which the trust instrument makes inconsistent provision, subsections (2) to (4) apply to a trustee if—
-   (a) there is a provision in the trust instrument entitling him to receive payment out of trust funds in respect of services provided by him to or on behalf of the trust, and
-   (b) the trustee is a trust corporation or is acting in a professional capacity.

(2) The trustee is to be treated as entitled under the trust instrument to receive payment in respect of services even if they are services which are capable of being provided by a lay trustee.

(3) Subsection (2) applies to a trustee of a charitable trust who is not a trust corporation only—
-   (a) if he is not a sole trustee, and
-   (b) to the extent that a majority of the other trustees have agreed that it should apply to him.

(4) Any payments to which the trustee is entitled in respect of services are to be treated as remuneration for services (and not as a gift) for the purposes of—
-   (a) section 15 of the Wills Act 1837 (gifts to an attesting witness to be void), and
-   (b) section 34(3) of the Administration of Estates Act 1925 (order in which estate to be paid out).

(5) For the purposes of this Part, a trustee acts in a professional capacity if he acts in the course of a profession or business which consists of or includes the provision of services in connection with—
-   (a) the management or administration of trusts generally or a particular kind of trust, or
-   (b) any particular aspect of the management or administration of trusts generally or a particular kind of trust,

and the services he provides to or on behalf of the trust fall within that description.

(6) For the purposes of this Part, a person acts as a lay trustee if he—
-   (a) is not a trust corporation, and
-   (b) does not act in a professional capacity.

29 Remuneration of certain trustees

(1) Subject to subsection (5), a trustee who—
-   (a) is a trust corporation, but
-   (b) is not a trustee of a charitable trust,

is entitled to receive reasonable remuneration out of the trust funds for any services that the trust corporation provides to or on behalf of the trust.

(2) Subject to subsection (5), a trustee who—

    (a)   acts in a professional capacity, but

    (b)   is not a trust corporation, a trustee of a charitable trust or a sole trustee,

is entitled to receive reasonable remuneration out of the trust funds for any services that he provides to or on behalf of the trust if each other trustee has agreed in writing that he may be remunerated for the services.

(3) "Reasonable remuneration" means, in relation to the provision of services by a trustee, such remuneration as is reasonable in the circumstances for the provision of those services to or on behalf of that trust by that trustee and for the purposes of subsection (1) includes, in relation to the provision of services by a trustee who is an authorised institution under the Banking Act 1987 and provides the services in that capacity, the institution's reasonable charges for the provision of such services.

(4) A trustee is entitled to remuneration under this section even if the services in question are capable of being provided by a lay trustee.

(5) A trustee is not entitled to remuneration under this section if any provision about his entitlement to remuneration has been made—

    (a)   by the trust instrument, or

    (b)   by any enactment or any provision of subordinate legislation.

(6) This section applies to a trustee who has been authorised under a power conferred by Part IV or the trust instrument—

    (a)   to exercise functions as an agent of the trustees, or

    (b)   to act as a nominee or custodian,

as it applies to any other trustee.

30 Remuneration of trustees of charitable trusts

(1) The Secretary of State may by regulations make provision for the remuneration of trustees of charitable trusts who are trust corporations or act in a professional capacity.

(2) The power under subsection (1) includes power to make provision for the remuneration of a trustee who has been authorised under a power conferred by Part IV or any other enactment or any provision of subordinate legislation, or by the trust instrument—

    (a)   to exercise functions as an agent of the trustees, or

    (b)   to act as a nominee or custodian.

(3) Regulations under this section may—

    (a)   make different provision for different cases;

    (b)   contain such supplemental, incidental, consequential and transitional provision as the Secretary of State considers appropriate.

(4) The power to make regulations under this section is exercisable by statutory instrument, but no such instrument shall be made unless a draft of it has been laid before Parliament and approved by a resolution of each House of Parliament.

31 Trustees' expenses

(1) A trustee—

    (a)   is entitled to be reimbursed from the trust funds, or

    (b)   may pay out of the trust funds,

expenses properly incurred by him when acting on behalf of the trust.

(2) This section applies to a trustee who has been authorised under a power conferred by Part IV or any other enactment or any provision of subordinate legislation, or by the trust instrument—

    (a)   to exercise functions as an agent of the trustees, or

    (b)   to act as a nominee or custodian,

as it applies to any other trustee.

32 Remuneration and expenses of agents, nominees and custodians

(1) This section applies if, under a power conferred by Part IV or any other enactment or any provision of subordinate legislation, or by the trust instrument, a person other than a trustee has been—

    (a)   authorised to exercise functions as an agent of the trustees, or

    (b)   appointed to act as a nominee or custodian.

(2) The trustees may remunerate the agent, nominee or custodian out of the trust funds for services if—

    (a)   he is engaged on terms entitling him to be remunerated for those services, and

    (b)   the amount does not exceed such remuneration as is reasonable in the circumstances for the provision of those services by him to or on behalf of that trust.

(3) The trustees may reimburse the agent, nominee or custodian out of the trust funds for any expenses properly incurred by him in exercising functions as an agent, nominee or custodian.

33 Application

(1) Subject to subsection (2), sections 28, 29, 31 and 32 apply in relation to services provided to or on behalf of, or (as the case may be) expenses incurred on or after their commencement on behalf of, trusts whenever created.

(2) Nothing in section 28 or 29 is to be treated as affecting the operation of—

    (a)   section 15 of the Wills Act 1837, or

    (b)   section 34(3) of the Administration of Estates Act 1925,

in relation to any death occurring before the commencement of section 28 or (as the case may be) section 29.

Part VI
Miscellaneous and Supplementary

34 Power to insure

(1) For section 19 of the Trustee Act 1925 (power to insure) substitute—

19 "Power to insure

(1) A trustee may—

    (a)   insure any property which is subject to the trust against risks of loss or damage due to any event, and

    (b)   pay the premiums out of the trust funds.

(2) In the case of property held on a bare trust, the power to insure is subject to any direction given by the beneficiary or each of the beneficiaries—

    (a)   that any property specified in the direction is not to be insured;

    (b)   that any property specified in the direction is not to be insured except on such conditions as may be so specified.

(3) Property is held on a bare trust if it is held on trust for—

    (a)   a beneficiary who is of full age and capacity and absolutely entitled to the property subject to the trust, or

    (b)   beneficiaries each of whom is of full age and capacity and who (taken together) are absolutely entitled to the property subject to the trust.

(4) If a direction under subsection (2) of this section is given, the power to insure, so far as it is subject to the direction, ceases to be a delegable function for the purposes of section 11 of the Trustee Act 2000 (power to employ agents).

(5) In this section "trust funds" means any income or capital funds of the trust."

(2) In section 20(1) of the Trustee Act 1925 (application of insurance money) omit "whether by fire or otherwise".

(3) The amendments made by this section apply in relation to trusts whether created before or after its commencement.

35 Personal representatives

(1) Subject to the following provisions of this section, this Act applies in relation to a personal representative administering an estate according to the law as it applies to a trustee carrying out a trust for beneficiaries.

(2) For this purpose this Act is to be read with the appropriate modifications and in particular—

    (a)   references to the trust instrument are to be read as references to the will,

(b) references to a beneficiary or to beneficiaries, apart from the reference to a beneficiary in section 8(1)(b), are to be read as references to a person or the persons interested in the due administration of the estate, and

(c) the reference to a beneficiary in section 8(1)(b) is to be read as a reference to a person who under the will of the deceased or under the law relating to intestacy is beneficially interested in the estate.

(3) Remuneration to which a personal representative is entitled under section 28 or 29 is to be treated as an administration expense for the purposes of—

(a) section 34(3) of the Administration of Estates Act 1925 (order in which estate to be paid out), and

(b) any provision giving reasonable administration expenses priority over the preferential debts listed in Schedule 6 to the Insolvency Act 1986.

(4) Nothing in subsection (3) is to be treated as affecting the operation of the provisions mentioned in paragraphs (a) and (b) of that subsection in relation to any death occurring before the commencement of this section.

36 Pension schemes

(1) In this section "pension scheme" means an occupational pension scheme (within the meaning of the Pension Schemes Act 1993) established under a trust and subject to the law of England and Wales.

(2) Part I does not apply in so far as it imposes a duty of care in relation to—

(a) the functions described in paragraphs 1 and 2 of Schedule 1, or

(b) the functions described in paragraph 3 of that Schedule to the extent that they relate to trustees—

(i) authorising a person to exercise their functions with respect to investment, or

(ii) appointing a person to act as their nominee or custodian.

(3) Nothing in Part II or III applies to the trustees of any pension scheme.

(4) Part IV applies to the trustees of a pension scheme subject to the restrictions in subsections (5) to (8).

(5) The trustees of a pension scheme may not under Part IV authorise any person to exercise any functions relating to investment as their agent.

(6) The trustees of a pension scheme may not under Part IV authorise a person who is—

(a) an employer in relation to the scheme, or

(b) connected with or an associate of such an employer,

to exercise any of their functions as their agent.

(7) For the purposes of subsection (6)—

(a) "employer", in relation to a scheme, has the same meaning as in the Pensions Act 1995;

(b) sections 249 and 435 of the Insolvency Act 1986 apply for the purpose of determining whether a person is connected with or an associate of an employer.

(8) Sections 16 to 20 (powers to appoint nominees and custodians) do not apply to the trustees of a pension scheme.

37 Authorised unit trusts

(1) Parts II to IV do not apply to trustees of authorised unit trusts.

(2) "Authorised unit trust" means a unit trust scheme in the case of which an order under section 78 of the Financial Services Act 1986 is in force.

38 Common investment schemes for charities etc

Parts II to IV do not apply to—

(a) trustees managing a fund under a common investment scheme made, or having effect as if made, under section 24 of the Charities Act 1993, other than such a fund the trusts of which provide that property is not to be transferred to the fund except by or on behalf of a charity the trustees of which are the trustees appointed to manage the fund, or

(b) trustees managing a fund under a common deposit scheme made, or having effect as if made, under section 25 of that Act.

39 Interpretation

(1) In this Act—

"asset" includes any right or interest;

"charitable trust" means a trust under which property is held for charitable purposes and "charitable purposes" has the same meaning as in the Charities Act 1993;

"custodian trustee" has the same meaning as in the Public Trustee Act 1906;

"enactment" includes any provision of a Measure of the Church Assembly or of the General Synod of the Church of England;

"exempt charity" has the same meaning as in the Charities Act 1993;

"functions" includes powers and duties;

"legal mortgage" has the same meaning as in the Law of Property Act 1925;

"personal representative" has the same meaning as in the Trustee Act 1925;

"settled land" has the same meaning as in the Settled Land Act 1925;

"trust corporation" has the same meaning as in the Trustee Act 1925;

"trust funds" means income or capital funds of the trust.

(2) In this Act the expressions listed below are defined or otherwise explained by the provisions indicated—

asset management functions	section 15(5)
custodian	section 17(2)
the duty of care	section 1(2)
the general power of investment	section 3(2)
lay trustee	section 28(6)
power of intervention	section 22(4)
the standard investment criteria	section 4(3)
subordinate legislation	section 6(3)
trustee acting in a professional capacity	section 28(5)
trust instrument	sections 6(2) and 35(2)(a)

40 Minor and consequential amendments etc

(1) Schedule 2 (minor and consequential amendments) shall have effect.

(2) Schedule 3 (transitional provisions and savings) shall have effect.

(3) Schedule 4 (repeals) shall have effect.

41 Power to amend other Acts

(1) A Minister of the Crown may by order make such amendments of any Act, including an Act extending to places outside England and Wales, as appear to him appropriate in consequence of or in connection with Part II or III.

(2) Before exercising the power under subsection (1) in relation to a local, personal or private Act, the Minister must consult any person who appears to him to be affected by any proposed amendment.

(3) An order under this section may—

(a) contain such transitional provisions and savings as the Minister thinks fit;

(b) make different provision for different purposes.

(4) The power to make an order under this section is exercisable by statutory instrument which shall be subject to annulment in pursuance of a resolution of either House of Parliament.

(5) "Minister of the Crown" has the same meaning as in the Ministers of the Crown Act 1975.

42 Commencement and extent

(1) Section 41, this section and section 43 shall come into force on the day on which this Act is passed.

(2) The remaining provisions of this Act shall come into force on such day as the Lord Chancellor may appoint by order made by statutory instrument; and different days may be so appointed for different purposes.

(3) An order under subsection (2) may contain such transitional provisions and savings as the Lord Chancellor considers appropriate in connection with the order.

(4) Subject to section 41(1) and subsection (5), this Act extends to England and Wales only.

(5) An amendment or repeal in Part II or III of Schedule 2 or Part II of Schedule 4 has the same extent as the provision amended or repealed.

43 Short title

This Act may be cited as the Trustee Act 2000.

SCHEDULE 1
APPLICATION OF DUTY OF CARE

Section 2

Investment

1

The duty of care applies to a trustee—

(a) when exercising the general power of investment or any other power of investment, however conferred;

(b) when carrying out a duty to which he is subject under section 4 or 5 (duties relating to the exercise of a power of investment or to the review of investments).

Acquisition of land

2

The duty of care applies to a trustee—

(a) when exercising the power under section 8 to acquire land;

(b) when exercising any other power to acquire land, however conferred;

(c) when exercising any power in relation to land acquired under a power mentioned in sub-paragraph (a) or (b).

Agents, nominees and custodians

3

(1) The duty of care applies to a trustee—

    (a) when entering into arrangements under which a person is authorised under section 11 to exercise functions as an agent;

    (b) when entering into arrangements under which a person is appointed under section 16 to act as a nominee;

    (c) when entering into arrangements under which a person is appointed under section 17 or 18 to act as a custodian;

    (d) when entering into arrangements under which, under any other power, however conferred, a person is authorised to exercise functions as an agent or is appointed to act as a nominee or custodian;

    (e) when carrying out his duties under section 22 (review of agent, nominee or custodian, etc).

(2) For the purposes of sub-paragraph (1), entering into arrangements under which a person is authorised to exercise functions or is appointed to act as a nominee or custodian includes, in particular—

    (a) selecting the person who is to act,

    (b) determining any terms on which he is to act, and

    (c) if the person is being authorised to exercise asset management functions, the preparation of a policy statement under section 15.

Compounding of liabilities

4

The duty of care applies to a trustee—

(a) when exercising the power under section 15 of the Trustee Act 1925 to do any of the things referred to in that section;

(b) when exercising any corresponding power, however conferred.

Insurance

5

The duty of care applies to a trustee—

(a) when exercising the power under section 19 of the Trustee Act 1925 to insure property;

(b) when exercising any corresponding power, however conferred.

Reversionary interests, valuations and audit

6

The duty of care applies to a trustee—

(a) when exercising the power under section 22(1) or (3) of the Trustee Act 1925 to do any of the things referred to there;

(b) when exercising any corresponding power, however conferred.

Exclusion of duty of care

7

The duty of care does not apply if or in so far as it appears from the trust instrument that the duty is not meant to apply.

SCHEDULE 2
MINOR AND CONSEQUENTIAL AMENDMENTS

Section 40

Part I
The Trustee Investments Act 1961and the Charities Act 1993
The Trustee Investments Act 1961 (c 62)

1

(1) Sections 1, 2, 5, 6, 12, 13 and 15 shall cease to have effect, except in so far as they are applied by or under any other enactment.

(2) Section 3 and Schedules 2 and 3 shall cease to have effect, except in so far as they relate to a trustee having a power of investment conferred on him under an enactment—

(a) which was passed before the passing of the 1961 Act, and

(b) which is not amended by this Schedule.

(3) Omit—

(a) sections 8 and 9,

(b) paragraph 1(1) of Schedule 4, and

(c) section 16(1), in so far as it relates to paragraph 1(1) of Schedule 4.

The Charities Act 1993 (c 10)

2

(1) Omit sections 70 and 71.

(2) In section 86(2) in paragraph (a)—

(a) omit "70", and

(b) at the end insert "or".

(3) Omit section 86(2)(b).

Part II
Other Public General Acts
The Places of Worship Sites Act 1873 (c 50)

3

In section 2 (payment of purchase money, etc) for "shall be invested upon such securities or investments as would for the time being be authorised by statute or the Court of Chancery" substitute "shall be invested under the general power of investment in section 3 of the Trustee Act 2000".

The Technical and Industrial Institutions Act 1892 (c 29)

4

In section 9 (investment powers relating to proceeds of sale of land acquired under the Act) for subsection (5) substitute—
　　"(5) Money arising by sale may, until reinvested in the purchase of land, be invested—
　　　　(a) in the names of the governing body, in any investments in which trustees may invest under the general power of investment in section 3 of the Trustee Act 2000 (as restricted by sections 4 and 5 of that Act), or
　　　　(b) under the general power of investment in section 3 of that Act, by trustees for the governing body or by a person authorised by the trustees under that Act to invest as an agent of the trustees.
　　(6) Any profits from investments under subsection (5) shall be invested in the same way and added to capital until the capital is reinvested in the purchase of land."

The Duchy of Cornwall Management Act 1893 (c 20)

5

The 1893 Act is hereby repealed.

The Duchy of Lancaster Act 1920 (c 51)

6

In section 1 (extension of powers of investment of funds of Duchy of Lancaster) for "in any of the investments specified in paragraph (a) of section one of the Trustees Act 1893 and any enactment amending or extending that paragraph" substitute "under the general power of investment in section 3 of the Trustee Act 2000 (as restricted by sections 4 and 5 of that Act)".

The Settled Land Act 1925 (c 18)

7

In section 21 (absolute owners subject to certain interests to have the powers of tenant for life), in subsection (1)(d) for "income thereof" substitute "resultant profits".

8

In section 39 (regulations respecting sales), in subsection (2), in the proviso, for the words from "accumulate" to the end of the subsection substitute "accumulate the profits from the capital money by investing them and any resulting profits under the general power of investment in section 3 of the Trustee Act 2000 and shall add the accumulations to capital."

9

In section 73 (modes of investment or application), in subsection (1) for paragraph (i) substitute—
　　"(i) In investment in securities either under the general power of investment in section 3 of the Trustee Act 2000 or under a power to invest conferred on the trustees of the settlement by the settlement;".

10

(1) In section 75 (regulations respecting investment, devolution, and income of securities etc), for sub-section (2) substitute—

"(2) Subject to Part IV of the Trustee Act 2000, to section 75A of this Act and to the following provisions of this section—

(a) the investment or other application by the trustees shall be made according to the discretion of the trustees, but subject to any consent required or direction given by the settlement with respect to the investment or other application by the trustees of trust money of the settlement, and

(b) any investment shall be in the names or under the control of the trustees."

(2) For subsection (4) of that section substitute—

"(4) The trustees, in exercising their power to invest or apply capital money, shall—

(a) so far as practicable, consult the tenant for life; and

(b) so far as consistent with the general interest of the settlement, give effect to his wishes.

(4A) Any investment or other application of capital money under the direction of the court shall not during the subsistence of the beneficial interest of the tenant for life be altered without his consent.

(4B) The trustees may not under section 11 of the Trustee Act 2000 authorise a person to exercise their functions with respect to the investment or application of capital money on terms that prevent them from complying with subsection (4) of this section.

(4C) A person who is authorised under section 11 of the Trustee Act 2000 to exercise any of their functions with respect to the investment or application of capital money is not subject to subsection (4) of this section."

(3) Nothing in this paragraph affects the operation of section 75 in relation to directions of the tenant for life given, but not acted upon by the trustees, before the commencement of this paragraph.

11

After section 75 insert—

"75A Power to accept charge as security for part payment for land sold

(1) Where—

(a) land subject to the settlement is sold by the tenant for life or statutory owner, for an estate in fee simple or a term having at least five hundred years to run, and

(b) the proceeds of sale are liable to be invested,

the tenant for life or statutory owner may, with the consent of the trustees of the settlement, contract that the payment of any part, not exceeding two-thirds, of the purchase money shall be secured by a charge by way of legal mortgage of the land sold, with or without the security of any other property.

(2) If any buildings are comprised in the property secured by the charge, the charge must contain a covenant by the mortgagor to keep them insured for their full value against loss or damage due to any event.

(3) A person exercising the power under subsection (1) of this section, or giving consent for the purposes of that subsection—

(a) is not required to comply with section 5 of the Trustee Act 2000 before giving his consent, and

(b) is not liable for any loss incurred merely because the security is insufficient at the date of the charge.

(4) The power under subsection (1) of this section is exercisable subject to the consent of any person whose consent to a change of investment is required by the instrument, if any, creating the trust.

(5) Where the sale referred to in subsection (1) of this section is made under the order of the court, the power under that subsection applies only if and as far as the court may by order direct."

12

Omit section 96 (protection of each trustee individually).

13

In section 98 (protection of trustees in particular cases), omit subsections (1) and (2).

14

Omit section 100 (trustees' reimbursements).

15

In section 102 (management of land during minority or pending contingency), in subsection (2) for paragraph (e) substitute—

"(e) to insure against risks of loss or damage due to any event under section 19 of the Trustee Act 1925;".

16

(1) In section 104 (powers of tenant for life not assignable etc)—

(a) in subsection (3)(b) omit "authorised by statute for the investment of trust money", and

(b) in subsection (4)(b) for the words from "no investment" to "trust money;" substitute "the consent of the assignee shall be required to an investment of capital money for the time being affected by the assignment in investments other than securities, and to any application of such capital money;".

(2) Sub-paragraph (1) applies to the determination on or after the commencement of that sub-paragraph of whether an assignee's consent is required to the investment or application of capital money.

17

In section 107 (tenant for life deemed to be in the position and to have the duties and liabilities of a trustee, etc) after subsection (1) insert—

"(1A) The following provisions apply to the tenant for life as they apply to the trustees of the settlement—

(a) sections 11, 13 to 15 and 21 to 23 of the Trustee Act 2000 (power to employ agents subject to certain restrictions),

(b) section 32 of that Act (remuneration and expenses of agents etc),

(c) section 19 of the Trustee Act 1925 (power to insure), and

(d) in so far as they relate to the provisions mentioned in paragraphs (a) and (c), Part I of, and Schedule 1 to, the Trustee Act 2000 (the duty of care)."

The Trustee Act 1925 (c 19)

18

Omit Part I (investments).

19

In section 14 (power of trustees to give receipts) in subsection (1) after "securities," insert "investments".

20

In section 15 (power to compound liabilities), for "in good faith" substitute "if he has or they have discharged the duty of care set out in section 1(1) of the Trustee Act 2000".

21

Omit section 21 (deposit of documents for safe custody).

22

In section 22 (reversionary interests, valuations, and audit)—

(a) in subsection (1), for "in good faith" substitute "if they have discharged the duty of care set out in section 1(1) of the Trustee Act 2000", and

(b) in subsection (3), omit "in good faith" and at the end insert "if the trustees have discharged the duty of care set out in section 1(1) of the Trustee Act 2000".

23

Omit section 23 (power to employ agents).

24

Omit section 30 (implied indemnity of trustees).

25

In section 31(2) (power to invest income during minority) for "in the way of compound interest by investing the same and the resulting income thereof" substitute "by investing it, and any profits from so investing it".

26 ...²

The Administration of Estates Act 1925 (c 23)

27

In section 33, in subsection (3) (investment during minority of beneficiary or the subsistence of a life interest) for the words from "in any investments for the time being authorised by statute" to the end of the subsection substitute "under the Trustee Act 2000."

28

In section 39 (powers of management) after subsection (1) insert—
  "(1A) Subsection (1) of this section is without prejudice to the powers conferred on personal representatives by the Trustee Act 2000."

The Universities and College Estates Act 1925 (c 24)

29

In section 26 (modes of application of capital money) in subsection (1) for paragraph (i) substitute—
  "(i) In investments in which trustees may invest under the general power of investment in section 3 of the Trustee Act 2000 (as restricted by sections 4 and 5 of that Act);".

The Regimental Charitable Funds Act 1935 (c 11)

30

In section 2(1) (application of funds held on account of regimental charitable funds)—
  (a) in paragraph (a) for "in some manner" to "trusts" substitute "under the general power of investment in section 3 of the Trustee Act 2000";
  (b) in paragraph (b) after "the income" insert "or the other profits".

The Agricultural Marketing Act 1958 (c 47)

31

(1) In section 16 (investment of surplus funds of boards) for paragraph (a) substitute—
  "(a) the moneys of the board not for the time being required by them for the purposes of their functions are not, except with the approval of the Minister, invested otherwise than in investments in which trustees may invest under the general power of investment in section 3 of the Trustee Act 2000 (as restricted by sections 4 and 5 of that Act); and".
(2) Any scheme made under the 1958 Act and in effect before the day on which sub-paragraph (1) comes into force shall be treated, in relation to the making of investments on and after that day, as including provision permitting investment by the board in accordance with section 16(a) of the 1958 Act as amended by sub-paragraph (1).

The Horticulture Act 1960 (c 22)

32

In section 13 (miscellaneous financial powers of organisations promoting home-grown produce) for subsection (3) substitute—
  "(3) A relevant organisation may invest any of its surplus money which is not for the time being required for any other purpose in any investments in which trustees may invest under the general power of investment in section 3 of the Trustee Act 2000 (as restricted by sections 4 and 5 of that Act)".

---

² Repealed by the Land Registration Act 2002, s 135, Sch 13.

The House of Commons Members' Fund Act 1962 (c 53)

33

(1) In section 1 (powers of investment of trustees of House of Commons Members' Fund)—
    (a) in subsection (2) omit "Subject to the following provisions of this section";
    (b) omit subsections (3) to (5).
(2) In section 2 (interpretation etc) omit subsection (1).

The Betting, Gaming and Lotteries Act 1963 (c 2)

34

In section 25(1) (general powers and duties of the Horserace Betting Levy Board) for paragraph (e) substitute—
    "(e) to make such other investments as—
        (i) they judge desirable for the proper conduct of their affairs, and
        (ii) a trustee would be able to make under the general power of investment in section 3 of the Trustee Act 2000 (as restricted by sections 4 and 5 of that Act);".

. . .[3]

35

. . .[4]

36

. . .[5]

The Solicitors Act 1974 (c 47)

37

In Schedule 2, for paragraph 3 (power of Law Society to invest) substitute—
    "3 The Society may invest any money which forms part of the fund in any investments in which trustees may invest under the general power of investment in section 3 of the Trustee Act 2000 (as restricted by sections 4 and 5 of that Act)."[6]

The Policyholders Protection Act 1975 (c 75)

38

In Schedule 1, in paragraph 7, for sub-paragraph (1) (power of Policyholders Protection Board to invest) substitute—
    "(1) The Board may invest any funds held by them which appear to them to be surplus to their requirements for the time being—
        (a) in any investments in which trustees may invest under the general power of investment in section 3 of the Trustee Act 2000 (as restricted by sections 4 and 5 of that Act); or
        (b) in any investment approved for the purpose by the Treasury."

The National Heritage Act 1980 (c 17)

39

In section 6 for subsection (3) (powers of investment of Trustees of National Heritage Memorial Fund) substitute—

---

[3] Repealed by the Horserace Betting and Olympic Lottery Act 2004, s 38, Sch 6.
[4] Repealed by SI 2008/576, art 18, Sch 5, para 7.
[5] Repealed by SI 2008/576, art 18, Sch 5, para 7.
[6] repealed by the Legal Services Act 2007, s 210, Sch 23.

"(3) The Trustees may invest any sums to which subsection (2) does not apply in any investments in which trustees may invest under the general power of investment in section 3 of the Trustee Act 2000 (as restricted by sections 4 and 5 of that Act)."

The Licensing (Alcohol Education and Research) Act 1981 (c 28)

40

In section 7 (powers of investment of Alcohol Education and Research Council) for subsection (5) substitute—

"(5) Any sums in the Fund which are not immediately required for any other purpose may be invested by the Council in any investments in which trustees may invest under the general power of investment in section 3 of the Trustee Act 2000 (as restricted by sections 4 and 5 of that Act)."

The Fisheries Act 1981 (c 29)

41

For section 10 (powers of investment of Sea Fish Industry Authority) substitute—

"10 Investment of reserve funds

Any money of the Authority which is not immediately required for any other purpose may be invested by the Authority in any investments in which trustees may invest under the general power of investment in section 3 of the Trustee Act 2000 (as restricted by sections 4 and 5 of that Act)."

The Duchy of Cornwall Management Act 1982 (c 47)

42

For section 1 (powers of investment of Duchy property) substitute—

"1 Powers of investment of Duchy property

The power of investment conferred by the Duchy of Cornwall Management Act 1863 includes power to invest in any investments in which trustees may invest under the general power of investment in section 3 of the Trustee Act 2000 (as restricted by sections 4 and 5 of that Act)."

43

In—

(a) section 6(3) (Duchy of Cornwall Management Acts extended in relation to banking), and

(b) section 11(2) (collective citation of Duchy of Cornwall Management Acts),

for "Duchy of Cornwall Management Acts 1868 to 1893" substitute "Duchy of Cornwall Management Acts 1863 to 1868".

The Administration of Justice Act 1982 (c 53)

44

In section 42 (common investment schemes) in subsection (6) for paragraph (a) substitute—

"(a) he may invest trust money in shares in the fund without obtaining and considering advice on whether to make such an investment; and".

The Trusts of Land and Appointment of Trustees Act 1996 (c 47)

45

(1) In section 6 (general powers of trustees), in subsection (3) for "purchase a legal estate in any land in England and Wales" substitute "acquire land under the power conferred by section 8 of the Trustee Act 2000."

(2) Omit subsection (4) of that section.

(3) After subsection (8) of that section insert—

"(9) The duty of care under section 1 of the Trustee Act 2000 applies to trustees of land when exercising the powers conferred by this section."

46

In section 9 (delegation by trustees) omit subsection (8).

47

After section 9 insert—

"9A Duties of trustees in connection with delegation etc.

(1) The duty of care under section 1 of the Trustee Act 2000 applies to trustees of land in deciding whether to delegate any of their functions under section 9.

(2) Subsection (3) applies if the trustees of land—

(a) delegate any of their functions under section 9, and

(b) the delegation is not irrevocable.

(3) While the delegation continues, the trustees—

(a) must keep the delegation under review,

(b) if circumstances make it appropriate to do so, must consider whether there is a need to exercise any power of intervention that they have, and

(c) if they consider that there is a need to exercise such a power, must do so.

(4) "Power of intervention" includes—

(a) a power to give directions to the beneficiary;

(b) a power to revoke the delegation.

(5) The duty of care under section 1 of the 2000 Act applies to trustees in carrying out any duty under subsection (3).

(6) A trustee of land is not liable for any act or default of the beneficiary, or beneficiaries, unless the trustee fails to comply with the duty of care in deciding to delegate any of the trustees' functions under section 9 or in carrying out any duty under subsection (3).

(7) Neither this section nor the repeal of section 9(8) by the Trustee Act 2000 affects the operation after the commencement of this section of any delegation effected before that commencement."

48

Omit section 17(1) (application of section 6(3) in relation to trustees of proceeds of sale of land).

49

In Schedule 3 (consequential amendments) omit paragraph 3(4) (amendment of section 19(1) and (2) of Trustee Act 1925).

Part III
Measures
The Ecclesiastical Dilapidations Measure 1923 (No 3)

50

In section 52, in subsection (5) (investment of sums held in relation to repair of chancels)—

(a) for "in any investment permitted by law for the investment of trust funds, and the yearly income resulting therefrom shall be applied," substitute "in any investments in which trustees may invest under the general power of investment in section 3 of the Trustee Act 2000, and the annual profits from the investments shall be applied"; and

(b) in paragraph (iii) for "any residue of the said income not applied as aforesaid in any year" substitute "any residue of the profits from the investments not applied in any year."

The Diocesan Stipends Funds Measure 1953 (No 2)

51

In section 4 (application of moneys credited to capital accounts) in subsection (1) for paragraph (bc) substitute—

"(bc) investment in any investments in which trustees may invest under the general power of investment in section 3 of the Trustee Act 2000 (as restricted by sections 4 and 5 of that Act);".

The Church Funds Investment Measure 1958 (No 1)

52

In the Schedule, in paragraph 21 (range of investments of deposit fund) for paragraphs (a) to (d) of sub-paragraph (1) substitute—
"(aa) In any investments in which trustees may invest under the general power of investment in section 3 of the Trustee Act 2000 (as restricted by sections 4 and 5 of that Act);".

The Clergy Pensions Measure 1961 (No 3)

53

(1) In section 32 (investment powers of Board), in subsection (1), for paragraph (a) substitute—
"(a) in any investments in which trustees may invest under the general power of investment in section 3 of the Trustee Act 2000 (as restricted by sections 4 and 5 of that Act);".
(2) Omit subsection (3) of that section.

The Repair of Benefice Buildings Measure 1972 (No 2)

54

In section 17, in subsection (2) (diocesan parsonages fund's power of investment), for "who shall have the same powers of investment as trustees of trust funds:" substitute "who shall have the same power as trustees to invest in any investments in which trustees may invest under the general power of investment in section 3 of the Trustee Act 2000 (as restricted by sections 4 and 5 of that Act)."

The Pastoral Measure 1983 (No 1)

55

In section 44, for subsection (6) (Redundant Churches Fund's power of investment) substitute—
"(6) The powers to invest any such sums are—
(a) power to invest in investments in which trustees may invest under the general power of investment in section 3 of the Trustee Act 2000 (as restricted by sections 4 and 5 of that Act); and
(b) power to invest in the investments referred to in paragraph 21(1)(e) and (f) of the Schedule to the Church Funds Investment Measure 1958."

The Church of England (Pensions) Measure 1988 (No 4)

56

Omit section 14(b) (amendment of section 32(3) of the Clergy Pensions Measure 1961).

The Cathedrals Measure 1999 (No 1)

57

In section 16 (cathedral moneys: investment powers, etc), in subsection (1)—
(a) for paragraph (c) substitute—
"(c) power to invest in any investments in which trustees may invest under the general power of investment in section 3 of the Trustee Act 2000 (as restricted by sections 4 and 5 of that Act),",
and
(b) omit the words from "and the powers" to the end of the subsection.

SCHEDULE 3
Transitional Provisions and Savings

Section 40

The Trustee Act 1925 (c 19)

1

(1) Sub-paragraph (2) applies if, immediately before the day on which Part IV of this Act comes into force, a banker or banking company holds any bearer securities deposited with him under section 7(1) of the 1925 Act (investment in bearer securities).

(2) On and after the day on which Part IV comes into force, the banker or banking company shall be treated as if he had been appointed as custodian of the securities under section 18.

2

The repeal of section 8 of the 1925 Act (loans and investments by trustees not chargeable as breaches of trust) does not affect the operation of that section in relation to loans or investments made before the coming into force of that repeal.

3

The repeal of section 9 of the 1925 Act (liability for loss by reason of improper investment) does not affect the operation of that section in relation to any advance of trust money made before the coming into force of that repeal.

4

(1) Sub-paragraph (2) applies if, immediately before the day on which Part IV of this Act comes into force, a banker or banking company holds any documents deposited with him under section 21 of the 1925 Act (deposit of documents for safe custody).

(2) On and after the day on which Part IV comes into force, the banker or banking company shall be treated as if he had been appointed as custodian of the documents under section 17.

5

(1) Sub-paragraph (2) applies if, immediately before the day on which Part IV of this Act comes into force, a person has been appointed to act as or be an agent or attorney under section 23(1) or (3) of the 1925 Act (general power to employ agents etc).

(2) On and after the day on which Part IV comes into force, the agent shall be treated as if he had been authorised to exercise functions as an agent under section 11 (and, if appropriate, as if he had also been appointed under that Part to act as a custodian or nominee).

6

The repeal of section 23(2) of the 1925 Act (power to employ agents in respect of property outside the United Kingdom) does not affect the operation after the commencement of the repeal of an appointment made before that commencement.

The Trustee Investments Act 1961 (c 62)

7

(1) A trustee shall not be liable for breach of trust merely because he continues to hold an investment acquired by virtue of paragraph 14 of Part II of Schedule 1 to the 1961 Act (perpetual rent-charges etc).

(2) A person who—

(a) is not a trustee,

(b) before the commencement of Part II of this Act had powers to invest in the investments described in paragraph 14 of Part II of Schedule 1 to the 1961 Act, and

(c) on that commencement acquired the general power of investment,

shall not be treated as exceeding his powers of investment merely because he continues to hold an investment acquired by virtue of that paragraph.

The Cathedrals Measure 1963 (No 2)

8

While section 21 of the Cathedrals Measure 1963 (investment powers, etc of capitular bodies) continues to apply in relation to any cathedral, that section shall have effect as if—

(a) in subsection (1), for paragraph (c) and the words from "and the powers" to the end of the subsection there were substituted—

"(c) power to invest in any investments in which trustees may invest under the general power of investment in section 3 of the Trustee Act 2000 (as restricted by sections 4 and 5 of that Act).", and

(b) in subsection (5), for "subsections (2) and (3) of section six of the Trustee Investments Act 1961" there were substituted "section 5 of the Trustee Act 2000".

SCHEDULE 4
REPEALS

Section 40

Part I
The Trustee Investments Act 1961 and the Charities Act 1993

Chapter	Short title	Extent of repeal
1961 c 62.	The Trustee Investments Act 1961.	Sections 1 to 3, 5, 6, 8, 9, 12, 13, 15 and 16(1).
		Schedules 2 and 3.
		In Schedule 4, paragraph 1(1).
1993 c 10.	The Charities Act 1993.	Sections 70 and 71.
		In section 86(2) in paragraph (a), "70" and paragraph (b).

Note: the repeals in this Part of this Schedule have effect in accordance with Part I of Schedule 2.

Part II
Other repeals

Chapter	Short title	Extent of repeal
1893 c 20.	The Duchy of Cornwall Management Act 1893.	The whole Act.
1925 c 18.	The Settled Land Act 1925.	Section 96.
		Section 98(1) and (2).
		Section 100.
		In section 104(3)(b) the words "authorised by statute for the investment of trust money".
1925 c 19.	The Trustee Act 1925.	Part I.
		In section 20(1) the words "whether by fire or otherwise".
		Sections 21, 23 and 30.
1961 No 3.	The Clergy Pensions Measure 1961.	Section 32(3).
1962 c 53.	The House of Commons Members' Fund Act 1962.	In section 1, in subsection (2) the words "Subject to the following provisions of this section" and subsections (3) to (5).
		Section 2(1).
1965 c 14.	The Cereals Marketing Act 1965.	Section 18(3).
1967 c 22.	The Agriculture Act 1967.	Section 18(3).
1988 No 4.	The Church of England (Pensions) Measure 1988.	Section 14(b).
1996 c 47.	The Trusts of Land and Appointment of Trustees Act 1996.	Section 6(4).
		Section 9(8).
		Section 17(1).
		In Schedule 3, paragraph 3(4).
1999 No 1.	The Cathedrals Measure 1999.	In section 16(1), the words from "and the powers" to the end of the subsection.

APPENDIX 3

Will Instruction Form

Signature and date for all actions required from these instructions having been completed...

CLIENT(S)...

FILE REFERENCE(S)...

Interview information				
Date				
Time				
Place				
Those present				
Is the client already known to you? Is the client satisfactorily identified by other means?				
Are any factors known which make the preparation of will(s) urgent?				

Observations on the testator's
mental capacity (details concerning
specific issues or tests in a separate
attendance note)

Personal information:-	*[1]*	*[2]*
Full name of testator, include • *courtesy titles* • *any alternative names used that should be recited* • *variation of names and spellings, or aliases, that may be on the title to any assets*		
Full address including postcode		
Contacts: *home phone* *work phone* *fax* *mobile phone* *email*		
Is the testator *blind or* *illiterate or* *unable to understand written English?*		
Is the testator *deaf or* *unable to understand spoken English?* *N.B. if an interpreter is used record name qualification (if any) and relationship to the testator*		

Current marital/civil partnership status Date of marriages etc will assist See attendance note for any further details	*Married* *Civil Partner* *Separated* *Widow(er)* *Divorced* *Separated* *Single* *Cohabitant*	*Married* *Civil Partner* *Separated* *Widow(er)* *Divorced* *Separated* *Single* *Cohabitant*
Previous marital etc history Dates of marriage/civil partnership etc In the case of divorce, [a] if a decree absolute has been issued [b] whether or not maintenance is paid and how much [b] if the divorce was on clean break, terms (barring future I(PFD)A 1975 claims) are important		
Sex	*Male* *Female*	*Male* *Female*
Date of birth		
Where born?		
Maiden or former name(s)		
Nationality		
Tax residence		
Domicile (but if non-UK domiciled or possibly domicile of choice write up facts separately)		
Occupation If retired, previous occupation		

Dependants' information:	[1]	[2]
Children (record any other special factors concerning children in attendance note) N.B. [1] identify parentage of children in case not born to this marriage or partner [2] identify adoption	[a] date of birth? in education? living with testator? Married/civil partnership	[a] date of birth? in education? living with testator? Married/civil partnership
	[b] date of birth? in education? living with testator? Married/civil partnership	[b] date of birth? in education? living with testator? Married/civil partnership
	[c] date of birth? in education? living with testator? Married/civil partnership	[c] date of birth? in education? living with testator? Married/civil partnership
	[d] date of birth? in education? living with testator? Married/civil partnership	[d] date of birth? in education? living with testator? Married/civil partnership
Other dependants (write up any relevant background in attendance note)		

Previous will and codicil(s) *The details below will assist if available*	
Who prepared them?	
Dates of documents	
Are copies of executed documents available?	
Were any previous wills mutual wills?	
If so obtain details of the wills, the agreement and any subsequent wills	
Are there any powers of appointment *[a] general* *[b] special* *held by the testator?* *(if yes copies of powers are needed)*	
Did previous wills exercise any specific or general powers of appointment?	
Foreign wills	
Are there any existing foreign wills?	
Will a new foreign will be required to deal with non-UK assets?	
N.B. where more than one will is being prepared take steps to ensure that neither inadvertently revokes the other	

Asset information	[1] £	[2] £	[joint] £ N.B. record proportion of ownership and type of joint ownership
This financial information may not always be needed in this detail, but in others it will and in order to consider Banks v Goodfellow implications of the will instructions the size and extent of the estate must be considered			
Cashlliquid assets [1] [2] [3] [4]			
Chattels			
Investments [1] unit trusts [2] quoted [3] options [4]			
Life Policies [1] [2] [3] N.B. [1] Care, any written in trust? [2] Any charged with debts? [3] Whose life are they on?			

			Total
Matrimonial home Is this charged and if so to what extent and are any assets also pledged for repayment of charge?			
Other real and leasehold property Is this charged and if so to what extent and are any assets also pledged for repayment of charge?			
Business [1] business activity? [2] sole trade or partnership? [3] ownership of assets used in business? [4] BPR qualifing?			
Agriculture [1] Description of business [2] APR qualifying [3] Is land and business in same name? [4] Tenure			
Private Companies Business activity? Share structure and other shareholders if material			
Non-UK assets (including where situate)			
Other assets [1] [2] [3] [4]			
	Total	**Total**	**Total**

	Notes
Aggregable property [1] [2] [3]	
Any other factors, including • Potential inheritances • Pension policies (N.B. care over nominations) • Death in Service benefits (N.B. care over nominations) • Any recent inheritances where QSR or DoV might be appropriate? • Unused nil rate band(s) from prior death of spouse?	
	Total
Gifts (N.B. give dates and donees) [a] PETs [1] [2] [3] [b] Chargeable transfers [1] [2] [3] [c] Exempt gifts	
Total	**Total**

WILL INSTRUCTIONS:	[1]	[2]	
Is any special execution or attestation clause required and if so what type?			
Are wills to be mutual?			
N.B. formal agreement required if land is specifically bequeathed as required by s.2 Law of Property (MP) Act 1989			
Are wills to be made in expectation of marriage/civil partnership?			
If yes, are any terms to be conditional upon that marriage/civil partnership taking place or not?			
Other party to the intended marriage/civil partnership?			
Is will to be limited to certain geographical assets?			
If any class gifts/trusts are to include spouses check if client wants this to include civil partners			
Executors (including alternates)			
Trustees, if not executors?			

Funeral instructions			
Guardians (including alternates)			
Powers of appointment to be exercised?			
Specific Bequests *N.B. On which death are they to take effect?* [1] [2] [3] [4] [5] [6]			

Pecuniary Legacies *N.B. On which death are they to be payable?* *Consider contingencies and intermediate income* *[1]* *[2]* *[3]* *[4]* *[5]* *[6]*			
Charitable legacies *[1]* *[2]* *[3]* *N.B. are bodies selected charitable?* *Care non-charitable unincorporated associations*			
Devises			
Trust Devises			

N.B. for both types of devise consider any existing charges and whether or not they are to pass with gift or be discharged		
Trust Legacies		
Residue		

On the terms of the above instructions, consider if any of the following needs to be clarified with the testator:

[1] [a] Will any gift of real or leasehold property be **charged with existing debt** or is the debt to be repaid from elsewhere?..
....

[b] If insurance in place to clear mortgage on death is the beneficiary to take the benefit?..............

[2] Discuss the **age of vesting** for any gifts to minors and are parental receipts appropriate?...........
....

[3] Does *s.33 Wills Act 1837* need to apply or should it be negated for gifts to children and remoter issue?...

[4] Does the nature of any asset require executors' or trustees' **exoneration/indemnity** provisions and if so has the testator considered and expressly consented?.......................................
....

[5] Are any **gifts to executors** payable if they do not accept the office?......................................
....

[6] Do any trusts require **letters of wishes** to be prepared?..
....

[7] Are the terms as proposed by the testator compatible with the actual ownership and devolution of the assets, or do you need to discuss **severance** of any joint ownership?........................
....

[8] If **severance** is required how will this be achieved? (N.B. record detailed advice and agreed actions in an attendance note)..
....

[9] [a] Is it appropriate to discuss the **standard administrative provisions** that you would propose and should they be amended to meet the testator's wishes?...
....

[b] If published administrative provisions are to be included has a copy been given to the client and an explanation given?...

[10] If the terms proposed by the testator permit any significant risk of an *I(PFD)A 1975 claim*, record in a separate note full and accurate details of the advice that has been given and the testator's decision (including the reasons for rejecting any advice you have given)..
....

[11] Is **tax planning** advice appropriate?...
....

[12] If **tax planning** is to be given, have terms and time scale been agreed?.................................
....

[13] Is a **lasting power of attorney** needed?...
....

[14] If a **lasting power of attorney** is to be prepared, have terms and time-scale been agreed?............
....

[15] Is any advice for planning for **care fees** appropriate?..
....

[16] If **care fees advice** is to be given, have terms and time scale been agreed?...........................
....

[17] In the case of a **Trust Company** taking instructions for its own appointment as executor, has a copy of the standard terms and conditions of business been given to the testator?....................
....

[18] Is it appropriate to have written statements prepared to be placed with the will regarding

Non-provision for any family member or dependant?..

Domicile?..

ACTIONS	[1]	[2]
Any limitations of service to be provided explained and agreed?		
Appropriate client engagement letter *Handed over?* *To be sent later?* *N.B. the retainer letter should clearly reflect any modification or exclusions of duty agreed with the client*		
Will drafts to be sent? *When?*		
When will engrossment be ready?		
Will draftsman to supervise execution? *Where?* *When?*		
If engrossments by post *Address?* *When?*		
Will wills be returned to draftsman for checking?		
Where will wills be stored?		
Have you undertaken to do any other work as a result of this interview?		

If the testator is an existing client, check office records for any dealings for which correspondence exists for matters that may affect the will and of which you might be found to have knowledge				
Length of interview				
Signature(s) of interviewer(s)				

Additional comments:

APPENDIX 4

Execution of a Will

Part 1 Aide-memoire—Where the draftsman is to supervise execution of the will

Before execution:

1. Are the witnesses available?
2. Are the witnesses identified and have you checked that they neither take benefit under the will nor are married to a beneficiary or the civil partner of a beneficiary?
3. Is the will the correct one, with all pages there?
4. Has the testator been taken through the terms of the will with all necessary explanations given and all questions answered?[1]
5. Is the testimonium and attestation correct for the circumstances and method of execution?
6. Are the spaces for the testator's signature and the witnesses' signatures clearly marked?

After execution:

1. While testator and witnesses are still present, check that the executed wills are correctly executed and dated.
2. While testator and witnesses are still present, where more than one will has been executed, check that each testator has signed the correct one.
3. Where copies of the executed wills are to be given to the testator, ensure that [a] each testator is given the correct one and [b] that they are copies and that you still have the originals.
4. Have notes been made of any unusual circumstances of the execution, including any comments on perceived capacity of the testator?

Part 2 Specimen instructions for executing a will

1. Optional text and choices are shown in square brackets [ ].
2. The form is drafted so as to be printed on two sides of one sheet of paper when the appropriate options are selected and the other options are discarded.

---

[1] Bear in mind *Franks v Sinclair* [2007] WTLR 439.

IT IS MOST IMPORTANT THAT YOU READ THESE NOTES CAREFULLY BEFORE YOU START THE PROCESS OF EXECUTING YOUR WILL

The valid execution of a will involves three people, you (the person making it—usually called the "*testator*" if male or "*testatrix*" if female) and your two witnesses. All three of you should be present throughout the whole process, so the witnesses should be present *before* you sign your will.

If someone has to read these notes to you because you have sight difficulties or you are not able to read, you must make sure that the person who drew your will knows this and has drawn the will to reflect that you cannot read. Check this with them before you proceed.

The witnesses are there to witness your signature only and they need know nothing of the contents of the will.

A person should *not* be asked to act as a witness if they are

- Blind
- Not capable of understanding what is required or what they are doing.

It is preferable *not* to use a witness who is under 18 years old.

A person should *not* be asked to act as a witness if they are

- Someone who could benefit under your will
- Someone who is married to, or is the civil partner of, a person who could benefit under your will.

[After the death of a person sometimes a legal challenge is made to their capacity to have made their will. Such challenges can be expensive for an estate and time-consuming and distressing for the beneficiaries and, if successful, can produce a result which was not intended. Although it is up to the individual to decide whether or not to do so, we recommend that your doctor's opinion on your mental capacity to sign your will is obtained if

- You are elderly
- You are receiving medical treatment for an illness which could affect your capacity
- You habitually use alcohol or drugs (whether prescribed or not).]

Now see over for instructions on how to sign your will

PLEASE FOLLOW THIS PROCEDURE EXACTLY IN ORDER TO EXECUTE
YOUR WILL VALIDLY

FAILURE TO FOLLOW THIS PROCEDURE MAY WELL MEAN
THAT YOUR WILL IS INVALID

You should not start this process until you and your two witnesses are together and then you should follow the steps below in order and remain together until the process is completed.

[1] You should sign the will in the presence of both witnesses using your usual signature in ink or ballpoint, while the two witnesses watch you. You should sign where the will says *"Signature of testator"* or *"Signature of testatrix"*.

[2] One witness should then sign while you and the other witness watch them, using their usual signature in ink or ballpoint where the wills says *"Signature of first witness"*. The witness should then add their full name, address and occupation in the spaces provided by where they have signed.

[3] The second witness should then follow the same procedure as the first, using the spaces provided for the second witness.

[4] When this has been done, the date should be inserted into the space provided, which will either be at the start or the end of the will.

Example of what the completed execution of the will should look like

Dated this   day of   (year)

[Signed by the above-named testator as and for [his/her]

last will in our presence and then by us in [his/hers]]

OR

[Signed by the above-named testator in our presence and by us in his]

OR

[Signed first by the testator in our joint presence and then by each of us in the testator's presence]

            …XXXXXXXXXXXXXXXXXXXX.………………………..

            (Signature of testator/testatrix)

YYYYYYYYYYYYY.………….……..

(signature of first witness)

Full name.………………………………………...

Address.……………………………………..

………………………………………………….…

………………………………………………….…

Occupation.………………………………….…

ZZZZZZZZZZZZZ...........................
(signature of second witness)
Full name..
Address..
....
....
Occupation..

APPENDIX 5

Information Needed in an Emergency Will Pack

1. Firm's *standard retainer letter* for the preparation of a will with any modifications where the standard is not appropriate for an emergency will attendance or where any advice or duty is to be excluded under the terms of the retainer
2. *Standard will questionnaire* for recording assets, family and testator's wishes
3. *Template for a will*
4. *Template for a codicil*
5. *Testimonium clauses*, including versions of
   - Standard for will
   - Standard for codicil
   - Testator unable to read or write (execution by mark)
   - Testator unable to read or write (execution by another)
   - Testator can sign but not read
   - Testator can read but not sign
   - Illiterate testator
6. *Attestation clauses* for both will and codicil including variations to cope with issues in point 5 above
7. *Standard administrative provisions* (consider also some standard explanations as to why they are needed)
8. *Standard precedents* for
   - Specific legacies (including standard definition of chattels)
   - Pecuniary legacies
   - Charity legacies
   - Absolute gifts of residue
   - Life interest in residue
   - Residue on discretionary trusts
   - Nil rate band discretionary trust
   - Funeral/burial instructions to executors
9. Template for a *letter of wishes* for a discretionary trust
10. *Letter of severance* for joint property (including envelope and stamp in order to post it immediately)
11. *Guidance on execution* of wills/codicils
12. Guidance notes on matters or information to be considered if a *codicil* is to be prepared
13. Notes on current *salient features of IHT* (but this should be most clearly dated so that it is obvious if it has not been updated for later budget changes)
14. *Organ donor* consent form
15. Authority for *medical information* to be disclosed to you, particularly as it relates to the client's capacity to make a new will
16. Template for an *attendance note* to record the circumstances of the visit, time taken and what occurred as fully as possible

Actions before attending the client (as far as time permits)

1. Check with hospital/nursing home/hospice to see if their policy permits their staff to witness wills and if staff will be available for this.
2. Do you need to take another witness with you from your firm?
3. Check existing *client database/files* for existing information on client.
4. Check if a *previous will* is held by you or if there is a copy on file of such a will.
5. Any indication from file that any previous will was a *mutual will*?
6. Does the file show any *personal information* that might be relevant to the new will?
7. Check if previous will exercised any *power of appointment*, contained *funeral instructions* or had any unusual features that will help with the new will.
8. Do your records show if any *property is held jointly*, in whatever form, with another?
9. Do your records show any matters which will throw light on the client's *mental capacity* to make a new will?
10. Does your firm have any *outstanding work* for the client (particularly will instructions)?

BEFORE YOU LEAVE, DO YOU HAVE WITH YOU

1 THE EMERGENCY WILL PACK?

2 A COPY OF PREVIOUS WILL AND ANY CODICILS?

3 ANY RELEVANT OFFICE FILES?

4 THE NAME OF THE CLIENT?

5 THE ADDRESS OF THE CLIENT?

6 IDENTIFICATION?

7 MOBILE PHONE?

Estate Progress Control Sheet

Deceased (name).....................................

File reference....................................

[1] *Initial actions*

Instructed ....

Death certificate received ....

Client care letter sent ....

Notification to beneficiaries of interests in will ....

AML/identity checks ....

Asset insurance checked and amended ....

Enquiry/confirmation letters re assets/liabilities ....

Executors bank accounts opened ....

Valuations:

[1] Asset   *requested*   *rec'd*

[2] Asset   *requested*   *rec'd*

[3] Asset   *requested*   *rec'd*

s.27 notices to creditors:

London Gazette ordered: ....*published*.........*expiry*............

Local ordered: ....*published*.........*expiry*............

Figures for IHT return prepared ....

Cash position reviewed ....

Anticipated outgoings estimated ....

Loan for IHT:.. or

Funds for IHT obtained...................................

(*Where*............*Amount*............*undertaking*.....................)

Probate papers prepared ....

executed by PR

submitted

Copy grants   number required...............ordered...........

Deed of variation discussed (if appropriate)...................

[2] *Grant*

Date of Grant   issued...................received.................

Assets collected to clear loans..............reserve for testamentary expenses............

Loan for IHT repaid   ....

Debts paid—receipts obtained   ....

[3] *Distribution*

Legacies paid...................

Bankruptcy searches...................

Receipts...

Appropriate/realise remaining assets   ....

Interim distribution to residuary legatees   ....

Bankruptcy searches......................

Receipt...

Final distribution to residuary legatees   ....

[4] *Completion*

Tax returns and clearances...

Deceased's IT/CGT to d.o.d. submitted............finalised........

PR's IT/CGT submitted.............finalised..........

IHT Corrective Account submitted..............assessed........paid........

Clearance certificate submitted.............received..........

All testamentary expenses cleared

Estate Accounts   sent   approved

Final distribution to residuary beneficiaries.......................

Bankruptcy search..

Receipt...

Trust file ref if a continuing trust arises..............................

Fee Accounts

[1] amount..............submitted.............paid............

[2] amount..............submitted.............paid............

[3] amount..............submitted.............paid............

Summary of Key Dates:

Date of Death:...

Date of Grant:...

IHT due..(note 1)

s.27 expiry date...(note 2)

Time limit for I(PFD)A 1975 claim..........................(note 3)

Time limit for variation/disclaimer under will............(note 4)

Time limit for variation of pre-death benefit............

Notes

1. *6 months from end of month of death—thereafter interest runs.*
2. *Minimum of 2 months after advert appears.*
3. *10 months from Grant—s.20 I(PFD)A 1975 refers to 6 months, but this only refers to late applications; in practice therefore allow a further 4 months for the service of any writ after the 6-month period in s.4.*
4. *Within 2 years of death.*
5. *Files need to be reviewed regularly and clients updated on progress. These matters should also be recorded on the Progress Sheet. Files need to be reviewed regularly and clients updated on progress. These matters should also be recorded on the Progress Sheet.*
6. *The signature of the person carrying out these functions should be requested and logged on the Progress Sheet.*
7. *This form is indicative of the key information needed to control progress, but the information should be adapted to suit either business needs or the needs of the particular estate.*

APPENDIX 7

Sources of Information to be Considered for Account Preparation

1. *The letter file*—this should be read and any significant actions/issues that will have to be reflected in the format of the accounts noted. This also acts as a check that actions agreed on by the trustees have in fact been carried out and can be reflected in the accounts. Where this is not the case, consider what notes to the accounts will be appropriate.

2. *Previous year's accounts*—these provide the opening figures for the current year's accounts. Note any items which will affect this year's statements—these include matters in the notes to previous years' accounts (which should be reviewed and updated or omitted as appropriate). Review any reserves shown in the previous year's accounts.

3. *Synopsis of the trust* (at the front of the previous year's accounts)—does this appear to be correct and show the current trusts? (Even if it does, periodically recheck the trust deed(s) to make sure it is correct.)

4. *Bank statements*—should be reviewed (or any computer printouts of whatever cash accounts are maintained by the trustee) as this information will all need to be reflected in the accounts. Together with this the process of matching invoices and accounts against the payments made (this is a simple security check as well).

5. *Investment transaction file*—contract notes etc should be reviewed and matched against the transactions in the current year's accounts. Prices and dates of investment transactions are not essential information for accounts but they are very often useful for future reference when consulting the accounts. Consider any investment transaction not supported by contract notes (rights issues, scrip issues, mergers, etc).

6. *Tax file*—the returns and assessments, etc should be reviewed—is all the income reflected in the accounts and all the income in the accounts reflected in the tax returns and all the tax payments matched against the assessments? Similarly for CGT and IHT.

7. *Permanent trust deed file*[1]—should be obtained (for checking and review of the documents, where necessary, against events in the trust).

8. *Property deeds*—are they held for all properties in the trust; no rent reviews or lease expiries missed? Do those in occupation and paying the rent match those who have taken the leases? Insurances and repairs dealt with and the burden of the expenditure has followed the burden of the covenants?

9. *Investment certificates or receipts*—match the assets held in the accounts? Where necessary confirmation of holdings from nominees? Pay particular attention to assets purchased during the year and that nominal holdings and types of share/stock match what is in the account and that the transactions are complete. N.B. although the income tax returns should have declared all income it is a useful double check to ensure that the right dividends on the right due dates for the right nominal value holdings have been received. This may involve checking for XD or cum div status of dealing prices.

---

[1] A file that is kept under reasonable security (and fireproof safety) which contains

- the original trust deed and any subsequent deeds affecting the trusts
- all deeds of retirement and appointment of new trustees
- any assignments or charges of interests in the trust
- any other original papers that affect the way the trustee manages the trust or distributes the assets such as court orders
- the originals of all letters of wishes
- where it is necessary to establish who is a member of a class of beneficiaries, all the information obtained.

There should also be a second permanent file with original documents of title to all trust assets and a third permanent file with all previously issued accounts in it.

10. If the trust owns shares in a *private company* obtain that company's latest accounts and balance sheet. Check to see if the accounts reveal information which might need to be disclosed in the trust accounts. Are the latest M&AA held? Have all dividends due been received?

11. *Litigation file*—details of it to consider if provisions/notes are required to the current year's accounts and consider reserves for costs and/or outcome of the litigation.

Actions (in addition to those listed above)

1. Analyse transactions, draft account, trial balance.

2. All dividends received (checking particularly for dividends on holdings purchased or sold and on any automatic reinvestment of income)? Check also that all income (including deposit interest) has been received from any investment manager.

3. Check that all income has been disclosed on the relevant tax returns.

4. Check that tax returns, where required, have been submitted. Any unpaid taxes should be reserved for in the accounts.

5. Investment transactions conform to any restrictions in the deed or by law? Checking in particular for demergers, special dividends and scrip dividends having been allocated correctly between capital and income.

6. Any scrip issues due have been received and any rights issued received and dealt with (especially receipt of proceeds and payments of instalments)?

7. Are cash balances excessive and are there funds that should be invested, placed on deposit or distributed?

8. If income is being accumulated, check that the accumulation has not exceeded the permitted period.

9. All rent received? Is the rent received from the tenant named in the lease?

10. If rented properties have become vacant, is some action for sale or reletting being taken?

11. Insurance premiums paid on any policies (non-payment is probably an issue to be noted on the accounts if it cannot be rectified straight away) and where applicable have premiums been recovered from tenants?

12. Any outstanding creditors/debtors? Is a note to the accounts required for this?

13. Invoices held for all outgoings including professional fees and that all outgoings have been paid (compare with last year and with what you know from the file). If litigation or similar legal costs are being incurred consider if a reserve is required and a note to the accounts.

14. If a trust company, check that trustee fees calculation is in accordance with Standard Terms and Conditions of Business and correct fee scale and STCs are being applied.

15. Where trust property, such as chattels, are in the possession of the beneficiaries consider how often their continued existence should be verified (check trust deed for any requirements on this) and also how often compliance with any conditions is checked.

16. Any delegated authority, such as that to investment managers has been made according to the requirements of law/deed and that any conditions have been met. Make sure also that all transactions carried out by the investment managers are reflected in the accounts.

17. Minutes of trustee decisions should be reviewed and a check made that the actions decided on have been taken and are reflected in the accounts. Look particularly for decisions about distributions and accumulations.

18. Where assets are subject to regulatory obligations check if any work required has been carried out and if reports recommend action that the action has been taken.[2]

19. Fraud checks, i.e. payments are made correctly to beneficiaries' bank accounts. Check receipts if they were obtained. If payments made to a third party for a beneficiary, check the authorisations. Generally

---

[2] Gas installations in rented properties require mandatory inspections with criminal sanctions for breaches. Commercial premises also require regular inspections for Legionnaire's disease contamination in water systems.

do not lose sight of security and potential fraud against trusts—properly prepared trust accounts are an important part of anti-fraud measures.

20. All payments and receipts that required AML checks had AML checks made.

21. Preparation and trial balance.

In some cases accounts will not be produced annually—e.g. several of the big trust companies do not do so and provide information in other ways (portfolio valuations, schedules of investment changes, etc). This is acceptable, and it can save costs, in that accounts need not be prepared if beneficiaries do not require them—but accounts must be provided at a later stage if they are needed so do not become careless with the integrity of the basic accounting records.

N.B.

[1] The detail of these notes will vary between trusts, depending upon jurisdiction and types of assets held.

[2] Terminology and sources may vary between different accounting systems.

INDEX

taxation (*cont.*):
  administration of estates and (*cont.*):
    estimated values 17.10–17.15
    payment of tax 12.17–12.36
    PR's personal liability 17.01–17.04
    reserving estate for contingent legacies 17.36–17.40
    selling estate assets 17.27–17.29
  advice during lifetime of client 19.53–19.54
    capital gains tax 19.47–19.52
    client's circumstances 19.20–19.29
    defining the duty 19.04–19.11
    discharging duty 19.19
    explaining risk 19.01–19.03
    inheritance tax (IHT) 19.30–19.46
    limitation periods in negligence cases 21.22–21.30
    limiting duty 19.12–19.18
  advice to settlors 9.177–9.187
  residence and 18.43–18.44, 19.22–19.25
  trusts and 18.01, 18.49–18.50
    capital gains tax 18.12, 18.25–18.31
    exercise of discretion and 18.05–18.10
    foreign tax liabilities 18.45–18.48
    income tax 18.32–18.37
    inheritance tax (IHT) 18.15–18.24
    residence and deemed residence 18.43–18.44
    tax investigations/penalties 9.72–9.73
    trust migrating abroad 18.41–18.42
    trustee's liability 18.11–18.15
    trustee's position on retiring from trust 18.38–18.40, 18.41–18.42
  wills and tax advice 16.01–16.02
    case law as it stands 16.03–16.04
    common tax considerations in will drafting 16.25–16.36
    duty or best practice 16.05–16.08, 16.19–16.21
    exclusion of duty 16.14–16.18
    extent of duty 16.09–16.13
    gifts to charities and sports clubs 16.26–16.30
    impact of Finance Act 2008 16.22–16.24
    lower rate of inheritance tax 16.31
    nil rate band trusts 16.32–16.34
    providing for incidence of IHT 16.35–16.36
    see also **capital gains tax; income tax; inheritance tax (IHT)**
tenanted property 9.33
terrorist financing 9.155–9.158
testators 4.01–4.11
  capacity 3.23, 4.45–4.47, 8.24
    costs in probate actions and 4.87–4.90
    delusions and 4.54–4.56
    duty of practitioner 4.62–4.68
    foreign wills and 6.34–6.36
    medical opinion 4.69–4.82
    statutory test in Mental Capacity Act 2005 4.57–4.61
    test of 4.48–4.50
    timing of assessment 4.51–4.53
    undue influence 4.04, 4.83–4.86
    want of knowledge and approval 4.83–4.86
  duty of care in relation to will preparation and 2.35–2.41
    intention 3.01–3.07

    no duty while testator is alive and can rectify 3.38–3.39
  instructions from *see* **instructions**
  reluctant testators 6.79–6.86
third parties
  modern reform of privity of contract and rights of third parties 1.09–1.15
time limits *see* **limitation periods**
timing 12.01
  consequences of delay 12.39–12.41
  delays in collecting assets 12.15
  delays in locating executor 12.02–12.03
  delays in notifying beneficiary of his interest 12.04–12.07
  delays in obtaining grant of probate 12.08–12.14
  delays in payment of tax 12.17–12.36
  delays in settling debts 12.16
  delays in taking legal advice 12.37–12.38
  distributions 14.02–14.04
    appropriations of assets in satisfaction of interests 14.16–14.30
    capacity in which distribution is made 14.14–14.16
    money-laundering regulations and 14.33–14.37
    receipts for distributions 14.31–14.32
    statutory notices to creditors 14.05–14.13
  sale of assets/investments 13.190
  time taken in preparation of will 6.51–6.63
    control of time 6.87–6.90
    delay attributable to will-preparer 6.70–6.71
    internal audit of time taken 6.91
    standard or optimum times 6.66–6.69
    urgent and non-urgent wills 6.51, 6.56, 6.64–6.65
tracing beneficiaries 14.44–14.50
tracing claims 9.65
training for draftsmen of wills 5.15–5.17
transsexual people
  gender recognition certificate and 14.51–14.54
trials 20.85–20.87
trustees 9.02, 14.14
  applications by 10.49–10.52
    applications for directions 10.57–10.60
    Beddoe applications 10.61–10.64
    principles 10.53–10.56
    procedure 10.57–10.60, 10.65–10.66
  capital gains tax and 18.25–18.31
  consequences of sham trusts for 9.60
  custodians and 13.145–13.149
    bearer securities 13.160–13.165
    supervision 13.158–13.159
    terms of appointment 13.155–13.157
    who may be appointed 13.150–13.154
  delays in notifying beneficiary of his interest 12.04–12.07
  delegation by *see* **delegation by trustees to agents**
  duty of care 1.43–1.56, 15.17
    duty of care of adviser to trustee 15.28–15.33
    under general law 15.23
    modification or exclusion 15.24–15.27
    statutory duty of care 15.18–15.22
  exercise of discretion 18.05–18.10
  exercise of powers 15.01–15.12

Lightning Source UK Ltd.
Milton Keynes UK
UKOW02f1228280214

227341UK00001B/1/P